MAGILL'S ENCYCLOPEDIA OF SOCIAL SCIENCE

PSYCHOLOGY

MAGILL'S ENCYCLOPEDIA OF SOCIAL SCIENCE

PSYCHOLOGY

Volume 1
Ability tests – Cultural competence

Editor
Nancy A. Piotrowski, Ph.D.
University of California, Berkeley

Project Editor
Tracy Irons-Georges

SALEM PRESS, INC.
Pasadena, California
Hackensack, New Jersey

Editorial Director: Christina J. Moose
Project Editor: Tracy Irons-Georges
Copy Editor: Leslie Ellen Jones
Assistant Editor: Andrea E. Miller
Acquisitions Editor: Mark Rehn
Photograph Editor: Philip Bader
Research Supervisor: Jeffry Jensen
Production Editor: Cynthia Beres
Page Design/Graphics: James Hutson
Layout: Eddie Murillo

Some of the updated and revised essays in this work originally appeared in *Magill's Survey of Social Science: Psychology,* edited by Frank N. Magill (Pasadena, Calif.: Salem Press, Inc., 1993).

Library of Congress Cataloging-in-Publication Data

Magill's encyclopedia of social science: psychology/ editor, Nancy A. Piotrowski.
    p. cm.
Includes bibliographical references and index.
ISBN 1-58765-130-0 (set : alk. paper) — ISBN 1-58765-131-9 (v. 1 : alk. paper) —
ISBN 1-58765-132-7 (v. 2 : alk. paper)— ISBN 1-58765-133-5 (v. 3 : alk. paper) —
ISBN 1-58765-134-3 (v. 4 : alk. paper)
1. Psychology—Encyclopedias. I. Piotrowski, Nancy A.

BF31 .M33 2003
150'.3—dc21

2002151146

Fourth Printing

TABLE OF CONTENTS

PUBLISHER'S NOTE

For years, our *Survey of Social Science: Psychology* (1993) has been a standard and popular reference source on the fundamentals of psychology study. The publication of *Magill's Encyclopedia of Social Science: Psychology* represents a substantial redesign, revision, and update of that work. Essays in the older set were uniform in length and format, employing standard subheadings; some topics were highly specialized. This new encyclopedia streamlines many of the older topics by replacing them with helpful overviews, offers greater flexibility in length and format, and provides a more comprehensive view of the field. *Magill's Encyclopedia of Social Science: Psychology* covers not only the history of the field and the core aspects of behaviorism, cognitive psychology, and psychoanalytic psychology but also diagnoses, disorders, treatments, tests, notable people, and issues, including many popular concepts. For all these reasons, the encyclopedia serves its audience of general readers, such as high school and undergraduate students or mental health patients and their caregivers, even better than before.

Of the 452 entries in this encyclopedia, 177 were newly commissioned and 103 entries were revised, often because of advances in diagnosis and treatment or changes in standards from the revised third edition of the American Psychiatric Association's *Diagnostic and Statistical Manual of Mental Disorders* (1987, DSM-III-R) to the text revision of the fourth edition (2000, DSM-IV-TR). Every reused entry has been edited anew and reformatted with new top matter and tailored subheadings to guide the reader through the text. The "Sources for Further Study" sections that conclude all entries have been updated with the latest editions and most recent scholarship. This encyclopedia also introduces a number of helpful appendices and is fully illustrated with more than two hundred photographs, drawings, tables, graphs, textual sidebars, and lists of diagnostic criteria from the DSM-IV-TR.

Entries in *Psychology* range from one to eight pages in length. Every entry begins with standard information. Where relevant, a date is provided for when theories were first presented, organizations were founded, and tests were designed. The heading "Type of psychology" lists as many as apply from the following categories: biological bases of behavior, cognition, consciousness, developmental psychology, emotion, intelligence and intelligence testing, language, learning, memory, motivation, origin and definition of psychology, personality, psychological methodologies, psychopathology, psychotherapy, sensation and perception, social psychology, and stress. The heading "Fields of study" lists as many as apply from a list of sixty-one categories, including ability tests, adolescence, adulthood, aggression, aging, anxiety disorders, attitudes and behavior, classic analytic themes and issues, coping, depression, group processes, infancy and childhood, interpersonal relations, organic disorders, physical motives, prejudice and discrimination, problem solving, sexual disorders, sleep, substance abuse, and thought. Biographical entries include an "Identity" line indicating nationality and discipline or specialty, as well as birth/death date and place information. For topical entries, an abstract briefly defines the subject, summarizing its importance to psychology, and "Key concepts" lists five to ten of the most important issues to be discussed in the essay that follows.

The text of each article offers a clear and concise discussion of the topic. An entry on a mental illness addresses its cause, diagnosis, treatment, and impact. An entry on a theory or school examines its origin, history, and current status. An entry on an organization covers its history and functions. An entry on a psychological test discusses its development and applications. A biographical entry focuses on the life, career, and contributions of the individual. Informative, descriptive subheadings divide the text of longer essays. All terminology is explained, and context is provided to make the information accessible to general readers. Every entry ends with a section "Sources for Further Study," with annotations that discuss the content and value of these secondary sources. All essays are signed by the author and conclude with a list of cross-references to related articles within *Psychology*.

At the end of each volume are a Complete List of Entries and a Categorized List of Entries. The latter is divided into sixty-six groups, including such categories as Conditioning, Developmental psychology, Diagnosis, Experimentation, Men's psychology, Methodology, Nervous system, Organizations and publications, People, Personality disorders, Prosocial behavior, Psychobiology, Schizophrenias, Sexuality, Testing, Treatments, and Women's psychology.

Several valuable appendices can be found at the end of volume 4: a Glossary of crucial terms with concise definitions; an annotated general Bibliography of nonfiction works organized by category; an annotated Web Site Directory for support groups and organizations; a Mediagraphy discussing depictions of mental illness and psychology as a field in films and television series; a list of Organizations and Support Groups with contact information and a list of hot lines; a Pharmaceutical List of generic and brand-name drugs grouped by their uses; a Biographical List of Psychologists with brief profiles of major figures; and a list of Notable Court Cases that mark important legal milestones in the history of psychology. The encyclopedia concludes with a comprehensive subject Index.

We must express our thanks to the Editor, Nancy A. Piotrowski, Ph.D., of the University of California, Berkeley; her Introduction, which can be found at the beginning of volume 1, provides insights into the history and future of this dynamic field. We also thank the contributors to this encyclopedia—academicians from psychology, medicine, and other disciplines in the social and life sciences—for sharing their expertise with general readers; a list of their names and affiliations follows.

CONTRIBUTOR LIST

Christopher M. Aanstoos
State University of West Georgia

Norman Abeles
Michigan State University

Steven C. Abell
Loyola College of Chicago

Richard Adler
University of Michigan—Dearborn

C. Emmanuel Ahia
Rider University

Mark B. Alcorn
University of Northern Colorado

Charles N. Alexander
Maharishi International University

Jeffery B. Allen
University of Mississippi

Tara Anthony
Syracuse University

Richard P. Atkinson
Fort Hays State University

Bryan C. Auday
Gordon College

Stephen M. Auerbach
Virginia Commonwealth University

Bruce E. Bailey
Stephen F. Austin University

Stephen R. H. Beach
University of Georgia

Donald G. Beal
Eastern Kentucky University

Alan J. Beauchamp
Northern Michigan University

Brett L. Beck
Bloomsbury University

Susan E. Beers
Sweet Briar College

Tanja Bekhuis
TCB Research

Michael S. Bendele
Indiana University—Purdue University, Fort Wayne

Alvin K. Benson
Utah Valley State College

Krishna Bhaskarabhatla
Saint Joseph's Regional Medical Center, Mount Sinai School of Medicine

Virginiae Blackmon
Independent Scholar

Cathy J. Bogart
Avila University

Lyn T. Boulter
Catawba College

Mary Brabeck
Boston College

Barbara E. Brackney
Eastern Michigan University

Nyla R. Branscombe
University of Kansas

Lillian J. Breckenridge
Oral Roberts University

Barbara A. Bremer
Pennsylvania State University Harrisburg

Christiane Brems
University of Alaska

Bruce Bridgeman
University of California, Santa Cruz

T. L. Brink
Crafton Hills College

Victor K. Broderick
Ferris State University

David W. Brokaw
Azusa Pacific University

Leonie J. Brooks
Towson University

Gayle L. Brosnan-Watters
Vanguard University of Southern California

Dennis Bull
Dallas Theological Seminary

John T. Burns
Bethany College

Joan Bartczak Cannon
University of Lowell

Mary E. Carey
University of Oklahoma

Jack Carter
University of New Orleans

Karen Chapman-Novakofski
University of Illinois

Paul J. Chara, Jr.
Northwestern College

Garvin Chastain
Boise State University

Kausalya Chennapragada
Saint Joseph's Regional Medical Center, Mount Sinai School of Medicine

Judith M. Chertoff
Baltimore-Washington Institute for Psychoanalysis

Rebecca M. Chesire
University of Hawaiiù—Manoa

Richard G. Cormack
Independent Scholar

Salvatore Cullari
Lebanon Valley College

Kenneth G. DeBono
Union College

Everett J. Delahanty, Jr.
Manhattanville College

Jack Demick
Suffolk University

James R. Deni
Appalachian State University

Karen M. Derr
Airport Marina Counseling Service

Thomas E. DeWolfe
Hampden-Sydney College

Ronna F. Dillon
Southern Illinois University

Duane L. Dobbert
Florida Gulf Coast University

Stefan C. Dombrowski
Rider University

George Domino
University of Arizona

Roger A. Drake
Western State College of Colorado

Robert J. Drummond
University of North Florida

Dana S. Dunn
Moravian College

Christopher A. Duva
Eastern Oregon University

Ted Eilders
American Psychological Association

Russell Eisenman
McNeese State University

David G. Elmes
Washington and Lee University

Carolyn Zerbe Enns
Cornell College

Charles H. Evans
LaGrange College

Lawrence A. Fehr
Widener University

Leonard Feinberg
Iona College

Julie A. Felender
Fullerton College

Ellen C. Flannery-Schroeder
University of the Sciences in Philadelphia

John H. Fleming
University of Minnesota— Minneapolis

Roy Fontaine
Pennsylvania College of Technology

Karen Anding Fontenot
Louisiana State University

Michael J. Fontenot
Southern University at Baton Rouge

Katherine A. Fowler
Emory University

Margaret M. Frailey
American Association of Counseling and Development

Robin Franck
Southwestern College

Cynthia McPherson Frantz
Amherst College

Donna Frick-Horbury
Appalachian State University

Lisa Friedenberg
University of North Carolina at Asheville

Jerome Frieman
Kansas State University

Jim Fultz
Northern Illinois University

R. G. Gaddis
Gardner-Webb College

Judi Garland
Wilmington Family Counseling Service

Judith L. Gay
Chestnut Hill College

J. Ronald Gentile
State University of New York at Buffalo

Alan K. Gibson
Southern California College

Albert R. Gilgen
University of Northern Iowa

Virginia L. Goetsch
West Virginia University

Doyle R. Goff
Lee College

Sanford Golin
University of Pittsburgh

Diane C. Gooding
University of Wisconsin—Madison

Jeff Greenberg
University of Arizona

Laurence Grimm
University of Illinois at Chicago

Lonnie J. Guralnick
Western Oregon State College

Regan A. R. Gurung
University of Wisconsin, Green Bay

Elizabeth Haase
The New York Hospital

Ruth T. Hannon
Bridgewater State College

Phyllis A. Heath
Central Michigan University

Joanne Hedgespeth
Pepperdine University

Daniel Heimowitz
*National Psychological Association
for Psychoanalysis*

Carol A. Heintzelman
Millersville University

Jean S. Helgeson
Collin County Community College

James Taylor Henderson
Wingate College

Lindsey L. Henninger
Independent Scholar

Oliver W. Hill, Jr.
Virginia State University

Peter C. Hill
Grove City College

Robert A. Hock
Xavier University

David Wason Hollar, Jr.
Rockingham Community College

Brynda Holton
St. Mary's College of Maryland

Sigmund Hsiao
University of Arizona

Timothy L. Hubbard
Eastern Oregon State College

Loring J. Ingraham
George Washington University

Tiffany A. Ito
University of Southern California

Stanley D. Ivie
Educational Leadership

Jay W. Jackson
*Indiana University—Purdue
University, Fort Wayne*

Shelley A. Jackson
*Texas A&M University—
Corpus Christi*

Robert Jensen
*California State University,
Sacramento*

Craig Johnson
Syracuse University

Eugene R. Johnson
Central Washington University

Mark E. Johnson
University of Alaska, Anchorage

Robert D. Johnson
Arkansas State University

Jonathan Kahane
Springfield College

Laura Kamptner
*California State University,
San Bernardino*

William B. King
Edison Community College

Debra A. King-Johnson
Clemson University

Terry J. Knapp
University of Nevada, Las Vegas

Gabrielle Kowalski
Cardinal Stritch University

Carol A. Kusché
*Seattle Psychoanalytic Society and
Institute*

R. Eric Landrum
Boise State University

Kevin T. Larkin
West Virginia University

Ellen Lavelle
Teikyo Western University

Joseph C. LaVoie
University of Nebraska at Omaha

Richard Lettieri
Los Angeles Psychoanalytic Society and Institute

Leon Lewis
Appalachian State University

Scott O. Lilienfeld
Emory University

Gary T. Long
University of North Carolina at Charlotte

Martha Oehmke Loustaunau
New Mexico State University

Anna Lowe
Loyola University Chicago

Richard D. McAnulty
University of North Carolina at Charlotte

Deborah R. McDonald
New Mexico State University

Nancy E. Macdonald
University of South Carolina, Sumter

David S. McDougal
Plymouth State College of the University System of New Hampshire

Salvador Macias III
University of South Carolina, Sumter

Susan Mackey-Kallis
Villanova University

Paul D. Mageli
Independent Scholar

Amy Marcus-Newhall
Occidental College University of Southern California

Linda Mealey
College of St. Benedict

Linda E. Meashey
Pennsylvania State University, Harrisburg

Bernard Mergen
George Washington University

William M. Miley
The Richard Stockton College of New Jersey

Laurence Miller
Western Washington University

Norman Miller
University of Southern California

Rowland Miller
Sam Houston State University

Todd Miller
University of St. Thomas

Fathali M. Moghaddam
Georgetown University

Robin Kamienny Montvilo
Rhode Island College

Brian Mullen
Syracuse University

Karen D. Multon
University of Missouri—Columbia

Debra L. Murphy
Huston-Tillotson College

Michelle Murphy
Independent Scholar

Donald J. Nash
Colorado State University—Lamar

Elizabeth M. McGhee Nelson
Christian Brothers University

John W. Nichols
Tulsa Junior College

Steve A. Nida
Franklin University

Annette O'Connor
La Salle University

Cynthia O'Dell
Indiana University Northwest

Amy L. Odum
University of New Hampshire

Janine T. Ogden
Marist College

Nancy Oley
City University of New York, Medgar Evers College

Don R. Osborn
Bellarmine College

Randall E. Osborne
Phillips University

Gerard O'Sullivan
Felician College

Ronghua Ouyang
Kennesaw State University

Shirley A. Albertson Ownes
Southern California College

Linda J. Palm
Edison Community College

Beverly Palmer
California State University, Dominguez Hills

Robert J. Paradowski
Rochester Institute of Technology

Vicky Phares
University of South Florida

Nancy A. Piotrowski
University of California, Berkeley

Anthony R. Pratkanis
University of California, Santa Cruz

Frank J. Prerost
Midwestern University

Debra S. Preston
University of North Carolina, Pembroke

Judith Primavera
Fairfield University

R. Christopher Qualls
Emory and Henry College

Timothy S. Rampey
Victoria College

Lillian M. Range
University of Southern Mississippi

F. Wayne Reno
Mt. Vernon Nazarene College

Paul August Rentz
South Dakota State University

Ronald G. Ribble
University of Texas at San Antonio

Richard J. Ricard
Texas A&M University

Betty Richardson
Southern Illinois University at Edwardsville

Cheryl A. Rickabaugh
University of Redlands

Loretta A. Rieser-Danner
Pennsylvania State University, Ogontz

Jaclyn Rodriguez
Occidental College

Michael D. Roe
Seattle Pacific University

René R. Roth
University of Western Ontario, Canada

Daniel Sachau
Mankato State University

Denise S. St. Cyr
New Hampshire Technical College

James D. St. James
Millikin University

Frank A. Salamone
Iona College

David Sands
Maharishi International University

John Santelli
Fairleigh Dickinson University

Anthony C. Santucci
Manhattanville College

Tulsi B. Saral
University of Houston—Clear Lake

Elizabeth D. Schafer
Independent Scholar

Rosemary Scheirer
Chestnut Hill College

Rebecca Lovell Scott
College of Health Sciences

Pennie S. Seibert
Boise State University

Felicisima C. Serafica
The Ohio State University

Manoj Sharma
University of Nebraska at Omaha

Matthew J. Sharps
California State University, Fresno

Michael F. Shaughnessy
Eastern New Mexico University

Bonnie S. Sherman
St. Olaf College

R. Baird Shuman
University of Illinois at Urbana— Champaign

Harold I. Siegel
Institute of Animal Behavior, Rutgers University

Marilyn N. Silva
California State University, Hayward

Sanford S. Singer
University of Dayton

Virginia Slaughter
University of Queensland

Lesley A. Slavin
Virginia Commonwealth University

Charles V. Smedley
Charleston Southern University

Stephanie Smith
Indiana University Northwest

Janet A. Sniezek
University of Illinois at Urbana— Champaign

Sheldon Solomon
Skidmore College

Frank J. Sparzo
Ball State University

Gerald Sperrazzo
University of San Diego

Michael D. Spiegler
Providence College

Mark Stanton
Azusa Pacific University

Sharon Wallace Stark
Monmouth University

Michael A. Steele
Wilkes University

Stephanie Stein
Central Washington University

Joseph E. Steinmetz
Indiana University Bloomington

Faye B. Steuer
College of Charleston

Glenn Ellen Starr Stilling
Appalachian State University

Lloyd K. Stires
Indiana University of Pennsylvania

Leland C. Swenson
Loyola Marymount University

Kathleen A. Tallent
University of Wisconsin—Madison

Richard G. Tedeschi
University of North Carolina at Charlotte

Linda R. Tennison
College of Saint Benedict/Saint John's University

Thomas J. Thieman
College of St. Catherine

Harry A. Tiemann, Jr.
Mesa State College

Derise E. Tolliver
DePaul University

James T. Trent
Middle Tennessee State University

Marlene E. Turner
San Jose State University

John V. Urbas
Kennesaw State College

Susana P. Urbina
University of North Florida

Mary Moore Vandendorpe
Lewis University

Lois Veltum
University of North Dakota

Scott R. Vrana
Purdue University

John F. Wakefield
University of North Alabama

Elaine F. Walker
Emory University

Mary L. Wandrei
Marquette University

Daniel L. Wann
Murray State University
University of Kansas

Jennifer A. Sanders Wann
Murray State University

Allyson M. Washburn
Institute on Aging/Jewish Home

T. Steuart Watson
Mississippi State University

Ann L. Weber
University of North Carolina at Asheville

Marcia J. Weiss
Point Park College

George I. Whitehead III
Salisbury State University

Edward R. Whitson
State University of New York, College at Genesco

Michael Wierzbicki
Marquette University

April Michele Williams
Drury University

Bradley R. A. Wilson
University of Cincinnati

Gregory L. Wilson
Washington State University

Adam Winsler
Stanford University

Stephen L. Wolfe
University of California, Davis

Karen Wolford
State University of New York, College at Oswego

Edelgard Wulfert
State University of New York at Albany

Frederic Wynn
County College of Morris

Daniel L. Yazak
Montana State University—Billings

Debra Zehner
Wilkes University

Ling-Yi Zhou
University of St. Francis

MAGILL'S ENCYCLOPEDIA OF SOCIAL SCIENCE

PSYCHOLOGY

INTRODUCTION

I would like to introduce this encyclopedia of psychology in both its recent and more distant historical contexts. Additionally, I would like to focus the attention of readers on the scope and depth of the work of psychologists, their students, and their supporters. As reading these volumes will show, psychology is a diverse and large field. Finally, I would like to remind readers that most of the research described in these volumes is completed through the silent contributions of thousands upon thousands of volunteers, as well as nonhuman animal participants. Without such contributions, none of this work would be possible.

HISTORICAL CONTEXT

When I was first asked to assist with this project, I thought it would be fun to look at how far the field of psychology had come since the last publication of similar volumes by Salem Press in 1993. Things that immediately came to mind as relevant issues included the evolution of the *Diagnostic and Statistical Manual of Mental Disorders* (DSM) by the American Psychiatric Association; the dot-com boom and bust of the Internet and the growth of Internet psychology; several national elections, both public and professional, and how they illustrated affinity toward different examples of leadership; and some amazing discoveries in diverse areas of the field, such as the "tend and befriend" stress response in women, newly identified early signs of Alzheimer's disease, and even advances in the areas of psychopharmacology applications and training. Such prospects seemed obvious as things to highlight in the new volumes—and the project as a whole seemed like an endeavor that was going to be quite energizing as the planning process began.

Then came the events of September 11, 2001, soon labeled 9/11, in which thousands died when radical Islamic terrorists hijacked four commercial planes and flew them into the World Trade Center, the Pentagon, and a field in Pennsylvania. History was made by a tragedy of global proportions—and sudden changes in perspective about what was im-

portant were occurring everywhere. In practical terms, there were necessary scheduling adjustments to allow our writers a bit more time to complete their work. More generally, everyone seemed to be thinking about the psychology of terrorism, war, and issues such as post-traumatic stress disorder, bereavement, substance use disorders, depression, anxiety, sleeplessness, concentration difficulties, culture and communication, intergenerational loss, the costs of hypervigilance, and the meanings of intelligence, judgment, and prediction. Additionally, the wisdom of social and developmental psychologists suddenly became more important, especially with regard to their theories addressing the development of differences in moral values, why some people might choose violence as a means of expression, and how people become committed to extreme causes.

I cannot persuade myself that the events of 9/11 did not color the content of the articles contained in this encyclopedia. I think it is good, however, that the contributors to this work came together to create these volumes with such a unique historical context as footing, because it makes the strength and value of the field of psychology to humanity readily apparent. For instance, by looking over the topics included in these volumes, it is easy to remember that aspects of psychology are helpful for promoting tolerance, prosocial behavior, and cooperation. There are also theories that help us to understand behavior by psychopaths and others where the motivation seems incomprehensible. There are methods of healing and prevention that are very effective for many types of problems, as well as methods of learning, and relearning and, thankfully, of forgetting and forgiveness.

Even more comforting, other sections in these volumes stand timeless—things we have learned that remain true and unchanged, even by 9/11. For instance, we know that there are similarities to human facial expression for certain basic emotions, such as fear, anger, happiness, sadness, and disgust—and that these expressions offer bridges across the diversity of culture, gender, and age. They allow for common understandings and communication. We also know that, by and large, humans as a group have evolved to be interdependent. Simply stated, there is comfort in this kind of knowledge in times of distress—and the hard work of psychologists is to be recognized for such insights.

WHAT PSYCHOLOGY DOES

Many different ideas may come to mind when people hear the word "psychology." For some, word associations may be first: psychic, psychedelic, psychotic, psychogenic, psychosomatic, psychopath—words that have associations to psychology in one way or another. Others might think of concepts, such as the psyche, referring to the self and the soul. They may think of getting psyched, or prepared for action, with psyched up being good and psyched out being bad. Some may think about the classic 1960 film *Psycho*, starring Anthony Perkins, which featured a story about a murderous and odd man—sadly, adding stigma to the tragedy of mental illness and suffering by inadvertently reinforcing stereotypes of the mentally ill as violent and dangerous individuals.

When people think of psychology, they often think of clinicians, such as those portrayed on television and in films or heard on the radio—people who work with or otherwise counsel the troubled and mentally ill. Ideas about Sigmund Freud and his theories of the id, ego, and superego are also common associations with the field. Still others will ponder whether psychology is really about consciousness, the mind, psyche, or brain—and wonder how these entities are different and similar. Somewhat less frequently, people might think not about human psychology but instead about rats running mazes, pigeons operating machinery, monkeys using sign language, salivating dogs and ringing bells, and even the mating habits of ducks and other animals. A few people might see psychology as related to machines, for indeed there is psychology involved in the design of artificial intelligence systems and in the interface shared between humans and machines, such as when hands type on a computer, fly a plane, or perform microsurgery with the use of virtual reality-type cameras. All these examples reflect psychology and its research.

Indeed, what people think of when they hear the word "psychology" can vary widely by their personal experience. For some, their first exposure to the term may be through an elective course taken in high school or college. Others may first encounter it in their jobs, when they learn that there may be business value in considering psychological angles to advertising, product development, sales, or business organization management. Similarly, others may learn about it in careers such as medicine or law, when they find that it can enhance performance or improve communication with clients, colleagues, and trainees. Artists might approach the field as a means of learning more about creativity and how to foster it. Some may come to know psychology through a personal or family crisis, possibly through exposure to a counselor or self-help book. Others may learn about the concept through films, songs, current events, or advertising portraying psychological principles or themes.

Most commonly, though, psychology is recognized as the study of human behavior. The field is advanced by the work of many individuals applying the principles of psychology in diverse settings for the purposes of teaching, research, clinical work, organizational management, administration, advocacy, data analysis, and consultation. Psychologists work in many different settings, such as universities, colleges, clinics, forensics units, the armed services, social service agencies, hospitals, research groups, laboratories, government bodies, businesses, wilderness areas, and even space. The work of psychologists has far-reaching effects for diverse peoples and in diverse settings, contributing much in terms of practical solutions to both the large and the small questions of daily life.

Psychology has deep roots in applications related to military defense, medicine, and teaching. In terms of military defense, psychology assisted the U.S. government with organizational decisions determining job assignments in the early 1900's via its development of intelligence testing strategies. As a result of creating ways of ranking soldiers for assignment from very basic to very complex work tasks, increases in efficiency were gained. Principles of psychology are also useful for the military in terms of fostering cohesion among soldiers, training and teaching them what they need to know in an efficient manner, and helping soldiers (and their families) deal with the stresses of active military duty. Additionally, the field has made contributions to understanding the psychological aspects of warfare, such as persuading one's enemies to provide information and debriefing those who have been prisoners of war.

The roots of psychology in medicine are obvious. Basic applications began as the treatment of those who were considered ill, feeble minded, or possessed by spirits. With regard to spirituality, there should be no surprise in finding a strong historical thread linking psychology and religion when it comes to healing. This link spans at least from William James's classic book *The Varieties of Religious Experience* (1902) to current efforts in the field examining spirituality as it relates to illness, healing, diagnosis, resilience against stress, and various types of group support. Historically, those not cured by other methods of medicine were usually sent to healers of the mind and spirit. At some point, psychologists were enlisted to help count and categorize such individuals. As the field developed, methods such as behavioral pharmacology grew in prominence with the discovery of new drugs to treat mental disorders. More recently, the effect of psychology in the treatment and prevention of stress-related, lifestyle-related, chronic, and terminal health problems has been noteworthy. As examples, psychological interventions related to stress management have been found useful for preventing heart disease and stroke. Obesity is often treated with behavioral interventions designed to modify lifestyle from a biopsychosocial perspective. Chronic pain is often addressed with cognitive interventions for pain perception and management. Even conditions such as cancer may be better managed with psychological interventions such as group support, family therapy, and mood-enhancing interventions that facilitate adherence to medical interventions for the body.

With regard to teaching, psychology has played a large role in the structure and design of academic settings, the development of educational curricula, achievement and intelligence testing, and career advisement and placement. It has also touched practices such as preschool for young children, the learning of new career skills later in life, retraining after injuries to the body or brain, and behavioral learning (such as how one might learn to shoot a basketball or play the piano). More recently, studies have examined Internet-based learning and how it differs from face-to-face learning. Whether on-line learning formats can be effective and whether the socialization aspects of learning can take place on-line are some of the questions pursued.

In the United States, psychology has gained a foothold in government, with psychologists being elected and appointed to public offices and serving in high-level decision-making bodies. One example is the placement of psychologists in the National Institutes of Health (NIH), where they have been able to influence government spending related to research, health care, and problem prevention on many fronts. In 1995, an office was established in the NIH called the Office of Behavioral and Social Science Research (OBSSR), with a designated role of advancing behavioral science knowledge and applications in the activities fostered and otherwise supported by the NIH.

As these many examples illustrate, psychology has become a diverse field. In looking to the future, it is clear that the role of psychology in the workplace and in international communications and relationships will expand. Notable growth has been seen, for instance, in the numbers of studies examining cultural differences among groups defined in terms of age, gender, ethnicity, race, sexual orientation, socioeconomic status, and other markers of culture. Pick virtually any area of psychological study and look at the number of references for cultural variation or differences since the mid-twentieth century, and it will be easy to spot a trend of increasing publications by year over time. This trend has been inspired by a desire to create better understanding among different cultures, as well as to assist efforts in providing more culturally appropriate and culturally sensitive training, education, and medical care. No doubt, this area of study will increase in importance as the field of psychology continues to evolve and as humans, as a group, continue to understand the ideas of conflict and cooperation as we approach nearly seven billion in number.

I hope that these volumes on psychology allow the diversity and capability of this vibrant and valuable field to shine. I also hope that it encourages its readers to be inspired, curious, and mindful observers of human behavior more and more each day, as there is much to be learned.

Nancy A. Piotrowski, Ph.D.
University of California, Berkeley

A

Ability tests

DATE: The 1890's to the present
TYPE OF PSYCHOLOGY: Learning
FIELDS OF STUDY: Ability testing

Ability testing assesses the capabilities of people who are not mentally ill in comparison to their peers, in order to identify qualities such as intelligence.

KEY CONCEPTS
- ability
- intelligence
- intelligence quotient (IQ)
- nature versus nurture
- psychometrics
- testing

INTRODUCTION

Whatever intelligence may be, the first scientific attempts to measure it were conducted by French psychologist and physician Alfred Binet (1857-1911). From 1894 until his death, he was director of the psychology laboratory at the Sorbonne. Between 1905 and 1911, Binet and his colleague Théodore Simon (c. 1873-1961) devised a series of tests that became the basis for tests in many areas. The Stanford, Herring, and Kuhlmann tests are among the revisions to Binet and Simon's tests. Alfred Binet, unlike many of his contemporaries in psychology, was interested in how normal minds work, rather than in mental illness. It was his goal to discover inherent intelligence, apart from any educational influence.

Binet came to develop his tests through observation of his daughters. He was interested in how they solved problems that he set for them. Binet noted the existence of individual differences and the fact that not all thought processes use the same operational path. Binet argued that lack of ability in specific fields was not a mental illness. There were also, he noted, different types of memory. This discovery led to his work with Simon on achievement levels for "normal" children.

His first test, carried out in 1905, asked children to follow commands, copy patterns, name objects, and put things in order or arrange them properly. Binet administered the test to students in Paris. His standard was based on his data. Thus, if 70 percent of a certain age group succeeded on a given task, those who passed at that level were at that mental age level. It was Binet who introduced the term "intelligence quotient," or IQ. IQ is the ratio of "mental age" to chronological age, with 100 being average. For example, an eight-year-old who succeeds on the ten-year-olds' test would have an IQ of $10/8 \times 100$, or 125. Soon there was a widespread enthusiasm for testing and finding IQ scores. A number of measures were introduced. The United States Army used tests to sort out recruits in World War I. The tests assessed general knowledge rather than ability on specific tasks.

Binet's tests required modifications. The first, and perhaps most famous, was the Stanford-Binet test, developed in 1916 by Lewis Terman (1877-1956). It was immediately put to use by various educational, government, and other agencies. This test is mainly based on verbal ability and uses an IQ. Terman worked to overcome the limitations of the age-scale principle of testing. He wanted to measure the full range of intelligence. There were two major shortcomings of Binet's scales in measuring adult intelligence. First, an older person's score became meaningless when divided by his or her chronological age. Terman assigned the chronological age of fifteen to everyone over sixteen. Another major defect in Binet's scales was the absence of test items to test and measure high intelligence. Terman added such items, assigning them mental ages levels up to twenty-two. This enabled Terman to measure IQs of older children and young adults.

There were additional revisions of the Stanford-Binet test. In 1937, for example, Terman and Maude

Merrill (1888-1978) published a revision of the test based on the same principles as the 1916 examination. However, they improved the selection of items and method of standardization. Merrill published another revision in 1959. These revisions have found wide acceptance, also serving as models for other individual IQ tests and a means for checking their scales.

The Wechsler scale, introduced in 1939, includes both verbal and performance measures. These scores compare an individual's intelligence with those of others of the same age to yield an IQ score. The Wechsler-Bellevue adult scale uses a derived IQ to measure the intelligence of people between the ages of seven and seventy, comparing each person's scores with standards for his or her age group. Wechsler produced two other scales, the Wechsler Intelligence Scale for Children, published in 1949, designed for children five to fifteen, and the Wechsler Adult Intelligence Scale, published in 1955, for people from sixteen to sixty-four, including a special standardization for people aged sixty to seventy-five.

Originally, IQ tests were individual tests, not group tests. However, as the military and other large organizations became involved in testing, large-scale tests were given. Individual tests tend to be more accurate, because an individual examiner is more likely to note the mood of a test taker in a one-to-one setting than in the more typical group setting. Individual tests are more likely to be administered to those who are thought to be either gifted or retarded. Group tests are more common in educational and military setting. Originally, all intelligence tests were individual tests, meaning that they were given in a one-to-one situation.

There is a good deal of dispute regarding the nature of intelligence and whether it can be measured in a quantitative fashion. Additionally, since the 1930's, there have been a number of virulent disputes regarding the role of genetics and environment in determining IQ, often termed the nature-nurture debate. Most psychologists concede that since environments are never uniform and the expression of genes is elastic, the argument for one or the other element as the sole determination of intelligence is somewhat flawed. Thus, intelligence, whatever it may be, is a function of both nature and nurture, of environment and genetic makeup.

Twin studies estimating environmental effects put genetic factors pertaining to "intelligence" at some-where below 50 percent. However, wide variation exists according to the particular characteristic of intelligence under study. Indeed, current views of intelligence hold that many different abilities comprise intelligence. The question for those who seek to measure intelligence, the process of psychometrics, is how to measure specific and general intelligence. Current views of intelligence note that there are many skills involved in both academic and professional success. For example, spatial intelligence is related to success in mathematics, science, engineering, architecture, and related fields, while it is not as important in literature or music.

PSYCHOMETRICS

A number of theories of intelligence exist: psychological measurement, often called psychometrics; cognitive psychology, the merger of cognitive psychology with conceptualism; and biologic science, which considers the neural bases of intelligence. Psychometric theories have been most concerned with the quantification of intelligence and its parts. Psychometricians generally seek to understand the structure of intelligence, that is, the forms it may take and the relationship between any parts it may have. These theories are tested through paper-and-pencil tests. These tests include analogies, classifications, and series completions.

The psychological model on which these tests are based states that intelligence is made up of abilities that mental tests measure. Each test score is based on a weighted composite of scores taken from the underlying abilities. The mathematical model is additive and assumes that less of one type of ability can be compensated for by more of another ability.

Charles Spearman (1863-1945), who put forth the first psychometric theory, published his first major article on intelligence in 1904. Spearman noted that people who do well on one mental ability test generally do well on others and conversely those who do poorly on one test tend to do poorly on others. Spearman's factor analysis enabled him to posit that there are two major factors underlying intelligence. The first and more important factor is the "general factor," or *g*. The second factor is that which is specifically related to each particular test. Spearman was not sure what *g* was, but he did posit that it was "mental energy."

L. L. Thurstone (1887-1955) disagreed with both Spearman's theory and with his isolation of a single factor of general intelligence. Thurstone argued that Spearman's misapplication of his factor method led him to find just one factor, the *g* factor. He argued that there are seven primary mental abilities underlying intelligence: verbal comprehension, verbal fluency, number, spatial visualization, inductive reasoning, memory, and perceptual speed.

Psychologists such as Philip E. Vernon (1905-1987) and Raymond B. Cattell (1905-1998) argued that in some senses both Thurstone and Spearman were correct. Their reasoning is that abilities are arranged in a hierarchy. General ability, or *g*, is at the summit. The other abilities relate to ever more specific tasks as one descends the hierarchy. Cattell went on to suggest that there are two major categories of abilities, fluid and crystallized. Fluid abilities, reasoning and problem solving, are measured by tests such as the analogies, classifications, and series completions. Crystallized abilities, derived from fluid abilities, include vocabulary, general information, and knowledge about specific fields. Most psychologists agreed that a broader subdivision of abilities was needed than was provided by Spearman, but not all of these agreed that the subdivision should be hierarchical. Other psychologists disagreed with the hierarchical ordering of abilities. The structure-of-intellect theory devised by J. P. Guilford (1897-1987), for example, postulated 120 abilities. He later increased the number to 150.

In general, it was becoming obvious to many that there were problems with psychometric theory. The number of factors had gone from 1 to more than 150. There was no satisfactory explanation given for any of these factors that explained overall intelligence.

TWIN STUDIES

Twin studies use two methods to measure the effect of nature and nurture on overall intelligence. The first method examines identical twins reared apart, and the second looks at the differences between identical twins reared together and fraternal twins reared together. Identical, or monozygotic, twins are not totally identical, because they have had different experiences and are unique social and cultural products. Fraternal twins are formed from two different fertilized eggs, just as normal siblings are. Unrelated children reared together are also studied.

Although most identical twins studied show a 50 to 80 percent genetic contribution to intelligence, a closer examination reveals identical pairs with up to a twenty-point difference in IQ scores. This occurs when environment is drastically different. The closeness of most identical twins is a result of nature and nurture; that is, the twins being raised in similar settings.

It has been reasonably obvious that many of the skills measured by IQ tests can be taught just as any other skills can be taught. If these skills can be taught, then at least part of what is measured by ability tests, including IQ tests, is learned and not inherent.

SPECIFIC ABILITY TESTS

Among the more common ability tests is the School and College Ability Test (SCAT) and the Sequential Tests of Educational Progress (STEP). The SCAT measures specific abilities in verbal and quantitative areas. It is used to make general, overall decisions about level and pace of instruction. The SCAT focuses on aptitude, not specific educational goals. The STEP battery measures actual achievement in reading, written language, and mathematics. STEP measures actual mastery and is, therefore, useful in indicating skills a student is ready to master.

Both SCAT and STEP testing can be used for in-grade-level or above-grade-level testing. In-grade-level testing provides information compared with others in the same grade, while above-grade-level testing indicates probable success or failure compared with those in higher grades.

SCAT assesses both verbal and mathematical reasoning abilities, using verbal analogies and quantitative comparison items. STEP Mathematics Computation measures a broad variety of computational skills, including operations (with whole numbers, fractions, and percents) to evaluation of formulas and manipulations with exponents. STEP Mathematics Basic Concepts measures knowledge of various concepts, including those involving numbers and operations; measurement and geometry; relations, functions, and graphs; and proofs. It also includes knowledge of probability and statistics, mathematical sentences, sets and mathematical systems, and application. STEP Reading measures the capacity to read and appreciate a multiplicity of written materials. STEP English Expression measures the aptitude to assess the accuracy and efficiency of sentences by requiring the student to perceive mistakes in grammar and usage or to decide among rewording of sentences.

The Scholastic Aptitude Test (SAT) is a widely used aptitude test that attempts to measure both intelligence and ability to undertake college studies. There are verbal and mathematical components to the test. The mean score on each test is 500, and each has a standard deviation of 100. The test was standardized on a group of ten thousand students in 1941. However, when scores dropped in the 1990's, with a verbal mean of 422 and a mathematical mean of 474, there was a readjustment of means. Educators attributed these lower scores of the student population to television and to deterioration in home and school situations.

CONTROVERSIES

IQ and other ability tests have come in for a great deal of criticism, especially since the 1960's. These controversies have centered upon the Eurocentric nature of the tests; namely, they have been designed primarily for use with white, middle-class children. The tests, therefore, have drawn fire from critics for being culture-bound. Minorities have seen them as unfair to African Americans, Latinos, and members of other minority groups. However, attempts to create culturally neutral tests have failed, and the tests have withstood court challenges. In *Pase v. Hannon*, for example, an Illinois court case, it was settled that the tests were not culturally biased and could be used to place children in special education courses.

These concerns over cultural bias, however, have raised another, related issue. That issue goes to the heart of IQ testing and concerns exactly what the tests measure. Critics argue that the tests do not measure mental abilities. The tests, they aver, do not show how children arrive at their answers, only whether they are right or wrong. Knowing how a child arrives at an answer would better allow evaluators to gauge intelligence, for those who arrive at a right answer by guessing are not necessarily more intelligent than those who get the wrong answer but whose reasoning is sound. Additionally, people from different cultural backgrounds have different but equally valid ways of approaching problems. Westernized tests do not take these skills into account.

Moreover, there is still a debate concerning the relative impact of nature and nurture on intelligence, the old heredity versus environment controversy. Those who hold for the predominant role of heredity have used comparative test results to argue

for the dominant role of genetic differences between the various ethnic groups. In the early 1970's, the published research of Nobel Prize-winning physicist William Shockley of Stanford University and educational psychologist Arthur R. Jensen of the University of California concluded that heredity accounts for most differences in intelligence between different racial groups. This conclusion caused a great controversy, matched by the publication of *The Bell Curve* (1994) by Richard Herrnstein and Charles Murray, which came to much the same conclusions: Intelligence is primarily inherited, and there are different levels of intelligence among races.

Another controversy regards the tendency of most tests to take a holistic approach to intelligence. The Stanford-Binet test, for example, sees intelligence as a unified trait. In the minds of many critics, IQ tests are designed to measure a particular type of ability defined by the ruling class. Tests are culturally biased. Therefore, scores do not reflect an objective universal pattern of intelligence. Rather intelligence is socially constructed. J. P. Guilford devised a 180-factor model of intelligence, which classified each intellectual task according to three dimensions: content, mental operation, and product. This theory is the predecessor to Howard Gardner's theory of multiple intelligence, developed since 1985.

Thanks to the influence of those social scientists who have argued for the influence of cultural differences, the tests are not the only basis for evaluating intellectual performance. There is a much greater awareness on the part of most psychologists of motivational and cultural factors in the role of development.

RESPONSE TO CRITICISM

Intelligence tests seek to measure intellectual potential by using novel items forcing test takers to think on the spot. The point is to avoid tapping factual knowledge. It is understood by psychologists that people come from different backgrounds so it is difficult if not impossible to find items that are totally novel. Therefore, test makers require test takers to use relatively common knowledge. It is impossible to control for all of a test taker's prior knowledge. Thus, intelligence scores represent a blend of potential and knowledge.

IQ tests have reliability correlations in the range of .90 and above, which is higher than most other psychological tests. This fact does not mean that variations in motivation or anxiety do not lead to misleading scores. IQ tests are also valid when used to predict success in academic work. They are, therefore, great predictors of school success, but they are not good for predicting other types of success. People, unfortunately, have acquired the belief that these tests measure a general sense of mental ability. Instead, they focus on abstract reasoning and verbal fluency, the type of skills needed for academic success. They do not measure either social or practical intelligence. IQ tests do not stabilize until adulthood, and even then they can change. There is a good correlation between high IQ scores and being in a prestigious occupation. Specific success in any given occupation, however, is not predicted in more than a mediocre way.

Thus, far from merely measuring useless things, IQ tests not only are stable, reliable, and valid but also predict academic success and occupational status. They are one good measure of giftedness and can be used with measures of creativity to aid recognition of this type of intelligence. Moreover, they can be used to place less gifted students in remedial classes.

CONCLUSION

It is essential to note that no psychological test should be used in isolation, whether that test is diagnostic of psychological and behavioral problems or of ability. Each test result needs to be compared with and used in conjunction with results from other tests. Trained psychologists need to evaluate the test results in context, whether these are diagnostic tests, intelligence tests, tests for evaluating emotional depression, or personality tests.

Much progress has been made since the era of the dominance of psychometric theories. Then, the study of intelligence was dominated by investigations of individual differences in people's test scores. Lee Cronbach, a major figure in testing, bewailed the segregation of those who study individual differences and those who seek regularities in human behavior. He made his plea for a union of these studies in an address to the American Psychological Association in 1957. His call helped lead to the development of cognitive theories of intelligence.

Use of cognitive theories has aided in interpreting the results of ability tests, for they give an understanding of the processes underlying intelligence.

These processes allow an evaluator to understand why someone may do poorly on various tests. It may not simply be a matter of poor reasoning, for example, that leads to poor performance on an analogies test. It may be that the student does not understand the words in the analogies. The different interpretations may lead to different recommendations. Someone who is good at reasoning but does not understand basic vocabulary requires an intervention that is different from that needed for someone who is a poor reasoner.

For cognitive psychologists, intelligence is a combination of a set of mental representations and a set of processes that can operate on them. Thus, ability tests based on these principles have sought to measure the speed of various types of thinking. There is, moreover, an assumption that processes are executed in a serial fashion. There are a number of cognitive theories of intelligence, but all of them assume a mental process working on a mental representation.

A number of cognitive theories of intelligence have evolved. Among them is that of Earl B. Hunt, Nancy Frost, and Clifford E. Lunneborg. In 1973, they demonstrated that psychometrics and cognitive modeling could be combined. They started with tests that experimental psychologists used to study perception, learning, and memory. Individual differences in these tests were related to patterns of individual differences in IQ scores. They concluded that basic cognitive process could be the basic components of intelligence.

New developments led other psychologists to begin with the psychometric tests themselves and to investigate the cognitive components of the skills tested on the tests. When these basic components were isolated, they could be evaluated and tested in isolation to compute their relationship with intelligence. This was done for information processing and computer modeling. Computer modeling, such as that of Allen Newell and Herbert A. Simon, uses a "means-ends analysis" to determine how close a problem is to a solution. Newell and Simon propose a general theory of problem solving.

There are a number of psychologists who hold that information processing is parallel rather than serial. They argue that the brain processes information simultaneously, not in a serial fashion. It has proved difficult to construct ability tests to test this hypothesis. Moreover, the fact that intelligence differs from one culture to another, as Michael E. Cole has argued, has been ignored in psychometric tests. Additionally, psychometric tests are not good indicators of job performance.

SOURCES FOR FURTHER STUDY

Binet, Alfred, and T. Simon. *The Development of Intelligence in Children*. 1916. Reprint. Salem, N.H.: Ayer, 1983. This volume includes reprints of many of Binet's articles on testing.

Fancher, R. E. *The Intelligence Men: Makers of the IQ Controversy*. New York: W. W. Norton, 1985. A clear discussion of the development of the IQ test and the controversies that have followed it.

Fischer, C. S., et al. *Inequality by Design*. Princeton, N.J.: Princeton University Press, 1996. Discusses how IQ and other tests help perpetuate inequality.

Garber, L. *The Milwaukee Project*. Washington, D.C.: American Association on Mental Retardation, 1988. Examines ways to improve test scores.

Herrnstein, R. J., and C. Murray. *The Bell Curve*. New York: Free Press, 1994. Controversial work on the innateness of IQ scores and the inherent inferiority of entire groups of people.

Minton, H. L. *Lewis M. Terman: Pioneer in Psychological Testing*. New York: New York University Press, 1988. A biography of the author of the Stanford-Binet test.

Plomin, R., et al. *Behavioral Genetics*. 3d ed. New York: W. H. Freeman, 1997. The role of genetics in IQ scores.

Tucker, William H. *The Science and Politics of Racial Research*. Urbana: University of Illinois Press, 1994. Looks at the misuse of science in perpetuation inequality.

Frank A. Salamone

SEE ALSO: Assessment; Career and personnel testing; Career Occupational Preference System (COPS); College entrance examinations; Creativity: Assessment; General Aptitude Test Battery (GATB); Human resource training and development; Intelligence tests; Interest inventories; Kuder Occupational Interest Survey (KOIS); Peabody Individual Achievement Test (PIAT): Race and intelligence; Scientific methods; Stanford-Binet test; Strong Interest Inventory (SII); Survey research: Questionnaires and interviews; Testing: Historical perspectives; Wechsler Intelligence Scale for Children-Third Edition (WISC-III).

Abnormality
Biomedical models

TYPE OF PSYCHOLOGY: Psychopathology
FIELDS OF STUDY: Models of abnormality

Biomedical models of abnormality examine the roles of medical, neurological, and biochemical factors in creating psychological disturbances. Psychologists have come to realize that many disturbances have a significant biomedical component or are, in some cases, primarily organic. This had led to the development of more effective biomedical therapies, such as drug therapies, for these disorders.

KEY CONCEPTS
- antidepressant drugs
- antipsychotic drugs
- biogenic amines
- cerebrospinal fluid
- differential diagnosis
- limbic system
- neurotransmitter
- primary disorder
- tranquilizers

INTRODUCTION

The study of biomedical bases for mental illnesses and their treatment is called biological psychiatry or biopsychiatry. A basic premise of biopsychiatry is that psychiatric symptoms occur in many conditions—some psychological and some medical.

Inherent in this viewpoint is a new outlook on mental illness. Faced with a patient who is lethargic, has lost his or her appetite, cannot sleep normally, and feels sad, traditional psychotherapists may diagnose him or her as suffering from one of the depressive disorders. Usually, the bias is that this illness is psychological in origin and calls for treatment with psychotherapy. Biopsychiatrists, however, see depression not as a diagnosis but as a description of the patient's condition. The task of diagnosing, of finding the underlying illness, remains to be done.

After examining the patient and performing a battery of medical tests, the biopsychiatrist may also conclude that the condition is a primary mood disorder. Further tests may reveal whether it is caused by life stresses, in which case psychotherapy is called for, or by biochemical imbalances in the brain, in which case drug therapy—perhaps in concert with psychotherapy—is called for. The medical tests may indicate that the depression is secondary to a medical condition, such as Addison's disease or cancer of the pancreas, in which case medical treatment of the primary condition is called for.

PHYSIOLOGICAL BASES OF PSYCHIATRIC CONDITIONS

An important distinction must be made between psychiatric conditions resulting from the psychological stress of having a serious illness and psychiatric conditions resulting from chemical imbalances or endocrine disturbances produced by the illness. For example, the knowledge that one has pancreatic cancer can certainly lead to depression. This is a primary mood disorder that can be treated with psychotherapy. According to Mark Gold, a leading biopsychiatrist, however, depression occurs secondarily to pancreatic cancer in up to three-quarters of patients who have the disease and may precede physical symptoms by many years. In such a case, psychotherapy not only would be pointless but also would actually put the patient's life at risk if it delayed diagnosis of the underlying cancer.

According to Gold, there are at least seventy-five medical diseases that can produce psychiatric symptoms. Among these are endocrine disorders, including diseases of the thyroid, adrenal, and parathyroid glands; disorders of the blood and cardiovascular system; infectious diseases, such as hepatitis and syphilis; vitamindeficiency diseases caused by niacin and folic acid deficiencies; temporal-lobe and psychomotor epilepsies; drug abuse and side effects of prescription drugs; head injury; brain tumors and other cancers; neurodegenerative diseases such as Alzheimer's, Huntington's, and Parkinson's diseases; multiple sclerosis; stroke; poisoning by toxic chemicals, such as metals or insecticides; respiratory disorders; and mineral imbalances.

After medical illnesses are ruled out, the psychiatric symptoms can be attributed to a primary psychological disorder. This is not to say that biomedical factors are unimportant. Compelling evidence indicates that the more severe psychotic disorders are caused by biochemical imbalances in the brain.

GENETIC PREDISPOSITIONS AND BIOCHEMICAL IMBALANCES

The evidence of genetic predispositions for schizophrenia, major depressive disorder, and manic-depressive disorder is strong. The function of genes is to regulate biochemical activity within cells, which implies that these disorders are caused by biochemical abnormalities.

Research suggests that schizophrenia, in most cases, results from an abnormality in the dopamine neurotransmitter system in the brain. All drugs that effectively treat schizophrenia block the action of dopamine, and the more powerfully they do so, the more therapeutically effective they are. Furthermore, overdoses of drugs, such as amphetamines, that strongly stimulate the dopamine system often cause a schizophrenia-like psychosis. Finally, studies show that, in certain areas of the brain in schizophrenic patients, tissues are abnormally sensitive to dopamine.

In major depressive disorders, the biogenic amine theory is strongly supported. Biogenic amines, among which are dopamine, norepinephrine, and serotonin, are neurotransmitters in the brain that are concentrated in the limbic system, which regulates emotional responses. Biogenic amines were originally implicated by the observation that drugs that deplete them in the brain, such as reserpine, frequently cause depression, whereas drugs that stimulate them, such as amphetamines, cause euphoria. Studies of cerebrospinal fluid have revealed abnormalities in the biochemical activity of these amines in some depressed patients. In many suicidally depressed patients, for example, serotonin activity in the brain is unusually low. In other depressed patients, norepinephrine or dopamine activity is deficient. These patients often respond well to antidepressant medications, which increase the activity of the biogenic amine neurotransmitter systems.

Less severe neurotic emotional disturbances may also have biochemical explanations in some patients. Research suggests that mild or moderate depressions often result from learned helplessness, a condition in which the person has learned that his or her behavior is ineffective in controlling reinforcing or punishing consequences. Experiments show that this produces depletion of norepinephrine in the brain, as do other psychological stressors that cause depression. These patients also are sometimes helped by antidepressant drugs.

Finally, many anxiety disorders may result from biochemical imbalances in the brain. Drugs that alleviate anxiety, such as Librium (chlordiazepoxide) and Valium (diazepam), have powerful effects on a brain neurotransmitter called gamma-aminobutyric acid (GABA), as do other tranquilizers, such as alcohol and barbiturates. GABA is an inhibitory neurotransmitter that acts to keep brain activity from running away with itself, so to speak. When GABA is prevented from acting, the result is agitation, seizures, and death. Positron emission tomography (PET) scans of the brains of people suffering from panic attacks show that they have abnormally high activity in a part of the limbic system called the parahippocampal gyrus, an effect that might be caused by a GABA deficiency there.

IMPROVING DIAGNOSIS AND CARE

Understanding the biomedical factors that cause illnesses with psychiatric symptoms leads directly to improved diagnoses and subsequent patient care. Numerous studies have shown that psychiatric disorders are misdiagnosed between 25 percent and 50 percent of the time, the most persistent bias being toward diagnosing medical problems as psychological illnesses. A study published in 1981 by Richard Hall and colleagues found that, of one hundred psychiatric patients admitted consecutively to a state hospital, eighty had a physical illness that required medical treatment but had not been diagnosed in preadmission screening. In twenty-eight of these patients, proper medical treatment resulted in rapid and dramatic clearing of their psychiatric symptoms. In another eighteen patients, medical treatment resulted in substantial improvement of their psychiatric conditions. In an earlier study, Hall and colleagues found that 10 percent of psychiatric outpatients—those whose conditions were not severe enough to require hospitalization—had medical disorders that caused or contributed to their psychiatric illnesses.

Psychiatric symptoms are often among the earliest warning signs of dangerous, even life-threatening, medical illnesses. Thus, proper physical evaluation and differential diagnosis, especially of patients with psychiatric symptoms not obviously of psychological origin, is critical. In other cases, psychiatric illnesses result from biochemical imbalances in the brain. In any case, patients and therapists alike must be wary of uncritically accepting after-the-fact psychological explanations. A psychological bias can all too easily become a self-fulfilling prophecy, to the detriment of the patient's health and well-being.

Hall et al. found that a medical work-up consisting of psychiatric and physical examinations, complete blood-chemistry analysis, urinalysis and urine drug screening, electrocardiogram (EKG), and electroencephalogram (EEG) successfully identified more than 90 percent of the medical illnesses present in their sample of one hundred psychiatric patients. The authors recommend that such a work-up be done routinely for all patients admitted to psychiatric hospitals.

E. Fuller Torrey makes similar recommendations for patients admitted to psychiatric hospitals because of schizophrenia. He recommends that a thorough examination should include a careful and complete medical history and mental-status examination, with assistance from family members and friends if necessary. Physical and neurological examinations are also recommended. A blood count, blood-chemical screen, and urinalysis should be done to reveal conditions such as anemia, metal poisoning, endocrine or metabolic imbalances, syphilis, and drug abuse. A computed tomography (CT) scan may be necessary to clarify suspicions of brain abnormalities. Some doctors recommend that a CT scan be done routinely to detect conditions such as brain tumors, neurodegenerative diseases, subdural hematomas (bleeding into the brain resulting from head injuries), viral encephalitis, and other conditions that might be missed upon initial neurological screening. Torrey also recommends a routine examination of cerebrospinal fluid obtained by lumbar puncture, which can reveal viral infections, brain injury, and biochemical abnormalities in the brain, and a routine electroencephalogram, which can reveal abnormal electrical activity in the brain caused by infections, inflammations, head injury, or epilepsy.

If any medical disorder is discovered, it should be treated appropriately. If this does not result in clearing the psychiatric symptoms, Torrey recommends that antipsychotic medications be given. If the initial drug trial is unsuccessful, then the dosage may have to be adjusted or another drug tried, since a patient's response to medication can be quite idiosyncratic. About 5 percent of patients react adversely to medication, in which case it may have to be discontinued.

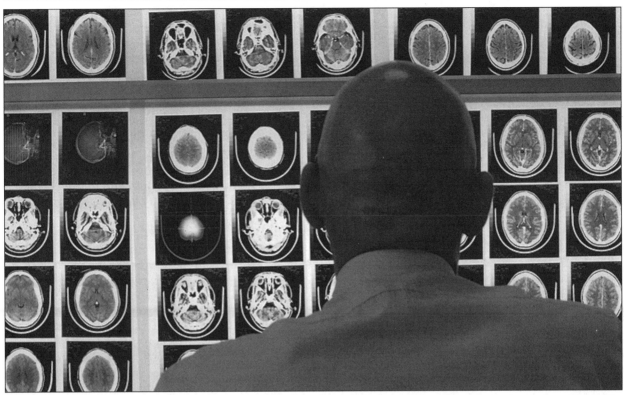

In some cases, a computed tomography (CT) scan may be recommended to rule out possible organic causes of psychiatric distress. (Digital Stock)

Mark Gold makes parallel recommendations for patients with depressive and anxiety disorders. In patients who have depressive symptoms, tests for thyroid function are particularly important. Perhaps 10 to 15 percent of depressed patients test positive for thyroid disorder. Hypothyroidism, especially before the disease is fully developed, may present only psychiatric, particularly depressive, symptoms. Hyperthyrodism may be indicated by depression, mania, or psychosis. Blood and urine screens for drug abuse are also indicated for patients with depression.

Patients who are found to have a primary mood disorder may be candidates for antidepressant drug therapy. Since responses to these medications are highly idiosyncratic, careful monitoring of patients is required. Blood tests can determine whether the drug has reached an ideally effective concentration in the body.

In some cases, even biological depressions can be treated without drugs. Seasonal affective disorder (SAD), also called winter depression, may be treated with exposure to full-spectrum lights that mimic sunlight. Studies suggest that this alters activity in the pineal gland, which secretes melatonin, a hormone that has mood-altering effects. Similarly, some depressions may result from biological rhythms that are out of synchronization. Exposure to light is often helpful in such cases, as is sleep deprivation.

In anxious patients, tests for endocrine function, especially hyperthyroidism, are called for, as are tests of the cardiovascular system and tests for drug abuse. In patients in whom no primary medical disorder is identified, the use of antianxiety medications may be indicated. Patients on medication should be closely monitored. Psychotherapy, such as behavior therapy for avoidant behaviors engendered by panic attacks and phobias, is also indicated.

As the public becomes more knowledgeable about the biomedical factors in psychiatric illnesses, malpractice lawsuits against therapists who misdiagnose these illnesses or who misapply psychotherapy and psychoactive drug therapy are becoming more common. In the future, it is likely that all manner of mental health providers will have to become more medically sophisticated and rely more on medical testing for the purpose of the differential diagnosis of illnesses presenting psychiatric symptoms.

HISTORY OF PSYCHIATRIC CARE

Theories of abnormal behavior have existed since prehistoric times. At first, these centered on supernatural forces. Behavior disturbances were thought to result from invasion by evil spirits. Treatment was likely to consist of trephining—drilling a hole in the skull to allow malevolent spirits to escape. The threat of trephination must have motivated many psychotic individuals to stay out of public view or to comply as nearly as possible with social expectations.

In the fourth century B.C.E., the Greek physician Hippocrates proposed the first rudimentary biomedical theory. He proposed that illnesses, including mental illnesses, resulted from imbalances in vital bodily fluids. His break with supernatural explanations resulted in more humane treatment of the mentally ill. Unfortunately, this trend proved to be abortive. By medieval times, theories of abnormality had reverted to demonology. Mental illness was often attributed to demoniac possession, and "treatment" was sometimes little less than torture.

The Renaissance, with its revival of learning and interest in nature, initially saw little change in this attitude. People whose behavior was considered peculiar were often accused of witchcraft or of conspiring with the devil. As knowledge of the human organism increased, however, superstitions again gave way to speculation that "insanity" resulted from physical illness or injury. The mentally ill were consigned to asylums where, it was hoped, they would be treated by physicians. In most cases, unfortunately, asylums were essentially prisons, and medical treatment, when available, was rarely effective.

Two historical movements were responsible for restoring humane treatment to the mentally ill. The first was a moral reform movement ushered in by such individuals as Philippe Pinel in France, William Tuke in England, and Dorothea Dix in America.

The second was continuing research in chemistry, biology, and medicine. By the nineteenth century, the brain was recognized as the seat of human reasoning and emotion. Once thought to be a place of supernatural happenings, the brain was finally re-

vealed to be an organ not unlike the liver. Like the liver, the brain is subject to organic disturbances, and the result of these is similarly predictable—namely, psychological abnormalities. Discovery of diseases, such as advanced syphilis, that cause brain deterioration and are characterized by psychological symptoms supported this organic model.

By the mid-twentieth century, little reasonable doubt remained that some psychological disturbances have biomedical causes. Interest centered especially on schizophrenia, major depressive disorder, and manic-depressive psychosis (later called bipolar disorder). Genetic studies strongly indicated that organic factors existed in each of these illnesses, and research was directed toward finding the biomedical fault and effecting a cure.

Paradoxically, effective treatments were found before medical understanding of the disorders was achieved. Therapeutic drugs were developed first for schizophrenia, then for depression, and finally for anxiety. These drugs proved to be important research tools, leading directly to discovery of neurotransmitter systems in the brain and helping to elucidate the biochemical nature of brain functioning. Much neuroscience research is still motivated by the desire for a better biomedical understanding of psychological disorders, which will ultimately lead to more effective treatments and patient care for these conditions.

SOURCES FOR FURTHER STUDY

Andreasen, Nancy C. *The Broken Brain: The Biological Revolution in Psychiatry.* New York: Harper & Row, 1984. An excellent introduction to biopsychiatry for the general reader. Andreasen's summary of brain structure and function, and their relationship to mood and behavior, is one of the best in a book of this type. Highly recommended.

Gold, Mark S. *The Good News About Depression: Cures and Treatments in the New Age of Psychiatry.* Rev. ed. New York: Bantam, 1995. Written in a light, easy-to-read style, this book discusses the myriad biomedical conditions that can lead to depression and describes how they can be diagnosed and treated. Especially valuable for someone who is contemplating psychiatric treatment for depression or who has a loved one who is.

_____. *The Good News About Panic, Anxiety, and Phobias.* New York: Random House, 1989. Written for the nontechnical reader, this book offers a good general summary of anxiety disorders, their diagnosis (and misdiagnosis), and their treatment. The second half deals specifically with the biopsychiatric approach to anxiety. Gold's books also include extensive bibliographies and state-by-state listings of experts in the field.

Gottesman, Irving I. *Schizophrenia Genesis: The Origins of Madness.* New York: W. H. Freeman, 1991. An excellent, well-written resource on the causes of schizophrenia that can be understood without a technical background. Highly recommended.

Torrey, E. Fuller. *Surviving Schizophrenia: A Family Manual.* 4th ed. New York: Quill, 2001. An excellent book for the general reader on schizophrenia. It should be read by everyone interested in the disorder, including every mental health worker.

Willner, Paul. *Depression: A Psychobiological Synthesis.* New York: John Wiley & Sons, 1985. This book was written for the specialist in the field but is not beyond the reach of readers with a solid background in science, especially chemistry (but keep a medical dictionary close by). The bibliography is very extensive.

William B. King

SEE ALSO: Abnormality: Legal models; Abnormality: Psychological models; Anxiety disorders; Bipolar disorder; Depression; Madness: Historical concepts; Neurons; Schizophrenia: Background, types, and symptoms; Schizophrenia: Theoretical explanations; Seasonal affective disorder.

Abnormality

Legal models

TYPE OF PSYCHOLOGY: Psychopathology
FIELDS OF STUDY: Models of abnormality

The law assumes rationality. Abnormality is a departure from this rationality, including the incapacity to have criminal intent (insanity) and the inability to understand legal responsibilities (incompetence). Legal trends in recent decades have been directed toward a more restricted use of these exemptions from rational expectations and the expansion of procedural safeguards against their abuse.

KEY CONCEPTS
- American Law Institute (ALI) rule
- civil commitment
- guilty but mentally ill verdict
- incompetency
- insanity
- M'Naghten rule
- *parens patriae*
- police power

INTRODUCTION

In the United States, three broadly based legal principles and their elaboration by judicial interpretation (case law) and by legislatures (statutory law) reflect the law's core assumptions about normal and abnormal behavior. These principles are rationality, the protection of the incompetent, and protection from the dangerous.

The first of these concerns is the importance of rational understanding. The normal person is, the law assumes, sufficiently rational that the person can base his or her choices and actions upon a consideration of possible consequences, of benefits and costs. In the civil law, two people making a contract or agreement are expected to be "competent" to understand its terms. In the criminal law, a destructive act is deemed much worse and punishable if it is intentional and deliberate. Concern about motivation extends through the normal range of illegal acts, and offenses resulting from malice (that is, intentional offenses) are generally dealt with more harshly than those that result from mere negligence. Under the civil law, those incapable of understanding simple business transactions with ordinary prudence may be deemed "incompetent." Under the criminal law, in a principle that dates back to Roman times, persons who are deprived of understanding are considered incapable of intent and the corresponding guilty mind (*mens rea*). In the words of the 1843 M'Naghten rule (named for Daniel M'Naghten, also spelled McNaughton), if the accused is laboring under such a defect of reason from a disease of the mind as not to know the nature and quality of the act he was doing, or, if he did know it, he did not know what he was doing was wrong, then this accused person is "insane" and cannot be found guilty.

Two other basic legal principles justify society's special attention to helpless people and to dangerous people. The doctrine of *parens patriae* as early as

1324 authorized King Edward II of England to protect the lands and profits of "idiots" and "lunatics." Under this doctrine, the state may appoint a guardian for the harmless but helpless mentally ill—that is, those incapable of managing their ordinary business affairs. Since the mentally incompetent cannot make an informed decision about their need for treatment, the protection of the state allows the commitment of such people to hospitals, regardless of their own wishes.

The third doctrine that has been applied to the abnormal is the police power of the state. Inherent in the very concept of a state is a duty to protect its citizens from danger to their personal safety or property. This duty is considered to include the right to remove from society those abnormal people who are dangerous and to segregate them in institutions. In the United States, the laws of all fifty states authorize the restraint and custody of persons displaying aberrant behaviors that may be dangerous to themselves or others.

These principles of law, all based upon logically derived exemptions from assumptions concerning rational intent and understanding, have changed slowly in response to influences from the public and from the mental health professions. In institutionalization decisions, the *parens patriae* power of the state became more widely used beginning in the mid-nineteenth century as judges and the public became more accepting of the mental health enterprise. Hospitals were considered protective, nonstressful environments where the harmless insane would be safe.

The insanity exemption from legal responsibility also has been adjusted and modified. The central concern of the professionals was that strict M'Naghten-rule insanity included only the small minority of offenders who had no understanding whatsoever that their offense was unlawful, the sort of offender who shot the victim thinking he was a tree. An offender could be mentally ill by psychiatric standards but still be considered sane. As a response

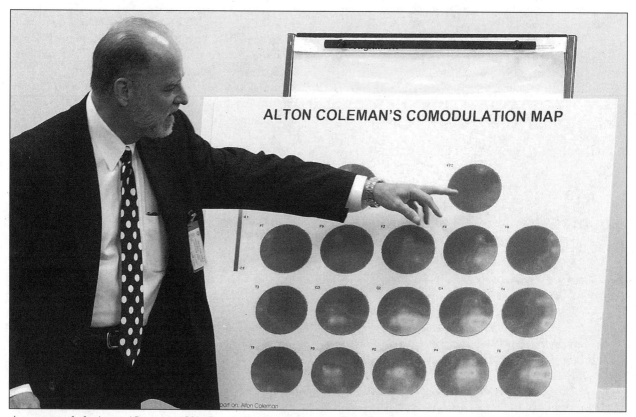

A neuropsychologist testifies at an Ohio Parole Board hearing in 2002 about the brain activity patterns of death row inmate Alton Coleman, who was executed ten days later. (AP/Wide World Photos)

to these criticisms, new legal tests that expanded the meaning of insanity were somewhat experimentally adopted by a few courts. The irresistible impulse rule, stating that a person would not be considered responsible if driven by an impulse so strong it would have occurred had there been "a policeman at his elbow," supplemented the M'Naghten rule in some states.

In 1954, the federal courts, in the case of *United States v. Durham,* adopted an even simpler rule: Insanity involves simply the illegal act being "the product of mental disease or defect." This Durham rule was quickly attacked for turning a legal decision over to mental health professionals, some of whom seemed to consider virtually all deviancy a disease. Stung by such criticisms, the federal courts, along with twenty-six states, adopted a rule proposed by the American Law Institute (the ALI rule) that seemed to incorporate aspects of each of the preceding rules: Because of mental disease or defect (Durham rule), the defendant lacks the substantial capacity to appreciate the criminality of his or her conduct (a softening of M'Naghten "know") or to conform this act to the requirements of law (the substance of the irresistible impulse test).

In endorsing an illness-caused "inability to conform to the requirements of law" as a standard for insanity, the ALI rule encouraged a definition that extended the parameters of insanity beyond those used to describe obviously disoriented people and not incidentally continued a major diagnostic role for the mental health professional.

PSYCHIATRIC SCIENCE AND LEGAL TRADITION

Legal traditions that precede by centuries the scientific study of abnormal psychology or psychiatry, therefore, mandated special legal treatment for citizens who did not meet the law's assumption of at least minimal rationality. Most people, the legal model assumed, are rational in that they can foresee the immediate consequences of their decisions. Those incompetent to comprehend a legal proceeding, those unable to care for themselves, or those unable to understand the wrongfulness of a criminal act must be treated differently. Abnormality in the legal sense was any condition that involved the incapacity to make rational decisions with an awareness of the consequences. There was a sharp dividing line between "normality" and the rare condition of abnormality. Exceptional treatment for this ex-

ceptional category, limited to the senseless acts of bizarre people, was mandated by clear principles that could be deduced from a concept of justice.

With the emergence of areas of learning that explored scientifically the same sort of cases referred to by the law, it appeared obvious to some that the new professions could aid the legal process by making more discriminating, accurate, and sensitive appraisals of these categories of individuals. In practice the concept of mental illness proved to be an elastic one. The boundaries of the concept could be easily expanded to include new conditions. In examining individuals for mental illness, one looked for the causes of their symptomatic behavior in antecedent events such as emotional trauma in childhood or chemical imbalances within the body. Once such causes were looked for, they were often found. In contrast to the legal model that interpreted such unwanted or inadequate human behavior as bad decisions willfully undertaken, the mental illness model implied that this behavior was caused by events in the past and beyond the individual's control.

The least restricted use of psychiatric standards by the law occurred in the decades of the 1950's and 1960's, when faith in the potential of the new science of psychiatry appeared unbounded. The ALI rule, by the 1960's used in federal courts throughout the United States, premised an underlying condition of mental illness manifested by a lack of control as insanity, a phrase which could easily encompass an expanding category of conditions. The thrust of theory and research during the final decades of the twentieth century involved a questioning of this mid-century optimism concerning the potential of psychiatry. Current trends reflect some retrenchment from the role of psychiatric decision making in the law with the adoption of procedural safeguards and a return to more restricted legal definitions.

CRITICISM AND DOUBTS

Theory, research, and events in the latter half of the twentieth century conspired to raise doubts about the potential of psychiatry to contribute to legal definitions. In the decades of the 1960's and 1970's, psychiatrist Thomas Szasz argued that mental illnesses were little more than metaphors for problems in living, myths that were used harmfully to deprive individuals of their feelings of responsibility. Erving

Goffman charged that institutionalization was not a health-restoring, protective sanctuary but rather a degrading, dependency-producing process. John Monahan reviewed research that suggested that the prediction of dangerousness, a primary reason for commitment to institutions, even under the best conditions involved more failures than successes.

No event was more important in stimulating public criticism of psychiatric influence upon the law than some well-publicized cases where otherwise criminal actions were defended by arguing the offender was insane. Especially influential was the acquittal by reason of insanity of presidential assailant John Hinckley in 1982. Hinckley's act had many of the characteristics of one resulting from mental illness. An aimless wanderer who had been diagnosed as schizophrenic, he shot and wounded President Ronald Reagan under the fantastic assumption this would win admiration from and a date with an actress he had never met. He was committed to a mental hospital after his trial. Nevertheless, his crime seemed premeditated and particularly heinous. The possibility he might be someday "cured" and released struck many as outrageous. In other well-publicized cases it was argued, often unsuccessfully, that otherwise criminal behavior resulted from such antecedent events as contamination by excessive television viewing, premenstrual syndrome (PMS), or hyperglycemia from eating snack cakes such as Twinkies. It appeared to many ordinary citizens that a concept so elastic as "mental illness" manifested by irrational, uncontrolled behavior could be used to excuse practically any type of crime or, in other situations, condemn practically anybody to arbitrary hospitalization.

PROCEDURAL AND DEFINITIONAL ADJUSTMENTS

As a result of such criticisms, civil commitment decisions were subject to increasing procedural safeguards. According to the illness model, such decisions should be left to the doctors, the experts who diagnosed the patient as "sick" and pronounced the patient "cured." From another perspective, however, civil commitment was more like incarceration in prison, depriving the mental patient of cherished freedoms. Increasingly, the legal system began to focus on commitment to a mental hospital in terms of the freedoms denied rather than health benefits conferred. Reasons for such enforced hospitalization were narrowed. Laws and judges demanded that

the disability had to be grave and the inability to care for oneself life-threatening before the *parens patriae* powers of the state could be invoked. "Dangerousness" increasingly meant dangers that were imminent, such as suicide or physical violence against others. Emergency detention, a loose procedure invoked during an emotional crisis, became limited in time to a few days. In the landmark decision of *Addington v. Texas* (1979), the Supreme Court decreed that civil commitment required a formal hearing, adversarial in nature. In such a hearing the prospective patient should be permitted counsel and the cross-examination of witnesses. The state must demonstrate clear and convincing evidence of the need for such commitment. Furthermore, the legislatures of most states enacted legislation requiring that inpatient hospitalization should be employed only as a last resort. Such "least restrictive alternative" laws compelled judges to consider placement of the mentally ill outside hospitals whenever possible. Outpatient commitment became common, an arrangement whereby a patient who continued to take medication was permitted to live under supervision in the community. Patients could no longer simply be warehoused in hospitals. In the case of *Wyatt v. Stickey*, the Supreme Court held that institutionalized mental patients must be actively treated.

In a similar vein, the rules concerning the determination of legal incompetency were tightened in the last decades of the twentieth century. Ordinary citizenship requires many important decisions in willing property to heirs, in handling everyday purchases, in selecting alternative medical treatments, and in standing trial for an alleged offense. Each situation requires specific abilities to appraise benefits and risks and the comprehension of specific knowledge. Few courts any longer considered an assigned diagnosis such as schizophrenia or mental retardation as sufficient evidence of incompetence in any legal situation. Legal tests for incompetence have, accordingly, focused upon the specific decision-making skills demanded in specific situations or their lack.

Procedural and definitional changes in evaluating a defendant's competence to stand trial, or adjudicative competence, offers a case in point. Such competence demands that defendants in criminal trials possess the ability to understand the charges against them, the nature of a court, the role of various participants (judge, prosecutor, defense lawyer, jury), and the consequences of being found guilty or innocent. Throughout the earlier years of the twentieth century, defendants who had been diagnosed as psychotic might be automatically considered to lack such understanding and be institutionalized for an indefinite period. By the 1980's and 1990's, the specific required understandings were investigated, often by psychologists. Tests were developed that measured quantitatively defendants' capacity to understand courtroom procedures or the lack thereof. Procedural safeguards were developed against using such incompetence as a pretext for indefinite hospitalization. The Supreme Court ruled in the case of *Jackson v. Indiana* that confinement of defendants incompetent to stand trial could last only for a limited period necessary to determine whether such competence could be restored. Thereafter, if competence was restored, defendants should stand trial. Otherwise, they must be formally committed or released.

Similar trends occurred in the criminal law, where definitions of insanity narrowed and the conditions under which an insanity defense could be employed were restricted. No matter that the insanity defense is employed in only about 1 percent of criminal cases, that most contested attempts to employ this defense fail, and that many cases involve defendants so clearly impaired that they are uncontested by the prosecution. No matter that most defendants decreed insane spend many years in mental hospitals. Because of a very few, highly publicized cases such as that of Hinckley, public opinion moved sharply to a concern that the insanity defense was a convenient loophole permitting wealthy defendants to escape punishment as "mentally ill." Closing this loophole became of public concern.

In 1984, Congress enacted the Insanity Defense Reform Act, which removed the "inability to conform to the requirements of law" phrase from the definition of insanity and returned to the narrower "inability to appreciate the wrongfulness of one's acts" of the M'Naghten rule. This act further specified that only in cases of a severe mental illness could an insanity defense be considered. The Insanity Defense Reform Act applied to the federal courts. The scope of the insanity defense was reduced by at least twelve states in another way. These states added a "guilty but mentally ill" alternative to strict M'Naghten-rule insanity. Under this alternative, mentally ill but not "insane" defendants might serve part of their sentence in a hospital rather than a prison.

Only institutional placement, not the length of the sentence, would be affected by the presence of mental illness or its cure. It was presumed that juries, with an alternative way to treat a defendant with an obvious mental illness, would reserve insanity verdicts for only the most extreme cases.

PSYCHOLOGY IN THE SERVICE OF LAW

All in all, the era of the law's enchantment with the science of abnormal psychology seems to be over. Forensic psychologists and psychiatrists remain important to the law's functioning. Yet their own concepts applied in diagnosing specific conditions of mental illness have receded in importance as legal safeguards have reduced their discretion. Ancient legal principles have endured much as they did the centuries before. The law's allegiance to its assumption of a rational citizen who makes rational decisions endures. Necessary exceptions to this rule also endure. Citizens incompetent to make legal decisions or citizens too much prisoners of their delusions to know the difference between right and wrong continue to be treated as special cases. In 2002, the U.S. Supreme Court ruled that it was unconstitutional to execute mentally retarded murderers. Forensic scientists are essential in operationalizing these conditions and in applying the legal rules to individual cases, but they function within the legal framework as servants of the law.

SOURCES FOR FURTHER STUDY

Bartol, Curt R., and Anne M. Bartol. *Psychology and Law: Research and Application.* Belmont, Calif.: Wadsworth, 1994. Like other law and psychology texts, competence, civil commitment, and insanity issues are discussed. Particularly strong in its treatment of the legal traditions and the philosophical rationale for current legal rules.

Borum, R. "Improving the Clinical Practice of Violence Risk Assessment." *American Psychologist* 51 (1996): 945-956. A major article reviewing psychological research on the prediction of "dangerousness." Using the right indicators, the research suggests, future violent behavior can be predicted above chance levels.

Davison, Gerald C., and John M. Neale. *Abnormal Psychology.* 8th ed. New York: John Wiley & Sons, 2001. Many, if not most, college textbooks on abnormal psychology have a chapter that discusses in summary fashion the law pertaining to psychological abnormality. The first part of chapter 18 offers a discussion of competency, insanity, and civil commitment issues.

Elliot, Carl. *The Rules of Insanity: Moral Responsibility and the Mentally Ill Offender.* Albany: State University of New York Press, 2000. An extensive discussion of the philosophical and ethical issues that underlie the rules of insanity. Written by a physician. The philosophical issues are related to actual cases.

Gaylin, Willard. *The Killing of Bonnie Garland.* New York: Penguin, 1982. A passionate and well-written discussion of an actual case in which the alleged mental illness of the defendant was the primary issue. A sensitive presentation of the various views of participants and of those from varying philosophical perspectives.

Melton, Gary B., J. P. Petula, G. Norman, and C. Slobogin. *Psychological Evaluation for the Courts: A Handbook for Mental Health Professionals and Lawyers.* 2d ed. New York: Guilford, 1997. An extremely comprehensive review of the current state of the mental health law. Covers legal commitment, mental competence, and civil commitment with special thoroughness.

Wrightsman, Lawrence S., Edie Greene, Michael T. Nietzel, and William H. Fortune. *Psychology and the Legal System.* 5th ed. Belmont, Calif.: Wadsworth, 2002. A standard college-level text on the law and psychology. Chapter 11, "Forensic Assessment in Criminal Cases," and chapter 12, "Forensic Assessment in Civil Cases," cover the issues with reference to actual cases.

Thomas E. DeWolfe

SEE ALSO: Abnormality: Biomedical models; Abnormality: Psychological models; Law and psychology.

Abnormality

Psychological models

TYPE OF PSYCHOLOGY: Psychopathology; psychotherapy

FIELDS OF STUDY: Behavioral and cognitive models; evaluating psychotherapy; humanistic-phenomenological models; models of abnormality

Abnormal behavior is typically defined as behavior that is harmful to the self or others and/or that is dysfunctional. Three models of abnormality stress medical or biological roots; psychological aspects, such as unconscious conflicts, inappropriate learning, blocking of full development, or maladaptive thoughts; and social and cultural context.

KEY CONCEPTS
- behavioral model
- cognitive model
- humanistic model
- medical model
- psychoanalytic model
- sociocultural model

INTRODUCTION

Prehistoric humans believed that evil spirits, witchcraft, the full moon, or other supernatural forces caused mental disorders. In modern times, people have more naturalistic ideas. The models of abnormality can be divided into three types: medical, psychological, and cultural. Medical models hold that mental disorders take on a psychological appearance, but the underlying problems are physical in nature. Psychological models hold that mental disorders are caused and then maintained by a person's past and present life experiences, which can result in inner conflicts, learned responses that are problematic, blocked efforts to grow and achieve self-actualization, or pessimistic, distorted thinking. Cultural models stress the sociocultural context of stress.

MEDICAL MODELS OF ABNORMALITY

Medical or biological models of abnormality stem back to Greek physician Hippocrates (c. 470-c. 377 B.C.E.), who proposed that psychological disorders are caused by body-fluid imbalances. Greeks believed that uterus could move around a woman's body, attaching itself at different places and causing the symptoms of hysteria, a disorder in which a person has physical symptoms without the usual organic causes.

The medical model gained support when people realized that some bizarre behaviors were due to brain damage and other identifiable physical causes. For example, people with scars in certain areas of the brain may have seizures. Also, people who contract the sexually transmitted disease syphilis, which is caused by microorganisms, can develop aberrant behavior ten to twenty years after the initial infection. Syphilis moves through the body and attacks different organs, sometimes the brain.

In contemporary times, biological researchers use modern research techniques to explore the brain chemistries of mentally disturbed people. They suspect that changes in the workings of neurotransmitters may contribute to many psychological disorders. For example, depression can be associated with abnormally low levels of norepinephrine and serotonin.

The medical model of abnormality is pervasive and can been seen in the language that is often used to describe mental problems. In this language, a patient is diagnosed with a mental disorder. This illness needs treatment that might include hospitalization and therapy to relieve symptoms and produce a cure.

The medical model ushered in humane treatment for people who hitherto had been persecuted as agents of the devil. Some of the advances in treatment for psychological problems include antipsychotic medication, which can reduce hallucinations and help a person with schizophrenia avoid hospitalization; lithium, which can moderate the debilitating mood extremes of bipolar disorder; antidepressants, which can relieve the chronic pain of depression; and antianxiety drugs, which can relieve the acute stress of anxiety disorders. These kinds of advances help the day-to-day lives of many people.

Also, the medical model has focused research attention on the genetic inheritance of mental illness. One way to study the genetic basis of behavior is to compare identical twins and fraternal twins. An identical twin of a schizophrenic who was adopted into an entirely different family and never even met the other twin is still twice as likely to be schizophrenic as a person identified randomly from the general population. Another way to study the genetic basis of behavior is to compare adopted children to their adoptive parents and to their biological parents. Using these types of research, scientists have implicated heredity in a number of mental disorders, including schizophrenia, depression, and alcoholism.

However, it may not be appropriate to view all psychological disorders in medical terms. Some disorders can be directly tied to life experiences. Also, the medical model has promoted the idea that people who behave abnormally are not responsible for their actions. They are mentally sick, therefore not in control of themselves. Some people disagree with this notion. In *The Myth of Mental Illness* (1961), American psychiatrist Thomas Szasz argued that mental illness is a socially defined, relative concept that is used to cast aside people who are different. In 1987, Szasz charged psychologists, psychiatrists, and other mental health professionals with being too quick to guard society's norms and values, and too slow to take care of the people who are in some way different. Further, Szasz claimed that the label "sick" invites those with problems to become passively dependent on doctors and drugs rather than relying on their own inner strengths.

PSYCHOLOGICAL MODELS OF ABNORMALITY

The psychological model of abnormality also stems from ancient Greece. In the second century C.E., the Greek physician Galen described a patient whose symptoms were caused either by an inflammation of the uterus or by something about which she was troubled but which she was not willing to discuss. He tested these two hypotheses and concluded that the patient's problem was psychological in origin.

The psychological model gained support when French physician Jean-Martin Charcot (1825-1893) used hypnosis to distinguish hysterical paralysis (with no organic cause) from neurologically based paralysis. When Charcot hypnotized patients, those with hysterical paralysis could use their supposedly paralyzed body part. One of his students, Austrian physician Sigmund Freud (1856-1939), expanded this approach. Freud and others believed that mental disorders usually begin with a traumatic event in childhood and can be treated with psychotherapy, a form of "talking cure." Today, there are four main psychological models of abnormality: psychoanalytic, behavioral, humanistic, and cognitive.

PSYCHOANALYTIC MODEL. A psychoanalytic model, stemming from Freud, emphasizes the role of parental influences, unconscious conflicts, guilt, frustration, and an array of defense mechanisms that people use, unconsciously, to ward off anxiety. According to this view, people develop psychological problems because they have inner conflicts intense enough to overwhelm their normal defenses.

Freud thought that all people have some aspects of their personality that are innate and self-preserving (the id), some aspects of their personality that are learned rules or conscience (the superego), and some aspects of their personality that are realistic (the ego). For example, the id of a person who is hungry wants to eat immediately, in any manner, regardless of the time or social conventions. However, it may be time to meet with the supervisor for an important review. The superego insists on meeting with the supervisor right now, for as long as necessary. The ego may be able to balance personal needs and society's requirements by, for example, bringing bagels for everyone to the meeting with the supervisor. People must somehow harmonize the instinctual and unreasoning desires of the id, the moral and restrictive demands of the superego, and the rational and realistic requirements of the ego.

Conflicts between the id, ego, and superego may lead to unpleasant and anxious feelings. People develop defense mechanisms to handle these feelings. Defense mechanisms can alleviate anxiety by staving off the conscious awareness of conflicts that would be too painful to acknowledge. A psychoanalytic view is that everyone uses defense mechanisms, and abnormality is simply the result of overblown defense mechanisms.

Some of the most prominent defense mechanisms are repression, regression, displacement, reaction formation, sublimation, and projection. In repression, a person forgets something that causes anxiety. For example, a student who genuinely forgets her meeting with her professor about a make-up test has repressed the appointment. In regression, a person reverts back to activities and feelings of a younger age. For example, a toddler who reclaims his old discarded bottle when a new baby sister comes on the scene is regressing. In displacement, a person has very strong feelings toward one person but feels for some reason unable to express them. Subsequently, she finds herself expressing these feelings toward a safer person. For example, a person who is extremely angry with her boss at work may keep these feelings to herself until she gets home but then find herself very angry with her husband, children, and pets. In reaction formation, people have very strong feelings that are somehow unacceptable, and they react in the opposite way. For example, a person who is campaigning against adult bookstores in the community may be secretly fascinated with pornography. In sublimation, a person rechannels energy, typically sexual energy, into socially acceptable outlets. For example, a woman who is attracted to the young men in swimsuits at the pool may decide to swim one hundred laps. In projection, people notice in others traits or behaviors that are too painful to admit in themselves. For example, a person who is very irritated by his friend's whining may have whining tendencies himself that he cannot admit. All defense mechanisms are unconscious ways to handle anxiety.

The psychoanalytic model opened up areas for discussion that were previously taboo and helped people to understand that some of their motivations are outside their own awareness. For example, dissociative disorders occur when a person's thoughts and feelings are dissociated, or separated, from conscious awareness by memory loss or a change in identity. In dissociative identity disorder, formerly termed multiple personality, the individual alternates between an original or primary personality and one or more secondary or subordinate personalities. A psychoanalytic model would see dissociative identity disorder as stemming from massive repression to ward off unacceptable impulses, particularly those of a sexual nature. These yearnings increase during adolescence and adulthood, until the person finally expresses them, often in a guilt-inducing sexual act. Then, normal forms of repression are ineffective in blocking out this guilt, so the person blocks the acts and related thoughts entirely from consciousness by developing a new identity for the dissociated bad part of self.

The psychoanalytic model views all human behavior as a product of mental or psychological causes, though the cause may not be obvious to an outside observer, or even to the person performing the behavior. Psychoanalytic influence on the modern perspective of abnormality has been enormous. Freudian concepts, such as Freudian slips and unconscious motivation, are so well known that they are now part of ordinary language and culture. However, the psychoanalytic model has been criticized because it is not verifiable, because it gives complex explanations when simple and straightforward ones are sufficient, because it cannot be proven wrong (lacks disconfirmability), and because it was based mainly on a relatively small number of upper-middle-class European patients and on Freud himself.

BEHAVIORAL MODEL. A behavioral model, or social-learning model, stemming from American psychologists such as John B. Watson (1878-1958) and B. F. Skinner (1904-1990), emphasizes the role of the environment in developing abnormal behavior. According to this view, people acquire abnormal behavior in the same ways they acquire normal behavior, by learning from rewards and punishments they either experience directly or observe happening to someone else. Their perceptions, expectations, values, and role models further influence what they learn. In this view, a person with abnormal behavior has a different reinforcement history from that of others.

The behavioral model of abnormality stresses classical conditioning, operant conditioning, and modeling. In classical conditioning, a child might hear a very loud sound immediately after entering the elevator. Thereafter, this child might develop a phobia of elevators and other enclosed spaces. In operant conditioning, a mother might give the child a cookie to keep him quiet. Soon, the child will notice that when he is noisy and bothersome, his mother gives him cookies and will develop a pattern of temper tantrums and other conduct disorders. In modeling, the person might notice that her mother is very afraid of spiders. Soon, she might develop a phobia of spiders and other small creatures.

The behavioral model advocates a careful investigation of the environmental conditions in which people display abnormal behavior. Behaviorists pay special attention to situational stimuli, or triggers, that elicit the abnormal behavior and to the typical consequences that follow the abnormal behavior. Behaviorists search for factors that reinforce or encourage the repetition of abnormal behaviors.

The behavioral model helped people realize how fears become associated with specific situations and the role that reinforcement plays in the origin and maintenance of inappropriate behaviors. However, this model ignores the evidence of genetic and biological factors playing a role in some disorders. Further, many people find it difficult to accept the view of human behavior as simply a set of responses to environmental stimuli. They argue that human beings have free will and the ability to choose their situation, as well as how they will react.

HUMANISTIC MODEL. A humanistic model, stemming from American psychologist Carl Rogers (1902-1987) and others, emphasizes that mental disorders arise when people are blocked in their efforts to grow and achieve self-actualization. According to this view, the self-concept is all-important and

people have personal responsibility for their actions and the power to plan and choose their behaviors and feelings.

The humanistic model stresses that humans are basically good and have tremendous potential for personal growth. Left to their own devices, people will strive for self-actualization. However, people can run into roadblocks. Problems will arise if people are prevented from satisfying their basic needs or are forced to live up to the expectations of others. When this happens, people lose sight of their own goals and develop distorted self-perceptions. They feel threatened and insecure and are unable to accept their own feelings and experiences. Losing touch with one's own feelings, goals, and perceptions forms the basis of abnormality. For example, parents may withhold their love and approval unless a young person conforms to their standards. In this case, the parents are offering conditional positive regard. This causes children to worry about such things as, "What if I do not do as well on the next test?" "What if I do not score in the next game?" and "What if I forget to clean my room?" In this example, the child may develop generalized anxiety disorder, which includes chronically high levels of anxiety. What the child needs for full development of maximum potential, according to the humanistic view, is unconditional positive regard.

American psychologist Abraham Maslow (1908-1970) and other humanistic theorists stress that all human activity is normal, natural, rational, and sensible when viewed from the perspective of the person who is performing the behavior. According to this model, abnormality is a myth. All abnormal behavior would make sense if we could see the world through the eyes of the person who is behaving abnormally.

The humanistic model has made useful contributions to the practice of psychotherapy and to the study of consciousness. However, the humanistic model restricts attention to immediate conscious experience, failing to recognize the importance of unconscious motivation, reinforcement contingencies, future expectations, biological and genetic factors, and situational influences. Further, contrary to the optimistic self-actualizing view of people, much of human history has been marked by wars, violence, and individual repression.

COGNITIVE MODEL. A cognitive model, stemming from American psychologists Albert Ellis and Donald Meichenbaum, American psychiatrist Aaron Beck, and others, finds the roots of abnormal behavior in the way people think about and perceive the world. People who distort or misinterpret their experiences, the intentions of those around them, and the kind of world where they live are bound to act abnormally.

The cognitive model views human beings as thinking organisms that decide how to behave, so abnormal behavior is based on false assumptions or unrealistic situations. For example, Sally Smith might react to getting fired from work by actively searching for a new job. Sue Smith, in contrast, might react to getting fired from work by believing that this tragedy is the worst possible thing that could have happened, something that is really awful. Sue is more likely than Sally to become anxious, not because of the event that happened but because of what she believes about this event. In the cognitive model of abnormality, Sue's irrational thinking about the event (getting fired), not the event itself, caused her abnormal behavior.

Beck proposed that depressed people have negative schemas about themselves and life events. Their reasoning errors cause cognitive distortions. One cognitive distortion is drawing conclusions out of context, while ignoring other relevant information. Another cognitive distortion is overgeneralizing, drawing a general rule from one or just a few isolated incidents and applying the conclusion broadly to unrelated situations. A third cognitive distortion is dwelling on negative details while ignoring positive aspects. A fourth cognitive distortion is thinking in an "all-or-nothing" way. People who think this way categorize experiences as either completely good or completely bad, rather than somewhere in between the two extremes. A fifth cognitive distortion is having automatic thoughts, negative ideas that emerge quickly and spontaneously, and seemingly without voluntary control.

The cognitive and behavioral models are sometimes linked and have stimulated a wealth of empirical knowledge. The cognitive model has been criticized for focusing too much on cognitive processes and no enough on root causes. Some also see it as too mechanistic.

The cognitive model proposes that maladaptive thinking causes psychological disorders. In contrast, the psychoanalytic model proposes that unconscious conflicts cause psychological disorders; the humanistic model proposes that blocking of full development causes psychological disorders; and the behavioral model proposes that inappropriate conditioning causes psychological disorders. These psychological models of abnormality stress the psychological variables that play a role in abnormal behavior.

SOCIOCULTURAL MODELS OF ABNORMALITY

A sociocultural model of abnormality emphasizes the social and cultural context, going so far as to suggest that abnormality is a direct function of society's criteria and definitions for appropriate behavior. In this model, abnormality is social, not medical or psychological. For example, early Greeks revered people who heard voices that no one else heard because they interpreted this phenomenon as evidence of divine prophecy. In the Middle Ages, people tortured or killed people who heard voices because they interpreted this same proclivity as evidence of demonic possession or witchcraft. Today, people treat those who hear voices with medicine and psychotherapy because this symptom is viewed as evidence of schizophrenia.

Social and cultural context can influence the kinds of stresses people experience, the kinds of disorders they are likely to develop, and the treatment they are likely to receive. Particularly impressive evidence for a social perspective is a well-known study, "On Being Sane in Insane Places"(1973) by American psychologist David Rosenhan. Rosenhan arranged for eight normal people, including himself, to arrive at eight different psychiatric hospitals under assumed names and to complain of hearing voices repeating innocuous words such as "empty," "meaningless," and "thud." These pseudopatients responded truthfully to all other questions except their names. Because of this single symptom, the hospital staff diagnosed all eight as schizophrenic or manic-depressive and hospitalized them. Although the pseudopatients immediately stopped reporting that they heard voices and asked to be released, the hospitals kept them from seven to fifty-two days, with an average of nineteen days. When discharged, seven of the eight were diagnosed with schizophrenia "in remission," which implies that they were still schizophrenic but simply did not show signs of the illness at the time of release. The hospital staff, noticing that these people took notes, wrote hospital chart entries such as "engages in writing behaviors." No staff member detected that the pseudopatients were normal people, though many regular patients suspected as much. The context in which these pseudopatients behaved (a psychiatric hospital) controlled the way in which others interpreted their behavior.

Particularly impressive evidence for a cultural perspective comes from the fact that different types of disorders appear in different cultures. Anorexia nervosa, which involves self-starvation, and bulimia nervosa, which involves binge eating followed by purging, primarily strike middle- and upper-class women in Westernized cultures. In Western cultures, women may feel particular pressure to be thin, and have negatively distorted images of their own bodies. Amok, a brief period of brooding followed by a violent outburst that often results in murder, strikes Navajo men and men in Malaysia, Papua New Guinea, the Philippines, Polynesia, and Puerto Rico. In these cultures, this disorder is frequently triggered by a perceived insult. Pibloqtoq, a brief period of extreme excitement that is often followed by seizures and coma lasting up to twelve hours, strikes people in Arctic and Subarctic Eskimo communities. The person may tear off his or her clothing, break furniture, shout obscenities, eat feces, and engage in other acts that are later forgotten. As researchers examine the frequency and types of disorders that occur in different societies, they note some sharp differences not only between societies but also within societies as a function of the decade being examined and the age and gender of the individuals being studied.

The sociocultural model of abnormality points out that other models fail to take into account cultural variations in accepted behavior patterns. Understanding cross-cultural perspectives on abnormality helps in better framing questions about human behavior and interpretations of data. Poverty and discrimination can cause psychological problems. Understanding the context of the abnormal behavior is essential.

The medical, psychological, and sociocultural models of abnormality represent profoundly different ways of explaining and thus treating people's problems. They cannot be combined in a simple way because they often contradict each other. For example, a biological model asserts that depression is due to biochemistry. The treatment, therefore, is medicine to correct the imbalance. In contrast, a behavioral model asserts that depression is learned. The treatment, therefore, is changing the rewards

and punishers in the environment so that the person unlearns the old, bad habits and learns new healthy habits.

One attempt to integrate the different models of abnormality is called the diathesis-stress model of abnormality. It proposes that people develop disorders if they have a biological weakness (diathesis) that predisposes them to the disorder when they encounter certain environmental conditions (stress). The diathesis-stress approach is often used to explain the development of some forms of cancer: a biological predisposition coupled with certain environmental conditions. According to this model, some people have a predisposition that makes them vulnerable to a disorder such as schizophrenia. They do not develop schizophrenia, however, unless they experience particularly stressful environmental conditions.

It is unlikely that any single model can explain all disorders. It is more probable that each of the modern perspectives explains certain disorders and that any single abnormal behavior has multiple causes.

SOURCES FOR FURTHER STUDY

Alloy, Lauren B., Neil S. Jacobson, and Joan Acocella. *Abnormal Psychology: Current Perspectives.* 8th ed. Boston: McGraw-Hill, 1999. This comprehensive textbook discusses the medical (biological), psychodynamic (psychoanalytic), and cognitive models of abnormality.

American Psychiatric Association. *Diagnostic and Statistical Manual of Mental Disorders: DSM-IV-TR.* Rev. 4th ed. Washington, D.C.: Author, 2000. This listing of all psychological disorders includes for each a description, associated features and disorders, prevalence, course, and differential diagnosis. It is revised every five to ten years as new information becomes available.

Gotlib, I. H., and C. L. Hammen. *Psychological Aspects of Depression: Toward a Cognitive-Interpersonal Integration.* New York: John Wiley & Sons, 1992. This book provides a summary of the symptoms of depression as well as theoretical explanations.

Gottesman, Irving I. *Schizophrenia Genesis: The Origins of Madness.* New York: W. H. Freeman, 1991. Gottesman, an active researcher in the field of schizophrenia, wrote this book for nonprofessionals interested in schizophrenia, and included first-person accounts written by people diagnosed with schizophrenia.

Kesey, Ken. *One Flew over the Cuckoo's Nest.* New York: Viking, 1962. This novel, and the 1975 film based on it, made the point that psychiatric diagnosis and treatment can be used to control behavior considered undesirable in a hospital and yet healthy from other perspectives.

Rosenhan, David L. "On Being Sane in Insane Places." *Science* 179 (1973): 250-258. The original report of a classic study of the effect that context has on perceptions of behavior.

Lillian M. Range

SEE ALSO: Abnormality: Biomedical models; Behavioral assessment; Borderline personality; Feminist psychotherapy; Histrionic personality; Narcissistic personality; Psychoanalytic psychology; Psychosexual development.

Achievement motivation

TYPE OF PSYCHOLOGY: Motivation
FIELDS OF STUDY: Motivation theory; personality theory; social motives

The study of achievement motivation examines crucial ingredients in the accomplishment of desirable goals. Studies have included a wide variety of domains, providing new insights into academic achievement, economic and other work-related achievement, gender and ethnic differences regarding achievement orientation, and individual personality differences.

KEY CONCEPTS
• academic success
• achievement motivation
• achievement need
• expectancy-value theory
• explanatory style theory
• extrinsic motivation
• goal orientation
• intrinsic motivation
• locus of control
• trait theory

INTRODUCTION

Achievement motivation can be understood simply as the tendency to strive for success or to attain a desirable goal. Embedded within this definition are a number of important implications. First, it is suggested that achievement motivation involves an inclination on the part of the individual. Historically, this included a consideration of the individual's personality and how that personality influences a motivational state, given the presence of certain environmental factors. Since the 1980's, the focus of achievement motivation research has shifted from individual differences in personality to the cognitive, situational, and contextual determinants of achievement. Second, achievement usually involves a task-oriented behavior that can be evaluated. Third, the task orientation usually involves some standard of excellence that may be either internally or externally imposed.

Henry A. Murray, in his influential book *Explorations in Personality* (1938), conceived of personality as a series of needs which involve a "readiness to respond" in certain ways under specific conditions. One of these needs is the need for achievement. He defined the need as a desire or tendency to "overcome obstacles, to exercise power, to strive to something difficult as well as and as quickly as possible." Thus, achievement is a generalized need. Like many later motivational theorists, Murray argued that the pleasure of achievement is not in attaining the goal but rather in developing and exercising skills. In other words, it is the process that provides the motivation for achievement. David McClelland and his many associates at Harvard University have furthered the idea of needs in over four decades' worth of work in learned needs theory. McClelland argues that people, regardless of culture or gender, are driven by three motives: achievement, affiliation, and influence. The need for achievement is characterized by the wish to find solutions to problems, master complex tasks, set goals, and obtain feedback on their level of success. McClelland proposed that these needs were socially acquired or learned.

John Atkinson, who collaborated with McClelland in some early work, developed a distinctively cognitive theory of achievement motivation that still retained the basic ideas of McClelland's theory, that people select and work toward goals because they have an underlying need to achieve. Atkinson made two important additions. First, he argued that the achievement motive is determined by two opposing inclinations: a tendency to approach success and a tendency to avoid failure. The first tendency is manifested by engaging in achievement-oriented activities, while the second tendency is manifested by not engaging in such activities. Second, Atkinson suggested that these two fundamental needs interact with expectations (the perceived probability of success or failure of the action) and values (the degree of pride in accomplishment versus the degree of shame in failure).

Several modifications were subsequently offered by Atkinson and others. For example, an important distinction between extrinsic motivation (engagement in a task for an external reward, such as a school grade or a pay raise) and intrinsic motivation (engagement in a task as a pleasure in its own right, with some standard of performance as a goal in itself) was developed to explain why some people may still engage in achievement activities, such as attending school or accepting a demanding job, even when their tendency to avoid failure is greater than their tendency to approach success.

Bernard Weiner's *Explanatory Style Theory* (1972) grows out of the observation that people have different explanations for success and failure. He postulates that success and failure at achievement tasks may be attributed to any of four factors: ability, effort, task difficulty, and luck. These four factors can be classified along two dimensions: locus of control (internal versus external) and stability (stable versus unstable). Internals believe that their successes and failures result from their own actions. Whether they succeed or fail, they attribute the outcome to their ability or to the effort they expended. Externals, in contrast, tend to believe that success or failure is beyond their control. They succeed because they had an easy task or they were lucky. They fail because they had a difficult task or were unlucky.

In *Self-Theories* (1999), Carol Dweck and her associates suggested that differences in achievement can be understood through the implicit theories that people have about the origins of their competency. People who adopt a performance orientation tend to attribute their successes and failures to unchanging personal traits such as ability. They also tend to pursue extrinsic rewards. People who adopt a mastery orientation tend focus less on ability and more on the process of overcoming obstacles and solving problems. They tend to find internal rewards very appealing and seek out and enjoy the challenge posed by difficult tasks.

PRACTICAL ACHIEVEMENT

Achievement motivation is an important psychological concept, and it is useful in explaining why some people are more successful in attaining goals than are others. In general, people with a higher need for achievement, people with a more internal locus of control, and people who pursue mastery goals tend to do better than their performance-oriented, external-locus-of-control, low-achievement-need counterparts.

McClelland, Dweck, and Weiner and their associates have studied the relation between achievement motivation and academic and vocational performance. Their conclusions are remarkably similar. High achievement motivation is generally a desirable trait that leads to more successful performance. Students who are higher in achievement motivation maintain higher grades, enjoy school and academic challenges more, and show greater persistence than students with low achievement motivation. In business, it appears that entrepreneurs require a high need for achievement to function successfully.

One of the most interesting applications in the study of achievement motivation has involved gender differences. Women and men may experience achievement motivation in considerably different ways. Most of the research conducted by McClelland and Atkinson during the 1950's and 1960's was with men only, in part on the basis of the belief that men need success and women need approval. With women's changing roles in society, however, the study of achievement motivation in women has flourished since the late 1960's.

Early research indicated that women show less need for achievement than do men. One explanation was derived from Atkinson's expectancy-value model, which suggested that women fear success out of concern for the negative social consequences they may experience if they achieve too much. An example would be a girl who lets her boyfriend win when they play tennis. In part, she may be concerned about his feelings, but she may also believe that she will be better accepted (by him and others) if she loses. While it is clear that some people, especially some women, may not find as much delight in winning as do others, subsequent research has suggested that some of the original conclusions may have been overstated. In fact, in terms of Janet Spence and Robert Helmreich's three-factor model of achievement motivation, it appears that the structure of men's and women's achievement motives are more similar than they are different. When sex differences do emerge, women tend to be slightly higher than men in work orientation, while men seem to be slightly higher in mastery and considerably higher in competitiveness.

Another interesting application has centered on ethnic differences in achievement. It has commonly been noted that children from ethnic minority groups perform much lower than average in a variety of achievement-oriented measures. These findings are frequently presented in terms of "deficits." The central comparison group is middle-class white students. Much of this work is confounded by a failure to consider socioeconomic status. When ethnicity and socioeconomic status are investigated in the same study, social class is a far better predictor of achievement than ethnicity. Further research suggests that encouraging low socioeconomic ethnic minority children to pursue mastery goals leads to improvements in academic success.

McClelland has also attempted to demonstrate the potential benefits of increasing achievement motivation in certain populations. Through various educational programs, increasing achievement motivation has helped raise the standard of living for the poor, has helped in the control of alcoholism, and has helped make business management more effective. McCelland has also developed, with apparent success, an elaborate program designed to increase achievement motivation among businesspeople, especially in so-called Third World countries.

HISTORIC ACHIEVEMENT

The study of achievement motivation grew out of two separate perspectives in the study of personality. The first perspective is the psychoanalytic tradition of Sigmund Freud (1856-1939). Henry Murray was a committed Freudian in his theory of personality, stressing an unconscious dynamic interaction of three personality components: the id, the ego, and the superego. Psychoanalytic thought stresses the similarity of motives among all people by focusing on these driving forces from the unconscious domain of the personality. Murray's contribution to the psychoanalytic tradition is the concept of need, which is understood as an entity that unconsciously organizes one's perception of and one's action ori-

entation toward the world. One of these needs is the need for achievement.

The second major perspective is the trait, or dispositional, tradition in personality theory. This perspective assumes that there are measurable individual differences between people in terms of their needs and motives; that these individual differences are relatively stable over time and manifest themselves in a wide variety of behaviors; and that motives (including the achievement motive), as dispositions within people, provide the basis of behavior. Thus, the emphasis within the trait tradition is on individuals' differences of motives. The psychoanalytic and trait approaches intersect in Murray's theory, which is one reason his theory is so important in psychology.

In addition, developments in industrial and postindustrial twentieth century societies made the time ripe for the study of achievement. McClelland has suggested that achievement motivation may explain economic differences between societies. In his book *The Achieving Society* (1961), McClelland attempted to predict the economic growth of twenty-three countries from 1929 to 1950 on the basis of images of achievement found in children's stories in those countries in the decade of 1920 to 1929. He found that those societies which emphasized achievement through children's stories generally experienced greater economic growth. While direct cause-and-effect relationships could not be established in a study such as this, subsequent research using experimental studies provided some support for McClelland's position.

Finally, developments in academic achievement testing and vocational performance testing since the early part of the twentieth century have provided a natural setting for measuring attainment in these domains. As more and more tests were developed, and as they became increasingly sophisticated in measuring achievement, it became readily apparent that a conceptual model of achievement was necessary.

SOURCES FOR FUTHER STUDY

Atkinson, John William, and D. Birch. *An Introduction to Motivation.* 2d ed. New York: Van Nostrand, 1978. Very readable. Does an effective job of discussing motivational concepts in general. Because of the first author's interest and research, a heavy emphasis is placed on achievement motivation, focusing particularly on elaborations of the expectancy value model.

Atkinson, John William, and Joel O. Raynor, eds. *Motivation and Achievement*. New York: Halsted Press, 1974. Reprints some of the most important research on achievement motivation. Many of the articles are too technical for the nonprofessional, but chapters 1, 2, 15, 19, and 20 are acessible to the college student and are outstanding reviews of prior theory and application to academic achievement and career striving.

DeCharms, Richard. *Enhancing Motivation in the Classroom*. New York: Irvington, 1976. Designed primarily for teachers, with applications at all levels. Nicely incorporates prior research on achievement motivation. More than a "how-to" book. Provides a challenge to the reader to think about factors involved in differing levels of achievement motivation in students.

Dweck, Carol S. *Self-Theories: Their Role in Motivation, Personality, and Development*. Philadelphia: Psychology Press, 1999. Summarizes her extensive work on individuals' own theories about the origins of their successes, failures, and abilities. Accessible to a general audience at the high school level and above.

McClelland, David. *Human Motivation*. Glenview, Ill.: Scott Foresman, 1985. Summarizes his extensive contributions to the field. Applies the methods of the behavioral sciences to provide a psychological basis for evaluating economic, historical, and sociological explanations of the achievement need. Accessible to the general reader at the college level and beyond.

Spence, Janet T., ed. *Achievement and Achievement Motives: Psychological and Sociological Approaches*. San Francisco: W. H. Freeman, 1983. Applies theoretical developments in achievement motivation to topics such as gender differences, children from one-parent households, social mobility, and cultural differences. Though scholarly and thorough, this excellent book is acessible to the general audience at a college level, but not without effort.

Peter C. Hill;
updated by Cynthia O'Dell

SEE ALSO: Birth order and personality; Coaching; Giftedness; Leadership; Motivation; Personality theory; Personology: Henry A. Murray; Sport psychology; Work motivation.

Addictive personality and behaviors

TYPE OF PSYCHOLOGY: Psychopathology

FIELDS OF STUDY: Attitudes and behavior; critical issues in stress; personality disorders; personality theory; substance use

There are many types of personalities and personality features associated with problems related to addictive behavior. No single personality type or disorder stands alone in this relationship. Further, personality and addictive behavior may influence each other: Personality may cause some addictive behavior, and some addictive behavior may lead to the development of certain personality features or even to personality disorders.

KEY CONCEPTS
- addiction
- compulsion
- generalization
- obsession
- personality
- self-regulation
- symptom

INTRODUCTION

Addiction is a condition in which individuals engage in habitual behaviors and/or the use of substances of abuse in a way that is maladaptive and causes them harm or distress. Fascination with the idea of an addictive personality and related behavior dates back to 950 B.C.E., to the works of Homer, the Greek poet, and perhaps before that to the writings of Lao-tzu, a Chinese philosopher and imperial adviser. These men studied human nature and sometimes wrote about the uncontrollable allure of certain desires which led to behaviors that were likely to cause personal and cultural destruction. In these cases, they were exploring the realm of personality: the intellectual, emotional, interpersonal, and intrapersonal structure of an individual that is exhibited through consistent patterns of thinking and behavior.

Some researchers have asked whether a single psychological predisposition or a multilevel series of complications is involved in the addictive personality—or whether virtually any personality is vulnerable to addiction. Researchers administering personality tests to individuals with addictive behavior problems have found a variety of notable personality traits. Sometimes these traits precede the addiction, and sometimes they seem to be caused by or exacerbated by the addiction. These findings are highly controversial and have fueled many heated discussions.

Symptoms, or indications of a problem, with personality are varied. For some individuals with addictive behavior problems, aggressive energy and antiauthority issues seem to be at the core of their personality. Indulgence in the addictive behavior is accompanied by the release of aggressive impulses, resulting in a feeling of euphoria. This feeling of relief is then associated with the outlet used, and it seduces the user to attempt a duplication of the original process, thus reexperiencing the euphoria.

Inadequate self-esteem is another psychological predisposition thought to be a common source of imperceptible pain, and the inability to handle the pain can lead to striving for a pain-reducing outlet. Some individuals with addictive behavior problems seem to have the desire to control the pain but lack the necessary social, psychological, and biological tools to follow through. Other symptoms that may be identified early enough to allow preventive measures to be taken include poor impulse control; intolerance and low frustration level, leading to a need for control; and rigidity and extremes in action and thoughts.

Behavior with addictive characteristics may involve alcohol, other drugs, food, work, sex, gambling, exercise, video-game playing, television watching, or Internet use. The notion of an addictive personality partially came about because many individuals display more than one behavior with addictive characteristics or, when they give up one addictive behavior, quickly find another to replace it. Some have seen this process of substituting one addiction for

---

DSM-IV-TR Criteria for Dependence and Abuse

SUBSTANCE DEPENDENCE

Maladaptive pattern of substance use, leading to clinically significant impairment or distress

Manifested by three or more of the following, occurring at any time in the same twelve-month period

Tolerance, as defined by either:
- need for markedly increased amounts of substance to achieve intoxication or desired effect
- markedly diminished effect with continued use of same amount of substance

Withdrawal, as manifested by either:
- characteristic withdrawal syndrome for substance
- same (or closely related) substance taken to relieve or avoid withdrawal symptoms

Substance often taken in larger amounts or over longer period than intended

Persistent desire or unsuccessful efforts to cut down or control substance use

Great deal of time spent in activities necessary to obtain substance, use substance, or recover from its effects

Important social, occupational, or recreational activities given up or reduced because of substance use

Substance use continues despite knowledge of persistent or recurrent physical or psychological problem likely to have been caused or exacerbated by substance

Specify if with Physiological Dependence (evidence of tolerance or withdrawal) or Without Physiological Dependence (no evidence of tolerance or withdrawal)

Course specifiers: Early Full Remission; Early Partial Remission; Sustained Full Remission; Sustained Partial Remission; on Agonist Therapy; in a Controlled Environment

SUBSTANCE ABUSE

Maladaptive pattern of substance use leading to clinically significant impairment or distress

Manifested by one or more of the following, occurring within a twelve-month period:
- recurrent substance use resulting in failure to fulfill major role obligations at work, school, or home
- recurrent substance use in situations in which it is physically hazardous
- recurrent substance-related legal problems
- continued substance use despite having persistent or recurrent social or interpersonal problems caused or exacerbated by the effects of the substance (such as arguments with spouse about consequences of intoxication, physical fights)

Criteria for Substance Dependence not met for this class of substance

another as a form of generalization in which behaviors form an addictive behavior pattern. Problems such as manipulation, denial of responsibility, displacement of emotions, and general dishonesty in lifestyle may provoke this process. In general, the addictive process can be periodic, cyclic, sporadic, or continuous, depending upon a person's life patterns, resources, and basic personality.

PERSONALITY THEORIES

Different personality theories present conflicting ideas about addiction, adding to the controversy-surrounding this topic. Psychoanalysts believe that the addictive personality is a result of unconscious-conflicts and of fixation on the pleasure principle,which states that one's energy in life is directed toward reducing pain and that one's innate drives control one's actions. Although some neo-Freudians disagree with the cause of the pain, most agree with the basic concept. Social learning and behavioral psychologists believe that an addictive personality is molded through shaping—the slow and continual development of a behavior, with continuous reinforcement along the way, based on the social mores prevalent when the individual grew up. The need to be accepted becomes the driving force.

Cognitive psychologists hold that an addictive personality is formulated by the way a person receives, processes, stores, and retrieves information received through the senses. If the action taken produces a positive effect, then the person is likely to repeat the process so that the effect can be duplicated. In essence, people become addicted to the pleasurable results before they become addicted to the particular path taken to achieve them.

Humanistic psychologists concentrate on the here and now, focusing on the fact that people have choices, yet many people do not know how to make them because of trauma they experienced while growing up. To the humanist, the idea of the family becomes very important, particularly how love was expressed and experienced, because through love, people can believe in themselves enough to be able to make a positive choice.

The proponents of trait theory contend that people are born with certain tendencies and preferences of action, which may or may not be genetic; the evidence is inconclusive. Trait theorists seem to agree, however, that society and the family have a strong influence on people and that some people are predisposed toward compulsive behavior from an early age.

Biological studies have been conducted to explore the suspected link between addictive behavior and genes, suggesting that, at least in part, the addictive personality may be inherited. Studies suggest that certain people may have inherited an impaired neurological homeostasis, which is partly corrected by their addiction—such as to alcohol. The sons of alcoholic fathers have a higher "body sway" (the degree to which a person sways when standing upright with the eyes closed) than do nonalcoholics; it decreases when they are intoxicated. Sons of alcoholics have a higher rate of addiction than do daughters, no matter which parent reared the children.

People with "familial essential tremor," an inherited disorder, have less tremor when drinking and have a higher rate of alcohol dependence. Also, while alcohol-dependent people do not have higher levels of arousal at rest, they become more aroused when stressed, as measured by heart rate, and are slower to return to rest.

Other studies have suggested that people who are at high risk have abnormal brain-wave activity, suggesting an inability to concentrate or a reduced brain capacity. High-risk people have shown normal to slightly above normal intelligence quotient (IQ) test scores, but low scores on verbal subscales and attention. They also show delayed language development. Moreover, they seem to produce a heroinlike tranquilizing substance which is released and soothes the person when using an addictive substance or pursuing addictive behavior.

The majority of controlled scientific studies on genetics have been conducted on the alcoholic population. Consequently, they are inconclusive when discussing the addictive personality overall. They do, however, add evidence to the possible link between biology and behavior.

SELF-REGULATION

It seems clear from the research that addiction is a multilevel problem with complex roots, dispersed throughout psychology, sociology, biology, and genetics. Among the symptoms of addictive behavior are tendencies toward excessiveness, compulsion, and obsessions. Compulsions are impulses that are difficult to resist, while obsessions are compelling ideas or feelings that are usually somewhat irrational. These tendencies have prompted many to won-

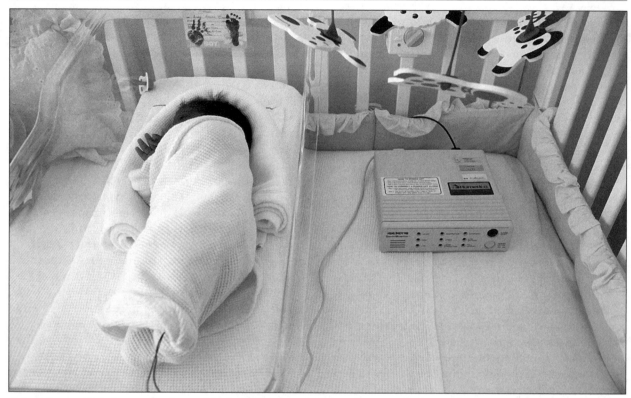

A baby born addicted to cocaine is monitored closely; women who continue to take drugs during pregnancy put their unborn children at risk. (PhotoDisc)

der about the existence of an addictive personality, as they seem generalized to other behaviors for some individuals.

For some, this tendency can be traced back to childhood and used as a warning sign. If it is identified in advance, efforts can be made to alter the child's first impulse and slowly, over time and with much positive reinforcement, show the child alternative, acceptable behavior. When the child can be taught to achieve self-regulation in a positive way, within acceptable social limits, there is a better chance for positive achievement as an outcome. Self-regulation is a process whereby individuals manage their feelings, reactions, and thoughts in response to internal and external events.

One question that arises regarding excessiveness is how to teach a person balance when American society in general does not know how to achieve this goal. The United States has been called a nation of overachievers for profit, success, and power. People are rewarded highly for these motives and are considered well adjusted by their fellow citizens if they

achieve them. A problem arises when one considers that addictive personalities are a mass of excessive desires. These individuals lack impulse control, and there is a strong need to achieve self-validation any way they can.

Whether addictive behavior is learned for survival, genetically passed on, or an intricate combination of both, it appears that a set of personal features can predispose a person toward addiction—or, at the least, can place a person in a high-risk group. If these symptoms can be identified early enough, the chance to teach potential addicts the path toward balance increases, and the compulsive lifestyle can be decreased or channeled in a healthy way.

ADDICTION TREATMENTS

Addictions and their victims have been studied and described at least since the beginning of written language, and probably since humanity first communicated by storytelling. A concentrated effort was made in Ohio in 1935 by Robert Smith and William Wilson to help the persons with addictive tendencies through the organization of Alcoholics Anonymous (AA), a self-help group of alcoholics in various stages of recovery.

The success of Alcoholics Anonymous is world renowned, and it is considered by most professionals and nonprofessionals who have contact with it to be one of the more complete recovery programs in the world. The twelve-step program, an idea that AA started, transcends the boundaries of alcohol abuse and has been applied to many addictions. AA is run by recovering alcoholics who are nonprofessionals, simply individual humans helping others. Yet it was not until the early 1970's that addictive people gained national and international attention.

In 1971, the National Institute on Alcohol Abuse and Alcoholism conducted research that showed addiction to be threatening American society. Since then, a concentrated effort has been made to study individuals addicted to alcohol and other drugs, with an attempt to find symptoms that would predict individuals at high risk for developing such problems. The federally funded studies, it was hoped, would find ways to help prevent and reduce the tremendous health, social, and economic consequences of addiction in the United States. Assessing dependence potential and discovering vulnerability or high-risk factors through demographic characteristics, psychological status, and individual drug history became its focus. The funding of these studies has become a critical component in the fight to better understand addiction.

Internationally, it has been surmised that advanced, technological societies seem to give rise to more kinds of dependency than do more slowly developing countries, a fact which could help researchers focus on some societal misconceptions of overall health. For example, in the United States and some other technologically advanced societies, there seems to be a belief pattern, propagated by the mass media, that supports instant gratification. People who are tense should take a pill. People who are lonely can call a certain number for conversation. People who are bored should have an alcoholic drink. People who want to be part of the in-crowd can smoke. People who are unhappy can eat. Societies, governments, and researchers must unite in a desire to unveil all possible symptoms of addiction, to identify those at high risk for addiction, and to employ successful recovery methods.

SOURCES FOR FURTHER STUDY

Khantzian, Edward J. *Treating Addiction as a Human Process.* Northvale, N.J.: Jason Aronson, 1999. This book provides a discussion about the universality of human vulnerabilities and addictive suffering, highlighting the delicate balance between forces encouraging human beings toward pleasure and self-destruction.

Mule, S. Joseph, ed. *Behavior in Excess: An Examination of the Volitional Disorders.* New York: Free Press, 1981. This set of nineteen chapters is a must for the beginning student of addictive personalities and behavior. Explains the many drugs of choice available to the addictive person as well as the societal addictions of eating, work, gambling, sports, television, sex, and smoking. Explores the environment influence on excessive behaviors and psychodynamic and behavioral treatments. An excellent group of writings.

Orford, Jim. *Excessive Appetites: A Psychological View of Addictions.* 2d ed. New York: John Wiley & Sons, 2001. This internationally focused, easily read book discusses addiction as an excessive appetite that may extend to behaviors beyond those of addictive substances.

Twerski, Abraham J. *Addictive Thinking: Understanding Self-Deception.* 2d ed. Center City, Minn.: Hazelden, 1997. This book discusses common thinking errors encountered in individuals with problems related to addictive behavior and how these errors may cause and maintain problems with addiction.

Wilson, Bill. *Alcoholics Anonymous.* 3d ed. New York: Alcoholics Anonymous World Services, 1976. In this compilation of stories, words of wisdom, and insights into the world of the addicted person, the cofounders of Alcoholics Anonymous have been the impetus for an inspiring group of writings that put into words the heart and soul of an addictive person's behavior—physically, emotionally, and spiritually. An essential part of any student's reading in the field of compulsive behavior.

Frederic Wynn;
updated by Nancy A. Piotrowski

SEE ALSO: Alcohol dependence and abuse; Codependency; Coping: Social support; Hunger; Obesity; Motivation; Self-esteem; Substance use disorders.

Adler, Alfred

BORN: February 7, 1870, in Vienna, Austria
DIED: May 28, 1937, in Aberdeen, Scotland
IDENTITY: Jewish Austrian psychoanalyst
TYPE OF PSYCHOLOGY: Individual psychology
FIELDS OF STUDY: Classic analytic themes and is-
sues; personality theory

Adler posited the inferiority complex as a source for
understanding human motivation and founded the
school of individual psychology.

Alfred Adler was born in suburban Vienna of middle-
class Jews. He began his medical career as an oph-
thalmologist, then became a general practitioner,
and finally became a psychiatrist in 1907. He had
become interested in the manner in which people
overcame organ inferiorities and compensated for
them. His work came to the attention of Sigmund
Freud, and Adler became a member of Freud's inner circle.

At first Adler's work was in agreement with
Freud's general doctrines. However, Adler began to
launch out in his own direction. He wrote a paper
concerning what he termed an aggression instinct.
Adler then followed up that paper with one on children's inferiority complexes, arguing that Freud's
notions of infantile sexuality be treated more as
metaphors than as reality.

In spite of the differences, Freud chose Adler as
president of the Viennese Analytic Society and
coeditor of the organization's newsletter. However,
Adler continued to attack Freud's ideas, resigning
with a number of his supporters to form the Society
for Free Psychoanalysis in 1911. In 1912 this group
became the Society for Individual Psychology.

Adler's experiences during World War I turned
his concerns to social interest. He became convinced that to survive, humans had to undergo reform, and that individual psychology had a major
role to play in that change. Adler turned increasingly to social projects, including clinics affiliated
with state schools and the training of teachers. A
1926 lecture tour led to a visiting position at the
Long Island College of Medicine. Adler and his
family left Austria in 1934.

Adler gave many different names to his single
drive or motivation for human behavior. He originally termed it an aggressive drive. He later came to

term it the striving for perfection, a notion close to
Abraham Maslow's theory of self-actualization. The
term "aggression drive," first used for the drive, referred to humans' frustration when their needs are
blocked. When blocked, people compensate for
their frustration. Adler argued that personalities
could be explained by the manner in which people
compensate for their problems.

Adler offered an alternative to Freud's sexual theory of human development. His theory of personality is grounded in holistic empiricism. He sought to
discern social practices as well as innate influences.
His concern for social interests led him to look at
cultural factors in personality development.

Adler died at Aberdeen, Scotland, where he was
giving a series of lectures at the university, on May
28, 1937.

SOURCES FOR FURTHER STUDY

Handlbauer, Bernard. *The Freud-Adler Controversy.*
Rockport, Mass.: Oneworld, 1998. A history of
the growing rift between Adler and Freud.
Hoffman, Edward. *The Drive for Self: Alfred Adler and
the Founding of Individual Psychology.* Reading,
Mass.: Addison-Wesley, 1994. The first major biography of Adler.
Kottman, Terry. *Partners in Play: An Adlerian Approach to Play Therapy.* Alexandria, Va.: American
Counseling, 1995. Application of Adler's theories.
Ludin, Robert W. *Alfred Adler's Basic Concepts and Implications.* Muncie, Ind.: Accelerated Development, 1989. A concise summary and assessment
of Adler's theories.

Frank A. Salamone

SEE ALSO: Adlerian psychotherapy; Cognitive therapy; Freud, Sigmund; Humanism; Individual psychology: Alfred Adler; Play therapy.

Adlerian psychotherapy

TYPE OF PSYCHOLOGY: Psychotherapy
FIELDS OF STUDY: Cognitive therapies; humanistic
therapies; psychodynamic therapies

Adlerian psychotherapy covers the assessment and
therapeutic techniques developed by Alfred Adler and

followers of his individual psychology school. This approach can be seen as a precursor of later forms of brief, humanistic, empathic, and cognitive psychotherapy.

KEY CONCEPTS

- early recollections
- individual psychology
- inferiority
- organ dialect
- private logic
- transference

INTRODUCTION

Alfred Adler's individual psychology, his approach to psychotherapy, starts with the assumption that all people suffer from a feeling of inferiority. Though most people outgrow this complex by developing healthy compensations through their career, family, and friends, many individuals turn inward and attempt to compensate with a private logic. This is a personal and unconscious "fictional" way of understanding self and reality in order to assuage the feelings of inferiority. Reliance on private logic impairs the individual's ability to cope.

The concept of private logic underlies Adler's understanding of psychopathology. Each disorder represents a different approach to private logic. For example, schizophrenics cope with the inferiority complex by believing their own private logic so thoroughly that they separate from external reality and live in a delusional world in which they are intensely talented and important. The schizophrenic's neologisms (invented words) can be seen as evidence of creativity. On the other hand, the critical auditory hallucinations often experienced by schizophrenics can be understood as the schizophrenic's inability to master totally the internal world.

The obsessive-compulsive patient has focused attention exclusively on some private issue of no real objective importance; in the person's private logic, however, the issue has a great importance, perhaps conferring on the person some special status. The paranoid's private logic allows the person to believe that he or she is the most important person in the world—why else would the Mafia, CIA, or Martians persecute the person so?

Adler began his practice of medicine not as a psychiatrist but as a general practitioner. As such, he saw all sorts of patients, most of whom did not define their various diseases and problems as mental. Psychosomatic, hypochondriacal, and somatoform patients illustrate what Adler called organ dialect, in which their bodies' problems reflect their dysfunctional approaches to life. Such physical disorders (real or imagined) mitigate feelings of inferiority by serving as an excuse for failure and/or a plea for sympathy.

Depressed patients suffer from low self-esteem, which may include feelings of hopelessness, helplessness, and guilt. The private logic of such a patient may be inadequate to lift the patient out of the inferiority complex. Some depressed patients even seem to rely upon their own suffering as a sham sense of merit: "I suffer, therefore I am worthy." Personality disorders, delinquency, and crime may spring from the attempt to overcome feelings of inferiority through defiance and a facade of toughness rather than meaningful contributions to society. Prostitutes and chemically dependent individuals have an unresolved inferiority complex coupled with an ambivalent attitude toward dependency.

What unifies people with different kinds of mental disorders, according to Adler, is that their private logic gives them a mistaken understanding of themselves and the world. They persist in their dysfunctional behaviors and attitudes in order to preserve their sham sense of self-esteem, but at the price of effective coping. When Adler set out to diagnose a patient, he was less interested in labeling that patient with a specific disorder than reaching a deeper understanding of who that person was: It is not so important what disease the patient has, but what kind of person has the disease. Therefore, Adler's approach to diagnosis was more qualitative than quantitative, more tailored to the individual situation than systematic and structured. However, Adler regularly employed about a half dozen techniques.

DIAGNOSTIC TECHNIQUES

Adler's first diagnostic technique was to observe the patient's body language. This included not only the organ dialect of the presenting (physical) problem but also all sorts of nonverbal behaviors: how the patient walked into the room, how he or she wiggled or slouched in the seat, the kind of handshake, the degree of eye contact, and so on. Adler once said that one can learn more from patients in a minute of watching them as if they were mimes (and ignoring anything they say) than one can in an hour of listening to them.

A second approach was the use of direct and specific questions, not only about the manifest symptoms but also about the patient's background. Since Adler was convinced that the formative stage of personality development is the first six years of life, he was most interested in asking about early childhood: relations with parents, siblings, teachers, and others, as well as a lifetime history of medical problems. Adler believed that people are purposive creatures and that mental disorders (and possibly physical disorders as well) are means to the end of assuaging feelings of inferiority; he would sometimes directly ask his patients: "If you were cured of this disorder, what would happen to you?" The answer could reveal what the patient most feared—sometimes that he or she would have higher expectations of his or her own performance in the areas of interpersonal relations and career.

During his ten-year association with Sigmund Freud, Adler learned to use dreams as a way of exploring the patient's unconscious. He believed that dreams were ways in which the patient rehearsed coping for waking life. The behavior of the dreamer reflects his or her real-life coping patterns and private logic.

One diagnostic technique that originated with Adler was the use of early recollections. Recalling such recollections is a projective technique in which the patient attempts to remember things that happened in the distant past. They would be elicited by the question "What is the farthest back that your memory can go?" Adler realized that such recollections would be hazy on the facts, but they would provide excellent vehicles for expressing the patient's private logic. Such recollections, like the patient's dreams or works of art, could be seen as projective techniques, rich with the markings of the patient's personality. Additionally, the patient's current mood would color the mood of the recollection, and conflicts currently on the patient's mind would be projected into the story. As the patient improved in psychotherapy, the early recollections would change to a more positive tone, reflecting more effective coping strategies.

Adler's own character is evident from the earliest recollection of his childhood. Young Alfred was lying in bed, very ill, and overheard the doctor out in the hall telling his father that Alfred would not make it through the night. Adler recalls that he resolved to live and prove the doctor wrong, and to become a doctor and fight death. The memory shows Adler's tremendous willpower as well as a desire to overcome suffering.

THERAPY TECHNIQUES

The first step in Adlerian psychotherapy was to use diagnostic techniques to comprehend the patient's underlying private logic. The next step was to use empathy to develop the patient's trust. (This was not to be allowed to evolve into a transference, or the transferring of emotions that a patient feels about other people onto the therapist treating the patient. Adler regarded transference as a childish dependency that would lengthen therapy and delay progress.) Then, patients had to be led to the identification of their own guiding private logic and to an insight that it was truly dysfunctional. This might include direct confrontation of the patient's misfocusing, abstractness, closed-mindedness, or excessive self-expectations. The last stage of therapy was the cultivation of the patient's social interest and involved encouraging the patient to venture forth into interpersonal relations and the world of work—emerging from the protective shell of the private logic and into the normal world's challenges.

Unlike Freudian psychoanalysis, Adler's approach to psychotherapy was directive. In addition to direct confrontation, Adler sometimes attempted to shake up the patient's guarded structure of private logic by answering with the unexpected. When one patient called him at home at three o'clock in the morning to report some trivial symptom, she ended by apologizing for awakening him; Adler responded that he had been sitting by his telephone awaiting her call. She thus gained the insight that she was behaving like a pampered child. Another patient was obsessed with the idea that he had contracted syphilis. He had compulsively sought the attention of many physicians around Vienna, all of whom had reported no evidence of the disease. Adler immediately agreed with the patient that he did, indeed, have the dreaded disease, thus pushing the patient to accept the validity of the previous diagnoses.

A variant of this technique was developed by one of Adler's protégés, Rudolf Dreikurs, who became one of the foremost apostles of individual psychology in America. Dreikurs used antisuggestion, urging patients who complained of an uncontrollable urge to give in to it and even practice it.

Unlike practitioners of classical psychoanalysis, Adler believed that therapy should be brief. Progress should be apparent in weeks, and termination should be possible in less than a year. Even after their sessions have ended, patients often continue to progress on their own. Unlike the humanistic and emotional therapies of the 1960's, Adlerian psychotherapy tries not to provoke abreaction (the expression of repressed emotions or thoughts) but to build the patient's capacity for self-control.

CASE STUDIES

Case studies of diagnosis and counseling with three very different patients can illustrate Adlerian techniques. Jay, age forty, had a psychophysiologic disorder (an ulcer) and was mildly depressed. He attributed his problems to organizational changes at the small firm by which he had been employed for a dozen years. An outstanding engineer with an earned doctorate and M.B.A. and numerous patents, Jay was convinced that his own efforts had helped the company grow and survive. As vice president for research and development, Jay advocated several new projects to get the firm's sales moving again; however, the other major figures in the company largely ignored Jay's plans and lurched from one budget-cutting scheme to another. "I am working eighty-hour weeks and worrying about the company all the time, but I just can't get things moving."

Jay's body language included averting his gaze and slouching, which he attributed to Vietnam War wounds. Upon direct questioning, he said that he was an only child: His father, fifty-five when Jay was born, wanted no children and resented the "accident" of Jay's conception, while his mother wanted more children and had to be satisfied with one son. Jay found that his mother was extremely encouraging and loving, perhaps spoiling Jay somewhat, while his father tended to ignore him except when some major accomplishment got his father's attention. Jay's guiding private logic was "I must work hard and accomplish something great; then I will get attention." This drove Jay to earn his degrees, invent new products, and work hard at the company. His frustration came from the fact that the old formula was not working in his changing corporate culture.

Jay was most angry at his company's chief executive officer and board of directors, whom he regarded as intellectually inferior to him. The CEO was an incredibly charming (and handsome) M.B.A. from the sales division who rejected most of Jay's suggestions for new products but had few ideas of his own. Jay admitted feeling envious of the CEO's sustained popularity, "especially considering that he has been running the company into the ground for seven years."

The earliest childhood recollection that Jay produced was that he was watching his mother use the toilet, sitting down on the bowl with the seat up, and that Jay was telling her that it was dangerous to do it that way. When the therapist encouraged Jay to ask his parents what had really happened, Jay found out that he was toilet trained early, and because he would urinate on the floor (through the crack between the seat and the bowl), his mother encouraged him to sit down on the bowl. His mother recalled that Jay then developed a fear of falling backward into the toilet. The interesting thing about Jay's recollection is that he inverted his role with his mother's: He was the one warning her of the danger. While a Freudian would say something about the Oedipus complex or anal fixation here, Adlerians are more concerned with the power quality of the interpersonal relations. Jay saw himself as the one who pointed out the danger; he was also very frustrated when the parental figures (the CEO and members of the board of directors) failed to heed his warnings.

Jay's ulcer was a badge of merit, like his earned degrees or patents ("Look at how much I have suffered for this company!"). Sacrifice and success had been Jay's strategy for winning the attention of his "parents," but now that strategy was not working, so he had become depressed.

An intelligent man, Jay rapidly gained insight into his private logic. After four sessions, he had the following dream: "I am going through one of my rental houses, and I discover a room that I did not remember before—a living room that looked so comfortable, I just wanted to sit and read for pleasure." Jay enjoyed the dream and agreed that it reflected his ongoing resolution of his problem. The dream represented new possibilities in Jay's life: a more mellow lifestyle in which he saw less need to push himself on the fast track in order to maintain his self-esteem.

Jay terminated after eight sessions, having made plans to seek a position with another firm. After two years in the new position, Jay reported that he made almost as much money, had slightly less status, worked half as many hours, but had twice as much enjoyment. His ulcer and depression had not recurred.

Dan was also a forty-year-old engineer when he began counseling. He met most, though not all, of the criteria for a narcissistic personality (a disorder characterized by a grandiose sense of self, lack of empathy, and other criteria). Although a brilliant computer programmer, Dan had never obtained a college degree. He had never remained with one company for more than a year, and most of his work history had been with "job shops" or as an independent consultant. The presenting problem for Dan was that he had gotten his girlfriend pregnant, and he was ambivalent about getting married and becoming a father.

Direct questioning revealed that Dan was the third of four children. His grandfather had been a famous politician, his father was an attorney, and an older brother was an accomplished (and very wealthy) surgeon. Dan directly denied feeling inferior to these male family members, for he was convinced that he was smarter than any of them and had a broader range of knowledge. Dan's private logic worked something like this: "Everyone else needs to get a degree and work in one career line for twenty years in order to be a success; I don't have to, because I am more brilliant than anyone else. Finishing my education or sticking with one company would be an admission that I am not more brilliant."

During the first few sessions, Dan used big words and attempted to impress the therapist with his knowledge of psychology. While Dan claimed an inability to come up with an early recollection, he was able to remember a dream: "I am at a new restaurant, and I am given a table next to the kitchen; although the waiters go back and forth, they ignore me. Finally, I am given the check and realize that I do not have enough money." After much resistance and intellectualization, Dan agreed that the dream exposed his dissatisfaction with his life: the fear that the honors and accomplishments of the other males in his family would pass him by and that he would be unable to achieve as much.

The cultivation of Dan's social interest took eight months, but it did progress. He accepted a position (which he initially thought to be beneath his talents) offering stable employment and advancement. He married his pregnant girlfriend and reported to be satisfied with his role of father, although he found his wife to be a little too "naggy." He did not try so hard to impress people with his intelligence.

Alicia, a sixty-four-year-old widow of fifteen years, went into therapy complaining of depression and suicidal thoughts. Her feeling of inferiority was expressed primarily as helplessness and ruminations of guilt. Direct questioning and discussion engendered by dreams indicated that she still blamed herself for her husband's fatal heart attack ("I cooked food that was too rich"), for her son's accidental death ("I encouraged him to follow his heart and become a pilot"), and for her daughter's upcoming marriage to a former priest ("I did not instill enough religion in her"). The function of her depressive illness was that her daughter was talking about delaying her marriage until her mother got better.

Her earliest recollection was that her parents would punish her for wetting the bed by making her sit in a tub of cold water; one time when her parents were out of the house, she wet the bed. When her parents returned they found her sitting in a tub of cold water, telling herself "You sit there." This consolidated the identification of her private logic: "I am responsible for things that go wrong, and I must punish myself when things go wrong."

Alicia developed the insight that her private logic was dysfunctional and her own depression was a manipulative, though effective, way of reacting to her daughter's forthcoming marriage. The facilitation of social interest in this case focused on getting Alicia out of the enmeshed relationship with her daughter and more involved with activities outside the home, such as religion and charity work.

UNIQUE CONTRIBUTIONS

Most of Sigmund Freud's patients were "hysterical" women (with what would now be called somatoform or dissociative reactions) from the middle and upper classes of Viennese society. Most of Adler's patients were from the poor and working classes; they were not as articulate as Freud's, so Adler had to assume a more directive stance. Adler remained in general medical practice, treating all kinds of physical illnesses and injuries as well as mental problems. Although he probably saw more patients in any given month than Freud saw in his professional lifetime, the brevity of Adler's counseling may have given only a superficial understanding of their problems.

Adler, like Joseph Breuer, Carl Jung, and Otto Rank, broke with Freud and came up with an alternative to psychoanalysis. He redefined Freud's use of dreams and interpretation of patient resistance as a reaction against the threat to the private logic which assuages inferiority feeling. Adler rejected transference as an artificial by-product of therapy and as a license for the patient to continue infantile behavior. He redefined the unconscious, not as a repository of sexual energy, but as the limitations of consciousness to understand one's own private logic.

Adler's emphasis on empathy and appreciating the uniqueness of each individual patient can be seen as a precursor to the humanistic approaches (such as that of Carl Rogers) that surfaced in the 1950's and 1960's. Adler's focus on the patient's private logic and coping strategies was echoed in the growth during the 1970's and 1980's of the cognitive approach (exemplified by Aaron Beck and Albert Ellis).

Some of Adler's ideas have been challenged by modern research. The correlation between birth order and personality, for example, is lower than Adler believed. Adler's notion that healthy people have no need to dream has been challenged by evidence from sleep laboratories that all people dream several times a night, though they might not remember their dreams. Nevertheless, Adler's specific techniques of diagnosis and therapy are useful tools that eclectic therapists often add to their collection.

Sources for Further Study

Adler, Alfred. *The Individual Psychology of Alfred Adler*. Edited by Heinz L. Ansbacher and Rowena R. Ansbacher. New York: HarperCollins, 1977. A definitive account of Adler's important contributions to psychology.

_____. *Superiority and Social Interest*. Edited by Heinz L. Ansbacher and Rowena R. Ansbacher. Evanston, Ill.: Northwestern University Press, 1964. There is no standard edition or comprehensive collection of Adler's writings; however, the above two edited works by the Ansbachers take representative excerpts from Adler's numerous books and, together with editorial comments, present a good picture of the techniques Adler developed for assessment and therapy.

Dinkmeyer, Don C., and W. L. Pew. *Adlerian Counseling and Psychotherapy*. 2d ed. Columbus, Ohio: Charles E. Merrill, 1987. This is a good summary of different Adlerian techniques for psychotherapy. It is written for the practitioner at al levels, from youth guidance counselor to psychiatrist.

Dreikurs, Rudolf. *Fundamentals of Adlerian Psychology*. 1950. Reprint. Chicago: Adler School of Professional Psychology, 1989. The author was an Adlerian disciple who became the leader of the Adlerian movement in the United States after World War II. His simple style and straightforward advice are very much in keeping with the style of Adler himself. Dreikurs's own expertise was in the area of child development.

Grey, Loren. *Alfred Adler, the Forgotten Prophet*. Westport, Conn.: Praeger, 1998. Illustrates the wide impact Adler's theories have had on American cultural understanding of psychology.

Mozak, Harold H., and Michael Maniacci. *A Primer of Adlerian Psychology: The Analytic-Behavioral-Cognitive Psychology of Alfred Adler*. Chicago: Brunner/Mazel, 1999. A straightforward introduction to the basic concepts of Adlerian psychology.

T. L. Brink

See also: Abnormality: Psychological models; Birth order and personality; Clinical interviewing, testing, and observation; Cognitive therapy; Dreams; Individual psychology: Alfred Adler; Psychoanalysis; Psychoanalytic psychology; Psychotherapeutic goals and techniques.

Adolescence
Cognitive skills

Type of psychology: Developmental psychology
Fields of study: Adolescence; cognitive development

Adolescence brings the potential for logical and theoretical reasoning, systematic problem solving, and acquisition of abstract concepts; adolescent cognitive skills are reflected in social and personality development as well as in learning and problem-solving behavior.

KEY CONCEPTS
- concrete operations stage
- developmental approach
- egocentrism
- formal operations stage
- hypothetical-deductive reasoning
- imaginary audience
- information-processing approach
- personal fable
- psychometric approach

INTRODUCTION

Psychologists approach the study of adolescent cognitive skills from three perspectives: the psychometric, the developmental, and the information-processing. The psychometric approach focuses on defining and measuring intellectual skills. Psychometric research typically involves studies of performance on intelligence tests. The developmental approach seeks to identify the types of cognitive skills that are unique to the adolescent years. This approach has been heavily influenced by the cognitive stage theory of Swiss psychologist Jean Piaget. The information-processing approach examines the characteristics of memory and problem solving. It views adolescent cognitive skills as parameters that determine how the brain stores and analyzes information.

PSYCHOMETRIC APPROACH

In the psychometric view, adolescence is a period of cognitive stability. Intelligence quotient (IQ) scores show little change during adolescence. Although IQ scores often fluctuate during early childhood, scores generally stabilize about age eight. It is common to find temporary periods of instability in IQ scores after age eight, such as at the onset of puberty or during other stressful times, but dramatic and long-term score changes are rare. According to this perspective, adolescence does not bring significant changes in cognitive skills.

Theory and research on cognitive skills began with the development of modern intelligence tests, such as Alfred Binet's 1916 test; however, the intelligence-testing, or psychometric, approach has contributed little to an understanding of adolescent cognitive skills. Intelligence tests are best suited to the study of individual differences, or how people compare to others of their age. It is difficult to use intelligence testing to compare and contrast cognitive skills at different ages.

Intelligence tests also are used to study the stability of intellectual level and the likelihood it will change in later years. Research indicates, however, that intelligence test scores in adolescence generally are similar to scores during childhood, although scores may fluctuate during childhood as a function of changes in factors such as diet, socioeconomic status, and education. Again, the psychometric approach seems poorly suited to the study of adolescent cognitive skills.

DEVELOPMENTAL APPROACH

The developmental approach seeks to identify the cognitive skills of adolescence and to contrast them with the skills found at other ages. This approach addresses both the qualities of thought and the process of change. In 1958, Piaget and his coworker Barbel Inhelder published *The Growth of Logical Thinking from Childhood Through Adolescence*, a detailed account of his four stages of cognitive development. In addition to proposing that specific cognitive skills emerge in each stage, Piaget proposes that the move from one stage to the next is largely maturational.

This statement may be confusing. Clearly, sixteen-year-olds must "know more" than eight-year-olds, and adolescents have the capacity to learn school subjects beyond the grasp of elementary school children. The psychometric approach, however, is not designed to contrast the nature of cognitive skills at different ages. Intelligence tests are scored by comparing a specific person to other people of the same age. A score of 100 at age eight means that a person performs similarly to the average eight-year-old; a score of 100 at age eighteen means that a person performs similarly to the average eighteen-year-old. IQ score is expected to remain the same if the person matures at a relatively normal rate.

Two of Piaget's stages are of particular importance to the study of adolescence: the concrete operational stage (ages seven to twelve) and the formal operational stage (age twelve and up). During the concrete operational stage, children acquire basic logical concepts such as equivalence, seriation, and part-whole relations. Children also master reversibility, a skill allowing them mentally to restore a changed object or situation to its original state. With reversibility, children can recognize that a small glass of juice poured into a taller and thinner

---

Neural Basis of Adolescent Cognition

Interest has been growing in the prospect of uniting brain and cognitive development during adolescence. With the use of magnetic resonance imaging (MRI), researchers now have a better understanding of how the adolescent brain actually functions. A surprising discovery is the fact that there are changes in the structure of the brain that appear relatively late in child development. Of special note during the teenage years is the second wave of synapse formation just before puberty, along with a pruning back during adolescence. It had already been known that prior to birth and during the first months after birth there was an overproduction of connections, but it was not known that a second spurt occurred. This time of rapid development of synapses followed by the pruning of connections determines the cells and connections that will be hardwired. From stud-

ies of growth patterns of the developing brain, it has also been found that fiber systems which influence language learning and associative thinking develop more rapidly just before puberty and for a short period of time just after puberty. Changes in the prefrontal cortex increase the adolescent's potential to reason with more accuracy, show more control over impulses, and make more effective judgments. Even the cerebellum is still developing into adolescence. Although commonly associated with physical coordination, the cerebellum also plays a role in processing mental tasks, such as higher thought, decision making, and social skills. In summary, it is now known that an important part of the growth of the brain is happening just before puberty and well into adolescence.

Lillian J. Breckenridge

---

glass may look like more juice but is actually the same amount. During concrete operations, children can think logically as long as their reasoning is in reference to tangible objects.

The formal operational stage follows the concrete operational stage and is the final stage of cognition according to Piaget. Beginning at adolescence, thinking becomes more logical, more abstract, more hypothetical, and more systematic. Unlike their concrete operational counterparts, formal thinkers can study ideologies, generate a variety of possible outcomes to an action, and systematically evaluate alternative approaches to a problem. Formal thinkers also are better able to adopt a new course of action when a particular strategy proves unsuccessful. In the Piagetian model, adolescents are compared to scientists as they utilize hypothetical-deductive reasoning to solve problems. Although children during the concrete operational stage would solve problems by trial and error, adolescents could be expected to develop hypotheses and then systematically conclude which path is best to follow in order to solve the problem.

INFORMATION-PROCESSING APPROACH

The information-processing approach provides additional information about these child/adolescent contrasts. According to John Flavell, cognitive growth is the acquisition of increasingly sophisticated and efficient problem-solving skills. For example, ado-

lescents can hold more information in memory than children, which enhances their ability to solve complex problems. Improvements in memory reflect more than changes in capacity. Adolescents are better able to develop associations between words and ideas, which in turn facilitates remembering them. Part of their improvement is a result of the fact that adolescents know more than children. Adolescents also are better able to think abstractly and develop hypotheses. These skills in part reflect improvements in generalization, identifying similarities between previous situations and new ones. Changes in thinking and hypothesizing also enable adolescents to generate a wider variety of problem-solving strategies, which also enhances their performance. Finally, adolescents know more about the nature of thought and memory. This metacognition, or ability to "think about thinking," increases the planning in their problem-solving behavior.

Information-processing research has helped explain some of the inconsistencies that appear in Piagetian research. According to Piagetian theory, people are located within particular cognitive stages and will reason at those levels of maturity in all problem-solving situations. Why, then, do most people show features of several stages, depending on the type of problem presented? According to information-processing research, variability in performance across different problem types is to be expected. The more one knows, the easier it is to use efficient cognitive processes. People will appear more cognitively mature performing tasks about which they are knowledgeable.

APPLICATION OF RESEARCH

The research on adolescent thinking has been applied to the study of learning, personality, and social behavior during adolescence. For example, research on adolescent cognition has influenced the development of both curricula and teaching methods at the middle-school and high-school levels. As individuals who are entering the stage of formal thinking, adolescents are better equipped to handle abstract topics such as geometry and physics. Their emerging ability to consider systematically the effects of several factors when solving a problem make adolescents good candidates for laboratory science courses.

Some applications of research on adolescent cognitive skills are the subject of much debate, however; ability tracking is a case in point. Psychometric research indicates that intellectual functioning becomes relatively stable in preadolescence. From this point onward, children continue to perform at the same level relative to their age-mates on standardized measures such as IQ tests. The stability of test performance has been used to support the creation and maintenance of ability tracks beginning in the middle-school years. Proponents of tracking maintain that ability grouping or tracking enables teachers to challenge more able students without frustrating less capable students. Opponents of tracking maintain that less able students benefit from both the academic challenges and the competent role models provided by superior students in ungrouped classrooms. In fact, critics of tracking charge that the level at which performance stabilizes actually results from subtle differences in how teachers interact with their students, differences often based on inaccurate assumptions about student potential. Perhaps students with low test scores, many of whom are poor or minority students, perform poorly because people expect them to be less capable.

ADOLESCENTS AND SOCIAL COGNITION

Although Piaget primarily limited his research of adolescent reasoning to mathematical and scientific concepts, he did consider the role that formal oper-

ations play in the adolescent's social life. David Elkind continued research in this area by noting that features of formal thinking are reflected in adolescent personality characteristics. According to Elkind, the ability to think abstractly and hypothetically enables adolescents to develop their own idealistic, theoretical views of the world. The ability to distinguish between reality and theory, however, can lead to disillusionment and the recognition that adolescents' idols have "feet of clay." Elkind identified an adolescent egocentrism that he equates with the heightened self-consciousness of adolescence. This egocentrism demonstrates itself in two types of social thinking—personal fable and imaginary audience.

In personal fable, young adolescents see themselves as unique and special. Personal fable may lead adolescents to take unnecessary risks because they believe they are so different from others: "I can drink and drive." "Only other people get pregnant." Personal fable also makes adolescents believe that no one else can understand how they feel or offer any useful suggestions: "No one has ever had a problem like mine." In imaginary audience, adolescents believe that "everyone" is watching them. Elkind sees this self-consciousness as an application of hypothetical thinking: "If my characteristics are so obvious to me, they must also be obvious to everyone else."

Cognitive changes also affect social behavior by inducing changes in social cognitive development. Social cognition refers to an individual's understanding of people and of interactions between people. According to Piaget, changes in cognition are reflected in the way people think about themselves and other people. The thinking of preadolescents (seven to eleven years) begins to focus less on the obvious features of objects, events, and people. They are better able to translate patterns of behavior into psychological characteristics, such as concluding that a particular person is "nice" or "rude." They are becoming less egocentric, better able to appreciate that people have different points of view. It is not surprising, then, that they are better able to see the world from the perspective of another person. As they enter formal operations (eleven or twelve years and older), adolescents are able to think in more logical and abstract ways. These changes are reflected in their ability to describe people in abstract terms, such as "cooperative" or "uncoordinated," and compare people along psychological dimensions.

Robert Selman has observed that changes in social cognition occur in stages that closely parallel Piaget's stages of cognitive development. According to Selman's research, most concrete operational preadolescents (ages ten to twelve) recognize the existence of different points of view. Many of them, however, have difficulty evaluating conflicting perspectives or understanding how perspectives relate to membership in different social groups. As adolescents become more fully formal operational (twelve to fifteen years and older), they become able to understand the relationship between another person's perspective and their membership in social systems. For example, the difference between two people's points of view may reflect their membership in different racial or ethnic groups. Progress through Selman's stages also is influenced by social experiences. In other words, it is possible for a person to mature intellectually and to become less egocentric without becoming skillful at adopting others' points of view.

FORMAL OPERATIONS CONTROVERSY

Piaget believed that formal operational thought, entered between eleven and fifteen years of age, was a fourth and final stage of cognitive development, although he did say that adults are quantitatively more knowledgeable than adolescents. Some experts argue that young adults demonstrate a fifth, postformal stage that is different from adolescent thinking. Postformal thought is characterized by an understanding that the correct answer to a problem requires reflective thinking that may vary from one situation to another. Truth is viewed as an ongoing, never-ending process. Critics of this view argue that research evidence is lacking to document this as a qualitatively more advanced stage than formal operational thought.

Research has called into question the link between adolescence and the stage of formal operational thought. It is estimated that only one in three young adolescents is a formal operational thinker. Many adolescents think in ways characteristic of concrete operations or use formal thinking only part of the time. In fact, even many adults have not mastered formal operations. Critics argue that individual differences and cultural experiences may play a greater role in determining formal operations than Piaget envisioned.

Piagetian theory has been notoriously difficult to evaluate. Research indicates that performance on Piagetian tasks depends on understanding the instructions, being able to attend to the relevant aspects of the problems, and being interested in the problems themselves. Adolescents who perform best on formal operational tasks are often those with interests in the natural sciences—an unlikely finding if cognitive change is largely maturational.

Adolescents who do use formal operations may experience development in two phases, one early and the other during late adolescence. The initial stage is primarily assimilation, and involves the incorporating of new information into existing knowledge. Rather than using hypothetical-deductive thinking, adolescents at this point may simply be consolidating their concrete operational thinking. They tend to perceive their world in subjective and idealistic terms. During the later phase, adolescents are more likely to accommodate, restoring intellectual balance after a cognitive upheaval occurs.

Although the popularity of Piagetian theory has declined, it remains one of the most influential theories in developmental psychology. In fact, it was Piagetian theory that led information-processing psychologists to become interested in cognitive development. In a summation, understanding adolescent cognitive skills requires some familiarity with all perspectives, in spite of their respective weaknesses. Each has made a unique historical contribution to current views of cognition.

SOURCES FOR FURTHER STUDY

Byrnes, James P. *Minds, Brains, and Learning; Understanding of the Psychological and Educational Relevance of Neuroscientific Research.* New York: Guilford, 2001. Provides a stimulus for rethinking assumptions regarding the connection between mental and neural processes. The author challenges some of Piaget's ideas on formal operational thought. Gives a clear and readable overview of current neuroscientific work, especially for those relatively new to the field.

Elkind, David. *The Child's Reality: Three Developmental Themes.* Hillsdale, N.J.: Lawrence Erlbaum, 1978. Discusses the ways in which adolescent cognitive skills are reflected in personality and in social behavior. Excellent presentations on egocentrism, ideologies, personal fable, and imaginary audience.

Flavell, John, Patricia Mill, and Scott Miller. *Cognitive Development*. Rev. ed. Englewood Cliffs, N.J.: Prentice-Hall, 2001. Presents theory and research on cognitive development from an information-processing approach. Discusses relationship between information-processing and Piagetian theory. An excellent effort to compare and contrast these two perspectives.

Ginsburg, Herbert, and Sylvia Opper. *Piaget's Theory of Intellectual Development*. Englewood Cliffs, N.J.: Prentice-Hall, 1988. In its latest edition, this now classic work contains an updated presentation of Piaget's theory of cognitive development, including a detailed analysis of formal operational thinking.

Kuhn, D. "Adolescence: Adolescent Thought Processes." In *Encyclopedia of Psychology*, edited by Alan E. Kazdin. New York: Oxford University Press, 2000. This is an outstanding reference source for cognitive development in general. Kuhn provides a good evaluation of Piaget's work.

Muuss, R. E. "Social Cognition: Robert Selman's Theory of Role Taking." *Adolescence* 17, no. 67 (1982): 499-525. Discusses the relationship between adolescent cognitive skills and the ability to adopt another person's point of view. Includes an overall summary of Robert Selman's model of social cognitive development.

Pruitt, David B., ed. *Your Adolescent: Emotional Behavioral and Cognitive Development from Early Adolescence Through the Teen Years*. New York: HarperCollins, 2000. Written with the parent in mind, this resource covers a wide range of concerns and issues. It is published by the American Academy of Child and Adolescent Psychiatry and complements a similar book written for the childhood years. The approach is more practical than scholarly.

Lisa Friedenberg;
updated by Lillian J. Breckenridge

SEE ALSO: Adolescence: Cross-cultural patterns; Adolescence: Sexuality; Cognitive ability: Gender differences; Cognitive development: Jean Piaget; Identity crises; Learning; Problem-solving stages; Problem-solving strategies; Social perception; Teenage suicide; Violence by children and teenagers.

Adolescence
Cross-cultural patterns

TYPE OF PSYCHOLOGY: Developmental psychology
FIELDS OF STUDY: Adolescence

Adolescence, generally considered to be the years between the ages of twelve and eighteen, is a time of rapid development and confusion, both physically and emotionally. Adolescence is viewed differently in different cultures; although certain characteristics seem to be widespread, they are not necessarily universal.

KEY CONCEPTS
- formal operations
- gender-role orientation
- identity crisis
- self-esteem

INTRODUCTION

Adolescence is a time of rapid and difficult changes unlike any other period in a human's life. Both physical development and cognitive development enter dramatic new stages. The physical changes of puberty signal the onset of sexuality; cognitive abilities progress to the sophistication needed for mathematics and complex word use. Social relationships outside the family become much more important than before. Adolescents frequently enter a stage of rebellion against parental authority. It is no wonder that this time is widely regarded as the most turbulent period of life and that adolescents restlessly seek their own identity (psychoanalyst Erik Erikson referred to the process as the identity crisis stage of development).

Both psychological and general Western cultural views of adolescence reflect the way this period is perceived in Western society. Two of the most widely discussed psychological models of adolescence—Jean Piaget's cognitive stage of formal operations and Erikson's view of the identity crisis—exemplify this Western orientation. Piaget's model of the stages of cognitive development (beginning in infancy), in particular, has been studied cross-culturally; that is, researchers have explored whether the stages apply equally well to various different cultures. It has been found that the stages do not universally occur in the order that Piaget suggested.

RITES OF PASSAGE

Historically, the idea of adolescence as a separate stage is a relatively new idea. Before the mid-nineteenth century, in fact, a person was simply considered to pass from childhood to adulthood. Historically, and in different cultures, there have been various types of initiation rituals or rites of passage to mark this transition. In contemporary American society, one event that typically occurs in adolescence that could be considered such a rite of passage is learning to drive. This event embodies some of the complexities of modern society in that learning to drive symbolizes a new autonomy, yet the adolescent is still dependent on parents (or parent): The first car driven is usually theirs, they often pay the necessary insurance, and they set restrictions such as curfews.

Many tribal cultures have puberty rituals that reflect the way puberty is viewed in the culture. The Arapesh, a society in New Guinea, have a ceremony at a girl's first menstruation in which a menstrual hut is built for her; she is rubbed with stinging nettles by the older women, and she fasts for a number of days. Among the Mano of Liberia, boys participated in a pubertal ceremony in which they underwent a symbolic death, complete with chicken's blood to make it seem that they were punctured by a spear. The Pueblo Indians' traditional puberty ceremony for boys involves whipping, a largely ceremonial event in which no blood is drawn. During the initiation, children are supposed to be very frightened; they are not ashamed to cry aloud. Taking a psychoanalytical approach to studying male initiation ceremonies across cultures, John Whiting, Richard Kluckholm, and Albert Anthony noted that, in some cultures, mother and newborn infant share a bed exclusively for a year or more after childbirth. They concluded that such societies are more likely to have a ceremony of transition from boyhood to manhood, with the ritual helping to sever the boy's emotional bond with his mother. In various cultures, hazing, harsh endurance tests, and genital operations have all been performed in the name of initiation protocol.

Cultural attitudes and expectations of adolescence, as well as adolescent behaviors and skills, show both similarities and differences in different cultures. Much has been learned about this by studying the conflicts and difficulties experienced by adolescents of minorities and adolescents whose families have immigrated to the United States. These youths often have conflicting role models (or worse, no effective role models). The experiences of Asian American youths from Southeast Asia have been discussed by J. F. Nidorf. Living in the United States, the youth feels that he or she must develop autonomy from parents in order to attain a personal identity and sense of worth. Yet the parents believe that the adolescent should remain "indefinitely in a position of mutual interdependence with family members" and that a sense of self-worth comes from subordinating one's own needs and assuming greater responsibility for the needs of other family members. In other words, the adolescent hears that one should "become a success in the United States, but find a way to do it without becoming an American." In another example, in traditional Chinese families, dating, as practiced in the United States, does (or did) not exist. As B. L. Sung puts it, in China, teenagers are kept "under wraps" until they are married; in the United States, they are "titillated."

ADOLESCENCE IN ISRAEL

Among the cultures in which various aspects of childhood and adolescent development have been studied are Israel and Japan. The Israeli kibbutz is a collective settlement, either agricultural or industrial. The profits that are generated supply the members' basic needs as well as medical and social services. Approaches to child rearing vary among kibbutzim; children are often reared as much by other supervising adults and by the community as a whole as by their biological parents. Traditionally, adults have their own living quarters, but children often live separately from their parents in special children's housing (this is by no means true of all kibbutzim). Cooking and dining are communal activities.

Psychoanalyst Edith Buxbaum practiced in Israel in 1965-1966 at Oranim, the child guidance clinic of the kibbutzim; she wrote of her experiences there in "Problems of Kibbutz Children" in *Troubled Children in a Troubled World* (1970). She noted that behavior considered to be delinquent was not usually reported as such, but that it occurred in connection with other symptoms. The peer group has a very strong influence on kibbutz adolescents (as on kibbutz children of all ages), in part because of the fact that the children are together so much of the time. The peer group is as much a consistent factor in a child's life as are the child's parents; the group is together from infancy until graduation from high school. The group is a primary source of security as well as of rules and demands. From about the age of ten, children are often given work to do on the adult farm, and shirking one's duty is looked upon very unfavorably by the peer group.

Although adolescence in most cultures is a time of belonging to groups, they are most frequently voluntary groups. This is not true of kibbutz adolescents, Buxbaum points out, and she compares the general attitude of loyalty and helpfulness among teenagers there to that among students at institutions such as boarding schools. In most adolescent groups, the voluntary aspect gives the group much of its character; it leads to a sense of assertion and rebelliousness. This rebellious quality is largely missing from the kibbutz adolescent group; here, individual rebellion must be directed against the group itself. In its extreme cases, rebellion may cause an adolescent or young adult to leave the kibbutz altogether—often for a different kibbutz.

Possibly the biggest rite of passage for a person reared on a kibbutz occurs at the end, not the beginning, of adolescence. At the age of eighteen, both men and women leave the kibbutz temporarily to perform Israel's compulsory military service. For some, this will be their first extensive experience with the "outside" world. Some who leave do not return, although leaving can involve challenges caused in part by a lack of preparedness for living outside the kibbutz. The purpose of kibbutz upbringing and education is primarily to help the child reach his or her potential while preparing the individual for life on the kibbutz. It is not necessarily designed to promote success in the wider society, since the kibbutz prefers that the young person return.

ADOLESCENCE IN JAPAN

In Japan, it has only been since the 1950's that the concept of an adolescent, or teenager, in the Western sense, has become popular. Its arrival has largely been attributable to Western, especially American, influences, and to an increase in affluence. Historically, a young person passed from childhood to adulthood. There is no real Japanese-language equivalent for the word "teenager." High school students are commonly referred to as children (young people age seven or eight through fourteen are called *shonen*, and those fifteen to twenty-four are called *seinen*). The skepticism and questioning attitude toward society that have come to be associated with late adolescence also came to Japan relatively re-

cently, and typical Japanese adolescent rebellions pale in comparison with Western proportions and standards.

Japanese adolescents associate mostly with same-sex friends, tending to associate with people their own age (as opposed to spending time with their elders) much more than previous generations have. The changes wrought by technological advances have increased the importance of the nuclear family structure in Japan, although adolescents spend most of their nonschool time with their friends. The family's primary demand on the adolescent is for academic achievement. Students spend several hours a day on homework. Values such as diligence, endurance, dedication, and the willingness and ability to choose a difficult task play important roles in education. Socialization is also very important in Japanese culture, generally much more so than in American society.

A 1984 study that looked at self-concept and sex-role development in Japan concluded that major inequalities exist between girls' and boys' levels of self-esteem, which proved to be considerably lower in girls. An even greater discrepancy was found in sex roles, self-concepts, and perceived sex-role norms. Girls are much more conditioned to conform to traditional sex-role expectations. Educational institutions demand, either explicitly or implicitly, that students—especially girls—conform to traditional sex-role stereotypes. In a 1989 study of Japanese and German students' own perceptions of socialization and gender, it was noted that the Japanese students reported significantly more parental acceptance and parental control than their German counterparts. Traditional gender-role orientations were also more apparent in Japanese students.

PSYCHOLOGY AND ANTHROPOLOGY

The study of behavior in different cultures has traditionally been the province of anthropology and sociology rather than psychology. A few psychological theorists in the 1960's, however, did begin to question psychology's nearly total reliance on Western cultural values for its models of normality and abnormality, noting, for example, the similarities between symptoms of "madness" and types of religious experiences such as shamanistic trances.

One of the first widely read works dealing with adolescence in a non-Western society was anthropologist Margaret Mead's *Coming of Age in Samoa* (1928). Causing something of a sensation when it first appeared, the book described puberty and adolescence in a simple Pacific island culture (her study focused only on girls). Mead's methodology and findings have since been reexamined and called into question by such researchers as Derek Freeman, who wrote a 1983 volume intended to "right the wrongs" committed by Mead and present a more accurate picture of traditional Samoan society. Nevertheless, her work, flawed though it may have been, was influential in focusing interest on other societies' approaches to life stages and to sexuality.

The study of adolescence in American society began in earnest in the 1950's, an era of postwar prosperity in which teenagers as a group had increasing visibility and mobility, attributable in part to the automobile. There was a growth of behavior labeled juvenile delinquency—illegal antisocial behavior, including gang activity—that caused concern among sociologists, law-enforcement agencies, and parents alike. The image of rebellious teenagers riding motorcycles and listening to rock and roll caught the public imagination and became the fodder for many motion pictures.

In many cultures, adolescence is a time of strong peer-group attachments. Moreover, cognitive abilities reach new levels of sophistication (Piaget's "formal operations" stage). Therefore, as adolescents are being formally or informally initiated into the ways of adulthood, they are also able to question those ways; the types of questions asked, the satisfaction with traditional answers, and the levels of actual rebellion that occur vary from culture to culture and from time to time. Similarly, the skills and behaviors necessary for success in a society vary, depending on the society's complexity and stratification. In technological societies, such as exist in the United States and Japan, formal education becomes tremendously important. Whatever the needs of a particular society, however, the period of adolescence is a critical time for learning what the necessary skills are and discovering one's ability to acquire them.

SOURCES FOR FURTHER STUDY

Alsaker, Françoise D., August Flammer, and Nancy Bodmer, eds. *The Adolescent Experience: European and American Adolescents in the 1990's.* Hillsdale, N.J.: Lawrence Erlbaum, 1999. A collection of papers making cross-national comparisons of the experiences of adolescents in Europe and North America.

Barnouw, Victor. *Culture and Personality.* 4th ed. Belmont, Calif.: Wadsworth, 1985. Presents a historical view of various dimensions of culture as they relate to personality. Examines correlational studies, specifically cross-cultural surveys.

Buxbaum, Edith. *Troubled Children in a Troubled World.* New York: International Universities Press, 1970. Buxbaum takes a psychoanalytical approach to children's and adolescents' psychological problems. Two chapters, "The Group in Adolescence" and "Problems of Kibbutz Children," are especially relevant to adolescence. The latter looks at kibbutz children generally and at a few particular case studies.

Feldman, S. Shirley, and Glen R. Elliott, eds. *At the Threshold: The Developing Adolescent.* Cambridge, Mass.: Harvard University Press, 1993. A comprehensive collection of essays on adolescence that presents the findings of a Carnegie Foundation study. Primarily concerned with American society, it does include interesting references to minority adolescents and other cultures as well as historical perspectives. Well indexed and has an exhaustive list of references.

Freeman, Derek. *Margaret Mead and Samoa.* Cambridge, Mass.: Harvard University Press, 1983. Freeman's primary purpose is to "right the wrongs" that Mead committed in her *Coming of Age in Samoa.* He presents detailed empirical evidence to advance his arguments and remove readers' doubts about his point of view.

Fukuzawa, Rebecca, and Gerald K. Letendre. *Intense Years: How Japanese Adolescents Balance School, Family, and Friends.* New York: Routledge, 2001. Examines the transition from childhood to adolescence that takes place during the middle-school years in Japanese society.

White, Merry. *The Japanese Educational Challenge.* New York: Free Press, 1987. Clear and compelling investigation of the Japanese educational system. Explores the concept of a system that focuses on parental guidance and the development of strong human relationships outside the home.

Denise S. St. Cyr

SEE ALSO: Adolescence: Cognitive skills; Adolescence: Sexuality; Cultural competence; Identity crises; Juvenile delinquency; Teenage suicide; Violence by children and teenagers.

Adolescence

Sexuality

TYPE OF PSYCHOLOGY: Developmental psychology
FIELDS OF STUDY: Adolescence

Adolescent sexuality examines the physical, psychological, and behavioral changes that occur as the individual leaves childhood, acquires sexual maturity, and incorporates the various aspects of sexuality into his or her identity.

KEY CONCEPTS
- contraception
- development of sexual identity
- levels of sexual activity
- psychological effects
- puberty

INTRODUCTION

Perhaps no single event during the adolescent years has as dramatic or widespread effects as the realization of sexuality. The lives of both males and females become wrapped in this new dimension. Adolescence is a time of sexual exploration and experimentation, of sexual fantasies and sexual realities, of incorporating sexuality into one's identity. These processes determine adolescents' comfort with their own emerging sexuality as well as with that of others. Adolescents are also beginning to be involved in intimate relationships, which is a context where sexual activity often occurs.

In recent decades, many of the milestones by which adulthood is defined and measured—full-time employment, economic independence, domestic partnership/marriage, and childbearing—are attained at later ages in people's lives than they were in earlier generations, while puberty begins at earlier ages. Thus, adolescents face many years between the onset of puberty, fertility, and the natural intensification of sexual feelings, on one hand, and committed relationships and economic independence, on the other hand. As a result, young people have sexual intercourse earlier in life, and there are a greater percentage of adolescents who are sexually experimenting at every age level, a greater number of acts of premarital intercourse, and a greater number of sexual partners before marriage.

PHYSICAL CHANGES

Adolescence is the life stage between childhood and adulthood. Its age limits are not clearly specified, but it extends roughly from age twelve to the late teens, when physical growth is nearly complete. Puberty, a term often confused with adolescence, occurs at the end of childhood and lasts from two to four years. It is the period of adolescence during which an individual reaches sexual maturity.

Human beings grow most rapidly at two times during their lives: before they are six months old and again during adolescence. The second period of accelerated growth is often referred to as the adolescent growth spurt. Adolescents grow both in height and weight, with the increase in height occurring first. As they gain weight, the amount and distribution of fat in their bodies change, and the proportion of bone and muscle tissue increases. In girls, the adolescent growth spurt usually begins between the ages of nine and eleven and reaches a peak at an average of twelve and a half years. Then growth slows and usually ceases completely between the ages of fifteen and eighteen. The growth spurt in boys generally begins about two years later than it does in girls and lasts for a longer time. It begins between the ages of eleven and fourteen, reaches a peak at about age fifteen, and slowly declines until the age of nineteen or twenty.

The teenager's body grows at differing rates, so that at times adolescents look a bit awkward. Big feet and long legs are the early signs of a changing body, but even these changes do not occur at the same time. First the hands and feet grow, then the arms and legs; only later do the shoulders and chest grow to fit the rest of the developing body. Changes in body proportion become obvious. The trunk widens in the hips and shoulders, and the waistline narrows. Boys tend to broaden mostly in the shoulders, girls in the hips.

Puberty is chiefly characterized by sexual development. Sexual development can be best understood by examining the maturation of primary and secondary sex characteristics. Primary sex characteristics are the physiological features of the sex organs. For males, these organs are the penis and the testes; for females, they are the ovaries, uterus, clitoris, and vagina. Secondary sex characteristics are not directly related to the sexual organs but nevertheless distinguish a mature male from a mature female. Examples of secondary sex characteristics are the male beard and the female breasts.

In girls, the onset of breast development is usually, but not always, the first sign that puberty has begun. This typically occurs between the ages of ten and eleven, but can occur as late as ages thirteen and fourteen. There is simultaneous development of the uterus and vagina, with enlargement of the labia and clitoris. Menarche (the first menstrual period), although perhaps the most dramatic and symbolic sign of a girl's changing status, occurs relatively late in puberty, after the growth spurt has reached its peak velocity. The first menstrual periods tend to be irregular, and ovulation (the release of a mature egg) does not usually begin until a year or so after menarche. Onset age of first menarche has decreased as body weight has increased in the modern era, with girls on average reaching menarche at ten and a half to eleven years of age.

The first noticeable change in boys is usually growth of the testes and scrotum. The growth of the genitals begins, on average, about the age of twelve and is completed, on average, by about the age of fifteen. Boys generally become capable of ejaculation about a year after the penis begins to grow. These first emissions may occur as a result of nocturnal emissions, the ejaculation of semen during sleep. Nocturnal emissions are a normal phase of development and are frequently caused by sexual excitation in dreams or by some type of physical condition, such as a full bladder or even pressure from pajamas.

As adolescents' bodies become more adult, their interest in sexual behavior increases sharply. They must learn the necessary behavior to satisfy that interest, and they must face the issue of a mature gender identity. This includes the expression of sexual needs and feelings and the acceptance or rejection of sex roles. The onset of dating and the beginning of physical intimacies with the opposite sex can provoke frustration and anxiety. As this unfamiliar territory is explored, the adolescent is often very underinformed and overly self-conscious. Conflicting sexual values and messages are frequently encountered, accentuating the problem of integrating sexual drives with other aspects of the personality.

PSYCHOLOGICAL ADJUSTMENT

Adolescents are acutely aware of the rapid changes taking place in their bodies. How they react to such

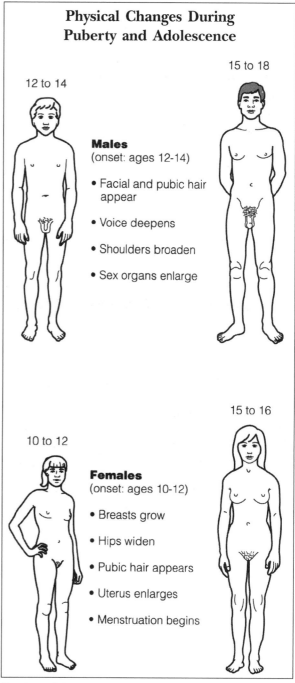

Physical Changes During Puberty and Adolescence

12 to 14

15 to 18

Males
(onset: ages 12-14)

• Facial and pubic hair appear

• Voice deepens

• Shoulders broaden

• Sex organs enlarge

10 to 12

15 to 16

Females
(onset: ages 10-12)

• Breasts grow

• Hips widen

• Pubic hair appears

• Uterus enlarges

• Menstruation begins

During adolescence, the physical changes of puberty result in relatively rapid sexual development. (Hans & Cassidy, Inc.)

changes greatly affects how they evaluate themselves; it is in this manner that physical and psychological development are related.

Physical changes may cause psychological discomfort. Adolescents are particularly concerned about whether they are the "right" shape or size and whether they measure up to the "ideal" adolescent. Rapid growth, awkwardness, acne, voice changes, menarche, and other developments may produce emotional distress. Therefore, it is not surprising that the timing of physical and sexual maturity may have an important influence on psychosocial adjustment. Adolescents are generally concerned about anything that sets them apart from their peers. Being either the first or last to go through puberty can cause considerable self-consciousness.

In general, boys who mature early have a distinct advantage over those who mature late. They tend to be more poised, easygoing, and good-natured. They are taller, heavier, and more muscular than other boys their age. They are also more likely to excel in sports, achieve greater popularity, and become school leaders. The ideal form for men in American society, as represented by the media, is that of the postpubescent male. Therefore, early entry into puberty draws boys closer to the male "ideal." In contrast, late-maturing boys not only are smaller and less well developed than others in their age group but also not as interested in dating. When they do become interested in girls, they often lack social skills; they are more likely to feel inadequate, anxious, and self-conscious. These personality characteristics tend to persist into early adulthood, although they may become less marked and often disappear as time goes by.

For girls, early maturation appears to be a mixed blessing. Girls who mature early grow taller, develop breasts, and go through menarche as much as six years before some of their peers. Their larger size and more adult physique may make them feel conspicuous and awkward, while at the same time they may be popular with boys and experience more dating opportunities. They also may have to deal with parents and other caregivers who have reacted to their early sexual development by being overly restrictive. The beauty ideal for women in American society, as portrayed by the media, is that of a prepubescent female. Changes in body fat related to puberty thus may lead to body image problems, as entry into puberty increases the distance from the beauty ideal just as girls become most interested in it. As with boys, the consequences of early and late maturation decrease over time. However, either early or late start of menarche seems significantly more difficult to deal with than if more typical.

SEXUAL BEHAVIOR

Sexual maturation has other psychological consequences as well. In particular, patterns of sexual behavior change tremendously with the arrival of sexual maturity. As adolescents' bodies become more adult, their interest in sexual behavior increases sharply; as they explore their sexual identities, they develop a sexual script, or a stereotyped pattern for how individuals should behave sexually.

The sexual script for boys is frequently different from the sexual script for girls. As a result, males and females generally think differently about sex. This discrepancy can cause problems and confusion for adolescents as they struggle with their sexual identities. For males, the focus of sexuality may be sexual conquest, to the point that young men who are nonexploitative or inexperienced may be labeled with negative terms such as "sissy." Males are more likely than females to see intercourse as a way of establishing their maturity and of achieving social status. As a consequence, boys are more likely to have sex with someone who is a relative stranger, to have more sexual partners, and to disassociate sex from love and emotional intimacy.

Adolescent girls are much more likely than adolescent males to link sexual intercourse with love. The quality of the relationship between the girl and her partner is a very important factor. Most females would agree that sexual intercourse is acceptable if the two people are in love and is not acceptable if they are not in a romantic relationship. Consequently, females are less likely than males to list pleasure, pleasing their partner, and relieving sexual tension as reasons for having sex.

During the past several decades, attitudes toward sexual activity have changed dramatically. Views regarding premarital sex, extramarital sex, and specific sexual acts are probably more open and permissive today than they have been at any other time in recent history. Young people are exposed to sexual stimuli on television and in magazines and motions pictures to a greater extent than ever before. Effective methods of birth control have lessened the fear of pregnancy. All these changes have given the adolescent more freedom. At the same time, the rise of acquired immunodeficiency syndrome (AIDS) in the late 1970's, the sharp increases in AIDS cases among hetersexual teenagers in the 1990's and the increased concern over antibiotic-resistant gonorrhea and other sexually tranmitted diseases have only produced more conflict, since guidelines for "appropriate behavior" are less clear-cut than they were in the past. In some families, the divergence between adolescent and parental standards of sexual morality is great.

Research specifically directed toward the exploration of adolescent sexuality was not seriously undertaken until the 1950's and 1960's. Even then, the few studies that were conducted handled the topic delicately and focused on attitudes rather than behavior. When behavior was emphasized, age at first intercourse was generally selected as the major variable. Later studies have been more detailed and expansive; however, a paucity of research in this area still exists.

In *Facing Facts* (1995), Debra W. Haffner categorizes adolescent sexuality into three stages; early, middle, and late. In early adolescence (ages nine to thirteen for girls, eleven to fifteen for boys) experimenting with sexual behavior is common, although sexual intercourse is usually limited. A 1994 national telephone survey of ninth- to twelfth-grade students found that nearly all had engaged in kissing; more than 70 percent had engaged in touching above the waist and more than 50 percent below the waist; 15 percent had engaged in mutual masturbation. This time period is characterized by the beginning of the process of separating from the family and becoming more influenced by peers. During middle adolescence (thirteen to sixteen for girls, fourteen to seventeen for boys) sexual experimentation is common, and many adolescents have first intercourse during this stage of life. Fifty percent of ninth- through twelfth-grade students report having had sexual intercourse, with percentages from 38 percent of ninth-graders to 65 percent of twelfth-graders. A slightly higher percentage of young men than young women reported having had sexual intercourse. In late adolescence (women sixteen and older; men seventeen and older), the process of physical maturation is complete. There is autonomy from family as well as from the peer group as adult roles are defined. Sexuality often becomes associated with commitment and planning for the future.

Awareness of sexual orientation often emerges in adolescence. A study, conducted by Margaret Rosario and her colleagues, of fourteen- to twenty-one-year-old lesbian, gay, and bisexual youths reports that the average age at which girls were certain of being gay was approximately 16, and the average age for boys was 14.6, with the majority reporting a history of sexual activity with both sexes.

Boys appear to initiate intercourse earlier than girls, but girls catch up by the late teens. The timing of puberty is important for boys, while for girls, social controls exert a greater influence than the onset of puberty. Girls who are academically engaged, with higher self-esteem, and with interests outside the dating culture are more likely to delay the onset of sexual activity. For both boys and girls, dual-parent families, higher socioeconomic status, parental supervision, and close relationship with parents are all associated with delayed onset of sexual activity.

Contraceptive use among adolescents continues to increase. Two-thirds of adolescents report using some method of contraceptive, usually condoms, the first time they have sexual intercourse. The older they are at first intercourse the more likely they are to use a contraceptive as well. Programs that improve teen access to contraceptives have not produced increased rates of sexual activity, but do increase condom use.

Social concerns such as teenage pregnancy, sexually transmitted diseases, and sex education have focused attention on the need to understand clearly the dynamics of adolescent sexuality. This awareness should continue to encourage broader perspectives for the study of teenage sexual behavior and produce detailed knowledge of sexuality as it occurs in the adolescent experience.

Sources for Further Study

Alan Guttmacher Institute. *Sex and America's Teenagers.* New York: Author, 1994. The report of a study conducted by the Alan Guttmacher Institute on teenage sexual activity in the 1990's. It is presented in written and graphical forms and provides a good look at the latest information on adolescent sexuality.

Bell, Ruth, et al. *Changing Bodies, Changing Lives: A Book for Teens on Sex and Relationships.* 3d ed. New York: Random House, 1998. Written specifically for a teenage audience. Teens from around the United States were surveyed in order to determine the book's contents, and they share their unique perspectives on sexuality. This is perhaps one of the best resources available for teens.

Columbia University Health Education Program. *The Go Ask Alice Book of Answers: A Guide to Good Physical, Sexual, and Emotional Health.* New York: Owl Books, 1998. Inspired by Columbia's award-winning and hugely popular Q&A Web site, this book is packed with straightforward, nonjudgmental, comprehensive answers to the toughest, most embarrassing questions teens and adults have about sexual, emotional, and physical health.

Haffner, Debra W., ed. *Facing Facts: Sexual Health for America's Adolescents.* New York: Sexuality Information and Education Council of the United States, 1995. A guide for policymakers, health professionals, and parents to use when developing policies on adolescent sexual health.

Madaras, Lynda, with Area Madaras. *The What's Happening to My Body? Book for Girls: A Growing Up Guide for Parents and Daughters.* 3d rev. ed. New York: Newmarket, 2000. Written especially for adolescents and their parents. The author is a leading sex educator, and she is joined by her daughter. The primary focus is on female puberty; however, topics such as sexual feelings and sexual intercourse are also discussed. Well written, with illustrations that enhance the text.

Madaras, Lynda, with Dane Saavedra. *The What's Happening to My Body? Book for Boys: A Growing Up Guide for Parents and Sons.* 3d rev. ed. New York: Newmarket, 2000. Written by a leading sex educator with the assistance of an adolescent male. The book deals primarily with male puberty but includes information about sexual feelings and sexual intercourse. A very useful and informative book, written in a conversational style.

Rosario, Margaret, et al. "The Psychosexual Development of Urban Lesbian, Gay, and Bisexual Youths." *The Journal of Sex Research* 33, no. 2 (1996): 113-126. Fills one of the gaps often left by general reference sources that often treat adolescent sexuality as strictly heterosexual in nature. Provides current information on alternative sexuality choices made by adolescents.

Strasburger, Victor C., and Robert T. Brown. *Adolescent Medicine: A Practical Guide.* 2d ed. Philadelphia: Lippincott-Raven, 1998. This book addresses the physical and psychosocial problems of teenagers that physicians are most likely to treat.

The emphasis is on practical information. Applied diagnostic and treatment guidelines cover conditions such as asthma, diabetes mellitus, developmental problems, headaches, sexually transmitted diseases and pregnancy, depression, and eating disorders.

Doyle R. Goff;
updated by Cynthia O'Dell

SEE ALSO: Adolescence: Cognitive skills; Adolescence: Cross-cultural patterns; Child abuse; Drives; Homosexuality; Identity crises; Psychosexual development; Sex hormones and motivation; Sexual behavior patterns; Violence and sexuality in the media.

Adrenal gland

TYPE OF PSYCHOLOGY: Biological bases of behavior
FIELDS OF STUDY: Endocrine system

The paired adrenal glands situated above the kidneys are each divided into two portions, a cortex and a medulla. The cortex produces steroid hormones, involved in the control of metabolism, inflammation, and other important processes; the medulla produces the amino acid-derived catecholamines, which are thought to be important in brain behavior.

KEY CONCEPTS
- affective disorders
- endocrine gland
- hormone
- protein
- receptor
- steroid hormone
- target organ

INTRODUCTION

The adrenal glands are a pair of triangular endocrine glands, one lying on top of each of the kidneys. These glands secrete several hormones that are essential to life in that they regulate the body's metabolism of fats, carbohydrates, and proteins; help to maintain appropriate amounts of body fluids, thus participating in blood-pressure regulation; fight the effects of stress and injury on the body; participate in the immune response; and function in nerve-impulse transmission and brain function.

By definition, endocrine glands produce one or more hormones and secrete them into the blood so that they can serve as intercellular messengers. In contrast, exocrine glands secrete their chemical products through ducts (such as the kidney, pancreas, or stomach). Hormones themselves are trace chemicals—present in tiny amounts—that act as extracellular messengers, controlling body processes in target organs far from the endocrine gland that produced them. A target organ is one that responds to a hormone by changes in its biological capabilities.

ADRENAL CORTICOSTEROIDS

The adrenal gland is divided into an outer cortex and an inner medulla. The cortex produces about three dozen hormones, all fatlike steroids. These adrenal corticosteroids are divided into two main groups, glucocorticoids and mineralocorticoids; the adrenal cortex also produces steroid sex hormones. Glucocorticoids, whose production is controlled mostly by the pituitary gland (via the protein pituitary hormone adrenocorticotropin, or ACTH), mediate the ways in which the body breaks down and uses fats, carbohydrates, and proteins. The most abundant and potent of these hormones is cortisol (hydrocortisone). In times of stress (such as injury, extreme temperature change, illness, surgery, or ingestion of toxic chemicals), ACTH will stimulate production of glucocorticoids. The glucocorticoids also have tremendous ability as anti-inflammatory agents, fighting inflammation caused by arthritis and allergic reactions. For this reason, they are utilized medically to combat allergy, asthma, and arthritis. In some instances, overdosage of glucocorticoids can cause abnormal mental behavior.

The second major group of adrenal corticosteroids is the mineralocorticoids. These hormones control the body's salt levels (sodium and chloride ions), which are important to the maintenance of body water balance and to the cellular import and export of both nutrients and wastes. If too much sodium chloride is retained in blood and tissues, the total fluid volume in the blood vessels increases and produces high blood pressure. Mineralocorticoids also control potassium levels, important because this ion is essential to nerve-impulse transport. The main mineralocorticoid, aldosterone, interacts with a kidney protein (called renin) to maintain appropriate blood volume by controlling the rate of salt

and water excretion. Diseases of underproduction or overproduction of adrenal steroids, including the sex hormones, can have serious consequences.

The adrenal steroids all act by forming complexes with special receptor proteins in target organs, transporting hormone-receptor complexes to cell nuclei, and stimulating the production of key cell proteins by interaction with the hereditary material (gene derepression) in cell nuclei. Proteins are amino acid polymers that have many biological functions, including acting as enzymes (biological catalysts) and hormone receptors. Receptors are proteins that interact with a specific hormone to enable it to carry out messenger functions in target organs.

The adrenal medulla—which arises from fetal nervous tissue—produces amino acid-derived hormones called catecholamines, stores them, and releases them on receiving an appropriate signal. The main catecholamines are epinephrine (adrenaline), norepinephrine (noradrenaline), and dopamine. These chemicals are linked with the nervous system in several ways. First, epinephrine and norepinephrine are hormones that control the fight-or-flight responses that enable the body to respond to emergencies (by anger or fear reactions). Such responses are partly attributable to linkage between the adrenal medulla and the sympathetic nervous system, which can produce the signals that cause release of catecholamines in times of stress.

Such release has many useful effects, including the dilation of eye pupils to allow better sight; elevation of the blood pressure and increasing of the heartbeat to allow better transport of energy-producing food; release of energy reserves of sugar from liver and muscle; and contraction of blood vessels near the skin, to minimize bleeding if wounds should occur. Epinephrine, norepinephrine, and dopamine also heighten the reactions of the central nervous system, acting as neurotransmitters in different parts of the brain and evoking responses needed for fight, flight, and normal brain function.

These actions of catecholamines can be harmful, as shown in a disease called pheochromocytoma, in which adrenal medullary hormones are overproduced because of tumors of the medulla or the sympathetic nervous system. Afflicted persons exhibit symptoms that include high blood pressure, heart palpitations, nervousness, anxiety, and neurotic symptoms. Abnormalities of catecholamine levels are implicated in a primary fashion in many psychological disorders. Catecholamine actions, like those of steroid hormones (a hormone that is a fatlike chemical derived from cholesterol), involve specific receptors; however, catecholamine-related processes do not involve hormone-receptor interactions with the hereditary material. Rather, they utilize a "second messenger" mechanism in which already existing proteins are activated.

RELATIONSHIP TO MENTAL DISORDERS

Mental illness is frequently divided into two basic types: organic and functional disorders. Organic mental illness is a consequence of a known disease, such as diabetes or a tumor of the adrenal gland, that alters the structure of the brain or its ability to function correctly, or produces a malfunction of some other part of the nervous system. Cure of organic mental illness uses surgery or other methods that eradicate the causative disease. In contrast, the exact basis for functional mental illness has often evaded understanding and has long been viewed as being caused by operational flaws of mental function. Among the most widely publicized mental disorders are schizophrenia and manic-depressive psychosis (bipolar disorder).

Relatively clear understanding has begun to develop for bipolar disorder, wherein afflicted persons alternate rapidly between an excessively happy (manic) state and a severely depressed (depressive) state, thus being unable to cope with the world around them. This understanding begins with consideration of the function and malfunction of the human nervous system, composed of a central computer—the brain—and a network of neuron wires—nerves—that communicate with the rest of the body via nerve impulses. When nerve impulses pass through the nervous system correctly, they allow recognition and appropriate response to the world. Malfunction of nerve-impulse generation and passage through the nerves or brain is believed to produce some functional mental illness.

The terms "synaptic gap" and "neurotransmitter action" should be explained. Nerve cells (neurons) are separated from one another by minute synaptic gaps, and the passage of nerve impulses through a nerve requires the impulses to cross thousands of such gaps. Nerve-impulse transport across synaptic gaps is mediated by biochemicals called neurotransmitters. The best known of these is ace-

tylcholine, which acts in cholinergic nerves. The dysfunction of cholinergic nerves, via disruption of acetylcholine action, is believed to be a major component of functional mental disease. This idea came partly from observation of impaired mental function in people exposed to nerve gases and insecticides that act by disrupting acetylcholine production and use.

Other neurotransmitters associated with mental disorders include catecholamines and chemicals called indoleamines. The main catecholamine neurotransmitters are the adrenal medulla hormones epinephrine and norepinephrine and their close cousin, dopamine (also made by the adrenal medulla). The catecholamines control nerve-impulse transmission by adrenergic portions of the nervous system. The indoleamines (especially serotonin) act in neurons related to sleep and sensory perception.

ROLE IN DEPRESSION

Some theories of depression and mania have arisen from the catecholamine (actually, norepinephrine) hypothesis of Joseph Schildkraut and others. The theory proposed that depression is attributable to suboptimum production or utilization of norepinephrine (decreased noradrenergic activity) and that mania arises from increased noradrenergic activity. Its acceptance led to the examination of norepinephrine levels in normal and mental disease states; use of observed levels of the neurotransmitter to explain how existing drugs, electric shock, and other psychiatric treatments affected functional mental illness; choice of new therapeutic drugs on the basis of their effects on norepinephrine levels; and study of effects of other catecholamines and related "biogenic amines."

These efforts soon showed that dopamine, a catecholamine cousin of norepinephrine, was implicated in central nervous system function. Then it was observed that several important tranquilizers (among them reserpine) decreased both norepinephrine and dopamine levels. Consequently, the catecholamine hypothesis was expanded to include dopamine. In fact, low levels of dopamine were shown to be more intimately involved in depression than are low epinephrine levels.

The biogenic indoleamine serotonin was next implicated in depression, because it is also depleted by tranquilizers such as reserpine. It was then shown that the action of therapeutic drugs called tricyclic antidepressants is also related mostly to alteration of serotonin levels. Because of this, an indoleamine (serotonin) corollary was added to the catecholamine hypothesis of affective disease.

In 1972, David Janowsky and coworkers at Vanderbilt University's psychiatry department proposed a new hypothesis of affective disease. Their hypothesis focused on the cholinergic neurotransmitter acetylcholine but expanded the conceptual basis for functional mental illness. Unlike preceding concepts, it recognized the importance of interaction between the various systems participating in nerve-impulse transmission and suggested that the affective state of any individual represents a balance between adrenergic and cholinergic activity. Furthermore, the hypothesis proposed depression as a disease of "relative cholinergic predominance," while mania was said to be attributable to "relative adrenergic predominance."

THERAPEUTIC DRUGS

Until the advent of the catecholamine (and later indoleamine) hypothesis of affective mental disorder and the realization of the adrenal medullary involvement in psychiatric disorders, the primary treatments attempted for functional mental disease included procedures such as lobotomy, electroconvulsive (shock) therapy, and insulin coma. These procedures are now viewed as being imprecise at best, though some use of each has persisted, most often as part of mixed psychotherapy (that adds them to psychoanalysis and treatment with psychotherapeutic drugs) or therapy involving patients extremely difficult to treat.

Much of the basis for use of such drugs evolved from examination of therapeutic drugs for the ability to alter catecholamine and indoleamine levels. Among the first psychotherapeutic drugs were the tricyclic antidepressants, organic chemicals that affected catecholamine and serotonin levels. Another useful family of these drugs is a group of chemicals called monoamine oxidase inhibitors (MAOIs). MAOIs prevent biological modification of catecholamines by the enzyme monoamine oxidase, prolonging their presence in the body. In addition, the importance of lithium-containing chemicals in fighting functional mental illness is also believed to be attributable to a mechanism that includes alterations of catecholamine and indoleamine concentrations in the nervous system.

CONTRIBUTIONS

The developing understanding of the role of the adrenal medulla in both normal and pathological processes in the nervous system has led to a more complete understanding of the basis for the utility of major tranquilizers in treatment of the severely mentally ill. It has also enabled better differentiation of schizophrenia from affective disorders—functional mental disorders associated with emotions or feelings—and led to explanations of the causes of (and some useful treatments for) the psychogenic manifestations of many illegal addictive drugs. Understanding of the adrenal gland has also led to the discovery of additional neurotransmitter chemicals that promise better understanding of the nervous system. Furthermore, examination of the steroid hormones of the adrenal cortex has shown that they can produce some psychopathology.

SOURCES FOR FURTHER STUDY

Janowsky, David S., Robert N. Golden, Mark Rapaport, John Cain, and J. Christian Gillian. "Neurochemistry of Depression and Mania." In *Depression and Mania*, edited by Anastasios Georgotas and Robert Cancro. New York: Elsevier, 1988. Reviews development of modern concepts of the neurochemistry of these mental diseases, including norepinephrine and the catecholamine hypothesis; acetylcholine and the cholinergic-adrenergic hypothesis; and serotonin, dopamine, neuropeptides, and other neurotransmitters.

Janowsky, David S., M. Khaled el-Yousef, John M. Davis, and H. Joseph Sekerke. "A Cholinergic-Adrenergic Hypothesis of Mania and Depression." *The Lancet* 2 (September, 1972): 632-635. This landmark article recognizes the importance of the several systems of nerve-impulse transmission and proposes that the affective state represents balance between noradrenergic and cholinergic activity. Depression and mania are viewed as attributable to relative cholinergic and adrenergic predominance, respectively. Manic-depression is seen as overreaction by part of the nervous system.

Lehninger, Albert L. *Lehninger Principles of Biochemistry*. New York: Worth, 2000. Offers a survey of the steroid hormones and related chemicals. Includes their structures, their biochemistry, their biological properties, and their interactions with receptors.

Valenstein, Elliot S. *Great and Desperate Cures: The Rise and Decline of Psychosurgery and Other Radical Treatments for Mental Illness*. New York: Basic Books, 1986. Describes the basis for the development, rise, and decline of psychosurgery. Its coverage also includes other therapeutic methods used at the time, the theories of mentation that led to such techniques, and reasons for technique replacement or retention. Many useful illustrations and references are included.

Sanford S. Singer

SEE ALSO: Bipolar disorder; Brain structure; Depression; Endocrine system; Gonads; Hormones and behavior; Nervous system; Pituitary gland; Psychosurgery; Seasonal affective disorder; Sex hormones and motivation; Stress: Physiological responses; Synaptic transmission; Thyroid gland.

Advertising

TYPE OF PSYCHOLOGY: Cognition; motivation; social psychology

FIELDS OF STUDY: Cognitive processes; social motives; social perception and cognition

Advertising is a psychological process of persuasion through attitude change. Advertisers create change in consumer beliefs, emotions, and intentions to act in regard to their products. Effective advertising draws on knowledge of narrative script, information processing, miscomprehension, psychological appeals, classical conditioning, and subliminal messages.

KEY CONCEPTS
- attitude
- classical conditioning
- encoding
- information processing
- miscomprehension
- narrative script
- needs
- persuasion
- psychological appeal
- subliminal advertising

INTRODUCTION

Advertising is a process of persuading an audience to buy products, contract services, or support a candidate or issue. Advertising creates a reality for the consumer—both the image of the product, company, or candidate and the need for a product or service. Advertisements try to change consumer attitudes toward a product, company, or candidate. Attitudes consist of three components: belief, affect (emotion), and intention to act. The ultimate goal of the advertiser is to persuade the consumer to act—to buy the product, support the candidate or company, or use the service.

Advertising is one form of mass communication. A classified ad from around 1000 B.C.E. offered a reward (a gold coin) to anyone finding and returning a runaway slave. Johannes Gutenberg, an inventor and metallurgist, invented movable type in the fifteenth century, which allowed for the printed mass communication of advertising. The Industrial Revolution of the nineteenth century cultivated commercialism and transportation of national publications, including a large number of magazines. Advertising proliferated on radio after 1920, on television after 1945, and on the Internet in the mid-1990's.

Psychologists study advertising as a form of communication in the context of cognition and psycholinguistics. Consumers read advertisements, whether in print, on television, or online, similarly to the way they read books. Therefore, one way to examine how consumers understand and react to advertisements is by researching comprehension of narrative scripts. For advertisements to effectively change consumer attitudes, their message must be understood. Psychologists study how consumers process the information in the advertisement. Sometimes information processing leads to miscomprehension which, often unintentionally, can create in the consumer false ideas about the product.

From a more social cognitive and humanistic perspective, psychologists look at the appeals advertisers make to human needs. Advertisements associate basic needs and natural responses to those needs with their products. Advertisers classically condition consumers to respond to their products as they would to any stimulus naturally satisfying a need. Sometimes these associations are not consciously made.

Even before the arrival of television, advertising had become pervasive by the 1940's, with billboards vying for the attention of consumers. (Hulton Archive)

NARRATIVE SCRIPT

The first step in changing consumer attitudes toward an advertised product is to persuade the consumer that the informational content of the advertisement is true. One way advertisers create belief in the consumer is to follow the narrative script, a simple plot such as a child might hear when a parent reads a story.

The narrative script is a knowledge structure composed of exposition, complication, and resolution. The exposition introduces the characters and settings of the story. The complication is a developing problem. The resolution is the solution to the problem. Many advertisements take the form of the narrative script in order to facilitate comprehension and belief. For example, John, Jane, and their daughter Judy are playing at the park (exposition). While swinging, Judy falls on the ground, scraping her knee (complication). Jane soothes Judy and dresses her wound by applying a plastic bandage coated with an antibacterial agent (resolution). The consumer is comfortable with the narrative script as

an understandable and entertaining format. The advertiser is able to hold the audience's attention. The resolution is associated with the product (bandages).

INFORMATION PROCESSING

The consumer's belief in the advertisement is affected by how the consumer processes the information presented in it. There are eight stages of information processing involved in the comprehension of advertisements. The belief component of the consumer's attitude toward the product can be formed or modified at any stage. The first stage is exposure. The consumer must have the opportunity to perceive the advertisement. The second stage is attention. The consumer may pay attention to part or all of an advertisement. The third stage is comprehension. The consumer must understand the information in the ad. The fourth stage is evaluation. The consumer assesses the information presented in the ad. The fifth stage is encoding. The consumer encodes, or saves, the advertised information in long-term memory. Later, the sixth stage, retrieval, can occur: The consumer retrieves the encoded information. The seventh stage is decision. The consumer decides to buy (or not buy) the advertised product. The final stage is the action of buying the product.

MISCOMPREHENSION

Advertisers may persuade consumers to buy their product by intentionally inducing miscomprehension. The basis of the miscomprehension is the tendency for people to encode inferences, or interpretations, of stated advertising claims. Therefore, the consumer later remembers inferences made, but not explicitly stated, about a product. At no point is the advertiser presenting false information. However, the advertisement is structured in a way that induces the consumer to draw a specific inference. An advertisement might use hedge words such as "may" or "could." For example, pain reliever Brand A "may help" prevent heart attacks. Other advertisements contain elliptical comparatives. In a comparison, the standard that something is being compared to is intentionally left out. The consumer naturally completes the comparison with the most logical standard. However, the true standard might not be the most logical. For example, cereal Brand A "gives you more." More what? A logical standard might be "more vitamins." The true standard might be "more heartburn." An advertisement might imply causation when in actuality the relationship is correlational. Juxtaposing two imperative statements implies that the first statement leads to, or causes, the next statement: Buy tire Brand A. Drive safely.

PSYCHOLOGICAL APPEALS

Advertisers use psychological appeals directed to basic human needs. Abraham Maslow, the American humanist psychologist who developed a hierarchy of needs in the 1960's, theorized that all humans have needs that must be met in order to achieve self-fulfillment. The most basic are the physiological needs, such as food, water, and shelter. People also need security. Humans need to belong and to be loved. All people need self-esteem. The final need is self-actualization, the highest form of self-fulfillment. Advertisements focus on any one, or combination, of these needs.

Psychological appeals in advertising influence the emotional component of people's attitudes. The ad-

vertised product is associated with positive emotions such as fun, love (and the need for belonging), warmth, excitement, and satisfaction. Advertisements can also be based on fear. The advertisers try to convince consumers that there will be negative consequences if they do not buy their product, focusing on the need for safety. For example, buying any tire other than the one advertised will increase the risk of an automobile accident.

Advertisements also appeal to the human need for self-esteem, which is heightened through power and success. An ad may aim to associate the product with the consumer being the best or having the most.

CLASSICAL CONDITIONING

Russian physiologist Ivan Pavlov discovered the process of classical conditioning in the early twentieth century. An unconditioned stimulus (US) produces naturally an unconditioned response (UR). For example, the image of a baby may naturally produce pleasant, even maternal or paternal, feelings. In classical conditioning, the US is paired with a neutral stimulus (one that does not normally produce the UR). For example, a can of soda (neutral stimulus) can be paired with a picture of a baby (US). With several pairings, the neutral stimulus will become the conditioned stimulus (CS), eliciting the UR without the actual association with the US. Once conditioning occurs, the UR becomes the conditioned response (CR). The can of soda becomes the CS when it alone produces pleasant feelings (CR). Advertisers use classical conditioning to associate a product with a stimulus that elicits the desired responses (belief in the product, positive emotions about the product, intent to buy the product) in the consumer. While shopping, a consumer sees the advertised can of soda, associates it with positive feelings, and therefore is more likely to purchase this brand of soda.

SUBLIMINAL ADVERTISING

Stimuli that are subliminal are below the threshold of conscious perception. Consumers are not normally aware of subliminal stimuli unless they consciously look for them. For example, an image on a product package may contain the shape of sexual organs. A popular rock song, if played backward, may contain phrases such as "smoke marijuana" or "suicide is fun." There is some weak evidence that subliminal messages in advertising may positively affect the emotional quality of consumer attitudes toward a product. However, there is no evidence that subliminal messages affect consumer behavior toward a product.

SOURCES FOR FURTHER STUDY

Cialdini, Robert B. *Influence: Science and Practice.* New York: Allyn & Bacon, 2000. Examines the psychology of compliance. The author combines research results with anecdotal evidence.

_____. *Influence: The Psychology of Persuasion.* Gardnerville, Nev.: Quill, 1993. This is an essential book on the science of persuasion and the psychological foundations of marketing.

Day, Nancy. *Advertising: Information or Manipulation?* Berkeley Heights, N.J.: Enslow, 1999. Discusses the effects of advertising on children, liquor and tobacco advertisements, and ways advertisements catch consumers' attention.

Harris, Richard J. *A Cognitive Psychology of Mass Communication.* Hillsdale, N.J.: Lawrence Erlbaum, 1999. This textbook deals with the effects of mass communication on its consumers. The author provides the reader with an objective and comprehensive look at years of scholarly writings.

Hogan, Kevin. *The Psychology of Persuasion: How to Persuade Others to Your Way of Thinking.* Gretna, La.: Pelican, 1996. Author teaches persuasion, using techniques derived from hypnosis, neurolinguistics, and the Bible.

Maddock, Richard C., and Richard L. Fulton. *Marketing to the Mind.* Westport, Conn.: Greenwood, 1996. Combines marketing and advertising with science.

Mills, Harry A. *Artful Persuasion: How to Command Attention, Change Minds, and Influence People.* New York: AMACOM, 2000. Advertisers depend on the fact that consumers respond to advertisements in just two ways: thoughtfully or mindlessly. The author uses case studies and examples to show the reader how persuaders create convincing messages.

Pratkanis, Anthony R., and Elliot Aronson. *Age of Propaganda: The Everyday Use and Abuse of Persuasion.* New York: W. H. Freeman, 2001. Drawing on the history of propaganda and research in social psychology, this book reveals why the tactics of mass persuasion work so well, and how consumers can protect themselves from manipulation.

Schumann, David W., and Esther Thurson, eds. *Advertising and the World Wide Web.* Hillsdale, N.J.: Lawrence Erlbaum, 1999. Discusses Web advertising and consumer reactions.

Sugarman, Joseph, Dick Hafer, and Ron Hugher. *Triggers: How to Use the Psychological Triggers of Selling to Motivate, Persuade, and Influence.* Las Vegas: Delstar, 1999. The authors explain sales tools that can control the mind of a consumer through effective use of motivation, influence, and persuasion.

Elizabeth M. McGhee Nelson

SEE ALSO: Attention; Concept formation; Conditioning; Consumer psychology; Drives; Emotions; Media psychology; Motivation; Pavlovian conditioning; Reinforcement.

Affiliation and friendship

TYPE OF PSYCHOLOGY: Social psychology
FIELDS OF STUDY: Interpersonal relations; social motives

Affiliation is the tendency to seek the company of others; people are motivated to affiliate for several reasons, and affiliation also meets many human needs. Friendship is an important close relationship based on affiliation, attraction, and intimacy.

KEY CONCEPTS
- affiliation
- attraction
- communal relationship
- complementarity
- consensual validation
- exchange relationship
- propinquity
- proselytize
- social comparison

INTRODUCTION

Affiliation is the desire or tendency to be with others of one's own kind. Many animal species affiliate, collecting in groups, flocks, or schools to migrate or search for food. Human affiliation is not controlled by instinct but is affected by specific motives. One motivation for affiliation is fear: People seek the company of others when they are anxious or frightened. The presence of others may have a calming or reassuring influence. Research in 1959 by social psychologist Stanley Schachter indicated that fear inducement leads to a preference for the company of others. Further work confirmed that frightened individuals prefer the company of others who are similarly frightened, rather than merely the companionship of strangers. This preference for similar others suggests that affiliation is a source of information as well as reassurance.

SOCIAL COMPARISON THEORY

The value of obtaining information through affiliating with others is suggested by social comparison theory. Social comparison is the process of comparing oneself to others in determining how to behave. According to Leon Festinger, who developed social comparison theory in 1954, all people have beliefs, and it is important to them that their beliefs be correct. Some beliefs can be objectively verified by consulting a reference such as a dictionary or a standard such as a yardstick. Others are subjective beliefs and cannot be objectively verified. In such cases, people look for consensual validation—the verification of subjective beliefs by obtaining a consensus among other people—to verify their beliefs. The less sure people are of the correctness of a belief, the more they rely on social comparison as a source of verification. The more people there are who agree with one's opinion about something, the more correct one feels in holding that opinion.

INFLUENCES ON AFFILIATION

Beyond easing fear and satisfying the need for information or social comparison, mere affiliation with others is not usually a satisfactory form of interaction. Most people form specific attractions for other individuals, rather than being satisfied with belonging to a group. These attractions usually develop into friendship, love, and other forms of intimacy. Interpersonal attraction, the experience of preferring to interact with specific others, is influenced by several factors. An important situational or circumstantial factor in attraction is propinquity. Propinquity refers to the proximity or nearness of other persons. Research by Festinger and his colleagues has confirmed that people are more likely to form friendships with those who live nearby, especially if they have frequent accidental contact with them.

Further research by social psychologist Robert Zajonc indicated that propinquity increases attraction because it increases familiarity. Zajonc found that research subjects expressed greater liking for a variety of stimuli merely because they had been exposed to those stimuli more frequently than to others. The more familiar a person is, the more predictable that person seems to be. People are reassured by predictability and feel more strongly attracted to those who are familiar and reliable in this regard.

Another important factor in attraction and friendship is physical attractiveness. According to the physical attractiveness stereotype, most people believe that physically attractive people are also good and valuable in other ways. For example, physically attractive people are often assumed to be intelligent, competent, and socially successful. Attraction to physically attractive persons is somewhat modified by the fear of being rejected. Consequently, most people use a matching principle in choosing friends and partners: They select others who match their own levels of physical attractiveness and other qualities.

Matching implies the importance of similarity. Similarity of attitudes, values, and background is a powerful influence on interpersonal attraction. People are more likely to become friends if they have common interests, goals, and pastimes. Similar values and commitments are helpful in establishing trust between two people. Over time, they choose to spend more time together, and this strengthens their relationship.

Another factor in interpersonal attraction is complementarity, defined as the possession of qualities that complete or fulfill another's needs and abilities. Research has failed to confirm that "opposites attract," since attraction appears to grow stronger with similarities, not differences, between two people. There is some evidence, however, that people with complementary traits and needs will form stronger relationships. For example, a person who enjoys talking will have a compatible relationship with a friend or partner who enjoys listening. Their needs are different but not opposite—they complete each other.

FRIENDSHIP

Friendship begins as a relationship of social exchange. Exchange relationships involve giving and returning favors and other resources, with a short-term emphasis on maintaining fairness or equity. For example, early in a relationship, if one person does a favor for a friend, the friend returns it in kind. Over time, close friendships involve shifting away from an exchange basis to a communal basis. In a communal relationship, partners see their friendship as a common investment and contribute to it for their mutual benefit. For example, if one person gives a gift to a good friend, he or she does not expect repayment in kind. The gift represents an investment in their long-term friendship, rather than a short-term exchange.

Friendship also depends on intimate communication. Friends engage in self-disclosure and reveal personal information to one another. In the early stages of friendship, this is immediately reciprocated: One person's revelation or confidence is exchanged for the other's. As friendship develops, immediate reciprocity is not necessary; long-term relationships involve expectations of future responses. According to psychologist Robert Sternberg, friendship is characterized by two experiences: intimacy and commitment. Friends confide in one another, trust one another, and maintain their friendship through investment and effort.

Comfort in a Group

Theories of affiliation explain why the presence of others can be a source of comfort. In Stanley Schachter's classic 1959 research on fear and affiliation, university women volunteered to participate in a psychological experiment. After they were assembled, an experimenter in medical attire deceived them by explaining that their participation would involve the administration of electrical shock. Half the subjects were told to expect extremely painful shocks, while the others were assured that the shocks would produce a painless, ticklish sensation. In both conditions, the subjects were asked to indicate where they preferred to wait while the electrical equipment was being set up. Each could indicate whether she preferred to wait alone in a private room, preferred to wait in a large room with other subjects, or had no preference.

The cover story about electrical shock was a deception; no shocks were administered. The fear of painful shock, however, influenced the subjects' preferences: Those who expected painful shocks preferred to wait with other subjects, while those who expected painless shocks expressed no prefer-

ence. Schachter concluded that (as the saying goes) misery loves company. In a later study, subjects were given the choice of waiting with other people who were not research subjects. In this study, subjects who feared shock expressed specific preference for others who also feared shock: Misery loves miserable company.

The social comparison theory of affiliation explains the appeal of group membership. People join groups such as clubs, organizations, and churches to support one another in common beliefs or activities and to provide one another with information. Groups can also be a source of pressure to conform. One reason individuals feel pressured to conform with group behavior is that they assume the group has better information than they have. This is termed informational influence. Cohesive groups— groups with strong member loyalty and commitment to membership—can also influence members to agree in the absence of information. When a member conforms with the group because he or she does not want to violate the group's standards or norms, he or she has been subjected to normative influence.

Factors in Friendship

Studies of interpersonal attraction and friendship have documented the power of circumstances such as propinquity. In their 1950 book *Social Pressures in Informal Groups*, Leon Festinger, Stanley Schachter, and Kurt Back reported the friendship preferences of married students living in university housing. Festinger and his colleagues found that the students and their families were most likely to form friendships with others who lived nearby and with whom they had regular contact. Propinquity was a more powerful determinant of friendship than common background or academic major. Propinquity appears to act as an initial filter in social relationships: Nearness and contact determine the people an individual meets, after which other factors may affect interpersonal attraction.

The findings of Festinger and his colleagues can be applied by judiciously choosing living quarters and location. People who wish to be popular should choose to live where they will have the greatest amount of contact with others: on the ground floor of a high-rise building, near an exit or stairwell, or near common facilities such as a laundry room. Zajonc's research on the power of mere exposure confirms that merely having frequent contact with others is sufficient to predispose them to liking.

Mere exposure does not appear to sustain relationships over time. Once people have interacted, their likelihood of having future interactions depends on factors such as physical attractiveness and similarity to one another. Further, the quality of their communication must improve over time as they engage in greater self-disclosure. As friends move from a tit-for-tat exchange to a communal relationship in which they both invest time and resources, their friendship will develop more strongly and satisfactorily.

LOVE

Research on love has identified a distinction between passionate love and companionate love. Passionate love involves intense, short-lived emotions and sexual attraction. In contrast, companionate love is calmer, more stable, and based on trust. Companionate love is strong friendship. Researchers argue that if passionate love lasts, it will eventually calm down and become transformed into companionate love.

Researcher Zick Rubin developed a scale to measure love and liking. He found that statements of love involved attachment, intimacy, and caring. Statements of liking involved positive regard, judgments of similarity, trust, respect, and affection. Liking or friendship is not simply a weaker form of love, but a distinctive combination of feelings, beliefs, and behaviors. Rubin found that most dating couples had strong feelings of both love and liking for each other; however, follow-up research confirmed that the best predictor of whether partners were still together later was how much they had liked—not loved—each other. Liking and friendship form a solid basis for love and other relationships that is not easily altered or forgotten.

RESEARCH

Much early research on affiliation and friendship developed from an interest in social groups. After World War II, social scientists were interested in identifying the attitudes and processes that unify people and motivate their allegiances. Social comparison theory helps to explain a broad range of behavior, including friendship choices, group membership, and proselytizing. Festinger suggested that group membership is helpful when one's beliefs have been challenged or disproved. Like-minded

fellow members will be equally motivated to rationalize the challenge. In their 1956 book *When Prophecy Fails*, Festinger, Henry Riecken, and Schachter document the experience of two groups of contemporary persons who had attested a belief that the world would end in a disastrous flood. One group was able to gather and meet to await the end, while the other individuals, mostly college students, were scattered and could not assemble. When the world did not end as predicted, only those in the group context were able to rationalize their predicament, and they proceeded to proselytize, spreading the word to "converts." Meanwhile, the scattered members, unable to rationalize their surprise, lost faith in the prophecy and left the larger group.

Research on propinquity combined with other studies of interpersonal attraction in the 1960's and 1970's. Friendship and love are challenging topics to study since they cannot be re-created in a laboratory setting. Studies of personal relationships are difficult to conduct in natural settings; if people know they are being observed while they talk or date, they behave differently or leave the scene. Natural or field studies are also less conclusive than laboratory research, since it is not always clear which factors have produced the feelings or actions that can be observed.

Friendship has not been as popular a topic in relationships research as romantic love, marriage, and sexual relationships. Some research has identified gender differences in friendship: Women communicate their feelings and experiences with other women, while men's friendships involve common or shared activities. Developmental psychologists have also identified some age differences: Children are less discriminating about friendship, identifying someone as a friend who is merely a playmate; adults have more complex ideas about friendship forms and standards.

As research on close relationships has gained acceptance, work in communication studies has contributed to the findings of social psychologists. Consequently, more is being learned about the development and maintenance of friendship as well as the initial attractions and bonds that encourage people's ties to others.

SOURCES FOR FURTHER STUDY

Festinger, Leon, Stanley Schachter, and Kurt Back. *Social Pressures in Informal Groups.* Stanford, Calif.:

Stanford University Press, 1950. This classic work documents the authors' research on housing and friendship preferences and ties work on friendship to theories of group structure and function.

Hendrick, Clyde, and Susan Hendrick. *Close Relationships: A Sourcebook.* Thousand Oaks, Calif.: Sage, 2000. A wide-ranging sourcebook of current theory, research, and practical application of the psychology of friendship.

_____. *Liking, Loving, and Relating.* 2d ed. Monterey, Calif.: Brooks/Cole, 1991. The Hendricks provide a thorough review of the processes of affiliation and interpersonal attraction. They include a discussion of issues in contemporary relationships, such as separation and divorce, blended families, changing sex roles, and dual-career couples.

Yager, Jan. *Friendshifts: The Power of Friendship and How It Shapes Our Lives.* 2d ed. Stamford, Conn.: Hannacroix Creek Books, 1999. A practical book on the structures and sustenance of friendships.

Ann L. Weber

SEE ALSO: Affiliation motive; Attraction theories; Cooperation, competition, and negotiation; Group decision making; Groups; Intimacy; Love; Self-disclosure.

Affiliation motive

TYPE OF PSYCHOLOGY: Motivation

FIELDS OF STUDY: Interpersonal relations; motivation theory; social motives

The affiliation motive is the tendency for individuals within a society to form groups or associations that are recognized components of the society's cultures. Affiliation may be based on cooperation, friendship, mutual interests, age, sex, protection, acquisition of physical resources, and social pressures to conform; affiliations transcend the usual kinship organizational structures of most societies.

KEY CONCEPTS

- affiliation
- aggregation
- altruism
- association
- caste
- dominance hierarchy
- drive
- incentive
- kinship

INTRODUCTION

Social behavior is a characteristic of animals having highly developed nervous systems, in particular the vertebrates (mammals, birds, reptiles, amphibians, fish) and the invertebrate social insects (ants, termites). In all these species, there are behaviors that are exclusively instinctive (endogenous); however, in mammals and birds, the process of learning from environmental experiences (exogenous behaviors) becomes pronounced. In mammalian and bird species, complex social interactions have evolved in which individuals aggregate and work together for the benefit of the group as a whole.

Such highly social species form aggregations composed of both males and females. These aggregations usually are migratory, as the individuals of the aggregate search for food, or are territorial, in areas of abundant food supply. Aggregation can be defined as a grouping of members of a species for mutual protection and acquisition of resources. Social aggregation is thus designed to find food for the sustenance of the group, to reproduce, and to protect the group members from predators. Single individuals or very small groups generally have more difficulty in finding food and in defending themselves than do large groups. This easily can be seen in birds or cattle, which flock and herd, respectively, at the approach of a predator.

DOMINANCE HIERARCHIES

Within such aggregates or societies, male and female associations develop; both associations are based upon dominance hierarchies. Association can be defined as an accepted social organization into which individuals affiliate based upon common interests for the attainment of the society's cultural goals.

A dominance hierarchy, or pecking order (as in chicken societies), is a precisely ranked ordering of individuals from most dominant to most subordinate. Dominance hierarchies are important features of practically all mammalian and avian (bird) societies. They are dynamic social structures which are constantly changing because of continual interactions, encounters, and conflicts between individuals and groups of individuals. Several less dominant males may cooperate to usurp the power of the dominant male, for example. Young males or females usually start at the bottom of a dominance hierarchy and gradually work their way up the scale of dominance. Older individuals generally fall down the dominance scale as they weaken from intergroup competition. The overall format of the dominance hierarchy guarantees the best territory, the most mates, the most and best food supply, and the best protection from predators for the most dominant individuals. The most subordinate individuals usually have the worst territory, few if any mates, poor nutrition, and great susceptibility to predation.

Such dominance hierarchies permeate human societies, although their presence is often subtle within the context of much more complex social and cultural systems. Human societies, whether primarily technological, agricultural, or hunting, consist of institutions, organizations, religions, clubs, and other groups with which individuals become affiliated, or involved. To some extent, many of these groups serve the same purposes as do groups in other animal societies: food assimilation, reproduction, and protection from predators, enemies, or other "undesirable" people. Human societies, however, employ unique rationales for individual affiliation. Affiliation is defined as the joining of an individual to a group of individuals, many of whom may be unrelated, based upon such things as cooperation, mutual interests, friendship, age, gender, and protection.

The affiliation motive behind an individual's joining a particular group lies within all these factors. Nevertheless, lurking beneath these factors are some very basic sociobiological principles. It is the individual's advantage to affiliate with other individuals. Through interactions with others, one can assert one's position within the existing dominance hierarchy, thereby gaining recognition for oneself not only in terms of dominance relationships but also in terms of meeting the society's views of acceptable behavior. Outcasts and other individuals who fail to affiliate within the accepted social institutions are frowned upon by their peers and are subject to prejudicial treatment. Antisocial behavior is strongly discouraged and is often punished in many societies.

The dominance hierarchy is without question a major evolutionary adaptation for the survival of social animal species. In every association of individuals, the dominance hierarchy is expressed in the power structure of the group as well as in the peer pressure aimed at forcing all societal members to conform. Conformity means affiliation with acceptable societal groups and submission to the dominance hierarchy.

SOCIAL MOTIVES

An individual's drive, or motivation, to affiliate with other individuals may be attributable to common interests or characteristics, but often this drive is tempered by social pressures to conform to the stability of the existing dominance structure. In many instances, the motivation to affiliate is influenced by societal incentives—a motivating force or system of rewards that is presented to an individual if he or she behaves or successfully performs specified tasks according to the norms of society. Affiliation with some groups may bring prestige, a better standard of living, and other benefits. Such affiliations usually are easier when kinship (the primary social organizing force in many human and animal societies, based upon the relatedness of individuals) with group members exists. Otherwise, the individual may have to make certain sacrifices.

Human societal groups include organizations such as elitist country clubs and social clubs or special interest groups (gem clubs, astronomy clubs), professionally related organizations, women's clubs, men's clubs, teen groups, elderly groups, churches, volunteer rescue squads and fire departments, and sports teams. Even youth gangs, mobsters, and hate groups fall within such categories. Affiliation is a social behavior in which practically everyone participates in some way, either willingly or unwillingly.

One phenomenon of affiliation behavior that is prevalent in numerous groups is altruism, an unselfish contribution on the part of an individual for others even if they are not genetically related to the individual. Altruism occurs in numerous species, although it usually occurs between related individuals. Humans exhibit an unusual level of altruism even toward unrelated individuals. There is some philosophical debate over whether such behavior in humans is truly unselfish. A number of investigators seek other underlying motives in such behavior and dismiss the notion that people help others purely out of a sense of caring.

Affiliation motives, therefore, are based upon mutual interest and characteristics between people, altruistic behavior, and peer pressure associated with existing social dominance hierarchies. Affiliation is an important component of the stable structuring of society. It is of major concern in specific cases where individuals are barred from groups because of intelligence, family background, political affiliation, religious beliefs, race, or personal wealth.

STUDY OF AFFILIATION

Affiliation is a major subject of study for psychologists, sociologists, and social-cultural anthropologists. A critical behavior in the formation of the complex societies which characterize mammalian and bird species, it is very pronounced in human societies. Psychologists and anthropologists study group associations in many different human societies, comparing the characteristics of these different groups to ascertain the importance of affiliation and other group interactions in the development of the individual, the development of culture, and the evolution of human civilization. Studies are also made of group behaviors in primates and other closely related species to arrive at the sequence of evolutionary events leading to group adaptations.

Affiliation motives and drives reveal the psychological background of various individuals and, as a result, enable the researcher to understand differences between people in achievement of goals. Such knowledge can be of great value in uncovering the psychological and physical blocks which prevent some people from reaching their maximum intellectual and physical potential. Dominance hierarchies, while representing a very central, structured component of practically all societies, are stumbling blocks to many people. Understanding how they operate can be of great use in assisting the smooth, nonviolent interaction of differing peoples. It also can be used to unravel the roots of antisocial behavior.

CULTURAL DIFFERENCES AND SIMILARITIES

Social and cultural anthropologists have studied the structure and organization of hundreds of different societies throughout the world. These societies exhibit many of the same social processes and patterns of organized behavior. They all exhibit dominance hierarchies, acceptable rules of individual and group behavior, and strong orderliness based upon kinship. Some such societies (Hindu, for example) relegate their members to separate castes, permanent

divisions based upon genetic inheritance and particular trades maintained by descendants of specific castes. In advanced technological societies, large populations, fast-paced lifestyles, and high regional mobility result in social structures based less upon kinship and more upon other factors, such as mutual interests, age, gender, and race.

The study of social groups and affiliation motives for such groups provides an informative analysis of human social evolution within the context of rapidly changing societies. The psychological impact of such changes upon the individual and upon the group as a whole can provide an understanding of societal problems such as crime, social inequality, and intergroup tensions. Underlying all these situations is the natural biological tendency for individuals to aggregate for the common good of all members, thereby reducing the chance of danger to individual members. Humans, like all animals, have a need to interact and associate with other members of their own species. The drive to affiliate is related to the need for acceptance and the subsequent goals of recognition, power, protection, and mating.

MOTIVATIONAL THEORIES

Societal pressures to conform and to affiliate are great. Numerous psychologists have propounded theories describing the psychological bases behind an individual's motives to affiliate with other individuals. These theories are in agreement as to the goals of affiliation—objectives such as friendship, mutual interests, mating, acquiring food, and ensuring protection. These theories differ, however, in the psychological mechanisms behind the affiliation motive.

Among the most famous of these motivational theories comes from the work of the psychoanalytical pioneer Sigmund Freud (1856-1939). Freud proposed that all motivational drives within an individual center on two principal components of the individual psyche: the libido and the Eros instinct. The libido is an aspect of one's psychological makeup whose prime focus is sexual reproduction, whereas the Eros instinct is one's inner need to survive. Influenced by Darwinian evolutionary theory, Freud maintained that all motives, including the affiliation motive, are aimed at satisfying one's sexual and survival needs.

The analytical psychologists Kurt Goldstein (1878-1965) and Abraham Maslow (1908-1970) maintained that an individual's psyche organizes itself about a tiered arrangement of personal needs and goals. These tiers include basic bodily needs such as food, protection, the need to be loved, and "self-actualization." According to their theories, different individuals focus upon different aspects of these psychological needs. They further maintained that one's psychological needs all emerge from the need for self-actualization, the need to be recognized as an important member of society. Psychological disorders were believed to occur as a result of conflicts within these inner needs.

Other theories of social involvement and motivation include those of Carl Jung (1875-1961) and Alfred Adler (1870-1937). Jung concentrates upon individuals as being introverts or extroverts. Adler concentrates upon inferior people overcompensating to become superior, with inferiority complexes arising when inferior individuals choose socially unacceptable means of becoming superior. All these theories and others employ many of the same basic concepts. They generally center on basic instinctive desires (sexuality, food acquisition, protection from danger) and the need for recognition (dominance, personal achievement). Consequently, they reflect the biological basis of behavior that has evolved in animals over the past few hundred million years.

ROLE OF SOCIOBIOLOGY

The psychological theories of motivation and the cultural manifestations of association and affiliation fall within the domain of sociobiology, a branch of biological thought advanced by numerous behaviorists and analytical psychologists that has been considerably refined and compellingly presented by Harvard University entomologist Edward O. Wilson. The motive of individual affiliation in any animal society, including human society, is the achievement of personal and group needs, which essentially boil down to views of survival and reproduction similar to those expressed by Freud.

Psychology and animal behavior have isolated the basis of affiliation and of behavior as one's instinctive needs as a living organism. This rationale stems from the fact that humans are animals and are the products of at least 3.8 billion years of evolutionary change on Earth. The nature of all life is to survive and to reproduce. Therefore, the activities of all organisms are centered on the achievement of these goals. In sociobiology theory, animal behavior and animal societies are driving forces in the survival, reproduction, and evolution of any given animal species. This theory has produced much controversy and debate; however, there is considerable evidence supporting it.

Affiliation is one of the foci of social behavior. Animals have a need to associate with other individuals of their own species. In so doing, they ensure their own safety and enhance their own reproductive potential. An individual's behavior is directed toward these ends. Another sociobiological viewpoint is that of the "selfish gene," a concept developed by modern molecular biologists and advanced by Richard Dawkins in his 1976 book of that name. The selfish gene concept maintains that evolution occurs at the level of the gene and that individual organisms are the means by which genetic information is copied and transmitted to future generations. All aspects of the organism and populations of organisms are geared to this end. Biochemical changes within an individual's nervous and endocrine systems facilitate such motivations. The physiology of motivation is an object of intense study.

SOURCES FOR FURTHER STUDY

Carter, C. Sue, I. Izja Lederhendler, and Brian Kirkpatrick, eds. *The Integrative Neurobiology of Affiliation.* Cambridge, Mass.: MIT Press, 1999. Looks at the biological effects of affiliation and other social behaviors on the brain.

Chagnon, Napoleon A. *Yanomamo: The Fierce People.* 5th ed. Belmont, Calif.: Wadsworth, 1996. Chagnon's anthropological study of the Amazonian Yanomamo people is a classic in the field of social and cultural anthropological research. Devotes considerable attention to group behaviors and individual motives for affiliation. Chapter 3, "Social Organization," is an extensive analysis of Yanomamo kinship, marriage patterns, division of labor, status differences, and individual social life.

Hall, Edward T. *The Hidden Dimension.* Reprint. Garden City, N.Y.: Doubleday, 1990. Hall's insightful work, first published in 1966, is an anthropological and psychological analysis of human individual and group interactions, primarily in modern technological societies. Concentrates primarily on personal and private distance levels between individuals in individual-individual and group-group encounters. Chapter 10, "Distances in Man," describes such levels and their significance upon individual behavior. From these studies, Hall draws important conclusions and recommendations for improving human society.

Manning, Aubrey, and Marion Stamp Dawkins. *An Introduction to Animal Behavior.* 5th ed. New York: Cambridge University Press, 1998. Manning's work is a concise, through survey of important animal behavior research. He cites numerous research studies on many different animal species, and he compares competing theories and models aimed at describing these behaviors. The chapter on motivation is a detailed analysis of animal drives based upon biological principles, including group cohesiveness, aggressiveness, sexual and feeding needs of the individual, and hormonal influences. An extensive reference list is provided for further research.

Skinner, B. F. *Science and Human Behavior.* New York: Macmillan, 1953. This outstanding discussion of human behavior, written by one of the great psychologists/behavioral scientists of the twentieth century, thoroughly and clearly presents all principal aspects of human behavior to a general audience. Chapter 15, "Self-Control," is a study of the behavioral and physiological mechanisms by which an individual regulates conduct. Chapter 27, "Culture and Control," analyzes sociocultural restraints upon human impulses and drives.

Vela-McConnell, James A. *Who Is My Neighbor? Social Affinity in a Modern World.* Albany: State University of New York Press, 1999. A sociological approach to affinity motives in Western society. Divides the concept into the aspects of social consciousness, sentiment, and action, and their constitutive elements.

David Wason Hollar, Jr.

SEE ALSO: Achievement motivation; Affiliation and friendship; Aggression; Groups; Motivation; Self; Social identity theory; Social networks; Social perception.

Ageism

TYPE OF PSYCHOLOGY: Developmental psychology
FIELDS OF STUDY: Adulthood; aging; prejudice and discrimination

Ageism refers to prejudice and discrimination directed toward persons because they are elderly. These negative attitudes and perceptions affect the ways that individuals and society treat the elderly and may determine one's own reactions to growing older.

KEY CONCEPTS
- discrimination
- gerontophobia
- negative ageism
- positive ageism
- prejudice
- prevalence
- stereotyping

INTRODUCTION

The term ageism was coined by Robert Butler, the first director of the National Institute on Aging. Like racism and sexism, ageism involves prejudice and discrimination directed toward a specific segment of the population. When someone claims that blacks are inferior to whites or that females are less intelligent than males, the listener usually realizes that racist and sexist attitudes are being presented. Many persons, however, will accept the notion that the aged are senile, asexual, inflexible, poverty-stricken, and incapable of learning, without recognizing the prejudicial nature of such statements. In most instances, the stereotypical elderly person is viewed negatively; the prevailing attitude in the United States is that young is good and old is inferior. According to sociologist Erdman Palmore, ageism differs from racism and sexism in two major ways: All people become targets of ageism if they live long enough, and people are often not aware that ageism exists.

Surveys and other research indicate that ageist attitudes are widely held in American culture. Any attitude must be learned, and there are many sources available in American society. On television and in motion pictures, there are comparatively few older characters. The few older persons portrayed are typically depicted as either bumbling, forgetful souls who beget laughter and ridicule (negative ageism) or saintly paragons of virtue who possess great wisdom (positive ageism). Neither portrayal is realistic. In actuality, these are stereotypes—what people believe old persons should be. Magazines and television present innumerable images of healthy, attractive young adults laughing, exercising, dancing, playing sports, and generally having a good time. It is not surprising that children begin to associate youth with goodness and old age with decrepitude.

The media also report cases of elderly persons who are found living in isolation, abandoned by relatives, and who are so poor that they resort to eating things such as cat food. Such cases are news precisely because of their rarity. There are destitute older persons, but reports produced by the federal government indicate that the percentage of aged persons (those above sixty-five years of age) below the official poverty line is actually less than the percentage in the general population. The elderly poor tend to be persons who have been impoverished for most of their lives. According to Palmore, a minority of the elderly are actually lonely and deserted by relatives; surveys indicate that most older persons live within a thirty-minute drive of at least one child and

Ageism can result in misconceptions about the abilities and interests of the elderly. (PhotoDisc)

have frequent contact with offspring. Also, less than 10 percent of those over the age of sixty-five report that they do not have enough friends. Only about 5 percent of the aged are in a nursing home at any one time.

AGE AND AGEISM

Children and others hear many "jokes" told about the aged. Analysis indicates that these jokes are usually derogatory and concern topics such as sexual behavior, physical ailments, and cognitive deficits. As is the case with "ethnic" jokes, whether the jokes are funny depends on the listener. A person seldom laughs at jokes that ridicule his or her own social group; persons who are racist or ageist, however, will find these jokes amusing and perceive them as being accurate.

Another factor in the ubiquity of ageism is that there may be less contact with the elderly in modern life than in the past. Families are more mobile today, and the extended family, in which several generations live in the same dwelling, is much less common. Many youngsters grow up in nuclear families without interacting extensively with aged persons; those with such limited contact are very likely to believe the ageist notions presented by others or by the media. In contrast, persons who have close relationships with several older individuals usually realize that most aged individuals are healthy and productive. A study by Melinda Kennedy and Robin Montvilo indicated that children who have close contact with older adults on a regular basis are more likely to view the elderly in a positive manner than children who have infrequent contact with the elderly. Degree of daily contact in adults did not seem to influence attitudes toward the elderly. Education to improve attitudes toward aging and the elderly appears more useful in the young.

Ageism is not restricted to young persons or the uneducated. Ageist attitudes are often maintained even into old age. Ironically, this means that an older person may be prejudiced against his or her own age group. Resolution of this dilemma often focuses on the person's refusal to label himself or herself as "old" or "elderly." Age identification studies typically find that the majority of persons over the age of sixty-five identify themselves as being "middle-aged." Even among subjects over eighty years of age, there is a considerable percentage (10 to 30 percent) who deny that they are "old." This denial allows the aging person to maintain ageist beliefs. Conversely, ageism may contribute to the denial. If one believes that old persons are all senile and so on, and one is obviously not that way oneself, then it follows that one must not be old.

PHYSICIANS AND AGEISM

Research suggests that ageist attitudes have been prevalent even among physicians and other professionals. Until the late twentieth century, geriatrics, the branch of medicine that deals with disorders and diseases of the aged, was not a popular specialty among doctors. In Robert Butler's *Why Survive? Being Old in America* (1975), demonstrates that the elderly have been given very low priority by physicians. In part, physicians are paid more by private health insurers than they are by Medicare. Additionally, younger adults are seen as having fewer health problems are taking up less time. Less thorough physical examinations are given to older patients. Psychiatrists and clinical psychologists report very little contact with aged clients and may be prone to believe that older persons cannot really suffer from the same mental disorders that younger clients do or believe that they need to be treated with medication as a quick fix. Senility (an ambiguous term that is not a clinical diagnosis) is not a normal aspect of aging. Alzheimer's disease and other organic brain syndromes are diseases which afflict only a small proportion of the aged. Most cases of confusion and disorientation in the aged are produced by drug intoxication or poor blood circulation to the brain. Nevertheless, such patients may be viewed as suffering from irreversible disorders and given little professional attention other than medication, which often exacerbates the symptoms. In spite of the negative stereotypes associated with aging, by the beginning of the twenty-first century, many physicians were going into geriatrics to meet the increasing demand occasioned by the aging of so-called baby boomers born in the middle of the twentieth century.

SOCIAL POLICY AND AGEISM

Varying beliefs and attitudes concerning the aging process have existed throughout the history of Western civilization. Indeed, in the Old Testament, longevity is granted to those who are faithful to God, and the elders are viewed as a source of great wisdom. Contemporary views toward aging, which typically are much more negative, have been influenced significantly by social policies. In an attempt to help end the Depression, the federal government initiated the Old Age and Survivors' Program (Social Security) in 1935 to encourage retirement and reduce unemployment among younger workers. This program was intended to help support people though the last three to four years of their lives. Medicare and Medicaid began in the mid-1960's. These measures served to identify older Americans as a homogeneous group of persons in need of special aid from the rest of society; old age thus became a distinct stage of development.

As mentioned previously, studies have found that the aged, as a group, are as well off financially as the general population (although often living on fixed incomes). Nevertheless, most states and the federal government grant tax relief in various forms to all aged citizens, rich and poor. Many businesses such as pharmacies, restaurants, and hotels give discounts to elderly customers. Some banks offer higher interest rates on savings and free checking to "senior citizens." Despite the fact that such practices might seem discriminatory against the young, there is little public protest. The general acceptance of these policies may be based on the mistaken belief that most aged persons are living in or near poverty.

Older persons often confront ageist attitudes when trying to obtain, or continue, employment. Widely held perceptions about the aged are that they cannot learn new skills, miss many workdays because of illness, are prone to work-related accidents, and work significantly more slowly than younger workers. Each of these notions is inaccurate, according to Palmore. Research involving a variety of occupations has determined that older persons are productive employees who actually have fewer accidents at work and miss fewer workdays than younger workers. Although motor responses are slowed with age, most workers increase their productivity as a result of increased experience. Learning new skills does usually require slightly more time for older workers, but they can, and do, learn.

Despite these research findings, many employers have discriminated against older applicants and have refused to hire them because of their advanced age. In response, the U.S. Congress passed the Age Discrimination in Employment Act (ADEA) in 1967, which outlaws age discrimination in hiring practices and sets seventy years as the age of mandatory retirement for most occupations. Fortunately, many companies have begun to realize the efficacy of older workers and have encouraged them to become employees. The "McMasters Program," established by the McDonald's fast food chain, is one example of a business welcoming older applicants.

GERONTOPHOBIA

Gerontophobia—a fear of the elderly or of the aging process—is closely related to ageism. Believing that the aged are decrepit, lonely, and likely to be senile makes one fear growing older. Many companies produce products that play upon this fear; indeed, these businesses have a financial stake in perpetuating gerontophobia. Commercial advertisements bombard consumers with messages indicating that to be old is to be ugly, and Americans spend enormous sums of money trying to look younger through cosmetic surgery, hair dye, "wrinkle removers," and so on. People are even encouraged by friends to try to look young. Many gerontologists, however, view these efforts as costly and futile attempts; these procedures can alter one's appearance, but they do not stop or retard the aging process.

Gerontophobia may also reflect the association often made between old age and death. In the past, many babies and young persons died of infectious and communicable diseases. Infant mortality is much lower today, and life expectancy has increased dramatically. Therefore, death in old age is typical, and this fact may well increase the fear of growing old that many persons experience.

Ironically, holding ageist views may adversely affect one's own aging. Indeed, many psychologists think that beliefs or expectations may be self-fulfilling. More simply put, an expectation may affect one's behavior so that eventually one acts in accordance with the expectation. A common example involves sexual behavior. An ageist view persists that older persons are no longer sexually viable. Males, especially, seem to accept this notion and to worry about their sexual performance. If, for example, a sixty-year-old man does experience an inability to achieve orgasm during intercourse, he may attribute this "failure" to aging; he may then be extremely anxious during his next sexual episode. This anxiety may cause further sexual problems and preclude orgasm. Believing that he is now too old for sex, this male may even terminate coital activity. In contrast, if he attributes his initial problem to stress or some other transitory variable, then his future sexual behavior may be unimpeded, especially in a society that now has anti-impotence drugs such as Viagra available.

CHANGES IN AGEISM SINCE 1960

The late 1960's were years of tremendous political and social unrest, as numerous minority groups clamored for greater power and fairer treatment. The aged had been delineated as a special-interest group with distinct needs. As the aged began to be defined solely by their age, a group consciousness began to emerge. Older persons, as a group, are more interested in politics and more likely to vote than their younger counterparts. Politicians became aware of and became more sensitive to elderly issues. Out of this milieu, Robert Butler helped to make these concerns salient by inventing the term ageism.

Ageism has been heightened by medical advances, and the concomitant increased life expectancy enjoyed in technologically advanced societies has altered views about aging. It has also led to a life expectancy close to seventy-seven years in the United States. Social Security and Medicare are now available to people for nearly a dozen years on the average. This places a drain on society and makes the elderly seem a burden. As a higher percentage of people now live into old age, death has become increasingly associated with growing old. Without doubt, the fear of death causes some people to shun the elderly and to view them as being "different from us." To admit that one is old is tantamount to confronting one's own mortality squarely. Many gerontologists and sociologists argue that the United States is a death-denying society. Death is a taboo topic in most circles; the majority of deaths in the United States occur in institutions. The denial and fear of death may encourage ageist notions.

Palmore has developed a survey instrument consisting of twenty items to assess the types and prevalence of ageism in the United States today. The most frequent types of ageism found using this tool were disrespect for older people and assumptions made about ailments and frailty caused by age. In an initial study, 77 percent of the elderly assessed reported having experienced ageism. This tool may be used to help reduce the prevalence of ageism in society by allowing it to be identified and by educating those in need.

Ageism may decline in the near future, simply because the median age of Americans is increasing. The baby boomers, a large and influential segment of society, are aging, and their impact is likely to be substantial. People in this age group have dramatically changed society as they have developed. When they were children, more schools had to be built, and education was emphasized. Their adolescence produced a rebellious period in the late 1960's, and a lowering of the voting age. As young adults, they touched off a boom in construction, as many new houses were needed. As the baby-boomers become senior citizens, their sheer numbers may cause a shift toward more positive attitudes toward the elderly. Also, more aged persons are maintaining good health and active lifestyles today than in the past. This trend will undoubtedly help counteract stereotypical ideas about the infirmities of the elderly.

Sources for Further Study

Achenbaum, W. A. "Societal Perceptions of Aging and the Aged." In *Handbook of Aging and the Social Sciences*, edited by Robert H. Binstock and Linda George. 5th ed. San Diego, Calif.: Academic Press, 2001. Examines attitudes toward aging from a historical perspective and assesses the impact of modern innovations such as technology and bureaucratization upon these attitudes. An extensive reference list containing more than one hundred entries is provided.

Birren, J. E., and K. Warner Schaie. *Handbook of the Psychology of Aging*. 5th ed. San Diego, Calif.: Academic Press, 2001. This reference book is the definitive source for material dealing with adulthood and aging. Comprehensive reviews of research are provided.

Butler, Robert N. "Ageism." In *The Encyclopedia of Aging*, edited by G. Maddox. 2d ed. New York: Springer, 1995. A brief overview and update of the field in the twenty years since his Pulitzer Prize-winning book.

_____. *Why Survive? Being Old in America*. New York: Harper & Row, 1975. This Pulitzer Prize-winning book is written for lay readers and provides a comprehensive overview of the prejudices and other problems faced by older Americans. Strongly critical of the fashion in which physicians, nursing home operators, politicians, and others deal with the elderly.

Ferraro, Kenneth F. "The Gerontological Imagination." In *Gerontology: Perspectives and Issues*. New York: Springer, 1990. Provides an overview of seven themes within research on aging, pointing out that "aging frequently gets a bad name for things it did not cause." Describes a three-year project in which a young female disguises herself as an elderly woman in order to note the ageist reactions of others.

Kennedy, Melinda J., and Robin Kamienny Montvilo. "Effects of Age and Contact on Attitudes Toward Aging and the Elderly." *The Gerontologist* 40 (2000): 147. This research based study focuses on factors affecting attitudes of elementary school children and college students toward aging and the elderly.

Oberleder, Muriel. *Avoid the Aging Trap*. Washington, D.C.: Acropolis Books, 1982. Examines many of the myths concerning aging in the light of research. Offers practical suggestions to attenuate the actual effects of aging. Numerous exercises, such as a test to compute one's "Aging Quotient," maintain reader interest. Especially recommended for the middle-aged reader.

Palmore, Erdman. *Ageism: Negative and Positive*. 2d ed. New York: Springer, 1999. An update on research in the field of ageism by one of its leading authorities. This book reviews the extensive literature on ageism, and makes a clear distinction between positive and negative forms of ageism. It makes clear the distinction between prejudice and discrimination as well.

Charles H. Evans;
updated by Robin Kamienny Montvilo

See also: Aging: Cognitive changes; Aging: Physical changes; Aging: Theories; Prejudice; Prejudice reduction; Racism; Retirement; Sexism.

Aggression

Type of psychology: Biological bases of behavior; emotion; personality; psychopathology
Fields of study: Aggression; biology of stress; childhood and adolescent disorders; coping; critical issues in stress; personality disorders; stress and illness

Aggression is an emotional response to frustration that often leads to angry and destructive actions directed against individuals, animals, or such organizations as corporate bureaucracies, social and religious groups, or governments.

KEY CONCEPTS
- anger
- defensive aggression
- frustration
- hostility
- offensive aggression
- predatory aggression
- regression
- social immaturity
- socialization
- stress
- tantrum

INTRODUCTION

Aggression, as the term is applied to humans, occurs as an emotional reaction to dissatisfactions and stress resulting in behaviors that society considers antagonistic and destructive. The term as used in common parlance has broad meanings and applications. In psychological parlance, however, aggression generally refers to an unreasonable hostility directed against situations with which people must cope or think they must cope. On a simple and relatively harmless level, people may demonstrate momentary aggressive behavior if they experience common frustrations such as missing a bus, perhaps reacting momentarily by stamping their foot on the ground or mouthing an oath subvocally. The moment passes and no one is hurt by this sort of aggression, which most people demonstrate with fair frequency as they deal with frustration in their daily lives.

People with tattered self-images may direct their aggression toward themselves, possibly in the form of expressing or thinking disparaging things about themselves or, in extreme cases, harming themselves physically, even to the point of suicide. Such internalized forms of aggression may remain pent up for years in people who bear their frustrations silently. Such frustrations may eventually erupt into dangerous behavior directed at others, leading to assaults, verbal and/or physical abuse, and, in the most extreme cases, to massacres. Such was the case when Timothy McVeigh blew up the Alfred P. Mur-

rah Federal Building in Oklahoma City on April 19, 1995, as an act of civil protest, killing 167 people, none of whom he knew.

Infants and young children make their needs known and have them met by crying or screaming, which usually brings them attention from whoever is caring for them. Older children, basing their actions on these early behaviors, may attempt to have their needs met by having tantrums, or uncontrolled fits of rage, in an effort to achieve their ends. In some instances, adults who are frustrated, through regression to the behaviors of infancy or early childhood, have tantrums that, while disconcerting, frequently fail to succeed in anything more than emphasizing their social immaturity. Socialization demands that people learn how to control their overt expressions of rage and hostility.

TYPES OF AGGRESSION

Hugh Wagner, a behavioral psychologist concerned with the biology of aggression, has identified three types: offensive aggression, defensive aggression, and predatory aggression. Offensive aggression occurs when the aggressor initiates aggressive behavior against one or more nonaggressors. The response to offensive aggression is likely to be defensive aggression that generally takes the form of self-defense.

Predatory aggression differs from offensive or defensive aggression, although it is basically a form of offensive aggression. It is characterized by, for example, such phenomena as the lurking of predatory animals that make themselves as inconspicuous as possible until their prey is within striking distance. They then pounce on the prey with the intention of killing it as quickly as they can so that they can eat it. Among humans, hunters are examples of predatory aggressors, although not all contemporary hunters consume their prey.

BIOLOGICAL ROOTS OF AGGRESSION

Although aggressive acts are usually triggered by environmental factors, laboratory research suggests that aggression has biological roots. Various experiments point to the fact that the three basic types of aggression are controlled by different mechanisms in the midbrain. It has been demonstrated in laboratory animals that offensive aggression has intimate connections to neurons in the ventral tegmental area of the midbrain. When lesions occur in this section of the brain, offensive aggression decreases markedly or disappears altogether, although defensive and predatory aggression are not affected.

Conversely, when parts of the anterior hypothalamus are stimulated, offensive behavior increases and attack may ensue. The brain appears in these experiments to be programmed in such a way that defensive aggression is controlled by the periaqueductal gray matter (PAG) found in the midbrain. So specialized are the neural activities of the midbrain that defensive aggression involving perceived threats emanates from a different part of the brain than defensive aggression that involves an actual attack. Acid-based amino neurons from the medial hypothalamus are known to trigger defensive aggression.

Alcoholic intake often intensifies aggressive behavior because alcohol reduces the inhibitions that the cerebral cortex controls while stimulating the neural pathways between the medial hypothalamus and the PAG. Although alcohol does not increase aggressive behavior in all humans, many people react aggressively when they consume alcoholic beverages.

AGGRESSION AND BODY CHEMISTRY

In most species, including humans, males are more aggressive than females. This is thought to be because of the testosterone levels present in varying degrees in males. The higher the testosterone level, the more aggressive the male. Aggressive behavior that threatens the welfare of the species is often controlled in humans by medication that reduces the testosterone levels and pacifies aggressive males.

It is notable that young males tend to be considerably more aggressive than older males, presumably because as men age, their testosterone levels decrease considerably. Prisons are filled with young males unable to control their aggressions sufficiently to stay out of trouble with the law. Many of these prisoners mellow into relatively benign older men not because prison has reformed them but because their body chemistry has undergone significant changes through the years.

At one time, aggressive behavior was controlled by electric shock therapy (which is used at present in some extreme cases) or by the more drastic surgical procedure known as lobotomy. Lobotomies often left people in virtually catatonic states from which they could never emerge. Drugs and psychiat-

---

DSM-IV-TR Criteria for Intermittent Explosive Disorder (DSM code 312.34)

Several discrete episodes of failure to resist aggressive impulses resulting in serious assaultive acts or destruction of property

Degree of aggressiveness expressed during episodes grossly out of proportion to any precipitating psychosocial stressors

Aggressive episodes not better accounted for by another mental disorder and not due to direct physiological effects of a substance or general medical condition

---

ric treatment have replaced most of the more devastating procedures of the nineteenth and twentieth centuries.

ROAD RAGE AND AIR RAGE

Two of the most common forms of offensive aggression in contemporary society are road rage and air rage. Road rage, which generally occurs on crowded, multilane highways or freeways, is often committed by otherwise civilized individuals who, when behind the wheel of a car that weighs well over a ton, are transformed into irrational monsters. If someone cuts them off in traffic, drives slowly in the lane ahead of them, or commits some other perceived roadway insult, perpetrators of road rage may bump the rear of car ahead of them, pass the car and shoot at the offending driver, or force the offending driver off the road and onto the shoulder, where a fight, a stabbing, or a shooting may occur.

Air rage is somewhat different. Some people who have been flying for long periods in cramped conditions, often passing through several time zones, may suffer from disorientation. Often this feeling is intensified by the consumption of alcohol before and/or during the flight. Such people, if refused another drink or if asked to return to their seats and buckle their seat belts, may strike out at flight attendants or at fellow passengers.

AGGRESSION IN ANIMALS

Although humans exhibit aggression in its most subtle and complicated forms, other species of animals also manifest aggressive behaviors. Most animals will fight if they are attacked because self-defense and self-preservation are inherent in most species. Within their own social constructs, some animals will attack those outside their group, even those of the same species, although few animals turn on their own species to nearly the extent that humans do. Carnivorous animals exhibit aggressiveness in preying on other animals as food sources, the large overpowering the small, the swift overtaking the slow, the strong killing and consuming the weak. Most animals also aggressively defend the areas in which they forage and build their nests or dens.

The less aggressive species of animals have been domesticated by humans as sources of food, notably poultry, cattle, and fish. More aggressive animals are sometimes used in sports such as bullfighting or cockfighting. In these instances, the animals are taught aggressive behaviors that are not instinctive in most of them. They are trained to perform, and satisfactory performance on their parts is rooted in aggression.

AGGRESSION AND PROCREATION
Aggressive behavior in nearly all species is rooted in sexuality. The male is usually more aggressive than the female. The sexual act is fundamentally an act of male aggression. Males during their sexual prime maintain the high levels of testosterone that assure the continuance of their species but that also result in aggressive, sometimes antisocial behavior.

The offensive aggression of one species, such as the predatory birds that feed on newborn turtles in the Galápagos Islands, evokes defensive aggressive behavior on the parts of those seeking to protect their young and to assure the continuance of their species. The species that demonstrates defensive aggression in a situation of this sort may demonstrate offensive aggression in pursuing and attacking a weaker species. All of these aggressions among nonhumans are, in the final analysis, directed at preserving the species.

CAN HUMAN AGGRESSION BE CONTROLLED?
Aggression is so inherent in nearly every species that it is doubtful that it can ever be fully controlled, nor would it necessarily be desirable to control it. When aggression among humans reaches the point of threatening the social fabric, however, steps must be taken to control or, at least, to redirect it. The adolescent male who wants to beat everyone up probably is suffering from extreme anger. It may be possible to redirect this anger, which is a form of energy, into more socially acceptable channels. It may also be possible to control elements in the environment—home life, being bullied at school, being rejected by peers—in such ways as to reduce the anger and resentment that have led to aggressive behavior.

The management of aggression through psychotherapy and medication may prove effective. The aggressive individual, however, may resist the treatment that could succeed in controlling the socially unacceptable aggressive behavior that he or she engages in. Attempts to control aggression often run counter to the very nature of human beings as they pass through the various developmental stages of their lives.

SOURCES FOR FURTHER STUDY
Anderson, Daniel R., et al. *Early Childhood Television Viewing and Adolescent Behavior.* Boston: Blackwell, 2001. Of particular relevance to those interested in aggression are chapters 6 ("Aggression") and 9 ("Self-Image: Role Model Preference and Body Image"). The five coauthors of this valuable study seek to explore the roots of aggression in teenagers in terms of their exposure to violence through television viewing in their formative years.

Archer, John, and Kevin Browne. *Human Aggression: Naturalistic Approaches.* New York: Routledge, 1989. The approach is that of the social psychologist who is much concerned with environmental factors affecting aggression. A worthwhile book for the beginner.

Blanchard, Robert J., and Caroline D., eds. *Advances in the Study of Aggression.* New York: Academic Press, 1984. Dan Olweus's chapter, "Development of Stable Aggressive Reaction Patterns in Males," and John Paul Scott's chapter, "Advances in Aggression Research: The Future," are particularly compelling. The book as a whole is well constructed, although it may be more appropriate to those experienced in the field than to beginners.

Englander, E. K. *Understanding Violence.* Mahwah, N.J.: Lawrence Erlbaum, 1997. The author presents a panoramic view of violence and human aggression, condensing effectively the major research in the field over the past half century.

Feshbach, Seymour, and Jolanta Zagrodzka, eds. *Aggression: Biological, Developmental, and Social Perspectives*. New York: Plenum, 1997. This comprehensive collection, although somewhat specialized, covers the two major factors in aggression (the biological roots and social determinants) thoroughly and accurately, interpreting recent research in the field extremely well.

Hoffer, Eric. *The True Believer: Thoughts on the Nature of Mass Movements*. New York: Harper & Row, 1951. One of the most compelling and readable accounts of mass movements and their relation to aggressive behavior in individuals.

Lesko, Wayne A. *Readings in Social Psychology: General, Classic, and Contemporary Selections*. 4th ed. Boston: Allyn & Bacon, 2000. Chapter 11, "Aggession," is clear and forthright. A desirable starting point for those who are not experienced in the field.

Lorenz, Konrad. *On Aggression*. 1963. Translated by Marjorie Kerr Wilson. New York: Harcourt, Brace, & World, 1966. This classic and revolutionary study posits a killer instinct in both animals and humankind.

Scott, John Paul. *Aggression*. Chicago: University of Chicago Press, 1958. Although it is somewhat outdated, this book remains especially valuable for its chapters on the physiology of aggression (chapter 3) and on the social causes of aggression (chapter 5). The book is well written and easily understandable for those who are new to the field.

Wagner, Hugh. *The Psychobiology of Human Motivation*. New York: Routledge, 1999. Chapter 7 focuses on aggression and explores productively possible biological origins of the three types of aggression (offensive, defensive, and predatory) that he employs in making his classifications.

R. Baird Shuman

SEE ALSO: Aggression: Reduction and control; Anger; Battered woman sydrome; Conduct disorder; Defense reactions: Species-specific; Domestic violence; Emotions; Fight-or-flight response; Hormones and behavior; Impulse control disorders; Jealousy; Misbehavior; Psychotic disorders; Road rage; Stress: Behavioral and psychological responses; Violence and sexuality in the media; Violence by children and teenagers.

Aggression
Reduction and control

TYPE OF PSYCHOLOGY: Social psychology
FIELDS OF STUDY: Aggression

Aggressive behavior has been a problem for humans since before the beginning of recorded history. Psychologists have developed many theories of aggression, and there are many different ideas as to how—or whether—aggression might be controlled.

KEY CONCEPTS
- behaviorism
- catharsis
- frustration-aggression hypothesis
- social learning theory
- sociobiology

INTRODUCTION

Aggression has been humankind's steady companion throughout history—in life, literature, and art. Many hypotheses have been suggested by psychologists and other scientists concerning the nature of aggression; some have suggested that it is learned behavior, others that it is an innate, genetically inherited drive. The fields of ethology and sociology have mustered evidence to support the evolutionary (genetic) basis of aggression. Theories based on these viewpoints hold that at some point in humankind's past, aggressiveness was an adaptive trait—that is, aggression helped ensure the survival of the individual who possessed that quality, thereby enabling the aggressive trait to be passed on to future generations. Social psychologists, on the other hand, have studied the effects of modeling aggressive behavior. When children, for example, have been exposed to aggressive behavior modeled (acted out or demonstrated in some way) by others, they have shown an increase in aggressive behavior. In other words, the children observe and learn the behavior. Albert Bandura's social learning theory describes this concept of aggression.

The frustration-aggression hypothesis, as described by John Dollard, holds that both violence and aggression are the result of being frustrated in an attempt to reach a goal. When basic needs have been thwarted, aggression appears. As Leonard Berkowitz stated it in *Roots of Aggression* (1969), "If a person is aggressive, he has been frustrated. If a person is frustrated, he has become aggressive." Negative environmental factors are also believed by many to have a major impact on aggression. Studies have found links, for example, between the number of violent crimes and air temperature. Overcrowding and economic hard times are also associated with higher crime rates. These studies tend to support negative affect theory, which holds that exposure to stimuli that create discomfort leads to aggression.

The amount of hope one holds for the possibility of reducing or controlling aggression depends, to some extent, on the theory of aggression that one believes to be most accurate. If aggressive behavior is an integral part of the genetic makeup of the human species, the outlook is not nearly as promising as it is if aggression is primarily a behavior learned from others and reinforced by certain rewards. In the former case, aggressive actions can perhaps be controlled by societal strictures, but the aggressive instinct will always remain within. In the latter case, decreasing the modeling of aggression or increasing the modeling of and rewards for nonaggressive behavior could conceivably produce effective results. Different studies have produced different results concerning the effectiveness of various attempts to reduce aggressive behavior.

Another complication in understanding and controlling aggression is that different people will react very differently when in similar circumstances. When frustrated, some people will react aggressively, while others will become withdrawn and depressed. Depression itself can lead to aggression, however, and this type of delayed aggression can produce seemingly unpredictable acts of violence. Psychologists simply do not have all the answers to why some people react aggressively and others do not when faced with identical predicaments.

TREATMENT TECHNIQUES

Psychologists Matthew McKay, Martha Davis, and Patrick Fanning adapted Donald Meichenbaum's concept of stress inoculation training to produce one technique that allows an aggressive person to control his or her own aggressive behavior. McKay and his colleagues present simple, concise, step-by-step directions to deal with aggression. Because aggression is often fueled by emotional distress, they offer a technique of "covert assertion" through the development of two separate skills: thought interrup-

tion and thought substitution. When becoming angry or frustrated, the potential aggressor thinks of the word "stop" or some other interrupting device. The void suddenly created is then filled with a reserve of previously prepared positive, nonaggressive thoughts. This technique can be mastered, the authors maintain, if it is practiced conscientiously throughout the day for three days to a week.

The creation of an "aggression stimulants structure" gives the individual who is compelled to be negatively aggressive the opportunity to take a personal inventory of who (or what) the targets of his or her aggression are, what the feelings associated with those people are, and what would occur if a plan of "attack" against them were to be put into action. This type of analysis lends itself well to self-accountability; it allows the individual to "own" the problem and to believe that it can be controlled if he or she chooses to control it. It also allows, through its identification of specific targets and imaging of the act of aggression, a global perspective on what can otherwise seem a very fragmented problem.

Aggression in the work environment can be damaging and disruptive both for individuals and for organizations. In a 1987 article in the *Journal of Occupational Psychology*, Philip L. Storms and Paul E. Spector claimed that high frustration levels of organizational employees were positively related to interpersonal aggression, sabotage, and withdrawal. Suggestions for dealing with aggression in the workplace have included such strategies as training courses and the use of humor to defuse tensions. Diane Lamplugh notes that aggression in this arena can range from whispered innuendo to harassment to violence. She maintains that a training course that focuses on tension control, relaxation techniques, customer-relations orientation, assertiveness practice, aggression-centered discussions, and self-defense training can be helpful. She also states that support from management in identifying problem areas and formulating guidelines for staff support is crucial. William A. Kahn promotes humor as a means for organizational members to make statements about themselves, their groups, or their organization. Humor, he notes, is a nonthreatening vehicle that allows people to say things that might otherwise insult or offend coworkers, thereby making them defensive and threatening working relationships.

Written or unwritten laws, rules, and codes of conduct are established in an attempt to curb unacceptably aggressive behavior. A company may terminate an employee who does not adhere to certain standards of behavior; athletes are benched for aggression or violence. Society as a whole formulates laws to control its members' aggressive behavior. When individuals act in ways that are damagingly aggressive to other people or to the property of others, law enforcement agencies step in to safeguard the population. Perpetrators are fined or sentenced to prison terms.

Studies disagree as to the most effective means of rehabilitating offenders, but many studies do suggest that rehabilitation is possible. One avenue that is frequently explored is the use of various techniques founded in behaviorism. In *Psychological Approaches to Crime and Its Correction* (1984), edited by Irving Jacks and Steven G. Cox, Stanley V. Kruschwitz investigates the effectiveness of using a voluntary token reinforcement procedure to change the behavior of inmates who are difficult to manage. In the same volume, Albert F. Scheckenbach makes an argument for behavior modification as it relates to adult offenders. Modeling positive behaviors and holding group discussions have been found at least somewhat effective in rehabilitating juvenile delinquents, as has the development of behavioral contracts. John Lochman and his colleagues, using what they called an "anger coping mechanism," explored cognitive behavioral techniques for reducing aggression in eleven-year-old boys. The boys treated with this procedure showed vast improvements—a reduction of disruptive classroom behavior and an increase in perceived social competence. Such techniques, used with young people, might reduce their high-risk status for later difficulties.

THEORETICAL EXPLANATIONS

Acts of aggression have been central in human history, myth, literature, and even religion. In the biblical account, for example, humankind has barely come into existence when Cain kills his brother Abel. Almost as old are questions concerning the causes of aggression and the debate over how to control it.

Sigmund Freud (1856-1939) saw aggression as the result of struggles within the psyche of the individual; the tension produced in the struggle between the life instinct and the death instinct creates outward aggression. Alfred Adler (1870-1937), another psychodynamic theorist, stated that aggression represents the most general human striving and is a necessity of life; its underlying principle is self-assertion. Humanistic theorist Rollo May (1909-1994) notes that attention to aggression has nearly universally focused on its negative aspects. In *Power and Innocence* (1972), May wrote that "we have been terrified of aggression, and we assume—delusion though it is—that we can better control it if we center all our attention on its destructive aspects as though that's all there is."

It was first the behaviorist school, then social learning theorists (such as Albert Bandura), who explored ways to reduce and control aggression. The frustration-aggression hypothesis, for example, was developed in the 1930's. Behaviorists tended to approach aggressive behavior in terms of stimuli, responses, and reinforcement. In a general sense, any approaches that seek to punish unacceptably aggressive behavior or to reward positive behavior are related to the behavioral view. Bandura and other social learning theorists found that, in some situations, children would respond to viewing aggressive acts by performing aggressive acts themselves. The implications of this have been widely argued and debated; one aspect concerns the effects of viewing television and motion-picture violence. Viewing violence on television does seem to cause increased aggressive behavior, although because of the nature of the types of studies most often performed, it can be difficult to draw incontestable cause-and-effect relationships.

The debate over whether aggression is learned, innate, or both (and, if both, over the relative importance of the two aspects) is not likely to end soon. Debates over how to control aggression will also continue. As in many areas of psychology, bridging the gap between the theoretical and the practical is difficult. As only one example, negative affect theory suggests that noxious environmental stimuli can produce negative emotions and, therefore, aggression; however, it is virtually impossible to remove such stimuli, except on a very small scale. Yet another area that will be increasingly explored is the relationship between aggression and biochemical factors. Studies have found correlations, for example, between aggressiveness and high levels of norepinephrine and low levels of serotonin, two important neurotransmitters. The significance of such chemical findings remains to be ascertained.

SOURCES FOR FURTHER STUDY

Bach, George R., and Herb Goldberg. *Creative Aggression*. Stevens Point, Wisc.: National Wellness Institute, 1975. A guidebook, still in print in 2002, for people who cannot confront conflict as well as for those who choose to seek conflict. Helps the reader to assess himself or herself honestly and to approach aggressiveness in new ways.

Berkowitz, Leonard, ed. *Roots of Aggression*. New York: Atherton Press, 1969. Revisits the frustration-aggression hypothesis. Examines such areas as catharsis, frustration, and conditions facilitating the occurrence of aggression.

Green, Russell G., and Edward Donnerstein, eds. *Human Aggression: Theory, Research, and Implications for Social Policy*. San Diego, Calif.: Academic Press, 1998. An up-to-date survey of current thinking on the psychology of aggression.

May, Rollo. *Power and Innocence*. 1972. Reprint. New York: W. W. Norton, 1998. Probes the sources of violence. Advances solutions for contemporary society, examining the concept of innocence and challenging traditional views of aggression.

Robbins, Paul R. *Anger, Aggression, and Violence: An Interdisciplinary Study*. Jefferson, N.C.: McFarland, 2000. Draws on psychology, anthropology, sociology, and history to suggest ways in which anger and aggression can be channeled into useful behaviors before exploding in violence.

Simmons, Rachel. *Odd Girl Out: The Hidden Culture of Aggression in Girls*. San Diego, Calif.: Harcourt Brace, 2002. A perceptive study of the coded aggression expressed by American girls and the ways in which hidden anger leaks through cultural expectations that girls be "nice."

Denise S. St. Cyr

SEE ALSO: Aggression; Emotions; Instinct theory; Psychoanalytic psychology and personality: Sigmund Freud; Violence and sexuality in the media.

Aging

Cognitive changes

TYPE OF PSYCHOLOGY: Cognition; intelligence and intelligence testing; learning; memory; psychopathology; sensation and perception

FIELDS OF STUDY: Aging; behavioral and cognitive models; cognitive processes; social perception and cognition; thought

Behavioral scientists have become increasingly interested in studying the cognitive changes that occur in the elderly across time. These studies have been conducted in order to assist individuals in their adjustment to aging as well as to unlock the secrets of the aging process itself.

KEY CONCEPTS
- attention
- cognition
- environmental influences
- information processing
- learning
- long-term memory
- mild cognitive impairment (MCI)
- pacing of instruction
- sensoriperceptual changes
- short-term memory

INTRODUCTION

Cognitive changes refer to those changes which occur in overall mental functions and operations. Cognition encompasses all mental operations and functions, including attention, intelligence, memory, language and speech, perception, learning, concept formation, thought, problem solving, spatial and time orientation, and motor/behavior control. Psychologists have worked hard to define and measure various areas of cognitive functioning, even though there has been no consensus about these areas. Understanding the progression of cognitive functioning requires an understanding of brain structure and those human functions emanating from the brain and its fullest human potentiality, the mind. There is considerable debate within the scientific community about what type of cognitive functions actually exist as well as the nature of the mental mechanisms that are necessary to understand cognitive functioning.

A common belief that cognitive abilities decline markedly in older individuals. More and more, however, this idea is being shown to be exaggerated. Studies have shown that the diminishment of cognitive skills with age may not be significant, especially before the age of about seventy-five. Aging has been found to have different effects on long-term and short-term memory processes. The capacity of short-term memory (which is quite limited in all age groups) remains essentially the same for older people. Long-term memory, however, does show a decline. This decline can be minimized by various strategies; the use of mnemonic devices is very effective, as is taking extra time in learning and remembering.

Both biological and environmental factors have been studied in regard to aging and cognition. An environment that induces apathy or depression has been found to have a lowering effect on cognitive abilities. Environments that provide stimuli to interest the individual can reduce cognitive decline. Moreover, at least one study has found that providing challenging stimuli can even reverse cognitive declines that have been observed. There is a tremendous range of aging effects from individual to individual, with some showing virtually no changes and others showing serious decay of functions. It should be noted that this discussion concerns cognition in healthy individuals; diseases such as Alzheimer's disease and Parkinson's disease and events such as strokes (cardiovascular accidents) have effects on memory that are considered separately from the normal effects of aging.

Contemporary research on cognitive changes caused by aging emphasizes the information-processing capabilities of individuals as reflected in memory capacities. Memory is a basic psychological function upon which higher-level psychological processes such as speech, learning, concept formation, and problem solving are based. Lester Sdorow describes the brain's information-processing capacities as the human being's active acquisition of information about the world. Sensory stimuli are transmitted to the brain, where replicas of the external world are stored briefly in the sensory registry (one second for visual stimuli and four seconds for auditory memory). Information is then transferred to short-term memory for about twenty seconds, unless it is actively rehearsed, then into long-term memory, where it is potentially retained for a lifetime.

INFORMATION PROCESSING AND MEMORY

Information processing is a view of cognitive development that is based on the premise that complex cognitive skills develop as the product of the integration of a hierarchy of more basic skills obtained through life experience and learning. According to this view, prerequisite skills are mastered and form the foundation for more and more complex skills.

Information-processing theories emerged as psychologists began to draw comparisons between the way computers operate and the way humans use logic and rules about the world as they develop. Humans use these rules for processing information. New rules may be added and old rules modified throughout childhood and adulthood as more information is obtained from interactions with the world. The cognitive changes that occur throughout adult life, as more useful and accurate rules are learned, are every bit as important as the cognitive advances that occurred during childhood, as long as the basic rules acquired in childhood were not distorted by aberrant experiences. Each advance refines the ability to process information. Elizabeth F. Loftus points out that the terms "cognition" and "information processing" have supplanted the term "thinking" among contemporary cognitive scientists. Similar efforts have been made to redefine other human abilities such as problem solving (by H. A. Simon) and intelligence (by Robert Sternberg) in order to describe greater specificity of function.

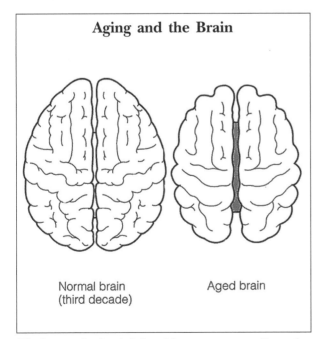

Aging and the Brain

Normal brain (third decade)   Aged brain

The human brain shrinks with age as nerve cells are lost and brain tissue atrophies. Cognitive changes in the elderly can range from mild forgetfulness to dementia. (Hans & Cassidy, Inc.)

Researchers have spent much time and effort defining and redefining memory constructs, although theorists remain in the early stages of understanding memory. Much debate has focused on naturalistic versus laboratory methodologies, with few resolutions as to how the results of both can contribute to a permanent knowledge base of memory.

The mediation school of thought suggests theoretical mechanisms of encoding, retention, and retrieval to explain memory functioning. Consequently, concerted efforts have been made to attribute memory changes across the life span to the specific deterioration of such mechanisms. Researchers continue to debate the importance, even existence, of such constructs. Similarly, the dichotomy of long-term versus short-term memory continues to be debated. In order to test the empirical validity of such theories, constructs must be able to be disproved if false, and these metaphorical constructs have proved difficult or impossible to test because of their abstract nature.

The greatest controversy in memory research focuses on laboratory versus naturalistic experiments; some researchers, such as M. R. Banaji and R. G. Crowder, state that naturalistic experiments have yielded no new principles and no new methods of memory research and should be abandoned. Others, such as H. P. Bahrick, however, claim that the naturalistic approach has provided in ten years what the laboratory has not in a hundred years. Banaji and Crowder criticize naturalistic experiments for their lack of control and thus their lack of generalizability. Yet confining a study to a specific population in a contrived laboratory setting does not seem to generalize any further. S. J. Ceci and Urie Bronfenbrenner emphasize the need to focus on the process of understanding, whatever that process might be. As Endel Tulving notes, the polemics that have ensued from this debate are not going to advance the science of memory. He concludes that there is no reason to believe that there is only one correct way of studying memory.

INFORMATION PROCESSING IN THE ELDERLY

Learning, memory, and attention are all aspects of cognition. Learning is the acquisition of information, skills, and knowledge measured by improvement in responses. Memory involves retaining and retrieving information for later use. Attention is the mechanism by which individuals process information. Cognition is how sensory input is transformed, stored and retrieved from memory.

Major stages of information-processing models of learning and memory include registration (input), storage (retention), and retrieval (process input for response). Attention is a major component of registration in that focusing on stimuli and processing of information begin at this stage. Environmental influences, age-related sensoriperceptual changes, and pacing of instruction affect the processing of information.

Environmental influences can produce negative responses from the elderly because older adults are less comfortable in unfamiliar settings, with unfamiliar people, and have difficulty performing multiple tasks. Additionally, the ability to block out extraneous information and to focus on multiple instructions decreases with age.

Sensoriperceptual changes include age-related vision deficits such as altered color perception as a result of yellowing of the eye lens, difficulty seeing at various distances as a result of presbyopia, difficulty adjusting from light to dark, and decreased peripheral vision and depth perception. Sensorineural hearing loss affects the ability to hear high-frequency sounds and consonants and hinders communication. Also, excessive noise interferes with the ability to hear in the elderly.

Pacing of instruction includes both the time it takes to present and the amount of information presented. With age there is slowing of physiological and psychological responses. Reaction time increases. Studies have shown that the elderly learn more efficiently when they are able to learn and respond at their own pace.

STUDIES IN AGE-RELATED COGNITION

In examining cognitive changes in aging populations, aside from the theoretical debates, researchers have reported that cognitive processes progressively decline as chronological age advances. Studies have tended to describe the cognitive declines as gradual and general, rather than being attributable to discrete cognitive losses in specific areas of functioning.

Several studies have supported the existence of age-related cognitive decline, while other studies dispute the severity of such declines. Research interest is increasing in the areas of identifying factors related to cognitive decline and interventions to abate them. Under the direction of Ronald C. Petersen and Michael Grundman, the National Institute on Aging is studying whether daily doses of vitamin E or donepezil can prevent those with mild cognitive impairment from developing Alzheimer's disease. Other studies are investigating cholinesterase inhibitors and anti-inflammatory agents as a means to slow the progression of mild cognitive impairment.

Psychologists who studied memory change identified diminished memory capacity in the elderly as attributable to a number of processes, such as slowed semantic access and a reduced ability to make categorical judgments. Other researchers concluded that older subjects were slower in mental operations but were not less accurate. Some researchers hypothesized that slower speed tied up processing functions, resulting in apparent memory impairment. Still others hypothesized that older adults have more trouble with active memory tasks because of increased competition for a share of memory processing resources, whereas others linked the aged's poor performance on working memory tasks to an actual deficiency in processing resources. Finally, some researchers concluded that older adults might simply have less mental energy to perform memory tasks. These studies accept gradual memory decline, or a slowing of processing, as a normal by-product of aging.

There are some who believe that mild cognitive impairment is a neurological disorder. This belief stems from the identification of atrophy of the left medial lobe and small medial temporal lobe, low parietal/temporal perfusion, and asymmetry of the brain as revealed by computed tomography. One study identified those with small hippocampi as prone to developing Alzheimer's disease. Additionally, electroencephalogram tracings of the brains of patients with mild cognitive impairment and patients with Alzheimer's disease showed similarities.

R. A. Hock, B. A. Futrell, and B. A. Grismer studied eighty-two elderly persons, from sixty to ninety-nine years of age, who were living independently in the community. These normal adults were tested on a battery of eight tasks that were selected to reflect cognitive functioning, particularly measuring primary and secondary memory, memory for nonverbal material, span of attention, the capacity to divide attention between competing sources of stimulation, and two motor tasks requiring psychomotor

integrity. This study found a gradual, progressive decline in cognitive functioning but found that the decline did not reach statistically significant levels. The decline was general, suggesting that it may have been a function of reduced attention rather than more discrete losses. This finding appears to be consistent with the notion that crystallized intellectual or abstract processes are well maintained across time. There were suggestions that speed of information processing is a sensitive measure of the aging process.

It is possible, however, that the tasks selected for this study did not discriminate between younger and older aging adults because the tasks may be more reliable for assessing brain injuries and psychologically impaired persons, who were not included in the population studied. Consequently, further studies on the same cognitive tasks with impaired aged adults would be necessary to see if the same relationships and conclusions would apply. Individuals with impaired cognitive functioning offer a unique opportunity to determine if the brain continues to show the same propensity to function as a unitary, global system as is observed with individuals who experience the normal aging process.

Although the brain does exhibit localization of functions, with specialization of certain brain cells for specific functions, its overall mode of operation is as a total unit. The brain has an exceptional capacity to compensate for the loss of some specific functions and continue the rest of its mental operations. This capacity or flexibility in brain function has been termed equipotentiation. Further studies of individuals with brain impairments will help to show how the brain attempts to carry out its overall functions when more specific impairments have been sustained. When cognitive disorders result in faulty information processing, actual observable changes may occur in a person's daily behavior. The previously neat person, for example, may neglect personal hygiene. The person who previously exhibited exceptional verbal abilities may speak in a socially inappropriate manner. The staid conservative businessperson may act impulsively or even make unreasonable decisions about personal finances, and may show impaired social judgment.

MILD COGNITIVE IMPAIRMENT
Studies of cognitive changes across the life span must distinguish between normal gradual change in

the elderly and change that is associated with disordered functioning. Studies must also respect the complexity of the human brain. Morton Hunt notes that cognitive scientists have concluded that there may be 100 billion neurons in the interior of the brain. Each of these neurons may be interconnected to hundreds of others by anywhere from one thousand to ten thousand synapses, or relay points. This may enable the average healthy person to accumulate five hundred times as much information as is contained in the entire *Encyclopedia Britannica*, or 100 trillion bits of information. The circuitry in one human brain is probably sixty times the complexity of the entire United States telephone system. Given this complexity, even the daily estimated loss of 100,000 brain cells from the aging process may leave human beings capable of sound cognitive functioning well into old age.

"Mild cognitive impairment" is a term used to describe isolated memory losses without changes in activities of daily living. There is some support for the theory that mild cognitive impairment represents a transitional stage between normal aging and Alzheimer's disease and may be a precursor to Alzheimer's disease. However, a significant proportion of patients with mild cognitive impairment do not progress to Alzheimer's disease. One research study followed a group of mildly cognitively impaired patients and reported they developed Alzheimer's disease at a rate of 10 percent to 15 percent per year, while individuals without mild cognitive impairment developed Alzheimer's disease at a rate of 1 percent to 2 percent per year. Individuals who have a memory problem but do not meet clinical criteria for Alzheimer's disease are considered to have mild cognitive impairment with memory loss. This is an important group for Alzheimer's disease research because up to 40 percent of those who are mildly cognitively impaired develop Alzheimer's disease within three years. One study supported that those who carried the gene apolipoprotein E-4 (APOE-4) were more likely to develop Alzheimer's disease. Studies involving molecular brain activity have contributed to understanding normal and abnormal memory activities. Another study linked poor performance on a memory test that provided cues to help participants at time of recall indicated a cognitive decline. To date there are no treatments to prevent or manage mild cognitive impairment. Therefore, awareness, understanding the implications, and early identifi-

cation are important in management and education about mild cognitive impairment.

Paul Baltes notes that it used to be considered "common knowledge" that cognitive abilities decline with age, but today this view is highly debatable. When the effects of disease and injury are separated out in studies of the healthy elderly, no drastic decline in cognitive ability is found. This conclusion may be one reason that studies of cognition and aging have begun to make a distinction regarding intelligence. The distinction is between crystallized intelligence, involving the accumulation of facts and knowledge, which holds up with age, and fluid intelligence, which is the rapid processing of new information, a function that appears particularly associated with the young and vulnerable to the effects of age or disease. Studies of neurologically healthy aging adults have revealed no consistent evidence of a reduced ability to learn. Studies have further shown that very little practice may be required to improve substantially an elderly person's ability to perform some cognitive tasks, reflecting a motivational factor. Studies of mentally active persons in their eighties have concluded that loss of cognitive ability stemmed more from intellectual apathy or boredom than from actual physical deterioration.

John Darley and his colleagues concluded that on average, the decline of intellectual capability with age is slight and probably does not occur before age seventy-five. When declines do occur, they do not occur equally across cognitive functions. Vocabulary and verbal skills may actually improve with age, whereas skills involving spatial visualization and deductive reasoning are more likely to diminish. In general, verbal skills and accumulated knowledge are maintained with aging, while tasks that require quick responses are more susceptible to aging.

SOURCES FOR FURTHER STUDY

Bahrick, H. P. "A Speedy Recovery from Bankruptcy for Ecological Memory Research." *American Psychologist* 46, no. 1 (1991): 76-77. This article addresses the controversy between those who favor naturalistic memory studies and those who favor strict experimental studies; Bahrick favors the naturalistic approach.

Banaji, Mahzarin R., and Robert G. Crowder. "The Bankruptcy of Everyday Memory." *American Psychologist* 44, no. 9 (1989): 1185-1193. This article addresses the controversy between naturalistic and experimental research; the authors favor more controlled experimental approaches.

Ceci, S. J., and Urie Bronfenbrenner. "On the Demise of Everyday Memory." *American Psychologist* 46, no. 1 (1991): 27-31. Addresses the naturalistic versus experimental memory study issue, offering a balanced perspective and inviting scientific inquiry regardless of the type of methodology.

Craik, Fergus I. M., and Timothy Salthouse, eds. *The Handbook of Aging and Cognition.* 2d ed. Mahwah, N.J.: Lawrence Erlbaum, 2000. A collection of review essays on all aspects of the aging brain.

Friedrich, M. J. "Mild Cognitive Impairment Raises Alzheimer Disease Risk." *Journal of the American Medical Association* 282 (1999): 621-622. Discusses link between cognitive impairment and developing Alzheimer's disease.

Lindsay, Heather. "Delaying, Treating Mild Cognitive Impairment." *Clinical Psychiatry News* 27 (1999): 18. Addresses consequences of not treating mild cognitive impairment early.

Loftus, Elizabeth F. *Memory: Surprising New Insights into How We Remember and Why We Forget.* Reading, Mass.: Addison-Wesley, 1988. Loftus discusses the development of the cognitive sciences in seeking greater specificity for human abilities such as thinking and memory.

Park, Denise, and Norbert Schwarz, eds. *Cognitive Aging: A Primer.* Philadelphia: Psychology Press, 2000. An upper-level college and graduate text covers all aspects of cognition in aging brains at an introductory level.

Petersen, Ronald. "Mild Cognitive Impairment or Questionable Dementia?" *Archives of Neurology* 57 (2000): 643-644. Differentiates between mild cognitive impairment and dementia.

Petersen, Ronald C., G. E. Smith, S. C. Waring, R. J. Ivnik, E. Tangalos, and E. Kokmen. "Mild Cognitive Impairment: Clinical Characterization and Outcome." *Archives of Neurology* 56 (1999): 303-308. Speaks of symptoms and consequences of untreated mild cognitive impairment.

Shah, Yogesh, Eric Tangalos, and Ronald Petersen. "Mild Cognitive Impairment: When Is It a Precursor to Alzheimer's Disease?" *Geriatrics* 55 (2000): 62-67. Discusses relationship between memory decline, mild cognitive impairment, and Alzheimer's disease.

Robert A. Hock;
updated by Sharon Wallace Stark

SEE ALSO: Ageism; Aging: Physical changes; Aging: Theories; Cognitive maps; Coping: Terminal illness; Dementia; Alzheimer's disease; Forgetting and forgetfulness; Long-term memory; Memory; Memory: Physiology; Memory storage; Parkinson's disease; Short-term memory.

Aging
Physical changes

TYPE OF PSYCHOLOGY: Developmental psychology
FIELDS OF STUDY: Adulthood; aging; stress and illness

Physical aging involves a process of change. These changes proceed at different rates for different people, and at different rates in the various systems of the same people.

KEY CONCEPTS
- arthritis
- gerontology
- immune system
- life expectancy
- life span
- metabolism
- osteoporosis
- reaction time

INTRODUCTION

The human life span (the length of time people may live under optimal conditions) is about 120 years. While this figure has not changed over the last century, life expectancy has. The amount of time an American baby can be expected to live has increased from under sixty years in 1900 to nearly seventy-seven if born in 2002. As people have begun to live longer, they have become aware of many changes that occur in people as they age. The scientists who study aging are called gerontologists; they do not know exactly what the aging process is or why it proceeds differently in different people. It is known that predictable changes occur in the body as it gets older. Some are easily noticed, such as hair turning gray, hair loss, and wrinkles. Other changes, such as a tendency toward rising blood pressure, are not visible.

In general, research on aging has emphasized losses. More recently, increased interest in the aging process has stimulated physiological, sociological, and psychological research on aging. Although many physiological variables show major losses with advancing age, it is important, when looking at the average, to note that there is substantial variability at all ages throughout life. Scientists are finding that some changes in blood pressure and cholesterol levels that had originally been interpreted as age specific are common in industrial societies but not in agricultural ones.

CHANGES IN BODY SYSTEMS WITH AGE

One of the major physical changes that occurs with age is an increase in reaction time. As one gets older, it takes longer to respond to a stimulus. This increased reaction time is due to a number of factors, including changes in sensory function, an increased concern for accuracy, a slower response (often due to arthritis), and a slowing of transmission of neural impulses. This slowdown in the transmission of impulses through the nervous system is due in large part to demyelinization. As the axons lose their fatty covering (myelin sheath), saltatory conduction is impaired, and slowing of the neural impulse occurs.

Advancing age is associated with progressive impairments in the capacity to metabolize glucose. Again, there is substantial variability of the results in successive age groups, with many older individuals metabolizing glucose as well as their younger counterparts. The carbohydrate intolerance of aging may carry substantial risk, even in the absence of disease. Attempts have been made to determine which components of the age-associated alterations in carbohydrate intolerance are related to aging itself and which components might be related to diet, exercise, or medications. It is thought that factors such as physical fitness may decrease the likelihood of carbohydrate intolerance with advancing age. Metabolism also begins to slow at around age twenty-five. For each decade thereafter, the number of calories required to maintain one's weight drops by at least 2 percent. Muscle mass gradually shrinks, so that people tend to have more body fat than they did when younger.

Aging is also associated with a decline in bone density in both males and females, but primarily females. In 2001, 10 million Americans had osteo-

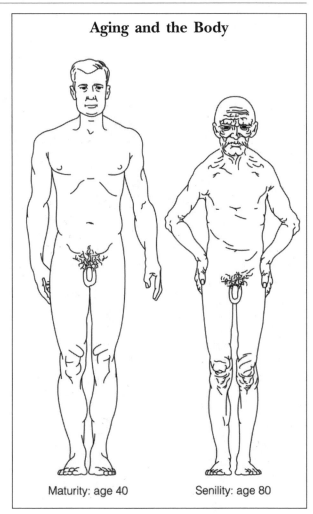

Aging and the Body

Maturity: age 40   Senility: age 80

Among the most obvious effects of aging are reduced body mass, a "shrinking" of height with loss of bone mass, sagging and wrinkling skin, and graying or loss of hair. (Hans & Cassidy, Inc.)

porosis, a condition in which the bones become dangerously thin and fragile. Osteoporosis is a major problem for the elderly. Bone mass reaches its peak in the thirties for both men and women, then begins to drop by about 1 percent per year. Brittle bones are the major cause of the fractures that cripple many of the elderly. It is estimated that by age sixty-five, one-third of women will have fractures of the vertebrae in the spinal column, and by age eighty-one, one-third of women and one-sixth of men will have suffered a hip fracture. A number of studies suggest that bone loss can be reduced in advanced age by adherence to moderate exercise programs, in addition to adequate calcium intake throughout life. Drugs such as Calcitonin and Fosimax have been developed to treat osteoporosis.

Arthritis (inflammation of the joints) is one of the common complaints of middle-aged and elderly adults. Osteoarthritis is the type that most commonly develops with age. It leads to stiffening of the joints, along with pain. As a result, people may tend to exhibit decreased mobility and slowing of their responses. Arthritis has long been treated with corticosteroids. Pain is often treated using nonsteroidal anti-inflammatory drugs (NSAIDs). Recent research has focused on the use of glucosamine and chondroitin to treat arthritis. Joint replacement is available as an option to treat advanced arthritis.

The sense organs of the elderly also go through changes. Taste diminishes as the nose loses its sense of smell. Odors account for most of the overall sensation of flavors, so taste is lost as a function of loss of smell. Loss of taste can lead to lack of appetite and to serious nutritional deficiencies. Hearing fades, particularly in the high-frequency range, resulting in presbycusis. This high-frequency hearing loss with age begins at age twelve, and involves a loss of 50 cycles per second per year (beginning with a maximum frequency of 20,000 cycles per second). Pathological hearing loss also is found as one ages, with 25 percent of individuals over the age of sixty having hearing loss that interferes with everyday communication. This pathological hearing loss seems to relate to exposure to noise pollution. As a result, it has been seen more commonly in males (due to participation in wars and noisy work environments) and is expected to increase in frequency in the future (due to the use of loud electronic equipment and headphones). Pathological hearing loss is of great concern to gerontologists and geriatricians because it is often denied by the elderly, who then do not seek treatment, and often develop interpersonal isolation and paranoid behavior as a result.

Vision changes also commonly occur with age. Beginning at about age forty, people become aware that they have difficulty reading and seeing close-up. By the age of forty-five, seven out of eight adults wear glasses or contact lenses to correct for presbyopia (farsightedness that develops with age). Other visual disturbances that may occur with advancing age include cataracts (opacity of the lens of the eye) and glaucoma (increasing intraocular pressure). Additionally, the elderly lose the ability to see color at the shorter wavelengths, so that violet and navy come to be seen as black.

As adults get older, they also become less sensitive to pressure, and therefore more likely to develop bedsores or skin ulcerations. Temperature regulation also becomes impaired, so that the elderly are often too hot or too cold. Sense of balance is also less precise, so presbystasis (lack of sense of balance with age) occurs, making falls more likely. Changes occur in the skin: The topmost layer, or epidermis, becomes dry, whereas the middle layer, or dermis, becomes thin and less elastic. Along with loss of fat from the underlying subcutaneous layer, these changes cause the skin to sag and become wrinkled.

There are other physiological changes that accompany aging. For example, the immune system starts to decline in young adulthood. The white blood cells that fight off invaders such as viruses and bacteria lose some of their effectiveness as a person gets older. Antibody production in people over the age of sixty-five is less than 10 percent of what it was in adolescence. As a result, the older adult is much more susceptible to illness than the adolescent or young adult. Thus, the elderly are urged to get flu and pneumonia shots to help keep themselves healthy.

The respiratory system undergoes many changes with age. There is a reduction in breathing efficiency because the lungs no longer expand to take in as much air. In fact, lungs lose on the average 30 to 50 percent of their maximum breathing capacity between ages thirty and eighty. There is a diminished uptake of oxygen in the lungs, so less oxygen is carried by the blood, which has health ramifications since oxygen is necessary for the synthesis of amino acids and fatty acids, and for the production of energy.

THEORIES OF AGING

Virtually all systems of the body, including cardiovascular, circulatory, endocrine, excretory, and gastrointestinal systems, show changes with age. Several theories attempt to explain the aging process. The aging of cells is a complex process that scientists still do not completely understand. There are genetic theories, as well as nongenetic and physiological ones. Genetic and nongenetic theories of aging both explain aging at the cellular or molecular level.

Genetic theories assume that a problem occurs in cell formation with age. This problem occurs at the level of the ribonucleic acid (RNA) or deoxyribonucleic acid (DNA). Error theory is the genetic theory best supported by evidence, and assumes that aging is most likely to occur due to a change in RNA.

Nongenetic theories assume that cell formation occurs normally with age, but that something interferes with cell functioning as one ages. Wear-and-tear theory and accumulation theory are two of the best-supported nongenetic theories. The buildup of free radicals in the cell (which fits accumulation theory) has led to the popular use of antioxidants (nutritional supplements) to try to slow the aging process.

Physiological theories assume that aging occurs at the molar level—the level of tissues, organs, or systems. These theories attribute aging to a breakdown in the integration and function of systems. Current evidence indicates support for some genetic, nongenetic, and physiological theories, indicating that each may play a role in bringing about the physical changes of aging.

TRENDS IN AGING

The number of elderly people in the United States has increased rapidly in recent years. In the second half of the twentieth century, the number of Americans sixty-five or older more than doubled. Americans are living longer than ever before. The Bureau of the Census predicts that by 2030, the number of elderly Americans will grow to nearly 65 million and will make up more than 20 percent of the population. It is estimated that by 2050, one in twenty Americans will be older than eighty-five years of age.

One popular misconception disputed by recent research is the idea that aging means inevitable physical and sexual failure. While some changes necessarily occur, many of the problems associated with old age fall into the category of secondary aging. Secondary aging means that the problems are not the result of age but of abuse and disuse, which often can be controlled by the individual. Researchers have found that people wear out faster from disuse than they wear out from overuse. This also applies to sexuality. Studies from the time of Alfred Kinsey's work in the 1940's and 1950's to the present show

that sexual interest and activity decrease with age, but the drop varies greatly among individuals. Psychologist Marion Perlmutter reported that one of the best predictors of continued sexual intercourse is past sexual enjoyment and frequency. People who have never enjoyed sexuality much may consider age a good reason to give up sex.

Psychosocial factors have been studied, and they sometimes reveal how older men and women feel about the physical changes happening to their bodies. It is important that family members and members of the helping professions, along with the elderly themselves, come to understand that the physical changes that occur with passing time produce needs that are real, and that elderly people are not simply trying to make demands for attention. Elderly people must be helped to retain their dignity and allowed to remain as active and independent as possible. No one, whatever his or her age, likes to be helpless or to be perceived as a helpless person. As a result of helplessness, researchers find lowered self-esteem, health problems, depression, and sometimes death.

Several lines of research on psychosocial factors and health focus on the idea of social support. Empirical research has found consistent relationships between social support and various indicators of health and well-being. Social networks and support are persistent conditions that affect the mortality of older people. Support-disrupting life events have specific negative effects on both mortality and morbidity. The positive effects of social support have been demonstrated by means of intervention studies. Most of the intervention has involved supportive behaviors by health care professionals. Positive effects include increased rate and completeness of recovery from injuries, a smaller number of heart attacks, decreased incidence of cancer, and fewer physical illnesses.

STUDIES ON AGING

Important early studies of aging were performed in the 1950's, including the Human Aging Study, conducted by the National Institute of Mental Health; the Duke Longitudinal Studies, done by the Center for the Study of Aging and Human Development at Duke University; and the Baltimore Longitudinal Study of Aging. These pioneering studies and hundreds of others have benefitted from growing federal support.

The Human Genome Project (especially Project Chronos) is among studies important in the field of aging today. These studies continue to investigate the changes that take place in aging, as well as attempting to find ways to stop or delay these changes. Today, many people reaching one hundred years of age (centenarians) continue to function very well, showing minimal physical change with age. As these people are studied in projects such as Chronos, perhaps humankind will find an answer to the biological changes in aging, as well as finding ways to delay such changes.

SOURCES FOR FURTHER STUDY

Birren, James E., and K. Warner Schaie, eds. *Handbook of the Psychology of Aging.* 5th ed. San Diego, Calif.: Academic Press, 2001. Presents information on the psychology of adult development and aging in an edited handbook format. Provides the reader with chapters written by experts on a wide range of topics. An authoritative review, serving as a definitive reference source for students, researchers, and professionals.

Hoyer, William J., John M. Rybash, and Paul A. Roodin. *Adult Development and Aging.* 4th ed. Boston: McGraw-Hill, 1999. This college-level text covers all aspects of human aging with two chapters focusing on physiological changes and physical health.

Masoro, Edward J., and Steven N. Austad, eds. *Handbook of the Biology of Aging.* 5th ed. San Diego, Calif.: Academic Press, 2001. A definitive source reviewing biological changes with aging. It covers the most interesting topics in biomedical gerontology.

Schulz, Richard, and Timothy Salthouse. *Adult Development and Aging: Myths and Emerging Realities.* 3d ed. Englewood Cliffs, N.J.: Prentice Hall, 1998. This college-level text provides an overview to the field of human aging focusing on physical aspects in part 2 of the text.

Deborah R. McDonald;
updated by Robin Kamienny Montvilo

SEE ALSO: Ageism; Aging: Cognitive changes; Aging: Theories; Alzheimer's disease; Death and dying; Dementia; Hearing; Memory: Physiology; Parkinson's disease; Stress: Physiological responses; Stress-related diseases.

Aging
Theories

TYPE OF PSYCHOLOGY: Developmental psychology
FIELDS OF STUDY: Aging; endocrine system; stress and illness

Aging is an entropic (energy-disorder) phenomenon that is exhibited by most multicellular organisms. Three major theories have been suggested to explain the mechanisms of aging: the free radical theory, the genetic program theory, and the error catastrophe theory. While each theory emphasizes different aspects of the aging process, they almost certainly are interrelated.

KEY CONCEPTS
- entropy
- error catastrophe theory
- free radical theory
- genetic program theory
- longevity

INTRODUCTION

The aging process occurs in all living organisms, although it is most pronounced in vertebrate animals, animals having a cartilaginous, bony endoskeleton, an efficient heart, and a highly developed nervous system. It is part of the basic sequence of animal development from conception to reproductive maturity to death. It follows the second law of thermodynamics, a physical principle of the entire universe which maintains that the disorder (entropy) of the universe is constantly increasing because of the dissipation of energy and the gradual transfer of energy from system to system. Living organisms age because of the inefficiency of the chemical reactions within their cells, thereby creating disorder as is evidenced by breakdowns in physiological rhythms (for example, nerve cell functioning, blood pressure changes, and reduced kidney filtration) and physical structure (for example, bone deformations, muscle weakness, and hair loss). The second law of thermodynamics maintains that no machine is 100 percent efficient; therefore, energy will be lost continuously with accompanying decay of the system, or body.

PHYSIOLOGICAL AGING

In humans and other mammalian species, the process of aging follows a very predictable pattern. An individual is conceived by the union of genetic information from the mother via egg and the father via sperm, thereby producing a single-celled zygote. By the connected processes of mitosis (chromosome duplication followed by separation) and cytokinesis (cell division), the zygote divides into two cells, which later divide to make four cells, then eight cells, and so on until an individual composed of approximately 100 trillion cells is produced. Very early in development (for example, a few hundred cells), different cells in various locations begin to specialize, or differentiate, by hormonally initiated changes in gene expression within these cells, thereby giving rise to specialized structures such as nerves, muscle, skin, bone, eyes, and fingers.

After the individual organism is fully developed and can survive in the environment on its own, it will either exit the mother's body or hatch from a protective egg case, or shell. Subsequent juvenile development will include brain neuronal changes (plasticity) as a result of learning and social interactions, and physiological changes, leading to sexual maturity, or adulthood. Development up to adulthood does technically constitute aging, although there is little evidence of physiological decay. Various hormones, particularly steroid hormones, are prominent during an individual's sexual stage when the individual is capable of sexual reproduction. The individual is at his or her physical peak during the reproductive period. At the end of the critical reproductive period (menopause in females), the degenerative physical effects of true aging become very evident and accelerate with time as the individual becomes older. In a biological sense, the purpose of an organism is to reproduce and continue the transfer of genetic information. By age fifty or so, both males and females should have achieved this objective and estrogen (females) and testosterone (males) begin a more rapid decline. Consequently, the individual organism begins a progressive deterioration after age fifty or so toward death, thereby making room in the environment for its descendants. This is a harsh, but real, view of an organism's life. The key to understanding why deteriorative aging occurs lies in the hormones, chemicals, and cellular changes that are present in the organism just before this stage.

Among the physiological effects of aging that are evident very early are heart and respiratory changes. Upon birth, the average human newborn has a pulse of 120 heartbeats per minute, a breathing rate of 40 to 45 breaths per minute, and a blood pressure of 60/30. These data indicate a very high metabolic rate in individuals during early development. As humans age, both pulse and breathing rates decrease, whereas blood pressure increases. The average healthy adult has a pulse of approximately 60 to 80 heartbeats per minute, a breathing rate of approximately 8 to 12 breaths per minute, and a blood pressure somewhere around 120/70. Neuronal plasticity of the brain and, therefore, learning peak during the early reproductive years and decline around the age of forty-five to fifty. Most physiological processes undergo a steady decline from age twenty or so, with steeper declines occurring near age fifty, although large individual variation exists.

THREE THEORIES

When an organism dies, the electrical activity of billions of brain neurons ceases along with cessation of heart and respiratory muscle contractions. In more than 80 percent of human deaths by "natural causes," however, the exact cause of death cannot be determined. The physiological causes of aging and death remain poorly understood, although more than three hundred theories have been proposed to explain the process. Of all the theories proposed, three have withstood vigorous testing and continue to be widely studied: the free radical theory, the genetic program theory, and the error catastrophe theory. While the theories emphasize different aspects of cellular aging, they are complementary. All three may be correct in their combined interpretations.

FREE RADICAL THEORY. The role of free radicals in cell damage and aging was first proposed by Denham Harman in 1972. The free radical theory of aging maintains that the degenerative events which occur within the cell and the entire organism during aging are caused by the toxic effects of oxidizing free radical molecules. Free radicals are molecules that have a free extra electron per molecule that can be donated to another molecule. As a result, free radicals are highly reactive with most substances that they encounter. Their chemical reaction with a recipient molecule may effect the structure and function of that molecule so that it does not function properly. In a living cell, such an event could have disastrous consequences. The deoxyribonucleic acid

(DNA) nucleotide sequence of any gene could be mutated, or altered, by a free radical, thereby altering the structure or function of the protein encoded by that gene and affecting all cellular functions controlled by that specific protein. If the protein is essential for the cell's survival, the result could be cellular death or cellular transformation to the cancerous state.

Free radicals such as superoxide, hydroxyl radical, and hydrogen peroxide are naturally produced as by-products of the cell's metabolic activities. The cells of most living organisms produce antioxidant enzymes such as catalase, glutathione peroxidase, and superoxide dismutase to scavenge and inactivate free radicals wherever they occur. No such capture operation is 100 percent efficient, however. Some free radicals react with cellular molecules; the accumulated effects of these reactions over time may be responsible for cellular aging.

GENETIC PROGRAMMED THEORY. The genetic programmed theory of aging maintains that the cells of all living organisms contain genes that encode signaling protein hormones. These hormones, when produced, elicit aging-related changes within the cells at specific times during the organism's development, including death. Another viewpoint within this theory is that the cells of various tissues within living organisms are programmed to die after undergoing a specified number of genetically encoded divisions.

ERROR CATASTROPHE THEORY. The error catastrophe theory of aging is based on the likelihood of an error occurring somewhere in the complex process of protein synthesis. In 1963, Leslie Orgel suggested that those enzymes (proteins) which were involved in DNA transcription and translation of DNA into protein were critical to having "normal" proteins made, and that if these critical enzymes were created with an error, they in turn would cause the synthesis of most other proteins to also have an error—which would be a catastrophe. However, laboratory experiments have not supported this theory well.

APPLYING THEORIES TO HEALTH AND DISEASE

Active research into the mechanisms of the aging process is currently being conducted in laboratories throughout the world. The problem is being tackled from many different perspectives, including biochemical, genetic, physiological, gerontological, psychological, and sociological approaches. The topic is of particular interest in countries such as the United States where the overall population is becoming progressively older. Whereas much of the research is devoted to medical care for the elderly, many scientists are exploring the biochemistry of aging with hopes of understanding the process and possibly slowing or reversing it.

The three principal theories of aging (senescence), when combined, provide a very good working model for attacking the aging problem. The free radical theory of aging provides the cause, the error catastrophe theory provides the effects, and the genetic programmed theory provides an overall developmental view of the phenomenon. There can be no question that there are certain genes within all living cells that in a step-by-step manner control the sequential development of the entire organism. At the same time, free radical molecules are constantly being produced within body cells and these same cells are being exposed to mutagenic (mutation-causing) radiation and chemicals. These substances will cause accumulated cellular damage over time, even with the body's combined defenses of antioxidant enzymes, immune system cells, and kidney filtration of impurities from blood. These defenses work extremely well up to the end of the individual's reproductive period; then, they decline rapidly, almost as if they were programmed to do so.

Biochemical and genetic analyses of the aging process involve the study of the chemical reactivity of oxidizing free radicals, the measurement of the enzymatic action of antioxidant enzymes, the identification of substances that can enhance antioxidant enzyme activity, the location of antioxidant protein-encoding genes on chromosomes, the study of the effects of antioxidant gene mutations on the organism, the study of the effects of accumulated mutations on living cells, and the identification of genes and hormones that control major events within the cell. The properties and chemical reactivities of natural free radicals such as superoxide, hydroxyl radical, and hydrogen peroxide have been extensively studied. The mechanisms of action of antioxidant enzymes such as superoxide dismutase (which scavenges superoxide), catalase (which scavenges hydrogen peroxide), and glutathione peroxidase are fairly well understood. The chromosomal locations of the genes that encode these enzymes have been determined in several different animal, plant, and bacterial species. Mutations in antioxidant protein-encoding genes such as superoxide dismutase have been generated, and the effects of these mutations on their host organisms have been studied; such organisms usually are very sickly and have a reduced life span. Many nutrients act as antioxidants within the cell, including vitamin C, vitamin E, vitamin A, and selenium. In vitro, in vivo, and certain animal experiments suggest that supplementation with these nutrients will decrease oxidative damage. However, human studies fail to support these conclusions. Reducing substrate for oxidation by reducing the total calories consumed has increased longevity in animals. Because the restriction is quite harsh, the applicability of this strategy to delay aging in humans has been debated.

Among humans, several unusual pathologies exist that are of interest to scientists who research aging. Among these is the disease progeria, a condition in which the aging process is greatly accelerated. Individuals suffering from this apparently genetic disorder exhibit all of the symptoms of old age by the end of their first ten years. They die of old age usually before reaching their early teenage years. The mutated genes that contribute to this disorder have not been identified. Isolation of these genes would be of tremendous medical significance not only in terms of treating progeria but also in terms of extending the human life span. If a set of critical genes can be mutated to accelerate aging, as in progeria, then it would seem reasonable that the same genes could be modified to slow the aging process.

The aging process is also emphasized in acquired immunodeficiency syndrome (AIDS) and the genetic disorder autoimmune deficiency syndrome. In both situations, an individual's entire immune system is rendered useless, thereby leaving the individual's body defenseless against the continuous onslaught of usually harmless bacteria, viruses, and mutations. In AIDS patients, the immune system is inoperative because of the destruction of essential T lymphocytes by the human immunodeficiency virus (HIV). In autoimmune deficient patients, mutated genes have resulted in an inoperative immune system. In either case, aging is accelerated because of the removal of critical obstacles that routinely stop the action of free radicals and other error-generating substances. With a conservative estimate of ten million HIV-infected people worldwide, research in this area is intense and must continue to be so.

Cancer is one of the leading causes of death, and the incidence of cancer increases as people age. Cancer is essentially a disease of uncontrolled cell growth, which interferes with the normal functions of the body. There are several dozen types of cancer, based upon the affected tissues, site of the cancer in the tissue, and cell type that is affected. Causes of cancers are believed to be both genetically and environmentally defined; that is, some people are genetically more susceptible to environmental insults than others. Scientists believe that all cancers begin with one cell that becomes damaged and is not stopped from dividing and creating new damaged cells. An important scientific discovery has been the identification of certain genes involved in the development of cancerous cells: the proto-oncogenes and the tumor suppressor genes. How cancer relates to death is complex, and continues to be debated. Until more research is completed, it will not be know with certainty whether aging-related changes in cells and their systems make them more susceptible to cancer, or whether advancing time just allows more genetic hits to accumulate and produce cancerous cells.

The process of aging is difficult to measure, describe, or quantify, although it is a process which every organism experiences. Aging is a focus of many sciences, including physiology, chemistry, biochemistry, and genetics. As a scientific process, aging must have a beginning and an end, a substrate and a product, and a reason for the metabolic change. The scientific process of aging is not yet understood. There is worldwide research being conducted to find answers to the questions of why and how people age, and perhaps a substantiated explanation is not far away.

PSYCHOLOGICAL PERSPECTIVE

The process of aging occurs within all living organisms. Theories describing the mechanisms of aging are of relevance to psychology because the aging process is a developmental process that encompasses all bodily systems, including the brain and central nervous system. As conscious beings, humans are aware of their own aging. It is a fundamental focal point of consciousness, religious beliefs, and social structure. Humans are afraid of dying. As a result, aging is incorporated into human religions, behavior, and culture. Society stresses youthfulness, so humans go to great lengths and expense to reverse the effects of aging with skin creams, baldness cures or coverups, clothing, bodybuilding, and the like.

Psychology is a phenomenon of intelligent living organisms, and living organisms are complex entities consisting of intricate chemical reactions. These biochemical reactions, which are responsible for all aspects of life, follow the fundamental physical and chemical properties of the universe. One of these physical processes is the second law of thermodynamics, which maintains that any system loses energy due to inefficiency and therefore becomes more disordered, or entropic. Therefore, aging is an entropic process for the entire universe. Living organisms do undergo a building process during early development that is antientropic; however, after a certain time, specifically the end of the reproductive period, entropy takes over and accelerates. All aspects of the living animal, including the brain, deteriorate.

The free-radical, genetic programmed, and error catastrophe theories of aging have provided scientists with greater insights into the mechanisms of the aging process. These three theories also give researchers ideas for attacking aging as a disease that can be treated. While the so-called fountain of youth represents wishful thinking, research on aging realistically can lead to the prolongation of human life and the definite improvement of the quality of human life. The latter benefit of aging research includes the elimination or treatment of maladies such as heart disease, Alzheimer's disease, cancer, and general aging-related declines in most bodily functions.

One factor that permeates human biology in terms of aging, disease, and abnormal psychological behavior is stress. Research has repeatedly linked stress with accelerated aging, increased susceptibility to many diseases (including cancer), decreased mental agility and memory, and insanity. The accelerating explosion of human population and technological growth has been paralleled by a rapid increase in individual stress levels; stress-related diseases such as heart disease, stroke, and cancer; acts of violence, devastating wars, torture, exploitation, and destruction of human life; and the use of alcohol and illegal drugs to "relieve" stress. Reevaluation of the way that one treats fellow humans, a slowing of the fast-paced society, major social reforms, and medical advances in the treatment of stress all will be needed for decreasing stress, a major killer and contributor to the aging process.

Advances in biochemical and genetic medical research probably will produce the means for extending life within the next century. Whether or not human longevity is extended, aging will continue. As it does, researchers will continue to study how we age, why we age, and the consequences of an aging society for both the individual and the community.

SOURCES FOR FURTHER STUDY

Bergtson, Vern L., and K. Warner Schaie, eds. *Handbook of Theories of Aging*. New York: Springer, 1999. A multidisciplinary handbook for those interested in the social-psychological aspects of aging theory. After a brief introductory chapter on the biology of aging, the authors provide an informative overview of the psychological and social science concepts related to aging. The application of aging theories to public policy provides a thoughtful concluding chapter.

Karp, Gerald. *Cell Biology.* 2d ed. New York: John Wiley & Sons, 1998. An interesting discussion of the structure and biochemistry of the living cell. Includes an excellent discussion of the causes of both cancer and senescence in living cells, including the role of free radicals and mutation, in chapter 19.

Lewin, Benjamin. *Genes.* 7th ed. New York: Oxford University Press, 1999. Describes in great detail the major concepts of molecular biology and genetics. Much of the book is devoted to cutting-edge research studies on the identification and isolation of critical developmental genes. Chapter 33 discusses the processes of mutation in genes and how the cellular machinery combats these errors.

Masoro, Edward J., and Steven N. Austad, eds. *Handbook of the Biology of Aging*. 5th ed. San Diego, Calif.: Academic Press, 2001. Describes in great detail the research of investigators in biological gerontology. Directed primarily to researchers and instructors of the biology of aging, as well as toward geriatric clinicians. Details of recent cellular and systemic aging theories are presented, as well as the role of animal models in the study of aging.

Shapiro, Bennett M. "The Control of Oxidant Stress at Fertilization." *Science* 252 (April 26, 1991): 533-536. A summary of cellular regulatory systems that prevent damage to eggs by oxidizing free radicals during fertilization by sperm. Clearly describes the intracellular effects of oxidizing free radicals such as hydrogen peroxide and the cellular antioxidant activities of specific enzymes.

Wickens, Andrew P. *The Causes of Aging.* Amsterdam: Harwood Academic Publishers, 1998. An excellent reference for the beginning student or general reader, although also provides an interesting perspective for the teacher of aging or clinician. Genetics and the cellular basis of aging are presented in simple but thorough style. The author also covers metabolism and the hormonal and immunological aspects of aging with many examples of historical and recent scientific findings.

David Wason Hollar, Jr.;
updated by Karen Chapman-Novakofski

SEE ALSO: Aging: Cognitive changes; Aging: Physical changes; Alzheimer's disease; Brain structure; Coping: Chronic illness; Coping: Terminal illness; Death and dying; Dementia; Endocrine system; Neuropsychology; Parkinson's disease; Stress: Physiological responses; Stress-related diseases.

Agoraphobia and panic disorders

TYPE OF PSYCHOLOGY: Psychopathology
FIELDS OF STUDY: Anxiety disorders; biology of stress; cognitive therapies

Panic disorder with agoraphobia is a condition characterized by the presence of severe anxiety attacks coupled with avoidance of a wide range of situations. Considerable progress has been made toward understanding its cause and treatment.

KEY CONCEPTS
- depersonalization
- derealization
- fear of fear
- flooding
- habituation
- hyperventilation
- mitral valve prolapse syndrome
- palpitation
- paresthesia
- social phobia

INTRODUCTION

Panic disorder is a condition characterized by frequent panic attacks—that is, intense surges of anxiety. These attacks of anxiety often occur unexpectedly or "out of the blue"; the individual frequently is unable to identify an external trigger for them. Between attacks, the patient often ruminates about the possibility of additional attacks.

Panic attacks tend to be accompanied by a number of physical symptoms. Hyperventilation—overly rapid or deep breathing—is common, as are choking and smothering sensations, dizziness, faintness, and paresthesias—sensations of numbness and tingling, particularly in the extremities. Other common symptoms during panic attacks are sweating, trembling, nausea, abdominal distress, hot or cold flashes, accelerated heart rate, chest pain, and palpitations (feeling one's heart pound). Not surprisingly, many individuals who are having a panic attack believe that they are experiencing a heart attack.

Panic attacks are also frequently characterized by a number of psychological symptoms. Depersonalization and derealization are among the most common of these symptoms. Depersonalization is marked by feelings of unreality regarding oneself or one's body—sensations of being "disconnected" from oneself or of "watching" oneself as would an outside observer are frequent. Derealization refers to feelings of unreality concerning the external world; objects or people may seem somehow "strange" or unfamiliar. Also common during panic attacks are fears of dying (for example, from a heart attack or stroke), losing one's mind, or performing embarrassing behaviors (such as screaming uncontrollably).

The difficulties of many patients with panic disorder do not end here, however; many, but not all, of these patients develop an often debilitating syndrome known as agoraphobia. Agoraphobia is a fear of situations in which escape is difficult, inconvenient, or potentially embarrassing, or in which assistance might not be readily available. Specifically, what appears to occur is that many panic patients, dreading the possibility of a future attack, begin to fear and (in many cases) avoid situations that might precipitate such an attack. The situations feared or avoided by agoraphobics are extremely varied, but they include public transportation, open spaces, shopping malls, supermarkets, large social gatherings, elevators, driving in heavy traffic, passing over bridges or through tunnels, standing in long lines, and sitting in crowded theaters or churches.

In mild cases, agoraphobics may experience moderate discomfort while traveling or shopping alone, and may avoid those situations in only certain cases. In severe cases, agoraphobics may be unwilling to leave the house unaccompanied. The fears of an agoraphobic are generally alleviated by the presence of another individual, particularly one close to the patient, probably because this person could provide help in the event of an emergency, such as a heart attack.

The prevalence of panic disorder with agoraphobia in the general population of the United States has been estimated to be approximately 5 percent; an additional 2 percent have been estimated to have panic disorder without agoraphobia. Thus, panic disorder is relatively common and is perhaps the most frequent reason individuals seek outpatient psychiatric care. In addition, isolated panic attacks occur frequently among individuals in the general population. G. Ron Norton and his colleagues, for example, have found that approximately 34 percent of college students experience occasional panic attacks.

Panic disorder and agoraphobia have been reported to occur more frequently among females than males, although this difference is probably more marked for agoraphobia than for panic disorder. In addition, the prevalence of panic disorder appears to decline with age; its frequency has generally been reported to be highest among individuals under thirty and lowest among individuals over sixty-five. The course of panic disorder tends to be chronic but fluctuating. In other words, its symptoms often persist for many years, but they typically wax and wane depending upon the level of life stress and other factors.

In addition, panic disorder patients appear to have an elevated rate of several medical conditions. A subset of these patients, for example, has been reported to have mitral valve prolapse syndrome, a condition in which the heart's mitral valve bulges into the atrium. Because this syndrome results in physical symptoms such as palpitations and chest pain, it may be a risk factor for panic disorder in some individuals. In addition, a subset of panic patients appear to have disturbances of the vestibular system, an apparatus in the inner ear responsible for maintaining balance. As dizziness is a common symptom of panic attacks, vestibular dysfunction may be an important precipitant of some panic attacks.

A number of psychiatric conditions are commonly found among patients with panic disorder and agoraphobia. Depression is a particularly frequent complication of both syndromes; in many cases, it probably results from the distress produced by panic attacks and the constriction of activities produced by agoraphobia. This depression may have tragic consequences; panic disorder patients have been reported to be at greatly increased risk for suicide compared with individuals in the general population. In addition, many panic disorder patients turn to alcohol or other substances to alleviate their anxiety. Also commonly associated with panic disorder is social phobia, a condition characterized by fears of the possible scrutiny or criticism of others. Like patients with panic disorder patients, many social phobics experience panic attacks. Nevertheless, in social phobia these attacks are almost invariably triggered by situations in which the patient is the perceived focus of others' attention.

POSSIBLE CAUSES

A variety of models have been proposed for the causation of panic disorder and agoraphobia. Early explanations tended to focus largely or exclusively on physiological factors. In the 1960's, Donald Klein and his colleagues reported that panic disorder improved following administration of imipramine, a drug traditionally used to treat depression, whereas more sustained and long-lasting ("generalized") anxiety did not. Based upon this finding, Klein and his coworkers argued that panic is biologically distinct from other forms of anxiety. Although Klein's observation was important, it should be noted that making inferences about the nature of a disorder from the treatment of that disorder is logically flawed: A condition's treatment bears no necessary implications for its cause (for example, one would not be justified in concluding that headaches are caused by a lack of aspirin).

Nevertheless, it seems likely that physiological factors play an important role in panic disorder. Identical twins (who share all the same genes) with panic disorder are more likely than are fraternal twins (who share only half of their genes, on average) to have co-twins with panic disorder, suggesting that genetic factors play at least some role in this disorder. It is not known, however, whether these genetic factors predispose a person to panic disorder

DSM-IV-TR Criteria for Agoraphobia and Panic Disorders

AGORAPHOBIA WITHOUT HISTORY OF PANIC DISORDER (DSM CODE 300.22)

Presence of agoraphobia related to fear of developing panic-like symptoms (such as dizziness or diarrhea)

Criteria for Panic Disorder not met

Disturbance not due to direct physiological effects of a substance or general medical condition

If associated general medical condition present, fear clearly exceeds that usually associated with condition

PANIC DISORDER WITH AGORAPHOBIA (DSM CODE 300.21)

Recurrent unexpected panic attacks with at least one attack followed by one month or more of one or more of the following:

- persistent concern about having additional attacks
- worry about implications of attack or its consequences (losing control, having a heart attack, "going crazy")
- significant change in behavior related to attacks

Presence of agoraphobia

Panic attacks not due to direct physiological effects of a substance or general medical condition

Panic attacks not better accounted for by another mental disorder, such as Social Phobia, Specific Phobia, Obsessive-Compulsive Disorder, Post-traumatic Stress Disorder, or Separation Anxiety Disorder

PANIC DISORDER WITHOUT AGORAPHOBIA (DSM CODE 300.01)

Recurrent unexpected panic attacks with at least one attack followed by one month or more of one or more of the following:

- persistent concern about having additional attacks
- worry about implications of attack or its consequences (losing control, having a heart attack, "going crazy")
- significant change in behavior related to attacks

Absence of agoraphobia

Panic attacks not due to direct physiological effects of a substance or general medical condition

Panic attacks not better accounted for by another mental disorder, such as Social Phobia, Specific Phobia, Obsessive-Compulsive Disorder, Post-traumatic Stress Disorder, or Separation Anxiety Disorder

---

per se or to anxiety in general. In addition, there is evidence that the locus coeruleus, a structure in the pons (which is located at the back of the brain), is overactive during panic attacks. The locus coeruleus is a major center for norepinephrine, a chemical transmitter in the nervous system that appears to play a major role in the genesis of arousal and anxiety. Finally, it has been found that, in contrast to normals, many patients with panic disorder develop panic attacks following infusion of certain substances, such as sodium lactate and caffeine. It is possible, however, that this is simply attributable to greater arousal on the part of panic disorder patients; the infusion of these substances may provoke attacks in these patients because they are already on the verge of panicking.

Many subsequent models of the causation of panic disorder have attempted to move beyond physiological abnormalities to examine how panic disorder patients react to and construe their environment. One of the most influential of these might be termed the "fear of fear" model. According to Dianne Chambless, Alan Goldstein, and other pro-

ponents of this model, individuals who are afraid of their own anxiety are particularly prone to the development of panic disorder. During frightening experiences, this "fear of fear" can spiral into a panic attack.

A more recent theory of panic disorder is the "cognitive model" of David Clark, Aaron Beck, and other researchers. According to this model, panic attacks result from the catastrophic misinterpretation of unusual or unexpected bodily sensations. In other words, panic attacks may occur when a physical symptom (such as rapid heartbeat or dizziness) is misinterpreted as presaging a disastrous outcome (heart attack or stroke). Interestingly, many of the physical symptoms of anxiety, such a rapid heartbeat, can themselves be exacerbated by anxiety, as anyone who has felt his or her heart race uncontrollably while giving a speech can attest. Thus, the misinterpretation of certain physical sensations may set in motion a cycle in which these sensations progressively increase in intensity, giving rise to further misinterpretations and ultimately culminating in a panic attack. The cognitive model is also consistent with the evidence, mentioned earlier, that some panic patients have physiological abnormalities, such as mitral valve prolapse and vestibular dysfunction. These abnormalities might be chronically misinterpreted by some individuals as indicative of serious consequences, and thereby provide a repeated trigger for panic attacks.

There is good evidence that many cases of panic disorder and agoraphobia are treatable by means of either medication or psychotherapy. Imipramine, as well as several other antidepressant drugs, appears to ameliorate the symptoms of these syndromes. It is not clear, however, whether these drugs actually exert their impact upon panic or whether they instead work by alleviating the depressive symptoms so common to these patients. Alleviating depressive symptoms may then provide agoraphobics with the energy and confidence needed to confront previously avoided situations.

Panic disorder and agoraphobia also are amenable to interventions involving confrontation with feared situations. For example, many panic patients improve following flooding, a technique involving prolonged and intense exposure to feared stimuli. In the case of panic disorder, the patient is typically exposed, in graduated fashion, to increasingly anxiety-producing situations. The patient is typically encouraged to remain in the situation until his or her anxiety subsides.

The efficacy of flooding and related treatments for panic disorder and agoraphobia can be explained in at least two ways. One possibility is that flooding works by a process known as habituation. Habituation is a process in which physiological or psychological responses decline in intensity with repeated stimulation. For example, many parachute jumpers find that their anxiety reactions gradually decrease with each succeeding jump; habituation may be the basis of this phenomenon. A second possibility is that flooding works by means of the cognitive model. That is, prolonged exposure to feared stimuli may demonstrate to patients that these stimuli are not as dangerous as they had believed.

HISTORY

The term "panic" derives from the Greek god Pan, who let out a terrifying scream whenever he was awakened by passersby. Most of the earliest accounts of panic attacks emphasized their physiological nature. In 1871, Jacob DaCosta described a syndrome

he termed "irritable heart," which was characterized by palpitations, shortness of breath, dizziness, and other symptoms now recognized as typical of panic disorder. DaCosta observed this condition both in Civil War soldiers and in individuals not involved in military combat. Irritable heart syndrome became a frequent diagnosis among anxiety-stricken soldiers in the Franco-Prussian and Boer Wars. Other early terms for this syndrome were "effort syndrome" and "neurocirculatory asthenia"; again, both of these terms emphasized overexertion of the heart and circulatory system as the principal causes of panic symptoms.

At approximately the same time, Sigmund Freud was describing a syndrome he called "anxiety neurosis." Freud noted that this neurosis could occur in a diffuse, long-lasting form (what would today be called generalized anxiety) or in sudden, discrete attacks marked by symptoms such as excessive heartbeat and respiration (what would today be called panic disorder). In contrast to DaCosta and other writers of this period, Freud emphasized unconscious psychological factors as the primary determinants of panic disorder. According to Freud, anxiety attacks resulted from a massive damming up ("repression") of sexual impulses. In his later writings, Freud revised his position to assert that anxiety served as a signal to the individual that sexual impulses needed to be repressed. According to this later view, anxiety (including panic) is a cause, rather than a result, of the repression of sexual urges. Although many psychologists did not concur with Freud's conjectures, by World War II there was increasing appreciation that many of the panic reactions seen among soldiers were largely of psychogenic origin.

The term "agoraphobia" stems from the Greek *agora*, meaning marketplace. As noted earlier, however, although agoraphobics fear marketplaces and similar situations, their fears tend to be extremely varied. "Agoraphobia" was coined by Alexander Westphal in 1871, who observed that many patients experienced anxiety while walking across open spaces or deserted streets. Interestingly, Moritz Benedikt had observed a similar syndrome in 1870; he labeled in *Platzschwindel* (dizziness in public places), a term that presaged findings of vestibular dysfunction in some of these patients.

For many years, panic disorder and agoraphobia were believed to be two quite different, although often overlapping, conditions. In the third edition of the American Psychiatric Association's *Diagnostic and Statistical Manual of Mental Disorders* (DSM-III, 1980), for example, panic disorder and agoraphobia were listed as separate disorders. Nevertheless, research has increasingly indicated that agoraphobia is, in most cases, a consequence of panic attacks. Therefore, in the 1987 revision of DSM-III, a new diagnosis called "panic disorder with agoraphobia" was christened, thereby explicitly acknowledging a causal association between what were previously viewed as distinct conditions.

SOURCES FOR FURTHER STUDY

Barlow, David H. *Anxiety and Its Disorders: The Nature and Treatment of Anxiety and Panic.* New York: Guilford, 1988. Surveys the major theoretical issues relevant to anxiety (such as the relation of anxiety to other emotions, the biological origins of anxiety, and the classification of anxiety disorders) and discusses the literature on each anxiety disorder. This is one of the finest and most complete sources on anxiety disorders.

Chambless, Dianne L., and Alan J. Goldstein, eds. *Agoraphobia: Multiple Perspectives on Theory and Treatment.* New York: John Wiley & Sons, 1982. Contains several chapters on more specialized topics than are found in other texts on agoraphobia, such as agoraphobia and the marital relationship, and the association between agoraphobia and obsessions. Chambless's chapter, which summarizes the typical characteristics of agoraphobics, and Goldstein's chapter, which includes several detailed case histories, are especially useful.

Goodwin, Donald W., and Samuel B. Guze. "Panic Disorder (Anxiety Neurosis)." In *Psychiatric Diagnosis.* New York: Oxford University Press, 1989. A brief but excellent introduction to the most important psychiatric research on panic disorder. The reader will find a clear discussion of topics such as diagnosis, family studies, and differentiating panic disorder from other conditions. The reference section is a good resource for readers wishing to pursue research on panic disorder in greater depth.

Mathews, Andrew M., Michael G. Gelder, and Derek W. Johnston. *Agoraphobia: Nature and Treatment.* New York: Guilford, 1981. The authors review the literature on the symptomatology, assessment, and pharmacological treatment of agoraphobia, and discuss the behavioral treatment of this syndrome in depth. The appendices include a detailed self-help manual for agoraphobics and a brief package of assessment materials.

Walker, John R., G. Ron Norton, and Colin A. Ross, eds. *Panic Disorder and Agoraphobia: A Comprehensive Guide for the Practitioner.* Pacific Grove, Calif.: Brooks/Cole, 1991. Provides a thorough overview of the literature on the diagnosis, causation, and treatment of panic disorder and agoraphobia. Coverage of material on assessment and on psychotherapeutic and pharmacological interventions is especially complete. Although intended for the clinician, this volume is also a good reference for the layperson.

Scott O. Lilienfeld

SEE ALSO: Anxiety disorders; Cognitive therapy; Diagnosis; Emotions; Phobias; Stress: Behavioral and psychological responses; Stress: Theories.

Alcohol dependence and abuse

TYPE OF PSYCHOLOGY: Psychopathology
FIELDS OF STUDY: Substance use

Alcohol dependence is a psychiatric disorder characterized by a maladaptive pattern of alcohol use involving serious behavioral and physical consequences that may, in its most severe form, result in death.

KEY CONCEPTS
- cerebral cortex
- cirrhosis
- delirium tremens
- harm reduction
- Korsakoff syndrome
- neuritis
- psychosis
- relapse prevention

INTRODUCTION

Pure ethyl alcohol is a colorless, mild-smelling liquid that boils at 79 degrees centigrade and evaporates quickly at room temperature. It is made either by fermentation of grain mashed and suspended in water or fruit juice, followed by the distillation (boiling) of the beer or wine that is produced, or by chemical synthesis from the petrochemical ethylene. Ethyl alcohol—usually simply called alcohol—has many uses, including the sterilization of surgical instruments and inclusion in the fuel gasohol; it is the liquid in which many medicines are dissolved, serves as the main component of perfumes and colognes, and is used in the manufacture of many useful chemicals. The best-known use of alcohol, however, is in alcoholic beverages, viewed by many as recreational beverages because of the mood-altering properties of the alcohol they contain.

It is believed that alcoholic beverages have been made since prehistoric times. The oldest records of widespread brewing of beer and production of wine have been found in what were ancient Babylon and Egypt, respectively. According to historians, the main reasons for the preparation of alcoholic beverages by early civilizations were that their antimicrobial properties kept grape juice and other food sources from which they were prepared from spoiling, and the fact that drinking sparing amounts of fermented beverages was thought to prevent many illnesses that people contracted from contaminated drinking water or from other unfermented beverages.

The misuse of alcoholic beverages has certainly occurred since their discovery; however, it became widespread during the Middle Ages, when the art of distillation became more universal, producing hard liquors (containing five to ten times the alcohol of beer and wine) that made it much easier to attain alcoholic euphoria and stupor. In the United States, it has been estimated that nearly 70 percent of men and 60 percent of women use alcoholic beverages. At any given time, 5 percent qualify for a diagnosis of alcohol dependence. People who misuse alcohol to the point of severe physical consequences and conditions such as alcohol dependence are often called alcoholics. They may exhibit problems with controlling their use of alcohol, despite its severe negative consequences on their health, behavior, daily functioning, time management, and relationships.

Continued drinking over a long period of time, despite alcohol dependence, affects many body organs. Among them is the brain, where related mental disorders include delirium tremens (also known as the DTs), acute alcoholic hallucinations, and Korsakoff's syndrome. The DTs are a response

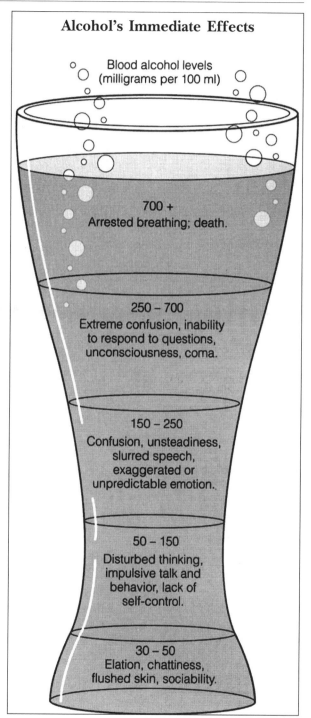

Alcohol's Immediate Effects

Blood alcohol levels (milligrams per 100 ml)

700 +
Arrested breathing; death.

250 – 700
Extreme confusion, inability to respond to questions, unconsciousness, coma.

150 – 250
Confusion, unsteadiness, slurred speech, exaggerated or unpredictable emotion.

50 – 150
Disturbed thinking, impulsive talk and behavior, lack of self-control.

30 – 50
Elation, chattiness, flushed skin, sociability.

The presence of 30-50 milligrams of alcohol per every 100 milliliters of blood represents one average drink (a glass of beer or wine or an ounce of hard liquor). People who abuse alcohol may not stop drinking until much higher levels result in confusion, unconsciousness, coma, or even death. (Hans & Cassidy, Inc.)

to severe alcohol withdrawal that includes anxiety attacks, confusion, depression, delirium, tremor, and terrifying hallucinations and other symptoms of psychosis. Psychosis is a severe mental state characterized by partial or complete withdrawal from reality. Korsakoff's syndrome is an alcohol-induced brain disorder that causes disorientation, impaired long-term memory, and the production of false perceptions to fill or make sense of memory gaps. Both the DTs and Korsakoff's syndrome may be accompanied by physical debility that can require hospitalization.

Alcoholic neuritis will develop when alcohol is the sole food eaten. In addition, alcohol dependence can lead to damage of the liver (causing cirrhosis that can be lethal), the kidneys, the heart, and the pancreas. Cirrhosis is a chronic liver disease characterized by the destruction of liver cells and their replacement by nonfunctional tissue. This ultimately causes blocked blood circulation, liver failure, and death. Furthermore, evidence suggests that severe alcohol dependence, combined with excessive cigarette smoking, greatly enhances the incidence of cancer of the mouth and throat.

There is no clear physical explanation for the development of alcohol dependence. Rather, it is most often proposed that alcohol dependence develops as the result of a genetic predisposition toward the disorder, social problems, and psychological stress. Much support is given to the high likelihood of alcohol dependence arising in the socioeconomic groups where consumption of alcoholic beverages is equated with manliness or sophistication. Other major bases proposed for the development of alcohol dependence include domineering or antisocial parents, adolescent peer pressure, personal feelings of inadequacy, loneliness, job pressures, and marital discord.

There is no known cure for alcohol dependence. Treatments for alcohol problems for the majority of individuals entering treatment demonstrate some benefit regardless of treatment orientations or treatment goals. Depending on the level of functioning of the individual prior to entering treatment for alcohol use disorders, rates of complete abstinence from drinking may range from 20 percent to 65 percent one year following treatment. Abstinence is only one treatment goal, however; relapse prevention and harm reduction approaches are also used sometimes. In relapse prevention, the goal is to have a person manage high-risk situations and lapses, where they might use, so that they do not turn into

relapses, or full-blown returns to pretreatment drinking. In harm reduction approaches, the goal might be to have the person not use in risky situations, such as driving or while taking medication, or to decrease the frequency or amount consumed, rather than quitting altogether. This latter approach is used to achieve some progress toward more adaptive behavior when, for whatever reasons, a client might not wish to abstain completely or might not be able to do so. The recognition of alcohol dependence as a medical problem has led to many alcohol-rehabilitation treatment centers, where psychiatric treatment, medication, and physical therapy—in various combinations—provide valuable treatments. Furthermore, many experts believe that Alcoholics Anonymous (AA) programs are effective deterrents to a return to maladaptive alcohol use.

CHANGING ATTITUDES

As pointed out by Andrew M. Mecca, before 1935 the main opinion on alcohol dependence was that it was criminal behavior that merited punishment. Around 1935, the identification of the problem as a disease began. Crucial to the successful treatment of alcohol dependence was the advent of Alcoholics Anonymous, founded in that year. This organization operates on the premise that abstinence is the best course of treatment for alcohol dependence, an incurable disease that can be arrested by cessation of all alcohol intake. The goal of the organization is sobriety: the permanent stoppage of a person's drinking.

The methodology of Alcoholics Anonymous is psychosocial. It brings individuals with alcohol problems to the realization that they cannot use alcoholic beverages without succumbing to alcohol dependence. It identifies the need for help from a higher power, and it develops a support group of people with the same condition. As stated by Mecca, "Alcoholics Anonymous never pronounces the disease cured. . . . [I]t is arrested." Estimates of the membership of the organization are between 1.5 million and 3 million, meaning that up to a third of Americans with alcohol problems are affected by its tenets. These people achieve results ranging from periods of sobriety (usually lasting longer and longer as membership in the organization continues) to lifelong sobriety. A deficit of sole utilization of Alcoholics Anonymous for treatment—according to many experts—is a lack of medical, psychiatric, and trained sociological counseling. This is especially

DSM-IV-TR Criteria for Alcohol Intoxication and Withdrawal

ALCOHOL INTOXICATION (DSM CODE 303.00)

Recent ingestion of alcohol

Clinically significant maladaptive behavioral or psychological changes (such as inappropriate sexual or aggressive behavior, mood lability, impaired judgment, impaired social or occupational functioning) developing during or shortly after alcohol ingestion

One or more of the following signs, developing during or shortly after alcohol use:
- slurred speech
- incoordination
- unsteady gait
- nystagmus
- impairment in attention or memory
- stupor or coma

Symptoms not due to a general medical condition and not better accounted for by another mental disorder

ALCOHOL WITHDRAWAL (DSM CODE 291.81)

Cessation of (or reduction in) alcohol use that has been heavy and prolonged

Two or more of the following, developing within several hours to a few days after symptoms:
- autonomic hyperactivity (such as sweating or pulse rate greater than 100)
- increased hand tremor
- insomnia
- nausea or vomiting
- transient visual, tactile, or auditory hallucinations or illusions
- psychomotor agitation
- anxiety
- grand mal seizures

These symptoms cause clinically significant distress or impairment in social, occupational, or other important areas of functioning

Symptoms not due to a general medical condition and not better accounted for by another mental disorder

Specify if with Perceptual Disturbances

---

true for the many individuals who may have alcohol problems in addition to other psychiatric disorders.

As to medical treatment aiming at abstinence via therapeutic drugs, two well-known drugs for enforcing sobriety are disulfiram (Antabuse) and citrated calcium carbonate (Abstem). These drugs may be given to alcoholics who wish to avoid using any alcoholic beverages and who require a deterrent to help them stop drinking. Neither drug should ever be given in secret by well-meaning family or friends because of the serious danger they cause in the presence of alcoholic beverages.

These dangers are attributable to the biochemistry of alcohol utilization via the enzymes (biological protein catalysts) alcohol dehydrogenase and aldehyde dehydrogenase. Normally, alcohol dehydrogenase converts alcohol to the toxic chemical acetaldehyde. Then aldehyde dehydrogenase quickly converts acetaldehyde to acetic acid, the main biological fuel of the body. Abstem or Antabuse turns off aldehyde dehydrogenase. This causes acetaldehyde buildup in the body, when alcohol is consumed, and quickly leads to violent headache, flushing, nausea, dizziness, heart palpitation, and vertigo.

Tranquilizers (and related sedative hypnotics)

are also used at times. However, this must also be done with great care, under the close supervision of a physician, for two main reasons: Many of these drugs can be addicting, with their abuse simply substituting another drug dependence for alcohol dependence, and alcohol and some of these drugs have additive effects that can be fatal if an alcoholic backslides during therapy.

The great value of therapists in alcohol dependence treatment has been identified by various sources. David H. Knott, in his book *Alcohol Problems: Diagnosis and Treatment* (1986), points out that while a psychotherapist cannot perform miracles, psychotherapy can be very valuable in helping the alcoholic patient by identifying factors leading to "destructive use of alcohol," exploring and helping to rectify problems associated with alcohol abstinence; providing emotional support that helps many patients to rebuild their lives, and interfacing in referring patients to Alcoholics Anonymous and other long-term support efforts. The psychotherapist also has irreplaceable experience with psychoactive therapeutic drugs, behavioral modification techniques, and identifying whether a given individual requires institutionalization.

Knott also points out the importance of behavioral modification as a cornerstone of alcohol psychotherapy and makes it clear that a wide variety of choices are available to alcoholics desiring psychosocial help. An interesting point made by A. E. Bennet, in *Alcoholism and the Brain* (1977), is that autopsy and a variety of sophisticated medical techniques, including computed tomography (CT) scans, identify atrophy of the cerebral cortex of the brain in many alcoholics. This damage is viewed as a factor in the inability of alcoholics to stop drinking, as well as in loss of motor skills and eventual development of serious conditions such as Korsakoff's syndrome.

TREATING AN EPIDEMIC

The excessive use of alcoholic beverages, with resultant alcohol dependence, has occurred for many centuries. Modern efforts to deal with alcohol dependence are often considered to have begun in the early twentieth century, with the activities of the American temperance movement that culminated with "Prohibition" upon the passage of the 1919 Volstead Act (Eighteenth Amendment) by the U.S. Congress. The idea behind the Volstead Act was that making liquor "impossible to get" would force sobriety on the nation. Prohibition turned out to be self-defeating, however, and several sources point out that it actually increased the incidence of alcohol dependence in the potential problem drinker. It was repealed in 1933.

The next, and much more useful, effort to combat alcohol dependence was the psychosocial approach of Alcoholics Anonymous, started in 1935 and still operating well. Yet that organization does not reach the majority of individuals with alcoholic problems, so other efforts needed to evolve as treatment methodologies. Among these have been the wide use of psychiatric counseling, alcohol rehabilitation centers, family counseling, and alcohol management programs in the workplace. These options—alone or in various combinations—have had considerable success in reaching alcoholics, and combined alcohol dependence therapy seems to work best; however, it has not yet been possible to stem the tide of increasing alcohol dependence or to cure the disease. Instead, these techniques—like those of Alcoholics Anonymous—can only arrest it. Part of the reason for this is the fact that the basis for alcohol dependence is not clearly understood by those attempting to eradicate it. One hope for curing alcohol dependence is ongoing basic research into the biochemistry, pharmacology, and physiology of alcohol dependence.

SOURCES FOR FURTHER STUDY

Bennett, Abram Elting. *Alcoholism and the Brain.* New York: Stratton Intercontinental Medical Book, 1977. Deals with relationships between brain function and alcohol dependence as a brain disease. Coverage includes the concept of alcohol dependence as a disease, alcohol actions in the brain, testing for alcoholic brain disease, constructive relationships between psychiatry and other aspects of alcohol dependence treatment, and rehabilitation methodology.

Connors, Gerard Joseph, Dennis M. Donovan, and Carlo DiClemente. *Substance Abuse and the Stages of Change.* New York: Guilford, 2001. This book discusses treatment for problems related to alcohol and other addictive behaviors from the perspective of considering the motivation of the affected person. Treatment approaches may vary depending on the stage of change of the individual.

Cox, W. Miles, ed. *The Treatment and Prevention of Alcohol Problems: A Resource Manual.* Orlando, Fla.: Academic Press, 1987. This edited work contains much information on many of the psychiatric, psychological, and behavioral aspects of alcohol. It is also widely useful in many other related alcohol dependence issues, including Alcoholics Anonymous, marital therapy, family therapy, and alcohol dependence prevention.

Fletcher, Anne M., and Frederick B. Glasser. *Sober for Good.* Boston: Houghton Mifflin, 2001. This book discusses alternative methods to stop drinking and provides detailed stories on how different drinkers changed their lives.

Hester, Reid K., and William R. Miller, eds. *Handbook of Alcoholism Treatment Approaches: Effective Alternatives.* Boston: Allyn & Bacon, 1995. This book gives an overview of alcoholism treatment approaches, ranging from traditional to more innovative, newer treatment strategies.

Knapp, Caroline. *Drinking: A Love Story.* New York: Bantam Dell, 1999. This book is a memoir of how drinking affected the life of one woman, and how her problems related to alcohol developed over time.

Knott, David H. *Alcohol Problems: Diagnosis and Treatment.* New York: Pergamon Press, 1986. Provides physicians with useful information on diagnosis and treatment of alcohol dependence. Topics include alcohol use and alcohol dependence; biochemical factors in alcohol use and abuse; epidemiology, diagnosis, and treatment of the disease; information on special populations affected by alcohol dependence; and perspectives on its control and prevention.

Mecca, Andrew M. *Alcoholism in America: A Modern Perspective.* Belvedere, Calif.: California Health Research Foundation, 1980. This interesting book covers the history of alcoholic beverages, the nature of alcohol dependence, effects of alcohol dependence on the body, its treatment, community alcohol dependence prevention, and future perspectives. Included are numerous sources of additional information and a useful glossary.

Sanford S. Singer;
updated by Nancy A. Piotrowski

SEE ALSO: Addictive personality and behaviors; Battered woman syndrome; Brain structure; Codependency; Coping: Social support; Group therapy; Motivation; Optimal arousal theory; Pain management; Self-esteem; Substance use disorders; Support groups.

Allport, Gordon

BORN: November 11, 1897, in Montezuma, Indiana
DIED: October 9, 1967, in Cambridge, Massachusetts
IDENTITY: American psychologist influenced by German thought
TYPE OF PSYCHOLOGY: Personality and social psychology
FIELDS OF STUDY: Personality assessment; personality theory; prejudice and discrimination; social motives

Allport rejected behaviorism, studied personality and self and practical aspects of social psychology as values, rumor, and prejudice, and promoted a humanistic psychology.

Gordon Willard Allport was the youngest of four boys in a Midwest family. His father was a physician; an elder brother, Floyd, became an important figure in social psychology. Gordon received his B.A. at Harvard in 1919, taught English in Turkey for a year, and received his Ph.D. at Harvard in 1922. The next two years he studied in Germany and England, making contacts that would influence him for a lifetime. He returned to spend the rest of his life teaching and doing research at Harvard University, except for a four-year hiatus from 1926 to 1930 at Dartmouth College. Influenced heavily by his European studies, he was one of the few to successfully resist both behaviorism and psychoanalysis as defining schools of thought. One of Allport's mentors was the German psychologist William Stern (1871-1938), whose personalistic psychology was seen by Allport as a step toward his own idiographic method (a study of the individual, as opposed to the study of the group, which is labeled nomothetic). Allport claimed that the closest counterpart of Stern's system of thought in the United States was the self psychology of Mary W. Calkins, a student of William James. Allport left a rich store of ideas about the personality and the self or the ego, which he finally designated as the proprium.

In 1937, Allport published his major work, *Personality: A Psychological Interpretation.* Here he introduced his concept of functional autonomy and gave prominent mention to Alfred Adler (1907-1980), the psychoanalyst who first stressed social variables. In the 1961 revision under the title *Pattern and Growth in Personality,* he elaborated on the concept of the proprium but followed his 1937 scheme of presenting the aspects of the self in a developmental context. He also enlarged his thinking on the mature person. In 1955, he published *Becoming: Basic Considerations for a Psychology of Personality.* Here he first introduced the term "proprium," addressing the question of whether the concept of self is necessary, and, making note of the valid criticisms, opted for a bare minimum of self functions.

His best-known and most popular work, *The Nature of Prejudice* (1954), represents a practical area in which he was interested. Others included studies on religion, expressive movement, social attitudes, rumor, and radio.

SOURCES FOR FURTHER STUDY
Evans, Richard I. *Gordon Allport: The Man and His Ideas.* New York: Praeger, 1981. Allport in the framework of a personal interview.

Monte, Christopher F. "Gordon W. Allport: Humanistic Trait and Self Theory." In *Beneath the Mask: An Introduction to Theories of Personality*, edited by Monte. 6th ed. New York: Harcourt Brace, 1999. Stresses the personal sources of Allport's ideas.

Everett J. Delahanty, Jr.

SEE ALSO: Adler, Alfred; Humanism; Humanistic trait models: Gordon Allport; Individual psychology; Alfred Adler; Prejudice; Prejudice reduction.

Altruism, cooperation, and empathy

TYPE OF PSYCHOLOGY: Social psychology
FIELDS OF STUDY: Interpersonal relations; prosocial behavior

Altruism and cooperation are types of prosocial behavior. Empathy involves identification with another, and it leads to increased prosocial behavior.

KEY CONCEPTS
- altruism
- cooperation
- empathy
- prosocial behavior

INTRODUCTION

Social psychologists, like other social scientists and social philosophers, have long been intrigued by what is called the altruism paradox. The altruism paradox arises from the fact that individuals sometimes engage in self-sacrificial acts that benefit another. This contradicts the assumption of most theories of motivation that individuals only engage in behavior that is beneficial to themselves. There are two basic ways to resolve the altruism paradox. One way is to try to identify the perhaps subtle self-benefits from helping that motivate seemingly altruistic prosocial behavior—behavior intended to benefit another. The second way is to assert that individuals do engage in behavior that benefits others, irrespective of any benefit to the self. Theories and research on prosocial behavior make use of both ways of resolving the altruism paradox.

THEORIES OF EGOISTIC MOTIVATION

Theories of egoistic motivation for helping assume that some form of self-benefit motivates individuals to act prosocially. The self-benefits from helping are most easily recognizable in the case of cooperation. Cooperation is a type of prosocial behavior in which the self-benefit is the same as the benefit to the person helped: Individuals mutually benefit by achieving a common goal. An individual's self-interest is often best served by cooperating with others because, without cooperation, the individual may be unable to achieve a desirable goal. Selfishness, then, may prompt cooperation; if it does so, the motivation to act prosocially is egoistic, not altruistic. The benefit to the other is a by-product of acting prosocially in order to benefit the self.

Theories of egoistic motivation for helping point out that cooperation is not the only type of prosocial behavior that can be mutually beneficial for both the persons giving and receiving help. The self-benefit for the person giving help also can be different from the benefit for the person receiving help. This principle forms the basis of the arousal-reduction explanation for helping developed by Jane Piliavin and her colleagues. Their theory proposes that individuals experience aversive physiological arousal when they encounter another person in need. One way to reduce this aversive arousal is to help the person in need, because alleviating the other's need terminates the stimulus causing the bystander's own distress. Thus, the theory proposes that bystanders will help as a way to reduce their own aversive arousal. The persons giving and receiving help benefit in different ways, but it is important to recognize that the egoistic desire to reduce aversive arousal motivates the bystander's helping, not unselfish regard for the other's welfare.

Other theories of egoistic motivation for helping propose that prosocial behavior can be based on factors different from the arousal caused by witnessing another's suffering. For example, the "negative state relief" explanation for helping developed by Robert Cialdini and his colleagues in the 1970's proposes that temporary depression or sorrow can motivate helping as way to dispel the negative mood state. This negative state, it is reasoned, produces helping because people learn through socialization that feelings of personal satisfaction accompany the performance of good deeds. Helping, therefore, occurs as a way to lift the spirits of the temporarily depressed individual. An important implication of this theory is that even affective states that are not caused by witnessing another's suffering can produce helping. A personal failure, thinking about a sad event, or watching a sad motion picture all can prompt helping as a way to relieve the negative mood state. Benefitting a person in need occurs as a way to benefit the self by dispelling a negative mood.

Additional theories of egoistic motivation for helping propose that many forms of selfishness can lead to helping. For example, motives to maintain a positive mood state, avoid guilt for failing to help, and gain social approval have been suggested to promote prosocial behavior. In general, theories of egoistic motivation for helping resolve the altruism paradox by proposing some form of self-benefit that motivates seemingly self-sacrificial behavior. In contrast, theories of altruistic motivation for helping propose that individuals do engage in behavior that benefits another, irrespective of any benefit to themselves. Such theories generally concur in assuming that empathy—an identification with another produced by similarity or attachment—is an important source of altruistic motivation, if it exists.

EMPATHY-ALTRUISM HYPOTHESIS

Conceptions of empathy, however, vary greatly. Although all assume that empathy involves identification with another, different approaches emphasize the cognitive, affective, or behavioral components of empathy, or some combination of each. In the study of the possibility of genuine human altruism, empathy is typically conceived as an emotional response to another's suffering that is characterized by feelings of sympathy, compassion, tenderness, and the like. The suggestion that this emotional response leads to prosocial behavior motivated by unselfish concern for the other's welfare has come to be called the empathy-altruism hypothesis.

The research efforts of C. Daniel Batson and his colleagues beginning in the 1980's are largely responsible for the advancement of the empathy-altruism hypothesis from a theoretical possibility to a plausible explanation for some, but certainly not all, prosocial behavior. Through their efforts, empathy has been shown to be an emotional response to another's suffering that is distinct from aversive arousal or temporary depression and that leads to motivation to help that is different from egoistic motivation to reduce aversive arousal or to relieve negative mood. A major challenge is to determine whether empathy leads to motivation to help that is different from all possible egoistic motives for acting prosocially.

PROSOCIAL MOTIVATIONS

The study of prosocial behavior has led to important insights into the determinants of the amount and the type of help that an individual provides to another when given the opportunity. Individuals often act apathetically or even antisocially toward one another because they lack sufficient incentives for acting prosocially. Competitive relationships involve situations in which one individual's gain is incurred at another individual's expense, so self-interest is best served by exploiting the other. Competitive relationships therefore often lead to antagonism and antisocial behavior. If it is possible to change the reward structure, however, this behavior can be changed. Instituting a superordinate goal, defined as a shared goal that can be achieved only through cooperation among individuals, reduces the antisocial behavior and increases the prosocial behavior of individuals in formerly competitive relationships. Prosocial behavior can be increased simply by making it more rewarding for individuals to act positively toward one another and less rewarding for them to act negatively toward one another.

Prosocial behavior can be increased by a variety of explicit material rewards (for example, money) or social rewards (for example, praise), but it also can occur in the absence of explicit rewards. For example, a bystander is often likely to intervene in an emergency when the emergency is unambiguous and there are no other potential helpers present. Research on the bystander effect, the phenomenon in which the presence of others decreases helping, has revealed several factors that contribute to the lack of responsiveness of large groups of bystanders. These factors include increased uncertainty about the need for help, potential embarrassment about offering help, and diffusion of the responsibility for helping. The absence of these factors, however, is insufficient for explaining the responsive behavior of a single witness to an emergency. If there are no material or social rewards for helping, and no punishments for not helping, why would an anonymous witness to an emergency stop to help?

One way to explain bystander intervention in the absence of explicit rewards for helping is to acknowledge that a victim's current state can affect the bystander's own state. Interestingly, the capacity to be affected by another's current state appears to be inborn. Even newborn babies respond emotionally to signs of distress in others. They often cry when they hear other babies cry. Adults also become more physiologically and emotionally aroused when exposed to another in need. The theory that arousal reduction serves as motivation for helping builds on the fact that people do respond emotionally to another's need. As the theory would predict, there is considerable evidence that people help rapidly and more vigorously the greater the arousal they experience in emergency situations.

There may be innate sources of motivation to help in emergencies, but much prosocial behavior occurs in nonemergency situations. The motivation to help in nonemergency situations is often assumed to result from socialization. In general, children become more helpful as they grow older. Developmental theories of prosocial motivations suggest that children's helpfulness is first encouraged by material rewards, later by social rewards, and finally by self-rewards produced by the internalization of social norms advocating helpfulness. The ability to reward oneself for helping leads the socialized individual to act prosocially even in the absence of explicit material or social rewards, because helping is accompanied by the positive feelings that become associated with doing good deeds during socialization. Helping thus acquires reinforcing properties and becomes particularly likely to occur when individuals are in need of reinforcement. It is well known that people self-indulge when they are saddened or depressed. People often treat themselves to a favorite dessert, a shopping trip, or a television show when they are sad, because self-indulgence relieves depression. Developmental theories of prosocial motivation would suggest that socialized individuals also use acting helpfully as a form of self-indulgence. Consistent with this suggestion, and with the prediction of the negative state relief explanation for helping, adults often act more prosocially when they are temporarily saddened than when they are in a neutral mood.

EGOISTIC MOTIVATIONS
Given that there are both innate and socialized sources of motivation to help, it may seem curious that people do not always act prosocially. Egoistic

theories of motivation to help, however, point out an important exception to the rule that people will help others in order to benefit themselves: Helping will occur only if it is a relatively uncostly, gratifying way to benefit the self. Thus, if helping is a more costly behavior than putting the victim's suffering out of sight and out of mind by leaving the scene, helping should not occur. Similarly, temporarily saddened individuals facing the prospects of large costs and small rewards for helping would not be expected to help because it would not be perceived as gratifying overall. Helping would be expected to occur only when the self-benefits of helping outweigh the costs. Egoistic theories of motivation for helping therefore provide a way to explain not only why people do help but also why they do not.

A problem for egoistic theories of motivation for helping is to explain the effects of feeling empathy (sympathy, compassion) on helping a person in need. Heightened empathy leads to increased prosocial behavior across a wide variety of both emergency and nonemergency situations. Furthermore, research testing the empathy-altruism hypothesis suggests that empathy does not lead to any of the more common types of egoistic motivation for helping. If the empathy-altruism hypothesis is valid, unselfish motives, as well as selfish ones, must be included in theories of why people act prosocially.

EMERGENCE OF SOCIAL PSYCHOLOGY
Social psychology emerged as a distinct field of psychology after World War II, during the years in which behaviorism was the dominant theoretical perspective in psychology. Initially, social psychologists devoted little attention to the study of prosocial behavior, perhaps because it was assumed that the general determinants of individual behavior would also apply to interpersonal behavior, as behaviorist theory would dictate. During the 1950's, some research on prosocial behavior was initiated. This research tended to focus on cooperation, however, to the exclusion of other forms of prosocial behavior. Behaviorist principles were often applied to determine, for example, if rewarding cooperation made it more likely to occur and competition less likely to occur.

In 1964, a troubling murder captured the attention of social psychologists and spurred interest in studying emergency intervention and other forms of prosocial behavior. In March of that year, a young woman named Kitty Genovese was attacked on the street near her home late at night. The attack continued for more than an hour and her screams woke many of her neighbors, but none of them left their homes to help her. Interest in the behavior of the unresponsive bystanders during this attack prompted social psychologists to investigate factors that lead people not to intervene in emergencies. This research led to demonstration of the bystander effect and revealed a number of factors that contribute to the unresponsiveness of groups of bystanders who witness an emergency.

Research on bystander intervention also revealed that certain circumstances make it quite likely for a bystander to offer help. The decline of behaviorism by the early 1970's provided a climate in which researchers could explore the effects of internal motives as well as external reinforcers on helping. Several influential egoistic theories of motivation for helping were developed during the 1970's. By the end of the decade, these theories clearly displaced earlier behaviorist theories as prominent explanations for prosocial behavior.

STUDY OF EMPATHY

Another trend to develop in the 1970's was the study of the effects of empathy on helping. By the 1980's, several theorists were proposing that empathy for a person in need leads to genuinely altruistic motivation for helping. Research during the 1980's quite consistently showed that empathy leads to helping even in situations in which egoistic motivation would not be expected to lead to help. Demonstrating that humans are capable of transcending selfishness and acting out of concern for another's welfare would have profound implications for psychological theories of motivation and views of human nature. It would be necessary to acknowledge that human behavior can be influenced by unselfish motives as well as by selfish ones.

SOURCES FOR FURTHER STUDY

Baston, C. D. "Prosocial Motivation: Is It Ever Truly Altruistic?" In *Advances in Experimental Social Psychology*, edited by Leonard Berkowitz. Vol. 20. San Diego, Calif.: Academic Press, 1987. A thorough and detailed chapter outlining the empathy-altruism hypothesis and its implications. Reviews the breakthrough research on the effects of empathy on helping, and discusses strategies for determining the nature of the motivation for helping.

Cialdini, Robert B., D. J. Baumann, and D. T. Kenrick. "Insights from Sadness: A Three-Step Model of the Development of Altruism as Hedonism." *Developmental Review* 1 (September, 1981): 207-223. A readable account of the development of the ability to self-reward for helping. Describes research showing how helping progresses from being externally determined to being internally motivated. Includes discussion of the negative state relief explanation for helping.

Eisenberg, Nancy, and Janet Strayer, eds. *Empathy and Its Development*. Cambridge, England: Cambridge University Press, 1987. Contributions by developmental, clinical, and social psychologists illustrate the multiplicity of approaches to the study of empathy. Many chapters review research on the effects of empathy on helping. Well referenced; an excellent source for those interested in pursuing research on empathy.

Hinde, Robert A., and Jo Groebel, eds. *Cooperation, Prosocial Behaviour, Trust, and Commitment*. Cambridge, England: Cambridge University Press, 1991. Authors from diverse disciplines contribute to this volume, bringing together knowledge about human prosocial activity at the individual, group, and international levels. Chapters are well integrated, relatively free from technical terms, and thought-provoking.

Kottler, Jeffrey A. *Doing Good: Passion and Commitment for Helping Others*. Philadelphia: Brunner/Mazel, 2000. An exploration of the realities of altruistic behavior, aimed at beginners in helping fields.

Ozinga, James R. *Altruism*. Westport, Conn.: Praeger, 2000. A well-rounded view, by a political scientist, of the sources of altruistic behavior.

Piliavin, Jane Allyn. *Emergency Intervention*. New York: Academic Press, 1981. A comprehensive treatment of research relevant to the arousal-reduction explanation for helping. Details the development of the arousal/cost model of helping into a comprehensive theory of human prosocial behavior. Discusses implications for structuring a more prosocial society.

Sober, Elliott, and David Sloan Wilson. *Unto Others: The Evolution and Psychology of Unselfish Behavior*. Cambridge, Mass.: Harvard University Press, 1998. An argument against the notion that humans are biologically programmed to be selfish.

Jim Fultz

SEE ALSO: Affiliation and friendship; Attraction theories; Bystander intervention; Cooperation, competition, and negotiation; Help-seeking; Helping; Love; Women's psychology: Carol Gilligan.

Alzheimer's disease

TYPE OF PSYCHOLOGY: Cognition; memory; psychopathology

FIELDS OF STUDY: Aging; cognitive processes; depression; interpersonal relationships; social perception and cognition; thought

Alzheimer's disease (AD) is the most frequent cause of dementia. Dementia is the loss of cognitive and social abilities to the degree that they interfere with activities of daily living (ADLs). AD is an irreversible and gradual brain disorder that occurs with aging.

KEY CONCEPTS
- activities of daily living (ADLs)
- cognitive function
- cognitive impairment
- dementia
- memory loss
- motor function
- neurofibrillary fibers
- plaques

INTRODUCTION

Alzheimer's disease (AD) and dementia are not a normal part of aging. Diseases that affect the brain such as genetic, immunologic, and vascular abnormalities cause AD. A defect in connections between the brain's cells causes gradual death of brain cells. AD advances progressively, from mild forgetfulness to a severe loss of mental function. It results in memory loss, behavior and personality changes, deterioration in thinking abilities, difficulty speaking (aphasia), declining motor function (apraxia), and disability recognizing objects (agnosia).

Forgetfulness and loss of concentration are early symptoms that may not be readily identified because they are considered normal signs of aging. Forgetfulness and loss of concentration may also result from use of drugs or alcohol, depression, fatigue, grief, physical illness, impaired vision, or hearing loss. The symptoms of AD usually occur after sixty years of age but may occur as early as forty. Symptoms often begin with recent memory loss, confusion, poor judgment, and personality changes. In later stages of AD, ADLs such as dressing and eating are affected. Eventually, AD sufferers are completely dependent on others for ADLs. They become so debilitated that they become bedridden, at which time other physical problems develop. Seizures may occur late in AD.

PREVALENCE AND IMPACT

AD accounts for 50 to 75 percent of all dementias. AD prevalence increases from 1 percent at age sixty-five to between 20 and 35 percent by age eighty-five. On average, AD sufferers may live from eight to twenty years following diagnosis. According to the World Health Organization (WHO), the number of people worldwide aged sixty-five years and older will reach 1.2 billion by 2025 and will exceed 2 billion by 2050. Of these, an estimated 22 million individuals will be afflicted with AD worldwide. The Alzheimer's Association speculates that if a cure is not found, AD will be diagnosed in 14 million Americans by the middle of the twenty-first century.

A study done in 1998 revealed that African Americans and Hispanic Americans might have a higher overall risk of AD. Socioeconomic status, health care, level of education, and culture may also influence the diagnosis of AD. Another study in 1998 estimated that the annual economic burden created by the cost of caring for a patient with mild AD is $18,000, for a patient with moderate AD $30,000, and for a patient with severe AD $36,000. More than half of AD patients are cared for at home, with almost 75 percent of their care provided by family and friends. In 2002 the Alzheimer's Association estimated that approximately $33 billion is lost annually by American businesses as a result of AD. Time taken by caregivers of AD sufferers accounts for $26 billion, and $7 billion is spent for health issues and long-term care related to AD. Additionally, AD costs the United States more than $100 billion annually.

HISTORY

AD is named after a German physician, Dr. Alois Alzheimer, who in 1906 found plaques and neurofibrillary tangles in the brain of a mentally disturbed woman. Today, these plaques and tangles in the brain are considered hallmarks of AD.

There is also evidence that Greeks and Romans recognized the disease, as there are writings dating from their time that appear to describe symptoms of AD. In the sixteenth century, playwright and poet William Shakespeare wrote that old age is a "second childishness and mere oblivion." In the past, terms such as "senility" and "hardening of the arteries" were commonly used to describe dementia. Until recently, AD was considered an inevitable consequence of aging. Researchers have discovered more about AD in the last quarter of the twentieth century.

RISK FACTORS

The major risk factors for AD are age and family history. Other possible risk factors include a serious head injury and lower socioeconomic status. There is speculation that genetics, environmental influences, weight, educational level, blood pressure and blood cholesterol levels are factors that may increase the risk for AD.

Dr. Konrad Maurer displays the handwritten file of Dr. Alois Alzheimer describing the first documented case of the disease named for him. (AP/Wide World Photos)

CAUSES

There are no definitive causes of AD. Some that have been identified include lesions caused by plaque, inflammation in brain cells, oxidative stress effects on brain cells, genetic factors, beta amyloid protein and senile plaques, tau protein and neurofibrillary tangles, estrogen effects on brain neurotransmitters, dysfunction in brain cell communication, autoimmune responses, viruses, and vessel anomalies.

PLAQUE. In AD, plaques develop in the areas of the brain that regulate memory and other cognitive functions. These plaques are deposits of beta-amyloid (a protein fragment from a larger protein called amyloid precursor protein, APP) intermingled with portions of neurons and with nonnerve cells such as microglia (cells that surround and digest damaged cells or foreign substances) and astrocytes (glial cells that support and nourish neurons). Plaques are found in the spaces between the brain's nerve cells. Researchers do not know whether amyloid plaques cause AD or are a by-product of the AD process.

AD consists of abnormal collections of twisted threads found inside nerve cells. The chief component is a protein called tau. In the central nervous system, tau proteins bind and stabilize brain cells' support structure by forming tubules that guide nutrients and molecules from the cells to the ends of the axon. Tau normally holds together connector pieces of the tubule tracks. In AD, tau threads twist around each other and form neurofibrillary tangles. Support to the cell is lost, causing cell death and leading to dementia.

GENETIC FACTORS IN AD DEVELOPMENT. Two types of AD have been identified: familial AD (FAD), which follows an inheritance pattern, and sporadic AD. The *Diagnostic and Statistical Manual of Mental Disorders* (4th ed., 1994, DSM-IV) describes AD as early-onset (younger than sixty-five years) or late-onset (sixty-five years and older). Only 5 to 10 percent of AD cases are early onset. Some forms of early-onset AD are inherited and often progress faster than late-onset AD.

ESTROGEN. Estrogen use has been associated with a decreased risk of AD and enhanced cognitive functioning. Its antioxidant and anti-inflammatory effects enhance the growth of processes of neurons for memory function. This has created intense interest in the relationship between estrogen, memory, and cognitive function in humans.

AUTOIMMUNE SYSTEM. The body's immune system may attack its own tissues and produce antibodies against essential cells. Some researchers postulate that aging neurons in the brain trigger an autoimmune response that causes AD. Antibodies have been identified in the brains of those with Alzheimer's disease.

VIRUSES. The finding of slow-acting viruses that cause some brain disorders has resulted in some researchers believing that a virus may also cause AD. As of 2002, no virus had been identified in the brains of those with AD.

VESSEL ANOMALIES. Defects in brain blood vessels such as cerebroarteriosclerosis or problems in the blood-brain barrier (which guards against foreign bodies or toxic agents in the blood stream from entering the brain) have not been identified as causes of AD.

GROWTH FACTORS. Some researchers believe that a decline in growth factors or an increase in factors that are toxic to neuronal cells causes AD. Researchers are investigating introducing naturally occurring nerve growth factor (NGF) into the brain to stimulate brain cell growth in rats.

CHEMICAL DEFICIENCIES. AD brains have lower levels of neurotransmitters responsible for cognitive functions and behavior. Acetylcholine is a neurotransmitter that is found in lower levels in the AD brain than in normally functioning brains. Scientists have seen slight, temporary cognitive improvement when acetylcholine levels in AD patients have been increased.

ENVIRONMENT. Metals such as aluminum and zinc have been found in brain tissue of people with AD. Researchers are studying these and other environmental factors to discover their relationship to AD development.

DIAGNOSIS

There is no single reliable biological test to diagnose AD; therefore, criteria to assist primary care

---

DSM-IV-TR Criteria for Dementia of the Alzheimer's Type

Development of multiple cognitive deficits manifested by both memory impairment (impaired ability to learn new information or recall previously learned information) and one or more of the following cognitive disturbances:
- aphasia (language disturbance)
- apraxia (impaired ability to carry out motor activities despite intact motor function)
- agnosia (failure to recognize or identify objects despite intact sensory function)
- disturbance in executive functioning (planning, organizing, sequencing, abstracting)

Cognitive deficits each cause significant impairment in social or occupational functioning and represent significant decline from previous level of functioning

Course characterized by gradual onset and continuing cognitive decline

Cognitive deficits not due to any of the following:
- other central nervous system conditions causing progressive deficits in memory and cognition (such as cerebrovascular disease, Parkinson's disease, Huntington's disease, subdural hematoma, normal-pressure hydrocephalus, brain tumor)
- systemic conditions known to cause dementia (such as hypothyroidism, vitamin B or folic acid deficiency, niacin deficiency, hypercalcemia, neurosyphilis, HIV infection)
- substance-induced conditions

Deficits do not occur exclusively during course of a delirium

Disturbance not better accounted for by another Axis I disorder (such as Major Depressive Episode, Schizophrenia)

Code based on presence or absence of clinically significant behavioral disturbance:
- Without Behavioral Disturbance (DSM code 294.10): Cognitive disturbance not accompanied by any clinically significant behavioral disturbance
- With Behavioral Disturbance (DSM code 294.10): Cognitive disturbance accompanied by clinically significant behavioral disturbance (such as wandering, agitation)

Specify with Early Onset (onset at age sixty-five years or younger) or with Late Onset (onset after age sixty-five)

---

providers in diagnosing AD have been established to differentiate between AD and other forms of dementia. One such guideline has been established by the Agency for Health Care Policy and Research (AHGPR). Any positive response to six identified areas warrants a work-up for dementia. New diagnostic tools and criteria make it possible for health care providers to make a positive clinical diagnosis of AD with around 90 percent accuracy.

Diagnostic criteria for AD includes dementia, history, physical and mental examinations consistent with AD, normal blood tests, and medications that are not the cause of dementia. Brain imaging study—computed tomography (CT) or magnetic resonance imaging (MRI)—is normal or shows brain atrophy.

A medical history provides information about mental or physical conditions, prescription drugs, and family health history. A physical examination evaluates nutritional status, blood pressure, and pulse. A neurological examination evaluates for neurological disorders. The Mini-Mental State Examination (MMSE) and Addenbrooke's Cognitive Examination (ACE) are instruments used to evaluate AD.

Blood and urine tests evaluate for other causes of dementia. Psychiatric evaluation assesses mood and emotional factors that mimic dementia. A neuropsychological assessment evaluates memory, sense of time and place, and ability to understand, communicate, and do simple calculations.

MRI and CT scans of the brain assess for the possibility of other potential causes of dementia, such as stroke, Huntington's disease, or Parkinson's disease.

Early diagnosis of AD is important to determine the proper treatment and to detect underlying diseases such as depression, drug interactions, vitamin deficiencies, or endocrine problems. These diseases may be reversible if detected early. A definitive diagnosis of AD can only be confirmed on autopsy.

FOUR STAGES OF AD

Early stage AD is recognized when one exhibits recent memory loss, mild aphasia, avoidance of the unfamiliar, difficulty writing, and necessity for reminders to perform ADLs such as dressing, washing, brushing one's teeth, and combing one's hair. Apathy and depression are common.

Middle stage AD is recognized when one exhibits routine recent memory loss, moderate aphasia, getting lost in familiar surroundings, repetitive actions, apraxia, mood and behavior disturbances, and necessity for reminders and help with ADLs.

Late stage AD is recognized when one misidentifies familiar people and places, is bradykinesic (exhibits slowness of movement and general muscle rigidity), frequently falls, has more frequent mood

and behavior disturbances, and needs help with all ADLs.

Terminal stage AD is recognized when one has no association to past or present, is mute or enunciates few coherent words, is oblivious to surroundings, has little spontaneous movement, is dysphagic (has difficulty swallowing), exhibits passive mood and behavior, and needs total care.

DSM-IV divides Alzheimer's disease into subtypes that represent the predominant features of the clinical presentation: with delirium, with delusions, with depressed mood, and uncomplicated. "With behavioral disturbance" can also be used to indicate the presence of difficulties such as wandering or combativeness.

TREATMENT

The principal goal of treatment is to slow AD progression, provide a safe environment, maintain function as long as possible, and provide emotional support for the patient and family through social services and support groups. However, the treatment of dementia varies according to the stage of the disease and is focused on management of symptoms because no cure exists. It is of utmost importance to educate the patient and family about AD, its course, ramifications, and treatment options. Treatment includes both patient and caregivers. In early stages of AD, patients and their families may need counseling to deal with a sense of loss; be made aware of support groups, respite care, and other social services that are available to them; and be introduced to legal considerations in making decisions about future care needs such as medical and financial powers of attorney and a living will. As more supervision is required, caregivers need to be aware of physical dangers that can result from memory loss, such as fires from unattended stoves or burning cigarettes, malnutrition from "forgetting" to eat and difficulty swallowing, increased risk for falls related to confusion, disorientation, and declining motor function, as well as issues about driving related to poor motor and cognitive function. Caregivers should also be aware of the patient's finances to assist in paying and recording bills, and planning for future care needs. During late stage AD, the family may need assistance in preparing for the patient's death. Hospice care should be discussed, as it provides for physical care and comfort for the patient and emotional support for the family.

PHARMACEUTICAL THERAPY

Pharmaceutical agents used to slow the progression of AD include acetylcholinesterase inhibitors (tacrine, donepezil, rivastigmine, and galantamine). These agents block the breakdown of neurotransmitters in the brain and are used to lessen symptoms of mild to moderate AD. Their action extends cognitive function and improves behavioral symptoms for twelve months up to two years. Vitamin E or selegiline delays the progression of AD. Estrogen has been associated with a decreased risk of AD and enhanced cognitive functioning. Its antioxidant and anti-inflammatory effects enhance the growth of processes of neurons for memory function. Ginkgo biloba has provided moderate cognitive improvement with few ill effects. Delusions and hallucinations often develop in moderately impaired patients. In the absence of agitation or combativeness, the best treatment is reassurance and distraction. Delusions and hallucinations accompanied by agitation and combativeness can be treated with low doses of antipsychotic or antidepressant medications. Medications may also be used to control wandering, anxiety, insomnia, and depression.

COMPLICATIONS

People with AD do not die from AD, but from complications that result from AD. The most common cause of death in AD is pneumonia. Difficulty swallowing increases the risk of inhaling foods and liquids into the lungs, which then may cause aspiration and pneumonia. The risk for falling is increased by disorientation, confusion, and declining motor function. Falls can lead to fractures and head injuries. Surgical intervention and immobilization also present risks for additional life-threatening complications in the elderly. Memory loss may result in fires from unattended stoves or burning cigarettes, or malnutrition from "forgetting" to eat.

PREVENTION

Studies have supported that regular use of non-steroidal anti-inflammatory drugs (NSAIDs) such as ibuprofen (Advil, Motrin, Nuprin), naproxen sodium (Aleve), and indomethacin (Indocin) may reduce AD risk by 30 to 60 percent.

Researchers are also studying the antioxidant affects of vitamin E and selegiline hydrochloride in preventing brain damage caused by toxic free radicals to slow the rate of progression of AD. Studies

of estrogen replacement therapy in menopausal women showed a reduced risk of developing AD by 30 to 40 percent. In 2002, a synthetic form of beta-amyloid protein (AN-1792) vaccine was being investigated in clinical trials.

RESEARCH FOR THE FUTURE

The National Institutes of Health's Alzheimer's Disease Prevention Initiative was organized to investigate pharmacological interventions and to identify factors that will assist in early recognition of AD and delay the development of AD. A collaborative association with federal and private agencies has allowed for diverse investigations that include biologic and epidemiologic research; instrument development to identify high-risk individuals, facilitating clinical trials; and researching alternate strategies to treat behavioral disturbances in AD patients.

New drugs to reduce symptoms of AD are being studied in clinical trials. Other research is being done to identify factors related to patients' and caregivers' coping and stress, as well as support mechanisms in dealing with progressive nature of AD.

SOURCES FOR FURTHER STUDY

Hamdy, Ronald, James Turnball, and Joellyn Edwards. *Alzheimer's Disease: A Handbook for Caregivers.* New York: Mosby, 1998. Causes, symptoms, stages, and treatment options for AD are discussed.

Karlin, Nancy, J., Paul, A. Bell, and Jody L. Noah. "Long-Term Consequences of the Alzheimer's Caregiver Role: A Qualitative Analysis." *American Journal of Alzheimer's Disease* (May/June, 2001): 177-182. Examines caregivers' adaptation to the role of caregiver, caregiver burden and coping, social support issues, and positive and negative experiences by created by unplanned changes brought on by AD.

Leon, J., C. Cheng, and P. Neumann. "Alzheimer's Disease Care: Costs and Potential Savings." *Health Affiliates* (November/December, 1998): 206-216. Identifies the economic impact for caring and treating those with AD and reasons for identifying a cure.

Mace, M., and P. Rabins. *The Thirty-six Hour Day: A Family Guide to Caring for Persons with Alzheimer Disease, Related Dementing Illnesses, and Memory Loss in Later Life.* Baltimore: The Johns Hopkins University Press, 1999. Discusses what dementia is, physical and psychological problems, effects on caregivers, financial and legal issues, and long-range care planning for AD suffers.

Powell, L., and K. Courtice. *Alzheimer's Disease: A Guide for Families and Caregivers.* Cambridge, Mass.: Perseus, 2001. Provides information about early signs, tests, diagnosis and treatment research for AD. Also provides insight into the emotional aspects experienced by caregivers, with advice on communication, safety, and long-term care issues for AD suffers.

St. George-Hyslop, Peter H. "Piecing Together Alzheimer's." *Scientific American* (December, 2000): 76-83. Good description of AD, symptoms, support, and ongoing research in the quest for a cure.

Terry, R., R. Katzman, K. Bick, and S. Sisodia. *Alzheimer Disease.* 2d ed. Philadelphia: Lippincott, Williams, & Wilkins, 1999. An in-depth review of hereditary links, signs and symptoms, diagnosis, and treatment for AD.

Sharon Wallace Stark

SEE ALSO: Aging; Cognitive changes; Aging: Physical changes; Brain structure; Coping: Chronic illness; Coping: Terminal illness; Dementia; Forgetting and forgetfulness; Parkinson's disease.

American Psychiatric Association

DATE: Founded in 1844

TYPE OF PSYCHOLOGY: Origin and definition of psychology; psychotherapy

FIELDS OF STUDY: Biological treatments; descriptive methodologies; general constructs and issues; methodological issues; models of abnormality; organic disorders

The Association of Medical Superintendents of American Institutions for the Insane, established in 1844, changed its name to the American Medico-Psychological Association in 1893 and to the American Psychiatric Association in 1921.

KEY CONCEPTS
- blood-letting
- chemical intervention
- drug therapy
- hydrotherapy
- political appointments
- psychiatric nursing
- psychiatric social work

INTRODUCTION

The Association of Medical Superintendents of American Institutions for the Insane (AAII), grandparent of the American Psychiatric Association, was established in 1844. At the time, there were twenty-four mental hospitals in the United States and two in Canada. The first of these was founded in Philadelphia, where Benjamin Rush, the acknowledged father of psychiatry in the United States, was instrumental in its establishment. Rush wrote the first psychiatric textbook, *Medical Inquiries and Observations upon Diseases of the Mind* (1812), which was the dominant textbook in the field for the next seven decades. He explored such methods of treating mental illness as blood-letting, control of diet, exercise, hydrotherapy, chemical intervention, diversion, and travel. He called for the humane treatment of mental patients.

Two other mental hospitals existed in the United States before 1800, the Eastern State Hospital in Williamsburg, Virginia, and Spring Grove Hospital in Catonsville, Maryland. During the nation's colonial period and long afterward, the care of the mentally ill fell largely to their families. In extreme cases that threatened community safety, however, public officials ordered people they considered dangerous confined, often holding them in prisons, sometimes chained to the walls or the floor. Disturbed people who did not have relatives to look after them were expelled from communities. If they stayed on, they might be put in the stocks and publicly whipped, after which they were forced to leave.

As mental hospitals were established, there were many more applicants for places than could be accommodated. Horace Mann, who conducted a legislative survey in 1829, identified 289 mentally disabled people in Massachusetts, of whom 138 were in almshouses, 141 confined in jails or treated at home, and a mere 10 cared for in mental hospitals. Mann's survey provided the impetus for the construction of the Worcester State Hospital in 1833. This institution became a model for other such institutions elsewhere in the country.

EARLY MEDICAL SCHOOLS AND SOCIETIES

In eighteenth century America, men could practice medicine simply by declaring themselves to be physicians. Many medical doctors received their training through apprenticeships provided by other doctors. Of 3,500 physicians in the country during the 1700's, about 400 had received formal training, usually gained by study in European medical schools. By 1840, about 35 percent of the physicians in New England had formal training.

Small medical schools existed in the United States during the eighteenth century, notably those established at the College of Philadelphia in 1756, King's College—now Columbia University—in New York City in 1767, Harvard University in 1782, and Dartmouth Medical School in 1797. These, however, were limited operations with meager faculties and few students.

In the 1820's, laws were passed permitting medical societies to establish standards for licensing physicians and to grant licenses. Such documents, however, were not required for those who wished to practice medicine, although unlicensed physicians were banned from suing in court to collect unpaid medical bills. At this time, no organization existed for physicians who specialized in treating the mentally ill.

In 1844, John M. Galt, a physician and grandnephew of James Galt, the first administrator of Eastern State Hospital in Williamsburg, Virginia, helped establish what became the American Psychiatric Association (APA). Twenty-five years old at the time, John Galt met in Philadelphia with twelve other superintendents of mental hospitals. The impetus for this meeting came partially from the establishment, in 1841, of the British Association of Medical Officers of Lunatic Asylums (later the Royal Society of Psychiatrists), which emphasized the need for superintendents of mental hospitals to share ideas about the management, treatment, and care of the mentally ill. There were superintendents of mental hospitals from Maine to Virginia present at the Philadelphia meeting, which began on October 16, 1844, and continued for four days. Thomas Kilbride, superintendent of the Philadelphia Hospital for the Insane, organized the conference and entertained the delegates in his residence on the grounds of the Philadelphia Hospital. As a result of this meeting, the AAII was established. Samuel B. Woodward was elected president and Samuel White, the oldest of the thirteen delegates, vice president.

EARLY OBJECTIVES OF THE AAII

A widely distributed AAII circular stated the objectives of the new organization, urging administrators of mental hospitals to communicate in order to share the results of their administrative experiences. This circular suggested that administrators should gather statistical information about mental illness and assist one another in finding ways to improve the treatment of the mentally ill.

To facilitate communication, it was decided that the organization should meet regularly. The second meeting was held in Washington, D.C., beginning on May 10, 1846. Ten superintendents who had not attended the first meeting were present for the second meeting, along with the thirteen original delegates. It was decided that subsequent meetings should be held in May, a time of year when travel was relatively easy. Membership was open to the medical superintendents of any incorporated or legally constituted institutions for the insane, and, where there was no medical superintendent because of different organizational patterns, the regular medical officer of such institutions might attend the scheduled meetings.

Between 1844 and 1861, meetings were held every year except 1845, 1847, and 1861. Meeting places were varied: Philadelphia, Boston, Washington, Baltimore, Cincinnati, Quebec, Utica, New York City, and Lexington, Kentucky. With rare exceptions, annual meetings have been held every May since the 1860's.

EARLY AAII INITIATIVES

As the AAII grew in size, it also grew in strength and influence. At its 1851 meeting, it set standards for the construction of mental hospitals, emphasizing such matters as ideal size, location, fire safety, and overall design. From its 1866 meeting came guidelines urging every state to provide facilities for the care of the mentally ill. Large states were to be divided into districts within which mental patients might be housed in residential facilities. The association called for those considered mentally ill but curable and those considered incurable to reside together. It called upon states to construct hospitals for the insane following closely the recommendations of its 1851 meeting.

In 1868, the association set forth twenty-one legal constraints relating to mental patients, emphasizing individual rights and dignity and designed for the protection of those with mental disorders. It had earlier condemned political appointments to super-intendencies of mental hospitals, demanding instead that the best person be chosen for such posts.

REORGANIZATION

Despite its influence, the AAII never had a large membership. Fewer than thirty delegates attended most of its annual meetings, although the fiftieth anniversary meeting in 1894 drew about one hundred delegates. At this time, the organization lacked a constitution and was run by a president, a vice president, and a secretary-treasurer.

Fourteen years earlier, the AAII had abolished its committees. In 1892, it established eight new committees that dealt with a broad range of mental disorders and related matters. It adopted its first constitution, which established a governing council and established three levels of membership: active, associate, and honorary. The proceedings of the meetings were to be published in *Transactions*. The following year, as the organization prepared for its fiftieth anniversary, its name was changed to the American Medico-Psychological Association (AMPA), the name it retained until 1920. In 1921, the organization changed its name again, to the American Psychiatric Association (APA), the name it retains to the present.

THE TWENTIETH CENTURY

The twenty-seven years of AMPA's existence were marked by phenomenal growth in modern psychiatry, impelled by the influence of such leading European theorists as Sigmund Freud (1856-1939), Alfred Adler (1870-1937), and Carl Jung (1875-1961). The association had earlier suggested guidelines for the training of psychiatrists. Now the field of child psychiatry came into being and such fields as psychiatric social work and psychiatric nursing were established.

The American Medical Association (AMA) had long sought to have the associations serving psychiatry join it, but it took until 1930 for the AMA to form a committee on mental health. This committee suggested an increased emphasis on psychiatry in medical schools, as well as on issues relating to the mentally ill and to legal aspects of their care and treatment.

Psychiatry received a boost during and immediately after World War II, when many enlisted men or returning veterans experienced psychiatric conditions caused by the stress of combat. During the late 1940's, two APA leaders, William Menninger and Daniel Blain, helped to establish new programs and obtained funding to strengthen the association. More advances in treating the mentally ill, particularly through drug therapy, occurred in the last half of the twentieth century than had been made in the preceding three centuries.

During the directorship of Daniel Blain, from 1948 to 1958, the APA moved into handsome headquarters at 1700 18th Street NW, in Washington, D.C., where a permanent staff ran the now-flourishing organization. Under Walter Barton's directorship, from 1963 to 1974, the permanent staff grew from 48 to 116 persons. The APA Museum was constructed and the headquarters building was renovated and expanded.

Following Barton as medical director was Melvin Sabsin, who assumed office on September 1, 1974. He founded the American Psychiatric Press and set about raising funds for the construction of the new, twelve-story headquarters building at 1400 K Street NW, in Washington, D.C., that was needed to serve an ever-increasing membership, which had spiraled from 5,856 members in 1950 to 18,407 by 1970 and 37,000 by 2002.

The organization continues to grow and contribute significantly to its medical subspecialty. It has a notable impact upon legislation regarding the mentally ill and is influential in directing the course of psychiatric training and licensure throughout the United States and Canada.

SOURCES FOR FURTHER STUDY

Barton, Walter E. *The History and Influence of the American Psychiatric Association*. Washington, D.C.: American Psychiatric Press, 1987. A comprehensive history of the APA that chronicles as well the development of American psychiatry from colonial times until the 1980's. Barton was the APA's ninetieth president (1961-1962) and medical director (1963-1974).

Bordley, J. B., and A. M. Harvey. *Two Centuries of American Medicine, 1776-1976*. Philadelphia: W. B. Saunders, 1976. A study of medicine in America, which includes the growth of care for the mentally ill and the role the APA played in establishing standards for delivering such care.

Deutsch, Albert. *The Mentally Ill in America*. Garden City, N.Y.: Doubleday Doran, 1937. Written at a popular level, this book, despite its age, offers interesting insights into the care of the mentally ill in America.

Grob, Gerald N. *Mental Illness and American Society, 1875-1940*. Princeton, N.J.: Princeton University Press, 1983. Grob traces the changing scene in American psychiatric care and shows how the APA helped to establish standards in the field.

Hall, J. K., Gregory Zilboorg, and Henry A. Bunker, eds. *One Hundred Years of American Psychiatry*. New York: Columbia University Press, 1944. This volume was published by the Columbia University Press for the APA to commemorate of its hundredth anniversary.

Kendrick, Douglas T., Steven L. Neuberg, and Robert B. Cialdini, eds. *Social Psychology: Unraveling the Mystery*. Boston: Allyn & Bacon, 1999. This excellent overview of social psychology contains brief but useful information on the role of the APA in establishing ethical standards for the profession.

Kolb, Lawrence C. *Modern Clinical Psychology*. 11th ed. Philadelphia: W. B. Saunders, 1982. This popular textbook traces the growth of clinical psychology in the United States and relates some of its development to the growth of the APA.

McGovern, Constance M. *Masters of Madness: Social Origins of the American Psychiatric Profession*. Hanover, N.H.: University Press of New England, 1985. Presents a solid, lucid overview of the origins and development of the APA.

R. Baird Shuman

SEE ALSO: American Psychological Association; Disaster psychology; Psychology: Fields of specialization.

American Psychological Association

DATE: Founded in 1892
TYPE OF PSYCHOLOGY: All
FIELDS OF STUDY: All

The American Psychological Association is the largest national organization of psychologists in the United States, representing the interests of over 155,000 *members, who are students, professors, practitioners, policy makers, and citizens who bring psychology to the American public, and the larger international community.*

KEY CONCEPTS
• advocacy
• directorates
• divisions
• lobbying
• policy
• practice

INTRODUCTION

The American Psychological Association (APA) is a professional organization that represents the interests of psychologists and psychological science in the United States. It has more than five hundred employees and is based in the District of Columbia, near the seats of government for the United States. It is also in close proximity to many other professional organizations and governmental bodies, such as the National Institutes of Health, the Institute of Medicine, and the National Science Foundation.

Through its work in promoting psychology as a science, as an area of clinical practice, as a field and tool of education, and as a matter of public policy and interest, the APA has the mission of advancing psychology as a scientific discipline and as a profession. Additionally, it maintains a mission of promoting human welfare and health through the work of psychologists as a whole. These goals are to be addressed in several ways. For instance, it does this by encouraging psychology as a field to develop into many forms and to forge new ways of doing research and improving research methods. Similarly, the fostering of high standards of achievement, education, ethics, and general conduct among psychologists is important in these regards. Finally, increasing the dissemination and use of psychological knowledge through collegial communications and communications with the public at large plays a central role in meeting these goals of the APA mission.

Advocacy, or the practice of supporting and advancing specific positions or viewpoints in a public fashion, is one task the APA encourages. It does this by fostering ethical standards among its members and also by taking positions on important public issues for the purpose of governmental decisions and debates. In some cases, this might include lobbying, encouraging members to contact governmental representatives or particular organizations, informing them of positions taken by the organization as a whole, or letting key officials know what their constituents wishes are. This also might be done through the participation of APA's members in various decision-making groups where policy, or decisions that may result in laws or guidelines about the directions of concerns such as health care, education, or scientific conduct, is determined.

Members may also influence clinical practice, or the delivery of services such as assessment, consultation, and psychotherapy, by participating on boards of psychology which oversee psychology in each state. In the larger organization of APA, structured subgroups are devoted to specific activities and areas of psychology to achieve similar tasks. One type of subgroup, the directorate, is devoted to a branch of psychology related to science, practice, public interest, or education. A second type of subgroup, with a special relationship to the directorates, is the division, a group designated to advance specific topical areas in psychology. Together, the directorates and divisions help to inform both the APA membership and the public at large about special events, themes, or decisions that might be important to the discipline and its influence on daily life.

HISTORY AND STRUCTURE

The organization is one that is managed by a formal set of bylaws and by a constitution. It is membership driven, meaning individuals who are members of the organization vote on how the organization adapts to contemporary social problems or needs for organizational development.

The bylaws of the APA provide an outline of the structure of the organization and describe this structure as including a central office with a chief executive officer, standing boards and committees, officers, a council of representatives, and a board of directors. The organization is also characterized by divisions, each of which has special interests in particular areas of psychological science, or the study of specific types of behavior. The relative size of the membership in each division determines the voting power and influence of the division on the larger whole of the organization in terms of the divisional input to the council of representatives, setting priorities, and votes for offices such as president. The majority of the work completed by the APA as a whole is actually done by volunteer members. These members, elected and appointed by the division members or the council, volunteer their time and energy to take on special projects, develop proposals for conferences, publications, or special projects, inform other members of important issues, and set strategic plans for the different areas of psychology in the organization. The organization is supported in part by membership dues and by monies it makes through other means. These other means include an annual convention for the membership and the development and sale of books and professional journals.

As an organization, the APA is diverse. The divisions are numerous and developed out of basic academic needs to have special discussion groups on specific topics in psychology, around relevant social issues, and also around relevant professional issues. In some cases, the divisions developed from organizational societies within the APA. In total, these division-type subgroups of the APA include the following: Society for General Psychology; Society for the Teaching of Psychology; Experimental Psychology; Evaluation, Measurement, and Statistics; Behavioral Neuroscience and Comparative Psychology; Developmental Psychology; Society for Personality and Social Psychology; Society for the Study of Social Issues (SPSSI); Psychology and the Arts; Society of Clinical Psychology; Society of Consulting Psychology; Society for Industrial and Organizational Psychology; Educational Psychology; School Psychology; Counseling Psychology; Psychologists in Public Service; Military Psychology; Adult Development and Aging; Applied Experimental and Engineering Psychology; Rehabilitation Psychology; Society for Consumer Psychology; Theoretical and Philosophical Psychology; Behavior Analysis; History of Psychology; Society for Community Research and Action: Division of Community Psychology; Pharmacology and Substance Abuse; Psychotherapy; Society of Psychological Hypnosis; State Psychological Association Affairs; Humanistic Psychology; Mental Retardation and Developmental Disabilities; Population and Environmental Psychology; Society for the Psychology of Women; Psychology of Religion; Child, Youth, and Family Services; Health Psychology; Psychoanalysis; Clinical Neuropsychology; American Psychology-Law Society; Psychologists in Independent Practice; Family Psychology; Society for the Psychological Study of Lesbian, Gay, and Bisexual Issues; Society for the Study of Ethnic Minority Issues; Media Psychology; Exercise and Sport Psychology; Society for the Study of Peace, Conflict, and Violence: Peace Psychology Division; Group Psychology and Group Psychotherapy; Addictions; Society for the Psychological Study of Men and Masculinity; International Psychology; Society of Clinical Child and Adolescent Psychology; Society of Pediatric Psychology; and the American Society for the Advancement of Pharmacotherapy.

This list of division-type subgroups shows the groups in the relative historical order they developed. As can be seen by looking at the list from beginning to end, it appears to have started with a focus on different types of basic psychological science. As the list developed, it transitioned and added more specialized branches of psychological work that grow from the earlier basic areas. Further development shows the emergence of numerous groups focusing on specific types of practitioners, populations, and settings. In many ways, this list shows the maturation of psychology as a discipline, showing growth from basic science to education, practice, and policy related to public interests.

FUNCTIONS

To understand some strategies the organization uses to reach its goals, it is helpful to take a closer look at each of the four major directorates of the APA (the Science Directorate, the Education Directorate, the Practice Directorate, and the Public Interest Directorate). Each has unique targets for change in terms of how the APA interacts with its members and the public at large.

The Science Directorate has a particular interest in advancing the study of psychology, such as through encouraging career development in the area of psychological science. Such work happens at all levels, from encouraging science students in their precollege years to think about psychology as a field of choice to attracting midcareer professionals who are thinking about a blended career where psychology plays a role. It may take the form of public announcements. For instance, disseminating new psychological research findings on important social problems such as Alzheimer's disease, why beeping mechanical sounds might distract military personnel, or pain relief in individuals with chronic health problems, or it might take the form of outreach, such as psychologists going into school systems and

talking about their work with interested students in science classes. Another important role the Science Directorate plays is in informing the members of APA about policy and governmental regulation changes that have the potential to affect the work of psychological scientist. Such topics might include rules about how animal or human research is conducted, plans for how tax dollars are distributed for research, or rules related to how data must be preserved.

The Education Directorate focuses on matters related to formal education. This includes issues around training psychologists, such as graduate education programs, program accreditation, and continuing professional education. Additionally, it focuses activities on how psychology is taught to undergraduates and younger students as well. For instance, the Education Directorate has an interest in gifted education and also advances efforts to engage young minds with interest in the field by making psychology more accessible to them. Finally, the Education Directorate encourages advocacy on the topic of education in general and also as it specifically relates to psychology.

The Practice Directorate plays the important role of focusing on helping professionals who provide psychological services get the information they need. For instance, this directorate provides tips on how to be an advocate of psychology as a profession and information on licensing and service provision for psychologists in independent practice. It also provides information to individuals in the community who might be seeking information on getting psychological help or assistance. During the months following the September 11, 2001, terrorist acts in the United States, for instance, the Practice Directorate provided public education materials about how to help children cope with terrorism, a disaster response network allowing psychologists to volunteer much needed services, and an advice column on how psychologists could maintain their own resilience in such professionally demanding times.

Finally, the Public Interest Directorate plays the role of facilitating the interface between psychology and public policy. Highlighting the needs of special populations and how psychology might better address the needs of those populations has been a very important focus of the Public Interest Directorate. Aging, children, youth, families, gender, disability, human immunodeficency virus (HIV) and acquired immunodeficiency syndrome (AIDS), sexual orientation, and ethnic and racial health disparities are just some of the areas where the Public Interest Directorate has concentrated its efforts. As with the other directorates, these efforts have taken the form of press releases, the provision of educational materials, and even conferences to bring these issues of policy to public attention.

As a whole, the directorates form the basic foci for APA in terms of how it interacts with its members and the general public. Their dynamic natures allow them to shift in response to pressing social issues and foster growth in the organization that is beneficial inside and out.

SOURCES FOR FURTHER STUDY

Dewsbury, Donald A., ed. *Unification Through Division: Histories of the Divisions of the American Psychological Association.* vol. 1. Washington, D.C.: American Psychological Association, 1996. This is the first volume in an ongoing series that covers the founding of the divisions of the organization, their function, and outlines their number, topic areas, and events responsible for their creation.

Kimble, Gregory A., Michael Wertheimer, and Charlotte White, eds. *Portraits of Pioneers in Psychology.* Volume 1. Washington, D.C.: American Psychological Association, 1991. This is the first volume in an ongoing series that interweaves the personal and professional backgrounds of the most influential psychologists of modern times.

Pickren, Wade E., and Donald A. Dewsbury, eds. *Evolving Perspectives on the History of Psychology.* Washington, D.C.: American Psychological Association, 2002. This work discusses the successes and failures of psychology in recent history by highlighting important transitions, controversies, and milestones of progress.

Puente, Antonio E., Janet Matthews, and Matthew Brewer, eds. *Teaching Psychology in America: A History.* Washington, D.C.: American Psychological Association, 1992. These authors provide a review not only of how psychology is taught, but why it has become an important educational topic and tool at this time in history.

Reiber, Robert W., and Kurt Salzinger, eds. *Psychology: Theoretical-Historical Perspectives: Second Edition.* Washington, D.C.: American Psychological Association, 1998. The history of psychology is presented across the major theories influencing its ongoing development across a broad number of practical applications areas.

Nancy A. Piotrowski

SEE ALSO: American Psychiatric Association; *Diagnostic and Statistical Manual of Mental Disorders* (DSM); Psychology: Fields of specialization.

Amnesia and fugue

TYPE OF PSYCHOLOGY: Psychopathology
FIELDS OF STUDY: Coping

The inability to totally or partially recall or identify a past experience is called amnesia. A fugue is an extensive escape from life's problems that involves an amnesiac state and actual flight from familiar surroundings. During a fugue, a new partial or entire identity may be assumed. Both fugue and amnesia involve the concept of dissociation.

KEY CONCEPTS

- behavioral explanation
- continuous amnesia
- dissociation
- dissociative disorders
- generalized amnesia
- localized amnesia
- psychodynamic explanation
- psychogenic amnesia
- selective amnesia

INTRODUCTION

Amnesia involves the failure to recall a past experience because of an anxiety that is associated with the situation. Fugue states take place when a person retreats from life's difficulties by entering an amnesic state and leaving familiar surroundings. During a fugue state, a person may assume a new partial or whole personality. Although amnesia may be caused by organic brain pathology, attempts to cope with anxiety can produce amnesia and fugue. The concept of dissociation refers to the ability of the human mind to split from conscious awareness. Through dissociation, a person can avoid anxiety and difficulty in managing life stresses. When stress and anxiety overwhelm a person, the mind may split from a conscious awareness of the troubling situations. When this takes place, the individual automatically loses memory of the event and may physically leave the stressful situation through a fugue state.

Amnesia and fugue are two of the dissociative disorders recognized by the American Psychiatric Association. The dissociative disorders are methods of avoiding anxiety through the process of pathological dissociation. In addition to amnesia and fugue, the dissociative disorders include dissociative identity disorder and depersonalization disorder. In the former, a person develops a number of alter identities. This disorder was previously called multiple personality disorder. Depersonalization disorder involves a process in which individuals suddenly feel that their bodies or senses of self have changed dramatically.

AMNESIA TYPES

Another term for dissociative amnesia is psychogenic amnesia. This conveys the concept that the amnesia is not due to organic brain pathology. Individuals developing psychogenic or dissociative amnesia often encounter a traumatic event or extreme stress that overloads their coping abilities. Four different types of psychogenic or dissociative amnesia can be identified. Localized amnesia is seen when a person cannot remember anything about a specific event. This is often seen after a person experiences a very traumatic event, such as a serious accident, and then does not recall what happened. The second type of amnesia is called selective amnesia and occurs when only some parts of a certain time period are forgotten. Infrequently, generalized amnesia takes place and the person forgets his or her entire life history. The fourth type of dissociative amnesia is the continuous type. This form of amnesia is seen when a person does not remember anything beyond a certain point in the past.

DIAGNOSIS

It is difficult to report reliable data on the prevalence of dissociative disorders, but it appears that females are diagnosed with the dissociative disorders at a rate five times that of males.

To make the diagnosis of dissociative amnesia, a doctor must identify a disturbance in memory that involves the appearance of one or more episodes of inability to recall important personal information

that is usually of a traumatic or stressful nature. The memory loss must be too extensive to be explained by ordinary forgetfulness. When people develop dissociative amnesia, they may not be able to remember their own names or the identities of relatives, but they retain a number of significant abilities. In psychogenic or dissociative amnesia, basic habits and skills remain intact. Thus, the person is still able to read a book, drive a car, and recognize familiar objects. The memories that are lost revolve around life events and autobiographical information.

The diagnosis of dissociative fugue requires the sudden unexpected travel away from home or customary place of work. Together with this travel, the person is unable to recall the past. During the fugue, the person shows confusion about personal identity or assumes a new one. The person's activities at the time of the fugue can vary extensively, from short-term involvement in new interests to traveling to distant locations and assuming a new identity and work roles. The fugue can last for days, weeks, or even years. At some point, the individual will leave the fugue state and be in a strange place without awareness of the events that took place during the dissociative period. When a fugue state is taking place, the person appears normal to others and can complete complex tasks. Usually, the activities selected by the person are indicative of a different lifestyle from the previous one.

The diagnosis of dissociative amnesia and fugue can be controversial since it often depends upon self-reports. The possibility that a person is faking the symptoms must be considered. Objective diagnostic measures for these disorders do not exist. The possibility of malingering or fabricating the symptoms must be considered in arriving at a diagnosis of dissociative amnesia and fugue.

When diagnosing dissociative amnesia and fugue, a number of other disorders and conditions have to be excluded. A number of medical conditions such as vitamin deficiency, head trauma, carbon monoxide poisoning, and herpes encephalitis can produce similar symptoms. Amnesia can also be found in conjunction with alcoholism and the use of other drugs.

POSSIBLE CAUSES

Normal dissociation is often differentiated from pathological dissociation. Normal dissociation can

DSM-IV-TR Criteria for Amnesia and Fugue

DISSOCIATIVE AMNESIA (DSM CODE 300.12)

Predominant disturbance is one or more episodes of inability to recall important personal information, usually of a traumatic or stressful nature, too extensive to be explained by ordinary forgetfulness

Disturbance not occurring exclusively during the course of Dissociative Identity Disorder, Dissociative Fugue, Post-traumatic Stress Disorder, Acute Stress Disorder, or Somatization Disorder and not due to direct physiological effects of a substance or a neurological or other general medical condition

Symptoms cause clinically significant distress or impairment in social, occupational, or other important areas of functioning

DEPERSONALIZATION DISORDER (DSM CODE 300.6)

Persistent or recurrent experiences of feeling detached from, and as if an outside observer of, one's mental processes or body (such as feeling in a dream)

During depersonalization experience, reality testing remains intact

Depersonalization causes clinically significant distress or impairment in social, occupational, or other important areas of functioning

Experience not occurring exclusively during the course of another mental disorder, such as Schizophrenia, Panic Disorder, Acute Stress Disorder, or another Dissociative Disorder, and not due to direct physiological effects of a substance or general medical condition

DISSOCIATIVE FUGUE (DSM CODE 300.13)

Predominant disturbance is sudden, unexpected travel away from home or one's customary place of work, with inability to recall one's past

Confusion about personal identity or assumption of new identity (partial or complete)

Disturbance not occurring exclusively during course of Dissociative Identity Disorder and not due to direct physiological effects of a substance or general medical condition such as temporal lobe epilepsy

Symptoms cause clinically significant distress or impairment in social, occupational, or other important areas of functioning

DISSOCIATIVE IDENTITY DISORDER (DSM CODE 300.14)

Presence of two or more distinct identities or personality states, each with its own relatively enduring pattern of perceiving, relating to, and thinking about the environment and self

At least two of these identities or personality states recurrently take control of person's behavior

Inability to recall important personal information too extensive to be explained by ordinary forgetfulness

Disturbance not due to direct physiological effects of a substance (such as blackouts or chaotic behavior during alcohol intoxication) or general medical condition (such as complex partial seizures); in children, symptoms not attributable to imaginary playmates or other fantasy play

---

be an adaptive way to handle a traumatic incident. It is commonly seen as a reaction to war and civilian disasters. In normal dissociation, the person's perception of the traumatic experience is temporarily dulled or removed from the conscious mind. Pathological dissociation is an extreme reaction of splitting the anxiety-provoking situation from consciousness.

There exist a limited number of research studies that seek to explain the causes of dissociation in certain individuals and predict what persons are vulnerable to the development of dissociative amnesia or fugue during periods of trauma or overwhelming stress. The psychodynamic explanation emphasizes the use of repression as a defense against conscious awareness of the stressful or traumatic event. Entire chunks of the person's identity or past experiences are split from the conscious mind as a way to avoid painful memories or conflicts. According to this explanation, some individuals are vulnerable to the use of dissociation because of their early childhood experiences of trauma or abuse. With the early experience of abuse, the child learns to repress the memories or engage in a process of self-hypnosis. The hypnotic state permits the child to escape the stress associated with the abuse or neglect. The abused child feels a sense of powerlessness in the face of repeated abuse and splits from this conscious awareness. This isolation of the stressful event leads to the development of different memory processes from those found in normal child development.

A behavioral explanation for the likely development of dissociation as a means to cope with stressful events focuses on the rewarding aspects of dissociative symptoms. The child learns to role-play and engage in selective attention to recognize certain environmental cues that provide rewards. Stressful circumstances are blocked out and disturbing thoughts ignored. Eventually, this process expands into a tendency to assume new roles and block out stressful situations.

The dissociative disorders appear to be influenced by sociocultural factors which are dependent upon social attitudes and cultural norms. Acceptance and toleration of the symptoms associated with dissociative disorders depend upon prevailing societal attitudes. Over time, cultures vary in the acceptance of dissociative symptoms and the manifestation of amnesia and fugue states. For example, historical reports of spirit possession can be interpreted as the experience of a fugue state.

TREATMENT

The symptoms associated with dissociative amnesia and fugue usually spontaneously disappear over time. As the experience of stress begins to lessen, the amnesia and fugue often disappear. When providing treatment for these individuals, it is important that caregivers provide a safe environment which removes them from the possible sources of stress. Some persons are hospitalized for this reason. The institutional setting allows them to regain comfort away from the traumatizing or stress-producing situation. Occasionally the memory loss can be retrieved through the use of specific medications. One such medication is sodium amytal, which can be used during an interview process that attempts to restore the lost memories. Hypnosis is also used as a means to put the person in a receptive state for questions that may overcome the amnesia.

Hypnosis is also used in the treatment of fugue states. The goal when using hypnosis is to access important memories that may have triggered the fugue. Medications are sometimes used with patients who have a history of fugue. Antianxiety medications called benzodiazepines have been utilized with individuals showing dissociative fugue. The medication helps to alleviate the feelings of worry and apprehension.

Since amnesia does not typically interfere with a person's daily functioning, few specific complaints about the lack of memory take place. Individuals may complain about other psychological symptoms, but not the amnesia. Consequently, treatment often does not focus on the lost memories. Some of the associated symptoms that occur with amnesia include depression and stress due to a fugue state. Treatment is often directed toward alleviating the depression and teaching a person stress management techniques.

SOURCES FOR FURTHER STUDY

Lewis, D., C. Yeager, Y. Swica, J. Pincus, and H. Lewis. "Objective Documentation of Child Abuse and Dissociation in Twelve Murderers." *American Journal of Psychiatry* 154 (1997): 1703-1710. This research study reports on the relationship between early child abuse and later dissociation. The article investigated a unique sample of murderers in coming to its conclusions.

Lowenstein, R. "Psychogenic Amnesia and Psychogenic Fugue." In *Review of Psychiatry*, edited by A. Tasman and S. Goldfinger. New York: American Psychiatric Press, 1991. This chapter provides a review of the scientific investigations into the causes of psychogenic amnesia and fugue.

Lynn, S., and J. Rhue. *Dissociation: Clinical and Theoretical Perspectives*. New York: Guilford, 1994. This volume comprises a number of chapters written by experts in the study of dissociation. The contributors place great emphasize on the role of trauma in producing vulnerability for dissociation as a defense in adulthood.

Michelson, L, and W. Ray. *Handbook of Dissociation: Theoretical, Empirical, and Clinical Perspectives*. New York: Plenum, 1996. This book provides an extensive explanation of dissociation with multiple examples. It is written for a reader who needs detailed research and clinical information.

Putnam, F. *Dissociation in Children and Adolescents*. New York: Guilford, 1997. This is a useful book for information on the manifestation of normal dissociation in children and teenagers and how normal dissociation can evolve into pathological dissociation, which signals the development of the dissociative disorders.

Sackeim, H., and W. Vingiano. "Dissociative Disorders." In *Adult Psychopathology and Diagnosis*, edited by S. Turner and M. Hersen. New York: John Wiley & Sons, 1984. The importance of treating other psychological symptoms is discussed in this chapter. Persons with dissociative disorders often show depression that should receive treatment.

Sadovsky, R. "Evaluation of Patients with Transient Global Amnesia." *American Family Physician* 57 (1998): 2237-2238. One of the medical conditions that has symptoms similar to those of dissociative amnesia is transient global amnesia. This article, which is written for physicians, provides the specifics for making a differential diagnosis.

Tulving, E. "What Is Episodic Memory?" *Current Directions in Psychological Science* 2 (1993): 67-70. This article is useful for understanding the different forms of memory loss that are seen in dissociative amnesia.

Tutkun, H., V. Sar, L. Yargic, and T. Ozpulat. "Frequency of Dissociative Disorders Among Psychiatric Inpatients in a Turkish University Clinic." *American Journal of Psychiatry* 155 (1998): 800-805. The dissociative disorders vary in incidence across countries. This article provides information concerning the reasons for the differences between cultural groups.

Frank J. Prerost

SEE ALSO: Aphasias; Brain damage; Brain structure; Forgetting and forgetfulness; Long-term memory; Memory; Memory: Animal research; Memory: Empirical studies; Memory: Physiology; Memory: Sensory; Memory storage; Short-term memory; Split-brain studies.

Analytic psychology

Jacques Lacan

TYPE OF PSYCHOLOGY: Personality

FIELDS OF STUDY: Classic analytical themes and issues; humanistic-phenomenological models; personality theory; psychodynamic and neoanalytic models; thought

Jacques-Marie Lacan, a pioneering psychoanalyst who emphasized the relationship between language and the unconscious, radically reinterpreted Freud in light of philosophy and structuralist linguistics. Lacan's theories of the unconscious (that it is "structured like a language") and the mirror phase have significantly reshaped the discourse of psychoanalysis and cultural theory.

KEY CONCEPTS
- desire
- falsifying character of the ego
- imaginary
- imaginary misidentification/ *méconnaissance*
- *jouissance*
- lack/*manque*
- little object *a*/ *objet petit a*
- mirror stage
- real
- symbolic

INTRODUCTION

According to Freudian psychoanalysis, desire is biological and driven by sexual force or libido. Jacques Lacan (1901-1981), on the other hand, regards desire as a drive for an original ontological unity which can never be achieved because of the psychic split resulting from what he called "the mirror stage" as well as the Freudian Oedipal phase. Desire emerges from this split or "lack" which it tries, continually, to fill. Desire expresses itself through language.

Lacan believed that his form of psychoanalysis was not a departure from, but a return to, the original principles of Freudian analysis. Lacan's readers have long complained about the difficulty of his prose, which is characterized by a seeming lack of linearity and an often impenetrable style. Many of Lacan's commentators have likened his discursive style to a rebus or puzzle, designed to communicate the idea that no "truth" about psychic life can ever be wholly and fully expressed through language because the psyche is always split against itself, and language is the result of absence and difference.

THE MIRROR STAGE

Central to Lacanian psychoanalysis is the celebrated "mirror stage." Lacan argues that a child's ego only begins to emerge in the ages between six and eighteen months, when the child first sees its own reflection in a mirror. This experience is illusory, according to Lacan, because the child's actual experience of its own body is never that of a clearly delineated whole in the child's full control. Lacan's observations on the so-called mirror stage relied heavily upon the earlier work of the American psychologist and philosopher James Mark Baldwin (1861-1934).

Desire emerges from the perceived distance between the actual or lived experience of the child's own body and the reflection it first sees in the mirror. The child envies the perfection of the mirror image or the mirroring response of its parents, says Lacan, and this lack or *manque* is permanent because there will always be a gap or existential distance between the subjective experience of the body and the complete image in the mirror, or the apparent wholeness of others.

Desire begins at the mirror stage in the psychic development of the young child. The apparent completeness of the reflected image gives the otherwise helpless child a sense of mastery over its own body, but this sense of self-mastery is as illusory as it is frustrating. Lacan urged his fellow psychoanalysts to reassess their focus on the patient's ego and turn their attention back to the unconscious because of what he termed "the falsifying character of the ego." Lacan argued that psychoanalysis should "return to Freud" and abandon its fascination with the ultimately untrustworthy ego of the patient.

Lacan believed that his theory of the "mirror stage" answered two fundamental questions raised by Sigmund Freud's 1914 essay, "On Narcissism": What "psychical action" takes place to bring the ego into being? If we are not narcissists from the earliest stages of life, what causes narcissism to emerge? According to Lacan, the mechanism of the mirror stage answers both of these questions.

THE OEDIPUS COMPLEX

Lacan, like Freud, believed that individuals are socialized by passing through the three stages of the Oedipus complex: seduction, the "primal scene," and the castration phase, the last of which Lacan reconfigured as "the Father's 'No'." In the so-called seduction phase, the child is attracted to the original object of desire, which is the body of the mother. In the "primal scene" or "primal stage" the child witnesses the father having sexual intercourse with the mother, and this is followed by the "castration phase," wherein the father restricts the child's access to the mother under threat of castration. The "Law of the Father" or "Father's 'No'" causes the child to redirect desire from the mother to what Lacan calls the "Other"—a hypothetical "place" in the unconscious which allows the individual to later project desire onto other persons—other, that is, than the mother.

Lacan holds that there are three "registers" in the child's psychosexual development: the imaginary, the symbolic, and the real. These correspond—

somewhat—to the Freudian oral, anal, and genital stages and are related, indirectly, to the three stages of the Oedipus complex.

At the level of the imaginary, the pre-Oedipal infant inhabits a world without clear subject-object distinctions. The child thinks that it is coextensive with the mother's body. While the child perceives the mother's body as nurturing and pleasurable, it also entertains fantasies that the mother's body might overwhelm and destroy it. This yields alternating fantasies of incorporation and assault, whereby the child is both blissful in its identification with the body of the mother and frightfully aggressive toward it. At this stage in its development, the child inhabits a world of images. The mirror stage is the most important moment of imaginary misidentification or *méconnaissance*.

It is the father who disrupts the closed dyadic relationship between mother and child, according to Lacan. The father signifies what Lacan calls "the Law" or "the Law of the Father," which is always, in the first instance, the incest taboo. The child's intensely libidinal relationship with its mother's body is opened to the wider world of family and society by the figure of the father. The father's appearance divides the child from the mother's body and drives the child's desire for its mother into the unconscious. Therefore "the Law" and unconscious desire for the mother emerge at the same time, according to Lacanian psychoanalysis.

The child's experience of the father's presence is also its first experience of sexual difference, and with it comes the dim awareness that there is someone else other than the mother in its world. The "Father's 'No'" deflects the child's desire from the mother to what Lacan calls the "Other." Lacan identified the "Other" as a hypothetical place in the unconscious which can be projected onto human counterparts by subjects. Lacan held that the "Other" is never fully grasped because the nature of desire is such that its object is always beyond its reach.

LANGUAGE AND THE SYMBOLIC

This is the point at which the child enters the register of the symbolic. It is at this stage, according to Lacan, that the child also enters the "language system." Absence, lack, and separation characterize the language system, according to Lacan, because language names things which are not immediately present ("signifieds") and substitutes words ("signifiers") for them. This is also the beginning of socialization, says Lacan. Just as the child realizes that sexual identity is the result of an originary difference between mother and father, it comes to grasp that language itself is an unending chain of "differences," and that the terms of language are what they are only by excluding one another. Signs always presuppose the absence of the objects they signify—an insight which Lacan inherited from structuralist anthropology and linguistics.

The loss of the precious object that is the mother's body drives desire to seek its satisfaction in incomplete or partial objects, none of which can ever fully satisfy the longing bred by the loss of the maternal body. People try vainly to settle for substitute objects, or what Lacan calls the "object little *a*." Lacan's thinking was heavily influenced by structuralist thinkers such as the anthropologist Claude Lévi-Strauss (b. 1908) and linguists Ferdinand de Saussure (1857-1913) and Roman Jakobson (1896-1982). Lacan's chief claim, based upon his readings of Saussure and Jakobson, is that the unconscious is "structured like a language." Lacan refashioned Freud's terminology of psychic condensation and displacement by translating them into what Lacan believed to be their equivalent rhetorical terms: metaphor and metonymy. Metaphor works by condensing two separate images into a single symbol through substitution, while metonymy operates by association—using a part to represent the whole (such as "crown" for "king") or using contiguous elements (such as "sea" and "boat").

The presence of the father teaches the child that it must assume a predefined social and familial role over which it exercises no control—a role which is defined by the sexual difference between mother and father, the exclusion of the child from the sexual relationship which exists between the mother and the father, and the child's relinquishment of the earlier and intense bonds which existed between itself and the mother's body. This situation of absence, exclusion, and difference is symbolized by the phallus, a universal signifier or metonymic presence which indicates the fundamental lack or absence which lies at the heart of being itself—the *manque à être*, as Lacan calls it.

THE REAL AND *JOUISSANCE*

Finally, Lacan posits a register called "the real"—not the empirical world, but the ineffable realm of constancy beyond the field of speech. According to Lacan, the "reality" which is given to consciousness is no more and no less than an amalgam of the imaginary (the specular and imagistic world of the rationalizing ego, with all of its self-delusions, defenses, and falsifications) and the symbolic (the meaningful social world of language). Lacan resists defining the real in any explicit or easily codifiable way. In his later work in the 1960's Lacan discussed the register of the real in light of his work on *jouissance*, a term which is loosely translated as "enjoyment" but which is much more complex.

According to Lacan *jouissance* is any experience which is too much for the organism to bear. More often than not it is experienced as suffering—an unbearable pain which is experienced as a kind of satisfaction by the unconscious drives. According to Lacan this is what lies at the heart of the Freudian "repetition compulsion," namely an unconscious, and unconsciously satisfying, wish to suffer. Healthy human life is about the regulation of *jouissance*. Children's bodies are prone to overexcitation and overstimulation because they are full of *jouissance*, which is slowly drained from the body of the child after its encounter with the "Law of the Father" and its entry into the register of the symbolic. Portions of *jouissance* linked to especially intense bodily memories from childhood can become "caught" or centered in the body and manifest as symptoms. Lacan reconfigured Freud's theory of castration by redefining it as the loss of *jouissance* from the body. More broadly, Lacan says that the entry into language itself is castration because it introduces the idea of lack or absence into the world.

LACANIAN CLINICAL PRACTICE

For Lacan, human subjects construct themselves through language. One of the chief goals of Lacanian clinical practice is to create a space wherein the patient can experience and release *jouissance* through speech without the disintegration of the his or her sense of self. The analyst will then determine where a patient lies on a diagnostic continuum—neurotic (obsessional or hysteric), perverse, or psychotic.

Psychotic patients, according to Lacanian analysis, are most greatly disconnected at the level of language, or the symbolic. The Lacanian analyst works with the disjointed speech of the psychotic to allow him or her to live within and to express, through language, the world of signifiers without significant discontinuity.

The perverse patient, on the other hand, is often drawn to a fetish object. The fetish object is a compliant one, and it allows the patient to experience *jouissance* without having to relive the experience of castration which was attendant upon the "Father's 'No.'" The perverse patient engages in an act of substitution, whereby a complicit object grants a sense of release—a real or simulated experience of *jouissance*—while allowing him or her to avoid the painful sense of separation from the Other, or the presymbolic mother.

The obsessional neurotic fears loss of control. Obsessional neurotics struggle to control and contain the upwelling of desire, and the accompanying experience of *jouissance*. The obsessional neurotic speaks the language of mastery and order, and attempts to exercise control well beyond his or her purview. The analyst is sensitive to dichotomizing tendencies in the patient's speech (order and disorder, right and wrong). According to Lacan, the patient's fantasy is that the upwelling of *jouissance* will alienate those around him or her and leave havoc in its wake. The analyst works with the obsessional neurotic to help the patient meet his or her needs without limiting defenses—to experience and speak desire without the fear of losing self-control.

Hysterics experience a deep and debilitating sense of lack which leads to a feeling of alienation from the Other. Once the hysteric obtains the imaginary object of the mother's desire, he or she wishes to be rid of it—sometimes almost violently. The goal of Lacanian analysis when working with hysterics is to move them beyond the dichotomy of having/not having to help them to achieve satisfactory levels of comfort with themselves, and to find a neutral space where the sense of lack is not all-consuming.

THE CASE OF AIMÉE

Lacan's early work on paranoia dealt with the case of a patient he called Aimée (Marguerite Anzieu) who was arrested by the Paris police in the attempted stabbing of a famous actress, Huguette Duflos. Lacan first encountered Aimée in 1931 at Sainte-Anne's Hospital, where he had begun his clinical training as a *légiste medicale,* or forensic psychiatrist, four years earlier. Lacan's patient, the subject of numerous press accounts and much public speculation, came to believe that her young son was about to be mur-

dered by Duflos. One night Aimée attended a play which featured the famous Parisian actress and suddenly lunged from the crowd of theatergoers brandishing a knife. Aimée was promptly arrested and given over to Lacan's care.

Lacan conducted an exhaustive number of analytic interviews with Aimée. Lacan was able to reconstruct the trajectory of Aimée's descent into what he termed self-punishment paranoia. Aimée both feared and admired Duflos, and she came to believe that the actress—really her ideal image of the actress—posed a danger to her and to her young child. Duflos's ideal image was the object of Aimée's intense hatred as well as her excessive fascination, writes Lacan, and in attacking Duflos the deluded woman was really punishing herself.

In one especially striking memory, Aimée recalled (falsely) reading an article in a newspaper in which the actress allegedly told an interviewer that she was planning to kill Aimée and her young son. Aimée therefore regarded her attack on Duflos as an act of preemptive self-defense based upon a misrecognition. Aimée finally found the real punishment she unconsciously craved (her *jouissance*) in her public humiliation, arrest, and confinement.

Lacan was struck by the relationship between memory (or, in this case, false memory) and identity. One sees in Lacan's early analysis of Aimée many of the most significant elements of his psychoanalytic theory, including the mirror stage, the imaginary, *jouissance* and its role in paranoia, and the power of misidentification.

Lacan's detailed analysis of "the case of Aimée" in his 1932 doctoral thesis, *De la psychose paranoiaque dans les rapports avec la personnalité* (paranoid psychosis and its relations to the personality), laid the groundwork for much of his later work on the nature of identity, the genesis of narcissism, the power of the image and the fundamentally social character of personality. From 1933 onward, Lacan was known as a specialist in the diagnosis and treatment of paranoia. His densely textured doctoral dissertation was widely circulated among artists and poets identified with the Surrealist movement, and Lacan wrote regularly for *Minotaure,* a Surrealist review published between 1933 and 1939 by Albert Skira. Many of Lacan's interpreters regard his work with philosopher Alexandre Kojève (1902-1968) as a theoretical turning point and the genesis of his thinking on the psychological significance of lack, loss, and absence.

In 1936 Lacan presented his paper "Le Stade du miroir" (the mirror stage) at the fourteenth International Psychoanalytical Congress, held at Marienbad in August of 1936 under the chairmanship of the preeminent British psychoanalyst Ernest Jones. It is in this seminal essay, since lost, that Lacan outlined his theory of the mirror stage. His theory of self-mastery through mimicry, in which the young child responds to its prematuration or defenselessness by identifying with images outside itself, was influenced by the anthropological insights of Roger Caillois (1913-1978).

Lacan's radical revision of psychoanalysis, which he regarded as a "return to Freud," led to his eventual ejection from the Société Française de Psychanalyse (SFP) in 1963. Lacan founded a new school, first called the École Française de Psychanalyse and then later the École Freudienne de Paris (EFP). Lacan dissolved the EFP in 1980 and died a year later, leaving behind a body of work which continues to influence psychoanalytic studies, philosophy, and literary and cultural theory.

SOURCES FOR FURTHER STUDY

Dor, Joel. *Introduction to the Reading of Lacan: The Unconscious Structured Like a Language.* New York: Other Press, 1998. A clearly written and accessible introduction. Includes a useful bibliography.

Evans, Dylan. *An Introductory Dictionary of Lacanian Psychoanalysis.* New York: Routledge, 1996. Evans defines over two hundred technical terms in their historical contexts.

Fink, Bruce. *A Clinical Introduction to Lacanian Psychoanalysis: Theory and Technique.* Cambridge, Mass.: Harvard University Press, 1997. A practicing psychoanalyst clearly introduces Lacan in theory and in clinical practice. Includes an extensive bibliography.

Lacan, Jacques. *Écrits: A Selection.* Translated by Alan Sheridan. New York: W. W. Norton, 1977. Lacan's own selection from his "writings"—really transcriptions of his lectures and seminars. An important collection of seminal works.

Leader, Darian, and Judy Groves. *Introducing Lacan.* New York: Toten Books, 1996. A concise, clearly written, and entertaining introduction to Lacan's most important concepts. Written by Leader, a practicing Lacanian analyst, for the general reader and wittily illustrated by Groves.

Muller, John P., and William J. Richardson. *Lacan and Language: A Reader's Guide to "Écrits."* New York: International Universities Press, 1982. One of the earliest and most comprehensive introductions to Lacan's work, coauthored by a practicing analyst and a philosopher with psychoanalytic training.

Gerard O'Sullivan

SEE ALSO: Lacan, Jacques; Language; Linguistics; Oedipus complex; Psychoanalytic psychology; Psychoanalytic psychology and personality: Sigmund Freud.

Analytical psychology
Carl G. Jung

TYPE OF PSYCHOLOGY: Personality
FIELDS OF STUDY: Psychodynamic and neoanalytic models

Analytical psychology is one of the most complex theories of personality. It attempts to improve on Sigmund Freud's work by deemphasizing sexual instincts and the abnormal side of human nature. Three of its more significant contributions are the notions of psychological types, the concept of the collective unconscious, and the depiction of the unconscious self as the most critical structure within the psyche.

KEY CONCEPTS
- anima and animus
- archetypes
- collective unconscious
- conscious ego
- persona
- personal unconscious
- self
- shadow

INTRODUCTION

Carl Gustav Jung (1875-1961) founded analytical psychology, perhaps the most complex major theory of personality. It includes the presentation and analysis of concepts and principles based on numerous disciplines within the arts and sciences. Because this complexity is combined with Jung's often awkward writing, the task of mastering his theory is a challenge even for experts in the field of personality. His key contribution was taking the study of psychology beyond the claims made by Sigmund Freud (1856-1939). Jung's emphasis on adult development and personality types and his willingness to break with strict Freudian teachings were major contributions within the history of psychology in general and personality in particular.

Jung's theory can best be understood by examining the key structures he proposes and the dynamics of personality. Jung divides the personality, or psyche, into three levels: At the conscious level, there is the conscious ego. The conscious ego lies at the center of consciousness. In essence, it is the conscious mind—one's identity from a conscious perspective. It is particularly important to the person whose unconscious self is not yet fully developed. As the unconscious self begins to develop, the importance of the conscious ego will diminish.

Beneath the conscious ego is the personal unconscious. This level involves material that has been removed from the consciousness of the person. This information may leave consciousness through forgetting or repression. Because the personal unconscious is close to the surface which is consciousness, items in it may be recalled at a later date. The personal unconscious is similar to Freud's notion of the preconscious. Material within the personal unconscious is grouped into clusters called complexes. Each complex contains a person's thoughts, feelings, perceptions, and memories concerning particular concepts. For example, the mother complex contains all personal and ancestral experiences with the concept of mother. These experiences can be both good and bad.

The deepest level of the psyche is called the collective unconscious. This level contains the memory traces that have been passed down to all humankind as a function of evolutionary development. It includes tendencies to behave in specific ways, such as living in groups or using spoken language. While each individual has his or her own personal unconscious, all people share the same collective unconscious. The key structures within the collective unconscious that determine how people behave and respond to their environment are labeled archetypes. Each archetype enables people to express their unique status as human beings.

ARCHETYPES

Archetypes are divided into major and minor archetypes. The major archetypes include the persona, animus, anima, shadow, and self. The persona is one's public personality, which one displays in order to be accepted by society. One's goal is to balance the needs of the persona with the desire to express one's true self. In contrast to the persona, the shadow represents the dark side of the psyche. It includes thoughts and feelings which the person typically does not express because they are not social. These cognitions can be held back on either a conscious or an unconscious level. The anima represents the feminine aspects of males, while the animus represents the masculine aspects of females. These archetypes have come about as a function of centuries of interactions between males and females. They have the potential to improve communication and understanding between males and fe-

Carl G. Jung, the founder of analytical psychology. (Library of Congress)

males. Finally, the most important psychic structure in Jung's theory is the self. It is the archetype which provides the whole psyche with a sense of unity and stability. The major goal of each person's life is to optimize the development of the self.

PSYCHIC STRUCTURES AND PERSONALITIES

In an effort to optimize the development of the self, each person develops his or her own psychological type. Each type (Jung conceived of eight types) consists of a combination of a person's basic attitude and basic function. Jung's two attitudes are extroversion and introversion. These terms follow societal stereotypes, with the extrovert being outgoing and confident and the introvert being hesitant and reflective. These attitudes are combined with four basic functions, or ways of relating to the world. These functions are thinking, feeling, sensing, and intuiting, which are consistent with a general societal view of these terms. Jung used the possible combination of the attitudes and functions to form the eight possible psychological types. Each person is thought to have dominance within one of the available types.

In addition to providing key psychic structures, Jung provides personality dynamics. He claimed that each person is endowed with psychic or libidinal energy. Unlike Freud, however, Jung did not view this energy as strictly sexual. Rather, he perceived it as life-process energy encompassing all aspects of the psyche. According to Jung, this energy operates according to two principles of energy flow: equivalence and entropy. The principle of equivalence states that an increase in energy within one aspect of the psyche must be accompanied by a decrease in another area. For example, if psychic energy is increasing in the unconscious self, it must decrease elsewhere, such as in the conscious ego. The principle of entropy states that when psychic energy is unbalanced, it will seek a state of equilibrium. For example, it would not be desirable to have the majority of one's psychic energy located in the conscious ego. The energy needs of the other levels of consciousness must also be met.

Jung's psychic structures, along with his views on the dynamics of personality, have provided psychologists with a wealth of information to consider, many complexities to address, and numerous possible ways to apply his ideas to human development and personality assessment.

REALIZATION OF SELF

Carl Jung made significant contributions to knowledge of areas such as human development and personality assessment. In terms of human development, Jung emphasized that personality development occurs throughout the life of the person. This was critical in that Freud's theory, the dominant theory at that time, emphasized the first five years of life in examining personality development. The overall goal of the person in Jung's approach to development is the realization of the self, which is a long and difficult process. Unlike Freud, Jung was particularly interested in development during the adulthood years. He emphasized the changes that occur beginning at the age of thirty-five or forty. He believed that this was often a time of crisis in the life of the person. This notion of a midlife crisis (which Jung experienced himself) has continued to be the source of significant theoretical and empirical claims.

Jung believed that the concept of a crisis during middle age was necessary and beneficial. Often, a person has achieved a certain level of material success and needs to find new meaning in life. This meaning can be realized by shifting from the material and physical concerns of youth to a more spiritual and philosophical view of life. The person seeks gradually to abandon the emphasis on the conscious ego which is dominant in youth. A greater balance between the unconscious and conscious is pursued. If this is successfully achieved, the person can reach a state of positive psychological health that Jung labels individuation. Perhaps the key to the midlife years in Jung's theory is that these are the years in which the person is attempting to discover the true meaning of life. Finally, Jung stated that religion can play an important role in life during the midlife and old-age years. During the midlife years, a sense of spirituality rather than materialism is important in personality development; looking at the possibility of life after death can be positive for the older adult.

ASSESSMENT TECHNIQUES

Jung made use of several interesting assessment techniques in addressing the problems of his patients. Like Freud, Jung was an advocate of the case-study method. He believed that much could be learned through an in-depth analysis of the problems of his patients. In his cases, Jung made extensive use of dream analysis. Jung maintained that dreams serve many purposes. They can be used to address and resolve current conflicts or to facilitate the development of the self. Dreams can therefore be oriented toward the future. While Freud focused his analysis on individual dreams, Jung would examine a group of dreams in order to uncover the problems of the patient. This examination of multiple dreams was viewed by Jung as a superior approach to gaining access to the deeper meanings of dreams, which could often be found in the collective unconscious.

Another important assessment device used by Jung which continues to have applications today is the word-association test. In this test, a person responds to a stimulus word with whatever comes to mind. Jung originally worked with a group of one hundred stimulus words and would focus on issues such as the response word given by the patient, the length of time it took the patient to respond, the provision of multiple responses, the repetition of the stimulus word, and the absence of a response. These and other factors could be used to establish the existence of an underlying neurosis as well as specific conflicts and complexes.

SPLIT WITH FREUD

The development of Carl Jung's analytical psychology can be traced to the development of his relationship with Sigmund Freud and the subsequent split that occurred between the two theorists. In 1906, Jung published a book which concerned the psychoanalytic treatment of schizophrenia. He sent a copy of this book to Freud, who was thoroughly impressed by Jung's work. Jung became one of the strongest Freudian advocates from 1907 to 1912. During this time he collaborated with Freud and was viewed by many within psychoanalytic circles as the heir apparent to Freud. Jung had in fact been elected president of the prestigious International Psychoanalytic Association. In 1913 and 1914, however, he abandoned Freud and his psychoanalytic theory. Three basic problems led to this split. The first was Freud's emphasis on sexuality. Jung believed that while sexual instincts did exist, they should not be emphasized at the expense of other relevant aspects of the psyche. Second, Jung believed that Freud overemphasized abnormality. He maintained that Freud appeared to have little to say about the normal aspects of human nature. Finally,

unlike Freud, Jung wished to emphasize the biology of the species rather than the biology of the individual.

The split between Freud and Jung was important for practical as well as theoretical reasons. Jung was rejected for a period of time by other analytically oriented thinkers because of his split with Freud. In addition, the break with Freud led Jung to experience a mental crisis which lasted for several years. This combination of factors eventually led Jung to conclude that he must develop his own view of the psyche, along with appropriate treatment techniques.

While the challenges encountered by Jung in his life were difficult to overcome, they clearly played a major role in his ability to develop the most complex theory of personality ever formulated. His key concepts and psychic structures, including the collective unconscious, personal unconscious, archetypes, self, and personality typology, continue to be among the most interesting theoretical contributions in the history of personality psychology.

SOURCES FOR FURTHER STUDY

Brome, Vincent. *Jung: Man and Myth*. New York: Atheneum, 1981. This is a sound biography of Jung and discussion of his work. Perhaps its main advantage is that it provides an analysis which is fair to both Jung and his critics.

Hannah, Barbara. *Jung: His Life and Work*. New York: Putnam, 1976. This positive biographical view of Jung is provided by a Jungian analyst who was a friend and colleague of Jung for three decades. While it may not be as objectively written as other accounts, it has the advantage of being written by a scholar who had firsthand knowledge of many of Jung's ideas.

Jung, Carl Gustav. *Memories, Dreams, Reflections*. New York: Pantheon Books, 1963. Jung's autobiography. It thoroughly portrays the evolution of Jung's thinking, including all those factors that were critical to his theoretical conceptions. Essential reading for anyone interested in gaining further insights into Jung and his work. It should be remembered, however, that Jung's writing is often difficult to follow.

_____. *Psychological Types*. Translated by Richard and Clara Winston. New York: Harcourt Brace, 1923. Provides both an overview of the basic principles of Jung's theory and an analysis of the derivation of the attitudes and functions that yield his psychological types. Particularly important to those who are interested in the derivation of Jung's view of typology.

McGuire, William, ed. *The Freud/Jung Letters*. Princeton, N.J.: Princeton University Press, 1974. Provides a unique analysis of the development of the relationship between Freud and Jung. Accurately portrays the promise of unity and collaboration within the relationship in its early years, beginning around 1907, and exposes the problems that eventually led to the Freud/Jung split, which was complete by 1914. Provides a context for examining the remainder of Jung's work and the personal problems that he was to encounter following his split with Freud.

Noll, Richard. *The Jung Cult: Origins of a Charismatic Movement*. New York: Free Press, 1997. Noll suggests that Jung's theories comprise not so much a psychology as a religious cult, based in nineteenth century occultism, neopaganism, and social Darwinism. Highly controversial.

Shamdasani, Sonu. *Cult Fictions: C. G. Jung and the Founding of Analytical Psychology*. New York: Routledge, 1998. A rebuttal to Noll's deconstruction of the "Jung Cult." Presents an accurate history of the foundation of analytical psychology both during and after Jung's life.

Lawrence A. Fehr

SEE ALSO: Abnormality: Psychological models; Analytical psychotherapy; Archetypes and the collective unconscious; Dreams; Midlife crises; Personality theory; Psychoanalytic psychology.

Analytical psychotherapy

TYPE OF PSYCHOLOGY: Psychotherapy
FIELDS OF STUDY: Psychodynamic therapies

Analytical psychotherapy is associated with the theory and techniques of Carl Gustav Jung. Similar to other psychodynamic therapies, it stresses the importance of discovering unconscious material. Unique to this approach is the emphasis on reconciling opposite personality traits that are hidden in the personal and collective unconsciouses.

KEY CONCEPTS
- collective unconscious
- compensatory function
- confession
- education
- elucidation
- method of active imagination
- method of amplification
- personal unconscious
- transference
- transformation

INTRODUCTION

Analytical psychotherapy is an approach to psychological treatment pioneered by Carl Gustav Jung (1875-1961), a Swiss psychoanalyst. A follower of Sigmund Freud (1856-1939), Jung was trained in the psychoanalytic approach, with its emphasis on the dark, inaccessible material contained in the unconscious mind. Freud was fond of Jung and believed that he was to be the heir to the legacy he had begun. Jung began to disagree with certain aspects of Freud's theory, however, and he and Freud parted ways bitterly in 1914.

Jung's concept of the structure of personality, on which he based his ideas of psychotherapy, was obviously influenced by Freud and the psychoanalytic tradition, but he added his own personal and mystical touches to its concepts. Jung believed that the personality consists of the ego, which is one's conscious mind. It contains the thoughts, feelings, and perceptions of which one is normally aware. Jung also proposed a personal unconscious that contains events and emotions of which people remain unaware because of their anxiety-provoking nature. Memories of traumatic childhood events and conflicts may reside in the personal unconscious. Jung's unique contribution to personality theory is the idea of a collective unconscious. This consists of memories and emotions that are shared by all humanity. Jung believed that certain events and feelings are universal and exert a similar effect on all individuals. An example would be his universal symbol of a shadow, or the evil, primitive nature that resides within everyone. Jung believed that although people are aware of the workings of the conscious ego, it is the unavailable material contained in the personal unconscious and collective unconscious that has the greatest influence on one's behavior.

Jung's analytical psychotherapy was a pioneering approach during the very early era of psychological treatment. He conformed to the beliefs of other psychodynamic therapists, such as Freud and Alfred Adler (1870-1937), in the importance of discovering unconscious material. The psychoanalysts would be followed by the behavioral school's emphasis on environmental events and the cognitive school's focus on thoughts and perceptions. Psychoanalysis brought a prominence to psychology it had not known previously.

PERSONALITY AND THE UNCONSCIOUS MIND

Jung believed that emotional problems originate from a one-sided development of personality. He believed that this is a natural process and that people must constantly seek a balance of their traits. An example might be a person who becomes overly logical and rational in her behavior and decision making while ignoring her emotional and spontaneous side. Jung believed this one-sided development eventually would lead to emotional difficulty and that one must access the complementary personality forces that reside in the unconscious. Even psychotherapists must be aware that along with their desire to help others, they have complementary darker desires that are destructive to others. Jung believed that emotional problems are a signal that one is becoming unbalanced in one's personality and that this should motivate one to develop more neutral traits.

The process of analytical psychotherapy, as in most psychodynamic approaches, is to make the patient conscious or aware of the material in his or her unconscious mind. Jung believed that if the conscious mind were overly logical and rational, the unconscious mind, to balance it, would be filled with equally illogical and emotional material. To access this material, Jung advocated a free and equal exchange of ideas and information between the analyst and the patient. Jung did not focus on specific techniques as did Freud, but he did believe that the unconscious material would become evident in the context of a strong, trusting therapeutic relationship. Although the patient and analyst have equal status, the analyst serves as a model of an individual who has faced her or his unconscious demons.

STAGES OF ANALYTIC PSYCHOTHERAPY

Analytic psychotherapy proceeds in four stages. The first stage is that of confession. Jung believed that it is necessary for the patient to tell of his or her conflicts and that this is usually accompanied by an emotional release. Jung did not believe that confession is sufficient to provide a cure for one's ills, however, nor did he believe (unlike Freud) that an intellectual understanding of one's difficulties is adequate. The patient must find a more neutral ground in terms of personality functioning, and this can only be accomplished by facing one's unconscious material.

The second stage of psychotherapy is called elucidation, and it involves becoming aware of one's unconscious transferences. Transference is a process in which a patient transfers emotions about someone else in his or her life onto the therapist; the patient will behave toward the therapist as he or she would toward that other person. It is similar to meeting someone who reminds one of a past relationship; for no apparent reason, one might begin to act toward the new person the same way one did to the previous person. Jung believed that these transferences to the analyst give a clue about unconscious material. A gentle, passive patient might evidence hostile transferences to the therapist, thus giving evidence of considerable rage that is being contained in the unconscious.

The third stage of analytic psychotherapy consists of education. The patient is instructed about the dangers of unequal personality development and is supported in his or her attempts to change. The overly logical business executive may be encouraged to go on a spontaneous vacation with his family with few plans and no fixed destinations. The shy student may be cajoled into joining a debate on emotional campus issues. Jung believed in the value of experiencing the messages of one's unconscious.

The final stage of psychotherapy, and one that is not always necessary, is that of transformation. This goes beyond the superficial encouragements of the previous stages and attempts to get the patient to delve deeply into the unconscious and thereby understand who he or she is. This process of understanding and reconciling one's opposites takes considerable courage and exploration into one's personal and cultural past. It is a quest for one's identity and purpose in life that requires diligent work between the analyst and patient; the result is superior wisdom and a transcendent calm when coping with life's struggles.

ANALYTIC TECHNIQUES

Jung developed several techniques aimed at uncovering material hidden in the unconscious. Like Freud, Jung believed that the content of dreams is indicative of unconscious attitudes. He believed that dreams have a compensatory function; that is, they are reflections of the side of personality that is not displayed during one's conscious, everyday state. The sophisticated librarian may have dreams of being an exotic dancer, according to Jung, as a way of expressing the ignored aspects of personality.

Jung gives an example of the compensatory aspects of dreams when describing the recollections of a dutiful son. The son dreamed that he and his father were leaving home and his father was driving a new automobile. The father began to drive in an erratic fashion. He swerved the car all over the road until he finally succeeded in crashing the car and damaging it very badly. The son was frightened, then became angry and chastised his father for his behavior. Rather than respond, however, his father began to laugh until it became apparent that he was very intoxicated, a condition the son had not previously noticed. Jung interpreted the dream in the context of the son's relationship with his father. The son overly idealized the father while refusing to recognize apparent faults. The dream represented the son's latent anger at his father and his attempt to reduce him in status. Jung indicated to the young man that the dream was a cue from his unconscious that he should evaluate his relationship with his father with a more balanced outlook.

AMPLIFICATION METHOD

Jung employed the method of amplification for interpreting dreams. This technique involved focusing repeatedly on the contents of the dream and giving multiple associations to them. Jung believed that the dream often is basically what it appears to be. This differs dramatically from Freudian interpretation, which requires the patient to associate dream elements with childhood conflicts.

The amplification method can be applied to a dream reported by a graduate student in clinical psychology. While preparing to defend his dissertation, the final and most anxiety-provoking aspect of receiving the doctorate, the student had a dream about his oral defense. Before presenting the project to his dissertation committee that was to evaluate its worth (and seemingly his own), the student dreamed that he was in the bathroom gathering his resources. He noticed he was wearing a three-piece brown suit; however, none of the pieces matched. They were different shades of brown. Fortunately, the pieces were reversible, so the student attempted to change them so they would all be the same shade. After repeated attempts he was unable to get all three pieces of the suit to be the same shade of brown. He finally gave up in despair and did not appear for his defense. With a little knowledge about the student, an analytical therapist would have an easy time with the meaning of this dream. This was obviously a stressful time in the young man's life, and the dream reflected his denied anxiety. In addition, the student did not like brown suits; one that does not match is even more hideous. It is apparent that he was unhappy and, despite his best attempts to portray confidence, the budding clinician was afraid that he was going to "look stupid." Jung would have encouraged him to face these fears of failure that were hidden in his unconscious.

ACTIVE IMAGINATION

A final application of analytical psychotherapy stems from Jung's method of active imagination. Jung believed that unconscious messages could come not only from dreams but also from one's artistic productions. He encouraged his patients to produce spontaneous, artistic material. Some patients sketched, while others painted, wrote poetry, or sang songs. He was interested in the symbols that were given during these periods, and he asked his clients to comment on them. Jung believed that considerable material in the unconscious could be discovered during these encounters. He also talked with his patients about the universal meanings of these symbols (as in his idea of the collective unconscious), and they would attempt to relate this material to the their own cultural pasts.

Many modern therapies, such as art, music, and dance therapy, draw heavily from this idea that one can become aware of unconscious and emotional material through association involving one's artistic productions. These therapists believe, as did Jung, that patients are less defensive during these times of spontaneous work and, therefore, are more likely to discover unconscious material.

CONTRIBUTIONS TO PSYCHOLOGY

Analytical psychotherapy is not considered a mainstream approach to psychotherapy, but it does have a small group of devoted followers. Some of Jung's techniques have been adapted into other, more common approaches. Many therapists agree with Jung's deemphasis on specific techniques in favor of a focus on the establishment of a supportive therapy relationship. Jung moved away from the stereotypical analyst's couch in favor of face-to-face communication between doctor and patient. Many psychotherapists endorse Jung's belief that the analyst and patient should have relatively equal status and input. Jung also reduced the frequency of meeting with his patients from daily (as Freud recommended) to weekly, which is the norm today.

Jung's analytical approach changed the focus of psychotherapy from symptom relief to self-discovery. He was interested not only in patients with major problems but also in those who were dissatisfied with their mundane existences. These people were usually bright, articulate, and occupationally successful.

Jung's most lasting contributions probably have been his insights into the polarity of personality traits. The Myers-Briggs Type Indicator, based on Jungian personality descriptions, is one of the most widely used personality tests in business and industry. Jung also believed that personality changes throughout one's life, and he encouraged a continual evaluation of oneself. The idea of a "midlife crisis," a period when one reevaluates personal and occupational goals, is a product of Jung's theory. He believed that individuals continually should strive to achieve a balance in their personality and behavior.

SOURCES FOR FURTHER STUDY

Bishop, Paul, ed. *Jung in Contexts: A Reader.* New York: Routledge, 2000. A collection of essays written between 1980 and 2000 on the evolution and theory of Jungian analytic psychology, placing it in its intellectual, literary, and historical contexts.

Hall, Calvin Springer, Gardner Lindzey, and John Campbell. *Theories of Personality.* 4th ed. New York: John Wiley & Sons, 1997. This is a classic text in personality theory and application, and it gives a detailed description of Jung's theory. Recommended for the serious student of Jung.

Hall, Calvin Springer, and Vernon J. Nordby. *A Primer of Jungian Psychology.* New York: New American Library, 1973. This paperback attempts to provide a comprehensive treatment of Jung's ideas. It is intended for the beginning student of Jung.

Hergenhahn, B. R., and Matthew Olsen. *Personality Theories: An Introduction.* 5th ed. Upper Saddle River, N.J.: Prentice Hall, 1998. Engler's chapter on Jung and his psychotherapy is easy to read and contains a good balance between theory and practical application.

Jung, Carl Gustav. *Man and His Symbols.* 1961. Reprint. New York: Laureleaf Books, 1997. Jung's own summary of his theories on dreams and dream analysis, aimed at a lay reader.

Mathers, Dale. *An Introduction to Meaning and Purpose in Analytical Psychology.* Philadelphia: Taylor & Francis, 2001. A guide aimed at therapists, counselors, and other mental health professionals, explaining the basic premises of analytical psychology.

Samuels, Andrew. *Jung and the Post-Jungians.* New York: Routledge, 1986. A comprehensive overview of both Jung's thought and the developments of his followers.

Stevens, Anthony. *Jung: A Very Short Introduction.* New York: Oxford University Press, 2001. A concise overview of Jung's analytical psychology theories, written by a prominent Jungian.

Brett L. Beck

SEE ALSO: Abnormality: Psychological models; Analytical psychology: Carl G. Jung; Archetypes and the collective unconscious; Dreams; Midlife crises; Psychoanalytic psychology.

Anger

TYPE OF PSYCHOLOGY: Emotion; personality; psychotherapy; stress

FIELDS OF STUDY: Aggression; attitudes and behavior; biology of stress; coping; endocrine system; stress and illness

Anger, a feeling of great displeasure and hostility toward others, has received modern research attention since the 1930's. The emotion is due to mental and physical processes related to perceived attacks on beliefs, values, and expectations, as well as to psychiatric conditions such as paranoia. Anger responds to psychological counseling and medication.

INTRODUCTION

The modern definition of anger is a feeling of great hostility, displeasure, or exasperation toward other persons. The experience of anger is perceived as being beyond any conscious reason, because emotions are reflexive, involuntary experiences rather than purposeful acts. To be angry is not a conscious choice. It happens when an experience changes biological and mental states. Anger is caused by both mental and physical stimuli. Its mental components are thoughts, beliefs, expectations, and values. Anger's physical components are changed biostatus, such as increased heart rate and blood pressure. These stimuli will differ in extent from person to person.

Anger occurs in all people. Psychologically, two things must occur to cause anger: first, a belief that others have committed misdeeds that have wronged the individual, and second, the assignment of blame to others, who are targeted for retribution. Anger is therefore a reaction to the actions of others and a judgment of the cause of those actions. To become angry, one must see an action of another person as intentional mistreatment. Whether this is true or not is irrelevant; the perception of mistreatment causes the anger response. The causes and expressions of anger vary with age and gender. Most frequently, anger is based on feeling unable to right wrongs committed against one; perceived violation of one's principles or values (such as honesty) and physical or verbal attacks on one's self-esteem; and actions preventing the attainment of goals that are perceived to be correct.

A great many situations can cause anger. Some are created by psychological disorders, while others are more normal but may become excessively severe. Anger in the case of psychological disorders includes the anger of paranoids and of some people experiencing depression. The more usual instances of anger include anger at a spouse, anger at an employer, anger at a friend, and anger due to a situation caused by a stranger (such as road rage). Manifestations of anger will range from rage responses to anger suppression. Rage leads to screaming at others, striking them, and destroying property. Suppressed anger can lead to depression. Rage and depression should be treated professionally.

THE BIOLOGY OF ANGER

Biologically, human anger is a response of the nervous system to stresses, demands, threats, and pressures. When one is faced with a threat to survival the nervous system quickly, automatically meets it by raising body defenses in a "fight-or-flight" mechanism (FFM). The FFM, identified by Harvard physiologist Walter Cannon in the 1930's, occurs whether life events require greatly changed lifestyle or are minor irritants. The nervous system does not await a conscious interpretation of an event, but simply reacts via the sympathetic nervous system, well designed for defense responses. The system trigger is the release of the hormone epinephrine (adrenalin), made by the adrenal glands located atop each kidney. Epinephrine causes dilation of the pupils, elevated heartbeat rate, increased blood pressure, rapid breathing, release of sugar into the blood by the liver, and movement of blood into the skeletal muscles.

These responses lead to arousal and readiness to fight or flee. Pupil dilation increases the ability to see danger and differentiate it from "normal" events. Increased heartbeat drives blood through the cardiovascular system more rapidly than usual. This hastens hormone and nutrient passage through the body, engendering swift signaling by hormones and bettering the ability of skeletal muscles for use in a fight or flight. The rerouting of blood and the increased heartbeat result in increased blood pressure which, over the long term, endangers the body. However, infrequently and over a short time period it is not dangerous.

Elevated blood sugar levels and rapid breathing are also related. Elevated blood sugar content, circulating rapidly to all the tissues, provides the energy needed for skeletal muscles to engender FFM responses and better allows the brain to coordinate these actions. The increase in the breathing rate is essential to the use of the energy in the blood sugar, because sugar is converted to energy most effectively through respiration, a process that requires a large amount of oxygen. Respiration results in the production of carbon dioxide, water, and energy—the latter consumed by the FFM.

It is crucial to find ways to handle or defuse anger because over the long term, mismanaged anger can lead to many disease conditions. These include heart disease, ulcers and other gastrointestinal disorders, frequent headaches, and susceptibility to microbial infection. The basis for such problems is the changed levels of hormones, other than epinephrine, caused by the experience of anger. Most often cited are the increased levels of testosterone (in men) and corticosteroids (in both genders). Long-term elevation of these hormones increases occurrence of atherosclerosis (coronary artery disease). Excessive amounts of body corticosteroids (such as cortisol) depress the action of the immune system, damaging the body's first line of defense against infectious diseases.

Problems related to epinephrine and its close relative norepinephrine are related to the FFM's ability to elevate heartbeat rates, blood pressure, release of liver sugar into the blood, and enhanced blood entry into skeletal muscle. When mismanaged or untreated anger causes these responses to occur too often, the liver is unable to remove blood cholesterol; this adds to the buildup of fat deposits in the heart and blood vessels (atherosclerosis). Elevated blood pressure results in a heart that overworks itself, becoming larger and less efficient.

DIAGNOSING ANGER

Almost everyone is angry at times, regardless of gender or age. Some individuals are subject to such frequent rage that they seek—or are sent to—a physician or psychotherapist for treatment. However, many individuals do not recognize their anger and blame reactions caused by it on job dissatisfaction, unsatisfactory marriages, dislike of minorities, and other life problems. Often, such anger will remain unnoticed until they visit a counselor or psychotherapist for help in such matters and it is suggested that they need to treat their anger with psychotherapy or medication.

There are many schools of thought on diagnosing and treating anger. Although the tools used for treatment differ, diagnosing, measuring, and evaluating anger are most often accomplished by administering assessment forms crucial to devising treatment. Diagnosis of severe anger is often occasioned when an enraged or depressed patient is admitted to a hospital emergency room or psychiatric ward and queries by physicians lead to psychiatric evaluation. More often, an angry individual seeks counseling for reasons ranging from marital or work-re-

lated problems to tiredness and general mental malaise. Psychotherapeutic consultation will then lead to diagnosis of anger. Some patients visit psychotherapists or counselors because they themselves recognize that they are angry too often, or excessively belligerent.

ANGER TREATMENT OPTIONS

In many cases, anger associated with depression, extreme rage and belligerence, and the passive-aggressive state may be treated with tranquilizers, hormones, and antidepressants. In such individuals, medication is often followed by combined psychotherapy and medication as an inpatient in a hospital ward. More often, it is accomplished by means of medication and periodic outpatient visits to a psychotherapist or counselor.

There are many different schools of thought concerning anger treatment for people who are not overly belligerent, severely depressed, or in other states in which they will severely harm themselves or other persons. Some therapists suggest that patients let out their anger, proposing that this will make them feel better and minimize aggressive tendencies. Others recommend leaving the site of an anger outbreak until calming down. Still others suggest psychotherapy that identifies the basis for the anger (such as events in childhood) and gives curative insights. Other psychotherapists, such as Albert Ellis and R. Chip Tafrate, propose techniques such as rational emotive behavior therapy and similar methods that can often be applied by self-treatment. Regrettably, there is no treatment consensus. This is likely to be due to the many and varied causes of anger.

THE HISTORY OF ANGER TREATMENT

Human anger has been reported since the beginning of written record keeping. For example, the emotion was discussed by the Greek physician Hippocrates (c. 460-c. 377 B.C.E.) and practitioners through the Middle Ages used herbs and bleeding to handle the emotion by bringing down the patient's blood pressure and "choler." Up until the twentieth century, members of the poorer classes who were encumbered with extremes of rage and other anger manifestations such as paranoia were chained in mad houses. In the twentieth century, development of modern psychoactive drugs and psychotherapy engendered treatment of afflicted individuals as described in the American Psychiatric Association's *Diagnostic and Statistical Manual of Mental Disorders* (DSM).

Walter Cannon's work in the 1930's on the FFM was essential to the conceptualization of appropriate treatment for anger. Hans Selye, in the 1970's and 1980's, proposed that Cannon's FFM was part of a general adaptation syndrome (GAS) used to handle all stresses a person encountered, from head colds to unexpected violence and anger. GAS was proposed to be nonspecific in humans, so the same basic reactions were deemed to occur due to good or bad news and regardless of the emotion currently being felt, whether fear, excitement, pleasure, or anger. The difference in the result, according to Selye, was not in the biology of the emotion but in the mindset that accompanied it.

From the late twentieth century on, treatment of uncontrollable physical anger against one's spouse, acquaintances, and others has been treated by combination of tranquilizers, hormones, antidepressants, psychotherapy, and hospitalization, when needed. Much of the treatment of milder anger is treated by psychotherapeutic methods conceptualized and used by psychiatrists and psychologists who often term themselves angerologists.

SOURCES FOR FURTHER STUDY

American Psychiatric Association. *Diagnostic and Statistical Manual of Mental Disorders: DSM-IV-TR.* Rev. 4th ed. Washington, D.C.: Author, 1994. This compendium gives useful insights into diagnosis and treatment of anger related to numerous psychiatric disorders

Cannon, Walter B. "The Stresses and Strains of Homeostasis." *The American Journal of the Medical Sciences* 189 (1935): 1-14. The article in which the fight-or-flight mechanism was first described and named.

Ellis, Albert, and Raymond C Tafrate. *How to Control Your Anger Before It Controls You.* New York: William Morrow, 1995. Covers topics related to the diagnosis and treatment of anger, such as the costs of anger; anger's rational and irrational aspects; rage-creating beliefs; and ways to feel or think oneself out of anger. Also presents a rational emotive behavior therapy for anger management treatment.

Gentry, W. Doyle. *Anger-Free: Ten Basic Steps to Managing Your Anger.* New York: William Morrow, 1999. Defines the toxic anger syndrome, how to assess it and how to treat it in ten steps. Includes discussion of self-assessment, psychobiological perspectives on angry dispositions, and how to "fix things up."

Kassinove, Howard, ed. *Anger Disorders: Definition, Diagnosis, and Treatment.* Washington, D.C.: Taylor & Francis, 1995. Essays by specialists in the field explore diagnosis of anger disorders, control of anger, anger and criminality, and treatments for children, adults, and adolescents.

Robbins, Paul R. *Anger, Aggression, and Violence.* Jefferson, N.C.: McFarland, 2000. The book probes anger, aggression, and violence from biological, sociological, and psychological approaches. Included are aspects of diagnosis, results of control and lack of control, and treatment of these related psychosocial phenomena.

Weisinger, Hendrie. *Anger at Work.* New York: William Morrow, 1995. The author discusses issues related to the basis, diagnosis, and treatment of anger at work. He also presents the means for anger management treatment. Informative without being too technical.

Sanford S. Singer

SEE ALSO: Aggression; Aggression: Reduction and control; Conduct disorder; Domestic violence; Emotions; Inhibitory and excitatory impulses; Jealousy; Mood disorders; Stress; Stress: Behavioral and psychological responses; Stress-related diseases; Violence and sexuality in the media; Violence by children and teenagers.

Animal experimentation

TYPE OF PSYCHOLOGY: Psychological methodologies
FIELDS OF STUDY: Experimental methodologies; methodological issues

Psychologists study animals and animal behavior as well as humans; sometimes the goal is to understand the animal itself, and sometimes it is to try to learn more about humans. Since there are many biological and psychological similarities between humans and other animals, the use of animal models can be extremely valuable, although it is sometimes controversial.

INTRODUCTION

Prior to the general acceptance of Charles Darwin's evolutionary theory in the late nineteenth century, animals were considered to be soulless machines with no thoughts or emotions. Humans, on the other hand, were assumed to be qualitatively different from other animals because of their abilities to speak, reason, and exercise free will. This assumption made it unreasonable to try to learn about the mind by studying animals.

After Darwin, however, people began to see that, even though each species is unique, the chain of life is continuous, and there are similarities as well as differences between species. Since animal brains and human brains are made of the same kinds of cells and have similar structures and connections, it was reasoned, the mental processes of animals must be similar to the mental processes of humans. This new insight led to the introduction of animals as psychological research subjects around the year 1900. Since then, animal experimentation has taught much about the brain and the mind, especially in the fields of learning, memory, motivation, and sensation.

Psychologists who study animals can be roughly categorized into three groups. Biopsychologists, or physiological psychologists, study the genetic, neural, and hormonal controls of behavior, for example, eating behavior, sleep, sexual behavior, perception, emotion, memory, and the effects of drugs. Learning theorists study the learned and environmental controls of behavior, for example, stress, stimulus-response patterns, motivation, and the effects of reward and punishment. Ethologists and sociobiologists concentrate on animal behavior in nature, for example, predator-prey interactions, mating and parenting, migration, communication, aggression, and territoriality.

REASONS FOR USING ANIMAL SUBJECTS

Psychologists study animals for a variety of reasons. Sometimes they study the behavior of a particular animal in order to solve a specific problem. They may study dogs, for example, to learn how best to train them as watchdogs; chickens to learn how to prevent them from fighting one another in hen houses; and wildlife to learn how to regulate populations in parks, refuges, or urban areas. These are all examples of what is called applied research.

Most psychologists, though, are more interested in human behavior but study animals for practical reasons. A developmental psychologist, for example, may study an animal that has a much shorter life span than humans so that each study takes a much shorter time and more studies can be done. Animals may also be studied when an experiment requires strict controls; researchers can control the food, housing, and even social environment of laboratory animals but cannot control such variables in the lives of human subjects. Experimenters can even control the genetics of animals by breeding them in the laboratory; rats and mice have been bred for so many generations that researchers can special order from hundreds of strains and breeds and can even obtain animals that are as genetically identical as identical twins.

Another reason psychologists sometimes study animals is that there are fewer ethical considerations as compared to research with human subjects. Physiological psychologists and neuropsychologists, in particular, may utilize invasive procedures (such as brain surgery or hormone manipulation) that would be unethical to perform on humans. Without animal experimentation, these scientists would have to do all their research on human victims of accident or disease, a situation which would reduce the number of research subjects dramatically as well as raise additional ethical considerations.

A number of factors make animal research applicable for the study of human psychology. The first factor is homology. Animals that are closely related to humans are likely to have similar physiology and behavior because they share the same genetic blueprint. Monkeys and chimpanzees are the animals most closely related to humans and thus are homologically most similar. Monkeys and chimpanzees make the best subjects for psychological studies of

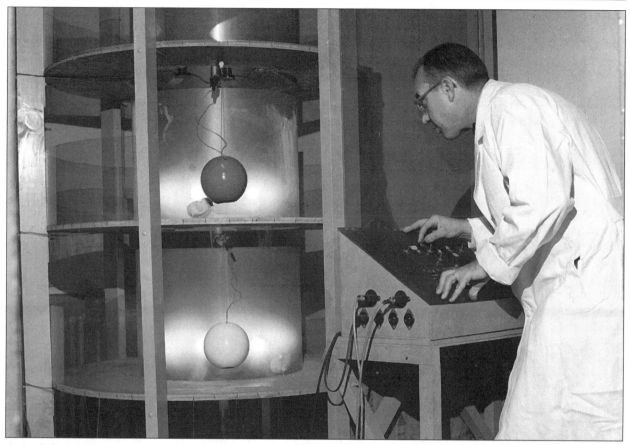

A psychologist observes the reactions of baby animals as he controls the light and sounds in a 1955 experiment. (Hulton Archive)

complex behaviors and emotions, but because they are expensive and difficult to keep, and because there are serious ethical considerations when using them, they are not used when another animal would be equally suitable.

The second factor is analogy. Animals that have a similar lifestyle to humans are likely to have some of the same behaviors. Rats, for example, are social animals, as are humans; cats are not. Rats also show similarity to humans in their eating behavior (which is one reason rats commonly live around human habitation and garbage dumps); thus, they can be a good model for studies of hunger, food preference, and obesity. Rats, however, do not have a similar stress response to that of humans; for studies of exercise and stress, the pig is a better animal to study.

The third factor is situational similarity. Some animals, particularly domesticated animals such as

dogs, cats, domestic rabbits, and some birds, adapt easily to experimental situations such as living in a cage and being handled by humans. Wild animals, even if reared from infancy, may not behave normally in experimental situations. The behavior of a chimpanzee that has been kept alone in a cage, for example, may tell something about the behavior of a human kept in solitary confinement, but it will not necessarily be relevant to understanding the behavior of most people in typical situations.

By far the most common laboratory animal used in psychology is *Rattus norvegicus*, the Norway rat. Originally, the choice of the rat was something of a historical accident. Since the rat has been studied so thoroughly over the past century, it is now often the animal of choice so that comparisons can be made from study to study. Fortunately, the rat shares many analogous features with humans. Other animals frequently used in psychological research include pigeons, mice, hamsters, gerbils, cats, monkeys, and chimpanzees.

SCIENTIFIC VALUE

One of the most important topics for which psychologists use animal experimentation is the study of interactive effects of genes and the environment on the development of the brain and subsequent behavior. These studies can only be done using animals as subjects because they require individuals with a relatively short life span that develop quickly, invasive procedures to measure cell and brain activity, or the manipulation of major social and environmental variables in the life of the subject.

In the 1920's, E. C. Tolman and Robert Tryon began a study of the inheritance of intelligence using rats. They trained rats to run a complex maze and then, over many generations, bred the fastest learners with one another and the slowest learners with one another. From the beginning, offspring of the "bright" rats were substantially faster than offspring of the "dull" rats. After only seven generations, there was no overlap between the two sets, showing that "intelligence" is at least partly genetic and can be bred into or out of animals just as size, coat color, or milk yield can be.

Subsequent work with selectively bred bright versus dull rats, however, found that the bright rats would only outperform the dull rats when tested on the original maze used with their parents and grandparents; if given a different task to measure their intelligence, the bright rats were no brighter than the dull rats. These studies were the first to suggest that intelligence may not be a single attribute that one either has much or little of; there may instead be many kinds of intelligence.

Traditionally, intelligence quotient (IQ) tests measure two kinds of intelligence: one related to verbal skills and one related to spatial skills. Newer theories and tests, however, attempt to address the possibility that there are dozens of different kinds of intelligence. The newer tests may help to identify special talents that may otherwise go unrecognized, undeveloped, and unrewarded in people who are not especially good at tasks measured by the more traditional tests. The new theories of multiple intelligences are also being used in the field of artificial intelligence to develop computer and robotic systems which utilize less sequential processing and more parallel systems or netlike processing, more like the human brain.

BRAIN STUDIES

Another series of experiments that illustrate the role of animal models in the study of brain and behavior is that developed by David Hubel and Torsten Wiesel, who study visual perception (mostly using cats). Hubel and Wiesel were able to study the activity of individual cells in the living brain. By inserting a microelectrode into a brain cell of an immobilized animal and flashing visual stimuli in the animal's visual field, they could record when the cell responded to a stimulus and when it did not.

Over the years, scientists have used this method to map the activities of cells in several layers of the visual cortex, the part of the brain that processes visual information. They have also studied the development of cells and the cell connections, showing how early experience can have a permanent effect on the development of the visual cortex. Subsequent research has demonstrated that the environment has major effects on the development of other areas of the brain as well. The phrase "use it or lose it" has some accuracy when it comes to development and maintenance of brain connections and mental abilities.

HARLOW'S EXPERIMENTS

Perhaps the most famous psychological experiments on animals were those by Harry Harlow in the 1950's. Harlow was studying rhesus monkeys and breeding them in his own laboratory. Initially, he would separate infant monkeys from their mothers. Later, he discovered that, in spite of receiving adequate medical care and nutrition, these infants exhibited severe behavioral symptoms: They would sit in a corner and rock, mutilate themselves, and scream in fright at the approach of an experimenter, a mechanical toy, or another monkey. As adolescents, they were antisocial. As adults, they were psychologically ill-equipped to deal with social interactions: Male monkeys were sexually aggressive, and females appeared to have no emotional attachment to their own babies. Harlow decided to study this phenomenon (labeled "maternal deprivation syndrome") because he thought it might help to explain the stunted growth, low life expectancy, and behavioral symptoms of institutionalized infants which had been documented earlier by René Spitz.

Results of the Harlow experiments profoundly changed the way psychologists think about love, parenting, and mental health. Harlow and his colleagues found that the so-called mothering instinct is not very instinctive at all but rather is learned through social interactions during infancy and adolescence. They also found that an infant's attachment to its mother is based not on its dependency for food but rather on its need for "contact comfort." Babies raised with both a mechanical "mother" that provided milk and a soft, cloth "mother" that gave no milk preferred the cloth mother for clinging and comfort in times of stress.

Through these experiments, psychologists came to learn how important social stimulation is, even for infants, and how profoundly lack of such stimulation can affect mental health development. These findings played an important role in the development of staffing and activity requirements for foundling homes, foster care, day care, and institutions for the aged, disabled, mentally ill, and mentally retarded. They have also influenced social policies which promote parent education and early intervention for children at risk.

LIMITATIONS AND ETHICAL CONCERNS

However, there are drawbacks to using animals as experimental subjects. Most important are the clear biological and psychological differences between humans and nonhuman animals; results one gets in a study using nonhuman animals simply may not apply to humans. In addition, animal subjects cannot communicate directly with the researchers; they are unable to express their feelings, motivations, thoughts, and reasons for their behavior. If a psychologist must use an animal instead of a human subject for ethical or practical reasons, the scientist will want to choose an animal that is similar to humans in the particular behavior being studied. Three factors can create similarity between animal and human behavior; each of these three must be considered.

For the same reasons that animals are useful in studying psychological processes, however, people have questioned the moral justification for such use. Since it is now realized that vertebrate animals can feel physical pain, and that many of them have thoughts and emotions as well, animal experimentation has become politically controversial.

Psychologists generally support the use of animals in research. The American Psychological Association (APA) identifies animal research as an important contributor to psychological knowledge. The majority of individual psychologists would tend

to agree. In 1996, S. Plous surveyed nearly four thousand psychologists and found that fully 80 percent either approved or strongly approved of the use of animals in psychological research. Nearly 70 percent believed that animal research was necessary for progress in the field of psychology. However, support dropped dramatically for invasive procedures involving pain or death. Undergraduate students majoring in psychology produced largely similar findings. Support was less strong among newer psychologists than older, and was also less strong in females than in males.

In addition, some psychologists would like to see animal experimentation in psychology discontinued. An animal rights organization called Psychologists for the Ethical Treatment of Animals (PSYETA), established in 1981, is highly critical of the use of animals as subjects in psychological research, and has strongly advocated improving the well-being of those animals that currently are used through publication of the *Journal of Applied Animal Welfare Science*. PSYETA is also a strong advocate for the developing field of human-animal studies, in which the relationship between humans and animals is explored. Companion animals (pets) can have a significant impact on psychological and physical health, and can be used as a therapeutic tool with, for example, elderly people in nursing homes and emotionally disturbed youth. In this field of study, animals themselves are not the subjects of the experiment; rather it is the relationship between humans and animals that is the topic of interest.

REGULATIONS

In response to such concerns, the U.S. Congress amended the Animal Welfare Act in 1985 so that it would cover laboratory animals as well as pets. (Rats, mice, birds, and farm animals are specifically excluded.) Although these regulations do not state specifically what experimental procedures may or may not be done on laboratory animals, they do set standards for humane housing, feeding, and transportation. Later amendments were added in 1991 in an effort to protect the psychological well-being of nonhuman primates.

In addition, the Animal Welfare Act requires that all research on warm-blooded animals (except those listed above) be approved by a committee before it can be carried out. Each committee (they are called Institutional Animal Care and Use Committees, or

IACUCs) is composed of at least five members and must include an animal researcher; a veterinarian; someone with an area of expertise in a nonresearch area, such as a teacher, lawyer, or member of the clergy; and someone who is unaffiliated with the institution where the experimentation is being done who can speak for the local community. In this way, those scientists who do animal experiments are held accountable for justifying the appropriateness of their use of animals as research subjects.

The APA has its own set of ethical guidelines for psychologists conducting experiments with animals. The APA guidelines are intended for use in addition to all local, state, and federal laws that obtain, including the Animal Welfare Act. In addition to being a bit more explicit in describing experimental procedures that require special justification, the APA guidelines require psychologists to have their experiments reviewed by local IACUCs and do not explicitly exclude any animals. About 95 percent of the animals used in psychology are rodents and birds (typically rats, mice, and pigeons), which are currently not governed by the Animal Welfare Act. It seems likely that federal regulations will change to include these animals at some point in the future, and according to surveys, the majority of psychologists believe that they should be. Finally, psychologists are encouraged to improve the living environments of their animals and consider nonanimal alternatives for their experiments whenever possible.

Alternatives to animal experimentation are becoming more widespread as technology progresses. Computer modeling and bioassays (tests using biological materials such as cell cultures) cannot replace animal experimentation in the field of psychology, however, because computers and cell cultures will never exhibit all the properties of mind that psychologists want to study. At the same time, the use of animals as psychological research subjects will never end the need for study of human subjects. While other animals may age, mate, fight, and learn much as humans do, they will never speak, compose symphonies, or run for office. Animal experimentation will always have an important, though limited, role in psychological research.

SOURCES FOR FURTHER STUDY

American Psychological Association. http://www. apa.org/ethics. Contains links to the Guidelines for Ethical Conduct in the Care and Use of Animals as well as a page describing the use and value of animal subjects in psychology.

Fox, Michael Allen. *The Case for Animal Experimentation.* Berkeley: University of California Press, 1986. Although the author is philosophically in favor of most animal experimentation, he gives a clear and thorough discussion of the entire context of animal experimentation from both sides. Includes sections on animal rights, similarities and differences between human and nonhuman subjects, the role of methodological considerations and replicability in scientific progress, and alternatives to animal testing. The author specifically addresses some of the uglier behavioral studies on animals, including some by Harry Harlow.

Gross, Charles G., and H. Philip Zeigler, eds. *Motivation.* Vol. 2 in *Readings in Physiological Psychology.* New York: Harper & Row, 1969. Although there are dozens of newer collections of articles in the area of physiological psychology, this one does a particularly good job of covering the broad diversity of topics in the field. In addition, all the work represented in this particular collection came from animal studies. This or a similar collection can be consulted for illustration of many specific methodologies utilized in research with animals.

Miller, Neal E. "The Value of Behavioral Research on Animals." *American Psychologist* 40 (April, 1985): 423-440. Good discussion of advances in the behavioral sciences that came from animal studies, including studies on effects of early experience on the brain and behavior, drug effects, eating disorders, and diseases of aging. Also includes some discussion of applied studies which benefit nonhuman species.

National Academy of Sciences and the Institute of Medicine. Committee on the Use of Animals in Research. *Science, Medicine, and Animals.* Washington, D.C.: National Academy Press, 1991. This thirty-page pamphlet answers commonly asked questions about the use of animals in biomedical research. Although not focusing specifically on psychology, it does address research in psychomedical areas such as brain research and drug addiction.

National Research Council. *Guide for the Care and Use of Laboratory Animals.* Washington, D.C.: National Academy Press, 1996. The primary reference on animal care and use for researchers, the Guide covers specific legal regulations regarding institutional responsibilities; animal housing and environment; veterinary care; and facility requirements. Also available online at http://www.nap.edu/readingroom/books/labrats/

Psychologists for the Ethical Treatment of Animals. http://www.psyeta.org. Informative page for this animal rights organization. Provides links to the table of contents of the journals they publish, as well as full text access to some articles.

Linda Mealey;
updated by Linda R. Tennison

SEE ALSO: Behaviorism; Conditioning; Emotions; Ethology; Experimental psychology; Hunger; Imprinting; Instinct theory; Memory: Animal research; Pavlovian conditioning; Reinforcement; Sexual behavior patterns; Skinner, B. F.; Visual system.

Anorexia nervosa and bulimia nervosa

TYPE OF PSYCHOLOGY: Psychopathology
FIELDS OF STUDY: Childhood and adolescent disorders

Anorexia and bulimia nervosa are disorders characterized by a distorted body image, an intense fear of becoming obese, and a desperate attempt to lose weight. These disorders most frequently occur in female adolescents, and they present serious health risks.

KEY CONCEPTS
- behavioral therapy
- binge eating
- cognitive behavior therapy
- distorted body image
- hypothalamus
- neurotransmitters
- psychoanalytic therapy
- purging
- weight phobia

INTRODUCTION
Anorexia nervosa and bulimia nervosa are two of several types of eating disorders—ways of managing food and/or weight that are unhealthy. "Anorexia" literally means a "severe loss of appetite," while "nervosa" means "nervousness." Actually, the word "anorexia" is somewhat of a misnomer, given that most people with anorexia nervosa have not lost their appetites. The syndrome of anorexia nervosa consists of four prominent symptoms, according to the American Psychiatric Association. The first symptom is a failure to maintain a normal weight for one's age and height such that one's weight is less than 85 percent of what is considered normal. The weight of most anorectics (persons with anorexia nervosa) is usually much less than 85 percent of their normal weight. For example, a 1988 review of treatment studies for anorexia nervosa by Christopher Qualls and Jeffrey Berman found that the average anorectic weighed 37 kilograms (82 pounds), 69 percent of normal weight.

The second symptom of anorexia nervosa is an intense fear of gaining weight that increases even as the anorectic continues to lose weight. This second symptom has been labeled weight phobia by some researchers because of the anorectic's anxiety toward food and the desperate attempts she (most documented anorectics have been girls or women) makes to avoid food. The third major symptom of the syndrome is distorted body image. Distorted body image involves the anorectic seeing herself as obese when in reality she is extremely underweight. For example, when an anorectic is asked to view her body in a mirror, she is likely to comment on how fat she looks. The final symptom for premenopausal women with anorexia nervosa is the absence of at least three menstrual cycles, which is caused by their being severely underweight.

Bulimia nervosa refers to the recurring cycle of binge eating, a period of excessive overeating, followed by purging or other compensatory behaviors, engaging in drastic efforts to lose the weight gained by binge eating. For the bulimic, episodes of binge eating may consist of consuming up to 15,000 calories, more than five times the recommended daily number, within a few hours. Purging may be accomplished through several means including vomiting (done either by gagging oneself or through the consumption of certain drugs) or the use of laxatives, diuretics, or enemas; other inappropriate compensatory behaviors include fasting or strict dieting and stringent exercising. In order to meet this first criterion of bulimia, one must engage in the cycle of binge eating and compensatory behaviors at least two times per week for three months.

DSM-IV-TR Criteria for Anorexia Nervosa and Bulimia Nervosa

ANOREXIA NERVOSA (DSM CODE 307.1)

Refusal to maintain body weight at or above a minimally normal weight for age and height

Intense fear of gaining weight or becoming fat, even though underweight

Disturbance in the way in which one's body weight or shape is experienced, undue influence of body weight or shape on self-evaluation, or denial of the seriousness of the current low body weight

In postmenarcheal females, amenorrhea (absence of at least three consecutive menstrual cycles, which occur only following hormone administration)

Types:
- Restricting Type: During the current episode, person has not regularly engaged in binge eating or purging behavior (self-induced vomiting or misuse of laxatives, diuretics, or enemas)
- Binge-Eating/Purging Type: During the current episode, person has regularly engaged in binge eating or purging behavior (self-induced vomiting or misuse of laxatives, diuretics, or enemas)

BULIMIA NERVOSA (DSM CODE 307.51)

Recurrent episodes of binge eating, characterized by both of the following:
- eating, in a discrete period of time, an amount of food definitely larger than most people would eat during a similar period of time and under similar circumstances
- sense of lack of control over eating during episode

Recurrent inappropriate compensatory behavior in order to prevent weight gain:
- self-induced vomiting
- misuse of laxatives, diuretics, enemas, or other medications
- fasting
- excessive exercise

Binge eating and inappropriate compensatory behaviors both occur, on average, at least twice a week for three months

Self-evaluation unduly influenced by body shape and weight

Disturbance does not occur exclusively during episodes of Anorexia Nervosa

Types:
- Purging Type: During the current episode, person has regularly engaged in self-induced vomiting or misuse of laxatives, diuretics, or enemas
- Nonpurging Type: During the current episode, person has used other inappropriate compensatory behaviors, such as fasting or excessive exercise, but has not regularly engaged in self-induced vomiting or misuse of laxatives, diuretics, or enemas

In addition to this cycle, other symptoms of bulimia nervosa include the feeling that one has no control over one's eating binges and constant concern regarding one's body shape or weight. In contrast to anorectics, who are grossly underweight, bulimics may be normal weight or even slightly obese. That is, the bulimic's weight-loss effects are often negated by the weight gained during binge eating.

HEALTH PROBLEMS

Numerous potential health problems may occur as a result of anorexia or bulimia. The health problems of anorectics include an abnormally low body temperature and blood pressure, irregular heart functioning, and bone thinning. Of those diagnosed with anorexia, approximately 4 percent die. The health complications of bulimia include the erosion of tooth enamel; sudden mineral depletions, particularly potassium reduction; irregular heart functioning; and a variety of disorders affecting digestive organs. A significantly lower number of people are thought to die from bulimia as compared to anorexia.

When compared to the most common eating disorder, obesity, anorexia and bulimia are rare. Approximately 30 percent of all Americans are reported to be obese. In contrast to the thirty out of one hundred who are obese, about one out of every one thousand Americans will have anorexia during his or her life. The incidence of anorexia among adolescent females, however, is about ten times higher than in the general population. In comparison, bulimia is estimated to occur in approximately three out of every one hundred Americans. Again, the incidence of bulimia among adolescent females is believed to be significantly higher.

CAUSES AND EXPLANATIONS

The proposed causes of anorexia and bulimia can be grouped into the following four categories: biological, sociocultural, familial, and psychological. The notion of biological causes of anorexia and bulimia involves the idea that anorectics and bulimics have specific brain or biochemical disturbances that lead to their inability to maintain a normal weight and/or eating pattern. The most popular biological explanation for the occurrence of anorexia and bulimia is the existence of an abnormal amount of certain neurotransmitters. Neurotransmitters are chemical messengers within the brain that transmit nerve impulses between nerve cells. Potential abnormal levels of the neurotransmitters norepinephrine and serotonin have received the most investigation as causes of anorexia and bulimia.

In contrast to biological explanations, sociocultural causes are factors that are thought to exist within a society that lead certain individuals to develop anorexia or bulimia. Joan Brumberg, a historian of anorexia, has outlined the sociocultural forces of the late nineteenth and twentieth centuries that many believe promoted the increased incidence of eating disorders among women. These societal forces included an emphasis on weight reduction, aesthetic self-control, and the regarding of women as sexual objects. The most prominent of these suggested cultural factors is the heightened (some would say obsessive) importance placed on being thin.

Some researchers believe that particular family types cause certain of their members to develop anorexia and bulimia. For example, family investigators believe that a family whose members are too emotionally close to one another may lead one or more family members to strive for independence by refusing to eat, according to Salvador Minuchin, Bernice Rosman, and Lester Baker. Other researchers believe that families whose members are controlling and express an excessive amount of hostility toward one another promote the occurrence of bulimia.

Psychological features make up the final category of causes for anorexia and bulimia. The most prominent of the suggested psychological causes for anorexia and bulimia are those expressed by researchers who take psychoanalytic or cognitive behavioral perspectives. For example, cognitive behavioral theorists emphasize the role of distorted beliefs in the development and continuation of anorexia and bulimia. These distorted beliefs include, "I am only attractive when I weigh _____ pounds [a number well below normal weight]," or "If I eat certain types of food [for example, carbohydrate-rich foods], I will become fat."

TREATMENTS

In general, the initial treatment for anorexia occurs within the hospital setting, given the risk of death associated with this disorder. Follow-up therapy for anorexia, as well as the typical treatment for bulimia, takes place on an outpatient basis. Numerous treatments have been used for individuals afflicted by these disorders. These treatments can be broadly grouped into the categories of medical and psychological therapies.

Prior to the 1960's, medical therapies for anorexia included such radical approaches as lobotomies and electroconvulsive therapy (ECT). The performing of a lobotomy involves the surgical removal of prefrontal portions of the brain. Electroconvulsive therapy, commonly known as "shock treatment," involves the introduction of an electrical current into a patient's body through electrodes placed on the patient's head. These treatments were shown to be of no benefit for anorectics. Although a controversial

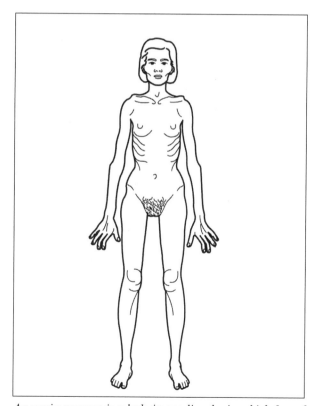

Anorexia nervosa is a body-image disorder in which fear of being fat results in undereating and other behaviors that lead to emaciation and, if unchecked, death. (Hans & Cassidy, Inc.)

treatment, various types of tube feeding continue to be used when a patient's malnutrition from anorexia poses an imminent risk of death. Tube feeding can be accomplished either intravenously or by inserting a tube via a patient's nasal cavity into the patient's stomach.

Since the 1960's, medications are used more often as the medical treatments of choice for anorexia and bulimia. These medications include such categories of drugs as antidepressants and major tranquilizers. For anorexia, these drugs are thought to increase eating behavior and promote weight gain by correcting imbalances in an individual's neurotransmitters. For bulimia, certain medications are thought to reduce carbohydrate cravings that precede the cycle of binge eating and compensation. In addition, antidepressant medication may be prescribed for bulimia because of the depression that often accompanies this cycle.

Different psychological interventions also have been attempted for anorexia and bulimia. These psychological treatments include individual, family, and group interventions. One type of individual therapy for anorexia is behavioral therapy. In behavioral therapy, weight gain is promoted through the use of positive reinforcers for increases in weight and negative consequences for weight decreases or the absence of weight gain. These positive reinforcers include such things as access to telephone and visitation privileges. Negative consequences for remaining the same weight or weight loss include confinement to bed and denial of all unit privileges. Besides behavioral treatment, other types of individual therapy include cognitive behavioral, Gestalt, hypnosis, and psychoanalytic interventions.

Another common treatment for both anorexia and bulimia is family therapy. The family treatment of an anorectic patient involves the therapist seeking to change the interactions among family members that serve to maintain the self-starvation of the patient. In attempting to correct faulty family interactions, the family therapist might address the overprotectiveness of the patient by her parents or the way that family members manipulate one another's behavior. For the bulimic patient, the family therapist would seek to lower the amount of family conflict or to redirect conflict between the parents away from the bulimic.

Another frequently employed method of treatment for bulimia is group therapy. Group treatment initially involves educating bulimics about their disorder, including its negative health consequences. The group experience provides members with the opportunity to share with fellow bulimics regarding their eating problems and to find support from one another in overcoming bulimia. In addition, the therapist or therapists initiate discussions regarding healthy eating and exercise habits as well as specific ways to curb the cycle.

A final issue involved in surveying the different interventions for anorexia and bulimia is the effectiveness of these treatments. The effectiveness of treatments for anorexia was addressed by Christopher Qualls and Jeffrey Berman in a 1988 study that grouped treatments reported in one hundred studies according to their type and then analyzed the effectiveness of each. The results of their study indicated that the average anorectic gains approximately 8 kilograms (18 pounds) during the initial phase of treatment and another 5 kilograms (11 pounds) by the time of a follow-up evaluation about four years later. There were only small differences between the various types of treatment for the amount of weight produced during therapy, although behavioral treatments appeared to work faster. Less research has been conducted investigating the effectiveness of different therapies for bulimia. No one therapy for bulimia, however, whether medical or psychological, has shown clear superiority in its effectiveness as compared to other interventions.

HISTORY OF THE DISORDERS

Anorexia is a disorder that can be traced as far back as seven hundred years ago. The disorder was specifically written about in 1874, when Sir William Gull published an article giving the disorder its present name. Bulimia nervosa, as a disorder separate from anorexia, has received meaningful attention only since the late 1970's. There is evidence to suggest that the incidence of both disorders has increased in the last two decades. As previously discussed, the increased emphasis being placed on thinness within current Western societies represents a likely explanation for the increase in eating disorders such as anorexia and bulimia.

Another area within the study of anorexia and bulimia that has begun to receive attention is the prevention of eating disorders. Catherine Shisslak and colleagues have suggested that preventive efforts should be targeted at adolescent females, given that they are at increased risk for developing an eating disorder. These efforts should focus on issues such as the physical as well as emotional and social changes that occur in maturation. Also, information regarding diet and exercise should be provided, and the connection between emotions and eating should be discussed, as should ways to resist the pressure to conform to peers' and societal expectations for one's appearance. It should also be recognized that there are those who oppose preventive efforts, including segments of the media, fashion, and exercise industries.

With evidence of the increasing prevalence of anorexia and bulimia, it is important to learn more regarding the causes and effective treatment methods of these disorders. In these areas, some of the questions that remain to be definitively answered are: Why do certain groups of people have a greater likelihood of developing anorexia and bulimia (notably, white adolescent females) as compared to other groups? Are the underlying causes of anorexia different from those of bulimia? Can a treatment with superior effectiveness be developed for those suffering with anorexia and bulimia? Anorexia and bulimia nervosa remain elusive syndromes for professionals and patients alike. It is hoped that present and future endeavors will answer these and other remaining questions regarding these disorders.

Sources for Further Study

Boskind-White, Marlene, and William C. White, Jr. *Bulimarexia: The Binge/Purge Cycle.* 2d ed. New York: W. W. Norton, 1991. A comprehensible overview of bulimarexia (more commonly referred to as bulimia). Takes a nonpathologizing, empathetic approach in addressing the problems of individuals with bulimia. Filled with illustrative patient histories.

Bruch, Hilde. *The Golden Cage: The Enigma of Anorexia Nervosa.* Reprint. Cambridge, Mass.: Harvard University Press, 2001. A classic work by a pioneer in the field of eating disorders. Portrays the development of anorexia nervosa as an attempt by a young woman to attain a sense of control and identity. Discusses the etiology and treatment of anorexia from a modified psychoanalytic perspective.

Brumberg, Joan J. *Fasting Girls: The History of Anorexia Nervosa.* Rev. ed. New York: Vintage, 2000. Outlines the history of anorexia nervosa. Examines the syndrome from multiple perspectives while leaning toward a cultural and feminist perspective. A well-researched and very readable work.

Gordon, Richard. *Eating Disorders: Anatomy of a Social Epidemic.* 2d rev. ed. New York: Blackwell, 2000. An up-to-date survey of current clinical practice in dealing with eating disorders, as well as thorough coverage of their history and social context.

Minuchin, Salvador, Bernice L. Rosman, and Lester Baker. *Psychosomatic Families: Anorexia Nervosa in Context.* Cambridge, Mass.: Harvard University Press, 1978. A classic work, still in print, which outlines the development and treatment of anorexia nervosa from a family systems perspective. Includes a description of Salvador Minuchin's famed "family lunch session," in which Minuchin conducts a family assessment and begins treatment of an anorectic patient while eating lunch with the patient and her family.

Sacker, Ira M., and Marc A. Zimmerman. *Dying to Be Thin: Understanding and Defeating Anorexia Nervosa and Bulimia.* Updated ed. New York: Warner Books, 2001. A practical approach, written by two medical doctors, to understanding the sources and causes of eating disorders and how to overcome them. Includes a guide to resources, treatment clinics, and support groups.

R. Christopher Qualls

See also: Abnormality: Psychological models; Cognitive behavior therapy; Eating disorders; Feminist psychotherapy; Hunger; Obesity.

Antisocial personality

Type of psychology: Psychopathology

Fields of study: Aggression; childhood and adolescent disorders; personality disorders; personality theory; prosocial behavior; social perception and cognition

Antisocial personality disorder is characterized by a pattern of behaviors and thinking that shows callous disregard for the welfare of others, conventional systems of rules, and authority figures. Although extensively researched, it is a controversial diagnostic

category because it takes into account criminal behavior. Crime is socially defined, not always prosecuted in a culture-fair manner, and not always a component of antisocial personality disorder.

KEY CONCEPTS
- arousal modification
- conduct disorder
- dyssocial psychopathy
- neurotic psychopathy
- oppositional defiant disorder
- personality disorder
- psychopathic personality
- somatization disorder
- successful psychopathy

INTRODUCTION

By personality disorder, psychologists mean a disorder where an individual's style of dealing with the world, relationship with self, problem solving, and managing emotions is inflexible to situations. As a result, the individual creates a maladaptive pattern of behavior and thinking that produces considerable impairment and distress. In the case of antisocial personality, these traits are thought to be manifested in criminal and otherwise irresponsible behaviors, which create problems for the individual and, more important, for society—hence the term "antisocial."

Individuals of all ages with an antisocial personality often have a childhood history of conduct disorder and/or oppositional defiant disorder. Conduct disorder is a pattern of behavior where both the rights of others and age-appropriate social norms or rules are repeatedly violated. Oppositional defiant disorder is characterized by a pattern of hostile behavior toward authority figures where the child is deliberately defiant, negative, hostile, annoying, and possibly vindictive, beyond what might be expected in children. Noteworthy antisocial behaviors include theft, school truancy, fire setting, vandalism, physical cruelty toward animals and people, financial irresponsibility, repeated lying, reckless driving, sexual promiscuity, and poor parenting. Not surprisingly, a large percentage of incarcerated criminals fulfill the criteria for antisocial personality disorder.

SYMPTOMS AND PREVALENCE

Many of the symptoms of antisocial personality were identified by the sociologist Lee Robins in her influential work *Deviant Children Grown Up* (1966).

Robins found that between 20 and 30 percent of children with conduct disorder develop antisocial personality in adulthood. There is also evidence that a subset of children with hyperactivity (attention-deficit hyperactivity disorder) develop antisocial personality in adulthood. Nevertheless, because many of these same children have conduct disorder, it may be conduct disorder, rather than hyperactivity, that is the major determinant of antisocial personality.

In addition to the behaviors mentioned above, persons with antisocial personality disorder have a number of other psychological and interpersonal difficulties. For example, they have high rates of alcohol and drug abuse, divorce, sexually transmitted diseases, out-of-wedlock pregnancies, and depression. In addition, individuals with this disorder are more likely than those in the general population to die prematurely from violent crimes and accidents. Antisocial personality is also associated with criminal recidivism: Individuals with this disorder who are released from prison are at high risk for subsequent incarceration.

In the United States, about 3 percent of males and 1 percent of females have antisocial personalities. The reason for this sex difference is unknown. Some researchers have speculated that men and women may express antisocial tendencies in different ways. For instance, men may commit crimes more likely to be visible and prosecuted than women. Others have speculated that females who are predisposed to antisocial personality may be likely to develop somatization disorder, a condition characterized by multiple physical complaints lacking any demonstrated medical basis. Indeed, somatization disorder is found among many of the female relatives of antisocial personalities. Thus, somatization disorder may be an alternative manifestation of antisocial personality that is found primarily among females, although considerably more research will be needed to corroborate this hypothesis. Finally, antisocial personality is also associated with low social class, although the causes of this relationship are unknown and controversial. For instance, it may be that individuals in lower social classes are more likely to be prosecuted for criminal behavior than those in upper classes and therefore more likely to get labeled as antisocial.

THE ANTISOCIAL LIFE

What happens to antisocial personalities over time? There is evidence that many such individuals "burn out" in middle age: Their antisocial behaviors decrease in frequency and severity in later adulthood. The reasons for this burnout phenomenon are unclear, but it may be a consequence of the decline in activity level and energy seen in most individuals with age. It is also important to consider that participation in dangerous activities such as crime and risk-taking may cause many individuals with antisocial personality disorder to die at young ages.

Little is known about the treatment of antisocial personality, except that no clearly effective treatment has been found. A number of therapies have been attempted, including psychoanalysis, behavior therapy, group therapy, and medication, but there is little evidence that any of them have been especially successful. As the symptoms of antisocial personality begin early in life and are easily identifiable, it may be prevention, rather than treatment, that holds the greatest promise for reducing the prevalence of this disorder.

Many individuals with antisocial personality disorder possess a constellation of personality traits known as the psychopathic personality. In his classic book *The Mask of Sanity* (1941), psychiatrist Hervey Cleckley provided a detailed description of this syndrome. According to Cleckley, psychopathic personalities (or, as they are sometimes called, psychopaths) tend to be superficially charming individuals who are relatively free of anxiety and seem possessed of excellent reason. Nevertheless, they also tend to be guiltless, callous, dishonest, and self-centered persons who rarely learn from their mistakes or take responsibility for their behavior.

Some psychologists believe that psychopathic personality is a more valid category than antisocial personality. According to these researchers, many antisocial personalities lack the traits characteristic of psychopathic personality, and instead exhibit antisocial behavior for a variety of other reasons. For example, some antisocial personalities may fall into a category known as dyssocial psychopathy, a syndrome in which antisocial behavior results from allegiance to a culturally deviant subgroup. Many gang delinquents or members of organized crime could probably be classified in this group. The behavior of still other antisocial personalities may result from neurotic psychopathy, a syndrome in which antisocial behavior is a consequence of internal psychological conflict and turmoil. Many neurotic psychopaths are probably socially anxious individuals who inhibit their anger for long periods of time and then erupt intermittently but violently.

Conversely, some critics of the antisocial personality diagnosis have argued that many psychopaths do not fulfill the criteria for antisocial personality. Indeed, some psychopaths may function highly in society, and would thus not be detected by the antisocial personality criteria in many cases. Cathy Spatz Widom has found that many persons who possess the traits described by Cleckley can be found outside prisons, and in some cases have socially valued occupations (for example, corporate executive). Further study of these "successful" psychopaths may shed light on factors that allow individuals at risk for antisocial personality to avoid legal and interpersonal problems. As a result, the diagnostic system used to identify this personality disorder has changed in recent years to bring in more of what Cleckley identified as problematic.

RESEARCH INTO CAUSES

One of the most active areas of research on antisocial personality concerns possible causes of the disorder. Psychologist David Lykken, for example, has theorized that the behavior of many antisocial personalities, particularly those who are psychopaths, can be traced to fearlessness.

Lykken has found that, compared with other individuals with antisocial behavior and with "normals," psychopaths tend to exhibit less sweating of the palms prior to a buzzer that has been repeatedly paired with a painful electric shock. Robert Hare has similarly shown that psychopaths tend to show relatively little palmar sweating during the countdown period prior to a painful electric shock or jarring blast of white noise. Because palmar sweating is often indicative of fear or arousal, the findings of Lykken and Hare can be interpreted to mean that psychopaths are not frightened or aroused by signals of impending punishment. This, in turn, might explain why many psychopaths engage in repeated antisocial behavior: The warning signs that would deter most people from performing such acts have little impact upon the psychopath. The average child or adult is prevented from committing antisocial acts largely by signals that punishment or danger is imminent: a parent or teacher saying "No" as a child reaches for a forbidden piece of candy, the watchful eye of a museum guard as one passes by a valuable painting, a light turning yellow as one approaches a busy intersection. If such signals arouse little or no fear in a person, however, his or her threshold for committing antisocial acts will surely be lowered.

Lykken also constructed a "mental maze" task, in which subjects were required to learn a complex series of lever presses. On each trial, some errors were punished with painful shock, whereas others were not. Lykken found that, compared with other subjects, psychopaths did not make more errors overall, indicating that they can learn certain tasks as well as other individuals. Nevertheless, Lykken found that psychopaths made more punished errors than other individuals, suggesting that they have difficulty learning from punishment. Again, this finding is consistent with the fearlessness hypothesis, because the capacity to benefit from punishment is largely dependent upon the capacity to become frightened of this punishment. Moreover, this finding has important implications; the psychopath's failure to learn from punishment in the laboratory may be a useful model for the antisocial personality's recidivism in the real world.

AROUSAL LEVELS

An alternative hypothesis for the behavior of antisocial personalities is that these individuals have unusually low levels of arousal. According to the Yerkes-Dodson law, moderate levels of arousal are optimal for performance and psychological functioning. Thus, as Herbert Quay and other psychologists have argued, many of the thrill-seeking and dangerous behaviors of antisocial personalities may represent attempts to bring their arousal to higher and thus more optimal levels. George Skrzypek has found that psychopathic delinquents, compared with other delinquents, have a greater preference for complex and novel stimuli. This is consistent with Quay's hypothesis, because such stimuli would be expected to increase arousal. Skrzypek also found that after both groups were placed in sensory isolation, psychopaths' preference for complex and novel stimuli increased more compared with nonpsychopaths.

One implication of these findings is that at least some antisocial personalities might benefit from treatments that boost their arousal levels. For example, antisocial personalities could be encouraged to find occupations (for example, combat soldier) or avocations (for example, skydiving) that might pro-

vide outlets for their risk-taking tendencies. Similarly, some researchers have explored the possibility that some antisocial personalities might be helped by stimulant medication. Stanley Schachter and Bibb Latan found that when psychopaths were asked to perform Lykken's mental-maze task while taking adrenaline, a stimulant drug, they were as successful as were nonpsychopaths at learning to avoid punishment. Nevertheless, as these "arousal modification" approaches have not been adequately researched, their potential as treatments for antisocial personality remains speculative.

There is considerable evidence that antisocial personality is influenced by genetic factors. Identical twins (who share all their genes) with antisocial personality are much more likely than are fraternal twins (who share only half their genes on average) to have co-twins with the disorder. Nevertheless, many of the co-twins of identical twins with antisocial personality do not have the disorder, which indicates that environmental factors play an important role in the development of antisocial personality. In addition, adopted children whose natural parents had antisocial personality are more likely to develop the disorder than are adopted children whose natural parents did not. Again, this is consistent with a genetic influence upon antisocial personality.

Nevertheless, several important questions concerning the genetics of antisocial personality remain. First, it is not known what factors are being genetically transmitted. Second, it is not known whether this genetic influence applies to all, or only some, individuals with antisocial personality. For example, this genetic influence might only play a role in individuals with psychopathic personality. Third, it is not known how environmental factors combine or interact with genetic factors to produce antisocial personality. These three questions are likely to occupy researchers for a number of years to come.

CHANGING LABELS

Although the term "antisocial personality" did not enjoy widespread currency until the latter half of the twentieth century, individuals with chronic antisocial symptoms have been described by a variety of labels over the years. In 1809, Philippe Pinel discussed a syndrome called *manie sans délire:* mania without delusion. Such individuals, according to Pinel, are driven by strong instinctual forces but maintain good contact with reality. In 1835, James

Pritchard coined the term "moral insanity" to refer to a condition characterized by severe deficits in ethical behavior.

In 1891, German psychiatrist August Koch referred to a group of conditions called "psychopathic inferiorities." In doing so, Koch broadened the concept of the disorder to include a diverse spectrum of abnormalities, not all of which were characterized by moral depravity. Koch's tradition was followed by the great German classifier Kurt Schneider, who in 1923 described a wide variety of psychopathic personalities, each of which was considered to be an exaggeration of a normal personality style. Thus, the German conceptualization was generally more inclusive than that of Morel and Pritchard, and viewed psychopathic personality as a set of conditions that created problems for the individual, society, or both.

It was authors such as Cleckley and Benjamin Karpman who were largely responsible for shaping contemporary notions of psychopathic personality. These authors emphasized personality traits as the key features of the disorder, and they deemphasized antisocial and criminal behaviors. This view was reflected in the second edition of the American Psychiatric Association's *Diagnostic and Statistical Manual of Mental Disorders* (DSM-II) in 1968, which focused upon personality traits such as guiltlessness and selfishness as the primary criteria for the disorder.

This personality-based approach, however, came under attack in the 1970's and 1980's for its subjectivity. After all, what one diagnostician might view as a pathological absence of guilt might be viewed by another as a healthy absence of self-criticism. Thus, in 1980, the third edition of the *Diagnostic and Statistical Manual of Mental Disorders* (DSM-III) introduced "antisocial personality disorder," a new diagnosis in which explicit references to personality traits were all but expunged. Instead, the emphasis in DSM-III (as well as in its 1987 revision, DSM-III-R) was upon easily agreed-upon transgressions against society. The advantage of this new approach was its objectivity: Clinicians could easily agree upon whether an individual had committed a robbery or driven while intoxicated. However, the fourth edition, DSM-IV (1994), and its text revision, DSM-IV-TR (2000), brought psychopathic personality traits back into the list of diagnostic considerations in order to allow for the diagnosis of individuals without extensive criminal behavior, but who were, nonetheless, threats to the well-being of others and likely to be causing themselves unnecessary impairment or distress.

SOURCES FOR FURTHER STUDY

Black, Donald W., and C. Lindon Larson. *Bad Boys, Bad Men: Confronting Antisocial Personality Disorder.* New York: Oxford University Press, 2000. This book is written in easy-to-understand language. It provides a discussion of warning signs of antisocial behavior and biological factors that may be important to consider with the presence of antisocial behavior.

Cleckley, Hervey. *The Mask of Sanity.* St. Louis: C. V. Mosby, 1941. In this classic work, Cleckley delineates the primary features of psychopathic personality in considerable detail, and provides a wealth of case history material that vividly illustrates the symptomatology of this disorder. Although many of Cleckley's speculations concerning the causation of this disorder are somewhat outdated, his clinical descriptions remain unparalleled in their depth and richness.

Hare, Robert D. *Psychopathy: Theory and Research.* New York: John Wiley & Sons, 1970. Perhaps the best overview of early research on the psychopathic personality. Reviews the evidence for a number of models of the causation of this disorder, and describes the research literature clearly, thoughtfully, and critically. An excellent primer for the layperson who wishes to learn more about psychopathic and antisocial personalities.

_____. *Without Conscience.* New York: Guilford, 1999. This book presents the notion that individuals with antisocial personality disorder are a type of predator. Stories of different individuals and their behaviors are described to illustrate this idea.

Hare, Robert D., and Daisy Schalling, eds. *Psychopathic Behaviour: Approaches to Research.* New York: John Wiley & Sons, 1978. Contains perhaps the finest collection of chapters on research issues relevant to psychopathic and antisocial personalities. Coverage of research on biological models is particularly impressive. Chapters on the history of the psychopathic personality concept and on assessment issues are also highly recommended.

Lykken, David T. *The Antisocial Personalities.* Hillsdale, N.J.: Lawrence Erlbaum, 1995. This book describes a range of personality features and types of individuals that may be observed in the category of antisocial personality, highlighting biological issues and key behaviors.

Reid, William H., John Ingram Walker, and Darwin Dorr, eds. *Unmasking the Psychopath: Antisocial Personality and Related Syndromes.* New York: W. W. Norton, 1986. This book provides a developmental perspective an antisocial behavior and links it to similar disorders that may have antisocial features.

Robins, Lee. *Deviant Children Grown Up.* Baltimore: Williams & Wilkins, 1966. Describes Robins's classic study of the long-term outcome of conduct disordered children, and provides a remarkably detailed examination of early risk factors for antisocial personality. Should be required reading for all individuals interested in the development of antisocial and criminal behavior.

Scott O. Lilienfeld;
updated by Nancy A. Piotrowski

SEE ALSO: Addictive personality and behaviors; Alcohol dependence and abuse; Attention-deficit hyperactivity disorder (ADHD); Borderline personality; Conduct disorder; Histrionic personality; Impulse control disorders; Juvenile delinquency; Narcissistic personality; Substance use disorders.

Anxiety disorders

TYPE OF PSYCHOLOGY: Psychopathology
FIELDS OF STUDY: Anxiety disorders; behavioral and cognitive models; psychodynamic and neoanalytic models

Anxiety is a central concept in many different schools of psychology, and there are many widely varying theories concerning it; theories of anxiety often have spawned approaches to treating anxiety disorders.

KEY CONCEPTS
- ego
- libido
- operant conditioning
- Pavlovian conditioning
- phobia
- preparedness
- repression
- three-systems approach
- two-factor theory
- vicarious transmission

INTRODUCTION

The concept of anxiety is one of the most often-used and loosely defined concepts in psychology. It can be used to describe a temporary state ("You seem anxious today") or an enduring personality trait ("He is an anxious person"). It is used to assign cause ("He stumbled over the words in his speech because he was anxious") and to describe an effect ("Having to give a speech sure makes me anxious"). It is seen as the result of discrete objects or situations such as snakes or heights, or as evolving from basic existential problems such as the trauma of birth or the fear of death. All major theories in psychology in some way confront anxiety.

Because of its preeminence in the field of psychology, there are many different theories about the nature and origin of anxiety disorders. The two most important and influential viewpoints on anxiety are the Freudian and the behavioral viewpoints. Although these theories attempt to explain many anxiety disorders, an examination of how they apply to phobias presents a good indication of how they work. A phobia can be defined as an anxiety disorder involving an intense fear of a particular thing (such as horses) or situation (such as heights).

FREUDIAN APPROACH

Sigmund Freud, who said that understanding anxiety "would be bound to throw a flood of light on our whole mental existence," had two theories of anxiety, an early one, in 1917, and a later one, in 1926. In the early theory, libido (mental energy, often equated with sexual drive) builds up until it is discharged by some pleasurable activity. Sometimes the energy cannot be discharged, for example, when the sexual object is not attainable or is morally unacceptable. This undischarged energy is anxiety, and remains even when its original, unacceptable object is repressed, or eliminated from conscious awareness. This anxiety may attach itself to an otherwise harmless object, resulting in a phobia. This theory is best illustrated in one of Freud's most famous cases, that of "Little Hans," a five-year-old who developed a phobia of horses. Freud believed that Hans had a sexual desire for his mother and wanted his father dead so that he could have his mother to himself. This desire for his mother and hatred of his father were unacceptable impulses, and so were repressed from consciousness, resulting in anxiety. This anxiety attached itself to horses, Freud thought, because the black blinders and muzzle of the horse symbolized his father's glasses and mustache.

In Freud's first theory, repression causes anxiety. In psychoanalytic theory, repression is a defense mechanism that keeps unacceptable thoughts and impulses from becoming conscious. In the later theory, the relationship between them has changed: Anxiety causes repression. In this theory, anxiety acts as a signal to the ego (in Freud's theory, the rational, conscious part of the mind) that a forbidden impulse (such as Little Hans's desire for his mother) is trying to force its way into consciousness. This signal alerts the ego to try to repress the unwanted impulse. If the ego cannot successfully repress the forbidden impulse, it may try to transfer the forbidden impulse to an irrelevant object (horses, in Little Hans's case). This object can arouse all the emotions associated with the forbidden impulse, including the signal anxiety. In this way, it becomes a phobic object.

TWO-FACTOR THEORY

One influential behavioral approach to anxiety is O. Hobart Mowrer's two-factor theory. It uses the principles of Pavlovian learning—in which two stimuli are presented one after the other, and the response to the first changes because of the response automatically elicited by the second stimulus—and operant conditioning—learning in which a behavior increases or decreases depending on whether the behavior is followed by reward or punishment—to explain fear and phobic avoidance, respectively. Fear is acquired through Pavlovian conditioning when a neutral object or situation is paired with something painful or punishing. For example, having an automobile accident can result in a fear of driving. At this point, operant learning principles take over to explain phobic avoidance. In operant learning, any action that leads to a reward is likely to be repeated. The person who is anxious about driving might avoid driv-

---

DSM-IV-TR Criteria for Generalized Anxiety Disorder (DSM code 300.02)

Excessive anxiety and worry (apprehensive expectation), occurring more days than not for at least six months, about a number of events or activities (such as work or school performance)
Person finds it difficult to control worry

Anxiety and worry associated with three or more of the following symptoms, with at least some present more days than not for previous six months (only one item required in children):
- restlessness or feeling keyed up or on edge
- being easily fatigued
- difficulty concentrating or mind going blank
- irritability
- muscle tension
- sleep disturbance (difficulty falling or staying asleep, or restless unsatisfying sleep)

Focus of anxiety and worry not confined to features of Axis I disorder
Anxiety and worry do not occur exclusively during Posttraumatic Stress Disorder
Anxiety, worry, or physical symptoms cause clinically significant distress or impairment in social, occupational, or other important areas of functioning
Disturbance not due to direct physiological effects of a substance or general medical condition and does not occur exclusively during a mood disorder, psychotic disorder, or pervasive developmental disorder

---

ing. Because this avoidance is rewarded by reduced anxiety, the person is more likely to avoid driving in the future. Continued avoidance makes it harder to get back behind the wheel again.

Many problems were found with two-factor theory, and many modifications have been made to it. Two problems will be discussed here to illustrate these changes. First, the theory predicts that people will be likely to fear things that are most often associated with pain. There are very few people in modern society, however, who are phobic of electrical sockets and end tables, even though almost everyone has received a shock from the former and stubbed a toe on the latter. On the other hand, many people are afraid of snakes and spiders, even if they have never been bitten by one. This has been explained through the concept of preparedness: Our evolutionary history has prepared us to learn that some things—such as reptiles, insects, heights, darkness, and closed spaces—are dangerous. These things are "easy" to learn to fear, and they account for a large proportion of phobias. On the other hand, our evolutionary ancestors had no experience with electric sockets or guns, so we are not prepared to become phobic of these objects even though they cause much more pain in modern society than do snakes or spiders.

Two-factor theory states that in order for something to cause fear, it must be paired with a painful or punishing experience. Yet people sometimes become phobic of objects or situations with which they have never had a bad experience. Indeed, many people who have never seen a live snake are afraid of snakes. Thus, there must be other ways in which fear is acquired. One of these is vicarious transmission: Seeing someone act afraid of something can lead to acquiring that fear. For example, whether an infant becomes afraid of being in a high place depends on whether its mother is smiling or has an expression of fear on her face. In an ingenious set of experiments, Susan Mineka and her colleagues showed that vicarious transmission of fear is influenced by preparedness. She showed that rhesus monkeys that watched a videotape of other monkeys acting afraid of a snake became afraid of snakes themselves. Monkeys that watched other monkeys act afraid of rabbits, however, did not become afraid of rabbits because they were not evolutionarily prepared to fear rabbits. Human beings also can acquire fear by being told that something is dangerous. A child can learn to avoid running in front of oncoming cars by being told not to do this by his or her parents; luckily, he or she does not have to be hit by a car or watch someone get hit in order to acquire this information.

TREATING ANXIETY

All theories of anxiety disorders attempt to explain and organize what is known about fear and anxiety. Some of the theories, including the ones described here, also have been applied in developing treatments for anxiety disorders. As might be expected, clinical psychologists with very different ideas about the cause of anxiety will recommend very different treatments to eliminate it.

In the case of Little Hans, Freud thought that his anxiety about horses was caused by repressed sexual impulses toward his mother and hatred of his father. From this, it follows that these repressed impulses would need to be brought out into the open and resolved before his anxiety about horses would diminish. This was the basic goal of the psychoanalytic therapy Freud recommended for Hans.

On the other hand, if Little Hans's parents had taken him to a behaviorally oriented therapist, the therapist would have assumed that the child's fear stemmed from a fright he suffered in the presence of a horse. In fact, Freud stated that the phobia began when Hans saw a horse fall while pulling a bus. Further, the therapist would assume that now Hans was rewarded for avoiding horses by anxiety reduction and by getting extra attention from his parents. Treatment would involve having the boy gradually think about, look at, and even pet horses, and it would include being rewarded for approaching (rather than avoiding) horses.

Presented with these vastly different theories and treatments, the question arises: Which is right? The theoretical issues are still debated, but it is clear that treatments based on a behavioral model of anxiety are much more successful in reducing fear than are treatments based on the theories of Freud or his followers.

COGNITIVE THEORIES

Cognitive theories of anxiety also illustrate how theory is applied to develop a treatment. There are many different cognitive models of anxiety, but all are similar in that they assume that there is a cognitive cause of the fear state. This cognitive step is sometimes called an irrational belief. A cognitive theorist might explain Little Hans's fear in the following way: Hans is afraid of horses because he has some irrational belief that horses are dangerous. The specific belief might be "The horse will bite me" or "The horse might get spooked and run into me" or even "Horses have germs, and if I go near one, I'll catch its germs and get sick." The theory assumes that anxiety will stop when the irrational belief is eliminated. Thus, a cognitive therapist would first carefully question Hans to find out the specific irrational belief causing his fear. Once that is determined, the therapist would use persuasion, logical reasoning, and evidence to try to change the belief. (Little Hans was used here only to continue with the same example. A therapist probably would not try to reason with a five-year-old, and a different treatment would be used. Cognitive therapies are more commonly used with adults.)

PHYSIOLOGICAL THEORIES

Physiological theories of anxiety are increasing in importance. As with behavioral, psychodynamic, and cognitive theories, there are many physiological theories. They differ with respect to the brain areas, pathways, or chemicals implicated in anxiety. It is likely that many physiological theories contain an element of truth. Anxiety is a complex state, involving multiple interacting parts of the nervous system, and it will take much additional research to develop a complete model of the brain's role in anxiety.

One physiological variable that has been integrated into many theories of anxiety is the panic attack. This is a sudden and usually short-lived attack that includes trouble with breathing, heart palpitations, dizziness, sweating, and fear of dying or going crazy. These attacks appear purely physiological in that they seem to come "out of the blue" at first; however, psychological factors determine whether they progress into a full-blown disorder. People can become anxious about having panic attacks, and this added anxiety leads to more attacks, producing panic disorder. Some people become afraid of having an attack in a place where they will be unable to cope or receive help. These people may progressively avoid more and more places. This is known as agoraphobia, which at its worst can result in people who are afraid to leave their homes.

The development of physiological theories also illustrates an important point in the relationship between theory and therapy. Thus far, it has been stressed that theories of anxiety help determine treatment. This relationship also works in reverse: Success or failure of treatments adds information used in theory development. This is most clear in physiological theories. For example, the physiological mechanisms of different types of anxiety-reducing tranquilizers have been investigated to provide clues as to how the brain is involved in anxiety.

IMPACT ON FIELD OF PSYCHOLOGY

Just as most theories in psychology have a view of anxiety, anxiety is an important concept in many areas of psychology. Obviously, anxiety is very important in the fields of psychopathology and psychotherapy. It also has been very important in learning theory; experiments with conditioned fear have advanced knowledge about Pavlovian and operant conditioning. Anxiety is also an important trait in theories of personality, and it figures in theories of motivation. It might be said that anxiety is everywhere in psychology.

Theoretical developments in anxiety have been incorporated into other areas of psychology. For example, in the early 1960's, Peter Lang described fear and anxiety as being composed of three systems—that is, there are three systems in which fear is expressed: verbal (saying "I'm anxious"), behavioral (avoiding or running away from a feared object), and physiological (experiencing an increase in heart rate or sweating). An important point in understanding the three systems of fear is that the systems do not always run along parallel tracks. A person may speak of being anxious about the condition of the world environment without any physiological arousal. Alternatively, a boy's heart might pound at the sight of a snake in the woods, but he reports no fear and does not run away in the presence of his friends. Describing fear in a three-systems framework presents an important challenge to any theory of anxiety. An adequate theory must explain why the three systems sometimes give the same information and sometimes do not. The three-systems approach not only has been very influential in anxiety theory and research, but also has been applied to many other areas of psychology, such as studying emotion, stress, and pain. This approach is an important concept in behavioral formulations of anxiety, stating that anxiety has behavioral, physiological, and verbal components and that they do not necessarily provide the same information.

Another major challenge for theories of anxiety is to begin to integrate different positions. The present theories are not all mutually exclusive. The fact that a behavioral theory of anxiety has some validity does not mean that cognitive approaches are wrong. Also, psychological theories need to be integrated with physiological theories that describe brain activity during anxiety. Although theory and research in anxiety has a long and fruitful history, there is much work to be done, and many important developments lie ahead.

SOURCES FOR FURTHER STUDY

Antony, Martin M., Susan M. Orsillo, and Lizabeth Roemer, eds. *Practitioner's Guide to Empirically Based Measures of Anxiety*. Plenum, 2001. Reviews more than two hundred instruments for measuring adult anxiety. Aimed at mental health professionals.

Barlow, David H. *Anxiety and Its Disorders.* 2d ed. New York: Guilford, 2001. The author, one of the leaders in the field of anxiety research, presents his integrative theory of anxiety. The book also describes assessment and treatment of anxiety and includes a separate chapter on each recognized anxiety disorder. The book's intended audience is graduate students and professionals in psychology, but it is very well written and worth the effort for anyone interested in an up-to-date and comprehensive presentation of anxiety disorders.

Freud, Sigmund. "Analysis of a Phobia in a Five-Year-Old Boy." In *The Standard Edition of the Complete Psychological Works of Sigmund Freud,* edited by James Strachey. Vol. 10. London: Hogarth Press, 1955. Originally published in 1909, this is Freud's description of the case of Little Hans, the most famous patient in the history of anxiety disorders. Freud is an excellent writer, and he presents many vivid details in this case history, making it interesting to read. One could also look up Joseph Wolpe and Stanley Rachman's behavioral interpretation of Little Hans's phobia, "Psychoanalytic 'Evidence': A Critique Based on Freud's Little Hans," in *Journal of Nervous and Mental Disease* 131, no. 2 (1960): 135-148.

_____. "Inhibition, Symptoms, and Anxiety." In *The Standard Edition of the Complete Psychological Works of Sigmund Freud,* edited by James Strachey. Vol. 20. London: Hogarth Press, 1959. In this paper, originally published in German in 1926, Freud describes his revised theory of anxiety. The paper covers a wide range of topics (including a redescription of Little Hans) and is not as readable as the initial presentation of the case. It is, however, an interesting illustration of the change in Freud's thinking about anxiety.

Marks, Isaac Meyer. *Living with Fear: Understanding and Coping with Anxiety.* 2d ed. New York: McGraw-Hill, 2001. This is a work written for the general public by Britain's foremost authority on fear and anxiety. It is accessible and provides a good introduction to theory and treatment of anxiety.

Stein, Dan J., and Eric Hollander, eds. *Textbook of Anxiety Disorders.* Washington, D.C.: American Psychiatric Press, 2002. An up-to-date clinical guide to anxiety and its treatment.

Tuma, A. Hussain, and Jack D. Maser, eds. *Anxiety and the Anxiety Disorders.* New York: Lawrence Erlbaum, 1985. This thousand-page book contains forty-three chapters of high quality, with most of the leaders in the field of anxiety represented. Every important theoretical approach to anxiety is covered. There are two hundred pages of references, an author index, and a subject index, making it easy to find information on specific topics.

Scott R. Vrana

SEE ALSO: Abnormality: Psychological models; Agoraphobia and panic disorders; Amnesia and fugue; Aversion, implosion, and systematic desensitization; Conditioning; Multiple personality; Observational learning and modeling therapies; Obsessive-compulsive disorder; Pavlovian conditioning; Phobias; Preparedness.

Aphasias

TYPE OF PSYCHOLOGY: Language
FIELDS OF STUDY: Cognitive processes

Aphasias include a variety of conditions in which a partial or total loss of the ability to understand or produce language-based material occurs; the deficits can be in speech, reading, or writing. Knowledge of aphasias can aid in the localization of brain injuries. An understanding of aphasias is also important because they cause communication problems that require treatment.

KEY CONCEPTS
- cerebral vascular disorders
- equipotentiality
- expressive (Broca's) aphasia
- global or mixed aphasia
- neuropsychology
- paraphasia
- primary progressive aphasia
- receptive (Wernicke's) aphasia

INTRODUCTION

Nearly all definitions of aphasia agree on the following four points: Aphasia refers to a condition in which a person suffers a loss in the ability to understand or produce language-referenced material; the deficits can be in speech, reading, and/or writing;

the impairment is assumed to be caused by cerebral rather than peripheral impairments; and aphasias represent a devastation of a previously manifested ability rather than a developmental failure.

A fifth point, included or implied in most descriptions of aphasias, is that they occur as a result of structural damage or disease processes that directly affect the brain—an organic etiology. This view is taken because functional mental disorders, such as major depression, that produce aphasic-like symptoms are best understood in the context of the psychological and environmental events that produce them. Aphasias, however, are best comprehended in relationship to the physical injuries and structural changes that cause their appearance. Furthermore, interventions that would be effective for the treatment of aphasias would have little or no relevance for the amelioration of aphasic-like symptoms that result from functional causes.

Vascular disorders, particularly strokes, are the most frequent cause of aphasia. Other conditions likely to lead to aphasia include traumatic head injuries, brain tumors, infections, toxins, and dementia.

It is left-hemisphere damage that is most commonly associated with aphasia. For most persons, language abilities are localized in the left hemisphere of the brain. Damage to the right side of the brain seldom results in any noticeable effect on language skills. The fact that left-handers sometimes show speech impairments following injury to the right side of the brain has often been taken as evidence that left-handers are right-brain dominant in regard to language. Research has failed to support this contention. Most left-handers show bilateral or left-hemisphere dominance for language, with no more than 15 percent showing primary control of speech via the right hemisphere.

Anyone can acquire aphasia, but most people who have this disorder are in their middle to late years. Men and women are equally affected; there are no apparent ethnic differences in the prevalence of aphasia. In 1999, nearly one million people in the United States were diagnosed with aphasia. The National Aphasia Association estimates that approximately eighty thousand Americans acquire aphasia each year.

MAJOR FORMS

Aphasias can be divided into three general categories: expressive aphasias, receptive aphasias, and mixed or global aphasias. Most persons with aphasia show a mixture of expressive and receptive symptoms.

Expressive aphasia is often referred to as Broca's aphasia, motor aphasia, nonfluent aphasia, executive aphasia, or verbal aphasia. Expressive aphasia can be considered to subsume subfluent aphasia, anarthric aphasia, expressive dysprosody, kinetic (efferent) motor aphasia, speech apraxia, subcortical motor aphasia (pure word-dumbness), transcortical motor aphasia (dynamic aphasia), conduction (central) aphasia, anomic (amnestic or nominal) aphasia, and agraphia, or the inability to write.

Expressive aphasia describes a condition in which language comprehension remains intact but speech, and quite often the ability to write, is impaired. People who suffer from expressive aphasia understand what is being asked of them, and their ability to read is unaffected; they have difficulty, however, communicating their understanding.

Verbal fluency, the capacity to produce uninterrupted phrases and sentences, is typically adversely affected in expressive aphasias. As a result of word-finding difficulties, speech may take on a halting and labored character. For example, a person with Broca's aphasia may say "Walk dog," meaning, "I will take the dog for a walk." The same sentence could also mean "You take the dog for a walk," or "The dog walked out of the yard," depending on the circumstances. When expressive aphasia is extreme, the affected person may be totally unable to speak (aphonia) or may be able to speak only in so distorted a way that he or she becomes incomprehensible. Still, as is the case with all other forms of aphasia, singing and swearing are generally preserved.

Paraphasias are a common form of expressive aphasia. Paraphasia differs from articulation problems, which are also quite prominent. When a person with expressive aphasia has difficulties with articulation, he or she has trouble making recognizable speech sounds. Paraphasia, on the other hand, refers to a condition in which articulation is intact but unintended syllables, words, or phrases are inserted. For example, one patient, in referring to his wife, always said "my dog."

Telegraphic speech, in which speech is reduced to its most elemental aspects, is frequently encountered in expressive aphasia. In telegraphic speech, the meaning is often clear; however, communications are reduced to the bare minimum and consist of simple noun-verb phrases.

Receptive aphasia is often referred to as Wernicke's aphasia, sensory aphasia, fluent aphasia, or agnosia. Receptive aphasia can be considered to subsume semantic aphasia, jargon aphasia, visual aphasia (pure word-blindness), transcortical sensory aphasia (isolation syndrome), syntactical aphasia, and alexia. In receptive aphasia, speech is generally fluent, with few, if any, articulatory problems; however, deficits in language comprehension are always present.

While fluent, the speech of a person with receptive aphasia is seldom normal. People who have receptive aphasia may insert nonwords, or neologisms, into their communications, and in severe cases their communications may contain nothing but jargon speech. For example, one patient, when asked what he had for breakfast, responded, "Eating and food. Got no more heavy come to there. No come good, very good, in morning."

Unlike people who have expressive aphasia, who generally show great distress in regard to their disorder, people who have receptive aphasia may appear oblivious to their disorder. They may produce lengthy nonsensical utterances and then look at the listener as if confused by the listener's lack of comprehension.

Global aphasia describes a condition in which there is a mixture of receptive and expressive deficits. Global aphasia is typically associated with less focalized brain injury. Although comprehension is generally less impaired than production in global aphasia, this disorder does not fit neatly into either the expressive or the receptive category. The prognosis is generally much poorer for persons with global aphasia than for those with purely receptive or expressive deficits.

DIAGNOSING

Determining the nature and extent of an aphasia in affected individuals facilitates the identification of disease processes that may be affecting cerebral functioning, assists in the localization of brain injuries, and provides information that should be considered in making post-discharge placements. In addition, and perhaps most important, a thorough understanding of the nature and extent of symptoms in individual cases is needed because aphasias cause significant communication deficits that require treatment.

There are a variety of conditions that can lead to aphasic-like symptoms: functional mental disorders, peripheral nervous system damage, peripheral motor impairments, congenital disorders, degenerative disease processes of the brain, cerebral vascular injury, central nervous system toxins, epilepsy, migraine, brain tumors, central nervous system infections, and cerebral trauma. Being able to discriminate between true aphasias (those caused by cerebral complications) and aphasic-like symptoms brought on by other causes can enable the selection of the most effective treatment and improve prognostic prediction. For example, depression, Parkinson's disease, and certain focal lesions can cause persons to appear emotionally unreactive (flat affect) and speak in a manner that lacks expres-

Primary Progressive Aphasia

The syndrome of primary progressive aphasia (PPA) was first defined in 1982 by M.-M. Mesulam and colleagues as a progressive disorder of language, with preservation of other mental functions and of activities of daily living, for at least two years. Most people with PPA maintain ability to take care of themselves, pursue hobbies and, in some instances, remain employed. The problem is a disorder of isolated language loss; signs and symptoms of other clinical syndromes are not found through tests routinely used to determine the presence of other conditions. PPA is not Alzheimer's disease.

Although PPA may take a number of forms, it commonly appears initially as a disorder of speaking (an articulatory problem), progressing to nearly total inability to speak in its most severe stage, while comprehension remains relatively preserved. A less common variety begins with impaired word finding and progressive deterioration of naming and comprehension, with relatively preserved articulation.

People with PPA will continue to lose their ability to speak, read, write, and/or understand what they hear. They may benefit, however, during the course of their illness by acquiring new communication strategies from speech-language pathologists. Some have also learned new communication strategies through participation in aphasia community groups.

Allyson Washburn

sive intensity and intonation (dysprosody). The treatments of choice for these disorders are substantially different, and some interventions that would be recommended for one disorder would be contraindicated for another. Similarly, knowing that cerebral hemorrhage is most often associated with global aphasia and diffuse tissue damage, whereas cerebral embolisms typically damage areas served by the left middle cerebral artery, resulting in more specific aphasias, has implications in regard to patient monitoring, treatment, and prognosis.

The interrelationships between aphasias and localized brain injuries have important ramifications. Among other implications, knowing the neural basis for language production and processing can facilitate the identification of the best candidate sites for surgical intervention and can provide clues regarding whether a disease process has been arrested or continues to spread. For example, an aphasia that begins with clear articulation and no identifiable deficits in language production would be consistent with conduction aphasia, and it might be assumed that damage to the arcuate fasciculus had occurred. If, over the course of time, the person began to manifest increasing difficulty with speech comprehension but articulation continued to appear intact, it could be inferred that damage was spreading downward and affecting a broader region of the temporal lobe. Such information would have important treatment and prognostic ramifications.

Given the importance of language and the ability to communicate in managing daily affairs, it can be seen that having information concerning the nature and the extent of aphasia is an important consideration that must be taken into account when making post-discharge plans. On the one hand, if the person's deficits are purely expressive in nature, it can be assumed that he or she will more likely be able to manage his or her daily affairs and will be more capable of managing independent placement. On the other hand, persons with receptive aphasia, despite wishes to the contrary, may have to be referred to a more restrictive environment. Not being able to understand the communications of others and perhaps manifesting deficits in safety and judgment require that the person with receptive aphasia be carefully assessed to ascertain the degree to which he or she is competent to manage his or her affairs.

TREATING APHASIAS

Aphasias cause significant communication problems that require treatment and amelioration. While there is no doubt that considerable spontaneous recovery takes place in regard to aphasia, research shows that treatment can have a facilitating effect. Furthermore, the earlier treatment is initiated, the more profound its effects.

Under most circumstances, therapy for aphasia is one element of a more comprehensive treatment process. Aphasia seldom occurs in isolation, and, depending on the type of damage, one is likely to see paresis, memory deficits, apraxias, agnosias, and various difficulties related to information processing occurring in conjunction with the aphasia. As a result, the person with aphasia is likely to be treated by an interdisciplinary team. The team will typically consist of one or more physicians, nurses, nursing support personnel, physical therapists, occupational therapists, speech therapists, a rehabilitation psychologist or neuropsychologist, a clinical psychologist, and one or more social workers. Each team member is expected to have an area of expertise and specialization, but the team approach requires that team members work together and, individually and collectively, support each discipline's treatment goals.

Common treatments for the aphasic person are systematic stimulation, behavioral teaching programs, deblocking, and compensation therapy. Systematic stimulation involves the use of everyday objects and everyday situations to stimulate language production and to facilitate language comprehension. Behavioral teaching programs are similar to systematic stimulation but are more organized, are designed more precisely to take into account known structural damage, and frequently employ behavior modification techniques. Deblocking, a less frequently used therapy, consists of stimulating intact language functions as a vehicle for encouraging rehabilitation of damaged processes. Compensation therapy includes teaching the person alternative communication strategies and utilizing intact abilities to circumvent the functional limitations that result from her or his aphasia.

The use of computers in aphasia treatment is being studied. One approach incorporates natural-language-understanding software, which enables a computer to understand spoken utterances. Another approach uses a "processing prosthesis" that allows aphasic persons to construct computer-generated spoken sentences piecemeal and store sentences already produced. Researchers exploring computer-based methods believe that these new methods will play complementary roles with existing aphasia therapies such as systematic stimulation.

The possibility of using medication to prevent or reduce the severity of aphasia following a stroke is being explored. Strategies include administration of drugs to restore compromised levels of neurotransmitters, to minimize the extent of cell loss in the brain, or to restore blood flow to regions of the brain that have become ischemic following stroke. The most promising approach appears to be one that combines several drugs to counteract the cognitive impairments that produce aphasia.

STUDYING OF APHASIAS

The study of aphasias dates back more than four thousand years. An Egyptian papyrus dated between 3000 and 2500 B.C.E. provides a case example of language deficits following traumatic head injury.

The Greeks variously subscribed to hypotheses that mental processes were located in the brain or the heart. Not until the time of the physician Galen (129 C.E. to 199 C.E.) did the brain hypothesis gain full sway. Galen based his arguments on dissection and clinical experience—he spent five years as a physician to the gladiators of the Roman circus, where he was exposed to multiple cases of traumatic head injury.

Over the next thirteen hundred years, little progress was made in relation to an appreciation of cerebral anatomy or physiology. With the anatomical observations of Andreas Vesalius (1514-1564) and the philosophical speculations of René Descartes (1596-1650), however, the stage was set for a new understanding of cerebral functioning.

In the early nineteenth century, phrenology, which postulated that specific areas of the brain controlled particular intellectual and psychological processes, became influential. Although it was subsequently discredited, phrenology provided the foundation for the localizationist position in neuropsychology.

Paul Broca (1824-1880) can be credited with raising the study of cerebral localization of speech to a scientific level. Broca's first case study was "Tan," a patient with apparently intact receptive abilities whose expressive skills had been reduced to utter-ing the word "tan" and a few colorful oaths. According to Broca, "Tan" was shown in an autopsy to have a lesion of the left anterior lobe of his brain, which caused his speech problems. Subsequently, the syndrome he described became known as Broca's aphasia. Furthermore, the posterior third of the left third frontal convolution of the left hemisphere of the brain became known as Broca's area.

Carl Wernicke (1848-1905) was the next person to make major contributions to the understanding of cerebral organization and language functioning. Wernicke proposed a sequential processing model that held that several areas of the brain affected language development, production, and expression. Following his work, the left first temporal gyrus was named Wernicke's area, and the particular type of receptive aphasia that resulted from damage to this area became known as Wernicke's aphasia.

Over the ensuing years, arguments raged regarding whether the localizationist position was tenable. As a general rule, researchers supporting equipotentiality (sensory input may be localized, but perception involves the whole brain) held sway. By the 1950's, interactionist theory had gained the ascendancy. Interactionist theory holds that basic functions are localized; however, there is redundancy in regard to function. Therefore, damage to a specific area of the brain may or may not cause a deficit in higher-order behaviors, since the damaged functions may be assumed by redundant or parallel backup components.

Recent years have seen notable advances in the understanding and treatment of aphasias. Psychometric instruments founded on modern principles of test construction have become available. Experimental techniques that take into account known aspects of cerebral functioning have been developed. Furthermore, advances in brain imaging have done much to aid in understanding cortical function and the effects of injury as they relate to the development of aphasias. These procedures include PET (positron emission tomography), CT (computed tomography), and MRI (magnetic resonance imaging). Functional magnetic imaging (fMRI), identifies areas in the brain that are used during activities such as speaking. This imaging technique may enable the field to address previously unanswerable questions, including the role of the right hemisphere in recovery from aphasia, how individual differences in brain organization for language contribute to recovery from aphasia, and how rehabilitation from aphasia alters brain organization for language.

SOURCES FOR FURTHER STUDY

Benson, D. Frank, and Alfredo Ardila. *Aphasia: A Clinical Perspective*. New York: Oxford University Press, 1996. This book presents an integrated analysis of the different aspects of the language disturbances associated with brain pathology. The authors cover the historical background of the aphasias, as well as recovery, management, and rehabilitation.

Broida, Helen. *Coping with Stroke: Communication Breakdown of Brain Injured Adults*. San Diego, Calif.: College-Hill Press, 1979. Broida provides a nontechnical introduction to stroke and aphasia. Answers many questions regarding functional deficits, treatment, and prognosis.

Brubaker, Susan Howell. *Sourcebook for Aphasia: A Guide to Family Activities and Community Resources*. Detroit: Wayne State University Press, 1982. Brubaker describes activities that relatives of aphasia patients can use to enhance the recovery process. The absence of an introduction to aphasia and minimal guidance regarding which exercises are appropriate for particular symptom presentations are limiting factors in this text.

Collins, Michael. *Diagnosis and Treatment of Global Aphasia*. San Diego, Calif.: College-Hill Press, 1986. Collins focuses on the practical implications of what is known about global aphasia. The text is somewhat technical, but it is valuable for persons who want to learn more about this disorder.

Ewing, Susan Adair, and Beth Pfalzgraf. *Pathways: Moving Beyond Stroke and Aphasia*. Detroit: Wayne State University Press, 1990. The authors summarize the experiences of six families that attempt to cope with the aftermath of a stroke. Practical and emotional problems that must be confronted by the patient and the family are discussed.

Fitch, James L. *Clinical Applications of Microcomputers in Communication Disorders*. Orlando, Fla.: Academic Press, 1986. Fitch provides an entry-level introduction to the use of computers in audiology and speech pathology. The text lacks an adequate discussion of the use of computers as adaptive devices, but many potential applications are discussed.

Murdoch, B. E. *Acquired Speech and Language Disorders: A Neuroanatomical and Functional Neurological Approach*. London: Chapman and Hall, 1990. Murdoch provides a comprehensive description of the various types of aphasia and dysarthria. Additionally, the author supplies an extended discussion of agnosia and apraxia. Furthermore, the author elucidates how neurological damage and disease processes affect language production and comprehension.

Sarno, Martha Taylor, ed. *Acquired Aphasia*. 2d ed. San Diego, Calif.: Academic Press, 1991. Contributions to this volume tend to be technical, but the book contains valuable information concerning neurological and linguistic factors associated with aphasia. The chapters on intelligence, artistry, and social sequelae are unique offerings.

Taylor, Martha, ed. *Acquired Aphasia*. 3d ed. San Diego, Calif.: Academic Press, 1998. This book provides a thorough update of the latest research and development in the area of acquired aphasia. Coverage includes the symptoms of aphasia, assessment, neuropsychology, the specific linguistic deficits associated with aphasia, related disorders, recovery, and rehabilitation.

Bruce E. Bailey;
updated by Allyson Washburn

SEE ALSO: Alzheimer's disease; Brain injuries; Brain specialization; Dementia; Dyslexia; Language; Neuropsychology; Parkinson's disease; Speech disorders; Speech perception.

Archetypes and the collective unconscious

TYPE OF PSYCHOLOGY: Analytical psychology
FIELDS OF STUDY: Personality theories; psychotherapy

Swiss psychologist Carl Jung, the founder of analytical psychology, proposed the theory of archetypes—universal human images, such as the Mother, Child, Trickster, and Wise Old Man, that reside in the unconscious—and the existence of a collective unconscious whose contents are shared by all human beings.

KEY CONCEPTS
- analytical psychology
- anima and animus
- archetypes
- Child archetype
- collective unconscious
- ego-identity
- individuation
- mandalas
- mother complex
- Mother archetype
- personal unconscious
- rebirth
- Shadow
- transcendent function

INTRODUCTION

Analytical psychology, founded by Swiss psychologist Carl Jung (1875-1961), is based on the idea that the key to psychological adjustment and growth lies in making unconscious material conscious through hypnosis, active imagination (free association and guided imagery), and dream interpretation. For Jung, such psychological maturation is defined as individuation, "the process by which a person becomes a psychological 'individual,' that is, a separate, indivisible unity or 'whole.'" For the developing individual, this involves the emergence of ego from a pre-egoic state of being. Children, for example, develop a growing sense of themselves as separate from their mothers as they move from childhood into adulthood. Erik Erikson, in *Identity and the Life Cycle* (1959), refers to this as the achievement of ego-identity. It represents the "comprehensive gains which the individual, at the end of adolescence, must have derived from all of his preadult experiences in order to be ready for the task of adulthood." According to Jung, however, ego-identity is not a final stage in the individuation process, but simply a step along the way. Full adult maturity implies a movement beyond ego-identity toward awareness of the collective, undivided nature of being and our unity with all things. Achievement of psychological maturity, or individuation, requires an integration of both conscious and unconscious energy.

DREAMS

Jung believed that dreams provide a window into the individual's unconscious, and thus are central to the process of individuation. According to Jung, there are, however, two types of dreams, personal and archetypal dreams, just are there are two types of unconscious, the personal and the collective unconscious. The personal dream arises from the personal unconscious, which consists of repressed personal memories and experiences, including the Shadow (which represents everything that the individual refuses to acknowledge about himself or herself, specifically negative character traits or tendencies).

The archetypal dream, by contrast, arises from the collective unconscious, which is made up of archaic or "primordial types," "universal images that have existed since the remotest times" and that are shared by all. Thus, while the personal unconscious is specific to the individual, and involves a personal inventory of material that may have been forgotten (memories of birth, for example) or repressed from consciousness (child abuse, for example), the collective unconscious represents a vast reservoir of elemental configurations or archetypes that are outside space and time (the Rebirth archetype, for example). The collective unconscious, in other words, is inherited. It is, as Jung explains, identical and present in all individuals and represents "a common psychic substrate of a suprapersonal nature." Jung's support for the existence of the collective unconscious is based, in part, on his assertion that the realm of consciousness does not account for the totality of the psyche, a claim supported through many years of clinical observations of patients' dreams and visions, particularly those of schizophrenics. Thus, achieving individuation through the "therapeutic method of complex psychology," according to Jung, requires rendering conscious the energy of both the personal and collective unconscious, in order to reconcile the conflict between conscious and unconscious content. Jung refers to this union of opposites as the "transcendent function."

ARCHETYPES

Unconscious energy is made manifest through archetypes, the "language" of the collective unconsciousness, or the way in which unconscious material is articulated. Archetypes not only represent unconscious content rendered into consciousness, as prototypes or patterns of instinctual behavior; they also exist outside space and time and thus speak to the universal nature of human experience. The

Mother archetype, for example, is a preexistent form that is above and yet subsumes individual experiences of one's own mother. Archetypes may emerge in picture form (such as the universal mandala symbol, a squared circle)or in mythic narratives (such as a story of rebirth). Whether as pictures or stories, however, archetypes emerge during states of reduced intensity of consciousness, such as daydreams, visions, dreams, or delirium. In these states, according to Jung, "the check put upon unconscious contents by the concentration of the conscious mind ceases, so that the hitherto unconscious material streams, as through from opened sidesluices, into the field of consciousness." They can also emerge during strong emotional states brought on by, for example, intense anger, love, hate, confusion, or pain. Archetypes are spontaneous products of the psyche that seem to have a life of their own; as such, they can be neither permanently suppressed nor ordered to emerge. They are, as Jung says, *in potentia*, waiting to be revealed. Some examples of archetypes include the Child, the Hero, the Old Man, the Mother, and the Trickster.

IMPORTANT FUNCTIONS

Jung claims that it is dangerous to suppress or ignore the collective unconscious, particularly in important matters, because he believes that the individual's fate is predominantly determined by the unconscious. In extreme cases, suppression of the unconscious results in neurosis, a nervous disorder characterized by intense emotional instability. Indeed, Jung claims that "when an individual or social group deviates too far from their instinctual foundations, they then experience the full impact of unconscious forces." It is as if, as Jung explains, the unconscious "were trying to restore the lost balance." Although Jung asserts that archetypes are manifestations of instinctual behavior, such as the child's need to suck or the innate attraction to warmth and light over cold and darkness, he also asserts that they may speak to our spiritual nature, and thus may be manifestations of the divine. He writes of archetypes, for example, that they "are meant to attract, to convince, to fascinate, and to overpower. They are created out of the primal stuff of revelation and reflect the ever-unique experience of divinity." Jung goes so far as to assert that "our concern with the unconscious has become a vital question for us—a question of spiritual being and non being."

Whether divine or instinctual, Jung makes a compelling argument for cultures' need to continually explore the archetypes of the unconsciousness. Indeed, he even claims that the practice of psychology (by which he means analytical psychology) would be "superfluous in an age and a culture that possessed symbols." Cultures, particularly Western cultures, according to Jung, have experienced a "growing impoverishment of symbols." Despite the universal qualities of the unconscious, Jung explains that archetypes must constantly be reborn and reinterpreted for every generation or they will die. Jung, in fact, argues that the primary role of art is to "dream the myth outward," to continually find new interpretations of the archetypes of the collective unconscious in order to live the fully human life.

Archetypes and archetypal stories, then, are continually produced and reproduced in all cultures in all ages. Manifest in dreams and delirium as well as in art (most notably in myths and fairy tales), they articulate human experiences, offer resources for psychological maturation, and provide a guide for living the fully human life. What, then, are some of these archetypes? How have they evolved? To what urgencies do they speak?

THE ANIMA AND MOTHER ARCHETYPES

According to Jung, hidden inside of the unconscious of every man is a "feminine personality"; likewise, hidden in the unconsciousness of every woman is a "masculine personality." Jung labels these the anima and animus, respectively. The anima/animus concept is best illustrated in the Chinese yin/yang symbol, where yang, representing "the light, war, dry, masculine principle" contains within it "the seed of yin (the dark, cold, moist, feminine principle)." Jung supports such an idea with biology, explaining that although a majority of male or female genes determines an individual's sex, the minority of genes belonging to the other sex do not simply disappear once the sex has been determined in the developing fetus. The idea of the anima and animus is also reflected in "syzygies" or dually gendered deities, such as god the father and god the mother, and in god's human counterparts, the "godmother" and "godfather," and in the child's own mother and father. Jung links the anima personality, in particular, with its "historical" archetypes of the sister, wife, mother, and daughter, with particular attention paid to the Mother archetype.

The Mother archetype, or the image of the mother-goddess or Great Mother, is an archetype that spans the world's religions and cultures. In psychological practice, it is often associated with fertility, fruition, a garden, a cave, or a ploughed field. It is connected with birth, the uterus, or any round cavernous place and, by extension, rebirth, or magical transformation and healing. These are positive connotations, but the archetype also has negative ones, as in the witch, the devouring dragon, the grave, deep water, or any suffocating or annihilating energy. Thus the mother archetype represents both the nurturing-protecting mother, as in the Roman Catholic image of the Virgin Mary, and the punishing-devouring mother, as in Medea of classical Greek mythology. Sometimes she represents both the loving and the devouring mother, as in the dual-natured Indian goddess Kali.

In clinical practice, the Mother archetype is manifest in what Jung refers to as the mother-complex, which also has both positive and negatives aspects. For the daughter, the mother-complex can either unduly stimulate or inhibit her feminine instinct. The exaggeration of the feminine instinct, particularly the maternal instinct, is represented in the daughter whose only goal is childbirth, who views her husband primarily as an instrument of procreation, and who is self-defined as "living for others" while unable to make any true or meaningful sacrifices for others. A second manifestation of the mother-complex, according to Jung, is the daughter with an overdeveloped eros, or sexual instinct. In this case, the maternal instinct, potentially wiped out, is instead replaced with an overdeveloped sex drive, often leading to an unconscious incestuous relationship with the father driven by jealousy of the mother. By contrast, a third type of identification with the mother involves a complete paralysis of the daughter's feminine will, such that "everything which reminds her of motherhood, responsibility, personal relationships, and erotic demands arouses feelings of inferiority and compels her to run away—to her mother, naturally, who lives to perfection everything that seems unattainable to her daughter." Finally, the daughter who resists or rejects the mother and everything she represents exemplifies the extreme negative mother complex.

The Mother archetype in a man's psychology is entirely different in character from that of a woman. Jung claims that while the mother-complex exemplifies the daughter's own gendered conscious life, for the son, it typifies the alien, unknown, or yet-to-be-experienced, since it exists only as unconscious imagery. The mother complex for sons, in other words, is connected with the man's sexual counterpart, the anima. Jung's discussion of the mother-complex in sons is some of his most controversial work, primarily because he argues that it produces homosexuality, Don Juanism, or impotence. In the case of homosexuality or impotence, he argues that the man's heterosexuality is unconsciously tied to his mother, and thus is dormant. By contrast, in Don Juanism, which is marked by an overly developed sexual instinct, the "unconscious seeks his mother in every woman he meets." Jung supports the idea of the strong influence of the mother on the son's sexuality by explaining she is the first female with whom the man comes in contact. The man becomes increasingly aware of her femininity and responds to it instinctually or unconsciously.

THE CHILD AND REBIRTH ARCHETYPES

Another significant archetype of the collective unconscious, according to Jung, is the Rebirth archetype. Stories and images of rebirth, or about being twice born, abound in all cultures across time. Underlying all rebirth stories, according to Jung, is "dual descent," the idea of both human and divine parents. For example, just as Jesus Christ is twice born, from his mother Mary and by his baptism by John the Baptist in the river Jordan, he also has a dual descent from a heavenly father and an earthly mother. Rebirth, then, is about acknowledging and experiencing the divine through the corporeal. Jung explains that there are five forms in which the rebirth archetype manifests itself and there are two central ways to experience it. The five forms include reincarnation (the continuity of a personality, accessible to memory, that is successively reborn in various human bodies), metempsychosis (the transmigration of souls into successive bodies, possibly without the continuity of personality or memory, as in karma, or soul debt), resurrection (the reestablishing of human existence after death, usually in a resurrected body rather than a corporeal one), participation in the process of transformation (an indirect rebirth through involvement in a ritual of transformation, such as taking part in the Catholic Mass), and rebirth (rebirth within an individual's life span involving a renewal or transformation of personality). The two central ways of experiencing rebirth are through ritual, as in the aforementioned Catholic Mass, or through immediate experience, as in a divine revelation or a significant insight gained through hypnosis or dream therapy.

The Rebirth archetype may manifest itself in numerous ways, such as the diminution of personality, or "soul loss"; the enlargement of personality, through, for example, a divine revelation; a change in internal structure, a transformation brought about, for example, by possession, whether possession by the persona (the public self), the Shadow (the dark self), the anima or animus (the opposite-sex self), or even the "ancestral soul"; identification with a group, such that the individual identity is subsumed or transformed into that of the group (for example, mob psychology); identification with a cult hero, as in the Christian idea of rebirth and salvation through Jesus Christ; technical transformation, achieved through certain meditative practices such as yoga; and finally natural transformation, whereby the individual undergoes the death of the old personality and the birth of a new or greater personality (individuation). This last manifestation of rebirth, individuation, is the most important from the perspective of analytical psychology.

The Child archetype represents the potential for such a rebirth, since the child, according to Jung, is an individuation archetype. It signifies the preconscious (the childhood aspect of the collective psyche) and the past, while also representing future possibilities. The child, in other words, represents the idea of an "a priori existence of potential wholeness" while also anticipating future developments for the individual and the culture. In Jung's words, it "paves the way for future change of personality," and, in the largest sense, is a "symbol which unites opposites," as a "mediator, a bringer of healing, that is, one who makes whole." Analytical psychology, and the work of Carl Jung, is primarily responsible for drawing attention to this and other archetypes of the collective unconscious and their role in the process of psychological maturity, or individuation.

SOURCES FOR FURTHER STUDY

Jung, Carl. *The Archetypes and the Collective Unconscious.* Translated by R. F. C. Hull. 2d ed. Princeton, N.J.: Princeton University Press, 1981. Collected essays written between 1936 and 1955 discuss such concepts as the collective unconscious, archetypes of the collective unconscious, the psychological process of individuation, the anima and animus, as well as specific archetypes, including the Mother, the Child, the Trickster, the Spirit, mandalas, and archetypes of rebirth.

_____. *The Essential Jung.* Edited by Anthony Storr. Princeton, N.J.: Princeton University Press, 1983. Selected essays by Jung on such topics as his involvement with Sigmund Freud and the ways in which his theories diverge from Freud's, Jung's idea of archetypes and the collective unconscious, the development of the individual, and the concepts of integration, wholeness and the self, and discussion of specific archetypes, including the shadow, the anima and animus, the persona, and the old wise man.

_____. *The Practice of Psychotherapy.* Translated by R. F. C. Hull. 2d ed. Princeton, N.J.: Princeton University Press, 1966. A collection of essays that define psychotherapy, explain its aims, questions, principles, problems, and practice, and relate it to medicine and philosophy.

_____. *The Structure and Dynamics of the Psyche.* Translated by R. F. C. Hull. 2d ed. Princeton, N.J.: Princeton University Press, 1970. A series of collected essays ranging over such topics as the transcendent function, the nature and structure of the psyche, instinct and the unconscious, the nature of dreams and dream psychology, the stages of life, psychological foundation of the belief in spirits, and the soul and death.

_____. *Symbols of Transformation.* Translated by R. F. C. Hull. 2d ed. Princeton, N.J.: Princeton University Press, 1977. Discusses such concepts as the libido and its transformation, the hero myth, the rebirth myth, and symbols of the mother and the sacrifice.

Stevens, Anthony. *Jung: A Very Short Introduction.* New York: Oxford University Press, 2001. A concise introduction to Jung's theories by a respected Jungian analyst and scholar.

Susan Mackey-Kallis

SEE ALSO: Analytical psychology: Carl G. Jung; Dreams; Introverts and extroverts; Jung, Carl G.; Personality theory; Self.

Archival data

TYPE OF PSYCHOLOGY: Psychological methodologies
FIELDS OF STUDY: Descriptive methodologies; experimental methodologies; methodological issues

Archival data, or information already on record, offer several real advantages to resourceful researchers: saving of time, access to very large quantities of information, and avoidance of some ethical issues, to list a few. At the same time, use of such data carries with it several real risks, the worst of which is potential inaccuracy.

KEY CONCEPTS
- archival data
- experimentation
- observation
- reliability
- self-report measures
- validity

INTRODUCTION

A major part of any research enterprise is the gathering of data—the information from which conclusions will be drawn and judgments made. This gathering can be accomplished in many ways, each with its advantages and drawbacks. Often, by using a combination of methods, a skilled researcher can let the strengths of one method compensate for the weaknesses of another. Which method, or combination of methods, is most appropriate depends on several factors. If research is intended to be only descriptive, the scientist may find observation adequate; if the research is intended to establish cause-and-effect relationships clearly, experimentation is all but essential.

The methods mentioned—observation and experimentation—actively involve the scientist in the gathering of data to be used. This involvement allows considerable control over possible sources of error, but it also limits what can be accomplished. For example, a scientist cannot step back into the past, cannot observe (or experiment with) more than a fairly small number of subjects during most research, and cannot avoid the possibility that the subjects' knowledge that they are involved in research will distort the answers most people give or the behaviors they display. When they can be located and used, archival data eliminate many of these problems for descriptive research and may, because they extend across time, give hints of cause-and-effect relationships typically revealed only by experimentation.

The term "archival data" may first suggest only information shelved in public archives such as courthouse records. Indeed, such a location may hold much useful information, but it is only one of dozens of possibilities. Similarly, data may first suggest only collections of numbers; here again, however, many other possibilities exist. For example, almost sixteen hundred years ago, Aurelius Augustinus, better known as Saint Augustine, wrote his autobiography, *Confessions*, well aware that its contents would fascinate his own and later generations. It seems likely that he also realized that he was presenting more than information about himself to his readers. Personal documents may also be used by contemporary researchers in ways unlikely to have been anticipated by their source. Comparing many autobiographies written over the centuries, a developmental psychologist might today examine how earlier generations behaved during the period now known as adolescence. A career counselor might examine how people who changed their original occupations in midlife managed to do so.

In recent years, with worldwide distribution of printed material, films, and electronic media, mass communications have been able to serve well as archival data pertaining to hundreds of topics. One problem, however, may be the presence of so much information that a sampling procedure must be devised to decide what to use. A caution regarding the use of mass media as sources can also apply to personal documents and statistical data, to be discussed below. Researchers who today want to extract data from, for example, United States newspaper reports of 1945 must consider the reliability of what they find. If they plan to use the reports as indicators of national public opinion, they must select several newspapers published across the nation. A single newspaper might serve to suggest what its own editor and readers believed, but dozens might be required to suggest national beliefs, and even dozens might not provide what researchers originally sought. If different papers carried very different accounts of an event, or divergent editorials regarding it, researchers might have to focus on differences, rather than unanimity of belief.

In his *Confessions*, Saint Augustine discussed the possibilities that writers might not know something about themselves or might deceitfully state something they know to be untrue. This validity issue also applies to the electronic media and, like differences of opinion across several newspapers, must be dealt with by consulting several independent sources, if they can be located.

Statistical data—measurements or observations converted to numerical form—can be the most immediately useful, yet possibly the most dangerous, archival data for a researcher to use. Most typically in psychological research, information is converted to numbers, the numbers are processed in some manner, and conclusions are drawn. When researchers gather data themselves, they know where the numbers came from, whether they should be considered approximations or precise indicators, and a host of other facts essential to their interpretation. When researchers process archival data—information gathered by others for their own purposes—such information essential to their interpretation is often unknown and must be sought as part of the research.

For example, a psychologist seeking information about the education levels of employees in a company might find it directly available on application blanks on file. If those blanks recorded the applicants' stated education levels, however, and there was no evidence that those statements had been verified as a condition of hiring, it would be risky to consider them highly accurate data. Most archival data need to be verified in some manner; how fully this is done should depend upon the degree of certainty needed in the research.

USES AND DRAWBACKS

Sociologist Émile Durkheim's use of archival data in his classic work *Le Suicide* (1897; *Suicide*, 1951) illustrates how much a master researcher can learn from already available material. Hypothesizing that social factors are key bases for suicide, he first gathered years of suicide records from European countries where they were available, then examined these statistics in the light of additional archival data to evaluate several alternative hypotheses.

Noting that suicide rates increased from January to June, then fell off, he considered the possibility that suicide is influenced by temperature. Finding, again from records, that suicides did not vary directly with temperature increases and decreases, he was drawn back to his favored hypothesis that social factors were of key importance. To elaborate on such factors, he considered religion, family, and political atmosphere, again through archival data.

The advantages that Durkheim gained over limiting himself to data personally gathered were enormous. For example, had he personally interviewed families and friends of suicide victims, far fewer cases would have been available to him, probably ones restricted to a fairly limited geographic area. He also would have been limited by time factors: It seems unlikely that interviewing years after the event would have been possible for most of the cases. Unavoidably, he ran risks in accepting available records as accurate, but he judiciously chose records likely to have been carefully assembled and unlikely to have contained willful distortions. As the world has changed remarkably since Durkheim's day, so have the opportunities to apply archival data to research questions. Part of the change results from there now being more numerous and more varied archives; additionally, there are almost incredible new methods of searching them.

For Durkheim, information that existed in print or still photographs, or could be told to him from someone's memory, was all that was available. For today's researcher, those possibilities remain, and the addition of new, mainly electronic, media since the beginning of the twentieth century has dramatically changed both the form and the amount of archival data in existence. Silent motion pictures, phonograph records, radio (with transcription discs), sound motion pictures, audio recording wire and then tape, television (with video recording tape), and, most recently and most important, computer storage have increased available information almost immeasurably. They have also created the possibilities for finding obscure fragments of data not before available.

Researchers studying attitudes leading to war, for example, have for centuries been able to work with written sources—documents, books, and newspapers. From the early 1900's on, social psychologists could add to those archival sources newsreel footage of political leaders' participation in war-related events, as well as a few phonograph records of their speeches. From the late 1920's on, they could add transcriptions (disc recordings) of radio broadcasts and sound motion-picture coverage. From the late

1940's on, they could add films, then television broadcasts and videotapes of them.

Beginning in the mid-1980's, a new sort of archive emerged, one that allows enormous amounts of information to be saved, distributed worldwide, and searched electronically for desired information. Computer storage of data has created a change in the handling of information comparable to the change created centuries ago by the invention of the printing press. Pulling information from storage media ranging from magnetic tape to CD-ROM (compact disc read-only memory) storage, to Internet databases, researchers can gain access to libraries of information—from indexes to research literature to archival data—and can sort through it with speed and accuracy never before known.

For example, a researcher with a personal computer and an Internet connection can search the entire works of William Shakespeare, encyclopedias, atlases, *Bartlett's Familiar Quotations*, world almanacs, and more, in a fashion that can be considered a modern version of looking for "a needle in a haystack." The old phrase suggests looking for something that exists but is so hidden that chances of finding it are nil. Computer searching is the equivalent of searching the haystack with a powerful metal detector and electromagnet to pull the needle from the depths of the stack.

Studying attitudes toward old age, for example, a scientist could direct searches for many key words and phrases (old age, elderly, retiree, senile, respected, and so on), some only very remotely related to the topic. The speed and accuracy of digital technology make feasible "needle-in-haystack" searches that were impractical to consider by earlier methods. A world atlas might contain very few age-related references, but with a search at lightning-speed possible, the one or two references to "retirement" might be worth seeking.

ASSESSING RESOURCES

Although scientific psychology has always taught its students how to generate data through their own research, in no way has it denied them the right to use data already available if the data meet their needs. Like other data, archival data must meet reasonable standards of consistency (reliability) and accuracy (validity), standards not always easy to assess when several sources, perhaps over an extended span of time, have generated the data.

Researchers who use other researchers' data probably have the fewest worries. Since the 1920's, published research standards have been uniform enough that today's readers can clearly understand what was done to produce data, and from that understanding can judge their quality. Researchers who work from personal documents have a more difficult task in determining data quality. What the writers stated might be distorted for a variety of reasons, ranging from intentional deception through the writers themselves not understanding what they reported. If the new researcher is working to assess the personality of an author, for example, checking the internal consistency of the document may be a useful, if not definitive, way of evaluating data quality. If the new researcher is studying some historical event, comparing the diary of one observer with those of others could help validate data obtained.

Researchers who work from mass media, which may carry carelessly assembled or intentionally slanted information, or those who work from public records that might, a century or more ago, have ignored minority populations—or even those who work from an online database that contains only works written in the English language—have special problems of data accuracy, and each must devise ways of discovering and working around them.

As compensation for the special problems that archival data present, they possess an advantage that all but eliminates worry about "invasion of privacy," often a major ethical issue. By their very definition, archival data are already public, and rarely does new analysis by researchers produce sensitive conclusions. In the rare case where it does, the researcher can simply decide not to report a particular conclusion, and no one has been hurt. By contrast, in certain experimental research, when subjects reveal something that they prefer had remained unknown (perhaps that they would cheat to succeed at some task), the ethical harm is already done if the subjects realize that the experimenter knows of their failing. Not publishing the results cannot remove their discomfort.

SOURCES FOR FURTHER STUDY

Freud, Sigmund, and William C. Bullitt. *Thomas Woodrow Wilson, Twenty-eighth President of the United States: A Psychological Study.* Boston: Houghton Mifflin, 1967. Written between 1919 and 1932, then revised to the authors' greater satisfaction in 1939, this book was not published until after the death of the late president's wife. To have a "new" book by Freud almost thirty years after his death guaranteed that it would be noticed; not all notice was favorable. As archival research by a major scholar, however, it is unequaled.

Hilgard, Ernest Ropiequet. *Psychology in America: A Historical Survey.* San Diego, Calif.: Harcourt Brace Jovanovich, 1987. Although "archival data" is not found within Hilgard's index, chapter 15, "Developmental Psychology," discusses infant biographies and other archival sources of developmental data, and chapter 16, "Social Psychology," discusses topics for which archival data are often used. This encyclopedic text can serve to place the topic within the many other research methods available to psychologists.

Langer, Walter Charles. *The Mind of Adolf Hitler.* New York: Basic Books, 1972. A fascinating account of a World War II archival research project that attempted to generate a psychiatric profile of the German leader. (Writing "psychohistory," as this approach has come to be called, is a controversial activity, often condemned by psychologists and historians alike.)

Selltiz, Claire, Marie Johoda, Morton Deutsch, and S. Cook. *Research Methods in Social Relations.* New York: Holt, 1959. Still a rich source of information related to research, this book's ninth chapter, "The Use of Available Data as Source Material," offers excellent detail on the use of archival data. Three other chapters describe in detail other research methods, and one chapter discusses problems of data accuracy. The book should be available in most college and university libraries.

Harry A. Tiemann, Jr.

See also: Case-study methodologies; Developmental methodologies; Field experimentation; Observational methods; Scientific methods.

Artificial intelligence

Date: Beginning in 1956

Type of psychology: Biological bases of behavior; cognition; consciousness; intelligence and intelligence testing; language; learning; memory; sensation and perception

Fields of study: Behavioral and cognitive models; biological influences on learning; cognitive learning; cognitive processes; general issues in intelligence; nervous system; problem solving; vision

Artificial intelligence is a conceptual framework for how a system can be implemented to process information and behave in a manner considered intelligent. Artificial intelligence, from the perspective of cognitive psychology, provides a means for developing and testing computer models of human cognitive processes. This approach is useful in terms of theory development and modification.

Key concepts
- artificial life
- case-based reasoning
- Chinese room
- cognitive science
- computer simulation
- connectionism (parallel distributed processing, artificial neural networks)
- expert systems
- intelligent tutoring systems
- physical symbol system hypothesis
- strong AI
- subsumption architecture
- traditional AI (pure AI)
- Turing test
- weak AI

Introduction

Ideas proposed in cybernetics, developments in psychology in terms of studying internal mental processes, and the development of the computer were important precursors for the area of artificial intelligence (AI). Editors William Bechtel and George Graham, in their 1998 book *A Companion to Cognitive Science,* discuss several of the important events that led up to the development of intelligent machines. Cybernetics, a term coined by Norbert Wiener in 1948, is a field of study interested in the issue of feedback for artificial and natural systems. The main idea is that a system could modify its behavior based on feedback generated by the system and/or from the environment. Information, and in particular feedback, is important for a system in order to make intelligent decisions. During the 1940's and 1950's, the dominant school in American psy-

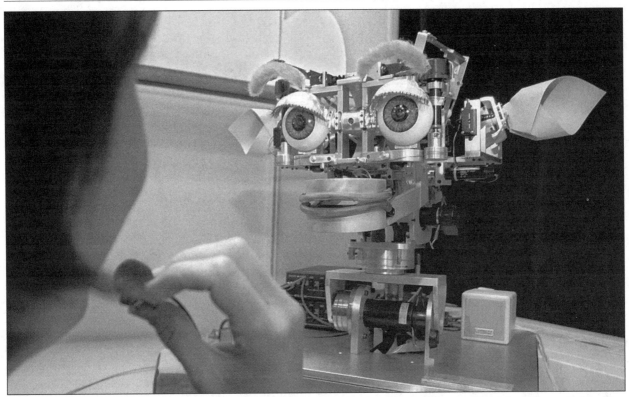

Kismet, an interactive robot, was created at the Massachusetts Institute of Technology's Artificial Intelligence Laboratory. (AP/Wide World Photos)

chology was behaviorism. The focus of research was on topics in which the behaviors were observable and measurable. During this time, researchers such as George Miller were devising experiments that continued to study behavior, but also provided some indication of internal mental processes. This cognitive revolution in America led to research programs interested in issues such as decision making, language development, consciousness, and memory, issues relevant to the development of an intelligent machine. The main tool for implementing AI, the computer, was an important development that came out of World War II.

The culmination of many of these events was a conference held at Dartmouth College in 1956, which explored the idea of developing computer programs that behaved in an intelligent manner. This conference is often viewed as the beginning of the area of artificial intelligence. Some of the researchers involved in the conference included John McCarthy, Marvin Minsky, Allen Newell, and Herbert Simon. Prior to this conference, Newell, Si-

mon, and Shaw's Logic Theorist was the only AI program. Subsequent projects focused on the development of programs in the domain of game playing. Games of strategy, such as checkers and chess, were selected, since they seem to require intelligence. The development of programs capable of "playing" these games supported the idea that AI is possible.

Cognitive science, an interdisciplinary approach to the study of the mind, was influenced by many of the same factors that had an impact of the field of AI. Some of the traditional disciplines that contribute to cognitive science are AI, cognitive psychology, linguistics, neuroscience, and philosophy. Each discipline brings its own set of questions and techniques to the shared goal of understanding intelligence and the mind.

TRADITIONAL AI VERSUS COMPUTER SIMULATIONS

"Artificial intelligence" is a general term that includes a number of different approaches to developing intelligent machines. Two different philosophical approaches to the development of intelligent systems are traditional AI and computer simulations. This term can also refer to the development of hardware (equipment) and/or software (programs) for an AI project. The goal remains the same for traditional AI and computer simulations: the development of a system capable of performing a particular task that, if done by a human, would be considered intelligent.

The goal of traditional AI (sometimes called pure AI) is to develop systems to accomplish various tasks intelligently and efficiently. This approach makes no claims or assumptions about the manner in which humans processes and perform a task, nor does it try to model human cognitive processes. A traditional AI project is unrestricted by the limitations of human information processing. One example of a traditional AI program would be earlier versions of IBM's chess program Deep Blue. The ability of this program to successfully "play" chess depended on its ability to compute a larger number of possible board positions based on the current positions and then select the best move. This computational approach, while effective, lacks strategy and the ability to learn from previous games. A modified version of Deep Blue in 1997 eventually won a match against Gary Kasparov, the reigning (human) chess champion at that time. In addition to the tradition AI approach, this particular version incorporated the strategic advice from Joel Benjamin (a former U.S. chess champion).

The goal of computer simulations is to develop programs that take into consideration the constraints of how humans perform various cognitive tasks and incorporate these constraints into a program (for instance, the amount of information that humans can think about at any given time is limited). This approach can take into account how human information processing is effected by a number of mechanisms such as processing, storing, and retrieving information. Computer simulations vary in the extent to which the program models processes that can range from a single process to a model of the mind.

THEORETICAL ISSUES FOR AI

A number of important theoretical issues influence the assumptions one makes in developing intelligent systems. Stan Franklin, in his book *Artificial Minds* (1995), presents these issues in what he labels the three debates for AI: Can computing machines be intelligent? Does the connectionist approach offer something that the symbolic approach does not? and Are internal representations necessary?

CAN COMPUTING MACHINES BE INTELLIGENT?

The issue is typically presented as "Can computers think in the sense that humans do?" There are two positions to this question: weak AI and strong AI. Weak AI suggests that the utility of artificial intelligence is to aid in exploring human cognition through the development of computer models. This approach aids in testing the feasibility and completeness of the theory from a computational standpoint. Weak AI is considered by many experts in the field as a viable approach. Strong AI takes the stance that it is possible to develop a machine that can manipulate symbols to accomplish many of the tasks that humans can accomplish. Some would ascribe thought or intelligence to such a machine because of its capacity for symbol manipulation. Alan Turing proposed a test, the imitation game (now called the Turing test), as a possible criterion for determining if strong AI has been accomplished. Strong AI also has opponents stating that it is not possible for a program to be intelligent or to think. John Searle, a philosopher, presents an argument against the possibility of strong AI.

Turing proposes a potential test of intelligence as criteria for determining whether a computer program is intelligent. The imitation game is a parlor game consisting of three people: an examiner, one male, and one female. The examiner can ask the male or female questions on any topic. Responses from the male and female are read. The man's task is to convince the examiner that he is the woman. The woman's job is to convince the examiner that she is the woman. Turing then proposes replacing either the man or woman with a computer. The examiner's task, then, is to decide which one is human and which one is the computer. This version of the imitation game is called the Turing test. The program (computer) passes the test if the examiner cannot determine which responses are from the computer and which ones are from the human. The Turing test, then, serves as a potential criterion for determining if a program is intelligent. Philosopher Daniel Dennett, in his book *Brainchildren: Essays on Designing Minds* (1998), discusses the appropriateness and power of the Turing test. The Loebner Prize competition, an annual contest, uses a modified version of the Turing test to evaluate real AI programs.

Searle, for his part, proposed a thought experiment he called the Chinese room. This thought experiment provides an argument against the notion that computers can be intelligent. Searle suggests a room from which information can be fed both in and out. The information coming into the room is in Chinese. Inside the room is a person who does not understand Chinese, but this person does have access to a set of instructions that will allow the person to change one symbol to another. Searle argues that this person, while truly capable of manipulating the various symbols, has no understanding of the questions or responses. The person lacks true understanding even though, over time, the person may become proficient in this task. The end results look intelligent even though the symbols carry no meaning for the person manipulating them. Searle then argues that the same is true for computers. A computer will not be capable of intelligence since the symbols carry no meaning for the computer, and yet the output will look intelligent.

CONNECTIONIST VERSUS SYMBOLIC APPROACH. The second debate deals with the approaches to the cognitive architecture, the built-in constraints that specify the capabilities, components, and structures involved in cognition. The classic approach, or symbol system hypothesis, and the connectionist approach are both different cognitive architectures. Cognitive architecture can be thought of in terms of hardware of a computer; it can run a number of different programs but by its nature places constraints on how things are conducted. The questions here is, does the contribution of connectionism differ from that of traditional AI?

The physical symbol system hypothesis is a class of systems that suggests the use of symbols or internal representations, mental events, that stand for or represent items or events in the environment. These internal representations can be manipulated, used in computations, and transformed. Traditionally, this approach consist of serial processing (implementing one command at a time) of symbols. Two examples of this approach are John R. Anderson's ACT* model (1983) and Allen Newell's Soar (1989). Both models are examples of architectures of cognition in which the goal is to account for all cognition.

The connectionist architecture is a class of systems that differ from the symbolic in that this model is modeled loosely on the brain and involves parallel processing, the ability to carry out a number of processes simultaneously. Other terms that have been used for this approach include parallel distributed processing (PDP), artificial neural networks (ANN), and the subsymbolic approach. The general makeup of a connectionist system is a network of nodes typically organized into various levels that loosely resemble neurons in the brain. These nodes have connections with other nodes. Like neurons in the brain, the nodes can have an excitatory or inhibitory effect on other nodes in the system. This is determined by the strength of the connection (commonly called the weight). Information then resides in these connections, not at the nodes, resulting in the information being distributed across the network. Learning in the system can take place during a training session in which adjustments are made to the weight during the training phase. An advantage that the connectionist approach has over the symbolic approach is the ability to retrieve partial information. This graceful degradation is the result of the information being distributed across the network. The system is still able to retrieve (partial) information even when part of the system does not work. This tends to be an issue for symbolic systems.

THE NECESSITY OF AN INTERNAL REPRESENTATION. Rodney Brooks, working at MIT, proposed in 1986 a different approach to traditional AI, a system that is reliant on a central intelligence responsible for cognition. Brooks's approach, a subsumption architecture, relies on the interaction between perception and actuation systems as the basis for intelligence. The subsumption architecture starts with a level of basic behaviors (modules) and builds upon this level with additional levels. Each new level can subsume the functions of lower levels and suppress the output for those modules. If a higher level is unable to respond or is delayed, then a lower level, which continues to function, can produce a result. The resulting action may not always be the most "intelligent," but the system is capable of doing something. For Brooks, intelligent behavior emerges from the combination of these simple behaviors. Furthermore, intelligence (or cognition) is in the eye of the beholder. Cog, one of Brooks's robot projects, is based on the subsumption architecture. Cog's movements and processing of visual information are not preprogrammed into the system. Experience with the environment plays an important role. Kismet, another project at MIT, is designed to show various emotional states in response to social interaction with other.

APPROACHES TO MODELING INTELLIGENCE

Intelligent tutoring systems (ITS's) are systems in which individual instruction can be tailored to the needs of a particular student. This is different from computer aided instruction (CAI's), in which everyone receives the same lessons. Key components typical of ITS's are the expert knowledge base (or teacher), the student model, instructional goals, and the interface. The student model contains the knowledge that the student has mastered as well as the areas in which he or she may have conceptual errors. Instruction can then be tailored to help elucidate the concepts with which the student is having difficulty.

An expert system attempts to capture an individual's expertise, and the program should then perform like an expert in that particular area. An expert system consists of two components: a knowledge base and an inference engine. The inference engine is the program of the expert system. It relies on the knowledge base, which "captures the knowledge" of an expert. Developing this component of the expert system is often time-consuming. Typically, the knowledge from the expert is represented in if-then statements (also called condition-action rules). If a particular condition is met, this leads to execution of the action part of the statement. Testing of the system often leads to repeating the knowledge acquisition phase and modification of the condition-action rules. An example of an expert system is MYCIN, which diagnoses bacterial infections based on lab results. The performance of MYCIN was compared to that of physicians as well as to that of interns. MYCIN's performance was comparable to that of a physician.

Case-based reasoning systems use previous cases to analyze a new case. This type of reasoning is similar to law, in which a current situation is interpreted by use of previous types of problems. Case-based reasoning is designed around the so-called four R's: Retrieve relevant cases to the case at hand; reuse a previous case where applicable; revise strategy if no previous case is appropriate; and retain the new solution, allowing for the use of the case in the future.

Other approaches to modeling intelligence have included trying to model the intelligence of animals. Alife is an approach that involves the development of a computer simulation of the important features necessary for intelligent behavior. The animats approach constructs robots based on animal models. The idea here is to implement intelligence on a smaller scale rather than trying to model all of human intelligence. This approach may be invaluable in terms of developing systems that are shared in common with animals.

SOURCES FOR FURTHER STUDY

Ashby, W. Ross. *Introduction to Cybernetics.* New York: John Wiley & Sons, 1956. Provides a tutorial to the area of cybernetics. Discusses the issue of feedback.

Bechtel, William, and George Graham, eds. *A Companion to Cognitive Science.* Malden, Mass.: Blackwell, 1998. Provides a history for the area of cognitive science as well as an exploration of many of the issues of interest today.

Clark, Andy, and Josefa Toribio. *Cognitive Architectures in Artificial Intelligence.* New York: Garland, 1998. A collection of papers dealing with the three types of architectures: physical symbol system, connectionist, and subsumption. Written by experts in the various areas.

Dennett, Daniel C. *Brainchildren: Essays on Designing Minds.* Cambridge, Mass.: MIT Press, 1998. Dennett, a philosopher, looks at issues such as what it means to be intelligent. He also takes a look at the appropriateness of the Turing test.

Franklin, Stan. *Artificial Minds.* Cambridge, Mass.: MIT Press, 1995. Franklin takes complicated subjects and presents them in a readable way even for people not professionals in the area.

Gardner, Howard. *The Mind's New Science: A History of the Cognitive Revolution.* New York: Basic Books, 1985. A good overview of the issues leading up to the cognitive revolution as well as the main issues of study for this area.

Michael S. Bendele

SEE ALSO: Brain structure; Computer models of cognition; Concept formation; Consciousness; Decision making; Grammar and speech; Hypothesis development and testing; Intelligence; Learning; Memory; Memory: Empirical studies; Memory storage; Pattern recognition; Problem-solving stages; Problem-solving strategies; Rule-governed behavior.

Assessment

TYPE OF PSYCHOLOGY: Psychological methodologies
FIELDS OF STUDY: Methodology issues

Assessment is a general term for a broad range of processes for testing, measuring, and evaluating performance. Standardized, alternative, and self-assessment methods are used for the purposes of replacement, diagnosis of performance, and the provision of formative and summative evaluation. The quality of an assessment depends on its validity and reliability.

KEY CONCEPTS

- alternative assessment
- diagnostic assessment
- formative assessment
- placement assessment
- self-assessment
- standard assessment
- summative assessment
- validity and reliability of assessment

INTRODUCTION

Every person has experienced some type of assessment. Those who have had public education in the United States are familiar with the Scholastic Aptitude Test (SAT) and the Iowa Test of Basic Skills (ITBS) administered in schools. Those whose native language is not English and have pursued education in the United States particularly know about Test of English as Foreign Language (TOEFL). Those who have applied to graduate schools are familiar with the Graduate Record Examination (GRE) or the Graduate Management Admission Test (GMAT). Assessment is used quite often, for different purposes, in daily life.

Assessment is a general term for a broad range of processes which include testing, measuring, and evaluation. Testing is simply a particular part of assessment, usually a set of questions that participants must answer in a fixed period time and under certain conditions. Measuring is a process that assigns numbers to assessment results, such as the number of correct or incorrect answers to a project or performance. A rubric rating scale is usually created to record quantitative or qualitative data. Evaluation is a process of assessment that emphasizes a value or a judgment to match with the correlated objectives of a project, an instruction, or a performance to see how well the project or performance is done.

STANDARD, ALTERNATIVE, AND SELF-ASSESSMENT

There are different types of assessment using specific tests, measurements, and ways of evaluation, used for different purposes. Generally, the assessment can be classified as standardized assessment, alternative assessment, or self-assessment.

Standardized assessment adopts standardized tests to measure and evaluate a performance. Standardized tests are always developed by a major test publisher for a large population and administered under the same conditions and time limits to all participants. The SAT is a typical example. Standard assessment is carried out to see how the results are norm-referenced for interpretation, that is, to compare an individual's performance with the performance of his or her peers. For example, one's SAT score can be ranked in percentile compared with others of the same age or grade. If one's percentile rank is 84, that means that 84 percent of all of the scores are lower than this individual's score.

According to educator James H. McMillan, alternative assessment and self-assessment are recent trends weighted more toward assessment of the process than assessment of a product or a performance. Individually created tests, portfolios, exhibitions, journals, and other forms of assessment are commonly used. Alternative assessment is intended to engage an individual in the process of learning and thinking, and in demonstrating during a performance. For example, a teacher who adopts a performance-based assessment will observe and make a judgment about the student's demonstration of a skill or competency in creating a product, constructing a response, or making a presentation. Self-assessment is a part of the learning process aimed at seeing where one is and how one is doing. Instead of relying on feedback from others, one is expected to self-assess: to think about and change what one is doing while doing it. Self-assessment is also a reflective practice to bring past events to a conscious level and to devise appropriate ways to think, feel, and behave in the future, through techniques such as an annual review portfolio or a self-checklist.

PLACEMENT, DIAGNOSTIC, FORMATIVE, AND SUMMATIVE ASSESSMENT

According to educator Donald Orlich, assessment can also be classified by the uses of tests: placement assessment, diagnostic assessment, formative assessment, and summative assessment. Either standardized tests or self-made tests can be adopted in the process of these assessments.

Placement assessment determines whether an individual has the required knowledge and skills to begin a new position. In education, placement assessment instruments are those pretests to see whether a student can be accepted or placed into a certain grade for instruction. Spontaneous, informal observations and interviews are also usually adopted in the placement assessment.

Diagnostic assessment tends to identify an individual's strengths and weakness. For example, the Kaufman Assessment Battery for Children (K-ABC) and Woodcock-Johnson Psychoeducational Battery-Revised (WJ-R) are two specific diagnostic assessment instruments. K-ABC is used to diagnose the learning potential and learning styles of children between 2.5 and 12.5 years old. WJ-R is used to assess the intellectual and academic development of individuals from preschool to adulthood.

Formative assessment monitors one's learning or working progress in order to provide feedback to enrich knowledge and skills. It is believed that formative assessments and feedback can play an important role in supporting a performance. The portfolio is one of the commonly adopted formative assessment instruments in education today. The data that are collected as part of the process of evaluating students' learning progress are used to help teachers provide feedback to students, make changes in teaching strategies, and inform parents of specific needs from family for students' success.

Summative assessment assesses final results, achievements, or projects for decision making. It occurs at the conclusion of instruction, such as at the end of a teaching unit or of an academic year. Instead of establishing students' proficiency in knowledge and skills, it provides an overview of achievement across the knowledge base and skills. Term papers, chapter achievement tests, final exams, and research projects are often adopted for a summative assessment in schools.

VALIDITY AND RELIABILITY OF ASSESSMENT

The quality of an assessment depends on its validity and its reliability. Validity refers to the appropriateness of the inferences, uses, and consequences that result from the assessment. It is the degree to which a test measures what it is supposed to measure. A specific test may be valid for a particular purpose and for a particular group. Therefore, the question is not whether a test is valid or invalid, but rather what it is valid for and for which group. However, it is important that a test is valid in order to measure or evaluate a typical situation or typical group of students. John Salvia and James E. Ysseldyke classify validity as content validity, criterion-related validity, or construct validity. Content validity is the degree to which a test's items actually represent the contents to be measured. Test items cannot measure each or every content area, but it is expected that the test items will adequately sample the content area. If a test does not measure what students are supposed to learn, the test score will not reflect a student's achievement. Criterion-related validity is the degree to which an individual's performance can be estimated on the assessment procedure being validated. Concurrent criterion-related validity and predictive criterion-related validity are commonly described. Concurrent criterion-related validity refers to how accurately a test score is related to the scores on another test administered or to some other valid criterion available at the same time. Predictive criterion-related validity refers to how accurately a test score can predict how well an individual will do in the future. Thus, since the validity of a test is related to a criterion, the criterion itself, either for the test or for its prediction for the future, must be valid.

Construct validity is the degree to which a test measures an intended theoretical construct or characteristic. The construct is "invented" to explain behavior; it cannot be seen, but its effect can be observed. For example, it is hypothesized that there is something called intelligence that is related to learning achievement; therefore, the higher the intelligence one has, the better the learning achievement one will make. A test is developed to measure how much intelligence an individual has. If the individual's test score and learning achievement were high, it would be evidence to support the construct validity of the test. However, if the higher score in the test did not indicate a higher learning achievement, it would not necessarily mean that the test did not measure learning achievement; the hypotheses related to the learning achievement of a high-intelligence individual might be incorrect.

Reliability refers to the dependability, trustworthiness, or consistency of the test results. It is the degree to which a test consistently measures whatever it measures. If a test is not reliable, then the results of the test will be expected to be different every time the test is administered.

There are three types of reliability: internal-consistency reliability, test-retest reliability, and inter-scorer reliability. When an individual is given a test with two similar but different groups of questions, the results of two parts should be the same. It means the two groups of tests are internal-consistency reliable. The results from one part of the test items can be generalized to the other group of test items. If a test is administered at two different times such as in a test and retest procedure, the results of the tests administered at different times should be quite stable. That means the results of a test and a retest are highly correlated. In this case, one test result can be generalized to the same test administered at a different time, for example, a week later. Inter-scorer reliability indicates that when two or more different scorers score a test, the results judged by different scorers are almost same and highly correlated. With high inter-scorer reliability, one individual scorer's judgment can be generalized to different scorers.

An interesting relationship exists between validity and reliability. A valid assessment is always reliable, because when an assessment measures what it is supposed to measure, it will be reliable every time the assessment is administered. However, a reliable assessment is not necessarily valid, since an assessment may consistently measure the wrong thing.

SOURCES FOR FURTHER STUDY

McMillan, James H. *Classroom Assessment: Principles and Practice for Effective Instruction.* 2d ed. Boston: Allyn & Bacon, 2001. This book provides prospective and practicing teachers with principles, current trends, and practical examples of assessment for more effective teaching.

Maroemau, C. "Self-Assessment at Work: Outcomes of Adult Learners' Reflections on Practice." In *Research Methods 01/02*, edited by Mary Renck Jalongo, Gail Gerlach, and Wenfan Yan. Guilford, Conn.: McGraw-Hill, 2001. This qualitative study examined the outcomes of engaging in self-as-

sessment as perceived by students in an experience-based graduate program.

Orlich, D., R. Harder, R. Callahan, and H. Gibbson. *Teaching Strategies.* Boston: Houghton Mifflin, 1998. Chapter 11 provides a very informative discussion on assessment, from basic concepts and assessment tools to instructional decision making.

Ruiz-Primo, M. A., S. E. Schultz, and M. Li. "Comparison of the Reliability and Validity of Scores from Two Concept-Mapping Techniques." *Journal of Research in Science Teaching* 38, no. 2 (February, 2001): 260-278. The authors discuss reliability and validity by comparing two concept-mapping techniques, one high-directed, "fill-in-the-map," and one low-directed, "construct-a-map-from-scratch."

Salvia, J., and J. E. Ysseldyke. *Assessment.* 7th ed. Boston: Houghton Mifflin, 1998. This is a good textbook to help readers understand the concepts and methods of assessment. A variety of tests are illustrated and analyzed.

Zeliff, N. D. "Alternative Assessment." *National Business Education Yearbook* (2000): 91-102. The author believes that business educators should use alternative as well as traditional assessment measures to best evaluate student progress and achievement. Alternative assessment strategies are well discussed.

Ronghua Ouyang

SEE ALSO: Ability tests; Career and personnel testing; Career Occupational Preference System (COPS); College entrance examinations; Creativity: Assessment; General Aptitude Test Battery (GATB); Human resource training and development; Intelligence tests; Interest inventories; Kuder Occupational Interest Survey (KOIS); Peabody Individual Achievement Test (PIAT): Race and intelligence; Scientific methods; Stanford-Binet test; Strong Interest Inventory (SII); Survey research: Questionnaires and interviews; Testing: Historical perspectives; Wechsler Intelligence Scale for Children Third Edition (WISC-III).

Attachment and bonding in infancy and childhood

TYPE OF PSYCHOLOGY: Developmental psychology
FIELDS OF STUDY: Infancy and childhood; interpersonal relations

Bonding and attachment are two theoretical con-structs that psychologists have used to describe and explain the intense emotional tie that develops be-tween a caregiver and child. Research has helped psychologists to explain the development of several common social behaviors in infancy and to use indi-vidual differences in infant behavior to predict as-pects of later development.

KEY CONCEPTS
- approach behaviors
- attachment behaviors
- avoidance
- felt security
- resistance
- separation protest
- signalling behaviors
- "strange situation"
- stranger anxiety

INTRODUCTION

Bonding refers to the development of an emotional tie of the mother to the infant. This biologically based process is believed to occur in mothers shortly after the birth of an infant, a time period during which the mother's intense emotional response is trig-gered by contact with her newborn. The ex-istence of such a bond is then evidenced in the mother's behavior. Attachment, on the other hand, refers to a relationship between the caregiver and infant that develops over the infant's first year of life; the quality of the attachment is apparent in the behavior of the infant.

Evidence for the biologically based bond-ing process has been inconsistent. In con-trast, there exists considerable scientific evi-dence to support the notion of attachment. Thus, the remainder of this discussion will focus on the development of the attach-ment relationship.

The work of British psychiatrist John Bowlby played an important role in the ac-ceptance and understanding of the notion of mother-infant attachment. Bowlby argued that the behaviors of infants are not ran-dom and that, in fact, some of the behaviors exhibited most commonly by infants actu-ally serve a single goal. Specifically, he ar-gued that the infant behaviors of crying, babbling, smiling, clinging, non-nutritional sucking, and fol-lowing all play an important role in bringing the in-fant into close contact with the caregiver. He be-lieved that, for the infant, seeking and maintaining proximity to the caregiver are essential for survival because the infant is dependent upon the caregiver for food, shelter, and protection. Thus, the infant's behavior is organized and goal-directed. During early infancy, however, this goal is neither understood nor learned by the infant. Rather, humans are born with a biological predisposition to engage in certain behaviors that aid in the maintenance of proximity to the caregiver. Thus, the goal of maintaining prox-imity is built into the human infant, as are some ini-tial behaviors that serve the function of achieving that goal. With further development, the infant be-comes more aware of the goal, and therefore his or her behaviors become more intentional.

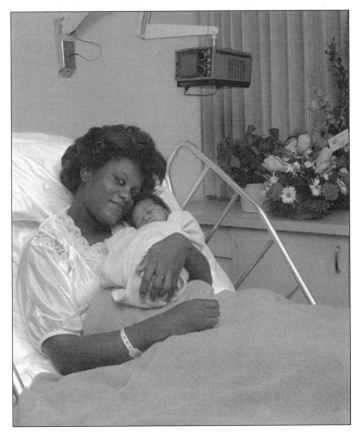

Bonding is an emotional and physiological process that begins at birth. (Digital Stock)

The infant's emotional state is also believed to play an important role in attempts to seek and maintain proximity to the caregiver. That is, the infant's behavior is dependent upon his or her sense of emotional security. For example, as long as a child is in the immediate presence of the attachment figure, or within easy reach, the child feels secure and may then attend to important developmental tasks such as exploration of the environment, using the mother as a secure base from which to explore. Upon the threat of loss of the attachment figure, however, the infant may lose that sense of security and may exhibit attachment behaviors designed to increase the proximity of the attachment figure. Thus, the infant's attempts to seek or maintain proximity to the caregiver are determined by how secure he or she feels with the caregiver in a specific environment.

The attachment relationship and the infant's sense of security develop over the period of infancy. Bowlby has described four phases in the development of the attachment to the caregiver. In phase one, the newborn shows limited discrimination among people and therefore exhibits no preferential or differential behaviors, thus behaving in a friendly manner toward all people. In phase two, the eight- to twelve-week-old infant shows the ability to discriminate the caregiver from others but exhibits no preferential behavior toward the caregiver. In phase three, which generally appears at approximately seven or eight months of age, the infant clearly discriminates the caregiver from other people and begins to show preferential treatment toward him or her. For example, the infant begins to follow a departing mother, greets mother upon her return, and uses her as a base from which to explore an unfamiliar environment. Furthermore, during phase three, the infant begins to treat strangers with caution and may withdraw from a stranger. In phase four, the child maintains a "goal-directed partnership" with the caregiver, a more complex relationship in which the child is acquiring some insight into the caregiver's own feelings and motives, and thus interacts with the caregiver as a partner. This final phase is not apparent in most children until after age two.

PATTERNS OF INFANT-MOTHER ATTACHMENT
During the second half of the first year of life (after about eight months of age), infants begin to show very clear attempts at exploration when their mothers are present. In fact, research reported by Mary

Ainsworth in the mid-1970's suggests that once an infant is able to crawl, he or she does not always remain close to the mother. Instead, the child begins to move away from the mother, more carefully exploring objects and people. From time to time he or she returns to her, as if to check her whereabouts or to check in with her. If the mother moves away, however, or if the infant is frightened by some event, he or she will either approach the mother or will signal to bring the mother in closer proximity. For example, the infant often fusses, cries, and clings to the caregiver at the first sign of the caregiver's possible departure, a response known as separation protest. At about the same time, infants begin to express stranger anxiety or stranger wariness by fussing and crying when an unfamiliar person enters the room or approaches.

Ainsworth designed a special laboratory technique, known as the "strange situation," that allows direct observation of the interactions between the behaviors associated with exploration, attachment, separation protest, and stranger anxiety. This situation places an infant in an unfamiliar setting with a stranger, both in the presence and in the absence of the mother. The procedure consists of a series of three-minute episodes (the process lasts a total of about twenty minutes) in which the child is exposed to an unfamiliar playroom containing a set of age-appropriate toys. During the initial episodes, the mother remains in the playroom with the infant. Mother and infant are then joined in the playroom by a female stranger, who first talks to the mother, then approaches the baby. Next, the mother leaves the room, and the baby and stranger are left alone together. Mother then returns and the stranger leaves, so that the baby is reunited with the mother. Following this episode, the baby is left alone in the room, then joined by the stranger; finally, the mother again returns and the stranger leaves.

This strange situation, therefore, exposes a child to three potentially upsetting experiences: separation from the caregiver, contact with a stranger, and unfamiliar surroundings. The episodes are arranged in such a way that they present a series of stressful experiences to the infant and thus present an opportunity to observe not only the infant's immediate response to a stranger and to separation from the mother, but also his or her ability to derive comfort from the mother and to use her as a secure base for exploration.

Ainsworth has reported that, while there are many similarities in infant responses to this strange situation, there are also important individual differences. In her initial study of twelve-month-old infants and their mothers, Ainsworth reported three distinct patterns of responding to the events of the strange situation, and the validity of these behavior patterns has been demonstrated by much additional research.

A majority of the infants exhibited active exploration of the new environment and the available toys when their mothers were present. Some of these infants showed distress during the first separation from mother, and by the second separation, the majority of these infants expressed distress. Upon reunion with their mother, they actively sought contact with her and were easily comforted by her, showing considerable signs of positive emotion but very little, if any, signs of negative emotion. Furthermore, these infants frequently returned to play and exploration after a period of contact with their mother. In general, then, these infants used their mothers as a secure base from which to explore the novel environment, exhibited appropriate attachment behaviors following her departure, and were easily comforted by the mother upon her return. Ainsworth suggested that this pattern of behavior reflects a secure attachment relationship.

A second group of infants showed a very different pattern of behavior. This minority group showed no evidence of distress during separation. They did sometimes show distress when left alone in the playroom but were easily comforted by the returning stranger. Furthermore, this group actually avoided or ignored their mothers when they returned. In essence, the mothers were treated very much as were the strangers. These infants showed virtually no signs of separation protest or stranger anxiety and exhibited very few attachment behaviors. Ainsworth suggested that this pattern of behavior reflects an insecure, avoidant attachment relationship.

Finally, a third group of children were extremely distressed upon separation yet, despite their obvious separation and stranger anxiety, resisted comfort from their mothers. Their behavior suggested an angry ambivalence—they objected to being left alone, but they refused to be consoled when reunited with their mothers. This group of infants often exhibited distress upon first entering the unfamiliar room with their mothers, and they rarely left her side to explore the toys or the environment, either before or after separation, suggesting a lack of a sense of security. Ainsworth suggested that this behavior pattern reflects an insecure, resistant, or ambivalent attachment relationship.

It is important to note that Ainsworth's research was done in the United States, in the 1970's. Follow-up work has demonstrated that various sociocultural factors can influence the patterns of attachment behavior seen in the "strange situation." For instance, studies done in North Germany in the 1980's revealed that as many as 60 percent of babies in that culture were classified as insecure-avoidant because of their lack of distress at separation from their mothers in the strange situation test. In contrast, studies of attachment carried out in Japan in the 1980's and 1990's indicate that up to 40 percent of Japanese infants are classified as insecure-ambivalent in the strange situation due to their tendency to cling to their mothers throughout the procedure. These differing cross-cultural patterns imply that the wider sociocultural context influences how mothers and infants interact: North German mothers expect their infants to be relatively self-sufficient and confident, even during short separations such as those characteristic of the "strange situation" procedure. Japanese mothers, on the other hand, expect their infants to be upset when they are out of close proximity, and in daily practice are unlikely to leave their infants alone even for short periods. These cross-cultural variations in patterns of attachment highlight the importance of considering mother-infant attachment in context.

The development of these distinct patterns of attachment is believed to be the result of the history of interaction between the caregiver and infant. Specifically, attachment theory suggests that responsive and consistent caregiving results in a secure mother-infant attachment, unresponsive caregiving results in an avoidant attachment, and inconsistent caregiving results in a resistant/ambivalent attachment. The "avoidant" mother has been described as cold and disliking physical contact with the infant, who responds by acting aloof and avoiding social interaction. The "resistant" mother, on the other hand, has been described as unpredictable, sometimes responding but sometimes not, and the infant often responds with anger and ambivalence.

As the infant matures, the specific behaviors that indicate the existence of the attachment relationship may change. The research evidence strongly suggests, however, that such individual differences in the quality of the mother-infant attachment relationship are predictive of later behavior. For example, infants who exhibit secure attachment patterns at one year of age have been found to be more cooperative with adults, to show greater enthusiasm for learning, to be more independent, and to be more popular with their peers during the preschool years. Thus, the quality of the mother-infant attachment relationship may have long-range effects. This does not mean that the child's future is determined solely by the quality of the attachment relationship. The evidence indicates that certain negative consequences of an insecure attachment relationship may be overcome by changes in the nature of the child's important relationships.

ATTACHMENT IN NONHUMAN PRIMATES

The existence of a mother-infant attachment relationship has been recognized for many years. For most of those years, however, psychologists explained the development of this attachment by way of traditional learning theory. That is, behaviorists argued that the infant-mother attachment develops because mothers are associated with the powerful, reinforcing event of being fed. In this way, the mother becomes a conditioned reinforcer. This reinforcement theory of attachment, however, came into question as a result of the work of Harry and Margaret Harlow in the early 1960's.

The Harlows' work was not with human infants but with infant rhesus monkeys. They removed newborn monkeys from their mothers at birth and raised them in the laboratory with two types of artificial or surrogate mothers. One surrogate mother was made of terrycloth and could provide "contact comfort." The other surrogate mother was made of wire. A feeding bottle was attached to one of the substitute mothers for each of the monkeys. Half of the monkeys were fed by the wire mother; the other half were fed by the cloth mother. This allowed the Harlows to compare the importance of feeding to the importance of contact comfort for the monkeys.

In order to elicit attachment behaviors, the Harlows introduced some frightening event, such as a strange toy, into the cages of the young monkeys. They expected that if feeding were the key to attachment, then the frightened monkeys should have run to the surrogate mother that fed them. This was not the case, however: All the young monkeys ran to their cloth mothers and clung to them, even if they were not fed by them. Only the cloth mothers were able to provide security for the frightened monkeys. The Harlows concluded that a simple reinforcement explanation of attachment was inaccurate and that the contact comfort, not the food, provided by a mother plays a critical role in the development of attachment.

This research provided the impetus for the development of Bowlby's ethological account of attachment. Since that time, research by Mary Ainsworth and Alan Sroufe, as well as many others, has provided important information for the continuing development of understanding of the complex relationship between caregivers and infants.

BIBLIOGRAPHY

Ainsworth, Mary D. Salter, Mary C. Blehar, Everett Waters, and S. Wall. *Patterns of Attachment.* Hillsdale, N.J.: Lawrence Erlbaum, 1978. Outlines, in general terms, the development of Bowlby's attachment theory. Describes in detail the procedures and scoring techniques for the strange situation and describes the patterns of behavior associated with the secure, avoidant, and resistant attachments. Discusses the research that addresses the antecedents of individual differences in the attachment relationship.

Bowlby, John. *Attachment and Loss.* 2d ed. New York: Basic Books, 1982. Examines the theoretical foundation of the attachment construct and discusses attachment behavior. Outlines the development, maintenance, and function of attachment in both humans and animals.

Cassidy, Jude, and Phillip R. Shaver, eds. *Handbook of Attachment: Theory, Research, and Clinical Applications.* New York: Guilford, 1999. A comprehensive collection of papers on modern attachment theory, including chapters on atypical attachment and implications for mental health.

Crittenden, Patricia McKinsey, and Angelika Hartl Claussen, eds. *The Organization of Attachment Relationships: Maturation, Culture, and Context.* New York: Cambridge University Press, 2000. A collection of papers examining important influences on attachment in infancy, childhood, and adulthood.

Loretta A. Rieser-Danner;
updated by Virginia Slaughter

SEE ALSO: Affiliation and friendship; Birth: Effects on physical development; Birth order and personality; Child abuse; Development; Father-child relationship; Gender-identity formation; Imprinting; Mother-child relationship; Parenting styles; Reactive attachment disorder; Separation anxiety.

Attention

TYPE OF PSYCHOLOGY: Consciousness
FIELDS OF STUDY: Cognitive processes

Humans are not able to be fully conscious of everything around them simultaneously; attention refers to a person's selection of only some of a number of things of which a person could be conscious. Studies have provided information on what things enter consciousness and how a person selects those things.

KEY CONCEPTS
- bottom-up
- early selection
- feature integration theory
- illusory conjunction
- late selection
- shadowing
- top-down

INTRODUCTION

Attention usually refers to concentrating upon a particular aspect of the external environment, although it is possible to attend to one's own thoughts and other internal states. The flavor of the typical use of the term is captured in a statement by nineteenth century German physiologist Hermann von Helmholtz, who noted that an observer may be steadily gazing at a fixation mark, yet at the same time can concentrate attention upon any given part of the visual field. The point in space to which one is directing one's eyes and the point to which one is attending thus are not necessarily the same, and one does not have to move the eyes to shift visual attention.

Attention has been of interest for a very long time. Hermann von Helmholtz wrote of attention in 1850, in a book on physiological optics. William James, a pioneer in the study of psychology, devoted much space to attention in his book published in 1890 titled *The Principles of Psychology.* He noted that attention can be involuntary and effortless, or else voluntary and effortful. According to James, attention allows people to perceive, conceive, distinguish, and remember better than they otherwise could. Edward Titchener, in his *Lectures on the Elementary Psychology of Feeling and Attention* (1908), reinforced this point by stating that attention determines what people are conscious of as well as the clarity of their conscious experience.

Other leading figures from the early history of psychology, such as Wilhelm Wundt, agreed with James that the issue of attention was of great importance. Titchener believed that attention determined both the quality and content of conscious experience, and regarded its prominence as one of the major achievements of experimental psychology. Interest was maintained through the period following World War I. Karl Dallenbach noted in the late 1920's that more studies had been reported on attention in the preceding three years than in any comparable period in history. After World War II the study of attention received an even greater boost with the increasing concern over human-machine interactions, especially in the military.

Attention can be drawn automatically (involuntarily and effortlessly) by certain characteristics of stimuli in the environment. These include abrupt brightness changes or vivid colors at particular locations; both intensity and clarity are important. Auditory attention is automatically drawn by changes in pitch or location. Such automatic attentional capture is often termed "bottom-up" or "data-driven." A person readily attends to familiar stimuli, although these more often invoke voluntary and effortful processing—that which is "top-down" or "internally driven." A person can voluntarily attend to any aspect of the environment the person chooses.

ATTENTION SELECTION

How does a person select the things to which he or she will attend? This question leads to a consideration of "early" (before meaning is analyzed) versus "late" selection. Donald Broadbent, in 1958, championed the view that selection is made early through a process analogous to filtering incoming information according to its sensory properties. For example, after a brief glimpse, a person can report the identity of items in the environment accurately if a cue indicating which items to report refers to their spatial location, but much less accurately if it refers to semantic properties (for example, asks for only the letters from a display of several letters and digits intermixed).

Other researchers, such as J. Anthony Deutsch and Diana Deutsch, have argued that people unconsciously analyze all incoming information for its meaning, although selection cannot be made on this basis as easily as on a sensory basis. Support for this process, termed late selection, is forthcoming in tasks such as naming the ink colors of printed letters. J. Ridley Stroop found that if the color of the letters from a word that is the name of a color is different from the ink color (for example, the word "blue" written in red ink), it takes much longer to name the ink color than if the combination of letters is meaningless (in the example, a row of red X's). People cannot avoid reading the word, no matter how hard they try. Thus, word meaning appears to be activated automatically, and people cannot selectively attend to the color. Nevertheless, if the color to be named appears as a patch, separated in space from the inconsistent color word, color naming is not slowed. Selection of what to attend to thus can be made easily on the basis of location, color, or brightness, but not on the basis of meaning.

VISUAL, SENSORY, AND SPATIAL ATTENTION

Attention is necessary because people do not have the capacity to be conscious of all aspects of their environment at once. Questions arise concerning the extent to which people can be conscious of more than one aspect simultaneously, and if so, of what aspects they can be simultaneously conscious. Because what is to be attended to can so easily be selected on the basis of its location, these questions often have been posed in relation to whether people can attend to nonadjacent areas simultaneously.

It is important first to point out that the observations of von Helmholtz, James, and Titchener have been verified in sensitive laboratory experiments. Subjects gazing at the center of a computer screen were first given information about the spatial location on the screen of a target that would later appear away from fixation. The correct location usually was indicated, but sometimes an incorrect location was indicated. In comparison with instances when no location information was shown, detection of the target was aided by valid information but harmed by invalid information. If the tar-

get did not appear in the indicated location, however, detection was better when it appeared near the indicated location than when it appeared farther away. The edges of the attended area thus are vaguely rather than sharply defined. Yet can attention be split between nonadjacent locations? Most research has shown that this is not possible; people cannot attend to two separate areas simultaneously, although a few studies have indicated that they can attend to ringlike areas with attention devoted to the ring but not the surrounding area or the center.

In contrast to splitting visual attention between two separate locations, dividing attention between two different senses is possible. People can, for example, listen (attend) to a conversation while watching (attending to) the road when driving. Nevertheless, unless one of the tasks is very easy or highly practiced, performance still suffers in comparison to when attention is dedicated to one sense.

Directing attention on the basis of spatial location appears to be very important. Ulric Neisser described the visual determination of what is present as occurring rapidly in two stages. The first he called "preattentive" because it involves only a rough, global analysis of information in the entire visual field, before attention is directed to any one location. People can detect simple visual features such as color, brightness, and the direction in which a straight line points on the basis of preattentive analysis. More precise determination of combinations of these simple features requires what is called focal attention, in which attention is focused on particular spatial locations containing the preattentively detected simple features. For example, seeing that a line in a particular orientation is of a certain color requires focal attention. Without it, a person could tell that the color is present somewhere, and that a line of that orientation is present somewhere, but not that the line is of that color. Focal attention therefore is required to combine simple features. This process has been termed feature integration theory, through which focused attention is described as the "glue" that binds separate features into a unitary object.

Feature integration theory has received experimental confirmation in the work of Anne Treisman and her colleagues. They found that when focal attention is diverted or cannot be applied because of an interfering task, simple features are often matched incorrectly to produce what they termed "illusory conjunctions." For example, when a red horizontal line and a green vertical one are shown, in the absence of focal attention, a subject is likely to be conscious of the horizontal line as green and the vertical line as red.

USE OF SCHEMATA

A person can direct attention on bases other than a spatial one. That is, even overlapping shapes can be selectively attended. Neisser has described a study in which a basketball game and a hand slapping game were shown simultaneously in outline form in the same location on a television screen. Observers could attend to only one game and indicate each occurrence of some event (for example, a throw of the ball from one player to another) as well when both games were shown as when only the relevant one was shown alone. Further, observers were largely unaware of events occurring in the unattended game. People can attend to only one game when both are being shown on the basis of expectations inherent in the way they understand and mentally represent the game. These mental representations are called schemata. Through them, attention has its effects as an alerting and sustaining process whereby receptivity to certain information can be maintained over the short or long term. Finally, consistent with results on tasks involving attempts to split attention spatially, observers were unable to attend to both games at once (and thereby indicate when a point had been scored in either one).

One additional phenomenon involves what Colin Cherry referred to as the "cocktail party phenomenon." The setting is a cocktail party or any gathering where people are engaged simultaneously in different conversations. A person can listen selectively to one conversation and apparently not be conscious of others. Auditory attention therefore seems fully focused on only one conversation; however, the listener might hear his or her name mentioned in any one of a number of other conversations and immediately shift attention to it. How can people attend fully to one source of information, yet simultaneously be sensitive to important information from other sources? Can their attention be focused and yet divided among a number of possible sources of information at the same time? The answer lies in the fact that stimuli outside the focus of attention are sometimes processed to the level of meaning, es-

pecially if they correspond to active and important schemata such as one's name.

PRACTICAL USES OF RESEARCH

Understanding how attention operates makes possible the design of environments that make it easier for people to attend to important characteristics. For example, hunters often are cautioned to wear a piece of clothing colored "blaze orange." A bright color is a simple feature that draws attention automatically. Another hunter's attention will be drawn to the blaze orange, and focusing attention on the color will allow it to be conjoined with other simple features, such as shape. The second hunter thus will almost immediately be conscious of the hunter wearing the blaze orange as a hunter and will be unlikely to misperceive this hunter as game (in addition, the color of game is never blaze orange). The same principle is applied when emergency vehicles such as fire trucks are painted bright red or yellow.

Principles stemming from basic research on attention have been applied in the development of what is known as "heads-up" displays in aircraft such as helicopters. Typically, a pilot faces a windscreen through which the environment can be seen, with a cluster of instruments designating altitude, speed, and so on nearby. With this configuration, the pilot must look away from the windscreen and at the instruments to check them. As helicopters are capable of traveling at a high rate of speed and often are flown close to the earth and to objects into which they might crash, it is important that looking away from the windscreen be minimized. In a heads-up display, the instruments are placed at an angle below the windscreen so that they reflect onto it. The pilot thus can check the instruments without having to divert his eyes from the windscreen.

Can the pilot attend to the instruments and the environment outside the windscreen simultaneously? They spatially overlap and thus are visible at the same time, yet studies of attention indicate that the pilot cannot attend to them both at once. The experiment described by Neisser in which two games were superimposed on a screen is relevant here. An observer could attend to one game or the other but not to both at the same time. This does not mean that heads-up displays are without value. Attention can be directed from the instruments to the environment or vice versa without the pilot's moving the head or eyes; and either type of physical movement is much more time-consuming than a relatively rapid shift of attention.

SHADOWING

One popular laboratory task is to have listeners "shadow" material presented to them. In shadowing, the listener hears a series of words spoken at a normal conversational rate and tries to repeat aloud each word as it is heard. The task is difficult, and subjects must devote considerable attention to the shadowing. Often a listener is asked to shadow material played with a tape recorder to one ear while different material is played by another tape recorder to the other ear (earphones are used). Certain characteristics of the material not being shadowed can be varied. After the task, the listener can be asked a number of questions regarding what he or she was conscious of in the unshadowed message.

Consistent with Cherry's cocktail party phenomenon, listeners are conscious of the presence of the unshadowed message and of whether there is an abrupt change of pitch (as in a change of voice from a man's to a woman's, or the introduction of a whistle). These global physical characteristics of the unshadowed message can be determined preattentively. Listeners are not conscious, however, of the contents or language of the unshadowed message, of whether the language changed during the message, or even of whether speech or nonsense sounds were presented, unless a change of pitch occurred. Many variations of this experiment have been performed, and all have produced the same results: Consciousness of the unshadowed material is limited to that which could be detected preattentively. There is no consciousness of the meaning of the unshadowed message, except that listeners sometimes are conscious of their own name if it appears as a result of powerful schemata for something as important as one's own name. The results are exactly what would be expected from what has been shown to be true of attention thus far and from the original description of the cocktail-party problem.

EMERGENCE OF ATTENTION THEORIES

The first complete theory of attention was not proposed until 1958, when Donald Broadbent introduced his concept of attention as a filter that admitted only certain information, selected on the basis of sensory characteristics, into the limited-capacity system. This marked the continuation of interest in attention by researchers in England, beginning with Colin Cherry in 1953. In 1963, J. Anthony Deutsch and Diana Deutsch of Oxford, England, proposed that all incoming information is analyzed to the level of meaning.

Many of the fundamental issues in attention, raised decades ago, have been recast somewhat, in the information-processing mode, beginning in the late 1960's. For example, attention is described in terms of "selection," "resources," "features," "input," and so on. Whereas the emphasis had been on hearing, visual attention began to receive more emphasis. Many of the findings were like those on hearing, although factors such as color and brightness were considered.

Attention remains central to the study of consciousness and cognitive psychology. As Michael Posner noted in 1975, "Attention is not a single concept, but the name of a complex field of study." Accordingly, questions about early versus late selection, automatic processing, and other issues in the control of attention have not yet been fully answered.

SOURCES FOR FURTHER STUDY

Gopher, Daniel, and Asher Koriat, eds. *Attention and Performance XVII.* Cambridge, Mass.: MIT Press, 1999. A collection of essays from a conference on attention, divided into sections covering the presentation and representation of information, cognitive regulation of acquisition and performance, consciousness and behavior, and special populations: aging and neurological disorders.

Humphreys, Glyn, John Duncan, and Anne Treisman, eds. *Attention, Space, and Action: Studies in Cognitive Neuroscience.* New York: Oxford University Press, 1999. A volume of papers presented at two linked conferences, utilizing psychological, physiological, and theoretical advances in neuroscience to understand attention.

Johnston, William A., and Veronica J. Dark. "Selective Attention." In *Annual Review of Psychology* 37. Stanford, Calif.: Annual Reviews, 1989. Provides a very thorough and well-organized review of the research on selective attention. Outlines eleven phenomena associated with attention, and the degree to which each of a number of theories accounts for these phenomena.

Parasuraman, R., and D. R. Davies, eds. *Varieties of Attention.* Orlando, Fla.: Academic Press, 1984. Includes articles by a variety of contributors. Many topics are covered, such as search, vigilance, levels of processing, and applications to industrial settings.

Treisman, Anne. "Features and Objects in Visual Processing." *Scientific American* 225 (November, 1971): 114B-125. Treisman provides a clear summary of feature integration theory and includes figures producing readily observable attention effects.

Garvin Chastain

SEE ALSO: Automaticity; Cognitive psychology; Consciousness; Memory: Sensory; Pattern recognition.

Attention-deficit hyperactivity disorder (ADHD)

TYPE OF PSYCHOLOGY: Psychopathology
FIELDS OF STUDY: Childhood and adolescent disorders

Attention-deficit hyperactivity disorder is one of the most common disorders of childhood and adolescence, but it is also one of the most disturbing and debilitating disorders that a child or adolescent can experience. Research into this disorder has identified its primary causes; however, it remains a difficult disorder to treat effectively.

KEY CONCEPTS
- impulsivity
- inattention
- overactivity
- treatment

INTRODUCTION

Attention-deficit hyperactivity disorder (ADHD) is one of the most extensively studied behavior disorders that begin in childhood. Thousands of articles, book chapters, and books have been published on the disorder. There are a number of reasons this disorder is of such interest to researchers and clinicians. The two primary reasons are, first, that

ADHD is a relatively common disorder of childhood, and second, that there are numerous problems associated with ADHD, including lower levels of intellectual and academic performance and higher levels of aggressive and defiant behavior (Although ADHD usually persists into adulthood, it is most commonly regarded as a childhood disorder.)

In national and international studies of childhood emotional and behavioral disorders, ADHD has been found to be relatively common among children. Although prevalence estimates range from 1 percent to 20 percent, most researchers agree that between 3 percent and 7 percent of children could be diagnosed as having ADHD. The revised fourth edition of the *Diagnostic and Statistical Manual of Mental Disorders* (DSM-IV-TR), which was published by the American Psychiatric Association in 2000, describes the diagnostic criteria for ADHD. In order to receive the diagnosis of ADHD according to DSM-IV-TR, a child must show abnormally high levels of inattention, hyperactivity-impulsivity, or both when compared with peers of the same age. The DSM-IV-TR lists two sets of behavioral symptoms characteristic of ADHD. The first list contains nine symptoms of inattention such as "often has difficulty sustaining attention in tasks or play activities," while the second list contains nine symptoms of hyperactivity-impulsivity such as "often talks excessively" and "often has difficulty awaiting turn." In order to be diagnosed with ADHD, a child must exhibit six to nine symptoms from at least one of the lists. Although many of these behaviors are quite common for most children at some point in their lives, the important point to consider in the diagnosis of ADHD is that these behaviors must be in excess of the levels of behaviors most frequently exhibited for children of that age and that the behaviors must cause functional impairment in at least two settings (for instance, at home and at school). Additionally, it is expected that these behaviors have been excessive for at least six months and that some of the problem behaviors were present by the time the child was seven years old.

Boys tend to outnumber girls in the diagnosis of ADHD, with the male:female ratio estimated at 2:1 to 9:1, depending on the source. ADHD boys tend to be more aggressive and antisocial than ADHD girls, while girls are more likely to display inattentive symptoms of ADHD.

ASSOCIATED PROBLEMS

There are a number of additional problems associated with ADHD, including the greater likelihood of ADHD boys exhibiting aggressive and antisocial behavior. Although many ADHD children do not show any associated problems, many ADHD children show deficits in both intellectual and behavioral functioning. For example, a number of studies have found that ADHD children score an average of seven to fifteen points below normal children on standardized intelligence tests. It may be, however, that this poorer performance reflects poor test-taking skills or inattention during the test rather than actual impairment in intellectual functioning. Additionally, ADHD children tend to have difficulty with academic performance and scholastic achievement.

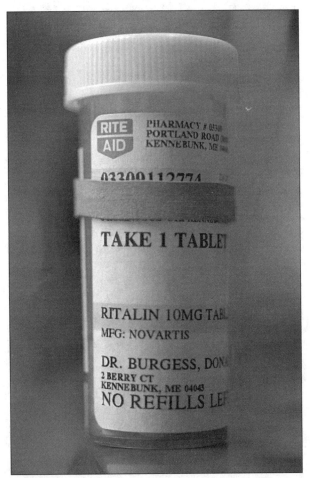

The drug Ritalin is becoming more widely used as increasing numbers of children are diagnosed with ADHD. (AP/Wide World Photos)

It is assumed that this poor academic performance is a result of inattention and impulsiveness in the classroom. When ADHD children are given medication to control their inattention and impulsiveness, their academic productivity has been shown to improve.

ADHD children have also been shown to have a high number of associated emotional and behavioral difficulties. As mentioned earlier, ADHD boys tend to show higher levels of aggressive and antisocial behavior than ADHD girls and normal children. Additionally, it is estimated that up to 50 percent of ADHD children have at least one other disorder. Many of these problems are related to depression and anxiety, although many ADHD children also have severe problems with temper tantrums, stubbornness, and defiant behavior. It is also estimated that up to 50 percent of ADHD children have impaired social relations; that is, they do not get along with other children. In general, there are many problems associated with ADHD, and this may be part of the reason that researchers have been so intrigued by this disorder.

Researchers must understand a disorder before they can attempt to treat it. There are a variety of theories on the etiology of ADHD, but most researchers now believe that there are multiple factors that influence its development. It appears that many children may have a biological predisposition toward ADHD; in other words, they may have a greater likelihood of developing ADHD as a result of genetic factors. This predisposition is exacerbated by a variety of factors, such as complications during pregnancy, neurological disease, exposure to toxins, family adversity, and inconsistent parental discipline. Although a very popular belief is that food additives or sugar can cause ADHD, there has been almost no scientific support for these claims. Since so many factors have been found to be associated with the development of ADHD, it is not surprising that numerous treatments have been developed for the amelioration of ADHD symptoms. Although numerous treatment methods have been developed and studied, ADHD remains a difficult disorder to treat effectively.

DRUG THERAPIES

Treatments of ADHD can be broken down into roughly two categories: medication; and behavioral or cognitive-behavioral treatment with the individual ADHD child, parents, or teachers. It should be noted that traditional psychotherapy and play ther-

DSM-IV-TR Criteria for Attention-Deficit Hyperactivity Disorder (ADHD)

Manifested as inattention or hyperactivity-impulsivity

INATTENTION

Six or more of the following symptoms, persisting for at least six months to a degree maladaptive and inconsistent with developmental level:

- often fails to give close attention to details or makes careless mistakes in schoolwork, work, or other activities
- often has difficulty sustaining attention in tasks or play activities
- often does not seem to listen when spoken to directly
- often does not follow through on instructions and fails to finish school work, chores, or duties in the workplace (not due to oppositional behavior or failure to understand instructions)
- often has difficulty organizing tasks and activities
- often avoids, dislikes, or is reluctant to engage in tasks that require sustained mental effort (such as schoolwork or homework)
- often loses things necessary for tasks or activities (such as toys, school assignments, pencils, books, tools)
- often easily distracted by extraneous stimuli
- often forgetful in daily activities

HYPERACTIVITY-IMPULSIVITY

Six or more of the following symptoms, persisting for at least six months to a degree maladaptive and inconsistent with developmental level:

Hyperactivity
- often fidgets with hands or feet or squirms in seat
- often leaves seat in classroom or in other situations in which remaining seated is expected
- often runs about or climbs excessively in situations in which it is inappropriate (in adolescents or adults, may be limited to subjective feelings of restlessness)
- often has difficulty playing or engaging in leisure activities quietly
- often "on the go" or often acts as if "driven by a motor"
- often talks excessively

Impulsivity
- often blurts out answers before questions have been completed
- often has difficulty awaiting turn
- often interrupts or intrudes on others

Some hyperactive-impulsive or inattentive symptoms cause impairment present before age seven

Some impairment from the symptoms present in two or more settings, such as school and home

Clear evidence of clinically significant impairment in social, academic, or occupational functioning

Symptoms do not occur exclusively during the course of a pervasive developmental disorder, schizophrenia, or other psychotic disorder and are not better accounted for by another mental disorder (mood disorder, anxiety disorder, dissociative disorder, personality disorder)

DSM code based on type:
- Attention-Deficit/Hyperactivity Disorder, Predominantly Inattentive Type (DSM code 314.00): Inattention, but not hyperactivity-impulsivity during the previous six months
- Attention-Deficit/Hyperactivity Disorder, Predominantly Hyperactive-Impulsive Type (DSM code 314.01): Hyperactivity-impulsivity but not inattention during the previous six months
- Attention-Deficit/Hyperactivity Disorder, Combined Type (DSM code 314.01): Both inattention and hyperactivity-impulsivity during the previous six months

---

apy have not been found to be effective in the treatment of ADHD. Stimulant medications have been used in the treatment of ADHD since 1937. The most commonly prescribed stimulant medications are methylphenidate (Ritalin), pemoline (Cylert), and dextroamphetamine (Dexedrine). Behavioral improvements caused by stimulant medications include impulse control and improved attending behavior. Overall, approximately 75 percent of ADHD children on stimulant medication show behavioral

improvement, and 25 percent show either no improvement or decreased behavioral functioning. The findings related to academic performance are mixed. It appears that stimulant medications can help the ADHD child with school productivity and accuracy, but not with overall academic achievement. In addition, although ADHD children tend to show improvement while they are on a stimulant medication, there are rarely any long-term benefits to the use of stimulant medications. In general, stimulant medication can be seen as only a short-term management tool.

Antidepressant medications (such as imipramine and Prozac) have also been used with ADHD children. These medications are sometimes used when stimulant medication is not appropriate (for example, if the child has motor or vocal tics). Antidepressant medications, however, like stimulant medications, appear to provide only short-term improvement in ADHD symptoms. Overall, the use or nonuse of medications in the treatment of ADHD should be carefully evaluated by a qualified physician (such as a psychiatrist). If the child is started on medication for ADHD, the safety and appropriateness of the medication must be monitored continually throughout its use.

BEHAVIOR THERAPIES

Behavioral and cognitive-behavioral treatments have been used with ADHD children themselves, with parents, and with teachers. Most of these techniques attempt to provide the child with a consistent environment in which on-task behavior is rewarded (for example, the teacher praises the child for raising his or her hand and not shouting out an answer), and in which off-task behavior is either ignored or punished (for example, the parent has the child sit alone in a chair near an empty wall, a "time-out chair," after the child impulsively throws a book across the room). In addition, cognitive-behavioral treatments try to teach ADHD children to internalize their own self-control by learning to "stop and think" before they act.

One example of a cognitive-behavioral treatment, which was developed by Philip Kendall and Lauren Braswell, is intended to teach the child to learn five "steps" that can be applied to academic tasks as well as social interactions. The five problem-solving steps that children are to repeat to themselves each time they encounter a new situation are the following: Ask "What am I supposed to do?"; ask "What are my choices?"; concentrate and focus in; make a choice; ask "How did I do?" (If I did well, I can congratulate myself; if I did poorly, I should try to go more slowly next time.) In each therapy session, the child is given twenty plastic chips at the beginning of the session. The child loses a chip each time he or she does not use one of the steps, goes too fast, or gives an incorrect answer. At the end of the session, the child can use the chips to purchase a small prize; chips can also be stored in a "bank" in order to purchase an even larger prize in the following sessions. This treatment approach combines the use of cognitive strategies (the child learns self-instructional steps) and behavioral techniques (the child loses a desired object, a chip, for impulsive behavior).

Overall, behavioral and cognitive-behavioral treatments have been found to be relatively effective in the settings in which they are used and at the time they are being instituted. Like the effects of medication, however, the effects of behavioral and cognitive-behavioral therapies tend not to be long-lasting. There is some evidence to suggest that the combination of medication and behavior therapy can increase the effectiveness of treatment. In the long run, however, no treatment of ADHD has been found to be truly effective, and in a majority of cases, the disorder persists into adulthood.

HISTORY AND CHANGING DIAGNOSTIC CRITERIA

Children who might now be diagnosed as having ADHD have been written about and discussed in scientific publications since the mid-1800's. Attention to ADHD began in the United States after an encephalitis epidemic in 1917. Because the damage to the central nervous system caused by the disease led to poor attention, impulsivity, and overactivity in children who survived, researchers began to look for signs of brain injury in other children who had similar behavioral profiles. By the 1950's, researchers began to refer to this disorder as "minimal brain damage," which was then changed to "minimal brain dysfunction" (MBD). By the 1960's, however, the use of the term MBD was severely criticized because of its overinclusiveness and nonspecificity. Researchers began to use terms that more specifically characterized children's problems, such as "hyperkinesis" and "hyperactivity."

The *Diagnostic and Statistical Manual of Mental Disorders* (DSM), published by the American Psychiatric Association, is the primary diagnostic manual used in the United States. In 1968, the second edition, called DSM-II, presented the diagnosis of "Hyperkinetic Reaction of Childhood" to characterize children who were overactive and restless. By 1980, when the third edition (DSM-III) was published, researchers had begun to focus on the deficits of attention in these children, so two diagnostic categories were established: "Attention Deficit Disorder with Hyperactivity (ADD with H)" and "Attention Deficit Disorder without Hyperactivity (ADD without H)." After the publication of DSM-III, many researchers argued that there were no empirical data to support the existence of the ADD without H diagnosis. In other words, it was difficult to find any children who were inattentive and impulsive but who were not hyperactive. For this reason, in 1987, when the revised DSM-III-R was published, the only diagnostic category for these children was "Attention-Deficit Hyperactivity Disorder (ADHD)."

With the publication of the fourth version of the manual, the DSM-IV, in 1994, three distinct diagnostic categories for ADHD were identified: ADHD Predominantly Hyperactive-Impulsive Type, ADHD Predominantly Inattentive Type, and ADHD Combined Type. The type of ADHD diagnosed is dependent upon the number and types of behavioral symptoms a child exhibits. Six of nine symptoms from the Hyperactivity-Implusivity list but fewer than six symptoms from the Inattention list lead to a diagnosis of ADHD Predominantly Hyperactive-Impulsive Type. Six of nine symptoms from the Inattention list but fewer than six symptoms from the Hyperactivity-Implusivity list lead to a diagnosis of ADHD Predominantly Inattentive Type. A child who exhibits six of nine behavioral symptoms simultaneously from both lists receives a diagnosis of ADHD Combined Type.

While the diagnostic definition and specific terminology of ADHD will undoubtedly continue to change throughout the years, the interest in and commitment to this disorder will likely continue. Children and adults with ADHD, as well as the people around them, have difficult lives to lead. The research community is committed to finding better explanations of the etiology and treatment of this common disorder.

SOURCES FOR FURTHER STUDY

Barkley, Russell A. "Attention-Deficit Hyperactivity Disorder." In *Treatment of Childhood Disorders*, edited by E. J. Mash and R. A. Barkley. New York: Guilford, 1989. This chapter provides a thorough discussion of different treatments for ADHD children, including stimulant medication, antidepressant medication, behavior therapy, parent training, teacher training, and cognitive-behavioral therapy. Each treatment modality is discussed in a fair and objective manner, and empirical research is provided to support the conclusions given.

_____. *Attention-Deficit Hyperactivity Disorder: A Handbook for Diagnosis and Treatment*. New York: Guilford, 1990. Provides comprehensive discussion of nearly all aspects of ADHD, including assessment, diagnosis, and treatment. Also notable for a thorough discussion of ADHD in older adolescents and adults. This excellent and comprehensive book is written by one of the leading researchers in the investigation of ADHD.

Kendall, Philip C. "Attention-Deficit Hyperactivity Disorder." In *Childhood Disorders*. Hove, East Sussex, U.K.: Psychology Press, 2000. A volume in the series Clinical Psychology, A Modular Course. A succinct but thorough discussion of ADHD, including current research on cognitive and neuropsychological performance of children with the disorder.

Wender, Paul H. *ADHD: Attention-Deficit Hyperactivity Disorder in Children and Adults*. New York: Oxford University Press, 2000. A comprehensive overview of ADHD history, diagnosis, treatment. Discusses strengths associated with ADHD as well as problems associated with the disorder.

Wodrich, David L. *Attention-Deficit/Hyperactivity Disorder: What Every Parent Wants to Know*. 2d ed. Baltimore: Paul H. Brookes, 2000. A book aimed at the general public, containing practical advice and clear descriptions of ADHD and related disorders, as well as resources for treatment.

Vicky Phares;
updated by Virginia Slaughter

SEE ALSO: Abnormality: Biomedical models; Cognitive behavior therapy; Conduct disorder; *Diagnostic and Statistical Manual of Mental Disorders* (DSM); Drug therapies.

Attitude-behavior consistency

TYPE OF PSYCHOLOGY: Social psychology
FIELDS OF STUDY: Attitudes and behavior

Research on attitude-behavior consistency examines the extent to which self-reported attitudes predict and guide behavior. It has outlined the conditions under which attitudes can and cannot be expected to be consistent with behavior, and has provided an understanding of the process by which attitudes may influence behavior.

INTRODUCTION

Most people would answer the following questions—Why does John go to see films often? Why will Sue not eat broccoli? Why does Mark read mystery novels? Why does Mary usually wear green?—by referring to the attitudes of the person in question. An attitude is defined as a positive or negative evaluation of a person, place, or thing. John goes to films because he likes them; Sue will not eat broccoli because she does not care for broccoli; Mark reads mystery novels because he enjoys them; Mary wears green because it is her favorite color.

Social psychologists have found that most people routinely explain other people's behavior, and their own, in terms of underlying attitudes. People tend to believe that attitudes influence and are predictive of most behaviors. Despite these intuitive notions, however, research has suggested that attitudes in general are actually very limited predictors of behavior. That is, there is generally not a high degree of consistency between people's attitudes and their behaviors. In fact, the extent to which attitudes predict and are consistent with behavior appears to depend on a number of variables, including what type of behavior is to be predicted, how the attitude was formed, what kind of personality the person has, and how easily the attitude can be recalled.

Imagine that a researcher wanted to predict whether people regularly attend religious services. He or she might reasonably ask them about their attitudes toward organized religion, expecting that those with more favorable attitudes toward organized religion would be more likely to attend services regularly than those with less favorable attitudes. If the researcher did this, however, he or she would not be likely to find much correspondence at all between attitudes and behaviors.

The reason for this is that the researcher is asking about a very general attitude and very specific behavior. For attitudes to predict behavior, both must be measured at the same level of specificity. If the researcher wants to predict a specific behavior, he or she needs to ask about an attitude specific to that behavior. In this example, he or she should not ask about general attitudes toward religion, but rather about attitudes toward attending religious services. These latter attitudes will be much more predictive of behavior. Attitudes that best predict behavior are attitudes about that specific behavior.

Sometimes, however, even specific attitudes will not correspond to specific behaviors. Icek Ajzen and Martin Fishbein, in their theory of reasoned action, propose that attitudes toward a behavior are only one influence on behavior. A second factor to consider, they suggest, is the subjective norm, which refers to individuals' beliefs about what important others (for example, parents, teachers, peers) think they should do. For some behaviors, the subjective norm is more important than attitude in predicting behavior. Even though someone might have a positive attitude toward attending religious services, he or she still might not go because of a belief that important others do not think that he or she should go.

FACTORS IN PREDICTING BEHAVIOR

Even in the case of behaviors for which attitude is the more important influence, however, there are other factors that determine the extent to which that attitude will predict behavior. One factor concerns how the attitude was formed, which generally is in one of two ways. Attitudes may be based on direct, personal experience with the object or person in question. A person may dislike religious services because he or she attended a few and had a number of unpleasant experiences. Alternatively, attitudes may be based on indirect, secondhand experiences. A person may dislike services because of what he or she has read and heard about them. In general, attitudes based on direct experience are much more predictive of behavior than are attitudes based on indirect experience.

A second concern is the type of person someone is. According to psychologist Mark Snyder, when deciding how to behave in a social situation, some people look to the environment and try to be the type of person called for by the situation; they are known as high self-monitors. If the situation calls for a quiet, introverted person, they will be quiet and introverted. If the situation calls for a loud, extroverted person, they will be loud and extroverted. In contrast, low self-monitors look inside themselves and ask, "How do I feel right now?" They base their behavior on their feelings regardless of what is called for in the situation. If they feel like being introverted, they will be introverted; if they feel like being extroverted, they will be extroverted. As might be expected, low self-monitors display a higher degree of attitude-behavior consistency than do high self-monitors.

A last, but perhaps most important, consideration is the ease with which an attitude can be recalled from memory, known as the degree of attitude accessibility. Simply put, the more accessible the attitude, the more likely it is that the attitude will predict behavior. Interestingly, attitudes based on direct experience tend to be more accessible than attitudes based on indirect experience, and low self-monitors tend to have more accessible attitudes than do high self-monitors. In general, any factor that increases attitude accessibility increases the extent to which that attitude will guide future behavior.

IMPACT ON POLITICS

One arena in which attitude-behavior consistency is an important concern is politics. Millions of dollars are spent on advertising during a political campaign. These funds are spent in an effort to influence attitudes, in the hope that attitudes will then influence behavior. The question arises as to whether these dollars are well spent—whether attitudes toward political candidates predict voting behavior.

To investigate this question, psychologists Russell Fazio and Carol Williams examined the relations between attitudes toward the two major-party candidates in the 1984 United States presidential election, Ronald Reagan and Walter Mondale, and various behaviors, such as perceptions of the televised presidential debates and voting. They assessed individuals' attitudes toward the candidates in June and July of the election year. The presidential debates were held in October, the election in November. As it turns out, overall, attitudes were indeed very predictive of behaviors. Attitudes toward the candidates predicted reactions to the presidential debates, with Reagan supporters believing he was more impressive than Mondale and Mondale supporters believing the opposite. Attitudes also generally predicted voting behavior very well. Those supporting Reagan tended to vote for him, and those supporting Mondale tended to vote for Mondale.

Although it is impressive that attitudes assessed in the summer months predicted behaviors three and four months later, so far the results may not be very surprising.

Fazio and Williams did not, however, simply examine the relations between attitudes and behaviors. When they assessed individuals' attitudes during the summer months, they also measured the accessibility of those attitudes—that is, how easily the subjects could call the attitudes to mind. To do this, they asked participants in their study to agree or disagree with different tape-recorded statements (for example, "A good president for the next four years would be Ronald Reagan") as quickly as possible by pressing one of five buttons on a computer; one button represented "strongly agree," one "agree," one "neutral," one "disagree," and one "strongly disagree." The computer then recorded how long it took the participants to respond after they heard the statements. Fazio and Williams reasoned that the more quickly people could respond, the more accessible their attitudes were.

Based on the results, Fazio and Williams classified some people as having highly accessible attitudes and others as having less accessible attitudes. When they then reexamined reactions to the presidential debates and voting behavior, they found that attitude-behavior consistency was much higher for those with highly accessible attitudes than for those with less accessible attitudes. That is, those with highly accessible attitudes were much more likely to act in a way consistent with their attitudes than were those with less accessible attitudes. For example, not everyone who agreed in June or July that Reagan would be a good president for the next four years voted for him in November. Those for whom this attitude could easily be brought to mind were much more likely to act on this attitude and vote for him than were those who had the same attitude but could not bring it to mind as quickly. It appears that, for attitudes to guide behavior successfully, they must be easily retrieved from memory.

FREQUENCY OF ATTITUDE EXPRESSION

Two of the factors that influence the ease with which attitudes can be recalled have already been discussed: how the attitude was formed, and whether one is a high or low self-monitor. An additional factor seems to be the number of times the attitude is expressed. In one study, students watched a videotape of five different puzzles and then expressed their interest in each of the puzzles. Some students were asked to express their attitudes once, while others were asked to express them three different times (on three different forms). When they were later asked to rate the puzzles along different dimensions as quickly as they could on a computer (just as in the voting study discussed above), those who had initially expressed their attitudes three times had quicker reaction times than those who had initially expressed their attitudes once, suggesting that repeated attitude expression makes attitudes more accessible. In a follow-up study, after students had seen the videotape of the puzzles and had expressed their attitudes toward the puzzles either one or three times, the researchers allowed the students actually to play with any or all of the puzzles. Attitudes toward the puzzles predicted playing behavior much better for those who had initially expressed their attitudes three times than for those who had initially expressed their attitudes once. The more often an attitude is expressed, the more accessible it becomes and the more likely it is to influence behavior.

EVOLUTION OF ATTITUDE-BEHAVIOR THEORIES

The extent to which attitudes predict and influence behavior is at the heart of social psychology. At its inception, social psychology was defined as the study of attitudes, and although the importance of attitudes has waxed and waned as the field has matured, most social psychologists would still consider attitudes to be a central concept. In fact, at least half the articles in any given scholarly journal in the field generally discuss some aspect of attitudes.

In this context, one can imagine the shock that the social psychological community felt when, in 1969, A. W. Wicker published a review of numerous studies examining the relations between attitudes and behaviors which concluded that attitudes generally bear little relation to overt behavior and do not predict behavior well at all. Historically, it is interesting to note that, about this same time, a personality psychologist named Walter Mischel was making similar conclusions about personality traits. In the research he reviewed, there did not seem to be much relationship between people's personality traits and their behavior.

The reaction to Wicker's review was mixed. Some called for social psychology to abandon attitudes as a focal point of research. After all, they argued, if attitudes cannot predict behavior, and since the goal of any field of psychology is to predict behavior, it would be foolish to spend more time and effort studying attitudes.

Although this type of reaction had many supporters, others took a more optimistic approach to addressing what became known as the attitude-behavior problem. Wicker's review, they suggested, concluded that on average attitudes do not seem to predict behavior; yet in some of the studies he reviewed, attitudes did predict behavior quite well. The question for these researchers, then, was not whether attitudes predict behavior—because in some cases, they clearly do—but rather, when and under what circumstances attitudes predict behavior. As a result, in the 1970's and 1980's, considerable research was directed at identifying those factors that seemed to increase or decrease the degree of attitude-behavior consistency. It was these efforts that shed light on the role of direct experience and self-monitoring.

In the 1970's and 1980's, social psychologists became convinced that, under certain circumstances, attitudes do predict and influence behavior. The next area to be explored is the process by which attitudes influence behavior. The pioneering work of Fazio has pointed out a direction in which to travel to answer this question, but much more research is needed before this remaining section of the attitude-behavior consistency puzzle can be solved.

SOURCES FOR FURTHER STUDY

Ajzen, Icek, and Martin Fishbein. *Understanding Attitudes and Predicting Social Behavior.* Englewood Cliffs, N.J.: Prentice-Hall, 1997. A very readable introduction to the authors' theory of reasoned action. Applied implications of the theory for specific areas such as political, consumer, and dieting behavior are also discussed, and more general implications for attitude change and persuasion are addressed.

Fazio, Russell. "How Do Attitudes Guide Behavior?" In *Handbook of Motivation and Cognition,* edited by Richard M. Sorrentino and E. Tory Higgins. Vol. 2. New York: Guilford, 1986. An excellent introduction to Fazio's initial work on the role of attitude accessibility. Also provides a brief history of the attitude-behavior consistency controversy and attempts to show how issues of attitude accessibility may help resolve parts of the controversy.

Fazio, Russell, and Mark P. Zanna. "Direct Experience and Attitude-Behavior Consistency." In *Advances in Experimental Social Psychology*, edited by Leonard Berkowitz. Vol. 14. New York: Academic Press, 1981. A thorough review of the research and theory on the role that attitude formation plays in the attitude-behavior relationship. Offers examples of both field research and laboratory research. Ideas presented here lay the foundation for Fazio's later work on attitude accessibility.

Terry, Deborah, and Michael Hogg, eds. *Attitudes, Behavior, and Social Context: The Role of Norms and Group Membership*. Hillsdale, N.J.: Lawrence Erlbaum, 1999. A collection of essays on the relationships of attitude and behavior.

Van der Pligt, Joop, Nanne K. de Vries, Antony S. R. Manstead, and Frenk van Harreveld. "The Importance of Being Selective: Weighing the Role of Attribute Importance in Attitudinal Judgment." In *Advances in Experimental Social Psychology*, edited by Mark P. Zanna. Vol. 32. San Diego, Calif.: Academic Press, 2000. A study of the process of maintaining attitude consistency.

Zanna, Mark P., E. Tory Higgins, and C. Peter Herman, eds. *Consistency in Social Behavior: The Ontario Symposium*. Vol. 2. Hillsdale, N.J.: Lawrence Erlbaum, 1982. Perhaps the most important single volume on attitude-behavior relations. The twelve chapters, written by the leading authorities on the topic, raise and discuss all the important issues about not only attitude-behavior relations but personality trait-behavior relations as well. Important for anyone who wishes to understand attitude-behavior relations thoroughly.

Kenneth G. DeBono

SEE ALSO: Attitude formation and change; Causal attribution; Cognitive dissonance; Crowd behavior; Personality theory; Self-perception; Violence and sexuality in the media.

Attitude formation and change

TYPE OF PSYCHOLOGY: Social psychology
FIELDS OF STUDY: Attitudes and behavior

Research has suggested many theories of attitude change; these theories have led to the development of numerous persuasion tactics and principles that find use in a variety of settings ranging from the mass media to consumer sales to organizational negotiations.

KEY CONCEPTS
- attitude
- central and peripheral routes
- cognitive dissonance theory
- cognitive response theory
- dual-mode processing model
- functional theories
- learning theory of persuasion
- persuasion
- self-perception theory
- social influence
- social judgment theory

INTRODUCTION

An attitude is a person's positive or negative evaluation of an object or thought; examples include "I support gun control," "I dislike brand X," and "I love the person next door." Much research finds that attitudes can influence a broad range of cognitive processes such as social inference, reasoning, perception, and interpretation, and can thereby influence behavior. In general, people favor, approach, praise, and cherish those things they like, and disfavor, avoid, blame, and harm those things they dislike. Given that attitudes can have pervasive effects on social behavior, it is important to understand how attitudes are formed and changed.

Attitudes can be formed directly through observation of one's own behavior or through experience with the attitude object. They may also be formed by exposure to social influences such as parents and peers, the mass media, schools and religious organizations, and important reference groups. William McGuire notes that attitudes are one of the most extensively studied topics in social psychology. Much of this research has centered on the question, Who says what to whom, with what effects?

For example, research has varied the source (or "who") of a message and found that people tend to be most persuaded by credible, trustworthy, attractive, and similar communicators. Research on message characteristics (or "what") has shown that fear appeals increase persuasion if accompanied by specific recommendations for how to avoid the fear; that there is a tendency for arguments presented first to have more impact, especially if there is a delay between hearing the arguments and making an evaluation; and that messages which present only one side of an issue are most effective when the recipient lacks the skills or motivation to process the information. In general, research shows that an audience (or "whom") is less persuaded if the message is wildly discrepant from original beliefs; such research also finds that an audience is less persuaded if it has been forewarned about the persuasion attempt and takes steps to prepare a counterargument. The effects of social influence are usually described in terms of compliance (attitude change, often short-lived, as a result of wanting to obtain rewards or avoid punishment), identification (change as a result of seeking to be similar to or distinguished from the source of a message), and internalization (change as a result of accepting a position on the basis of its merits).

EARLY RESEARCH

Perhaps social psychology's first theory of persuasion, the learning model is based on the research of Carl Hovland and his colleagues at Yale University in the 1950's. According to this model, a message is persuasive when it rewards the recipient at each of the following stages of psychological processing of a message: attention, comprehension, message learning, and yielding. For example, a highly credible source is persuasive because it is rewarding to attend to and comprehend what he or she says, and then to act on it.

One problem with the learning model of persuasion is that subsequent research in the 1960's found that persuasion could occur even if the message was only minimally comprehended and the message's content was forgotten or never learned. To account for these results, the cognitive response approach posited that the key determinant of persuasion was not message learning but the thoughts running through a person's head as he or she received a communication. Effective communications are ones that direct and channel thoughts so that the target thinks in a manner agreeable to the communicator's point of view.

Later research reversed the casual sequence of the learning model from one of "attitudes cause behavior" to "behavior causes attitudes." Two theories which utilize this counterintuitve approach are cognitive dissonance theory and self-perception theory. According to consistency theories such as cognitive dissonance theory, people attempt to rationalize their behavior and to avoid a state of dissonance, or simultaneously holding two dissonant cognitions (ideas, beliefs, or opinions). Persuasion occurs as a result of resolving this dissonance. For example, fraternity and sorority pledges often must perform embarrassing behavior to gain admission to the organization. The thoughts "I just ate a plate of grasshoppers as an initiation rite" and "It is stupid to eat grasshoppers" are dissonant with a positive view of oneself. One way to reduce this dissonance is to reevaluate the fraternity or sorority more positively: "I ate those grasshoppers because I wanted to join a great club."

Self-perception theory states that attitudes are based on observing one's own behavior and then attributing the behavior to underlying beliefs. For example, suppose a man is at a dinner party and is served brown bread, which he then eats. When asked, "Do you like brown bread?" he observes his eating behavior and concludes that he does (unless there is some other plausible reason, such as force or politeness). While dissonance theories serve to explain attitude change when existing attitudes conflict with one's current behavior, self-perception theory proposes that when there is no better available explanation for one's behavior, observing "what I do" is the best indication of one's attitudes.

Social judgment theory attempts to explain how attitude formation and change occur within a single social context. Attitude change can occur when the context for making judgments is changed. For example, in one study, males rated photographs of females as much less attractive after viewing the 1970's television show *Charlie's Angels*. In other words, the very attractive female stars of *Charlie's Angels* provided a highly positive context in which to rate the photographs, and thus made women of average attractiveness appear much less attractive.

DUAL-MODE PROCESSING MODELS

In an effort to synthesize the vast persuasion research, psychologists proposed a dual-mode processing approach to attitude formation and change. Dual-mode processing models emphasize two factors which influence the success of a persuasion attempt, both the recipient's motivation and the recipient's ability to process an argument.

Richard Petty and John Cacioppo have suggested there are two routes to persuasion. In the peripheral route, recipients give little thought to a message, perhaps because they have little motivation to think about it or lack the necessary skills, and persuasion is based less on the arguments made and more on simple persuasion cues or heuristics such as the credibility of the source and the number of other people who agree with the message. Cognitive dissonance, self-perception, and social judgment theory models of attitude change often emphasize peripheral routes, as anxiety reduction, the lack of alternative explanations, and contextual cues are the important determinants of persuasion as opposed to careful analysis of the message.

In the central route, where people are motivated and able to process the message, recipients carefully scrutinize the communication, and persuasion is determined by the quality and cogency of the arguments. The central route is emphasized in cognitive response theories of persuasion. Although cognitive responses can vary on a number of dimensions, two of the most important ones are evaluation and elaboration. Most cognitive responses to a message are either positive evaluations (support arguments) or negative evaluations (counterarguments) toward the message's conclusion. Studies that disrupt these cognitive responses and decrease the recipient's ability to process the argument using a mild distraction (for example, background noises or difficult-to-read print) have found that a distraction results in more persuasion when the recipient's natural tendency is to make arguments against the message, and less persuasion when the recipient normally would have supported the message. Elaboration refers to how much thought a recipient gives to a message. Recipients who are highly motivated to analyze an argument are likely to give it more thought.

Dual-process models of attitude change have led researchers to examine when and why recipients are motivated to process a message carefully. Three motivations have been suggested to influence persuasion attempts. Recipients are motivated to make sense of themselves and their world, to protect or defend existing self or worldviews, and to maintain or enhance their social status. When the message corresponds to an individual's immediate motiva-

tions, persuasion attempts are more effective. For example, individuals who are more image-conscious (motivated to enhance their social status) are more likely to be persuaded by arguments which emphasize the social consequences of a behavior while messages which emphasize the personal benefits of a behavior are more effective with those who are more internally guided.

Functional theories of attitude change incorporate these motivational goals. Functional theories posit that attitude formation and change are made when such change functions to serve a recipient's needs. For example, consider someone who is prejudiced against an ethnic group. This negative attitude helps the person interpret, often incorrectly, social reality ("Members of the ethnic group can do no good and often are the cause of problems"), helps the person maintain a positive view of self ("I am better than they are"), and may enhance the person's social status ("I'm a member of a superior social group"). Advertisers make use of functional theories when they market products to appeal to self-images; in such cases, a product is liked and used to obtain a desired image, such as appearing to be sophisticated, macho, a modern woman, and so on.

HISTORY OF PERSUASION RESEARCH

As early as 1935, Gordon Allport declared that attitude is social psychology's "most indispensable construct." Research on attitudes began in the 1920's in the United States as a response to changing social conditions. The period was marked by the rise of new mass media such as radio and mass-circulated magazines, the development of large-scale consumer markets, and the changing nature of political activity. Such developments required that the attitudes and opinions of citizens toward a variety of issues be measured and tracked. Academic researchers responded by developing techniques of attitude scaling and measurement and by laying the foundation for survey methodology. The first empirical research on attitudes sought to address questions such as "How are movies changing Americans' attitudes and values?" and "Has modern life changed traditional cultural attitudes?"

World War II changed the focus of attitude research from an interest in measurement to an interest in understanding attitude change and persuasion. Many of the post-World War II attitude researchers either had fled Nazi Germany or had worked for the Allies in an attempt either to defuse Nazi propaganda or to bolster their fellow citizens' attitudes toward the war effort. After the war, in the 1950's, many researchers attempted to explain the propaganda and attitude-change tactics used during the war and now increasingly employed in the mass media. This research resulted in the development of learning, functional, social judgment, and cognitive consistency theories of persuasion.

PRACTICAL APPLICATIONS

Research and theorizing on attitude change have led to the development of numerous tactics and principles of persuasion. These principles are useful for interpreting persuasion effects such as those that occur in mass media and interpersonal or organizational settings, and for directing persuasion attempts. Three of the more popular tactics will be discussed here.

One of the simplest and most surefire ways to ensure positive cognitive responses is to induce the target to argue for the message conclusion, a tactic known as self-generated persuasion. For example, in one study during World War II, women were asked to "help" a researcher by coming up with reasons that other women should serve organ and intestinal meats (brains, kidneys, and so on) to their families as part of the war effort. These women were eleven times as likely to serve such meats as those who were merely lectured to do so. In another study, consumers were asked to imagine the benefits of subscribing to cable television versus being told about those benefits. Those who imagined subscribing were two and a one-half times as likely to subscribe as those who were merely told about the benefits.

The "foot-in-the-door" technique makes use of cognitive dissonance theory. In this tactic, the communicator secures compliance to a big request by first putting his or her "foot in the door" by asking for a small favor that almost everyone will typically do. For example, in one study, residents were asked to place in their yards a large, ugly sign that read "Drive Carefully." Few residents complied unless they had been "softened up" the week before by an experimenter who got them to sign a petition favoring safe driving. For those residents, putting the ugly sign in the yard helped avoid cognitive dissonance: "Last week I supported safe driving. This week I will be a hypocrite if I don't put this ugly sign in my yard."

Another effective tactic is to add a decoy, or a worthless item that no one would normally want, to a person's set of choices. For example, a real estate agent may show customers overpriced, run-down homes, or a car dealer may place an old clunker of a used car on his or her lot. Consistent with social judgment theory, such decoys create a context for judging the other "real" alternatives and make them appear more attractive. An unsuspecting consumer is more likely to select and buy these "more attractive" items.

Attitude research since the 1960's has sought to test and develop the major theories of attitude change, to refine the principles of persuasion, and to apply these principles to an ever-expanding list of targets. For example, research on the relationship between attitude change and memory of a communication led to the development of a cognitive response analysis of persuasion in the late 1960's. Many of the compliance techniques described by Robert Cialdini and by Anthony Pratkanis and Elliot Aronson were first elaborated in this period. As knowledge of persuasion improves, the principles of persuasion are increasingly applied to solve social problems. Prosocial goals to which theories of persuasion have been applied include decreasing energy consumption and increasing waste recycling, slowing the spread of acquired immunodeficiency syndrome (AIDS) by changing attitudes toward safe sex practices, lowering the automobile death toll by increasing seat belt use, improving health by promoting practices such as good dental hygiene and regular medical checkups, improving worker morale and worker relationships, and reducing intergroup prejudice.

SOURCES FOR FURTHER STUDY

Allport, Gordon W. "Attitudes." In *Handbook of Social Psychology*, edited by Carl Allanmore Murchison. Worchester, Mass.: Clark University Press, 1935. The first review of the attitude concept. Provides a useful introduction to the historical origins of attitude research.

Cialdini, Robert B. *Influence: How and Why People Agree to Things.* 3d ed. New York: HarperCollins, 1993. This highly readable account provides a fascinating discussion of six of the most frequently used compliance tactics.

Eagly, A. H., and S. Chaiken. *The Psychology of Attitudes*. San Diego, Calif.: Harcourt Brace Jovanovich, 1992. A comprehensive analysis of a half century of research on attitudes and attitude change.

Hovland, Carl Iver, Irving L. Janis, and Harold H. Kelley. *Communication and Persuasion*. New Haven, Conn.: Yale University Press, 1953. This first research monograph on persuasion covers issues such as source credibility, fear appeals, and personality and persuasion.

Perloff, R. M. *The Dynamics of Persuasion*. Hillsdale, N.J.: Lawrence Erlbaum, 1993. Easy-to-read text with practical examples of persuasion from cults to mass media.

Petty, Richard E., and John T. Cacioppo. *Attitudes and Persuasion: Classic and Contemporary Approaches*. Boulder, Colo.: Westview, 1996. An excellent textbook that provides a description of major theories of persuasion and supporting research.

_____. *Communication and Persuasion: Central and Peripheral Routes to Attitude Change*. New York: Springer-Verlag, 1986. Provides a detailed description of the role of elaboration in persuasion and provides a useful summary of recent research in persuasion.

Petty, Richard E., and Duane T. Wegener. "Attitude Change: Multiple Roles for Persuasion Variables." In *Handbook of Social Psychology*, edited by Daniel T. Gilbert, Susan T. Fiske, G. Lindzey. 4th ed. New York: McGraw-Hill, 1998. A detailed review of persuasion research with a focus on the interaction of the multiple variables involved in attitude change.

Pratkanis, Anthony R., and Elliot Aronson. *The Age of Propaganda: The Everyday Use and Abuse of Persuasion*. Rev. ed. New York: W. H. Freeman, 2001. A popular treatment of the role of persuasion in society. Describes numerous persuasion tactics and provides the reader with an in-depth analysis of how they work and what can be done to prevent unwanted propaganda.

Pratkanis, Anthony R., Steven J. Breckler, and Anthony G. Greenwald, eds. *Attitude Structure and Function*. Hillsdale, N.J.: Lawrence Erlbaum, 1989. The papers in this volume summarize how attitudes influence social processes such as cognition and behavior, and update functional theories of attitude.

Zimbardo, Philip G., and Michael R. Leippe. *The Psychology of Attitude Change and Social Influence*. Philadelphia: Temple University Press, 1991. This textbook presents an engaging review of attitude-change techniques and analyzes their use in various social settings.

Anthony R. Pratkanis and Marlene E. Turner;
updated by Michelle Murphy

SEE ALSO: Attitude-behavior consistency; Cognitive dissonance; Consumer psychology; Decision making; Self-perception; Survey research: Questionnaires and interviews.

Attraction theories

TYPE OF PSYCHOLOGY: Social psychology
FIELDS OF STUDY: Interpersonal relations

Theories of interpersonal attraction attempt to specify the conditions that lead people to like, and in some cases love, each other. Attraction is a two-way process, involving not only the person who is attracted but also the attractor.

KEY CONCEPTS
- equity theory
- matching phenomenon
- mere exposure
- physical attractiveness stereotype
- proximity
- reciprocity
- reinforcement model
- social exchange theory

INTRODUCTION

Relationships are central to human social existence. Personal accounts by people who have been forced to endure long periods of isolation serve as reminders of people's dependence on others, and research suggests that close relationships are the most vital ingredient in a happy and meaningful life. In short, questions dealing with attraction are among the most fundamental in social psychology.

The major theories addressing interpersonal attraction have a common theme: reinforcement. The principle of reinforcement is one of the most basic notions in all of psychology. Put simply, it states that behaviors that are followed by desirable consequences (often these take the form of rewards) tend to be repeated. Applied to interpersonal relations, this principle suggests that when one person finds something rewarding in an interaction with another person (or if that person anticipates some reward in a relationship that has not yet been established), then the person should desire further interaction with that other individual. In behavioral terms, this is what is meant by the term "interpersonal attraction," which emerges in everyday language in such terms as "liking" or, in the case of deep romantic involvement, "loving." Appropriately, these theories, based on the notion that individuals are drawn to relationships that are rewarding and avoid those that are not, are known as reinforcement or reward models of interpersonal attraction.

The first and most basic theory of this type was proposed in the early 1970's by Donn Byrne and Gerald Clore. Known as the reinforcement-affect model of attraction ("affect" means "feeling" or "emotion"), this theory proposes that people will be attracted not only to other people who reward them but also to those people whom they associate with rewards. In other words, a person can learn to like others through their connections to experiences that are positive for that individual. It is important to recognize that a major implication here is that it is possible to like someone not so much because of that person himself or herself, but rather as a consequence of that person's merely being part of a rewarding situation; positive feelings toward the experience itself get transferred to that other person. (It also follows that a person associated with something unpleasant will tend to be disliked.) This is called indirect reinforcement.

For example, in one experiment done during the summer, people who evaluated new acquaintances in a cool and comfortable room liked them better than when in a hot and uncomfortable room. In another, similar, study subjects rating photographs of strangers gave more favorable evaluations when in a nicely furnished room than when they were in a dirty room with shabby furniture. These findings provide some insight into why married couples may find that their relationship benefits from a weekend trip away from the children or a romantic dinner at a favorite restaurant; the pleasant event enhances their feelings for each other.

There are other models of interpersonal attraction that involve the notion of rewards but consider the degree to which they are offset by the costs associated with a relationship. Social exchange theory suggests that people tend to evaluate social situations. In the context of a relationship, a person will compare the costs and benefits of beginning or continuing that relationship. Imagine, for example, that Karen is considering a date with Dave, who is kind, attractive, and financially stable but fifteen years older. Karen may decide that this relationship is not worth pursuing because of the disapproval of her mother and father, who believe strongly that their daughter should be dating a man her own age. Karen's decision will be influenced by how much she values the approval of her parents and by whether she has other dating alternatives available.

A third model of attraction, equity theory, extends social exchange theory. This approach suggests that it is essential to take into account how both parties involved in a relationship assess the costs and benefits. When each person believes that his or her own ratio of costs to benefits is fair (or equitable), then attraction between the two tends to be promoted. On the other hand, a relationship may be placed in jeopardy if one person thinks that the time, effort, and other resources being invested are justified, while the other person does not feel that way.

Considering the rewards involved in the process of interpersonal attraction provides a useful model, but one that is rather general. To understand attraction fully, one must look more specifically at what people find rewarding in relationships. Social psychological research has established some definite principles governing attraction that can be applied nicely within the reward framework.

FACTORS OF ATTRACTION

The first determinant of attraction, reciprocity, is probably fairly obvious, since it most directly reflects the reinforcement process; nevertheless, it is a powerful force: People tend to like others who like them back. There are few things more rewarding than genuine affection, support, concern, and other indicators that one is liked by another person.

The second principle, proximity, suggests that simple physical closeness tends to promote attraction. Research has confirmed what many people probably already know: People are most likely to become friends (or romantic partners) with others with whom they have worked, grown up, or gone to school. Other studies have shown that people living in dormitories or apartments tend to become friends with the neighbors who live closest to them. Simply being around people gives an individual a chance to interact with them, which in turn provides the opportunity to learn who is capable of providing the rewards sought in a relationship.

It seems, however, that there is yet another force at work, a very basic psychological process known as the mere exposure phenomenon. Research has demonstrated consistently that repeated exposure to something new tends to increase one's liking for it, and examples of the process are quite common in everyday life. It is not uncommon, for example, for a person to buy a new tape or compact disc by a favorite musical artist without actually having heard the new material, only to be disappointed upon listening to it. The listener soon discovers, however, that the album "grows" on him or her and finds himself or herself liking it quite a bit after hearing it a few times. Such occurrences probably involve the mere exposure phenomenon. In short, familiarity breeds liking, and physical closeness makes it possible for that familiarity to develop.

BEAUTY AND ROMANCE

Generally speaking, the same factors that promote the development of friendships also foster romantic attraction. The third principle of attraction, physical attractiveness, is somewhat of an exception, however, since it is more powerful in the romantic context.

In a classic study published by Elaine (Hatfield) Walster and her associates in 1966, University of Minnesota first-year men and women were randomly paired for dates to a dance. Prior to the date, these students had provided considerable information about themselves, some of it through personality tests. During the evening, each person individually completed a questionnaire that focused primarily on how much the person liked his or her date, and the participants were contacted for follow-up six months later. Despite the opportunity to discover complex facts about attraction, such as what kinds of personality traits link up within a couple to promote it, the only important factor in this

study was physical appearance. For both sexes, the better-looking the partner, the more the person liked his or her date, the stronger was the desire to date the person again, and the more likely the individual was actually to do so during the next six months.

The potent effect of physical attractiveness in this study sparked much interest in this variable on the part of researchers over the next decade or so. The earliest studies determined rather quickly that both men and women, given the opportunity to select a date from a group of several members of the opposite sex representing a range of attractiveness levels, almost invariably would select the most attractive one. Dating in real life, however, is seldom without the chance that the person asking another out might be turned down. When later experiments began building the possibility of rejection into their procedures, an interesting effect emerged, one that has been termed the "matching phenomenon." People tend to select romantic partners whose degree of attractiveness is very similar to their own.

Other research revealed that physically attractive people are often judged favorably on qualities other than their appearance. Even when nothing is known but what the person looks like, the physically attractive individual is thought to be happier, more intelligent, and more successful than someone who is less attractive. This finding is referred to as the "physical attractiveness stereotype," and it has implications that extend the role of appearance well beyond the matter of dating. Studies have shown, for example, that work (such as a writing sample) will be assessed more favorably when produced by an attractive person than when by someone less attractive, and that a cute child who misbehaves will be treated more leniently than a homely one. What is beautiful is also good, so to speak. Finally, one may note that physical attractiveness fits well with the reward model: It is pleasant and reinforcing both to look at an attractive person and to be seen with him or her, particularly if that person is one's date.

The last principle of attraction, similarity, is the most important one in long-term relationships, regardless of whether they are friendships or romances. An extremely large body of research has demonstrated consistently that the more similar two people are, especially attitudinally, the more they will like each other. It turns out that the old adage, "opposites attract," is simply false. (Note that the matching phenomenon also reflects similarity.) A friend or spouse who holds attitudes similar to one's own will provide rewards by confirming that one's own feelings and beliefs are correct; it is indeed reinforcing when someone else agrees.

EVOLUTIONARY THEORIES OF ATTRACTION

Evolutionary psychologists have provided an important new way to look at why individuals are attracted to others. Borrowing from the basic theorizing of the English biologist Charles Darwin, psychologists are paying increasing attention to the information provided by both physical and social features of living creatures. Everyone is influenced by what people look like, in that they form impressions of others before they even hear them speak. People often use the appearance and behavior of others to make a variety of judgments about them, and these judgments are made quickly, nonconsciously, and are fairly resistant to change. What sort of impressions are formed? What aspects of a person are focused upon? Evolutionary psychology has some answers to these questions.

Specifically, evolutionary psychologists suggest that the attractiveness of a person's body serves as a valuable and subtle indicator of social behavior, social relationship potential, fitness, quality, reproductive value, and health. Evolutionary psychologists place heavy emphasis on clearly observable features of human bodies and do not focus as much on internal, unobservable aspects of personality such as kindness or trustworthiness. There is a growing body of research that supports these ideas. For example, significant relationships were found between attractiveness and measures of mental health, social anxiety, and popularity, so the idea behind evolutionary theory does seem to be relevant.

Most work studying how body characteristics relate to attractiveness has focused on a single factor, such as the face, although many features of the body can influence attractiveness. Faces are often the first part of a person that is looked at. Furthermore, the face is almost always clearly visible (except for women in cultures that forbid it). Social psychologists have shown that people often make quick judgments about others based on their faces, and more than 80 percent of studies on judging attractiveness have focused on the face alone. The sex, age, culture, and past experiences of the perceiver, specific facial features such as large lips for women and strong jaws for men, body and facial symmetry, and specific body ratios such as the waist-to-hip ratio (WHR, the number attained by dividing the waist measurement by the circumference of the hips) all influence judgments of attractiveness. Consistent with this idea are findings that some standards of attractiveness are consistent across time and cultures. For example, people with symmetrical faces—those whose eyes and ears are of equal size and equal distances apart—are preferred over people who do not have symmetrical faces.

FEMALE SHAPELINESS

Another example of a body characteristic that is tied to attractiveness from an evolutionary perspective is women's WHR. Around the world, men prefer women with lower WHRs (between 0.7 and 0.8). Evolutionary psychology research emphasizes the importance of WHRs as a major force in social perception and attraction because shape is a very visible sign of the location of fat stores. This consequently signals reproductive potential and health. Low WHRs do indeed directly map onto higher fertility, lower stress levels, and resistance to major diseases. For example, women with WHRs of 0.8 are almost 10 percent more likely to get pregnant than women with WHRs around 0.9.

Although not as much research has focused on the female breast as a signaler of reproductive fitness, a variety of studies suggest that it is also an important factor, although the evidence is mixed. Some studies support the commonly held stereotype that men prefer larger breasts, although others seem to show no such preference. In contrast, some studies have showed that small and medium breasts are preferred to larger breasts, but much of this work focused either on the bust or on WHRs, not both together. The appeal of breast size should depend on overall body fat, waist, and hips, and both physical features should interact to influence ratings of attractiveness. In support of this idea, research now suggests women with lower WHRs and larger breasts are the ones considered most attractive. Unfortunately, methodological restrictions and poor stimulus materials limit the generalizability of most previous work using WHRs and other bodily features. For example, many studies used line drawings of figures or verbal descriptions of figures instead of pictures of real people. Research is currently under way to provide clearer tests of evolutionary psychology theories of attraction.

The most consistently documented finding on the evolutionary basis of attraction relates to gender differences in human mate choice. Consistent with Darwin's ideas that humans are naturally programmed to behave in ways to ensure that their genes will be passed on to future generations (ensuring survival), evidence indicates that men tend to prefer young, healthy-looking mates, as these characteristics are associated with the delivery of healthy babies. An examination of the content of more than eight hundred personal advertisements found that men stressed attractiveness and youth in mates more than did women, a finding supported by marriage statistics throughout the twentieth century. Women have been shown to place more emphasis on a prospective mate's social status and financial status, because these traits are often related to being able to take good care of children. The fact that women in Western societies are achieving higher economic positions, however, would suggest that this pattern of preferences may change in time.

HISTORICAL DEVELOPMENT

Although it would seem to be of obvious importance, physical appearance as a determinant of romantic attraction was simply neglected by researchers until the mid-1960's. Perhaps they mistakenly assumed the widespread existence of an old ideal that one should judge someone on the basis of his or her intrinsic worth, not on the basis of a superficial characteristic. Nevertheless, when the Minnesota study discussed earlier produced a physical attractiveness effect so strong as to eliminate or at least obscure any other factors related to attraction in the context of dating, social psychologists took notice. In any science, surprising or otherwise remarkable findings usually tend to stimulate additional research, and such a pattern definitely describes the course of events in this area of inquiry.

By around 1980, social psychology had achieved a rather solid understanding of the determinants of attraction to strangers, and the field began turning more of its attention to the nature of continuing relationships. Social psychologist Zick Rubin had first proposed a theory of love in 1970, and research on that topic flourished in the 1980's as investigators examined such topics as the components of love, different types of love, the nature of love in different kinds of relationships, and the characteristics of interaction in successful long-term relationships. Still other lines of research explored how people end relationships or attempt to repair those that are in trouble.

People view relationships with family, friends, and lovers as central to their happiness, a research finding that is totally consistent with common experience. One need only look at the content of motion pictures, television programs, musical lyrics, novels, and poetry, where relationships, particularly romantic ones, are so commonly a theme, to find evidence for that point. Yet nearly half of all marriages end in divorce, and the lack of love in the relationship is usually a precipitating factor. Whatever social psychology can teach people about what determines and maintains attraction can help improve the human condition.

SOURCES FOR FURTHER STUDY

Berscheid, Ellen. "Physical Attractiveness." In *Advances in Experimental Social Psychology*, edited by Leonard Berkowitz. New York: Academic Press, 1974. A very thorough review of the research examining the role of physical attractiveness in interpersonal attraction. This is a frequently cited and extensively documented chapter that includes interesting discussions of how people judge attractiveness and how attractiveness affects the individual.

Berscheid, Ellen, and Harry T. Reis. "Attraction and Close Relationships." In *The Handbook of Social Psychology*, Vol. 2, edited by Daniel T. Gilbert, Susan T. Fiske, and Gardner Lindsey. 4th ed. Boston: McGraw-Hill, 1998. An in-depth review of contemporary theories of attraction and a good summary of research findings.

Berscheid, Ellen, and Elaine Hatfield Walster. *Interpersonal Attraction*. 2d ed. Reading, Mass.: Addison-Wesley, 1978. Presents a solid overview of the psychology of attraction. Directed toward the reader with no background in social psychology, the book is quite readable; nevertheless, it is highly regarded and frequently cited within the field. Clever illustrations feature many cartoons.

Buss, David M. *Evolutionary Psychology: The New Science of the Mind*. Boston: Allyn & Bacon, 1999. A very readable book about the ways in which evolutionary science can help the study of social behavior. Good sections on mating strategies and the factors determining attraction.

Duck, Steve. *Relating to Others.* Chicago: Dorsey Press, 1988. Duck deals briefly with the traditional work on interpersonal attraction, but this book is most notable for being devoted primarily to reviewing the research on personal relationships, which became important in the 1980's. It covers thoroughly such topics as developing and maintaining relationships, exclusivity in relationships, and repairing and ending them. A good reference for taking the reader beyond the principal focus of the present article.

Hatfield, Elaine, and Susan Sprecher. *Mirror, Mirror: The Importance of Looks in Everyday Life.* Albany: State University of New York Press, 1986. An extremely thorough and very readable review of all the different effects of personal appearance. Explores how judgments of attractiveness are made and addresses the effects of beauty across the entire life span. Nicely supported with effective photographs and illustrations.

Langlois, Judith H., Lisa Kalakanis, Adam J. Rubenstein, Andrea Larson, Monica Hallam, and Monica Smoot. "Maxims or Myths or Beauty? A Meta-analytic and Theoretical Review." *Psychological Bulletin* 126, no. 3 (2000): 390-423. This article provides a wonderful resource by reviewing many articles that look at the factors that predict attractiveness. It also uses the evolutionary approach to explain some of the findings.

Myers, David G. *Social Psychology.* 6th ed. New York: McGraw-Hill, 1999. This very popular social psychology textbook features an unusually good chapter on interpersonal attraction. Offers a solid survey of the research relating to the principles of attraction and provides particularly good coverage of work on love. The author's engaging writing style makes this an excellent starting point for further exploration of the topic.

Steve A. Nida;
updated by Regan A. R. Gurung

SEE ALSO: Affiliation and friendship; Affiliation motive; Intergroup relations; Love; Prejudice reduction; Self-presentation; Social perception.

Attributional biases

TYPE OF PSYCHOLOGY: Social psychology
FIELDS OF STUDY: Social perception and cognition

Attributions about the causes of one's own behavior and the behavior of others play an important role in self-perception and the perception of others. Attributional biases are systematic errors that distort perceptions and attributions; the study of these provides insight into stereotyping, the blaming of victims, faulty decision making, conflict, and depression.

KEY CONCEPTS
- actor-observer bias
- attribution
- attributional bias
- defensive attribution
- depression
- expectancy confirmation bias
- fundamental attribution error
- generalization fallacy
- self-serving bias
- stereotype

INTRODUCTION

When trying to make sense of human behavior, one must be able to perceive behavior accurately and understand its causes. Theories that describe ways in which one can make these judgments about the causes of behavior are called attribution theories. An attribution can be defined as the process by which one gathers information and interprets it to determine the cause of an event or behavior.

Most attribution theories propose models that describe how people collect information and how attributions are formed from that information. Many specific attributions are possible, but generally these attributions can be grouped into two categories: personal and situational. If a situational attribution is made, the behavior is attributed to external forces or circumstances; for example, someone who trips may attribute his or her behavior to a slippery floor rather than to clumsiness. In a personal attribution, an internal cause, such as the person's personality, or an internal force, such as ability or effort, is seen as being the cause of the behavior. For example, if David observes Lois making a donation to charity, he may attribute her behavior to her generous personality rather than to some external circumstance. Attribution theories predict and explain the circumstances under which a personal or a situational attribution will be made.

Fundamental Attribution Error

Attribution theories provide logical models of how people gather and use information to form attributions, but people do not always seem to follow a logical process. Researchers have discovered that people frequently fall prey to attributional biases. These systematic errors teach much about human social cognition.

One attributional bias is so pervasive that it has earned the right to be called the fundamental attribution error. Social psychologist Lee Ross discovered that people tend to overestimate the role of personal, internal factors and underestimate the influence of situational factors; therefore, people make unwarranted personal attributions. In research demonstrating this bias, subjects were given essays supporting a particular position on an issue (in favor of abortion, for example). Despite the fact that the subjects were told that the authors had no choice but to take the stated position, the subjects rated the authors' attitudes as being in agreement with the essay.

Two explanations have been proposed for the fundamental attribution error. In 1958, Fritz Heider proposed that people are more aware of persons than situations because persons are the obvious, attention-getting figures, whereas situations are the more easily ignored background. Daniel Gilbert, in 1989, proposed that, contrary to what most attribution models propose, people do not initially use information to decide between personal and situational attributions; instead, they initially assume a personal attribution and then revise that attribution to include situational forces only if information that is inconsistent with a personal attribution forces them to do so. Supporting this hypothesis, he has found that if he keeps subjects too busy to use incoming information to revise their attributions, they are more likely to make personal attributions than are subjects who are allowed time to think about the information they are given.

Attribution Biases

The fundamental attribution error is related to the actor-observer bias. Research has shown that the fundamental attribution error pattern is often reversed when people are attributing their own actions; actors tend to overestimate situational factors and underestimate personal ones. This bias leads to situations in which people attribute their own actions to circumstances and others' often identical actions to personal factors, as in "I am late because of traffic, but you are late because you do not care about being punctual." This bias has been demonstrated in numerous studies; in one, researchers examined letters to "Ann Landers" and "Dear Abby" and found that the letter writers were more likely to attribute their own actions to situational factors and others' behavior to personal factors.

Perceivers are often motivated to make a particular attribution. One motivation that may affect attribution is the motive to be correct, which may lead the person making the attribution to interpret ambiguous information as being supportive of an initial expectation or attribution. This bias often takes the form of "seeing" a trait that one associates with another trait. For example, if Glenda has made the attribution that Jennie's astute decisions are the result of her intelligence, she may also assume that Jennie is exceptionally outgoing, not because she actually observed that trait, but because Glenda associates being intelligent with being outgoing. This expectancy confirmation bias is robust; unless the target person behaves in a way that is inconsistent with the assumption, the perceiver is unlikely to test the assumption.

One well-documented motivated attributional bias is the self-serving bias in attributing success and failure. When a person succeeds, he or she tends to attribute that success to personal, internal factors such as ability and effort; however, when that person fails, he or she is likely to attribute the failure to situational, external factors such as having a difficult task or bad luck. As its name implies, the self-serving bias is thought to be motivated by a desire to preserve or enhance self-esteem by taking credit for success and denying one's role in failure.

Another motivated bias is the tendency for observers to blame victims for their situations. This is called defensive attribution, because it has been found to be more likely to occur when the observer is similar to the victim than when the observer is dissimilar, and when the victim's harm is severe rather than mild. Kelly Shaver, the social psychologist who first discussed this bias, believes that it is motivated by fear. If observers blame the victims rather than their situations, the observers can also believe that they themselves are unlikely to be harmed. This is related to what Melvin Lerner calls the belief in a just world. People are motivated to believe that there is justice in the world and that people get what they deserve. This is comforting, because it leads to the conclusion that if one is good, one will get good outcomes; however, the belief in a just world also leads one to assume that victims deserve their outcomes.

Finally, people may fall prey to a group of biases that are collectively called the generalization fallacy. This fallacy is seen when people overgeneralize information from individual cases and personal experience and ignore more reliable information. One example of this bias is that many people believe that air travel is more dangerous than auto travel; in fact, the opposite is true. Because accidents involving airplanes are given greater attention than those involving automobiles, they are more vivid and therefore more memorable than the dangers associated with automobiles. As Heider suggested, vivid figures may be more salient than dull, statistical background information.

RELATIONSHIP TO CONFLICT

Because accurate attributions help perceivers negotiate complex social environments, attributional biases can interfere with that process. Therefore, it is not surprising that examples of attributional bias are found in situations in which there is conflict. One situation in which the fundamental attribution error and the actor-observer bias are often involved is arguments. If both parties believe that their own behavior is caused by circumstances but their partner's behavior is caused by his or her personality, they are likely to experience conflict. This can even be seen between nations; for example, each may attribute the other's cache of weapons to an aggressive personality but its own to necessity.

Another area of conflict that may involve attributional bias is stereotyping. Because stereotyping involves assuming the presence of other traits based on membership in some group, the expectancy confirmation bias has been used as a model for stereotyping. Further, if people act on stereotypes in ways that encourage the targets to behave in certain ways, they may behaviorally confirm the stereotype. For example, if a perceiver believes that all dark-haired men are hostile, she may act in ways that prompt hostility from them, thereby confirming her stereotype. The belief in a just world and defensive attribution may also play a part in stereotyping. In general, stereotypes of minority or less powerful groups are negative. The belief in a just world may lead people to reason that the targets of their stereotypes deserve their poorer outcomes because they have these negative traits. Defensive attributions may add to this by motivating perceivers to overestimate differences between themselves and the target group out of the fear that if they are similar, they may receive similar outcomes.

ROLE IN DECISION MAKING AND DEPRESSION

Researchers who investigate the generalization fallacy are often concerned that falling victim to it may lead to poor decisions. In one study, subjects who were given both reliable statistical information from a large group of car owners and the testimonial of one person tended to weigh the testimonial more heavily than the statistical information. Logically, a testimonial based on one car owned by one person is poorer data than information based on many cars owned by many people. Overreliance on unreliable but vivid data can lead to poor decisions.

Some psychologists believe that the absence of an attributional bias may be involved in depression. People who are depressed do not show the usual self-serving bias in attributing their successes and failures; severely depressed people can even show a reversal of the usual pattern, attributing failure to internal causes such as lack of ability, and success to external factors such as luck. In working with these patients, psychotherapists may help them learn to attribute their outcomes in ways that enhance their self-esteem.

EVOLUTION OF COGNITION STUDY

In the late 1800's, psychology was defined as the science of the mind, and human cognition was at the forefront of early psychologists' interests. Wilhelm Wundt and his followers relied on introspection for their data; they observed their own cognitive processes and reported on them. Hermann Ebbinghaus taught himself lists of words and tested his knowledge after varying time periods to investigate human memory. Beginning in 1913, however, this early cognitive research was largely ignored in America, as John B. Watson redefined psychology as the science of behavior. The main proposition of behaviorism, as this school of psychology is known, is that psychology should use scientific methods of observation and data collection. Behaviorists argue that since cognitive processes are not observable and behaviors are, behaviors are the only proper subject for psychological study. Behaviorism ruled psychology almost exclusively until approximately 1960; although it is still an important force in psychology, it is no longer the dominant force it once was.

As behaviorism's influence has lessened, cognition has become once again a topic of interest to psychologists. Behaviorism left its mark on cognition in the form of more rigorous experimental methods; introspection has been replaced by objective data collection using groups of subjects. As research methods in cognitive psychology continue to become more sophisticated, theories that might have been untestable in earlier years have become the subject of research. One indication of the strength of cognition in the academic world as a whole is that many universities have introduced interdisciplinary departments of cognitive science in which psychologists, neuroscientists, philosophers, linguists, and experts in artificial intelligence study different aspects of cognition.

Attribution played a significant part in the cognitive revolution; Fritz Heider's *The Psychology of Interpersonal Relations* (1958) was an important early work in social cognition. Attribution is one of the most researched topics in social psychology; in fact, some would argue that—especially since it has been found to be useful in applied areas such as health psychology, cognitive psychology, and clinical psychology, as well as social psychology—it is one of the most influential concepts in the field. One of the characteristics of the cognitive revolution is an interest in such topics as ambiguity, uncertainty, and the effects of emotion on cognition. This emphasis provides an interesting context for the study of attributional bias and opens new avenues of inquiry for theorists and researchers. Because of this and the applied areas that have adopted and adapted attributional bias, it has become an area of interest in its own right as well as being important for the refinement of attribution theories.

SOURCES FOR FURTHER STUDY

Brehm, Sharon S., and Saul M. Kassim. "Perceiving Persons." In *Social Psychology*. Boston: Houghton Mifflin, 1990. This chapter in a social psychology textbook provides an excellent overview of social perception and attribution, including a very complete discussion of attributional biases. Theory and research are presented clearly enough for a beginner to understand, yet in enough detail to be useful to the reader.

Fischoff, Baruch, and Ruth Beyth-Marom. "Hypothesis Evaluation from a Bayesian Perspective." *Psychological Review* 90 (July, 1983): 239-260. The authors of this article propose that social psychologists may be overestimating the occurrence of bias by ignoring the possibility that perceivers are using non-Bayesian logic. Their arguments are complex, although this article is clear and follows an orderly sequence of ideas; appropriate for more advanced students of the field.

Försterling, Friedrich. *Attribution: An Introduction to Theories, Research, and Applications*. Philadelphia: Psychology Press, 2001. A well-written introduction to the field of attribution, written for undergraduate students.

Harvey, J. H., and G. Weary. "Current Issues in Attribution Theory and Research." In *Annual Review of Psychology* 35. Stanford, Calif.: Annual Reviews, 1984. Reviews attribution theory and research from 1978 to 1983, a particularly fertile period in the area. Includes a section on the effects of motivation on attribution. Well organized and clear.

Hayes, Brett, and Beryl Hesketh. "Attribution Theory, Judgmental Biases, and Cognitive Behavior Modification: Prospects and Problems." *Cognitive Therapy and Research* 13 (June, 1989): 211-230. Discusses the use of attributional concepts in therapy. Techniques to reduce biases are presented, along with a discussion of the limits of these attributional retraining or debiasing techniques. For a journal article aimed primarily at professionals, this piece is quite accessible.

Ross, M., and G. J. O. Fletcher. "Attribution and Social Perception." In *Handbook of Social Psychology*, edited by Gardner Lindzey and Elliot Aronson. 3d ed. New York: Random House, 1985. This chapter, a comprehensive overview of attribution theory, is clear, engaging, and suitable for readers of all levels. Much of the chapter is devoted to research and the implications of that research on theory; despite this work's status as a review article in a book intended for both academicians and nonspecialists, the authors of this article manage to take a critical stance and ask intriguing questions.

Schneider, D. J. "Social Cognition." In *Annual Review of Psychology* 42. Stanford, Calif.: Annual Reviews, 1991. Reviews social cognition theories and research with an emphasis on categorization and the formation of trait attributions from behaviorial information. Bias is discussed, including a section titled "In Defense of Accuracy." An insightful presentation of research and ideas, this article is an excellent resource for advanced readers.

Brynda Holton

SEE ALSO: Causal attribution; Decision making; Depression; Emotions; Intergroup relations; Motivation; Self-perception; Social perception.

Autism

TYPE OF PSYCHOLOGY: Psychopathology
FIELDS OF STUDY: Childhood and adolescent disorders

Autism, a poorly understood, nonschizophrenic psychosocial problem, includes great social unresponsiveness, speech and language impairment, ritualistic play activity, and resistance to change. The causes of and treatments for autism have not been conclusively determined, although behavior therapy is a promising alternative.

KEY CONCEPTS
- affective
- cognitive
- dopamine
- echolalia
- electroencephalogram (EEG)
- epileptic seizure
- norepinephrine
- schizophrenia
- secretin
- serotonin

INTRODUCTION

The modern term "autism" was originated by Leo Kanner in the 1940's. In "Autistic Disturbances of Affective Contact" (1943), he described a group of autistic children; he viewed them as much more similar to one another than to schizophrenics, with whom they generally had been associated. Until that time, the classical definition for autism (still seen in some dictionaries) was "a form of childhood schizophrenia characterized by acting out and withdrawal from reality." Kanner believed that these children represented an entirely different clinical psychiatric disorder. He noted four main symptoms associated with the disease: social withdrawal or "extreme autistic aloneness"; either muteness or failure to use spoken language "to convey meaning to others"; an "obsessive desire for maintenance of sameness"; and preoccupation with highly repetitive play habits, producing "severe limitation of spontaneous activity." Kanner also noted that autism—unlike other types of childhood psychoses—began in or near infancy and had both cognitive and affective components.

Over the years, several attempts have been made to establish precise diagnostic criteria for autism. The criteria that were given in the American Psychiatric Association's *Diagnostic and Statistical Manual of Mental Disorders* (4th ed., 1994, DSM-IV) are onset prior to thirty-six months of age; pervasive lack of responsiveness to other people; gross deficits in language development; if speech is present, peculiar patterns (such as delayed echolalia and pronoun reversals); bizarre reaction to environmental aspects (resistance to change); and the absence of any symptoms of schizophrenia. These criteria are largely a restatement of Kanner's viewpoint.

The prevalence of autism is generally estimated at between 3 to 9 percent of the population of the United States. Study of the sex distribution shows that it is 2.5 to 4 times as common in males as in females. The causes of autism have not been conclusively determined, although the possibilities are wide-ranging and said to be rooted in both biology and environment. As an example of the latter, one of the most widely cited causes has been vaccination, particularly the mumps, measles, and rubella (MMR) vaccine that is given at approximately eighteen months of age and often corresponds with the earliest detected symptoms of autism. Still, researchers in the United States and Europe have determined that this vaccine does not cause autism, based on the fact that vaccination rates held steady throughout the 1990's at almost 97 percent of children, yet the rate of autism diagnosis increased sevenfold during the same time period.

Possible physiological causes include genetics (siblings of autistic children are two hundred times more likely than the general population to be diagnosed with autism themselves), neurochemistry (abnormal levels of the neurotransmitters norepinephrine, serotonin, and dopamine have been established in children with autism as well as their relatives), low birth weight, older mothers, and brain abnormalities such as reduction of tissue in the cerebellum and enlarged ventricles in the cerebrum.

Largely because of Kanner's original sample (now known to have been atypical), many people believe that autistic children come from professional families. Subsequent studies have indicated that this is not so. Rather, autistic children come from families within a wide socioeconomic range, and more than 75 percent of them score in the moderately mentally retarded range on intelligence tests prior to or in the absence of effective treatment.

The behavior that characterizes the autistic personality strongly suggests that the disorder is related to other types of neurologic dysfunction. Identified neurological correlations include soft neurologic signs (such as poor coordination), seizure disorders (such as phenylketonuria), abnormal electroencephalograms, and unusual sleep patterns. This emphasis on neurologic—or organic—explanations for autism is relatively new; autism was previously thought to be an entirely emotional disorder.

The difficulties that autistic children show in social relationships are exhibited in many ways. Most apparent is a child's failure to form social bonds. For example, such youngsters rarely initiate any interactions with other children. Moreover, unlike nonautistic children, they do not seek parental company or run to parents for solace when distressed. Many sources even point to frequent parental statements that autistic children are not as "cuddly" as normal babies and do not respond to their mothers or to affectionate actions. Autistic children avoid direct eye contact and tend to look through or past other people. In addition, autistic children rarely indulge in any cooperative play activities or strike up close friendships with peers.

Sometimes speech does not develop at all. When speech development does occur, it is very slow and

---

DSM-IV-TR Criteria for Autism

AUTISTIC DISORDER (DSM CODE 299.00)

Six or more criteria from three lists

1) Qualitative impairment in social interaction, manifested by at least two of the following:
- marked impairment in use of multiple nonverbal behaviors (eye-to-eye gaze, facial expression, body postures, gestures)
- failure to develop peer relationships appropriate to developmental level
- lack of spontaneous seeking to share enjoyment, interests, or achievements with others
- lack of social or emotional reciprocity

2) Qualitative impairments in communication, manifested by at least one of the following:
- delay in, or total lack of, development of spoken language, not accompanied by attempts to compensate through alternative modes of communication such as gesture or mime
- in individuals with adequate speech, marked impairment in ability to initiate or sustain conversation
- stereotyped and repetitive use of language or idiosyncratic language

- lack of varied, spontaneous make-believe play or social imitative play appropriate to developmental level

3) Restricted, repetitive, and stereotyped patterns of behavior, interests, and activities, manifested by at least one of the following:
- preoccupation with one or more stereotyped and restricted patterns of interest abnormal in either intensity or focus
- apparently inflexible adherence to specific, nonfunctional routines or rituals
- stereotyped and repetitive motor mannerisms (hand or finger flapping, complex whole-body movements)
- persistent preoccupation with parts of objects

Delays or abnormal functioning in at least one of the following areas, with onset prior to age three:
- social interaction
- language as used in social communication
- symbolic or imaginative play

Symptoms not better explained by Rett's Disorder or Childhood Disintegrative Disorder

may even disappear again. Another prominent speech pathology in autism is either immediate or delayed repetition of something heard but simply parroted back (such as a television commercial), phenomena called immediate and delayed echolalia, respectively. Yet another problem seen is lack of true language comprehension, shown by the fact that an autistic child's ability to follow instructions is often dependent on situational cues. For example, such a child may understand the request to come and eat dinner only when a parent is eating or sitting at the dinner table.

Behavior denoting resistance to change is often best exemplified by rigid and repetitive play patterns, the interruption of which results in tantrums and even self-injury. Some autistic children also develop very ritualistic preoccupations with an object or a schedule. For example, they may become extremely distressed with events as minor as the rearrangement of furniture in a particular room at home.

TREATMENT

Autistic children can be very frustrating to both parents and siblings, disrupting their lives greatly. Often, individuals with autism also cause grief and guilt feelings in parents. According to Mary Van Bourgondien, Gary Mesibov, and Geraldine Dawson, this can be ameliorated by psychodynamic, biological, or behavioral techniques. These authors point out that all psychodynamic therapy views autism as an emotional problem, recommending extensive psychotherapy for the individual with autism and the rest of the family. In contrast, biological methodology applies psychoactive drugs and vitamins. Finally, behavioral therapy uses the axioms of experimental psychology, along with special education techniques that teach and reinforce appropriate behavior.

Psychodynamic approaches are based on the formation of interpersonal relationships between the child and others. One example of these is holding therapy, which involves the mother holding the child for long periods of time so that a supposedly damaged bond between the two can be mended. Floor time, joining the child in his or her activities, is a more active method of establishing a bond with a child. However, both of these methods lack empirical verification of their effectiveness.

Biological methods, on the other hand, involve affecting how the brain receives and processes infor-

mation. Sensory integration is favored by occupational therapists from the perspective that the nervous system is attempting to regain homeostasis, causing the individual to behave oddly. The approach, an attempt to meet the sensory needs through a "sensory diet" of activities throughout the day, is not supported by scientific research and is not even implemented in an agreed-upon fashion by all of its practitioners. Auditory integration training (AIT) works in the same way as sensory integration with regard to the sensation of sound but is not generally accepted by professionals as being effective. Drug therapies include antiseizure medications, tranquilizers, stimulants, antidepressants, and antianxiety medications that have varying results. One of the most controversial drug therapies is the injection of the hormone secretin, which reportedly causes remarkable improvements in the symptoms of some children but no change in others. Dietary interventions include megadoses of vitamins and minerals that could have very harmful side effects and are not reliably beneficial. Some parents also follow a gluten-free and casein-free regimen with their children, effectively eliminating all milk and wheat products from their diets. Only anecdotal evidence exists of the effectiveness of this and other special diets.

The last category of therapies, behavioral or skill-based techniques, is the most empirically supported. The Treatment and Education of Autistic and Related Communication Handicapped Children (TEACCH) program emphasizes modification of the environment to improve the adaptive functioning of the individual given his or her unique characteristics and teaching others to accommodate autistic children at their particular level of functioning. In contrast, applied behavior analysis programs, such as those advocated by Norwegian psychologist Ivar Lovaas, involve manipulating the environment only for the initial purpose of shaping an individual's skills toward more normal functioning, with the eventual goal of mainstreaming the child with his or her typically developing peers in the regular education setting, an outcome that is estimated to be more likely for children whose treatment begins by two or three years of age.

CHANGING PERCEPTIONS OF AUTISM

It is widely reported that autistic children, as defined by Kanner in the 1940's, were at first perceived as victims of an affective disorder brought on by their emotionally cold, very intellectual, and compulsive parents. The personality traits of these parents, it was theorized, encouraged such children to withdraw from social contact with them, and then with all other people.

In the years that have followed, additional data—as well as conceptual changes in medicine and psychology—have led to the belief that autism, which may actually be a constellation of disorders that exhibit similar symptoms, has a biological basis that may reside in subtle brain and hormone abnormalities. These concepts have been investigated and are leading to definitive changes in the therapy used to treat individual autistic children. Although no general treatment or unifying concept of autism has developed, promising leads include modalities that utilize drugs which alter levels of serotonin and other neurotransmitters, as well as examination of patients by nuclear magnetic resonance and other techniques useful for studying the brain and the nervous system.

The evolution of educational methodology aimed at helping individuals with autism has also been useful, aided by legislation aimed at bringing severely developmentally disabled children into the mainstream. Some cities and states have developed widespread programs for educating autistic people of all ages. Instrumental here has been the development of the National Society for Autistic Children, which has focused some of its efforts on dealing with autistic adolescents and adults.

Combined therapy, biological intervention, and educational techniques have helped autistic persons and their families to cope, have decreased behavior problems in autists, have enhanced the scholastic

Members of the Masket family watch son Alex, who has autism, work with a bead project. Family support can have a significant impact in some cases. (AP/Wide World Photos)

function of a number of these people, and have produced hope for autistic adults, once nearly all institutionalized.

SOURCES FOR FURTHER STUDY

Herin, L. Juane, and Richard L. Simpson. "Interventions for Children and Youth with Autism: Prudent Choices in a World of Exaggerated Claims and Empty Promises. Part I: Intervention and Treatment Option Review." *Focus on Autism and Other Developmental Disabilities* 13 (1998): 194-211. Covers the specific interventions from the psychodynamic, biological, and behavioral categories and gives an overview of the research support for each.

Kalat, James W. *Biological Psychology.* 6th ed. Pacific Grove, Calif.: Brooks/Cole, 1998. A basic text that explains the role of physiological factors in behavior.

Kaye, James A., Maria del Mar Melero-Montes, and Hershel Jick. "Mumps, Measles, and Rubella Vaccine and the Incidence of Autism Recorded by General Practitioners: A Time-Trend Analysis." *British Medical Journal* 322 (2001): 460-463. Describes evidence refuting the hypothesis that the MMR vaccination causes autism.

Lonsdale, Derrick, and Raymond J. Shamberger. "A Clinical Study of Secretin in Autism and Pervasive Developmental Delay." *Journal of Nutritional and Environmental Medicine* 10 (2000): 271-280. Describes an experiment to measure the effectiveness of secretin injections for alleviating the symptoms of autism.

Lovaas, Ivar, and Tristam Smith. "Intensive Behavioral Treatment for Young Autistic Children." In *Advances in Clinical Child Psychology*, edited by B. B. Lahey and A. E. Kazdin. New York: Plenum, 1988. A more detailed description of ABA therapy and specific research findings relating to the topic.

Maurice, Catherine, Gina Green, and Stephen C. Luce, eds. *Behavioral Intervention for Young Children with Autism: A Manual for Parents and Professionals.* Austin, Tex.: Pro-Ed, 1996. Edited by the mother of two children who were diagnosed with autism and successfully treated with behavior therapy, it provides clear guidance for parents embarking on a search for effective treatment methods for their children and the professionals who are helping them. Included is information on the effectiveness of various treatments, funding behavior therapy, working with educators and other professionals, and what is involved in behavior therapy.

Murray, John B. "Psychophysiological Aspects of Autistic Disorders: Overview." *Journal of Psychology* 130 (1996): 145-158. Covers the symptoms and potential causes of autism.

Sundberg, Mark L., and James W. Partington. *Teaching Language to Children with Autism or Other Developmental Disabilities.* Pleasant Hill, Calif.: Behavior Analysts, 1998. Gives technical guidelines on applied behavior analysis techniques used to teach the different components of language in a skill-based intervention.

Van Bourgondien, Mary E., Gary B. Mesibov, and Geraldine Dawson. "Pervasive Developmental Disorders: Autism." In *The Practical Assessment and Management of Children with Disorders of Development and Learning*, edited by Mark L. Wolraich. Chicago: Year Book Medical Publishers, 1987. Succinctly and clearly describes autism, including its definition, incidence, etiologies and pathophysiologies, assessment and findings, and management. Also included are 133 useful references. Although technically written, the article is nevertheless very useful to the beginning reader.

Sanford S. Singer;
updated by April Michele Williams

SEE ALSO: Abnormality: Biomedical models; Abnormality: Psychological models; Attention; Brain injuries; Language; Schizophrenia: Background, types, and symptoms; Schizophrenia: Theoretical explanations.

Automaticity

TYPE OF PSYCHOLOGY: Consciousness
FIELDS OF STUDY: Cognitive processes

Automaticity refers to the ability to perform certain types of mental and motor skills with very little attention; skills become automatic when they are highly practiced under consistent conditions. The development of automaticity can improve human performance in many ways, but it can also lead to errors in responding when conditions change rapidly.

KEY CONCEPTS

* automatic process
* consistent mapping
* controlled process
* dual-task methodology
* reaction time
* varied mapping

INTRODUCTION

Psychologists have found it useful to classify many aspects of human mental and motor performance as either "automatic" or "controlled." Automatic processes are those that are carried out with ease, often requiring little or no attention. They can usually also be performed simultaneously with other tasks. Controlled processes, on the other hand, are more difficult and typically require a person's full attention. Because they require so much attention, it is difficult to do anything else at the same time. Research on automaticity has outlined the conditions under which each type of processing can develop, as well as the conditions under which each works best.

DEVELOPMENT OF AUTOMATICITY

To illustrate automaticity and its development, consider the task of driving an automobile. (Driving really involves many tasks, such as steering, looking out for traffic and pedestrians, checking for traffic lights and signs, changing speed, starting and stopping as traffic changes, and perhaps even discussing directions with a passenger.) When first learning to drive, most people have difficulty doing all these things at once. When they see a stop sign, for example, they may have to decide consciously and deliberately which pedal to push to stop the car. For novice drivers, holding a conversation while driving is also difficult—if they pay attention to their driving, they will not hear what their passenger says, but if they listen and respond to their passenger, they may be endangering themselves and others. After some experience, however, the same person (now a relatively expert driver) will stop at a stop sign, check for oncoming traffic, and proceed safely, all while holding up his or her end of a conversation.

What has changed that makes the response to a stop sign so much easier? Psychologists describe this phenomenon by saying that for the novice driver the act of stopping at a stop sign was controlled but,

through practice, has become automatic. Another example of this change occurs in reading, which is initially very difficult. With practice, however, a skilled reader no longer has to think about reading as a deliberate act. Instead, when one points one's eyes at a printed page, words are recognized automatically.

ROLE OF MAPPING

Walter Schneider and Richard Shiffrin have been active in working out the details of how (and under what conditions) a process changes from controlled to automatic. The change from controlled to automatic processing is a gradual one. Put another way, automaticity is a matter of degree. From the examples above, it is clear that practice is a key ingredient in automaticity. Their research has highlighted the relevance of the kind, as well as the degree, of practice. They have described two kinds of practice: practice with consistent mapping, which promotes automaticity, and practice with varied mapping, which does not. The term "mapping" here refers to the relationship between stimulus and response, or which response is "mapped" onto each stimulus. Varied mapping refers to a situation in which a stimulus should sometimes be responded to and sometimes ignored.

To pursue the example of driving, the difference between consistent and varied mapping can be likened to the difference between a stop sign and a yield sign. A stop sign involves consistent mapping, because the only response one should ever make to a stop sign is to stop. The sign never calls for any other response. These are the hallmarks of consistent mapping: A particular response is always (consistently) mapped to a particular stimulus. That is the only response to make to the stimulus, and the stimulus never appears under circumstances when it should be ignored. As a result of always stopping at stop signs, that response becomes automatic and can be executed without a pause in a conversation between the driver and a passenger. A yield sign, on the other hand, is an example of varied mapping. When a yield sign is seen, it sometimes means that one should continue without stopping (if no traffic is coming). If there is other traffic coming, however, it means that one should stop. A driver sometimes has to respond to a yield sign by stopping but at other times only needs to check quickly for other traffic.

To promote automatic processing, large amounts of practice with consistent mapping are needed. The mental or motor act thus practiced becomes automatic: It is now easy to perform and can easily be shared with other activities, but it is very difficult to change, in part because it calls so little attention to itself. There are costs to as well as benefits from automaticity. One cost is the large amount of practice required for the development of automaticity. The inflexibility of automatic processes can also lead to inappropriate responses if the situation changes. As an example, imagine the difficulties faced by drivers in Sweden when, in the 1960's, the nation switched from driving on the left side of the road (as in the United Kingdom) to driving on the right. Drivers setting off to work on the morning after the change might well have found themselves driving on the (now) wrong side of the road. That is an extreme example, but any time that flexibility of response is required, controlled processes, though somewhat slower, may be better. Where flexibility is not a problem and quick response is needed, automaticity should be encouraged.

DUAL-TASK METHODOLOGY

Much of the research conducted on the development of automaticity has involved a letter search task, in which a subject is seated before a computer monitor. Subjects are told to look for a letter (or several different letters). They start the task and begin seeing a series of letters on the screen. Whenever one of the items they are looking for appears, they are to press a key on the computer keyboard. Usually they do many such trials, divided into two types. On some series of trials, they always search for the same letters, such as P and C. This is consistent mapping, because any time they see a P or a C they are to press the key. On another series of trials, however, the letters for which they are to search change every few trials; a letter for which subjects searched a moment before may now appear on the screen but no longer be a target. This is varied mapping. Note that if the letters P and C were used for the consistently mapped condition they never appear as distractors (nontargets) in the varied mapping condition. The only time the subject sees them is when they are targets.

To test for the development of automaticity, a common approach is to employ a dual-task methodology. After considerable training at the task described above (typically twenty to thirty hours), a sec-

ond task is added, which is to be performed at the same time. One task that has often been used is a category search task, in which the subject (in addition to searching for certain letters) also sees words displayed on the screen and must decide whether the word fits into a certain category (for example, "pieces of furniture"). The typical finding is that subjects who are searching for the consistently mapped letters (P and C, in this example) will show little change in reaction time, or the time from when they see the letter to when they respond to it. They will continue to make rapid, accurate responses to the letter search task while also doing well at the category search task. On the other hand, subjects who are looking for target letters that were practiced with varied mapping will suddenly become slower and less accurate, and they will do poorly on the category search task. Just as the novice driver has to think about what to do when approaching a stop sign and will pause in a conversation, so the subject searching for varied targets will find sharing two tasks difficult.

One interesting example of the degree to which a task may become automatic was given by the concert pianist Charles Rosen. When practicing for a performance of a piano concerto that he knew well, he found that he became bored, so he began to read light novels while practicing. Reading is a relatively automatic task, which he could apparently combine easily with the (at least partially) automatic task of playing a well-practiced piece of music.

ROLE OF DRILL

In examining many skills, it becomes evident that at least some aspects of them are (and probably must be) automatic. Driving is composed of many component skills, some automatic (such as steering and braking at stop signs) and some controlled (such as choosing at which corner to turn). The same is true in other areas as well. One reason for drill in practicing sports is to increase automaticity so that responses are quick and reliable. In baseball, a base runner who has to stop to plan how to slide into base would have a short career. In education, one must be able to recall the multiplication tables quickly and accurately in order to use them easily at each step in multiplying two three-digit numbers.

One practical issue raised by research on automaticity is the degree to which drill is necessary in educational practice. At one time, educational practice relied heavily on large amounts of drill.

More recently, drill has been seen as boring and "irrelevant" to education. It is now clear, however, that drill, or repetitive practice, is absolutely essential to gaining many of the component skills necessary for success at larger skills. Without enough drill in algebra, for example, students find that their first course in calculus is mostly spent trying to figure out the algebra of the equations, with an accompanying reduction in understanding of the new material. Further research will provide more information about the optimum amount of drill: not enough to discourage people through boredom, but enough so that the skill being practiced can be easily integrated into more complex tasks.

EVOLUTION OF AUTOMATICITY STUDY

In *The Principles of Psychology* (1890), William James, who was a principal founder of American psychology, described the fact that some mental acts are so easy that one hardly notices them, while others require careful thought and attention. It is exactly this distinction that finds modern expression in the distinction between automatic and controlled processes. It was not until the 1970's that experimental psychologists, including Schneider and Shiffrin, developed ways to study automatic processes, and especially the acquisition of these processes.

The development of cognitive psychology, beginning in the 1950's, has shown the benefit to psychology of studying complex psychological processes by trying to identify and study their various components. By focusing on one part of the overall task at a time, more adequate experimental control can be gained, and each component skill can more easily be studied. By knowing the conditions under which automaticity develops, and by having approaches such as dual-task methodology to help measure automaticity, those parts of a complex task that are best performed automatically can be isolated. That isolation can lead to improvements in learning, because aspects of a complex skill that can be performed automatically can be subject to drill. It also can lead to improved understanding of complex mental processes (such as reading), which can result in the discovery of ways to help new learners understand what is required for mastery.

CONTRIBUTION TO ATTENTION STUDIES

The study of automaticity has added to the general study of phenomena of attention. Fully automatic processes, such as well-trained letter searches in a Schneider and Shiffrin experiment or braking at a stop sign, seem to require almost no attention at all. A popular view of attention is the "resource" approach, suggested by Daniel Kahneman, which treats attention as a limited resource that can be assigned fairly flexibly. When a task to which one is paying attention is fairly easy (that is, uses few attentional resources), it can often be performed at the same time as another task. If a task requires considerable attentional resources, however, one is unable to perform another task at the same time. For example, driving in a thunderstorm or on icy roads makes conversation difficult for the driver, who will probably not even respond if a passenger tries to start a conversation. In this case, the driver must attend and respond in a controlled manner to many aspects of driving that are usually automatic. Thus, the concepts of automatic and controlled processes fit well with one of the major approaches to the study of attention.

SOURCES FOR FURTHER STUDY

Kahneman, Daniel. *Attention and Effort*. Englewood Cliffs, N.J.: Prentice-Hall, 1973. This book first made the resource notion of attention widely popular among psychologists. It details many experiments that lend support to that view. Although written for an audience of psychologists, it is readable by a wider audience and provides the contextual background in which the ideas of automaticity were developed.

Schneider, Walter. "Training High-Performance Skills: Fallacies and Guidelines." *Human Factors* 27 (1985): 285-300. This paper provides an excellent overview of what is known about the practical application of knowledge concerning automaticity to training in high-level skills. The emphasis is on practice, rather than theory; the discussion is aimed at correcting some common errors made in training skilled personnel, including a tendency to ignore drill even when it is essential to learning.

Smyth, Mary M., et al. *Cognition in Action*. 2d ed. Hillsdale, N.J.: Lawrence Erlbaum, 1994. This very readable presentation of modern cognitive psychology includes a discussion of how automaticity comes about through training and how automaticity is demonstrated experimentally. A number of interesting experiments on dual-task performance are discussed. One of the more readable accounts of automaticity.

Solso, Robert L. *Cognitive Psychology.* 6th ed. Boston: Allyn & Bacon, 2000. Discusses automaticity within the context of resource models of attention. Solso includes several interesting descriptions of automaticity acting in everyday life.

Wickens, Christopher D., and Justin Hollands. *Engineering Psychology and Human Performance.* 3d ed. Upper Saddle River, N.J.: Prentice Hall, 1999. Wickens provides a general survey of engineering psychology, or the application of knowledge from experimental psychology to engineering objects and systems for human use. Treats attention at length, as well as issues of automatic and controlled processing and their implications for the design of systems for human use.

Wyler, Robert S., Jr., ed. *The Automaticity of Everyday Life.* Hillsdale, N.J.: Lawrence Erlbaum, 1997. A collection of fifteen essays on the theories and applications of automaticity in understanding human behavior.

James D. St. James

SEE ALSO: Attention; Cognitive maps; Consciousness; Pattern recognition; Reflexes; Reflexes in newborns.

Aversion, implosion, and systematic desensitization

TYPE OF PSYCHOLOGY: Psychotherapy
FIELDS OF STUDY: Behavioral therapies

Aversion, implosion, and systematic desensitization therapies are effective therapy techniques based on the principles of Pavlovian conditioning. The latter two are most effective in treating fear and anxiety; aversion therapy is most often used in treating habit disorders such as cigarette smoking or drug abuse.

KEY CONCEPTS
- aversion therapy
- covert sensitization
- desensitization hierarchy
- flooding

- implosion therapy
- Pavlovian conditioning
- systematic desensitization

INTRODUCTION

Systematic desensitization, implosion, and aversion therapy are all behavior therapy techniques that are based on Pavlovian conditioning. In Pavlovian conditioning, when one stimulus is paired with another, the response to the second stimulus can affect the response to the first. For example, if the presence of a dog is followed by a painful bite, the pain and fear that result from the bite can produce a conditioned response of fear toward dogs. An important process in Pavlovian conditioning is extinction: When the first stimulus is presented a number of times without the second stimulus, the response that became conditioned because of the pairing becomes extinguished. If, after having been bitten by a dog, a person spends time around dogs without being bitten, his or her fear of dogs will gradually disappear. Both systematic desensitization and implosion therapy use extinction to eliminate fear of an object or situation. Aversion therapy uses conditioning to attach a negative response to something pleasant but undesirable (such as cigarettes or alcohol) in order to eliminate a bad habit.

Systematic desensitization, implosion, and aversion therapy were among the first psychotherapies that were developed from principles discovered in the experimental psychology laboratory. During the 1960's, they also were the first therapies to have their effectiveness confirmed in controlled experimental studies. In the 1950's, a patient seeking treatment for a phobia might have received a course of psychoanalysis, potentially stretching hundreds of sessions over several years with questionable effectiveness. By the 1970's, a patient going to a psychologist for the same problem would probably receive systematic desensitization or flooding, treatments with proven effectiveness and lasting only a handful of sessions.

On a broader level, these therapies and the research done on them ushered in a new era of scientific standards for clinical psychology. They led the behavior therapy movement, which continued to develop therapy techniques from research done in experimental psychology and to test the effectiveness of these therapies. This led to an expectation that all therapies should have proven effectiveness.

These therapies, then, represent a large step forward for the importance of scientific principles in all areas of clinical psychology and psychiatry.

SYSTEMATIC DESENSITIZATION

Systematic desensitization, developed and described by Joseph Wolpe in the 1950's, is one of the most well-accepted and effective psychological treatments. It is most successful when used to eliminate phobias, which are fears of specific objects or situations. The goal of systematic desensitization is to put the patient into a relaxed state and gradually present him or her with the feared situation, so that very little anxiety is actually experienced during treatment. The therapist usually presents the feared situation to the patient by having the patient vividly imagine being in the situation. Systematic desensitization starts out with the patient briefly imagining a situation that provokes very little anxiety. This is repeated until no anxiety is produced by the image; then the patient moves on to a slightly more anxiety-provoking image. This continues until the person can imagine his or her most-feared situation with little or no anxiety.

IMPLOSION AND FLOODING

Implosion is similar to systematic desensitization in that a person repeatedly imagines a feared situation until the fear dissipates; however, while systematic desensitization is like lowering inch by inch into a cold pool, implosion is like diving headfirst into the deep end. Unlike systematic desensitization, which proceeds gradually and evokes little discomfort, implosion plunges the patient right into imagining his or her most intensely feared situation. Whereas systematic desensitization uses short image periods, implosion requires a person to keep imagining the feared situation for as long as it takes until the fear begins to decrease. Implosion works best with long sessions of imagining, sometimes two hours or more. As might be expected, flooding works faster than systematic desensitization but is more uncomfortable and is more likely to cause people not to want to try the treatment. Flooding is very similar to implosion, except that the image is restricted to the specific situations the client describes as fearful and does not include elements the therapist introduces from psychodynamic theory. Flooding is now a more commonly used therapy than implosion.

As originally described by Thomas Stampfl, implosion was a mixture of extinction and psychodynamic theory. In addition to imagining the situation that the patient presented as anxiety-provoking, the patient would imagine things the therapist thought were psychodynamic elements related to the anxiety, such as childhood fears or conflict. For example, the therapist might instruct the patient to imagine being rejected by his or her parents.

Both systematic desensitization and flooding can be done through exposure to the actual situation, as well as through imagining it. For example, a person with a phobia of dogs could approach a real dog rather than merely imagine it. Research has shown that confronting the actual fear situation is more effective than imagining it; however, sometimes there are practical constraints. It would be too expensive, for example, for a person who is afraid of flying to buy an airplane ticket every week to become desensitized to the situation; imagining an airplane trip costs nothing. In practice, treatment usually involves a combination of imagery and actual exposure. The flight phobic might imagine being on an airplane during therapy sessions and between sessions have a homework assignment to drive to an airport and watch planes take off.

AVERSION THERAPY

Whereas systematic desensitization and flooding try to extinguish a fear response, the goal of aversion therapy is to attach a new, aversive response to a currently positive stimulus. This is usually done to eliminate a bad habit such as drinking alcohol, smoking, or overeating. During treatment, the sight, smell, or taste of alcohol, cigarettes, or a favorite food might be followed by electric shock or a nausea-inducing drug. After experiencing a number of these pairings, the person begins to develop a negative response to the previously valued stimulus. Like flooding and systematic desensitization, aversion therapy can be performed either in actuality or through the use of imagery. The use of imagery in this case is called covert sensitization; an example would be an alcoholic who imagines becoming violently ill after sipping his favorite drink.

There are a number of concerns with using aversion therapy. First, there are always ethical concerns about any treatment that involves punishment or severe discomfort. Aversive procedures are preferred only when other effective treatments are not available or if other treatments have failed. A second concern with aversion therapy is its effectiveness. The alcoholic may avoid drinking when he is hooked up to the electric shock or has taken the nausea-producing drug, but aversion therapy may not be effective in stopping him from drinking after treatment, when no punishment will be suffered.

DESENSITIZATION TECHNIQUES

Systematic desensitization is most useful, as noted earlier, when applied to reduce fear. The application of systematic desensitization is straightforward. The first step in systematic desensitization is to establish a list of ten to fifteen feared situations (called a desensitization hierarchy), ordered from least to most anxiety-provoking. For example, the hierarchy for a person afraid to fly might start out with making an airplane reservation a month before a scheduled trip and end with actually being in a plane while it is taking off. Creating the desensitization hierarchy is one of the most important parts of treatment and involves finding out what is most important to the phobia: It might be fear of heights, fear of crashing, or fear of being in a closed space with no escape. Two people with the same phobia may have completely different desensitization hierarchies.

When the hierarchy is complete, desensitization can begin. The therapist first gets the patient or client to relax deeply, usually by teaching a specific muscle relaxation technique the patient can practice at home. While the patient is relaxed, the therapist instructs him or her to imagine vividly the item on the hierarchy that provokes the least anxiety. This image is held for only a few seconds, so very little anxiety is felt; then the patient returns to relaxing. This pattern is repeated until no anxiety is felt while imagining the scene; then the person imagines the next situation on the hierarchy. Over the course of a number of sessions, the patient progresses up the hierarchy until he or she can imagine the highest, most fear-provoking scene without feeling any fear. As noted earlier, treatment usually includes between-session homework assignments that involve confronting the fear situation.

FLOODING TECHNIQUES

Flooding is used in the treatment of similar problems. In this case, the client is immediately immersed in the most fearful situation he can imagine. The person with a fear of flying might be asked immediately to imagine being on a flight over the ocean while the plane is being jostled by severe turbulence. The phobic would continue to imagine this (sometimes for hours) until the anxiety reduces. One interesting and successful application of flooding has been in treating people with compulsive washing rituals. People with obsessive-compulsive disorder will often wash their hands until they are raw or bleeding, or will wash their clothes or clean house many hours a day, fearing unseen contamination and germs. Because of the time and energy this takes, the disorder can severely interfere with a person's life. Treatment involves having the person get his hands dirty by touching garbage or some other feared material (or put on dirty clothes), then not allowing the person to wash. This treatment is technically known as "exposure with response prevention." Because invisible germs are often what is most feared, the treatment also involves having the person imagine germs covering and infecting his skin. In severe cases, the person may need to be prevented from washing for days or even weeks before the anxiety goes away. This is obviously a very uncomfortable treatment for both patient and therapist, but it is one of the few long-lasting treatments for this disorder.

AVERSION TECHNIQUES

Aversion therapy is used much less frequently than systematic desensitization or flooding, and it is not used when other effective therapies are available. One relatively common application of aversion therapy is rapid smoking. In this technique a cigarette smoker will smoke one cigarette after another in a small, enclosed room until it causes a feeling of nausea. After a few sessions of this, the person begins to anticipate the nausea at the first cigarette, reducing the desire to smoke. Rapid smoking can be effective when used as one component of a treatment program and when there are no medical reasons for the person to avoid this technique.

Although aversion therapy is not used as often as systematic desensitization or flooding, an especially creative application of it, reported by Peter Lang and Barbara Melamed in 1969, illustrates its importance in certain situations. The case involved a nine-month-old infant who was failing to gain weight because he vomited his food ten minutes after every meal. No physical reason for this was found, despite three hospitalizations, many medical tests, and surgery. Several treatments were tried without success prior to beginning aversion therapy. When aversion therapy was begun, the child was in critical condition and was being fed through a nasogastric tube. Therapy involved giving an electric shock to the leg whenever the child was vomiting. Within three days, shocks no longer had to be given. His weight had increased 26 percent by the time he was discharged from the hospital thirteen days after treatment began. One year later, he was still progressing normally. This dramatic case shows that there is a place for aversion therapy in psychology.

TREATMENT PROBLEMS

Although systematic desensitization and flooding are standard and effective treatments, they are not 100 percent effective. Research continues to improve their effectiveness and to reach the percentage of people who do not seem to improve with these therapies. A particularly important area of research is to figure out how best to combine these therapies with drug therapies for fear and anxiety. Regardless of where this research leads, however, systematic desensitization and flooding will remain important therapy techniques in clinical psychology.

Aversion therapy also is important as one of the original scientifically derived and tested treatments, but it has more of a checkered history. One of its initial uses in the 1960's was to "treat" homosexual males by pairing pictures of attractive men with electric shock. It should be noted that this was in an era when society had a much different attitude toward homosexuality, and gay males voluntarily approached psychologists for this treatment. Nevertheless, aversion therapy contributed to an early popular view of behavior therapy as dehumanizing behavior control that took away free will and reduced individual rights. When used thoughtfully and ethically by competent psychologists, aversion therapy has an important role in psychological treatment; however, psychologists will surely continue to debate the ethics and effectiveness of aversion therapy.

SOURCES FOR FURTHER STUDY

Foa, Edna B., G. S. Steketee, and L. M. Ascher. "Systematic Desensitization." In *Handbook of Behavioral Interventions: A Clinical Guide*, edited by Alan Goldstein and Edna B. Foa. New York: John Wiley & Sons, 1980. This book was written as a "how-to" guide for the psychotherapist; however, the beginner will also find it readable and engaging. It is very well written and is filled with interesting case material and direct transcripts from therapy sessions. This is the best place to experience what systematic desensitization is actually like for the client and the therapist.

Levis, D. J. "Implementing the Techniques of Implosive Therapy." In *Handbook of Behavioral Interventions: A Clinical Guide*, edited by Alan Goldstein and Edna B. Foa. New York: John Wiley & Sons, 1980. This is another chapter from the book described above, and the positive comments above apply to this chapter as well. This book also contains an interesting chapter by Joseph Wolpe on how to gather information to plan treatment and chapters on how to apply exposure therapy to specific disorders such as agoraphobia and obsessive-compulsive disorder.

McMullin, Rian. *The New Handbook of Cognitive Therapy Techniques*. Rev. ed. New York: W. W. Norton, 2000. Discusses a wide variety of techniques; most of those discussed here are covered in chapter 4, "Countering Techniques: Hard."

Paul, Gordon L. *Insight vs. Desensitization in Psychotherapy*. Stanford, Calif.: Stanford University Press, 1966. This short book is a classic. It describes an early and very influential study that showed systematic desensitization to be superior to insight-oriented psychotherapy for treating public speaking anxiety. It was one of the first studies to evaluate therapy effectiveness and is a good illustration of how research to test the effect of therapy is done.

Wolpe, Joseph. *The Practice of Behavior Therapy*. 3d ed. New York: Pergamon, 1982. This book describes the practice of behavior therapy in detail, especially systematic desensitization. It includes chapters on aversion therapy and flooding as well as other therapy techniques, and illustrates how these techniques can be extended to treat problems other than fear and anxiety.

_____. *Psychotherapy by Reciprocal Inhibition*. Stanford, Calif.: Stanford University Press, 1958. The classic book in which Wolpe introduces and advocates systematic desensitization as an alternative to psychoanalytic treatment developed by

Sigmund Freud. Describes the basic principles and practice of systematic desensitization for psychiatrists of the late 1950's, who generally had no knowledge of these techniques.

Scott R. Vrana

SEE ALSO: Anxiety disorders; Behavior therapy; Conditioning; Habituation and sensitization; Learning; Obsessive-compulsive disorder; Operant conditioning therapies; Pavlovian conditioning; Phobias; Reinforcement; Taste aversion; Virtual reality.

B

Bandura, Albert

BORN: December 4, 1925, in Mundare, Alberta, Canada

IDENTITY: Canadian-born professor and psychological scientist

TYPE OF PSYCHOLOGY: Cognition; motivation; social psychology

FIELDS OF STUDY: Aggression; cognitive processes; physical motives; motivation theory; social motives; social perception and cognition; thought

Bandura became internationally recognized for his study of how beliefs are formed and how they influence behavior and motivation.

Albert Bandura was born in a small town in Alberta, Canada. He attended rural elementary and high schools staffed by resourceful and encouraging teachers and attended college at the University of British Columbia, where he earned his bachelor degree in psychology in 1949. Intrigued by the work of Kenneth Spence, he went to the University of Iowa to pursue his graduate degrees in psychology, studying under Arthur Benton. He received an M.A. in 1951 and a year later earned a Ph.D., focusing his attention on learning theory. Following graduation, he took a postdoctoral position in Kansas at the Wichita Guidance Center.

In 1953, Bandura began teaching at Stanford University in Northern California, becoming a full professor in 1964 and serving as chair of the psychology department in 1976 and 1977. He was named David Starr Jordan Professor of Social Sciences in Psychology. Throughout his teaching career, he wrote many books; his most notable contributions are *Aggression: Social Learning Analysis* (1973), *A Social Learning Theory* (1977), *Social Foundations of Thought and Action: A Social Cognitive Theory* (1985), and *Self-Efficacy: The Exercise of Control* (1997). He was the recipient of numerous honorary degrees, president to the American Psychological Association and Western Psychological Association, and honorary president of the Canadian Psychological Association.

Bandura's work on social cognitive theory is at the core of his prominence. In this theory, cognition plays a central role in the regulation of and motivation to behavior. Its key concepts include vicarious learning, symbolic thought, outcome expectancies, self-efficacy, self-reflection, and self-regulation. His arguments suggest that learning comes from more than trial and error. His emphasis on the importance of cognition as a motivational force to behavior was a major step forward for psychological theory and practice.

SOURCES FOR FURTHER STUDY

Evans, Richard Isadore. *Albert Bandura: The Man and His Ideas—A Dialogue.* Westport, Conn.: Praeger, 1989. Part of a series of interviews on influential psychologists designed to put a personal face on their work.

Maddux, James E. *Self-Efficacy, Adaptation, and Adjustment: Theory, Research, and Application.* New York: Plenum, 1995. Provides an overview of how self-efficacy theory relates to a variety of important everyday behaviors.

Miller, Neal, and John Dollard. *Social Learning and Imitation.* New Haven, Conn.: Yale University Press, 1941. A classic on social learning theory, foundational to the work done by Bandura that challenged and extended this theory substantially.

Nancy A. Piotrowski

SEE ALSO: Aggression; Learning; Social learning: Albert Bandura.

Battered woman syndrome

DATE: First described in the 1970's

TYPE OF PSYCHOLOGY: Psychotherapy; social psychology

FIELDS OF STUDY: Anxiety disorders; depression; interpersonal relations

Battered woman syndrome describes the common emotional, interpersonal, and behavioral patterns that develop in women who are abused by their intimate partners and has been argued to be a subcategory of post-traumatic stress disorder (PTSD). It is usually treated through empowering psychotherapy and community resources. When a woman kills her abuser, battered woman syndrome has been invoked as part of legal self-defense arguments.

KEY CONCEPTS

- cycle of violence
- learned helplessness
- post-traumatic stress disorder (PTSD)
- self-defense
- traumatic bonding

INTRODUCTION

As the women's movement raised social awareness of domestic violence in the 1970's, Lenore Walker, an American psychologist, began interviewing women who had been physically, sexually, and emotionally abused by their husbands and boyfriends. Contrary to the notion that battered women are masochistic, her interviewees abhorred the abuse and wished to be safe. Walker formulated the concept of battered woman syndrome to describe a constellation of reactions to domestic violence, especially traumatic responses, lowered self-esteem, and learned helplessness.

DIAGNOSTIC FEATURES

Walker and others argue that battered woman syndrome is a subtype of PTSD, in that it stems from an unusually dangerous, life-threatening stressor rather than personality, and that it involves traumatic stress symptoms, including cognitive intrusions (such as flashbacks), avoidant or depressive behaviors (such as emotional numbness), and arousal or anxiety symptoms (such as hypervigilance). American psychologist Angela Browne describes further correspondence between battered woman syndrome and PTSD, including recurrent recollections of some abusive events, memory loss for others, psychological or social detachment, and constricted or explosive emotions. Complex PTSD, as formulated by American psychiatrist Judith Herman, further

recognizes the multifaceted pattern of personality, relationship, and identity changes in the survivor.

The low energy and decreased self-care that come with depression, and associated coping mechanisms such as substance use, may impede a woman's ability to seek safety. Walker's research participants often developed learned helplessness when efforts to avoid abuse led to increased violence. However, American psychologist Edward Gondolf and others have found that battered women are more resourceful and persistent in their self-protection and help-seeking than Walker's sample suggested.

Walker's cycle of violence consists of a tension-building stage, an acute battering stage, and a loving contrition stage. The battered woman often becomes acutely aware of the warning signs of the first stage that signal imminent danger in the second stage. Canadian psychologists Donald Dutton and Susan Painter have found that while this cycle is not universal, the intermittence of battering often leads to traumatic bonding, in which the woman finds love, self-esteem, and even protection from the same person who alternately abuses and woos her.

INCIDENCE, PREVALENCE, AND RISK FACTORS

A task force of the American Psychological Association estimated in 1994 that 4 million women in the United States are victims of domestic violence each year, and one in three women will be assaulted by a partner sometime in their lives. Research in the 1990's found that between 31 percent and 89 percent of battered women meet the criteria for PTSD. Few individual predictors for becoming a victim of or being vulnerable to battered woman syndrome have been confirmed. Among those suggested are witnessing or experiencing violence in one's family of origin, leaving home at an early age, and holding traditional, nonegalitarian gender roles.

TREATMENT

Psychological treatments are usually most effective when integrated with community services that aim to eliminate the economic, legal, and social obstacles to women's safety by offering temporary shelter, support groups, and financial, job, and legal assistance. Partner violence often comes to light in the context of couples therapy, and then only with

A consultant offers support and advice to a battered woman on a confidential hot line at the Women's Crisis Center in Moscow. (AP/Wide World Photos)

appropriate assessment questions. Because of the power differential and coercion present when a partner is violent, batterer treatment should precede consideration of couples therapy.

Therapy for the survivor usually begins with danger assessment and safety planning, exploration of the abuse history, and screening for PTSD and other psychological reactions. It is vital that therapy empower the client to make her own decisions, in order to avoid recreating the powerlessness felt under the abuser's control. The therapist helps the woman recognize her strengths while providing an empathic, nonjudgmental space for her to tell her story and evaluate the patterns of abuse. Individual or group treatment may be recommended, and symptom management techniques or medication may be introduced. When the woman feels safer, treatment may move into a healing stage in which emotions, self-blame, body issues, childhood abuse, and power and intimacy issues are more fully addressed.

ROLE OF BATTERED WOMAN SYNDROME IN COURT

In cases in which a battered woman kills her abuser, battered woman syndrome has become admissible in many courts as part of the defense of provocation and/or self-defense. Expert testimony is used to combat misconceptions and provide information about battering, so that the jury can interpret the woman's perception that defensive action was necessary, much as in other self-defense arguments. The admissibility of expert testimony about battered woman syndrome has been challenged on the grounds that the experience and the symptom pattern of battered woman syndrome are not universal or adequately researched. However, evidence regarding battered woman syndrome has been admitted in the majority of cases in which it has been introduced in the United States.

SOURCES FOR FURTHER STUDY

Blowers, Anita Neuberger, and Beth Bjerregaard. "The Admissibility of Expert Testimony on the

Battered Woman Syndrome in Homicide Cases." *Journal of Psychiatry and Law* 22, no. 4 (1994): 527-560. A good review of battered woman syndrome and the appropriate use of expert witnesses in a battered woman's self-defense claim.

Dutton, Donald G., and Susan Painter. "The Battered Woman Syndrome: Effects of Severity and Intermittency of Abuse." *American Journal of Orthopsychiatry* 63, no. 4 (1993): 614-622. Offers empirical support for the concept of battered woman syndrome as a distinct, enduring syndrome.

Herman, Judith. *Trauma and Recovery.* New York: Basic Books, 1992. Presents survivor reactions to major categories of human-made trauma, including battered woman syndrome.

Walker, Lenore E. *Abused Women and Survivor Therapy.* Washington, D.C.: American Psychological Association, 1994. Treatment guidelines for working with abused women.

_____. *The Battered Woman.* New York: Harper & Row (1979). The original description of battered woman syndrome.

Mary L. Wandrei

SEE ALSO: Aggression; Aggression: Reduction and control; Anger; Child abuse; Codependency; Domestic violence; Feminist psychology; Law and psychology; Learned helplessness; Rape and sexual assault; Sexual variants and paraphilias; Support groups; Violence and sexuality in the media.

Beck, Aaron T.

BORN: July 18, 1921, in Providence, Rhode Island
IDENTITY: American psychiatrist
TYPE OF PSYCHOLOGY: Cognition; psychological methodologies; psychopathology
FIELDS OF STUDY: Anxiety disorders; behavioral and cognitive models; cognitive development; cognitive learning; cognitive processes; cognitive therapies; depression; nervous system; personality disorders

Beck developed a cognitive therapy for depression and several tests to assess depression.

From the time that he was a child, Aaron Beck always had a keen interest in psychiatry. His parents encouraged his learning and interest in science. While attending Brown University, he served as an associate editor of the Brown *Daily Herald* and earned many honors and awards for his writing and oratorical skills.

After graduating magna cum laude from Brown in 1942, Beck entered Yale Medical School, eventually serving a residency in pathology at the Rhode Island Hospital. Although still interested in psychiatry, Beck became attracted to neurology and served a residency at the Cushing Veterans Administration Hospital in Framingham, Massachusetts. During this residency, he became interested in psychoanalysis and cognition and earned a doctorate in psychiatry from Yale University in 1946. He gained substantial experience in conducting long-term psychotherapy while serving for two years as a fellow at the Austin Riggs Center in Stockbridge, Massachusetts. During the Korean War, Beck served as the assistant chief of neuropsychiatry at the Valley Forge Army Hospital.

In 1954, Beck joined the department of psychiatry at the University of Pennsylvania and graduated from the Philadelphia Psychoanalytic Institute in 1956. Initially, he explored the psychoanalytic theories of depression, but, finding no confirmation of these theories, he developed the cognitive therapy approach, including several well-known tests to assess depression, such as the Beck Depression Inventory and the Scale for Suicide Ideation. In 1959, he began to investigate the psychopathology of depression, suicide, anxiety disorders, panic disorders, alcoholism, and drug abuse. He also researched personality disorders and cognitive therapy for these disorders.

Beck served on many review panels for the National Institute of Mental Health and on the editorial boards of several journals, and he lectured throughout the world. He served as a consultant for psychiatric hospitals and managed care organizations and set up inpatient and outpatient programs organized according to the cognitive therapy model. A prolific writer, Beck published hundreds of articles and many books, including *Depression: Clinical, Experimental, and Theoretical Aspects* (1967), *Cognitive Therapy and the Emotional Disorders* (1979), *Cognitive Therapy and Depression* (1980, coauthor), *Cognitive Therapy of Personality Disorders* (1990), and *Prisoners of Hate: the Cognitive Basis of Anger, Hostility, and Violence* (1999).

SOURCES FOR FURTHER STUDY

Chadwick, Paul D., Max J. Birchwood, and Peter Trower. *Cognitive Therapy for Delusions, Voices, and Paranoia*. New York: John Wiley & Sons, 1996. A discussion of cognitive therapy treatments for serious mental disorders, focusing on the individual symptoms of delusions, voices, and paranoia.

Dattilio, Frank M., and Arthur M. Freeman, eds. *Cognitive-Behavioral Strategies in Crisis Intervention*. 2d ed. New York: Guilford, 2000. Discusses applications of Beck's cognitive therapy approach to a wide spectrum of crisis situations, including depression, panic disorders, and substance abuse.

Ingram, Rick E., Jeanne Miranda, and Zindel V. Segal. *Cognitive Vulnerability to Depression*. New York: Guilford, 1998. A cognitive approach based on Beck's research for determining what factors put individuals at risk for developing depression.

Alvin K. Benson

SEE ALSO: Beck Depression Inventory (BDI); Children's Depression Inventory (CDI); Cognitive behavior therapy; Cognitive psychology; Cognitive therapy; Depression; Personality rating scales; Suicide; Teenage suicide.

Beck Depression Inventory (BDI)

DATE: Developed in 1972

TYPE OF PSYCHOLOGY: Cognition; emotion; motivation; psychopathology; psychotherapy

FIELDS OF STUDY: Aging; cognitive processes; coping; depression; interpersonal relationships; social perception and cognition; thought

The Beck Depression Inventory is a self-rating scale for screening depression that measures the severity of depression. It can be used to assess progress as treatment for depression proceeds.

KEY CONCEPTS
- depression
- depression screening
- depressive disorders
- mental health
- suicide

INTRODUCTION

The Beck Depression Inventory is an assessment used to measure the presence and severity of depression. It was developed in 1972 by psychiatrist Dr. Aaron Beck. Beck earned his Ph.D. in psychiatry from Yale University in 1946. He became interested in psychoanalysis and cognition during his residency in neurology. Beck was the Assistant Chief of Neuropsychology at Valley Forge Hospital during the Korean War. He graduated from the Philadelphia Psychoanalytic Institute in 1956 and began research to validate psychoanalytic theories. However, his research did not support his hypotheses, so he began to develop cognitive therapy for depression. He developed several depression screening tests, including the Beck Depression Inventory.

THE NATURE OF DEPRESSION

Depression is a mental state characterized by extreme feelings of sadness, dejection, and lack of self-esteem. Depression affects men and women, young and old, of all races and socioeconomic statuses. According to statistics published by the National Institute of Mental Health in 2000, approximately 19 million Americans suffer from depression annually. Two out of three people who are depressed do not seek treatment. Almost 15 percent who do not seek treatment commit suicide. In the same year, the World Health Organization (WHO) asserted that by the year 2020, depression would be the second greatest cause of premature death in the world.

Depression is a common and costly mental health problem, seen frequently in primary care settings. Between 5 and 13 percent of those seen in a physician's office have a major depressive disorder. Depression is more prevalent in the young, female, single, divorced, separated, and seriously ill and those with a history of depression.

The United States Department of Health and Human Services' Center for Mental Health Services estimates that depression costs the United States $43 billion annually. According to a report by the Agency for Healthcare Research and Quality published in 2000, major depression is undiagnosed or not treated according to professional recommendations in almost 50 percent of adult patients who are seen in primary care offices. Therefore, it has been proposed that routine depression screening may be instrumental in early identification and improved treatment of depressive disorders. Side effects from medications, medical conditions such as infection, endocrine disorders, vitamin deficiencies, and alcohol or drug abuse can cause symptoms of depression. The possibility of physical causes of depressive symptoms can be ruled out through a physical examination, medical history, and blood tests. If a physical cause for depression is excluded, a psychological evaluation, called a depression screening, should be performed. This screening includes a history of when symptoms started, the length of time they have been present, the severity of symptoms, whether such symptoms have been experienced previously, and the methods of treatment, and whether any family members have had a depressive disorder and, if so, what methods were used to treat them.

The *Diagnostic and Statistical Manual of Mental Disorders: DSM-IV-TR* (rev. 4th ed., 2000) is the standard for diagnosing depression. DSM-IV-TR criteria for a major depressive episode require a depressed mood or loss of interest or pleasure, in addition to five or more of the following symptoms during a single two-week period that are a change from previous functioning: lack of energy, thoughts of death or suicide, sleep disturbances, changes in appetite, feelings of guilt and worthlessness, poor concentration, and difficulty making decisions. Depression screening questionnaires assist in predicting an individual's risk of depression.

SELF-RATING WITH THE BDI

The BDI is a self-rating scale that measures the severity of depression and can be used to assess the progress of treatment. It consists of twenty-one items and is designed for multiple administrations. Modified, shorter forms of the BDI have been designed to allow primary care providers to screen for depression. Each symptom of depression is scored on a scale of 0 for minimal to 3 for severe. Questions address sadness, hopelessness, past failure, guilt, punishment, self-dislike, self-blame, suicidal thoughts, crying, agitation, loss of interest in activities, indecisiveness, worthlessness, loss of energy, insomnia, irritability, decreased appetite, diminished concentration, fatigue, and lack of interest in sex. A score less than 15 indicates mild depression, scores from 15 to 30 indicate moderate depression, and a score greater than 30 indicates severe depression.

SOURCES FOR FURTHER STUDY

American Medical Association, ed. *Essential Guide to Depression.* New York: Pocketbooks, 1998. Discussion of the latest findings related to depression and a guide to resources in the diagnosis and treatment of depression.

American Psychiatric Association. *Diagnostic and Statistical Manual of Mental Disorders, Fourth Edition (DSM-IV): Primary Care Version.* 4th ed. Washington, D.C.: Author, 1995. The standard guide to symptoms and treatment of mental disorders.

Greden, J. "Treatment of Recurrent Depression." In *Review of Psychiatry*, edited by J. Oldham and M. Riba. Volume 20. Washington, D.C.: American Psychiatric Press, 2001. Discusses symptoms, impact and treatment and prevention of chronic recurrent depression.

Greist, J., and J. Jefferson. *Depression and Its Treatment.* 2d ed. Washington, D.C.: American Psychiatric Press, 1992. Provides an overview of depression, what may contribute to it, and the effectiveness of treatments.

Sharon Wallace Stark

SEE ALSO: California Psychological Inventory (CPI); Children's Depression Inventory (CDI); Clinical interviewing, testing, and observation; Depression; Diagnosis; *Diagnostic and Statistical Manual of Mental Disorders* (DSM); Minnesota Multiphasic Personality Inventory (MMPI); Personality interviewing strategies; Personality: Psychophysiological measures; Personality rating scales; State-Trait Anxiety Inventory; Thematic Apperception Test (TAT).

Bed-wetting

TYPE OF PSYCHOLOGY: Psychopathology
FIELDS OF STUDY: Behavior therapies; childhood and adolescent disorders

Bed-wetting, technically known as nocturnal enuresis, is a disorder characterized by the frequent failure to maintain urinary control by a certain age. It most frequently occurs in young children, although it may continue through adulthood.

KEY CONCEPTS
- arginine vasopression
- diurnal enuresis

- functional bladder capacity
- functional enuresis
- nocturnal enuresis
- organic enuresis
- primary type
- secondary type
- urine alarm

INTRODUCTION

Enuresis is a disorder characterized by an individual's repeated inability to maintain urinary control after having reached a chronological or developmental age of five years. Although enuresis may continue into adulthood, it most frequently occurs in young children. For example, at age five, approximately 15 percent of all children are nocturnally enuretic on a once-a-week basis. By age eighteen, however, only about 1 percent of adolescents are enuretic. Among children under the age of eleven, boys are more likely to be enuretic than girls. After age eleven, however, boys and girls have equal rates of enuresis. It should be noted that bed-wetting by children under five years of age and occasional bed-wetting by older children are common and usually not cause for concern.

Enuresis is a disorder that has probably existed since the beginning of humankind. In spite of the fact that since the 1960's considerable scientific research has been conducted examining enuresis, many misconceptions continue to exist. For example, many believe that children's bed-wetting is a result of laziness and not wanting to take the time to use the bathroom. This is not the case; most enuretic children desperately want to stop their bed-wetting.

Another misconception is that children will "outgrow" their bed-wetting. In fact, the yearly spontaneous remission rate for enuretic children, a measure of how many children stop wetting their beds without treatment during a year's time, is only about 15 percent. On average, it takes more than three years for enuretic children to stop wetting the bed on their own. During this time, the enuretic child may develop poor self-esteem and feelings of failure and isolation.

Misconceptions also continue regarding the effectiveness of different treatments for enuresis. For example, many parents believe that the bed-wetting will cease if they sufficiently shame or punish their child. This is not an effective approach; it exerts a negative influence on a child's self-concept and may actually worsen the problem. A more humane but also ineffective treatment technique is the restriction of fluids given to the child prior to bedtime. The bladder will continue to empty even when fluids are withheld for long periods of time.

One of the reasons for these continued fallacies is the secrecy that often accompanies the disorder. Because of embarrassment, the parents of enuretic children are often unwilling to ask others, including professionals, for assistance in dealing with an enuretic child. When the parents of an enuretic child do seek guidance, they are often given advice that is ineffective in treating the problem. For this reason, better efforts are needed to educate parents and professionals who work with enuretics. The basic message that should be delivered to parents is that enuresis is a treatable problem and that they should not be reluctant to take their child to a qualified professional for evaluation and treatment.

TYPES AND SUBTYPES

Because there are different types of enuresis, several distinctions should be made in discussing the disorder. The first distinction involves the cause of the disorder. If enuresis is the result of physical causes, such as a urinary tract infection or diabetes, it is referred to as organic enuresis. Although estimates vary, fewer than 5 percent of enuretic cases are thought to be the result of physical causes. The majority of the cases of enuresis are referred to as functional enuresis because no physical cause can be identified. Even though most cases are functional, a medical examination always should be conducted prior to treatment in order to make certain that the enuresis is not the result of a physical problem.

Another important distinction to make in discussing enuresis involves the time at which it occurs. Nocturnal enuresis, or bed-wetting, refers to lack of urinary control when an individual is sleeping. Diurnal enuresis refers to lack of urinary control during an individual's waking hours. Nocturnal enuresis occurs much more frequently than diurnal enuresis. A combined type consisting of both nocturnal and diurnal enuresis is very rare. Diurnal enuresis is more often the result of physiological causes, such as urinary tract infections.

A final useful distinction is that between primary and secondary enuresis. Primary enuretics are individuals who have never demonstrated bladder control. Secondary enuretics are individuals who, after a substantial period of urinary control (at least six months), become enuretic again. Approximately 80 percent of all nocturnal enuretics have never gained proper urinary control. Although professional differences of opinion exist, most researchers believe that the causes of primary and secondary enuresis are usually the same and that children with both types respond equally well to treatment. In order to avoid possible confusion, the remainder of this entry will focus on the most common type of enuresis in children: functional primary nocturnal enuresis.

POSSIBLE CAUSES

Over the years, numerous explanations have been given for the occurrence of nocturnal enuresis. These explanations can be grouped into three areas: emotional, biological, or learning. An emotional explanation for the occurrence of enuresis involves the idea that the enuretic is suffering from an emotional disorder that causes him or her to lose urinary control. Examples of these proposed emotional disturbances include anxiety disorders, poor impulse control, and passive-aggressive tendencies. Recent research indicates, however, that few enuretic children have emotional problems that cause their enuresis. In fact, among enuretic individuals who do have an emotional disturbance, it may be that their enuresis actually causes their emotional problems. In this regard, it is widely accepted that the occurrence of enuresis lowers children's self-esteem and increases family conflict.

Biological factors are a second suggested cause of enuresis. Included in these factors are genetic components, sleep disorders, small functional bladder capacity, maturational lag, and a deficiency of antidiuretic hormone. The evidence for a possible genetic component arises from research that suggests a strong link between parental enuresis and enuresis in offspring. If one parent was enuretic as a child, 44 percent of his or her offspring were diagnosed as enuretic. When both parents had a history of enuresis, 77 percent of their offspring were enuretic as well. If neither parent

was enuretic as a child, only 15 percent of their children were diagnosed with enuresis.

The relationship between sleep and enuresis is unclear. Early studies provided mixed results on the relationship between arousability and enuresis. A more recent study found that enuretic children awoke during only 8.5 percent of arousal attempts, whereas nonenuretic children awoke during 39.6 percent of arousal attempts. These differences in arousability may indicate that enuretic children sleep more deeply than nonenuretic children, a conclusion with which many parents of enuretic children would agree. Enuresis is not more likely to occur during one stage of sleep than another and rarely occurs during rapid eye movement (REM), or dream, sleep. If dreams do occur that involve urination, it is more likely that the dream was caused by urinating as opposed to the urinating being a product of the dream.

Functional bladder capacity (FBC) refers to the voiding capacity of the bladder. True bladder capacity (TBC) refers to the physical structure of the bladder. Research consistently suggests that the FBC of enuretic children is less than that of their nonenuretic siblings and peers. Although their TBCs are about the same, enuretic children urinate more frequently and produce less urinary volume than their nonenuretic siblings and peers.

There is strong evidence that delays in maturation may be related to enuresis. For instance, an inverse relationship exists between birth weight and enuresis; as birth weight decreases, the likelihood of developing enuresis increases. Children with lower

---

DSM-IV-TR Criteria for Bed-Wetting

ENURESIS (DSM CODE 307.6)

Repeated voiding of urine into bed or clothes (whether involuntary or intentional)

Behavior is clinically significant as manifested by one of the following:
- frequency of twice a week for at least three consecutive months
- presence of clinically significant distress or impairment in social, academic (occupational), or other important areas of functioning

Chronological age of at least five years (or equivalent developmental level)

Behavior not due exclusively to direct physiological effect of a substance (such as a diuretic) or a general medical condition (such as diabetes, spina bifida, seizures)

Types: Nocturnal Only, Diurnal Only, Nocturnal and Diurnal

developmental scores at one and three years of age are also more likely to develop enuresis than children with higher developmental scores. The fact that enuresis occurs more frequently in males than in females also points to delays in maturation being related to enuresis because boys tend to develop more slowly than girls.

Arginine vasopression is an antidiuretic hormone (ADH) produced by the pituitary gland. The theory behind ADH as a cause for enuresis is that insufficient amounts are produced during the day, which leads to increased urine production at night. Although a small body of research has shown that a subset of enuretic children do not exhibit normal daytime secretion of ADH, there is no physiological reason that the lack of ADH would prevent a child from awakening with the sensation of a full bladder.

The final explanation for enuresis is that the child has failed to acquire the skills necessary to maintain continence at night. These skills include attending to the sensation of a full bladder while asleep and either contracting the pelvic floor muscles to prevent the flow of urine or awakening to void in the toilet. The most effective treatments for enuresis are based on this etiology.

TREATMENT

Early treatments for enuresis, dating back some three thousand years, included such things as giving the child juniper berries, cypress, and beer or having the child consume ground hedgehog. Currently, drug and behavioral therapies are the two treatments that have been utilized and studied to the greatest extent.

One of the most common treatments for enuresis is drug therapy. Historically, imipramine, an antidepressant, has been the drug of choice. Imipramine helps to reduce enuretic episodes in 85 percent of cases within the first two weeks, although the exact mechanism is unclear. Despite this initial success, only about 50 percent of enuretic children stop wetting completely while on imipramine. More important, there is a 95 percent relapse rate when the drug is discontinued. Significant side effects are associated with the use of imipramine, including sleep disturbance, lethargy, and gastrointestinal distress.

More recently, the drug of choice for treating enuresis has been a synthetic version of ADH called desmopressin (DDAVP) that is administered intranasally. It reduces enuretic episodes by concentrating urine, which results in decreased urine output from the kidneys to the bladder. Despite immediate effects of DDAVP, only about 25 percent of children achieve short-term complete dryness and only 6 percent remain dry after discontinuing the drug. The major advantage of DDAVP over imipramine is that is has fewer side effects.

The most effective treatment for enuresis is the urine alarm. The alarm is attached to the child's underwear and is activated when moisture comes in contact with the sensors. When the alarm is activated, the child awakens, which momentarily halts the flow of urine and allows him or her the opportunity to get out of bed and void in the toilet. After voiding, children check their underwear, pajamas, and bedsheets for wetness. If there is any need to be changed, the child does so before returning to bed. If underwear is changed, the sensors are reattached. During the initial stages of treatment, parents may need to assist their child with awakening until he or she becomes conditioned to the sound of the alarm. It is also not unusual for a child to void completely before awakening to the sound of the alarm during the first weeks of treatment. The amount voided prior to awakening should decrease as treatment progresses. Use of the urine alarm alone has been shown to result in a 75 percent success rate after ten to twelve weeks of treatment, with only a 17 percent relapse rate when an intermittent alarm is used (the alarm rings after every other accident as opposed to every accident).

When the urine alarm is used, some type of positive reinforcement system is also utilized. Positive reinforcement programs will not cure enuresis, but they help to promote motivation and compliance with treatment. One example of an often-used positive reinforcement program is the dot-to-dot or grab-bag system. In this system, the child identifies a mutually agreed upon prize with his or her parents, who then draw a picture of the prize with dots circling the picture. Every third or fourth dot is larger than the others. For each night the child remains dry, two dots are connected. When a large dot is reached, the child obtains access to a grab bag containing small prizes such as gum, coins, games with a parent, or special privileges. The big prize is earned when the child completely connects the dots that encircle its picture.

The success rate of the urine alarm can be further increased and the relapse rate decreased when ancillary components are used with the alarm. Some of these components include retention control training (sometimes called "hold it and wait"), Kegel exercises (sometimes called "stop and go"), and responsibility training. In retention control training, which is designed to increase FBC, the child drinks extra fluids and is instructed to delay urination for as long as possible. Kegel exercises involve initiating and terminating the flow of urine at least once per day. Kegels strengthen the pelvic floor muscles that terminate urination. Responsibility training involves removing diapers or pull-ups at night and assigning age-appropriate duties associated with the urinary accidents.

SOURCES FOR FURTHER STUDY

Azrin, Nathan H., and Victoria A. Besalel. *A Parent's Guide to Bedwetting Control*. New York: Simon & Schuster, 1979. A self-help book written for parents with enuretic children in which Nathan Azrin's "dry-bed training" is described. Azrin's treatment is based on behavioral principles; the specific procedures are discussed in terms that most nonprofessionals will understand.

Azrin, Nathan H., and Richard M. Foxx. *Toilet Training in Less Than a Day*. New York: Simon & Schuster, 1974. Although over twenty-five years old, this book outlines the major behavioral components of successful toilet training, most of which form the basis for treating enuresis. An excellent guide for parents who are having difficulty in teaching their child to use the toilet successfully.

Friman, Patrick C., and Kevin M. Jones. "Elimination Disorders in Children." In *Handbook of Child Behavior Therapy*, edited by T. Steuart Watson and Frank M. Gresham. New York: Plenum, 1998. An excellent chapter that describes the major features of both enuresis and encopresis (soiling) and provides research data on treatment approaches.

Houts, Arthur C., and Hillel Abramson. "Assessment and Treatment for Functional Childhood Enuresis and Encopresis: Toward a Partnership Between Health Psychologists and Physicians." In *Child and Adolescent Disorders*, edited by Sam B. Morgan and Theresa M. Okwumabua. Hillsdale, N.J.: Lawrence Erlbaum, 1990. Summarizes work in the field of enuresis and encopresis, an elimination disorder involving involuntary soiling. Chapter sections include the assessment, causes, and treatment of enuresis. Reviews types and effectiveness of both behavioral and medical treatments.

Houts, Arthur C., and Richard M. Liebert. *Bedwetting: A Guide for Parents and Children*. Springfield, Ill.: Charles C Thomas, 1984. A self-help book intended for parents that outlines a treatment package for enuresis called the "full spectrum home training" system. This effective treatment approach is described in understandable terms, although the authors advise that it is best conducted under professional supervision.

Mills, Joyce C., and Richard J. Crowley. *Sammy the Elephant and Mr. Camel*. New York: Magination Press, 1988. An illustrated book for children that presents a metaphorical story regarding enuresis. Designed to promote self-esteem in enuretic children and to provide a way of discussing bedwetting with children in a nonthreatening way.

Ondersma, Steven J., and C. Eugene Walker. "Elimination Disorders." In *Handbook of Child Psychopathology*. Edited by Thomas H. Ollendick and Michel Hersen. 3d ed. New York: Plenum, 1998. A comprehensive chapter that provides a thorough overview of the possible etiologies of enuresis and encopresis.

R. Christopher Qualls;
updated by T. Steuart Watson

SEE ALSO: Behavior therapy; Childhood disorders; Conditioning; Development; Psychotherapy: Children; Sensation and perception; Sleep.

Behavior therapy

TYPE OF PSYCHOLOGY: Learning; psychotherapy
FIELDS OF STUDY: Anxiety disorders; behavioral and cognitive models; behavioral therapies; cognitive therapies; instrumental conditioning; Pavlovian conditioning; prosocial behavior; stress and illness

Behavior therapy consists of a wide array of therapeutic techniques that directly change abnormal behaviors by modifying the conditions that maintain them. Behavior therapy is further distinguished by four defining themes: scientific, action-oriented, present-focused, and learning emphasis.

KEY CONCEPTS
- behavior modification
- behavioral assessment
- behavioral medicine
- behaviorism
- cognitive behavioral therapy
- maintaining conditions
- target behavior

INTRODUCTION

Behavior therapy is a major field of psychotherapy comprised of a wide array of therapeutic techniques (or specific behavior therapies) that directly change problem behaviors by altering the conditions that presently maintain them. At the core of behavior therapy are four defining themes.

First and foremost, behavior therapy is scientific in its commitment to precision and empirical validation. Behaviors to be changed, goals for therapy, and procedures used to assess and change the problem behaviors are defined precisely. The validity or effectiveness of assessment and therapy procedures is evaluated through controlled studies that can be independently replicated by other researchers.

Second, behavior therapy is action-oriented, in that clients engage in specific behaviors to alleviate their problems rather than just talk about them (as in traditional, verbal psychotherapies). Generally, there is a collaboration between the therapist and the client throughout therapy, and sometimes key people in a client's life (such as a parent or spouse) are recruited to assist in the treatment. With the guidance of the behavior therapist, clients may actively plan, implement, and evaluate their therapy in their home environments.

Third, the focus of therapy is in the present, rather than in the past. The reason is simple: Clients' problems always occur in the present, and only present conditions can directly affect present behaviors. Although clients' problems may have begun at some time in the past, past conditions no longer exist; if they still are in effect, they are present conditions.

Fourth, learning is a major element in behavior therapy. Clients' problems frequently develop and are maintained by learning, and principles of learning, such as reinforcement, often are used in behavior therapy.

In addition to these defining themes, behavior therapies have four common characteristics. First, although standard treatment procedures are used, they always are individualized for each client's unique problems and circumstances. Second, therapy often proceeds in an incremental, stepwise progression, such as beginning with easier or less threatening elements of a problem. Third, treatment plans are likely to consist of more than one therapy to increase their effectiveness and efficiency. Fourth, in general, behavior therapies result in therapeutic changes in relatively brief time frames, especially compared to many "long-term" psychotherapies.

THE BEHAVIORAL MODEL

A simple but comprehensive theoretical model of human behavior underlies behavior therapy. It assumes that people are best understood in terms of their behaviors, both overt (actions others can directly observe) and covert (private behaviors, including thoughts and emotions). This perspective directly contrasts with the way in which people typically are viewed—namely, in terms of their personality traits. The behavioral model deals with specific behaviors, such as "working on a project until it is completed," rather than an assumed trait of "conscientiousness."

According to the behavioral model, the maintaining conditions, or causes of a client's problem behaviors, are found in their present antecedents and consequences. Antecedents, which occur before a behavior is performed, set the stage for and cue a person to engage in the behavior. Consequences, which occur after a behavior is performed, determine the likelihood that the individual will perform the behavior again. The chances are greater that the person will engage in the behavior again if the consequences are positive or favorable than if they are negative or unfavorable.

For a male college student who frequently gets drunk, the antecedents might include being at places where alcohol is readily available, observing others drinking, and feeling anxious or socially inhibited. The consequences might be reduced anxiety, being able to converse easily with women, and feeling like "one of the guys." To deal with this problem behavior, therapy would change one or more of the maintaining conditions, such as reducing the client's anxiety (which changes a maintaining antecedent) and teaching him social interaction skills (which changes a maintaining consequence).

THE PROCESS OF BEHAVIOR THERAPY

Behavior therapy proceeds in a series of seven interrelated steps. First, the client's presenting problems are clarified and, if there are multiple problems, prioritized. Second, the client and therapist establish the goals for therapy. Third, the problem is defined as a target behavior, a narrow, discrete aspect of the problem that can be unambiguously stated, can be measured, and is appropriate for the problem and the client. Behavior therapy generally involves treating just one or two target behaviors at a time; if several target behaviors are appropriate, each is dealt with successively rather than at the same time. Fourth, the current maintaining conditions of the target behavior are identified. Fifth, a treatment plan consisting of specific, individualized therapy procedures is specified to change the maintaining conditions of the target behavior, which, in turn, will change the target behavior and the client's presenting problem. Sixth, the treatment plan is implemented. Seventh, after the treatment plan has had time to have an effect, its success is evaluated. The evaluation is based on a comparison of the client's functioning before and after treatment. This is possible because measurement of the target behavior begins before treatment to provide a pretreatment baseline and continues throughout the treatment.

The success of behavior therapy is evaluated in terms of three criteria: The changes that occur in therapy must transfer to the client's everyday life, make a meaningful impact on the client's problem, and endure after the treatment ends.

BEHAVIORAL ASSESSMENT

Behavioral assessment procedures are an integral component of behavior therapy. They are used to gather information for identifying the maintaining conditions of target behaviors and measure the effectiveness of treatment. Like behavior therapy, behavioral assessment is individualized for each client; has a narrow focus (in contrast to broad, personality assessment); and focuses on assessing current (rather than past) conditions. Also like behavior therapy, there are many different behavioral assessment procedures, and more than one assessment procedure generally is employed. This practice results in comprehensive assessment of the client's problems. It also provides corroborative evidence from assessment procedures that tap different modes of behavior (overt actions, thoughts, emotions, and physiological responses) gathered through different methods. A brief description of eight methods of behavioral assessment follows.

BEHAVIORAL INTERVIEWS. Behavioral interviews are the most widely used assessment procedure because of their efficiency in gathering data. The behavior therapist asks "what," "where," "when," and "how" questions rather than "why" questions. The former questions yield specific, known information, whereas questions that ask "why" typically involve speculation. Moreover, from a behavioral perspective, the important issue of why a problem behavior is occurring (that is, what is causing it) is answered by the types of questions asked in a behavioral interview because the causes of behaviors are found in the current maintaining conditions that are tapped by those questions. For example, "where" and "when" questions concern the antecedent conditions under which the behavior is performed.

INVENTORIES. Direct self-report inventories are short questionnaires specifically related to the type of problem experienced by the client. They are efficient means of assessment, requiring little time for clients to complete and no therapist time. Hundreds of direct self-report inventories have been developed and standardized for particular problems, including depression, anxiety, sexual dysfunctions, eating disorders, and marital discord. Because they are standardized instruments, they provide information that may not be specific to a particular client. Accordingly, direct self-report inventories primarily are used for initial screening and to provide leads that can be followed by individualized assessment procedures.

SELF-RECORDING. Self-recording (or self-monitoring) involves clients' observing and keeping a record of their own overt and covert behaviors. A major advantage of self-recording is that the client is the observer and thus always is present. This is especially useful for recording behaviors that occur in private settings. Additionally, self-recording can assess a client's thoughts and emotions directly.

CHECKLISTS AND RATING SCALES. Interviews, inventories, and self-recording are based on clients' self-reports about themselves, which can result in a variety of unintentional and intentional errors and biases. Thus, there are behavioral assessment procedures that employ other people to assess clients' behaviors. The simplest of these are behavioral checklists and rating scales. Similar in format to self-report inventories, these paper-and-pencil measures are completed by someone who knows the client well, such as a parent, teacher, or spouse. Checklists consist of a list of behaviors related to the client's problem, and the observer merely indicates which of them the client engages in or are problematic for the client. With rating scales, the observer evaluates each behavior on a scale, such as rating how frequently or intensely the client performs a behavior. Standard behavioral checklists and rating scales have been developed for different problems, as with direct self-report inventories.

NATURALISTIC OBSERVATION. Systematic naturalistic observation may be the optimal method for gathering information about a clients' overt behaviors. One or more trained individuals observe and record predetermined behaviors as clients engage in the behaviors in their natural environments. For example, a child who has difficulty interacting appropriately with other children in play situations might be observed during recess to assess aspects of the child's peer interactions. Valid naturalistic observation requires agreement among observers (interobserver reliability) and that the observers remain as unobtrusive as possible so that they do not interfere with the client's behaving naturally.

SIMULATED OBSERVATION. Naturalistic observation may require a large investment in time for observers, especially when clients perform a target behavior infrequently and observers must wait a long time to observe the client engaging in it. A more efficient, though potentially less valid way to collect data about clients' overt actions is through simulated observation. Observations are made in contrived conditions that closely resemble the natural setting in which the client engages in the target behavior. The observations themselves are made in the same way as with systematic naturalistic observation. For example, the assessment of attention-deficit hyperactivity disorder might involve simulated observation of various predefined categories of on- and off-task behaviors as a child engages in schoolwork in a room that looks like a classroom. The simulated conditions are expected to elicit the target behavior, which means that observations are likely to be completed more quickly than with naturalistic observation. However, the key to valid simulated observation is that clients perform in the simulated conditions similarly to the way in which they perform in their natural environments.

ROLE PLAYING. Role playing is a form of simulated observation that is most frequently employed to assess clients' difficulties dealing with interpersonal situations. Clients are told to imagine that they are in a problematic situation and to act "as if" they were actually in it. The therapist plays the role of the other person(s) involved. For instance, a man who has difficulty expressing his concerns and needs to his supervisor would be asked to role play talking to his supervisor about an important issue, with the therapist's responding as the man's supervisor might. The specific ways in which the man talks and interacts with his "supervisor," including the content of what he says as well as his tone, body language, and presentation, can provide important data about the maintaining conditions of the man's difficulties in dealing with his supervisor.

PHYSIOLOGICAL MEASURES. With some problems, such as anxiety, physiological reactions are key components and may even be target behaviors. Physiological measures range from the simple and inexpensive, such as clients' taking their own pulse, to complex electroencephalography (EEG) recordings of brain activity that require elaborate and expensive equipment. Portable physiological recording devices that clients can use in their everyday lives are becoming increasingly available, affordable, and reliable.

TYPES OF BEHAVIOR THERAPY

Behavior therapies can be classified into four categories. One category, often referred to as behavior modification, primarily changes the consequences of behaviors. Reinforcement and punishment are employed to increase desirable behaviors and to decrease undesirable behaviors, respectively. For example, token economies employ token reinforcers (such as points or poker chips) that are earned for adaptive behaviors and can be exchanged for desirable goods and access to activities. Contingency contracts set up a written agreement detailing the target behaviors that the client is expected to perform and the consequences for performance and nonperformance. The responsibilities of the therapeutic agents (such as the therapist or parents) are spelled out, and all participants in the treatment plan sign the contract.

A second category of behavior therapies consists of exposure therapies for alleviating fear and anxiety-related disorders. In exposure therapies, clients confront previously threatening situations or engage in threatening behaviors without incurring negative consequences, which has the result of reducing or eliminating the fear or anxiety. The exposure can occur in a variety of ways. Joseph Wolpe, a South African psychiatrist, developed the first exposure therapy, systematic desensitization. Clients briefly and repeatedly imagine anxiety-evoking scenes while relaxed (which counteracts muscle tension associated with anxiety). The exposure begins with scenes that elicit little anxiety, and progressively more anxiety-evoking scenes are presented gradually. In contrast, in vivo flooding involves exposure to the actual anxiety-evoking stimuli for a prolonged period without any response that competes with the anxiety.

A third category consists of modeling therapies, in which clients observe other people engaging in adaptive behaviors that they need to learn or perform. Modeling therapies are used to teach clients adaptive skills (such as assertive behaviors) and to reduce debilitating fears and anxiety.

The fourth category, which represents the most widely practiced type of behavior therapy, is cognitive behavioral therapy. A wide array of techniques are used to directly and indirectly change maladaptive cognitions (thoughts, beliefs, or expectations) associated with psychiatric disorders. Cognitive restructuring changes maladaptive cognitions directly, such as when a client who views life crises as threats comes to view crises as opportunities. Stress-inoculation training provides clients with coping skills to handle stressors in their lives, which indirectly changes their perceptions of what is stressful.

Clients in behavior therapy are treated individually and in groups. The latter includes behavioral couples therapy and family therapy. Beyond the treatment of psychiatric disorders, behavior therapy principles and procedures have been harnessed for other practical ends. Prominent among these has been their widespread use in behavioral medicine, the interdisciplinary field devoted to the assessment, treatment, and prevention of physical disease. Behavioral procedures sometimes are employed to treat medical disorders less intrusively and less expensively than physical medical treatments, such as medication, and without negative side effects. Behavioral therapy is used to increase patients' adherence to medical treatments, such as engaging in physical exercises and maintaining a prescribed diet; to help patients cope with debilitating medical tests and

treatments, such as chemotherapy; and to prevent physical disease by increasing healthful behaviors, such as eating low-fat foods, and decreasing unhealthful behaviors, such as unprotected sexual activity. Other applications of behavior therapy principles and procedures beyond therapy have included classroom management, child rearing, coping with problems of aging, enhancing athletic performance, and solving community-related problems, such as safety and ecology.

HISTORICAL ROOTS OF BEHAVIOR THERAPY

The inspiration for behavior therapy came from behaviorism, the school of psychology that emphasized the influence of the environment on observable behaviors, and the experimental work on learning in the early nineteenth century by Russian physiologist Ivan Pavlov and in the twentieth century by American psychologists Edward Thorndike and John B. Watson. The modern practice of behavior therapy began simultaneously in South Africa, Great Britain, and North America in the 1950's. It developed, in part, as a reaction and alternative to psychoanalysis, the predominant psychotherapy at the time.

In South Africa, Wolpe, arguably the founder of behavior therapy, was disenchanted with psychoanalysis and developed treatments based on Pavlovian conditioning such as systematic desensitization. Similar reactions to psychoanalysis and experimentation with learning approaches to therapy occurred in Great Britain. In the United States, Ogden Lindsley and Nathan Azrin, students of Harvard operant-conditioning researcher B. F. Skinner, began to apply principles of operant conditioning to the treatment of severe psychiatric disorders, as did Teodoro Ayllon in Canada. These early applications were met by skepticism, criticism, and resistance from the established mental health community, which was still firmly ensconced in psychoanalysis.

In the 1960's, as empirical evidence supporting behavioral treatment methods mounted, behavior therapy began to be accepted. Also in this period, the idea of dealing with cognitions began to take root. Independently, psychiatrist Aaron Beck and psychologist Albert Ellis developed the first cognitive-behavioral therapies—cognitive therapy and rational-emotive therapy, respectively. The advent of cognitive-behavioral therapies, which broadened the domain of the field, increased acceptance of behavior therapy in general. Professional journals devoted exclusively to behavior therapy, including *Behaviour Research and Therapy*, *Journal of Applied Behavior Analysis*, and *Behavior Therapy*, commenced publication. The Association for Advancement of Behavior Therapy, the major professional organization in the field, was established. Behavior therapy was on its way to becoming the prominent field of psychotherapy that it is today.

SOURCES FOR FURTHER STUDY

Burns, David. *Feeling Good*. New York: William Morrow, 1980. Available in paperback, this is both a self-help book for depression using Aaron Beck's cognitive therapy and a lay reader's guide to the principles and practices of cognitive therapy.

Dobson, Kenneth S., ed. *Handbook of Cognitive-Behavioral Therapies*. 2d ed. New York: Guilford, 2000. Offers a discussion of a variety of cognitive-behavioral interventions for a wide array of problem behaviors. Although it is written for professionals, the volume will give the lay reader a broad picture of the practice of cognitive-behavioral therapies.

Kazdin, Allan E. *Behavior Modification in Applied Settings*. 6th ed. Pacific Grove, Calif.: Brooks/Cole, 2001. A survey of clinical and everyday applications of the principles of operant conditioning (reinforcement and punishment), which constitute a subset of behavior therapies.

_____. *History of Behavior Modification: Experimental Foundations of Contemporary Research*. Baltimore: University Park Press, 1978. The best comprehensive description of and commentary on the historical development of behavior therapy.

Spiegler, Michael D., and David C. Guevremont. *Contemporary Behavior Therapy*. 4th ed. Pacific Grove, Calif.: Brooks/Cole, 2003. This comprehensive introduction to behavior therapy can be read with no background in psychology or psychiatric disorders. Active learning exercises provide the reader with hands-on experience with behavior therapy principles and procedures.

Ullmann, Leonard P., and Leonard Krasner, eds. *Case Studies in Behavior Modification*. New York: Holt, Rinehart, and Winston, 1965. This classic collection of early studies in behavior therapy presents the bedrock of the field. The lengthy introduction provides firsthand insights into the early development of the behavior therapy by two of its earliest proponents in the United States.

Wolpe, Joseph. *The Practice of Behavior Therapy*. 4th ed. Elmsford, N.Y.: Pergamon, 1990. The classic explication of the theoretical and practical contributions of one of the founders of behavior therapy.

Michael D. Spiegler

SEE ALSO: Agoraphobia and panic disorders; Aversion, implosion, and systematic desensitization; Behavioral family therapy; Behaviorism; Conditioning; Habituation and sensitization; Learned helplessness; Learning; Operant conditioning therapies; Pavlovian conditioning; Phobias; Reinforcement.

Behavioral assessment

TYPE OF PSYCHOLOGY: Learning; Personality
FIELDS OF STUDY: Behavioral therapies; Personality assessment

Behavioral assessment uses reports by the person or others of observable behavior rather than making inferences from more subjective sources.

KEY CONCEPTS
- consequent variable
- discriminative stimulus
- organismic variable
- response variable
- triple-response system

INTRODUCTION

Behavioral assessment arose from behavioral research, which offered explanations of human behavior that differed from traditional theories. For example, early behaviorists believed that a person's behavior was the appropriate focus for understanding the person, while other psychologists believed that behavior is only a symbolic representation of an unconscious conflict. Rating scales were developed by psychologists interested in behavioral assessment and in determining the intensity of a behavior experienced by a person.

Traditional assessment approaches describe a person as having a particular trait or characteristic. For example, a person might be described as having an authority conflict or an anxious personality. In contrast, behavioral assessment describes the person's behavior in specific situations. For example, the behavioral assessment might say, "When the person is given an order by a superior, the person argues and makes sarcastic remarks." The behavioral assessment would go on to describe the consequences of arguing and talking back, which could be anything from the superior withdrawing the order to the superior punishing the person who argues.

Contemporary behavioral assessment is concerned with both internal and external events. Marvin Goldfried describes a model of behavioral assessment that includes a systematic analysis of internal and external events. Four classes of variables are assessed in this model: stimulus antecedents, organismic variables, response variables, and consequent variables. Stimulus antecedents refer to the environmental events that precede the occurrence of the target behavior. Sometimes called discriminative stimuli, they may be either external or internal. An example of an external event that serves as a stimulus antecedent is drinking a cup of coffee, which may serve as a discriminative stimulus for lighting a cigarette. An internal event that might serve as a prompt for an emotional response is thinking about taking a test, which may result in a feeling of anxiety. Both internal and external stimulus antecedents can produce behaviors that are experienced as either external (observable) or internal (unobservable).

This model of behavioral assessment includes a thorough description of organismic variables. These variables include anything that is personally relevant and could influence the response to the stimulus antecedents. Both acute and chronic medical conditions which may affect the perception of and/or response to the discriminative stimuli are noted. The influence of the person's genetic makeup is assessed when it seems relevant to the target behavior. Finally, the person's learning history is considered to be important in understanding the response to the antecedent stimuli. Organismic variables serve as mediators or filters between the stimulus antecedents and the responses.

Response variables are the person's behaviors in response to the stimulus antecedents and filtered through the organismic variables. The response variables are considered to be part of the triple-response system. The triple-response system requires the assessment of behavior in each of three domains: motor, physiological, and cognitive/emotional. Motor behavior refers to the observable actions of the person. Examples of motor behavior include lighting a cigarette, leaving a room, and throwing a temper tantrum. Physiological responses are unobservable behaviors that can be made observable by using specialized instruments. Heart rate is an unobservable physiological response until an instrument detects and displays it. Cognitive and emotional responses are also unobservable events. The behavioral assessment of these responses requires the person to report his or her own thoughts and feelings in the presence of the stimulus antecedents.

The triple-response system is important from the perspectives of both assessment and treatment. While behaviorists have historically focused on motor behavior, it is well known that people experience physiological changes and cognitive/emotional changes concurrently with the motor behavior in the presence of the stimulus antecedents. As behavioral assessment has become more sophisticated, it has become apparent that the relative importance of the components of the triple-response system varies in different people. Thus, treatment may focus on cognition in one person because it is the most important behavior and on physiological responses in another.

The final component of this model of behavioral assessment requires a consideration of consequent variables. The events that follow a response are the consequent variables. These variables are important in determining whether the response will be continued or discontinued. The consequences of a response also determine the strength of the response. Any consequence that leads to a reward for the person will strengthen the response it follows. Rewards may include getting something one wants (for example, studying results in a good grade on a test) or ending something that is unpleasant (for example, leaving a situation results in reduced anxiety). Consequences that do not reward the person lead to a weakening of the behavior.

The goal of behavioral assessment is to describe fully the problem behavior and the events that surround it. While earlier approaches tried to limit the assessment to one or two behaviors identified as problems, more recent approaches apply the assessment methodology to clusters of behaviors that may form syndromes or diagnostic categories.

A variety of approaches is used to gather the information that constitutes a behavioral assessment.

Naturalistic observation is used to observe the person's behavior in the settings most germane to the behaviors of interest. These settings may include home, school, work, and a hospital. In self-monitoring, the person observes and records each instance of the behavior of interest. Researchers use role playing and controlled observations to study the behaviors of interest while maintaining more control over the environment than is possible with naturalistic observation. Rating scales are also used to determine the intensity of the behavior under study.

USES AND INTERPRETATIONS

Behavioral assessment has many uses in psychology. There are three major ways of interpreting the data obtained from these assessment procedures. Client-referenced interpretation compares one performance on a task to another performance by the same person on the same task. The simplest example is a comparison of pretreatment and post-treatment performance on a task to see if the person improved after the intervention. There is no consideration of how other people perform the task. Criterion-referenced interpretation compares the person's performance to a previously established level of acceptable performance. Finally, norm-referenced interpretations compare an individual's performance to normative data; thus, it is possible to learn how a person compares to all others for whom norms are available. The comparison could be with everyone who has completed the task or taken the test in the normative sample, or with specific age or ethnic groups, genders, or occupational groups. Norm-referenced interpretations can be used to compare an individual to any group for which norms are available. It is up to the psychologist to ensure that the normative group used for comparison is one that is appropriate for the person being evaluated.

Behavioral assessment has been used in industrial and organizational settings. A 1990 study by Robert P. Bush and others described a procedure for developing a scale to assess the performance of people working in retail sales. A 1990 study by Richard Reilly and others described the use of a behavioral assessment procedure within the context of an assessment center. Assessment centers are established by businesses in order to simulate the tasks associated with different positions. It is assumed that superior performance in the assessment center will translate into superior performance on the job.

Reilly and others demonstrated that by incorporating behavioral assessment procedures—checklists—into the assessment center procedures, the validity of the assessment center results was improved.

The clinical use of behavioral assessment procedures is quite extensive and includes both children and adults. Thomas Ollendick and Greta Francis have reviewed the use of behavioral assessment techniques in the assessment and treatment of children with phobias. These authors provide examples of how to obtain information about fears and phobias from children by asking them questions in both direct and indirect ways. A variety of rating scales are reviewed, including the Fear Survey Schedule for Children and the Children's Manifest Anxiety Scale. The Fear Survey Schedule for Children consists of eighty items pertaining to childhood fears, which the child rates on a scale ranging from "none" to "a lot." Normative data are available for children between the ages of seven and sixteen years. It is possible to obtain information about fear of failure, fear of the unknown, fear of danger and death, and so on. The Children's Manifest Anxiety Scale measures the extent of anxiety that the child feels. This scale assesses the child's anxiety in the domains of physiological responsiveness, worry/oversensitivity, and concentration. It is appropriate for children between the ages of six and eighteen years.

Other scales for children, reviewed by Larry D. Evans and Sharon Bradley-Johnson, assess adaptive behavior. Adaptive behavior is the degree to which a child is able to cope effectively with the environment based upon the child's age. Deficits in adaptive behavior are an important part of the definition of mental retardation. These authors review several measures of adaptive behavior that are completed by teachers, caregivers, or psychologists. Comparisons are made to existing scales assessing adaptive behavior. Rating scales are used to measure various behaviors in adolescents and children. In addition to the behaviors mentioned above, there are rating scales for attention and distractibility, autism, and various psychiatric syndromes.

Randall Morrison describes a variety of rating scales that assess adult psychopathology. They include scales of schizophrenic symptoms that are completed by a psychologist who interviews and observes the person suspected of having schizophrenia. A scale of global adjustment is also reviewed by Morrison. This 100-point rating scale is useful with a wide variety of psychiatric patients. It focuses on the extent to which the person has coped effectively with environmental events during the past year. According to Morrison, it has some value in predicting how well a person will cope after treatment, as well as in assessing the effectiveness of the treatment.

There are many rating scales for children, adolescents, and adults. They assess a wide range of behaviors and vary in the degree to which they have been constructed with attention to the standards for test development and the compilation of appropriate norms.

THE DEVELOPMENT OF BEHAVIORAL ASSESSMENT

The history of psychological assessment is replete with examples of attempts to measure the characteristics and traits of people. These traits and characteristics are defined as underlying psychological processes that are pervasive aspects of personality. In fact, they define the personality for many psychologists. Traditional approaches to psychotherapy try to identify the traits in order to develop a therapeutic strategy that will reveal the unconscious conflicts.

Unlike traditional approaches to psychological assessment and psychotherapy, behavioral assessment arose from the need of behavior therapists to describe more completely the events surrounding the problem behavior. The history of behavior therapy is one of defining a target behavior and designing a program to change the behavior. As behavior therapy developed and became more sophisticated, it became apparent that more information was needed to identify the antecedent stimuli, the organismic filters that were operating, which aspect of the triple-response system was relevant, and what the consequences of the target behavior were. In response to that need, behavioral assessment was developed. Initially, behavioral assessment was rather straightforward and did not bother much with the procedures of psychological test construction, since the process itself was one of observing behavior rather than making inferences about behavior from test responses. As behavioral assessment has matured, it has become more concerned with meeting the standards of test construction applied to other assessment methods and has become more sophisticated and complex.

Behavioral assessment is used to measure clusters of behaviors and syndromes rather than merely isolated problem behaviors. More attention is paid to the extent to which standards of validity and reliability are met. Psychologists are putting behavioral assessment to the test of demonstrating its worth as an assessment procedure: It must add something to the understanding of the person being assessed in order to justify its use. The challenge is being met, and behavioral assessment continues to provide valuable information about the person being assessed. Information obtained is useful in determining the extent to which certain behaviors are problems. Other information is used in determining the personality of the individual, with all the attendant traits and characteristics.

SOURCES FOR FURTHER STUDY

Barrios, B. A. "On the Changing Nature of Behavioral Assessment." In *Behavioral Assessment: A Practical Handbook*, edited by Alan S. Bellack and Michel Hersen. 3d ed. New York: Pergamon, 1988. This chapter is a good review of the principles associated with behavioral assessment, which are put in both historical and methodological contexts. The book is a thorough description of behavioral assessment and how it is used in various settings.

Bush, Robert P., Alan J. Bush, David J. Ortinau, and Joseph F. Hair, Jr. "Developing a Behavior-Based Scale to Assess Retail Salesperson Performance." *Journal of Retailing* 66, no. 1 (1990): 119-136. A good article describing the development of a rating scale of salesperson performance. An example of the scale content is provided.

Evans, Larry D., and Sharon Bradley-Johnson. "A Review of Recently Developed Measures of Adaptive Behavior." *Psychology in the Schools* 25, no. 3 (1988): 276-287. A thorough review of six rating scales of adaptive behavior. They are compared to older scales that have been in use for a number of years.

Goldfried, Marvin R. "Behavioral Assessment: An Overview." In *International Handbook of Behavior Modification and Therapy*, edited by Alan S. Bellack, Michel Hersen, and Alan E. Kazdin. New York: Plenum, 1982. This chapter provides a good introduction to behavioral assessment. It is part of a book that includes many examples of assessment and therapy.

Kanfer, Frederick H., and W. Robert Nay. "Behavioral Assessment." In *Contemporary Behavior Therapy: Conceptual and Empirical Foundations*, edited by G. Terence Wilson and Cyril M. Franks. New York: Guilford, 1982. A well-written chapter that provides a detailed description of the procedure of behavioral assessment. A fairly advanced description in the context of a presentation of behavior therapy.

Ollendick, Thomas H., and Greta Francis. "Behavioral Assessment and Treatment of Childhood Phobias." *Behavior Modification* 12, no. 2 (1988): 165-204. A very informative review of the normal aspects of fear and the problems associated with abnormal fear. Children's fears and assessment devices for children are the focus of this article.

Phares, E. Jerry. *Clinical Psychology.* 4th ed. Pacific Grove, Calif.: Brooks/Cole, 1991. Includes a chapter on behavioral assessment within the context of a more comprehensive description of the duties of clinical psychologists.

Reilly, Richard R., Sarah Henry, and James W. Smither. "An Examination of the Effects of Using Behavior Checklists on the Construct Validity of Assessment Center Dimensions." *Personnel Psychology* 43, no. 1 (1990): 71-84. A technical description of a study testing the value of a behavioral assessment procedure in the assessment center.

James T. Trent

SEE ALSO: Behavior therapy; Behaviorism; Clinical interviewing, testing, and observation; Emotions; Observational methods; Personality: Psychophysiological measures; Personality rating scales.

Behavioral family therapy

TYPE OF PSYCHOLOGY: Psychotherapy
FIELDS OF STUDY: Group and family therapies

Behavioral family therapy is a type of psychotherapy that applies the principles of learning theory to the treatment of family problems. It is most frequently used to treat parent-child problems, with the parents being taught to apply behavioral techniques in order to correct their children's misbehavior.

KEY CONCEPTS
- circular causality
- classical conditioning
- contingency management
- learning theory
- linear view of causality
- operant conditioning
- positive reinforcement
- response cost

INTRODUCTION

Behavioral family therapy is a type of psychotherapy used to treat families in which one or more members are exhibiting behavior problems. Behavioral therapy was employed originally in the treatment of individual disorders such as phobias (irrational fears). Behavioral family therapy represents an extension of the use of behavioral techniques from the treatment of individual problems to the treatment of family problems. The most common problems treated by behavioral family therapy are parent-child conflicts; however, the principles of this type of therapy have been used to treat other familial difficulties, including marital and sexual problems.

ROLE OF LEARNING THEORY

The principles of learning theory underlie the theory and practice of behavioral family therapy. Learning theory was developed through laboratory experimentation largely begun by Ivan Pavlov and Edward L. Thorndike during the early 1900's. Pavlov was a Russian physiologist interested in the digestive processes of dogs. In the process of his experimentation, he discovered several properties regarding the production of behavior which have become embodied in the theory of classical conditioning. Pavlov observed that his dogs began to salivate when he entered their pens because they associated his presence (new behavior) with their being fed (previously reinforced old behavior). From this observation and additional experimentation, Pavlov concluded that a new behavior which is regularly paired with an old behavior acquires the same rewarding or punishing qualities of the old behavior. New actions become conditioned to produce the same responses as the previously reinforced or punished actions.

Another component of learning theory was discovered by Thorndike, an American psychologist. Thorndike observed that actions followed closely by rewards were more likely to recur than those not followed by rewards. Similarly, he observed that actions followed closely by punishment were less likely to recur. Thorndike explained these observations on the basis of the law of effect. The law of effect holds that behavior closely followed by a response will be more or less likely to recur depending on whether the response is reinforcing (rewarding) or punishing.

Building on the observations of Thorndike, American behaviorist B. F. Skinner developed the theory of operant conditioning in the 1930's. Operant conditioning is the process by which behavior is made to occur at a faster rate when a specific behavior is followed by positive reinforcement—the rewarding consequences that follow a behavior, which increase the rate at which the behavior will recur. An example that Skinner used in demonstrating operant conditioning involved placing a rat in a box with different levers. When the rat accidentally pushed a predesignated lever, it was given a food pellet. As predicted by operant conditioning, the rat subsequently increased its pushing of the lever that provided it with food.

Gerald Patterson and Richard Stuart, beginning in the late 1960's, were among the first clinicians to apply behavioral techniques, previously utilized with individuals, to the treatment of family problems. While Patterson worked primarily with parent-child problems, Stuart extended behavioral family therapy to the treatment of marital problems.

Given the increasing prevalence of family problems, as seen by the rise in the number of divorces and cases of child abuse, the advent of behavioral family therapy has been welcomed by many therapists who treat families. The findings of a 1984 study by William Quinn and Bernard Davidson revealed the increasing use of this therapy, with more than half of all family therapists reporting the use of behavioral techniques in their family therapy.

CONDITIONING AND DESENSITIZATION

The principles of classical and operant conditioning serve to form the foundation of learning theory. Although initially derived from animal experiments, learning theory also was applied to humans. Psychologists who advocated learning theory began to demonstrate that all behavior, whether socially appropriate or inappropriate, occurs because it is either classically or operantly conditioned. John B. Watson, an American psychologist of the early twentieth century, illustrated this relationship by producing a fear of rats in an infant named Albert by repeatedly making a loud noise when a rat was pre-

sented to Albert. After a number of pairings of the loud noise with the rat, Albert began to show fear when the rat was presented.

In addition to demonstrating how inappropriate behavior was caused, behavioral psychologists began to show how learning theory could be used to treat people with psychological disorders. Joseph Wolpe, a pioneer in the use of behavioral treatment during the 1950's, showed how phobias could be alleviated by using learning principles in a procedure termed systematic desensitization. Systematic desensitization involves three basic steps: teaching the phobic individual how to relax; having the client create a list of images of the feared object (for example, snakes), from least to most feared; and repeatedly exposing the client to the feared object in graduated degrees, from least to most feared images, while the individual is in a relaxed state. This procedure has been shown to be very effective in the treatment of phobias.

Behavioral family therapy makes the same assumptions regarding the causes of both individual and family problems. For example, in a fictional case, the Williams family came to treatment because their seven-year-old son, John, refused to sleep in his own bed at night. In attempting to explain John's behavior, a behaviorally oriented psychologist would seek to find out what positive reinforcement John was receiving in response to his refusal to stay in his own bed. It may be that when John was younger his parents allowed him to sleep with them, thus reinforcing his behavior by giving him the attention he desired. Now that John is seven, however, his parents believe that he needs to sleep in his own bed, but John continues to want to sleep with his parents because he has been reinforced by being allowed to sleep with them for many years. This case provides a clinical example of operant conditioning in that John's behavior, because it was repeatedly followed by positive reinforcement, was resistant to change.

TREATMENT PROCESS

Behavioral family therapy is a treatment approach that includes the following four steps: problem assessment, family (parent) education, specific treatment design, and treatment goal evaluation. It begins with a thorough assessment of the presenting family problem. This assessment process involves gathering the following information from the family: what circumstances immediately precede the problem behavior; how family members react to the exhibition of the client's problem behavior; how frequently the misbehavior occurs; and how intense the misbehavior is. Behavioral family therapy differs from individual behavior therapy in that all family members are typically involved in the assessment process. As a part of the assessment process, the behavioral family therapist often observes the way in which the family handles the presenting problem. This observation is conducted in order to obtain firsthand information regarding ways the family may be unknowingly reinforcing the problem or otherwise poorly handling the client's misbehavior.

Following the assessment, the behavioral family therapist, with input from family members, establishes treatment goals. These treatment goals should be operationalized; that is, they should be specifically stated in order that they may be easily observed and measured. In the example of John, the boy who refused to sleep in his own bed, an operationalized treatment goal would be as follows: "John will be able to sleep from 9:00 P.M. to 6:00 A.M. in his own bed without interrupting his parents during the night."

APPLYING LEARNING THEORY PRINCIPLES

Once treatment goals have been operationalized, the next stage involves designing an intervention to correct the behavioral problem. The treatment procedure follows from the basic learning principles previously discussed. In cases involving parent-child problems, the behavioral family therapist educates the parents in learning theory principles as they apply to the treatment of behavioral problems. Three basic learning principles are explained to the child's parents. First, positive reinforcement should be withdrawn from the unwanted behavior. For example, a parent who meets the demands of a screaming preschooler who throws a temper tantrum in the checkout line of the grocery store because he or she wants a piece of candy is unwittingly reinforcing the child's screaming behavior. "Time-out" is one procedure used to remove the undesired reinforcement from a child's misbehavior. Utilizing time-out involves making a child sit in a corner or other nonreinforcing place for a specified period of time (typically, one minute for each year of the child's age).

Second, appropriate behavior that is incompatible with the undesired behavior should be positively reinforced. In the case of the screaming preschooler, this would involve rewarding him or her for acting correctly. An appropriate reinforcer in this case would be giving the child the choice of a candy bar if the child were quiet and cooperative during grocery shopping, behavior inconsistent with a temper tantrum. In order for positive reinforcement to have its maximum benefit, prior to the beginning of the specific activity (for example, grocery shopping) the child should be informed about what is expected and what reward will be received for fulfilling these responsibilities. This process is called contingency management because the promised reward is made contingent upon the child's acting in a prescribed manner. In addition, the positive reinforcement should be given as close to the completion of the appropriate behavior as possible.

Third, aversive consequences should be applied when the problem behavior recurs. When the child engages in the misbehavior, he or she should consistently experience negative costs. In this regard, response cost is a useful technique because it involves taking something away or making the child do something unrewarding as a way of making misbehavior have a cost. For example, the preschooler who has a temper tantrum in the checkout line may have a favorite dessert, which he or she had previously selected while in the store, taken away as the cost for throwing a temper tantrum. As with positive reinforcement, response cost should be applied as quickly as possible following the misbehavior in order for it to produce its maximum effect.

DESIGNING TREATMENT INTERVENTION

Once parents receive instruction regarding the principles of behavior therapy, they are actively involved in the process of designing a specific intervention to address their child's behavior problems. The behavioral family therapist relates to the parents as cotherapists with the hope that this approach will increase the parents' involvement in the treatment process. In relating to Mr. and Mrs. Williams as cotherapists, for example, the behavioral family therapist would have the couple design a treatment intervention to correct John's misbehavior. Following the previously described principles, the couple might arrive at the following approach: They would refuse to give in to John's demands to sleep with them; John would receive a token for each night he slept in his own bed (after earning a certain number of tokens, he could exchange them for toys); and John would be required to go to bed fifteen minutes earlier the following night for each time he asked to sleep with his parents.

Once the intervention has been implemented, the therapist, together with the parents, monitors the results of the treatment. This monitoring process involves assessing the degree to which the established treatment goals are being met. For example, in the Williamses' case, the treatment goal was to reduce the number of times that John attempted to get into bed with his parents. Therapy progress, therefore, would be measured by counting the number of times that John attempted to get into bed with his parents. Careful assessment of an intervention's results is essential in order to determine whether the intervention is accomplishing its goal.

DETRACTIONS

In spite of its popularity, this type of therapy has not been without its critics. For example, behavioral family therapists' explanations regarding the causes of family problems differ from those given by the advocates of other family therapies. One major difference is that behavioral family therapists are accused of taking a linear (as compared to a circular) view of causality. From a linear perspective, misbehavior occurs because A causes B and B causes C. Those who endorse a circular view of causality, however, assert that this simplistic perspective is inadequate in explaining why misbehavior occurs. Taking a circular perspective involves identifying multiple factors that may be operating at the same time in order to determine the reason for a particular misbehavior. For example, from a linear view of causality, John's misbehavior is seen as the result of being reinforced for sleeping with his parents. According to a circular perspective, however, John's behavior may be the result of many factors, all possibly occurring together, such as his parents' marital problems or his genetic predisposition toward insecurity.

INTEGRATION WITH OTHER THERAPIES

Partially in response to this criticism, attempts have been made to integrate behavioral family therapy with other types of family therapy. Another major purpose of integrative efforts is to address the resistance often encountered from families during treatment. Therapeutic resistance is a family's continued attempt to handle the presenting problem in a mal-

adaptive manner in spite of having learned better ways. In the past, behavioral family therapists gave limited attention to dealing with family resistance; however, behavioral family therapy has attempted to improve its ability to handle resistance by incorporating some of the techniques used by other types of family therapy.

In conclusion, numerous research studies have demonstrated that behavioral family therapy is an effective treatment of family problems. One of the major strengths of this type of therapy is its willingness to assess objectively its effectiveness in treating family problems. Because of its emphasis on experimentation, behavioral family therapy continues to adapt by modifying its techniques to address the problems of the modern family.

SOURCES FOR FURTHER STUDY

Atwood, Joan, ed. *Family Therapy: A Systemic Behavioral Approach*. Chicago: Nelson-Hall, 1999. A thorough overview of behavioral family therapy, with chapters on specific problems as well as more general, theoretical, and historical treatments of the subject.

Clark, Lynn. *The Time-Out Solution*. Chicago: Contemporary Books, 1989. Provides the general reader with an excellent overview of the major techniques used in behavioral family therapy. A good resource for parents or others interested in correcting children's misbehaviors through the use of well-tested methods.

Falloon, Ian R. H., ed. *Handbook of Behavioral Family Therapy*. New York: Guilford, 1988. Provides a thorough review of the applications of behavioral family therapy; written primarily for persons familiar with behavioral therapy. Six chapters are devoted to general issues in behavioral family therapy; twelve chapters illustrate the use of its principles with families whose members have specific clinical problems.

Gordon, Thomas. *Parent Effectiveness Training*. Rev. ed. New York: Three Rivers Press, 2000. Written primarily for parents interested in successfully handling parent-child interactions. Contains sixteen easily understood chapters that address various topics which primarily relate to improving communication between parents and children as well as handling children's misbehavior.

Nichols, Michael P. "Cognitive-Behavioral Family Therapy." In *Family Therapy: Concepts and Methods,* by Michael P. Nichols and Richard C. Schwartz. 5th ed. Boston: Allyn & Bacon, 2000. A very readable, well synthesized chapter. Provides information regarding the leading characters, definitions of important terms, beliefs regarding causes of abnormal behavior, and techniques involved in behavioral family therapy. An excellent piece for the person interested in reading only an article about the topic.

Robin, Arthur L., and Sharon L. Foster. *Negotiating Parent-Adolescent Conflict: A Behavioral Family Systems Approach.* New York: Guilford, 1989. Illustrates the integration of behavioral family therapy with other types of family therapy. Fifteen chapters are nicely divided between assessment and treatment issues. For the person already familiar with the subject.

R. Christopher Qualls

SEE ALSO: Behavior therapy; Cognitive behavior therapy; Conditioning; Group therapy; Instrumental conditioning; Misbehavior; Operant conditioning therapies; Psychotherapy: Children; Strategic family therapy.

Behaviorism

DATE: Founded in 1912
TYPE OF PSYCHOLOGY: Learning
FIELDS OF STUDY: Behavioral and cognitive models; experimental methodologies; instrumental conditioning; methodological issues; nervous system; Pavlovian conditioning; thought

Behaviorism uses the methods of natural science to search for lawful relationships between behavior and the observable social and physical environment. The focus on observable and measurable behavior-environment relationships distinguishes behaviorism from other psychological perspectives that rely on unobservable and hypothetical explanations such as the mind, ego, the self, and consciousness.

KEY CONCEPTS
- classical conditioning
- operant behavior
- operant conditioning
- punisher
- reflex
- reinforcer
- stimulus control

INTRODUCTION

Behaviorism was founded in 1912 by the American psychologist John Broadus Watson (1878-1958). Watson's position was formed as a reaction to the then-current focus of psychology on consciousness and the method of research known as introspection, which Watson considered to be highly subjective. Using the research of the Russian Nobel Prize-winning physiologist Ivan Petrovich Pavlov (1849-1936), Watson argued that psychology could become a natural science only by truly adopting the methods of science. What Watson meant was that psychology must have an empirical, objective subject matter and that the events to be investigated as possible causes of behavior must also be described objectively and verified empirically through experimental research. This latter point meant that introspection would have to be abandoned, for it was unscientific. Watson therefore presented the goals of psychology as the prediction and control of behavior rather than as the understanding of the mind and consciousness.

Watson's behaviorism was an extension of Pavlov's discovery of the conditioning of stimulus-response reflexive relationships. The term "reflex" refers to the connection between some environmental event, or stimulus, and the response that it elicits. The response is involuntary—inborn or unlearned—and relatively simple. In addition, no prior learning is necessary for the response to occur when the stimulus is presented. What Pavlov had already demonstrated experimentally was how previously neutral parts of the environment could become effective in stimulating or eliciting an animal's salivation response. By repeatedly pairing a bell with food powder, which elicited salivation, and then presenting the bell alone, Pavlov showed that the bell by itself could then elicit salivation. This process, termed classical conditioning (the process is also known as Pavlovian or respondent conditioning), in turn offered Watson an explanation for behavior that relied on observable elements, thus eliminating the need to use unobservable and hypothetical mental explanations.

Watson's significant contribution resulted from his attempt to show how Pavlov's discovery of the conditioning process with animals could also explain the behavior of human beings. Watson assumed that human behavior and the behavior of animals were both governed by the same laws of nature. Given this assumption, the objective methods of study that were appropriate for the scientific study of nonhuman animals were therefore appropriate for the study of human beings as well. Watson demonstrated the application of these methods in the famous but ethically controversial case study of "Little Albert." In this study, Watson and his graduate student, Rosalie Rayner, showed how human emotional responses could come to be conditioned to previously neutral environmental stimuli. "Little Albert" was eleven months old at the time, and Watson and Rayner began their study by showing that Albert initially approached and smiled when he was shown a live rat. At a time when the rat was not present, Watson struck a metal bar with a hammer. Albert then flinched and began to cry. Next, the rat and the loud, unexpected sound were presented together on seven occasions. On these occasions, Albert reacted to the sound of the hammer striking the metal bar, withdrawing from the rat, moving away from the sound, whimpering, and then crying. Finally, the rat alone was shown to Albert. Now, when only the rat was placed before Albert, he would instantly move away from the rat, whimper, and then cry. Watson and Rayner had demonstrated through the process of classical conditioning that the once-neutral object, the rat, would now produce, or elicit, a strong emotional response.

Watson attempted to present an objective, behavioristic account of the full range of human behavior in *Behaviorism* (1924), written for a popular audience. In that book, Watson proposed that the stimulus-response reflex was the essential building block of all human behaviors. A collection of separate elemental reflexive responses, unlearned and as-yet unconditioned, could become integrated into a complex habit through the regular presentation of the appropriate stimuli by the physical and social environment by parents, siblings, teachers, and others. The result would be, in Watson's words, "habits, such as tennis, fencing, shoe-making, mother-reactions, religious reactions, and the like." The process by which these habits were formed was presumably the conditioning process discovered by Pavlov. In addition to such "habits," Watson attempted to show that the conditioning of neutral environmental stimuli to existing reflexive responses could also account for thinking and the personality.

B. F. SKINNER AND RADICAL BEHAVIORISM

A very different form of behaviorism came from the work of the American psychologist Burrhus Frederic Skinner (1904-1990). Skinner, too, focused his research on behavior. He also continued to search for lawful relationships between behavior and the environment. Skinner's thinking began with an acceptance of the stimulus-response approach of Watson, but Skinner ultimately took behaviorism in a fundamentally different direction. The first presentation of Skinner's approach was in *The Behavior of Organisms* (1938). In this book, Skinner described the methods and results of systematic research that demonstrated the key points of what was later to become known as radical behaviorism: Stimulus-response relationships, or reflexes, include only a narrow range of behavior; classical, or Pavlovian, conditioning could not account for the development of new behavior or the complexity of human behavior; behavior does show lawful relationships with the environment; the consequences immediately following a behavior determine the future strength of that behavior; new behavior can be acquired by the process of shaping (from existing behavior, elemental forms can be strengthened by consequences which follow the step-by-step approximations until the new behavior is present); once acquired, behavior is maintained by a particular arrangement of environmental consequences; and certain events are present when a behavior is strengthened. Often, one of those antecedent events is by design especially correlated with the behavior and the consequence that makes that behavior stronger in the future. At a later time, the presence of that antecedent event by itself will make the behavior more likely to occur.

Skinner named the process used to investigate these behavior-environment relationships operant conditioning. Skinner called the behavior in this process operant behavior, because it operates or acts on the environment. In operating or acting on the environment, the behavior produces consequences, or changes, in the environment. Consequences in turn affect the behavior for the future. Skinner was able to detect this relationship between present consequences to the behavior and their later effect on behavior by the method that he used for his research. This method, used initially with rats and later with pigeons, allowed Skinner to observe and measure the behavior of interest continuously and over long periods of time. Not only was the behavior observed at the time that the consequence to it occurred, but it was observed continuously subsequent to the consequence.

Skinner observed two effects of consequences on the future strength of behavior. Some consequences resulted in stronger behavior (reinforced the behavior), while other consequences resulted in weaker behavior (punished the behavior). It is important to note that for Skinner and his followers the consequent events to behavior that serve as reinforcers or punishers are defined only in terms of their effects on the future strength of some behavior. Events or things in themselves are not reinforcers or punishers. For example, a harsh command to a learner in the classroom ("Sit down and get to work!") is assumed by many teachers to "punish" wandering around the room and inattentiveness to seatwork. Yet in countless instances the teacher's consequence serves only to strengthen or maintain the learner's wandering and inattentiveness. In this case, the teacher's remarks function as a reinforcer irrespective of what the teacher believes.

Skinner also showed that once a behavior had been acquired and was maintained, the occurrence of the behavior could be made more or less probable by the presentation or removal of events that preceded the behavior. These antecedent events— for example, the ringing of a telephone—have been reliably present when one picks up the telephone and says "Hello." On the other hand, if one picks up the telephone and says "Hello" when the telephone has not rung, the voice of another person responding to the greeting is extremely unlikely. The term for this process is "stimulus control," defined as the effect that events preceding a behavior can have on the likelihood of that behavior occurring. Stimulus control comes about because of the presence of particular events when a behavior is reinforced.

THE CAUSES OF BEHAVIOR

For Skinner, the causes of behavior lie in humans' genetic endowment and the environment in which they live. The specific ways in which the environment causes behavior can be seen in the experimentally derived principles noted previously.

Skinner's approach differs sharply from most psychological theories that put the causes of behavior inside the person. Skinner believed that these internal causes were either not scientific explanations, were actually behaviors themselves in need of explanation, or were explanations taken from disciplines other than psychology.

Skinner regarded the "mind" as an unscientific explanation because of its status as an inference from the behavior that it was supposed to explain. While psychological theory has, since the 1970's, redefined the "mind" in two broad ways, Skinner continued to note that the redefining did not solve the problems posed by the requirements of science. On one hand, mental processes have become cognitive processes, a metaphor based on computer operations. Humans are said to "process" information by "encoding, decoding, storing, and retrieving" information. However, all these hypothesized activities remain inferences from the behavior that they are said to explain. There is no independent observation of these hypothetical activities.

On the other hand, the mind has been translated to mean the brain, which can be studied scientifically. Thus, the physiology of the brain is thought to explain behavior. Neither Skinner nor other radical behaviorists deny the role of the brain in a complete understanding of behavior. However, psychology and brain physiology look for the causes of behavior at different levels of observation. Psychology is viewed as a separate discipline with its own methods of scientific investigation leading to the discovery of distinct psychological explanations for behavior. In addition, research results suggest that rather than brain physiology explaining behavior, changes in the brain and changes in behavior appear to result from changes in the environment. Changes in behavior are correlated with changes in the brain, but changes at both levels appear to be the result of the environment.

Thoughts and feelings are also considered to be causes of behavior. One thinks about talking with a friend and then goes to the telephone and dials the number. These two people talk together on the telephone regularly because they feel affection for each other. Yet the "thinking" or "feeling" referred to as causes for the actions involved in dialing the telephone and talking with each other are themselves viewed as responses in need of explanation. What gave rise to thinking in early development, and what now makes thoughts of this particular friend so strong? How have feelings of affection become associated with this friend? From the radical behaviorist perspective, both the thoughts and the feeling are explained by the principles of operant or classical conditioning.

RADICAL BEHAVIORISM AND COMPLEX HUMAN BEHAVIOR

Some of the facts of human experience include talking, thinking, seeing, problem-solving, conceptualizing, and creating new ideas and things. A common point of view holds that behaviorism either rejects or neglects these aspects of human experience. However, a fuller reading of Skinner's works reveals that he offered a serious examination of these topics and demonstrated that behavioral principles could account for their presence in the repertoire of human behavior.

For example, Skinner's examination of verbal behavior resulted in *Verbal Behavior* (1957). In this book, Skinner showed that behavioral principles were capable of explaining the acquisition and continuation of behaviors such as talking, reading, and thinking. Basic processes such as imitation, reinforcement, shaping, and stimulus control were all shown to have likely roles in the various aspects of verbal behavior.

Behaviorism's analysis of verbal behavior is directly related to the more complex forms of human behavior often referred to as higher mental processes. For example, radical behaviorism views thinking as an activity derived from talking out loud. Parents and teachers encourage children to talk to themselves, initially by encouraging whispering, then moving the lips as in speaking but without making sounds. What results, then, is talking privately, "in our own heads." In a similar fashion, a parent asks a child to "think before you act" and a teacher asks learners to "think through" the solution to a problem in mathematics or ethics. The social environment thus encourages people to think, often shows them how to do so, and then reinforces them for doing so when the overt results of their thinking are praised or given high scores.

More complex behavior-environment relationships such as those found in concept formation have also been analyzed in terms of the principles of behaviorism. The term "concept" is defined as a characteristic that is common to a number of objects that are otherwise different from one another. People are said to have concepts in their heads which produce the behaviors they observe. A radical behavioral analysis, however, views concepts as the appropriate response to the common characteristic. The appropriate response has been reinforced only when it occurs in the presence of the specific characteristic. For example, a child is said to understand the concept of "red" when the child reliably says "red" in response to the question "What color are these objects?" in the presence of a red hat, red fire truck, red tomato, and red crayon.

APPLICATIONS OF THE PRINCIPLES OF BEHAVIORISM

The behaviorism of Watson has resulted in applications in psychology and many other disciplines. The most notable form of application of Watson's behaviorism is the psychological treatment known as systematic desensitization. This treatment was created by South African psychiatrist Joseph Wolpe (1915-1997). Systematic desensitization was designed to reverse the outcome of the classical conditioning process where extremely intense negative emotional responses such as fear or anxiety are elicited by everyday aspects of the environment. This outcome is referred to as a phobia. The treatment first requires training in relaxation. The second component of treatment takes a person through a hierarchy of steps beginning with a setting very distant from the feared stimulus and ending with the problem setting. At each step, the individual is asked to note and in some manner signal the experiencing of fear or anxiety and then is instructed to relax. Movement through the hierarchy is repeated until the person can experience each step, including the one that includes the feared stimulus, and report feeling relaxed at every step. This treatment has been employed in both the clinic and in real-life settings. Systematic desensitization has been shown to be an effective intervention for fears associated with, for example, dental treatment and flying, as well as the intense anxiety that accompanies social phobia and panic disorder.

Applied behavior analysis is the field of application that has arisen out of Skinner's behavioral principles. Applied behavior analysis was introduced first in educational settings. Applications in education have occurred at every level from preschool to university classrooms. Equally important has been repeated successful application to learners with autism, severe and profound delays in behavioral development, and attention-deficit-disorder with and without hyperactive behavior. The application of behavioral principles has been shown to be effective across behaviors, settings, individuals, and teachers.

Applications of behavioral principles have also been shown to be effective in reducing behaviors that pose a threat to public health, including smoking, overeating, essential hypertension, and domestic violence.

Finally, behavioral principles have found application in the arena of public safety. For example, researchers using techniques based on Skinner's science of behavior have increased seat belt usage by automobile drivers.

SOURCES FOR FURTHER STUDY

Alberto, Paul A., and Anne C. Troutman. *Applied Behavior Analysis for Teachers.* 5th ed. Upper Saddle River, N.J.: Prentice-Hall, 1999. A readable introduction to applied behavior analysis principles and methods for use in the classroom.

Baum, William J. *Understanding Behaviorism: Science, Behavior, and Culture.* New York: HarperCollins College Publishers, 1994. Written by a well-known radical behaviorist. A thorough review of Skinner's behaviorism in relation to philosophy of science and in its societal implications.

Johnson, Kent R., and T. V. Joe Layng. "Breaking the Structuralist Barrier: Literacy and Numeracy with Fluency." *American Psychologist* 47, no. 11 (1992): 1475-1490. Demonstrates the application of Skinner's principles to the design of maximally effective academic curricula for children and adults. Accessible reading that does not require a background in statistics.

Nye, Robert D. *The Legacy of B. F. Skinner: Concepts and Perspectives, Controversies and Misunderstandings.* Pacific Grove, Calif.: Brooks/Cole, 1992. An excellent starting point for a reader interested in Skinner's behaviorism.

Pierce, W. David, and W. Frank Epling. *Behavior Analysis and Learning.* 2d ed. Upper Saddle River, N.J.: Prentice-Hall, 1999. An excellent introduction at the college level to basic Skinnerian principles and experimental methods for basic behavioral research.

Skinner, B. F. *About Behaviorism.* New York: Alfred A. Knopf, 1974. Skinner's analysis of thinking, perceiving, emotions, and the self.

_____. *Walden Two.* New York: Macmillan, 1948. A fictional account of the application of behavioral principles in a utopian community.

Watson, John B. *Behaviorism.* Chicago: University of Chicago Press, 1930. Early behaviorism in the words of its founder.

Robert Jensen

SEE ALSO: Aversion, implosion, and systematic desensitization; Behavior therapy; Conditioning; Habituation and sensitization; Learned helplessness; Learning; Operant conditioning therapies; Pavlovian conditioning; Phobias; Radical behaviorism: B. F. Skinner; Reflexes; Reinforcement; Skinner, B. F.; Thought: Study and measurement.

Bilingualism

TYPE OF PSYCHOLOGY: Language
FIELDS OF STUDY: Cognitive development; cognitive processes

Bilingualism refers to the use of two or more languages by either an individual or a community. The psychological study of bilingualism has contributed to an understanding of language acquisition, brain organization, methods of educating language-minority children, and the relationship between language and cognition.

KEY CONCEPTS
- additive bilingualism
- balanced bilingual
- bilingual
- code-switching
- partial bilingual
- sequential bilingual
- simultaneous bilingual
- subtractive bilingualism

INTRODUCTION

Bilingualism refers to the use of two languages, by either an individual or a community. It is estimated that more than half of the world's population is bilingual, and there are sizable numbers of bilinguals in every country. Psychologists have long been interested in understanding the process of learning two languages, as well as the social, psychological, and intellectual consequences of being bilingual. Areas of inquiry have included how the mind of a bilingual differs from that of a monolingual and whether people learn a second language in the same way that they acquire their first language. The cognitive advantages and disadvantages of being bilingual have been investigated. One important question concerns what type of educational system is best for children who are exposed to more than one language.

At the community level, one can make a distinction between additive and subtractive bilingualism. Additive bilingualism generally occurs when members of a majority culture choose to learn a second language in addition to speaking the language used by the mainstream society. Both languages learned and used by bilinguals are viewed positively and supported by the society. Subtractive bilingualism, on the other hand, occurs when the acquisition of the majority language results in the weakening and possible loss of a minority group's native language, caused in part by the low status assigned to minority languages by the mainstream culture. Subtractive bilingualism is characteristic of many language-minority groups in the United States.

There is little agreement even among experts in the field as to how competent an individual has to be in a second language in order to be considered bilingual. Some believe that a minimal level of competence, such as being able to form a few grammatical sentences in a second language, is enough for a person to be called bilingual. Others believe that both nativelike fluency and functional literacy skills are necessary to be truly bilingual. Most people, however, would agree that bilingual individuals are those who have enough competence in a second language to function well with that language in a number of different contexts. Bilingualism is probably best thought of, then, as representing a range of second-language skills.

Language Acquisition

In contrast to first-language acquisition, there is considerable variation in how, when, and in what setting people learn a second language. Simultaneous bilingualism refers to the situation in which a child grows up learning two languages from the beginning (this is also known as early childhood bilingualism). Sequential or consecutive bilingualism describes individuals who acquire their second language after they have for the most part mastered their primary language. A balanced bilingual has approximately equal facility in both languages, while a partial or dominant bilingual is much stronger in one language.

Children who grow up learning two languages at the same time do not show any significant delays in language development compared to monolingual children, and they may even have advantages. For example, infants exposed to two languages are able to make more types of speech sounds than their monolingual counterparts. A common but unfounded fear is that language development will suffer as children become confused between the two languages. Before the age of two, children reared in bilingual environments do seem to treat both languages as if they were one system. They mix the two languages and use words in one language for certain things and words in the other language for other distinct things. In an effort to help the child keep the languages separate, many two-parent families wishing to rear a bilingual child use a one-parent/one-language method in which each parent speaks to the child exclusively in one language. This strategy, however, does not seem to be necessary, because children, regardless of the type of early bilingual language input, are able to differentiate between the two systems of language quite well by about the age of two. By age three, in addition to being able to differentiate between the languages and use them appropriately in different contexts, simultaneous bilinguals become aware of their two languages and begin spontaneously to translate from one to the other.

There is much more variation in the development of a second language in the case of consecutive bilingualism. The ease and speed with which people learn a second language depends on the context as well as on the learner's attitude, motivation, and language-learning aptitude. As a group, consecutive bilinguals tend to take longer in learning a second language than do simultaneous bilinguals, and their progress in a second language is more influenced by their first language. The amount and type of this "interference" depends upon the characteristics of the particular languages involved.

There is some evidence that a "sensitive period" exists for second-language acquisition; that is, because language specialization in the brain is basically completed by puberty, it is easier for a person to learn a second language as a child than as an adult. Although this is probably the case for some language skills, such as pronunciation, it is important to note that the context in which adults learn a second language is often quite different from that of children. Adults and older children, in a supportive context, with the right motivation and much exposure to the target language, can certainly learn a second language as well as young children.

BRAIN ORGANIZATION

Different types of bilinguals may have different types of brain organization for language and memory. For the most part, the brains of simultaneous bilinguals are thought to be structured in a compound organization, whereas consecutive bilinguals have a coordinate organization. Compound organization means that both languages are stored in roughly the same place in the brain and that a person has a single memory store for concepts in both languages. Coordinate organization means that the two languages and the two sets of concepts are stored separately in the brain. Brain-lesion studies have found that after specific damage to the brain, certain bilinguals lose both of their languages while other bilinguals lose only one language. Despite the speculation about differing brain structures, it is thought that all bilinguals must have at least some overlapping common store in their brains; it would seem to be required in order for them to do the rapid processing, the switching back and forth, and the translating that is characteristic of bilinguals.

Bilingual individuals also seem to have a different brain organization for language from that of monolinguals. For most monolinguals, language information is stored and processed primarily by the left hemisphere of the brain. Bilinguals who learn their two languages at different times appear to use more of the right hemisphere and tend to have a bilateral (both-sided) organization for both languages. This does not seem to be the case for early-childhood bilinguals, who actually show faster and more left-hemisphere lateralization than monolinguals do. A number of factors affect the degree to which bilinguals will either use the right hemisphere more or use both hemispheres in the processing of language. They include the type of languages learned (some languages naturally require more right-hemisphere processing), the setting in which the languages are learned (natural settings encourage right-hemisphere processing, whereas classrooms encourage the left hemisphere), the amount of time using the second language (the right hemisphere is favored at early stages of bilingualism, the left at later stages), the age at which the second language is learned (older learners use more right hemisphere), and the handedness and gender of the learner (left-handed people and females generally use more of both hemispheres for language processing).

COGNITIVE PROCESSING

Being able to speak more than one language has an effect on the way in which one can process cognitive information. Because of their access to two different systems of language, bilingual individuals are able to process different types of information and employ different types of strategies, and do so more flexibly than their monolingual counterparts. Bilinguals can think in two languages and switch back and forth as needed for a particular problem-solving situation. During speech, the switching back and forth between two languages within a single conversation or sentence is called code-switching. Although at one time it was thought to be a sign that the person was confusing the two languages, code-switching is now understood to be a complex and mostly deliberate social, cognitive, and linguistic process, and it is one which many balanced bilinguals use frequently.

The use of code-switching follows both grammatical rules and linguistic constraints, and it serves a variety of important functions for both the speaker and the listener, including signaling cultural identity and intimacy, placing emotional emphasis, conveying a more subtle or connotatively correct meaning, and role playing. Translating spontaneously from one language to another also demands a special type of simultaneous information-processing skill that monolinguals do not develop. Even very young bilingual children, especially those from language-minority groups, translate both extensively and proficiently. Because translating and code-switching are skills that require both language-processing systems to be operating simultaneously, it appears that both languages can be active at the same time in the mind of the bilingual. Most of the time, however, the bilingual individual thinks and processes information in only one language.

BILINGUAL EDUCATION

Psychologists who study bilingualism have made contributions in several areas. First, by applying their knowledge of second-language acquisition, psychologists have made helpful suggestions as to how to rear a child bilingually and how best to teach a foreign language. For example, works by François Grosjean and by Lenore Arnberg are excellent resources for interested parents and teachers. Another area in which the study of bilingualism has made an impact is in the understanding of, and behavior toward, language-minority groups in the United States. Because of an earlier lack of knowledge about bilingualism, minority children from homes where a language other than English was spoken have been misunderstood and treated as if they were somehow mentally handicapped. Now, however, it is becoming clear that knowing multiple languages is a valuable cognitive and cultural resource and that there is nothing about bilingualism, per se, that is detrimental to an individual.

Probably the most widespread application of the study of bilingualism has been in informing the planning and implementation of bilingual education programs for language-minority students. In the United States, the question of how best to educate students who do not speak English as a first language is a controversial, political, and emotional issue. As the number of immigrants living in the United States continues to rise, questions about whether schools should teach children in their native language and, if so, how much and for how long will become more and more critical. Psychologists who study bilingualism have been called upon to help answer many questions concerning bilingual education.

Because there are so many different types of bilingual education programs, it is difficult to talk about them as a single group in order to judge whether bilingual education is effective. Bilingual programs vary in how much time they spend giving instruction in the native language. While some programs use the minority language for the entire school day, most programs use some combination of the two languages, and some programs use exclusively English even though they are labeled "bilingual education" (presumably because of their high enrollment of minority children). Some classrooms use different languages for different subjects, while others alternate between both languages for all subjects. Most bilingual education programs are considered "transitional"—that is, their goal is to make children sufficiently proficient in English that they can enter all-English classes as soon as possible. Because these programs usually do not value the chil-

dren's native language, the result is often subtractive bilingualism, or the eventual loss of the child's native language. Other programs are more "maintenance-oriented" in that, in addition to promoting English skills, they value and attempt to maintain the students' first language.

Overall, good bilingual education appears to have positive consequences for language-minority children. Children who receive instruction in a language other than English have no long-term delays in the development of academic skills compared to children in regular classes, and often they seem to do better academically than those who had been in all-English classes. Children who learn a concept in one language have no problem transferring it to the other language when needed. Bilingual education seems especially beneficial for those language-minority children who are particularly at risk of doing poorly in regular classrooms.

BILINGUALISM AND CULTURAL ASSIMILATION

The first known systematic attempts to study the development of bilingualism took place in Europe during the early 1900's. Two scholars, German linguist Werner Leopold and French psychologist Jules Ronjat, published extensive diaries on the language development of their own infants who were being reared in a bilingual (German-English and French-German, respectively) environment. Both painted a positive picture of early-childhood bilingualism and concluded that young children have no problem growing up with two languages.

A different view of bilingualism, however, was forming in the United States at the same time. Coinciding with both the country's newly found fascination with intelligence quotient (IQ) tests and its keen desire to limit immigration at that time, researchers in the 1920's in the United States were demonstrating that "bilinguals" (immigrant minorities) had lower IQs and were mentally and linguistically handicapped, confused, and racially inferior. A series of poorly controlled studies was done in which researchers typically gave IQ tests (in English) to children of recent immigrants who were poor and spoke little English, then compared their results to the IQ scores of white middle-class children. It is not surprising that under these poor testing conditions, without measuring whether the immigrant children were actually bilingual and without controlling for differences in socioeconomic status, researchers found significantly lower test scores for the language-minority children. Unfortunately, the negative views of bilingualism that were advanced by these early studies persisted.

In the 1960's, a new wave of interest in the psychological study of bilingualism began, and psychologists have been steadily conducting research on the topic ever since. The study often credited for rekindling this interest was conducted by Elizabeth Peal and Wallace Lambert in 1962. Peal and Lambert compared balanced bilinguals to monolinguals who were from the same school system and socioeconomic background on a number of psychological tests, including IQ tests. They found that bilingual children performed better than their monolingual counterparts on nearly all the tasks, and they concluded that bilingualism is indeed positively associated with intelligence and cognitive skill. Since then, numerous investigations have examined in more detail the cognitive advantages of bilingualism. Studies suggest that, compared to monolingual children, bilingual children are more aware of and have more control over the subtle aspects of language, use more flexible problem-solving strategies, are better able to detect ambiguities and errors in language, are more original and creative, and are more sensitive to linguistic and social cues.

SOURCES FOR FURTHER STUDY

Albert, Martin L., and Loraine K. Obler. *The Bilingual Brain: Neuropsychological and Neurolinguistic Aspects of Bilingualism.* New York: Academic Press, 1978. An excellent, accessible, but somewhat dated account of the theory and research on the structure of bilingual individuals' brains and how they differ from those of monolinguals. Written from both a linguistic and psychological perspective. Good bibliography.

Arnberg, Lenore. *Raising Children Bilingually: The Pre-School Years.* Philadelphia: Multilingual Matters, 1987. An excellent resource for parents interested in rearing bilingual children. Based on the author's experience with her own children in Sweden, this book discusses the issues involved in all types of childhood bilingualism.

Bialystok, Ellen. *Bilingualism in Development: Language, Literacy, and Cognition.* New York: Cambridge University Press, 2001. Compares the process of language acquisition in monolingual and bilingual children.

Cummins, Jim. *Bilingualism and Special Education: Issues in Assessment and Pedagogy.* Clevedon, Avon, England: Multilingual Matters, 1984. Written by a leading expert in the field of bilingual education, this small book provides a thorough review of bilingual education programs and their corresponding theories. The author's popular perspective on the education of language-minority children is discussed.

Diaz, R. M. "Thought and Two Languages: The Impact of Bilingualism on Cognitive Development." In *Review of Research in Education,* edited by E. W. Gordon. Vol. 10. Washington, D.C.: American Educational Research Association, 1983. An excellent and well-written review of the history and status of the study of bilingualism and intelligence. Discusses problems with research designs and suggests a partial theory for understanding the relationship between intelligence and bilingualism.

Grosjean, François. *Life with Two Languages: An Introduction to Bilingualism.* Cambridge, Mass.: Harvard University Press, 1982. A very readable and nontechnical book about bilingualism. Using many examples, it provides a comprehensive and enjoyable review of the topic. Good bibliography.

Hamers, Josiane F., and Michel H. A. Blanc. *Bilinguality and Bilingualism.* 2d ed. New York: Cambridge University Press, 2000. A comprehensive but somewhat technical volume on bilingualism. Good coverage of social, psychological, and cognitive aspects.

Kecskes, Istvan, and Tunde Papp. *Foreign Language and Mother Tongue.* Hillsdale, N.J.: Lawrence Erlbaum, 2000. In contrast to most bilingual studies, which look at the influence of a first language on the acquisition of a second, this study looks at the effect of second language acquisition on the functioning of the first language.

Padilla, Amado M., H. H. Fairchild, and C. M. Valadez, eds. *Bilingual Education: Issues and Strategies.* Newbury Park, Calif.: Sage Publications, 1990. An excellent collection of articles about theories and types of bilingual education. Good discussion of the history of bilingual education in the United States from both a researcher's and teacher's perspective. Examples of model programs are given.

Peal, Elizabeth, and Wallace E. Lambert. "The Relation of Bilingualism to Intelligence." *Psychological*

Monographs 76 (1962): 1-23. This is the classic research study that transformed many scholars' and laypersons' negative views of bilingualism into positive ones. An excellent account of the relationship between bilingualism and intelligence.

Adam Winsler

SEE ALSO: Ability tests; Brain specialization; Communication; Grammar and speech; Language; Linguistics; Nonverbal communication; Neurons; Race and intelligence; Racism; Split-brain studies; Synaptic transmission; Thought: Study and measurement.

Biofeedback and relaxation

TYPE OF PSYCHOLOGY: Stress
FIELDS OF STUDY: Behavioral therapies; coping; stress and illness

Responses to stress by the body have traditionally been thought to be made up of involuntary reactions that are beyond the control of the individual. Some of these responses become maladaptive and may now be brought under control by using various relaxation techniques and biofeedback.

KEY CONCEPTS
- autogenic phrases
- cheating
- classical conditioning
- electroencephalography (EEG)
- electromyography (EMG)
- galvanic skin response (GSR)
- instrumental conditioning
- progressive muscle relaxation

INTRODUCTION

From the day that people are born, and even before, they are subjected to a variety of stressors from the environment around them. Each one of these exacts a certain toll on their bodies. Some stressors seem to affect individuals differently, while others seem to have a universal effect; in any case, both the mind and the body must mobilize to deal effectively with these factors. The individual is usually able to handle these problems by using various coping strategies to help alleviate the stress. The problem arises when too many stressors are present at

one time or when these stressors last too long. Individuals must adapt or change their coping strategies to return to a normal equilibrium. A coping strategy is a process that takes effort and is learned; the individual must acquire this coping skill as one acquires any skill. It must be practiced.

If the stressors are not dealt with adequately, fatigue and illness may result. In the most serious circumstances, the organism can die. Hans Selye reported on what he termed the general adaptation syndrome (GAS). As stressors affect an organism, a series of neurological and biological responses occur to protect the body. If these responses are prolonged and go unchecked, however, the body will begin to break itself down. In the first phase, the alarm phase, the body mobilizes itself. The adrenal glands enlarge and release epinephrine (adrenaline) and steroids in order to cope. After a while, the body adapts and seems to be normal; this is the resistance stage. In fact, the body is not normal. It is very vulnerable to further stress, and, if subjected to additional stressors, it will enter the third stage, exhaustion. The organism can then become extremely sick or die.

DEVELOPMENT OF COPING STRATEGIES

It becomes essential for the individual to adopt a successful coping strategy in order to avert this progression of events. Two such techniques will be discussed here. Biofeedback is a procedure whereby the individual is given information about how a variety of body responses are reacting in various circumstances. The individual is generally unaware of these reactions, but biofeedback technology allows the individual to monitor them and eventually bring them under control. Autonomic, visceral responses to stress have traditionally been thought to be involuntary and automatic. Biofeedback is a technique aimed at gaining control over these reactions. Voluntary responses can affect these visceral responses, and this fact complicates the ultimate effectiveness of biofeedback.

Neal E. Miller was one of the early pioneers in the field. His work has been applied to the control of a wide variety of stress-related problems through the use of biofeedback. The control of what have been termed "psychosomatic problems" has been accomplished using Miller's assumptions. Individuals have learned to control blood pressure, heart rate, muscle spasms, headaches, and myriad other ailments through biofeedback techniques.

Miller believed that these responses to stress can be changed through the use of instrumental conditioning and reinforcement. Instrumental conditioning refers to learning that occurs from reinforcing a response and is traditionally thought to be successful with voluntary responses mediated by the skeletal nervous system. When a machine makes this information available to a person, the responses can be reinforced (or they can reinforce themselves) when a therapeutic change occurs. The same principle is at work when an experimental rat learns to press a bar for food.

Another coping strategy that can be used to deal with stressors is the adoption of one of a variety of relaxation procedures. As odd as it may sound to some, people must learn to relax in many situations, and this takes practice. Relaxation techniques are often used in conjunction with biofeedback, which sometimes makes it difficult to determine which of the two procedures is responsible for the changes that occur and to what degree they are acting in relationship to each other.

There are several relaxation techniques, and different techniques are successful for different individuals. One of the most widely used techniques is progressive muscle relaxation, proposed by Edmund Jacobson. The individual is instructed to tense a particular muscle group and hold it for several seconds, paying attention to the feelings associated with this state. Then the individual is told to relax the muscle group and is asked to concentrate on the different feelings while the muscle is relaxed. The major muscle groups of the body are put through this procedure. Ultimately, the individual is able to reproduce the relaxed sensations when feeling tense.

Rhythmic breathing techniques are also used for relaxation in order to combat stress. The person learns to inhale through the nose to the count of three and exhale through the mouth to the count of five. Between each breath is a count of two. The breathing should be with the diaphragm as much as possible, as opposed to the chest. Meditation, another relaxation technique that often incorporates rhythmic breathing, may require that the person either visualize an object or repeat a word or phrase with each breath. This action prevents the person's mind from wandering to the anxiety-provoking stimuli.

In biofeedback therapy, patients monitor their own autonomic physiological responses, such as blood pressure or heart rate, in order to gain some control over them or to reduce stress. (Hans & Cassidy, Inc.)

BIOFEEDBACK EXPERIMENTS

One of the experiments that pioneered the use of biofeedback in a clinical setting was conducted by Neal Miller using white rats. Miller wanted to demonstrate that the animal was able to learn to increase the blood flow to one ear by dilating the capillaries in the ear. He needed to ensure that the animal was not using a skeletal response ("cheating") to influence this response. For example, a human can accomplish this task by covering the ear with the palm of the hand for a period of time. Miller asked whether this could be done without a skeletal response. He administered the drug curare to the rat to incapacitate the skeletal nervous system and kept the animal alive by using an artificial respirator. He attached a sensitive thermometer, which was able to detect slight changes in temperature caused by differential blood flow, to the animal's ear. When a slight increase in temperature was detected, the message was sent to a computer, which delivered an electrical reinforcement to the brain of the subject. This represents the same mechanism which establishes the bar-pressing response in a white rat: operant conditioning. The experiment was successful.

One of the first applications of this experiment to humans came when a woman who had suffered paralysis in an automobile accident was unable even to remain in a sitting position without her blood pressure dropping to dangerous levels. Miller and his staff assembled a biofeedback device that allowed the woman to determine the nature of her blood pressure from moment to moment. No external reinforcement (such as food) was necessary in this case; knowing that the response was therapeutic was reinforcement enough. The woman was able to learn how to raise and lower her blood pressure at will through the use of the biofeedback device. By learning to control her blood pressure (and eventually wean herself off the biofeedback machine), she was able to become more productive and do some tasks on her own.

BIOFEEDBACK APPLICATIONS

The concept of biofeedback, then, can be generalized to learning to control any of the visceral responses to accomplish a healthier state. As society's stressors increase, many of the visceral responses can cause clinical problems. Among the most common are headache symptoms, muscular (tension) and vascular (migraine). By using electromyography (EMG) biofeedback, a person can monitor the muscle tension in the forehead and learn to decrease the tension by obtaining constant auditory feedback. By the same token, thermal biofeedback machines can monitor blood flow to the cranial arteries and can teach a person how to reduce the volume of blood to this area and redirect it to the periphery of the body. This change often helps other problems associated with migraines such as Raynaud disease, in which the extremities are cold because of lack of blood flow.

The galvanic skin response (GSR) is one of the most common responses used to measure the degree of anxiety and stress. In fact, it is one of the measures in a lie detector, which assumes that when one lies, anxiety increases automatically. The GSR can be brought under control using biofeedback methods. For example, if a pregnant woman is anxious about the upcoming birth, she can receive constant feedback from a GSR biofeedback apparatus and learn to lower the GSR by attending to the machine. As she learns to accomplish this, she can apply these skills on her own and eventually use them during the birth process.

Yet another application of biofeedback in coping with stress has been the use of the technique in controlling brain waves through electroencephalography (EEG) biofeedback. EEG measures the electrical output of the brain, which may be brought under voluntary control by biofeedback and relaxation. It is thought that the brain's alpha wave (eight to thirteen cycles per second) represents the resting brain. By having a machine monitor the amount of alpha acitivity from moment to moment through electrodes on the scalp, a person can learn to increase alpha production and reduce stress by doing so.

USE OF RELAXATION TECHNIQUES

Prior to and during biofeedback training, various relaxation techniques are employed to help with the procedure. This arrangement actually leads to an academic problem: Which technique is working and to what degree? The use of Jacobson's progressive muscle relaxation with asthmatic children and adults helped to reduce the frequency and severity of the incidents. One of the common problems that arise from increased stress is insomnia; the use of Jacobson's technique has proved useful in combating this problem in several documented cases. Autogenic phrases—phrases used by the therapist to help the client while relaxing and performing biofeedback (for example, "Your hands feel heavy and warm")—are often employed with biofeedback as well. For muscular disorders, phrases such as "My leg is heavy" can be used. For cardiac problems, a common phrase is "My heartbeat is calm and regular."

Meditation has been shown to produce an increase in alpha-wave activity, as has biofeedback. Practitioners of yoga focus on a phrase or word (a mantra) and exclude everything else. The nervous system shows evidence of reduced stress and arousal. A variety of businesses have used meditation programs for their employees and have realized improved health and productivity from them.

IMPLICATIONS FOR THE FIELD OF PSYCHOLOGY

The ability to achieve voluntary control over autonomic nervous system responses in order to help cope with stressors is a valuable skill. The area of biofeedback has important implications for both the theoretical and the clinical sides of the field of psychology. First, it is traditionally thought that classical conditioning deals with the "involuntary" nervous system responses, while instrumental conditioning mediates the "voluntary" skeletal responses.

Classical conditioning refers to learning that occurs by contiguously pairing two stimuli, whereby the second stimulus comes to yield a response similar to the first; it is traditionally thought to be successful with involuntary responses mediated by the autonomic nervous system. Since biofeedback deals with visceral autonomic nervous system reactions and is basically a form of instrumental conditioning, this traditional dichotomy must be brought into question. Biofeedback, a phenomenon of the second half of the twentieth century, is still in its infancy. Biofeedback techniques ultimately aim toward bringing unconscious, previously uncontrolled body responses into conscious awareness in order to control them therapeutically. It is a wonderful example of the interaction of the mind and body and the complicated dilemma of how and when they interact.

Biofeedback therapy invariably uses other therapies, such as relaxation and meditation, in the clinical setting. This situation naturally raises the question of whether, and to what degree, biofeedback, relaxation, meditation, and their interactions are responsible for changes in the condition of the client. Many experiments are being conducted to determine the answers to these questions, and the results have been equivocal. It is also important to know what type of feedback, what type of feedback schedule, and what additional therapies are indicated for various problems.

The control of stress-related disorders without drugs or surgery is obviously a desirable goal, and biofeedback, relaxation, and meditation seem to hold some promise in this field for certain types of cases. The applications seem extensive. Hypertension, insomnia, sexual dysfunction, cardiac arrhythmias, asthma, and gastrointestinal disorders are but a few of the problems that have been addressed so far, with varying degrees of success. The degree of success of biofeedback and relaxation as coping strategies for dealing with stress is not yet clear. The results so far, however, are promising and are spawning much research.

SOURCES FOR FURTHER STUDY

Lazarus, Judith. *Stress Relief and Relaxation Techniques*. Boston: McGraw-Hill, 2000. Covers fifty approaches to stress relief and relaxation (including biofeedback), from a wide range of cultures and disciplines.

Robbins, Jim. *A Symphony in the Brain: The Evolution of the New Brain Wave Biofeedback*. New York: Grove, 2001. Surveys the emerging field of neurofeedback, an evolution of biofeedback methods.

Schwartz, Mark, and Frank Andrasik. *Biofeedback: A Practitioner's Guide*. 2d ed. New York: Guilford, 1998. A comprehensive guide for health care professionals in the practical applications of biofeedback techniques for a wide variety of conditions.

Jonathan Kahane

SEE ALSO: Adrenal gland; Cognitive behavior therapy; Coping: Strategies; Emotions; Endocrine system; General adaptation syndrome; Meditation and relaxation; Operant conditioning therapies; Pain management; Psychosomatic disorders; Stress: Physiological responses; Stress-related diseases.

Bipolar disorder

TYPE OF PSYCHOLOGY: Biological bases of behavior; psychopathology; psychotherapy
FIELDS OF STUDY: Biological treatments; depression

Knowledge about bipolar disorder, a serious mental illness that is characterized by depressive episodes and manic episodes, has grown extensively since the 1970's. Advanced neurobiological research and assessment techniques have shown the biochemical origins and the genetic element of this disorder. Recent research indicates the ways in which stress may play a role in precipitating recurrence of episodes. The main treatment interventions include lithium, mood stabilizing anticonvulsants, and psychotherapy.

KEY CONCEPTS
- diathesis-stress model
- lithium carbonate
- mania
- melatonin
- neurotransmitter
- psychotic symptoms
- seasonal affective disorder (SAD)

INTRODUCTION

Although mood fluctuations are a normal part of life, individuals with bipolar affective disorder experience extreme mood changes. Bipolar affective disorder, or bipolar disorder (also called manic-depressive disorder), has been identified as a major psychiatric disorder characterized by dramatic mood and behavior changes. These changes, ranging from episodes of high euphoric moods to deep depressions, with accompanying behavioral and personality changes, are devastating to the victims of the disorder and perplexing to the loved ones of those affected. Prevalence rates have been estimated at about 1.6 (0.8 to 2.6) percent of the American population. The disorder is divided fairly equally between males and females. Clinical psychiatry has been effective in providing biochemical intervention in the form of lithium carbonate to stabilize or modulate the ups and downs of this illness. However, lithium treatment has only been effective for approximately 70 percent of those administered the compound. Mood-stabilizing anticonvulsant medications such as Depakote, Tegretol, and Lamictal, are showing promise in helping some people with the disorder who were formerly referred to as lithium nonresponders. Psychotherapy is seen by most practitioners as a necessary adjunct to medication.

SYMPTOMS

In the manic phase of a bipolar episode, the individual may experience inappropriately good moods, or "highs," or may become extremely irritable. During a manic phase, the person may overcommit to work projects and meetings, social activities, and/or family responsibilities in the belief that he or she can accomplish anything; this is known as manic grandiosity. At times, psychotic symptoms such as delusions, severe paranoia, and hallucinations may accompany a manic episode. These symptoms may lead to a misdiagnosis of another psychotic disorder such as schizophrenia. However, skilled clinicians can make a differential diagnosis between schizophrenia and bipolar disorder.

The initial episode of bipolar disorder is typically

DSM-IV-TR Criteria for Bipolar I Disorder

BIPOLAR I DISORDER, SINGLE MANIC EPISODE (DSM CODE 296.0X)

Only one Manic Episode and no past Major Depressive Episodes

Manic Episode not better accounted for by Schizoaffective Disorder and not superimposed on Schizophrenia, Schizophreniform Disorder, Delusional Disorder, or Psychotic Disorder Not Otherwise Specified

Specify mixed if symptoms meet criteria for Mixed Episode

Specify for current or most recent episode: Severity/Psychotic/Remission Specifiers; with Catatonic Features; with Postpartum Onset

BIPOLAR I DISORDER, MOST RECENT EPISODE HYPOMANIC (DSM CODE 296.40)

Currently or most recently in Hypomanic Episode

Previously at least one Manic Episode or Mixed Episode

Symptoms cause clinically significant distress or impairment in social, occupational, or other important areas of functioning

Episodes not better accounted for by Schizoaffective Disorder and not superimposed on Schizophrenia, Schizophreniform Disorder, Delusional Disorder, or Psychotic Disorder Not Otherwise Specified

Specify: Longitudinal Course Specifiers (with and Without Interepisode Recovery); with Seasonal Pattern (applies only to pattern of Major Depressive Episodes); with Rapid Cycling

---

one of mania or elation, although in some people a depressive episode may signal the beginning of the disorder. Episodes of bipolar disorder can recur rapidly—within hours or days—or may have a much slower recurrence rate, even of years. The duration of each episode, whether it is depression or mania, varies widely among individuals but normally remains fairly consistent for each individual.

TYPES

According to the *Diagnostic and Statistical Manual of Mental Disorders: DSM-IV-TR* (rev. 4th ed., 2000), the diagnostic manual of the American Psychiatric Association, there are several types of bipolar disorder, which are categorized according to the extent of severity, the types of the symptoms, and the duration of the symptoms. Bipolar I disorder is characterized by alternating periods of mania and depression. At times, severe bipolar disorder may be accompanied by psychotic symptoms such as delusions and hallucinations. For this reason, Bipolar I disorder is also considered a psychotic disorder. Bipolar II disorder is characterized by alternating episodes of a milder form of mania (known as hypomania) and depression. Cyclothymia is a form of bipolar disorder in which hypomania alternates with a low-level, chronic depressive state. Seasonal affective disorder (SAD) is characterized by alternating mood episodes that vary according to seasonal patterns; the mood changes are thought to be related to changes in the amount of sunlight and accompanying effects on the levels of hormone melatonin. In the Northern Hemisphere, the typical pattern is associated with manic symptoms in the spring and summer and depression in the fall and winter. Manic episodes often have a shorter duration than the depressive episodes. Bipolar disorder must be differentiated from depressive disorders, which include major depression (unipolar depression) and dysthymia, a milder but chronic form of depression.

CAUSES

The causes of bipolar disorder are not fully understood, but genetic factors play a major role. Approximately 80 percent of individuals with bipolar disorder have a relative with some form of mood disorder, whether bipolar disorder or depression. It is not uncommon to see families in which several generations are affected by bipolar disorder. Serotonin, norepinephrine, and dopamine, brain chemicals known as neurotransmitters that regulate mood, arousal, and energy, respectively, may be altered in bipolar disorder.

A diathesis-stress model has been proposed for some psychosomatic disorders such as hypertension and ulcers. This model has also been applied to bipolar disorder. In a diathesis-stress model, there is a susceptibility (the diathesis) for the disorder. An individual who has a diathesis is at risk for the disorder but may not show signs of the disorder unless the there is sufficient stress. In this model, a genetic or biochemical predisposition toward the disorder (the bipolar diathesis) may lie dormant until stress triggers the emergence of the illness. The stress may be psychosocial, biological, neurochemical, or a combination of these factors.

A diathesis-stress model can also account for some of the recurrent episodes of mania in bipolar disorder. Investigators suggest that positive life events, such as the birth of a baby or a job promotion, as well as negative life events, such as divorce or the loss of a job, may trigger the onset of episodes in individuals with bipolar disorder. Stressful life events and the social rhythm disruptions that they cause can have adverse effects on a person's circadian rhythms. Circadian rhythms are normal biologic rhythms that govern such functions as sleeping and waking, body temperature, and oxygen consumption. Circadian rhythms affect hormonal levels and have significant effects on both emotional and physical well-being. For those reasons, many clinicians encourage individuals with bipolar disorder to work toward maintaining consistency in their social rhythms.

More recently, investigators have compared the course of bipolar disorder to kindling, a process in which epileptic seizures increase the likelihood of further seizures. According to the kindling hypothesis, triggered mood episodes may leave the individual's brain in a sustained sensitized state that makes the person more vulnerable to further episodes. After a while, external factors are less necessary for a

---

DSM-IV-TR Criteria for Bipolar II Disorder (DSM code 296.89)

Presence or history of one or more Major Depressive Episodes

Presence or history of at least one Hypomanic Episode

No Manic Episodes or Mixed Episodes

Mood symptoms not better accounted for by Schizoaffective Disorder and not superimposed on Schizophrenia, Schizophreniform Disorder, Delusional Disorder, or Psychotic Disorder Not Otherwise Specified

Symptoms cause clinically significant distress or impairment in social, occupational, or other important areas of functioning

Specify for current or most recent episode: Hypomanic (currently or most recently in Hypomanic Episode) or Depressed (currently or most recently in Major Depressive Episode)

Specify for current or most recent Major Depressive Episode (only if the most recent type of mood episode): Severity/Psychotic/Remission Specifiers; Chronic; with Catatonic Features; with Melancholic Features; with Atypical Features; with Postpartum Onset

Specify: Longitudinal Course Specifiers (with and Without Interepisode Recovery); with Seasonal Pattern (applies only to pattern of Major Depressive Episodes); with Rapid Cycling

mood episode to be triggered. Episode sensitization may also account for rapid-cycling states, in which the individual shifts from depression to mania over the course of a few hours or days.

IMPACT

The impact of bipolar disorder is considerable. Some believe that the illness puts people on an "emotional roller coaster" in which their ups and downs are so severe that resulting behavior can have its own disastrous consequences. For example, people suffering from episodes of mania sometimes use drugs, alcohol, money, or sex to excess, then later have to deal with an additional set of problems and trauma brought about by their behavior and impulsiveness.

Organizations such as the National Alliance for the Mentally Ill (NAMI) and support groups such as the Depressive and Manic Depressive Association (DMDA) have provided a way for people with bipolar disorder to share their pain as well as to triumph over the illness. Many people have found comfort in knowing that others have suffered from the mood shifts, and they can draw strength from one another. Family members and friends can be the strongest supporters and advocates for those who have bipolar disorder or other psychiatric illnesses. Many patients have credited their families' constant, uncritical support, in addition to competent effective treatment including medications and psychotherapy, with pulling them through the devastating effects of the illness.

TREATMENT APPROACHES

Medications have been developed to aid in correcting the biochemical imbalances thought to be part of bipolar disorder. Lithium carbonate is usually effective for approximately 70 percent of those who take it. Many brilliant and successful people have reportedly suffered from bipolar disorder and have been able to function successfully with competent and responsible treatment. Some people who have taken lithium for bipolar disorder, however, have complained that it robs them of their energy and creativity and said that they actually miss the energy associated with manic phases of the illness. This perceived loss, some of it realistic, can be a factor in relapse associated with lithium noncompliance.

Other medications have been developed to help those individuals who are considered lithium nonresponders and/or who find the side effects of lithium intolerable. Anticonvulsant medications, such as Depakote (valproic acid), Tegretol (carbamazepine) and Lamictal (lamotrigine), which have been found to have mood-stabilizing effects, are often prescribed to individuals with bipolar disorder. During the depressive phase of the disorder, electroconvulsive therapy (ECT) has also been administered to help restore the individual's mood to a normal level. Phototherapy is particularly useful for individuals who have SAD. Psychotherapy, especially cognitive-behavioral therapy or interpersonal social rhythm therapy, is viewed by most practitioners as a necessary adjunct to medication. Indeed, psychotherapy has been found to assist individuals with bipolar disorder in maintaining medication compliance.

DSM-IV-TR Criteria for Cyclothymic Disorder (DSM code 301.13)

For at least two years, numerous periods with hypomanic symptoms and numerous periods with depressive symptoms not meeting criteria for Major Depressive Episode

In children or adolescents, duration must be at least one year

During this two-year period (one year in children or adolescents), person has never been without symptoms for more than two months at a time

No Major Depressive Episode, Manic Episode, or Mixed Episode present during the first two years of disturbance

After initial two years (one year in children and adolescents) of Cyclothymic Disorder, possible superimposed Manic or Mixed Episodes (both Bipolar I Disorder and Cyclothymic Disorder may be diagnosed) or Major Depressive Episodes (both Bipolar II Disorder and Cyclothymic Disorder may be diagnosed)

Symptoms not better accounted for by Schizoaffective Disorder and not superimposed on Schizophrenia, Schizophreniform Disorder, Delusional Disorder, or Psychotic Disorder Not Otherwise Specified

Symptoms not due to direct physiological effects of a substance or general medical condition

Symptoms cause clinically significant distress or impairment in social, occupational, or other important areas of functioning

Local mental health associations are able to recommend psychiatric treatment by board-certified psychiatrists and licensed psychologists who specialize in the treatment of mood disorders. Often, temporary hospitalization is necessary for complete diagnostic assessment, initial mood stabilization and intensive treatment, medication adjustment, or monitoring of an individual who feels suicidal. As many as 15 percent of those with bipolar disorder commit suicide. This frightening reality makes early intervention, relapse prevention, and treatment of the disorder necessary to prevent such a tragic outcome.

SOURCES FOR FURTHER STUDY

Goldberg, J., and Martin Harrow, eds. *Bipolar Disorders: Clinical Course and Outcome.* Washington, D.C.: American Psychiatric Press, 1999. This edited volume summarizes recent research regarding the course and outcome of bipolar disorder. Chapters are written by experts in the field.

Goodwin, Frederick K., and Kay R. Jamison. *Manic Depressive Illness.* New York: Oxford University Press, 1990. This comprehensive book on bipolar disorder provides information on diagnosis, theories regarding the etiology of the disorder, and treatment options.

Jamison, Kay R. *An Unquiet Mind.* New York: Knopf, 1995. An insightful first-person account of a psychiatrist's experience with bipolar disorder. Offers descriptions of mania as well as depression and discusses relevant issues such as the genetic basis of the disorder.

Johnson, Sheri L., and John E. Roberts. "Life Events and Bipolar Disorder: Implications from Biological Theories." *Psychological Bulletin* 117, no. 3 (1995): 434-449. This theoretical article was written for psychologists but is readily accessible to laypeople. The authors review research and accounts for ways in which life events, both positive and negative ones, may trigger the onset of episodes in individuals with bipolar disorder.

Diane C. Gooding and Karen Wolford

SEE ALSO: Abnormality: Biomedical models; Anxiety disorders; Attention-deficit hyperactivity disorder (ADHD); Beck Depression Inventory (BDI); Borderline personality; Children's Depression Inventory (CDI); Clinical depression; Conduct order; Depression; Drug therapies; Histrionic personality; Hysteria; Madness: Historical concepts; Neurotic disorders; Obsessive-compulsive disorder; Paranoia; Personality disorders; Psychotic disorders; Schizophrenia: Background, types, and symptoms; Schizophrenia: High-risk children; Schizophrenia: Theoretical explanations; Seasonal affective disorder; Synaptic transmission.

Birth
Effects on physical development

TYPE OF PSYCHOLOGY: Biological bases of behavior; developmental psychology
FIELDS OF STUDY: Infancy and childhood

Birth represents a baby's transition from intrauterine existence to life outside the mother's womb. Although most births progress smoothly, some involve complications that can have an adverse impact on the physical and neurological development of the baby.

KEY CONCEPTS
- afterbirth
- anoxia
- breech position
- cervix
- cesarean section
- labor
- immature birth
- midwife
- miscarriage
- oxytocics
- premature birth

INTRODUCTION

Birth represents the culmination of an incredible journey from a single-celled fertilized egg to a newborn baby. Normal, uncomplicated childbirth does not have any significant physical impact of the development of the baby. Neurological or physical abnormalities following a smooth delivery are most likely attributable to disruptions during prenatal development. Prenatal disruptions may be chromosomal, environmental, or an interaction of the two and are studied in the field of teratology. Although the second and third trimesters of pregnancy are important, the first trimester of prenatal development is often considered most sensitive to disruptions. Disturbances during prenatal development can produce fetal death or severe abnormalities (such as deformed or missing limbs, cerebral palsy, mental retardation) as well as more subtle complications (such as mood disorders or learning disabilities) that may not manifest until later stages of development.

Most pregnancies in industrialized countries progress smoothly. When a mother experiences birth complications, however, the baby is at increased risk for adverse physical and neurological outcomes. Some of the more serious birth complications include anoxia, premature delivery, low birth weight, and contact with maternal genital herpes lesions at birth. In Third World countries, babies may be at greater risk for physical or neurological damage due to a lack of medical facilities or trained medical personnel. As a result, birth complications can lead to abnormalities ranging from fetal (and maternal) death to physical abnormalities such as paralysis or cerebral palsy and neurological abnormalities such as mental retardation or schizophrenia.

STAGES OF LABOR

"Labor" is the term used to describe the process of the birth of the baby. Labor has three stages and begins when the cervix dilates. The cervix is the opening in the women's vagina through which the baby passes. A common misconception is that labor begins with the onset of uterine contractions, but they are often present several hours prior to dilation. The duration of labor depends upon a number of factors, most important the mother's previous birth experience. First-time mothers experience longer labors (eight to fourteen hours) than mothers who have given birth previously (three to eight hours).

The first stage of labor is the longest and most uncomfortable for the mother. It officially begins when the uterine contractions occur within fifteen-minute intervals. The first stage of labor ends when the cervix is fully dilated so that the fetus can pass through. The second stage of labor represents the actual delivery of the baby. In vaginal childbirth (as opposed to cesarean section), the baby is pushed out through the expanding cervix, and delivery time ranges from thirty to forty minutes. The third stage of labor takes about ten minutes and involves expulsion of the afterbirth, which comprises the placenta

and other membranes. A physician will typically examine the afterbirth to ensure that all of it has been expelled. If not, the physician may scrape the uterus to remove the remaining portions and prevent infection.

The birth process is thought to be stressful on the baby but also adaptive. The contractions of the uterus during labor help push the baby out but may also restrict the oxygen supply to the fetus. This decrease of oxygen, called anoxia, can cause brain damage and fetal death if it persists beyond four minutes. In response to contractions during labor and the subsequent oxygen restriction, the fetus secretes hormones that increase blood flow to the brain and ensure that the baby will breathe on its own when it finally enters the extrauterine environment.

CHILDBIRTH POSITIONS AND SETTINGS

There are considerable cultural variations in the childbirth process. For some cultures, childbirth is a communal occasion. For others, childbirth takes place in isolation. In most non-Western societies, childbirth takes place in a vertical position, such as squatting or sitting, whereas in Western societies the mother is often placed on her back or side.

Before the 1800's in the United States, the birth of a child took place at home, where the expectant mother was surrounded by family, relatives, and friends. In contrast, today's setting is most likely a hospital. A majority of the births in North America (92 percent) occur in a hospital setting. This percentage is lower in some European countries such as Norway, where as few as 60 percent of births occur in a hospital setting.

Childbirth in a hospital setting is thought to have both advantages and disadvantages. The hospital setting is perceived to be less comfortable and less likely to allow extensive mother-baby contact at birth. However, this setting is the most appropriate for older mothers and mothers who are likely to experience birth complications. Freestanding birth centers are thought to be more flexible, less likely to use unnecessary medical procedures, and more likely to encourage early contact between parents and the baby. Some developmental psychologists argue that the first twelve hours following birth are a critical period in the bonding experience between mother and baby. Without such initial contact, some developmental psychologists argue that the baby's development will be suboptimal. The research in this area is inconclusive.

Home births are more frequent in Europe and Third World countries than in North America. Advantages include a familiar environment and a setting that is in a position to promote parent-infant contact. Advocates of this setting indicate that the benefits of early attachment to the caregiver and the comfort level of the mother during the birth process outweigh any possible risks of being away from a hospital setting in the event of an emergency. If complications occur, however, the mother and baby must be transported to the hospital, jeopardizing the physical health of the baby by delaying what could be critical intervention.

In the United States, a midwife accompanies approximately 6 percent of expectant mothers in any of the described settings. A midwife is an individual experienced in the process of childbirth who assists with the delivery of the baby and provides emotional as well as educational support to the expectant mother. Midwives are common in many countries around the world, assisting pregnant women not only through all stages of birth but also through all stages of pregnancy.

METHODS OF DELIVERY

There are three types of delivery: natural, medicated, and cesarean. Natural childbirth is a type of delivery that avoids medication and requires education of the expectant mother to reduce fear and anxiety. Fear and anxiety during childbirth are thought to increase the duration of labor and, as a result, the possibility of fetal complications. Prepared childbirth (the Lamaze method) was developed by French obstetrician Ferdinand Lamaze and is a type of natural childbirth. It includes not only education about childbirth to reduce fear and anxiety but also training in special breathing techniques to control pushing in the final stages of labor. Other natural childbirth techniques, such as the Bradley method, have been developed but are usually a variation of the

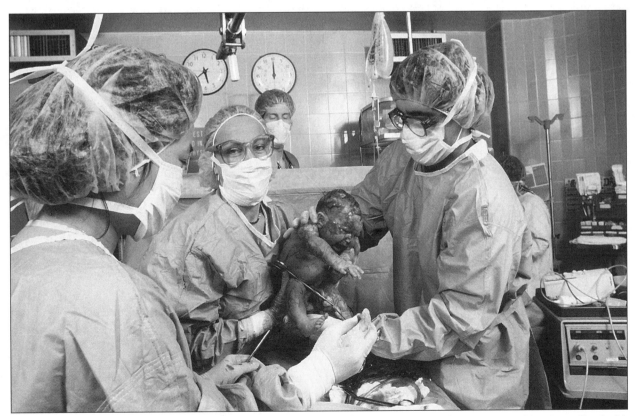

A baby is delivered by Cesarean section. Newborns tend to be less alert and have greater difficulty breathing immediately following cesarean delivery, but there appears to be no significant lasting impact. (PhotoDisc)

Lamaze method plus the anxiety-reducing educational component.

Medicated childbirth uses a nonsurgical approach to expedite the delivery of the baby and to decrease the mother's pain. Expectant mothers are commonly given oxytocics, synthetic hormones that expedite the birth process by stimulating uterine contractions. The American Academy of Pediatrics recommends the least possible use of medication (tranquilizers or pain medications) due to potential adverse impact of the medication(s) on the newborn baby. Although it is difficult to predict the precise effects of medication on the fetus, it is customary to use minimal medicinal therapy. A general anesthetic, such as Demerol, is sometimes given to relieve the mother's muscle tension and anxiety. This medication passes through the placenta and can lead to detrimental changes in the fetus such as decreases in heart rate, muscle tone, breathing, and general attentiveness. One commonly used alternative is an epidural block, which has fewer side effects on the fetus than intravenous or oral medications. An epidural block requires the insertion of a needle into the spinal canal of the mother and the introduction of local anesthesia that numbs the woman's body from the waist down. A cesarean section commonly involves epidural analgesia so that the expectant mother can remain alert to greet her newborn baby.

A cesarean delivery is a surgical birth. The physician makes an incision to the mother's abdomen and surgically removes the baby from her uterus. The indications for a cesarean section include previous cesarean births, abnormal labor, the presentation of the baby in breech position (buttocks first), and infant distress due to oxygen deprivation. In addition, a cesarean section might be necessary if there is serious maternal illness such as diabetes, premature separation of the placenta from the uterus (placenta abruptio), or maternal infection with genital herpes. Cesarean births require extra recovery time for the mother. Babies tend to be less alert and have greater breathing difficulties following cesarean delivery. However, there does not appear to be any significant lasting deleterious impact with cesarean delivery.

BABY'S PHYSICAL APPEARANCE

At the time of birth, the baby is covered with protective grease called the vernix caeosa. This covering serves to protect the baby's skin during birth. At birth the baby appears bluish in color (from oxygen deprivation) and may have a misshapen head, a flattened nose, and bruises. These characteristics are related to passage through the birth canal. The head is large compared to the rest of the body, and it has spaces between the skull bones (fontanelles) that allow it to contort slightly in order to fit through the birth canal. The fontanelles will close shortly after birth.

There are times during natural childbirth when a physician uses forceps or a vacuum extractor to deliver the baby. Forceps are a tonglike device used to pull the baby out of the mother's birth canal. A vacuum extractor is a suction device that attaches to the baby's head and pulls the baby out through the birth canal. Both forceps and vacuum extraction can contribute to transient bruises and misshapen features at birth.

ASSESSMENT OF THE BABY

There are two widely used approaches to assess the baby's physical and neurological status following birth. The Apgar test assesses the baby's vital functions within sixty seconds of birth and again five minutes after birth by looking at heart rate, respiratory effort, reflex irritability, muscle tone, and color. A low score suggests possible physical or neurological abnormalities. A more thorough assessment may be conducted using the Brazelton Neonatal Assessment Scale which is administered a few days after birth. Areas assessed by the Brazelton include reflex and respiratory responses and the infant's capacity to respond to stimuli in an interactive process. For the Brazelton, the baby is manipulated from sleep to wakefulness to crying and then back down to a quiet state. The baby's coping and adaptive strategies are thus examined, and the baby's physical and central nervous system functioning can be assessed.

BIRTH COMPLICATIONS

Although most births progress smoothly, some involve complications that can have a profound impact on the physical and neurological development of the baby. Premature birth is a significant risk factor for physical and neurological abnormalities. A baby's physical status may be classified along two dimensions: the length of time spent in the mother's womb and birth weight. A normal birth usually occurs between thirty-seven and forty-two weeks of pregnancy, and the baby averages 7.5 pounds. A fetus that is born prior to the twentieth week of pregnancy and/or weighing less than one pound will die. This type of birth is called a miscarriage. A fetus delivered between the twentieth and twenty-eighth week of pregnancy and weighing between one and two pounds is called immature. With the advancement of medical practices, it is possible for babies that are born as early as four months prematurely and weighing only 1.5 pounds to survive. A baby born between the twenty-ninth and thirty-sixth week of pregnancy and weighing between 2 and 5.5 pounds is termed premature. Both immature and premature births predispose a baby to a variety of adverse outcomes, ranging from death to severe physical and mental disabilities.

Low birth weight is another complication that predisposes a baby to adverse physical and neurological outcomes. Complications of low-birth-weight babies include a greater incidence of mental retardation and cerebral palsy and general intellectual and gross motor delay. Babies weighing less than two pounds at birth are at risk for the most severe outcomes should they survive beyond infancy. Research indicates that nearly a quarter of these children experience mental retardation, vision problems, and hearing difficulties. Babies weighing less than three pounds at birth continue to have a smaller physical stature and a significantly higher incidence of various illnesses throughout childhood. There is a clear relationship between premature birth, low birth weight, and adverse physical and neurological outcomes. A baby delivered prematurely is commonly a low-birth-weight baby. Both of these complications increase the baby's risk for abnormalities ranging from fetal death to physical abnormalities such as paralysis or cerebral palsy and neurological abnormalities such as mental retardation or schizophrenia.

Anoxia is another birth complication that is cause for particular concern. A cesarean section is used when the fetus is at risk for prolonged oxygen deprivation. Newly born babies can tolerate oxygen deprivation for as long as four minutes. Continued deprivation beyond that point can cause severe brain damage. There are several causes of anoxia. In many cases, the condition may occur as a result of constriction of the umbilical cord. This is common in a breech birth, in which the baby's buttocks present for delivery rather than the baby's head. A second cause of anoxia is associated with premature separation of the placenta from the uterus, which interrupts the supply of oxygen to the fetus. Sedation given to the mother during childbirth is another risk factor for anoxia. Sedation crosses the placenta and interferes with the baby's impetus to breathe. Anoxia may also occur as a result of airway obstruction from mucus inhaled during the birth process. This problem is typically alleviated through suctioning of the newborn's airway at birth.

Sources for Further Study

Berk, Laura E. *Infants, Children, and Adolescents.* Boston: Allyn & Bacon, 1999. A comprehensive text that devotes an entire chapter to the subject of childbirth. Berk is one of the leading scholars in the field of developmental psychology. Appropriate for all audiences, from the general public to graduate students.

Johnson, Robert V. *Mayo Clinic Complete Book of Pregnancy and Baby's First Year.* New York: William Morrow, 1994. A highly readable and comprehensive book intended for the general public but also appropriate for undergraduate students seeking a more involved understanding of the birth process.

Kail, Robert V., and John C. Cavanaugh. *Human Development: A Lifespan View.* Belmont, Calif.: Wadsworth/Thomson Learning, 2000. Provides a comprehensive, yet highly readable, account of not only the birth process but also human development across the life span. Illustrations and charts facilitate comprehension of the material. Appropriate for both the layperson and the undergraduate student.

Lansky, Vicki. *Complete Pregnancy and Baby Book.* Lincolnwood, Ill.: Publications International, 1996. Provides a thorough overview of all aspects of childbirth. A highly readable book that provides valuable information on the complications that may arise during childbirth.

Lefrancois, Guy R. *The Lifespan.* New York: Wadsworth, 1999. A comprehensive and scholarly text on life-span development that is accessible to both the layperson and the undergraduate student. Includes a chapter on prenatal development and birth, and covers research and trends in the field.

Moore, Keith L., and T. V. N. Persaud. *Before We Are Born.* Philadelphia: W. B. Saunders, 1993. A detailed and comprehensive text on the topics of prenatal development and teratology written by two leading scholars. Appropriate for undergraduate and graduate students who seek a more advanced understanding of prenatal development and teratology.

Santrock, John W. *Life-Span Development*. New York: McGraw-Hill, 2002. A comprehensive text on human growth and development. An entire chapter devoted to the topic of prenatal development and childbirth. Provides a very accessible overview with color illustrations and diagrams throughout. Appropriate for both the layperson and the undergraduate student.

Stefan C. Dombrowski

SEE ALSO: Attachment and bonding in infancy and childhood; Childhood disorders; Development; Developmental disabilities; Family life: Children's issues; Father-child relationship; Learning; Mother-child relationship; Parenting styles; Physical development: Environment versus genetics; Piaget, Jean; Reflexes in newborns.

Birth order and personality

TYPE OF PSYCHOLOGY: Developmental psychology
FIELDS OF STUDY: Infancy and childhood; personality theory

Although there is debate over the effects of birth order on personality, with some researchers claiming there is no effect, studies have found subtle differences between firstborn and later-born children; the order of children's births has also been found to influence how the parents treat them.

KEY CONCEPTS
- anxiety
- creativity
- scientific method
- self-image

INTRODUCTION

A child's order of birth into a family may influence how the parents treat the child. This treatment, in turn, can produce personality differences. Most research has focused on comparing the firstborn

child with later-born children. Thus, most of what is known about birth order has to do with ways in which firstborns and later-borns are different.

Parents tend to be overly anxious with regard to their first child. The birth of their first child is a major event in their lives, and it can be somewhat threatening. They have never been parents before, and they do not know what to do in many instances. Thus, many parents tend to be overly restrictive with their first child, having many fears of the terrible things that may happen if they do not monitor and care for their child constantly. This anxiety can influence the personality of the child. Firstborns often grow up to be more anxious than later-born children. By the time parents have a second, third, or fourth child, they are more comfortable caring for children and know that they do not have to be overly concerned with protecting their child from every imaginable harm. Thus, they relax and allow the later-born children more freedom.

It should be made clear that this does not mean that every firstborn child is more anxious than every later-born child. It only means that there is a tendency, greater than could be expected by chance, for firstborns to be more anxious than later-borns. There will be many exceptions, instances where a firstborn is not anxious or where a later-born is.

ACHIEVEMENT AND RISK TAKING

When the firstborn child is growing up, until the birth of a sibling, the child has the parents all to himself or herself. This situation probably accounts for another personality difference of firstborns relative to later-borns: Firstborns tend to score higher on intellectual measures. When the later-born children come, the parents will probably spend less time with them than they did with the first child; the later-born child will have as models the other children in the family. The first child had adults as models and thus may acquire a more adultlike interest in things—and therefore score higher on intellectual measures. This effect may account, in part, for the fact that firstborns achieve at a greater rate than later-borns. For example, there are more famous firstborn scientists (for their proportion in the population) than would be expected by chance.

Another difference in personality is found with the kinds of risks firstborns or later-borns will take. Firstborns will take risks if they believe that they can handle the situation safely but will be less likely to engage in behavior that exposes them to potential injury. Thus, firstborns are less likely than later-borns to be college football players. Football is a violent sport, and injury is unavoidable no matter how skilled one is. On the other hand, firstborns are over-represented among astronauts and aquanauts. They would seem to be potentially dangerous occupations, but firstborns probably believe that they can avoid harm via good training and high-quality skills. Thus, the issue may be perceived harm: Firstborns may believe that they can avoid harm as astronauts or aquanauts, while it is impossible to believe this about an inherently violent sport such as football.

CREATIVE DIFFERENCES

Differences in creativity have been found between firstborns and later-borns, but to understand them one must consider sex differences as well. It is only by looking at both birth order and gender that the creativity results become clear. Firstborn males tend to score higher on creativity measures than do later-born males. Creativity can be defined as the combination of originality and usefulness, and there are tests developed to measure it. When testing females, however, the results are the opposite: Later-born females score higher on creativity than firstborn females. This finding could be explained by the ways in which parents treat their firstborn child as well as how parents treat their female children. The first-born female child has two disadvantages. Not only are the parents anxious and restrictive because she is a firstborn, but the parents are also likely to re-strict female children more so than they do their male children. Thus, the firstborn female would be the most restricted of all the birth order and sex groupings. Other researchers have found that the firstborn female tends to grow up with traditional values. Traditional beliefs may be fine in many in-stances, but they tend to restrict creativity, which of-ten needs a challenging of society's views in order to occur. The creative person is often something of a rebel, at least as far as thoughts about traditional, accepted beliefs are concerned.

APPLICATIONS OF BIRTH ORDER RESEARCH

Knowledge of the effects of birth order often pro-motes greater self-understanding in those people who are most affected. For example, a firstborn male seeing his friends try out for the football team may have a dilemma. He knows that he does not wish to join them, but he feels like a "chicken." His self-image makes him feel inadequate because he is not like his friends. If he knew the research findings concerning firstborns, however, he would realize that he might be quite courageous and risk-taking in other pursuits but probably will not be when there is clear-cut physical danger. His personality was estab-lished long ago, as he grew up the firstborn child in his family. Thus, he would see the causes of his per-sonality and be more self-accepting.

When people are anxious, they tend to talk. This talking may be an attempt to relieve their anxiety. This fact and the findings about birth order could be used in group situations to foster effective discus-sion. Thus, a teacher or a group therapist could make sure that the group was composed of a combi-nation of firstborns and later-borns. The anxious firstborns will be likely to speak up, and discussion will be facilitated. If the group were all firstborns, there might be too many people talking at once, while if the group were all later-borns, there might be too little discussion. Thus, a mixture of firstborns and later-borns may produce the best group discus-sion.

Another application might be in changing peo-ple from their typical tendencies. Thus, if it is known that firstborn females tend not to be as creative be-cause of a predilection toward traditional beliefs, one could educate the firstborn female about differ-ent ways of thinking. Education could focus on chal-lenging some of the traditional beliefs by offering alternative, more questioning attitudes for the first-born female to consider. This approach might in-crease the chances that the firstborn female would come up with creative solutions and ideas.

Birth order and sex difference findings can also serve as a basis for making interventions to help people in all the different birth order and sex com-binations. The major recipient of help might be the firstborn female, since she has probably received an overly restrictive upbringing. Teachers or therapists, if aware of the tendency of some firstborn females to be inhibited in their challenging of society's con-ventional beliefs, might help these individuals to think more critically. Later-born males may also, to a lesser extent, be inclined toward this inhibited thinking, if generalizations from the research are correct. They, too, could benefit from training or as-sistance in greater critical thinking that challenges the conventional beliefs they have learned. It should be emphasized that conventional beliefs are not necessarily wrong; one should, however, learn to think for oneself and not accept everything one is told automatically.

Although firstborn males and later-born females perform the best on creativity measures, they are by no means immune to society's conventions, which in some cases lead to an inhibition of creativity. Firstborn males seem to have a high need for social approval, which at times may inhibit creativity and lead to conformity. When this conformity is undesirable or restricts creativity, it needs to be overcome. Later-born females, although scoring more creatively than firstborn females, still have the burden of being female in a society that places many inhibitions upon females. Everyone can use help to think more critically, to challenge what they have been taught, and in this way to increase the likelihood of creative thinking and of production of creative products.

EVOLUTION OF RESEARCH

Alfred Adler (1870-1937) was an Austrian psychoanalyst who was a follower of Sigmund Freud, the inventor of psychoanalysis. Adler, like several of Freud's early followers, believed that Freud neglected the social context of his research, and Adler broke away to establish his own school of psychology, which he called individual psychology. Among the many concepts which formed the basis of Adler's approach was his belief that birth order is worthy of study. He speculated in detail about how the ordinal position of the child affected the child's personality.

For many years, research psychologists did not study birth order to any extent. One reason is that birth order is an actuarial variable, like age, gender, or social class, and psychologists did not view it as worthwhile to study in and of itself. In 1959, however, Stanley Schachter published the book *The Psychology of Affiliation*, in which he showed that birth order is an important variable. Many other researchers started looking at birth order in their studies. Sometimes they had little understanding of what birth order should mean, but it was easy to ask subjects to list their birth order to see if any patterns became apparent. One problem was that the early researchers included only children (children with no siblings) as firstborns. It is now known that while these groups are sometimes similar, they are often different from one another. It is best to include only

children as a separate category. Unfortunately, there have been too few only children in the population for statistical testing. Thus, researchers often simply drop only children from their analysis. As a greater understanding of birth order has been gained, it has become possible to conduct research based on what is known rather than to treat birth order as simply one more variable.

SOURCES FOR FURTHER STUDY

Adler, Alfred. *What Life Should Mean to You.* Edited by Alan Porter. New York: Capricorn books, 1958. Adler, one of the most important people in establishing birth order as an idea worthy of study, spells out his views on birth order in this book, originally published in 1931. He believed that the place of the child in the family influences how the parents treat the child, which in turn creates personality differences among the various birth orders.

Blake, Judith. *Family Size and Achievement.* Berkeley: University of California Press, 1989. Discusses the effects of family size on achievement. The author found that only children and children from small families are more able intellectually and gain more education than children who are not the only child or who are from large families.

Eisenman, Russell. *From Crime to Creativity: Psychological and Social Factors in Deviance.* Dubuque, Iowa: Kendall/Hunt, 1991. In addition to detailed discussions of creativity, this book deals with birth order and shows how it can relate to other things. For example, the book discusses birth order and projection, which is the tendency to see things in others that are really in oneself. Firstborns scored higher in the projection of sex and aggression when viewing ambiguous figures.

Hann, Della M., and Howard J. Osofsky. "Psychosocial Factors in the Transition to Parenthood." In *New Perspectives on Prenatal Care*, edited by Irwin R. Merkatz and Joyce E. Thompson. New York: Elsevier, 1990. Hann and Osofsky discuss the problems of being a new parent and give examples of how things can go wrong. They also suggest interventions that can be made to help people be better parents. They cite research showing that depressed parents make their children depressed.

Schachter, Stanley. *The Psychology of Affiliation.* Stanford, Calif.: Stanford University Press, 1959. This book caused other researchers to begin birth-order studies. Schachter used female subjects and told them they were going to experience painful electric shocks. Firstborns preferred to wait for the alleged shocks with others who were also waiting to receive shocks. Thus, birth order was established as something which made a difference and could be studied.

Sulloway, Frank. *Born to Rebel: Birth Order, Family Dynamics, and Creative Lives.* New York: Vintage, 1997. A somewhat controversial study showing that first-born children tend to be conformists, while second-born children tend to be both more rebellious and more creative.

Wallace, Meri. *Birth Order Blues: How Parents Can Help Their Children Meet the Challenges of Birth Order.* New York: Owl Press, 1999. Offers parents practical advice on how birth order creates strengths and weaknesses in children's development, how to recognize birth-order related problems, and how to address them.

Russell Eisenman

SEE ALSO: Achievement motivation; Adolescence: Cognitive skills; Creativity and intelligence; Development; Family life: Children's issues; Parenting styles; Sibling relationships.

Borderline personality

TYPE OF PSYCHOLOGY: Personality; psychopathology
FIELDS OF STUDY: Personality assessment; personality disorders

Borderline personality is characterized by a long-standing pattern of instability in mood and interpersonal relationships. It is the most prevalent personality disorder and has been the focus of significant research attention.

KEY CONCEPTS
- cognitive-behavioral therapy
- dialectical behavioral therapy
- personality disorders
- self-mutilation

INTRODUCTION

Borderline personality disorder (BPD) is a psychological disorder characterized by chronic instability in mood and interpersonal relationships. It was not included in the American Psychiatric Association's *Diagnostic and Statistical Manual of Mental Disorders* (DSM) until the text's third edition was published in 1980. The term "borderline" was used to refer to people who, it was believed, displayed behaviors that fell on the borderline between neurosis and psychosis. Over the years, the term has come to refer to a collection of symptoms that constitute an unstable personality structure.

According to the DSM-IV-TR (rev. 4th ed., 2000), BPD is characterized by a longstanding pattern of instability in mood and relationships. A person with BPD develops intense and unstable relationships with others. They tend to vacillate between devaluing and overidealizing significant people in their lives. BPD is characterized by an intense fear of abandonment by others. A person with BPD may make frantic attempts to avoid real or imagined threats of abandonment; at an extreme, this may take the form of suicidal threats. According to the DSM-IV-TR, a person with BPD demonstrates an unstable sense of self, which may manifest as confusion about sexuality or the feeling that one does not exist. BPD is also reflected in impulsive behavior, such as drug or alcohol abuse, promiscuity, binge eating, or overspending. Data suggest that approximately 75 percent of people with BPD engage in self-mutilating behaviors, such as self-inflicted cigarette burns or self-inflicted cutting or stabbing. Another primary feature of BPD is chronic feelings of emptiness. People with BPD will often report that they self-mutilate due to these chronic feelings of emptiness in an effort to feel something. BPD is also characterized by emotional instability; a person with BPD may fluctuate quickly between mood extremes and engage in frequent inappropriate displays of anger. People with BPD frequently engage in conflict with others. Symptoms begin by early adulthood and are persistent.

CAUSES

A great deal of research has focused on the possible causes of BPD. The diathesis-stress model examines how the effects of stress, combined with a diathesis, or genetic vulnerability to develop a psychological disorder, may instigate the development of BPD. The underlying personality traits of BPD, such as impulsivity and emotional instability, are inheritable. According to the diathesis-stress model, a person with these personality traits, combined with in-

DSM-IV-TR Criteria for Borderline Personality Disorder (DSM code 301.83)

Pervasive pattern of instability of interpersonal relationships, self-image, and affects and marked impulsivity beginning by early adulthood and present in variety of contexts

Indicated by five or more of the following:
- frantic efforts to avoid real or imagined abandonment
- pattern of unstable and intense interpersonal relationships characterized by alternation between extremes of idealization and devaluation
- identity disturbance (markedly and persistently unstable self-image or sense of self)
- impulsivity in at least two areas that are potentially self-damaging (spending, sex, substance abuse, reckless driving, binge eating)
- recurrent suicidal behavior, gestures, or threats, or self-mutilating behavior
- affective instability due to marked reactivity of mood (intense episodic dysphoria, irritability, or anxiety usually lasting a few hours and only rarely more than a few days)
- chronic feelings of emptiness
- inappropriate, intense anger or difficulty controlling anger (frequent displays of temper, constant anger, recurrent physical fights)
- transient, stress-related paranoid ideation or severe dissociative symptoms

effective means of managing stress, may be at greater risk of developing BPD. Other researchers have explored the role of the limbic system in borderline patients. The limbic system is the part of the brain associated with the regulation of emotional responses. Research indicates that BPD patients report a higher incidence of sexual abuse, separation from or early loss of a parental figure, verbal and emotional abuse, and family chaos during childhood.

TREATMENT

Treatment for BPD is a challenging issue. People suffering from personality disorders such as BPD lack the insight that the dysfunction of their personality is the source of impairment. Many with BPD, therefore, may never seek treatment. When a person with BPD does seeks treatment, it is usually for a reason other than their BPD. There is a high risk that the borderline patient will end treatment prematurely due to their difficulties with relationship and emotional functioning.

American psychologist Marsha M. Linehan developed a treatment program called dialectical behavior therapy (DBT) to treat the borderline patient. DBT involves a combination of cognitive, behavioral, and Zen principles to develop a balance between acceptance and change. DBT treatment focuses on helping patients to develop tools to solve problems, regulate their emotions, reframe suicidal or destructive behaviors, and become more mindful of themselves and others. Linehan's therapy emphasizes the importance of the patient-therapist relationship in establishing progress. Linehan's DBT treatment model has gained widespread attention and has been implemented in treatment programs worldwide. DBT can be can be used in both individual therapy and group therapy. Individual therapy using the DBT model focuses on six core areas: suicidal behaviors, behaviors that are counterproductive to the therapy process, behaviors that compromise the quality of life, the development of behavioral skills, post-traumatic stress behavior, and self-respecting behaviors. Individual therapy with the borderline patient can be very emotionally demanding. The therapist needs to set clear limits with the borderline patient and to be consistent in abiding by those limits, as borderline patients are characteristically manipulative and emotionally demanding.

Cognitive-behavioral therapies for BPD are grounded in the belief that borderline patients have distorted and self-defeating thinking patterns, or schemas, which include themes about abandonment, mistrust, low self-worth, and guilt. University of Pennsylvania psychiatrist Aaron Beck states that dichotomous thinking (black-and-white thinking) is an essential problem among borderline patients and results in the extreme emotional responses displayed by them.

Psychopharmacological therapy involves a combination of therapy and medication in treating BPD. Certain antidepressant medications (selective serotonin reuptake inhibitors, or SSRIs) have been effective in alleviating some of the symptoms of depression in BPD.

SOURCES FOR FURTHER STUDY

American Psychiatric Association. *Diagnostic and Statistical Manual of Mental Disorders: DSM-IV-TR.* Rev. 4th ed. Washington, D.C.: Author, 2000. The standard source for diagnosis.

Linehan, Marsha M. *Cognitive-Behavioral Treatment of Borderline Personality Disorder.* New York: Guilford, 1993. The author provides an overview of borderline personality disorder followed by a thorough exploration of the foundations and applications of DBT treatment.

Livesley, W. John, Marsha L. Schroeder, Douglas N. Jackson, and Kerry L. Jang. "Categorical Distinctions in the Study of Personality Disorder—Implications for Classification." *Journal of Abnormal Psychology* 103, no. 1 (1994): 6-17. These authors explore the history of psychiatric classification and explore research about the diagnostic distinctions among the personality disorders.

Trull, Timothy J., J. David Useda, Kelly Conforti, and Bao-Tran Doan. "Borderline Personality Disorder Features in Nonclinical Young Adults 2: Two Year Outcome." *Journal of Abnormal Psychology* 106, no. 2 (1997): 307-314. The authors trace the functioning of individuals in a two-year study who were identified as having features of borderline personality disorder.

Janine T. Ogden

SEE ALSO: Anger; Behavior therapy; Emotional expression; Emotions; Histrionic personality; Narcissistic personality; Personality disorders; Stress; Suicide.

Brain damage

TYPES OF PSYCHOLOGY: Biological bases of behavior; cognition; consciousness; emotion; language; memory; personality; psychopathology

FIELDS OF STUDY: Aggression; anxiety disorders; attitudes and behavior; behavioral and cognitive models; cognitive processes; personality disorders; thought; vision

Brain damage can be localized, when nerve-cell destruction is centered in a part of the brain, causing specific behavioral defects, or it may be diffuse, when the injury causes deterioration throughout the brain, leading to severe physical or mental impairments.

KEY CONCEPTS

- aphasia
- cerebral cortex
- equipotentiality
- imaging techniques
- localizationism
- plasticity

INTRODUCTION

The brain, often called the final scientific frontier, has challenged investigators with its labyrinthine complexities, and much that is now known about its structure and functioning has been acquired through the study of the damaged brains of animals and humans. The brain structure most commonly affected by brain lesions is the cerebral cortex. A brain lesion is nervous-tissue damage that impairs the normal functioning of neurons (nerve cells). The cerebral cortex is the outer layer of the cerebrum, the rounded and fissured structure with two symmetric hemispheres occupying most of the cranial cavity. Damage to the cerebral cortex has been related to dysfunctions of perception, memory, language, and thought. Located in the depths of the cerebrum is the limbic system, a connected set of structures that includes the hippocampus, hypothalamus, and amygdala. Damage to the amygdala has been related to emotional dysfunctions. The story of how scientists used brain damage to discover the connections between brain parts and bodily behavior has been called the most astonishing in the history of medicine.

HISTORY OF RESEARCH ON BRAIN DAMAGE

Two centuries of research on brain-damaged animals and humans helped establish how brain components divide the work of sensing, learning, remembering, and thinking. This research also led to a number of theories, from an extreme reductionist view in which every human behavior is rooted in a highly localized brain component (localizationism) to an extreme holistic view in which every human function is rooted in all parts of the brain (equipotentiality). A researcher whose work supported both views was the French physiologist Pierre Flourens (1794-1867), who decided to test localization by the surgical removal, or ablation, of parts of the brains of animals. He found that ablations of small sections did not cause any change in behavior, which controverted strict localizationism. Very large ablations did result in the impairment of functions. Thus Flourens's experiments in the 1820's could be used to support both localization (since the removal of a certain large section of the brain caused the animals to become blind) and unity (since the animal returned to normal behavior after partial ablations).

Another French researcher who was interested in localization was Pierre Paul Broca (1824-1880). For thirty years he studied a patient who, despite a healthy vocal apparatus, could not talk. Finally, in 1861, after the patient's death, Broca was able to examine the man's brain, and he discovered a lesion in a frontal convolution on the left side (a region now known as Broca's area). This phenomenon— loss of speech due to a brain lesion—came to be called aphasia. Broca's pinpointing of a certain brain function stimulated so many other researchers that aphasia became the disease par excellence for studying cerebral localization.

Further evidence supporting localization was found by two German investigators, Gustav Fritsch (1838-1927) and Eduard Hitzig (1838-1907), who used the electrical stimulation of the cerebral cortex to discover the principle of contralateral representation, according to which the left hemisphere controls the right side of the body and vice versa. Their work had important neurophysiological implications. If specific cerebral areas controlled certain functions, then brain lesions could be localized by means of clinical observations.

The detailed brain mapping envisioned by localizationists encountered difficulties when scientists discovered that certain brain functions were not susceptible to localization. For example, in the twentieth century the American psychologist Karl Lashley (1890-1958) conducted experiments on rats to study how brain lesions affected a rat's ability to solve mazes. Although he found that lesions retarded learning, he also discovered no relation between this dysfunction and the locus of the lesion. All parts of the relevant region of the rat's brain seemed to be equivalent (or equipotential) in storing information.

Because of ethical concerns, the ablation of the cerebral cortex in humans was not as common as the use of this procedure in animals, but in the late 1920's and through the 1930's, the Portuguese neurosurgeon António Egas Moniz (1874-1955) developed prefrontal lobotomy, or leucotomy, in which he severed nerve tracts from the limbic system to a frontal lobe to mitigate the anxiety accompanying such conditions as schizophrenia. Though the anxiety of many patients lessened, serious side effects such as apathy, headaches, and memory difficulties also occurred.

In 1940, a neurosurgeon working in Rochester, New York treated several patients suffering from epilepsy by severing the nerve fibers connecting the right and left hemispheres of their brains. These operations lessed the severity of their seizures, but the patients also experienced serious side effects. Other split-brain studies in the second half of the twentieth century showed that certain surgically brain-damaged patients, despite profound impairment of their conscious knowledge, preserved access to their nonconscious knowledge. A good example is the phenomenon of "blindsight," where patients deny that they see an object but can in some way sense its location and other attributes.

Research on brain-damaged animals and humans has advanced scientific understanding of the cerebral cortex. Most scientists now accept that such functions as vision are related to such brain structures as the visual cortex. However, the goal of the localizationists, a highly detailed functional map of the brain, has not been fully achieved, nor will it, holists point out, since the functional units that have been discovered are also interconnected with the brain's information-processing system. Many scientists have abandoned extreme reductionist and holistic positions, believing instead that the truth lies between the extremes.

CAUSES

Brain damage can be caused directly or indirectly, suddenly or gradually. Direct causes include concussions, gunshot wounds, and surgical ablations. Cerebral tissue may be destroyed indirectly and gradually through tumors, viruses, syphilis, or epilepsy. One of the most common causes of brain injury is cerebral vascular accident, formerly called apoplexy and now commonly called stroke. Over two million Americans suffer strokes annually. A clot can cause a stroke by blocking blood flow to a part of the brain (an occlusive stroke) or by the rupture of a weakened blood vessel (a hemorrhagic stroke). The location of the damaged tissue is pivotal, since a large lesion in some areas of the cerebral cortex may have negligible consequences whereas a little lesion in the limbic system may have such devastating consequences as uncontrollable, violent behavior. After stroke, the most common cause of brain damage is cancer. Among the elderly, several brain-damaging illnesses are widespread, most notably Alzheimer's disease.

Among the young, the most common causes of brain injury are accidents and assaults. During wartime, bullets and shrapnel become major causes of brain injuries. During peacetime, traumatic brain injury from motor-vehicle accidents is the leading cause of death and disability in the first four decades of life. For the United States in the early twenty-first century, statisticians conservatively estimate half a million new cases of brain injury annually. By a three-to-one ratio, males are at greater risk of brain injury than females, and the costs of all brain injuries are estimated at about forty billion dollars per year.

EFFECTS

Because of the complex interconnectivity of various brain structures, the effects of brain damage on behavior have been difficult to quantify. Even in cases where the lesion is circumscribed and the deficit in function is well defined, a precise link between a lesion and behavioral problem cannot be securely deduced, since lesions in one area may cause interference in other areas. Nevertheless, patients with brain lesions exhibit behavioral problems that can be attributed to damaged areas of the brain. For example, lesions in the left hemisphere often lead to problems in understanding and remembering verbal information, whereas lesions in the right hemisphere often lead to impairment of visual and other nonverbal abilities. A stroke in the right hemisphere often leaves patients with their left side paralyzed, and sometimes patients even deny their paralysis, a phenomenon known as anosognosia.

Brain damage can have significant effects on consciousness. For example, damage to the brain stem frequently results in loss of consciousness. However, localizationists who once identified the frontal lobes of the cerebral cortex with intelligence had to retreat from this position when patients missing much of their frontal cortex tested normal for intelligence. These observations convinced holists of the plasticity of the cerebral cortex, which means that the cerebral cortex is not simply a permanent arrangement of neuronal circuits but a dynamic system that is constantly being changed and reorga-

nized by experiences and feedback. On the other hand, reductionists point to "diseases of consciousness" in which specific lesions cause specific disorders. For example, patients with midbrain lesions can manifest retrograde amnesia (the inability to recall information acquired just before the brain damage) but not anterograde amnesia (the inability to form new permanent memories after the brain damage).

DIAGNOSING BRAIN DAMAGE

Because of the structural complexities of the brain, determining the nature and amount of functional impairment after brain damage is difficult. A neurologist may diagnose the nature and extent of brain damage by an astute interpretation of the symptoms (the subjective manifestations of disease)—for example, a patient's complaint about her difficulties in speaking—and signs (objective manifestations of disease)—for example, the physician's observation that a patient can no longer move her right arm. In the early days of medicine, diagnosis of brain damage was mainly through simple observations of patients in natural situations, but the need to make diagnoses more scientific led psychiatrists, as early as the late 1800's, to construct batteries of tests to discover the details of various impairments. For example, some patients, called conduction aphasics, were unable to repeat correctly a word or phrase that they had just heard. Development of objective tests was problematic, however, because of interconnectivities among symptoms. For example, patients who had a dysfunction in speech might or might not have a parallel dysfunction in hearing.

In the late nineteenth and early twentieth centuries, instruments were invented that aided physicians in diagnosing brain damage. In the late 1890's, X rays, discovered by Wilhelm Röntgen (1845-1923), were used to locate tumors and other brain lesions, and this technique was refined in 1918 when Walter Dandy (1886-1946) invented pneumoencephalography. This technique involved replacing the fluid within certain brain cavities by such gases as oxygen or helium and then taking X-ray pictures of the brain. These pictures, called encephalograms, helped physicians to diagnose such localized lesions as tumors.

The diagnosis of brain-damaged patients was sharpened during the twentieth century's two world wars. Because of numerous head injuries, much material became available to scientists who were interested in the relationship between brain lesions and psychological disorders. Test batteries became highly sophisticated, and testers examined brain-damaged soldiers for such abilities as naming, repeating, visual-image recognition, and many others. In this way diagnosticians were able to understand more fully than before the many variations in aphasic disorders.

The person who devoted himself more than many others to the study of brain-damaged soldiers was Aleksandr Luria (1902-1977), a Russian neuropsychologist. He reported on a series of eight hundred cases of brain wounds sustained by soldiers during World War II. His evidence showed that such behavioral functions as perception, speech, or calculation are never lost in a patient with a circumscribed lesion. Furthermore, complex behavioral functions may be lost due to lesions in widely different areas of the brain. Luria's clinical data revealed to him how difficult precise diagnosis was since many specific brain structures are involved in even the simplest forms of mental activity.

After the war, diagnosis improved because of better test batteries and more sophisticated instruments. During the 1950's and 1960's, various psychological tests were developed that located brain lesions with a high degree of accuracy. Significant, too, was the development of advanced imaging techniques. Even before World War II, Hans Berger (1873-1941) used the brain's electrical activity to invent the electroencephalograph, an apparatus that records electric potentials of the brain. The record of the variations in electric potential, the electroencephalogram (EEG), helped physicians diagnose disturbances within the brain. Neurological disorders such as epilepsy, brain tumors, and acute brain trauma produced distinctive features in EEGs. During the final decades of the twentieth century, several new imaging techniques became important tools in the neurological diagnosis of brain damage. Such techniques as magnetic resonance imaging (MRI), magnetic resonance angiography (MRA), computed tomography (CT) scanning, and positron emission tomography (PET) have allowed diagnosticians to picture in detail noninvasively various brain structures, thereby facilitating the correlation between cerebral lesions and patient symptoms. Computers have also been used to create models of the cerebral cortex, and while these models vastly oversimplify complex realities, they nevertheless help scientists to understand how, for example, the brain reorganizes itself after a stroke.

HISTORY OF TREATMENT

The history of the care of the brain-damaged is intimately connected with the history of theories about brain function. What physicians do about brain damage depends on what they think it is. Throughout the early history of medicine, physicians relied on the healing power of nature, and cases certainly existed of brain-damaged patients who experienced spontaneous recovery. With the development of modern knowledge about the cerebral cortex, physicians were able, with reasonable confidence, to ascribe various disabilities in brain-damaged patients to lesions in particular cortical areas. This theory created a problem in treating these patients. Since scientists believed that neurons could not be regenerated, how could a patient restore a function if the brain location responsible for that function was destroyed? When Broca, a champion of localization, proclaimed in 1865 that "one speaks with the left hemisphere," physicians countered with examples of children with atrophied left hemispheres who grew up to be normal, not aphasic. It gradually became clear that when one part of the brain is damaged, resulting in the loss of a specific function, another brain area may take over and make possible a partial or complete recovery of that function. In short, the capacity for various functions is initially widely distributed throughout the brain. This explains why young people often recover from strokes completely, whereas older people sustaining the same brain injury may never speak normally again.

Just as the carnage of two world wars provided ways of improving diagnoses of brain-damaged patients, so these same wars provided new ways of rehabilitation. For example, some physicians who believed that recovery of function was the outcome of compensatory changes in the structure of the brain emphasized that rehabilitation of brain-damaged soldiers should not be focused on remedying specific impairments but rather on creating an environment in which soldiers could use their intact capacities to successfully complete tasks.

During the decades following World War II, observations were made and experiments performed that suggested a critical period existed for recovery from brain damage, and it was therefore important to use certain drugs and rehabilitation techniques as early as possible during the recovery period. As more was learned about brain damage, an entire continuum of specialized brain-injury rehabilitation programs developed. They helped dramatically increase the quantity and quality of restored functions after brain damage.

TREATMENT OPTIONS

Since clinicians' approaches to treatment are inextricably tied to their philosophy of rehabilitation, different treatment options for brain-damaged patients exist. However, the goal of all these treatments is the same: to restore patients to the normal life they had before the injury. Some scholars distinguish between two types of treatment, restoration and compensation. Those who practice restoration believe that damaged brain functions can be regenerated, even enhanced, by techniques that help the brain to become "reorganized." Those who favor compensation hold that the task of the rehabilitator is to encourage a different part of the brain to take over from the damaged part. Other scholars see an even larger number of models of recovery, from traditional and paternalistic through educational and empowering to biomedical models based on a reductionist view of the brain. In general, these different models conceptualize disease and disability within the context of the provider-patient relationship.

Brain damage often results in the impairment of physical, cognitive, behavioral, emotional, sexual, occupational, and social skills, and rehabilitating these skills is a complex task. Few therapists have training or experience in all these areas. Therefore, rehabilitation involves the efforts of many specialists.

Treatment begins as soon as the brain-damaged patient comes into the care of professionals, for example, at the scene of an accident. Basic life support is an important part of this prehospital phase of treatment. By using hemorrhage control and other techniques, paramedics can make sure that a patient with a brain injury enters a trauma center with the best possible chances for recovery. These trauma centers are usually part of a network of facilities equipped with modern medical technologies and staffed by teams of specialists. Rehabilitation can begin as early as the patient's stay in the intensive-care unit. During this early phase of recovery,

treatments include behavioral therapy as well as the use of such chemicals as nerve growth factors.

Treatment of the brain-injured patient is often long, and since the patient's problems change over time, so must the rehabilitation process. The places of treatment may be outpatient clinics, office buildings, group homes, or the patient's family setting. This last is particularly important, since studies have shown that the success of rehabilitation depends not only on professional treatment but also on the quality and amount of family support.

CONCLUSION

Since all that one experiences, feels, and knows depends on a healthy brain, damage to this crucial organ can have devastating consequences. The study and treatment of brain damage have deepened scientific knowledge of the mind-brain interaction. This knowledge has come from scientists who were materialists, holists, and interactionists (those who believe a dynamic relationship exists between cerebral structures and functions). As the sciences concerned with the brain have matured, traditional demarcations between specialties have blurred and a healthy cross-fertilization among disciplines has led to new insights that in turn have resulted in more effective treatment of brain-damaged individuals. Much still remains to be discovered about the brain, how it is structured, and how the brain-damaged can best be helped. The goal of a perfect understanding of the complexities of the human brain may be unattainable, as some critics contend, but everyone can certainly agree that a deep, detailed, and coherent knowledge of brain structures and functions will benefit all individuals, whether their brains are hurt or healthy.

SOURCES FOR FURTHER STUDY

Churchland, Patricia Smith. *Neurophilosophy: Toward a Unified Science of the Mind-Brain.* Cambridge, Mass.: MIT Press, 1986. The author provides an introduction to neuroscience from a philosophical point of view. She sketches the history of the mind-brain problem and uses research about brain lesions to argue for a unified science of mind and brain.

Damasio, Antonio R. *Descartes' Error: Emotion, Reason, and the Human Brain.* New York: Putnam, 1994. Drawing on his experiences with brain-damaged patients, Damasio shows how the absence of emotion in some of these patients can destroy rationality. His thesis is that emotions provide a bridge between the body and its "survival-oriented regulations," on one hand, and consciousness, on the other.

Gardner, Howard. *The Shattered Mind: The Person After Brain Damage.* New York: Alfred A. Knopf, 1975. The author, a Harvard-trained psychologist, worked with brain-damaged patients in Boston. In this book, intended for general audiences, he uses several case studies to cast light on what happens to the brain when it is diseased or injured.

Gazzaniga, Michael S. *Mind Matters: How Mind and Brain Interact to Create Our Conscious Lives.* Boston: Houghton Mifflin, 1988. A prolific researcher and writer on neuroscience, Gazzaniga describes how the mind and brain are bound together by guiding the reader through the best historical and modern research on the subject.

Levin, Harvey S., and Jordan Grafman, eds. *Cerebral Reorganization of Function After Brain Damage.* New York: Oxford University Press, 2000. This book uses the insights of neuroscientists to illuminate ways of rehabilitating brain-injured patients. The expert contributors to this volume lead the reader through the background, significance, practical applications, and potential future of "neuroplasticity" as a tool in the treatment of neurological impairments.

Mackay, Linda E., Phyllis E. Chapman, and Anthony S. Morgan. *Maximizing Brain Injury Recovery: Integrating Critical Care and Early Rehabilitation.* Gaithersburg, Md.: Aspen, 1997. This textbook, written with the endorsement of the Brain Injury Association, is intended to supply helpful information for people coming to terms with brain injury. The authors' chief theme is the necessity of an interdisciplinary approach in treating brain-injured patients and in returning them to some degree of normalcy.

Robert J. Paradowski

SEE ALSO: Abnormality: Biomedical models; Alzheimer's disease; Animal experimentation; Aphasias; Dementia; Developmental disabilities; Forgetting and forgetfulness; Incompetency; Memory: Animal research; Mental retardation; Motor development; Nervous system; Neuropsychology; Prenatal physical development; Shock therapy; Speech disorders; Split-brain studies; Synaptic transmission.

Brain specialization

TYPE OF PSYCHOLOGY: Biological bases of behavior
FIELDS OF STUDY: Nervous system

Brain specialization involves the relationships between different physical parts of the brain and abilities, behaviors, and types of thinking. The seemingly inseparable whole of the self is the product of blended inputs from a diverse collection of structures. Right and left brain hemispheres are capable of independent thought and have specialized abilities.

KEY CONCEPTS
- bilateral
- cerebral cortex
- cerebrum
- laterality
- limbic system
- mosaic theory
- neuron
- subcortical

INTRODUCTION

In the 1800's, practitioners of a pseudoscience called phrenology claimed that they could predict personality and abilities by examining bumps on a person's skull. The theory was that each part of the brain was responsible for a particular human characteristic. Larger brain areas were said to be related to stronger characteristics, and they raised the skull over those areas into a bump. Researchers showed this early version of the mosaic theory to be wrong in detail but correct in that different brain areas have specialized functions. Those who believed that all brain areas are equal and unspecialized, however, resisted the mosaic idea. Data from all over the world gathered for more than a hundred years have illustrated not only that different regions of the brain are specialized but also how they are specialized.

There are three particularly influential models of brain organization. Paul MacLean developed the theory of the triune brain to help researchers think about the overall functions of brain regions in humans. This model helps explain why primitive brain areas do not vanish when more advanced structures evolve; rather, they interact with the more recent structures that lie on top of them. First there was the reptilian brain, the primitive structures making up the bulk of the most developed part of a reptile's brain. They consist of the swollen ending of the spinal cord before it ends, called the brain stem, and primitive structures sitting on top of the brain stem. The most noticeable of these structures are called the thalamus and the hypothalamus. A lizard normally responds to immediate stimulation; when there is neither food nor an enemy, it usually does nothing. The human brain stem, thalamus, and hypothalamus perform similar functions.

In early mammals, a new structure called the cerebrum evolved on top of the thalamus. The cerebrum has neurons only on its outer surface, or cortex. The fibers carrying messages from those neurons are inside, in the medulla. The earliest cortex consisted of three to five layers of neurons and is called the paleocortex ("old cortex") and intermediate cortex. Later cortical areas six neurons thick, called the neocortex, evolved and covered the entire outer surface of the cerebrum. The paleocortex was relegated to the places where the two cerebral hemispheres come together and to clumps in the medulla of the cerebrum. These paleocortical and transitional areas, often collectively called the limbic system, control emotional responding and make behavior more flexible. When a mammal has no immediate stimulation, it rarely remains motionless, as does a lizard. Instead, it may go exploring for old enemies, old mates, or simply knowledge about its environment. MacLean called the limbic system the paleomammalian brain.

The neocortex is the most prominent brain structure seen when one examines a mammalian brain. It inhibits impulsive behaviors that would otherwise result from motives and feelings arising from the lower centers. Having a conscience, for example, depends on the parts of these areas in the front of the brain in humans. MacLean called these areas the neomammalian brain.

Aleksandr Luria, a noted Russian neuropsychologist famous for his work diagnosing and helping brain-damaged soldiers, proposed another three-part model of brain function. Subcortical and limbic structures, basically MacLean's reptilian and paleomammalian brain, serve reflexes, motives, emotions, and arousal. The cerebral cortex, or MacLean's neomammalian brain, can be divided. The front part consists of the frontal lobes, and the hind part consists of the temporal, occipital, and parietal lobes. The front part plans and executes ac-

tions. There is a gradient from abstract to concrete functions within the frontal lobes, running from the prefrontal structures that lie behind the forehead back to areas controlling talking and eye movement to areas in the back of the frontal lobes controlling voluntary muscle control.

The hind portion of the cerebral cortex processes sensory information and stores memories. It consists of three lobes with their own specializations. The temporal lobes specialize in hearing and higher-order processing of emotional information from the paleomammalian brain. The parietal lobes process information about touch, muscle position, and location in space. The occipital lobes process visual information. The place in the center of each side of the back part of the brain where all three lobes touch includes a fold of cortical surface called the angular gyrus and the parietal, occipital, and

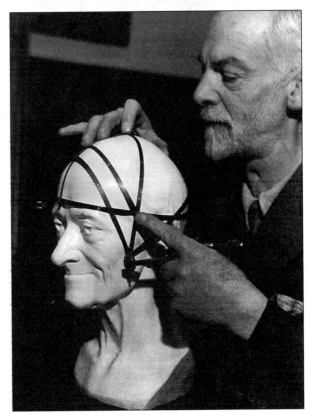

G. E. Sewell, president of the Phrenological Congress in 1934, demonstrates how to read "bumps" on the head to discern personality and abilities. Phrenology was discredited, but the concept of specialization in the brain proved correct. (Hulton Archive)

temporal (POT) association areas. A human processes sequences of information there, including the orders of words in sentences, and integrates information from multiple senses.

RIGHT AND LEFT BRAIN

A last theory that helps in understanding the brain is the right brain-left brain model. At one time, it was thought that the two hemispheres of the cerebral cortex were bilateral mirror images of each other. Today it is known that they have slightly different shapes and internal organizations, and they do somewhat different things. Roger Sperry, of the California Institute of Technology in Pasadena, California, cut the bundles of nerves connecting the two hemispheres of cats, including the largest bundle, the corpus callosum. He found that each hemisphere could process information independently and suggested that this operation might help humans with epileptic seizures. When the operation was performed on humans, it was successful in reducing the severity of epileptic seizures. Sperry found that the two hemispheres could each process information individually. Each developed its own memory and had special skills. Sometimes the hemispheres conflicted when researchers gave each side of the brain different information. If the information was visual, such as matching pictures of faces, the right hemisphere would win; if it was verbal, the left would dominate.

Hemispheric specialization is called lateralization. Most control of the muscles is lateralized, with the left hemisphere controlling the right hand and the right hemisphere controlling the left hand. The left hemisphere is best at verbal, detail, and sequential processing. For example, finding one's way around by sequences of right and left turns usually requires the left hemisphere. Strokes damaging the left hemisphere are more likely to cause loss of speech. The expression of speech is controlled by Broca's area in the left frontal lobe. Understanding speech requires Wernicke's area, located where the three hind cerebral lobes meet. A large nerve bundle called the arcuate fasciculus connects the two types of speech centers. Because the left hemisphere usually controls language and movements of the right hand, most people write with their right hand.

Damage to the right hemisphere causes problems in assembling puzzles, recognizing people, playing music, and painting. Finding one's way around by maps or landmarks requires the right hemisphere. Looking at someone's face and naming them requires both hemispheres. Each hemisphere has some abilities of the other; this has been found to be most apparent in females and in left-handed people.

BRAIN INJURY AND LATERALIZATION

Understanding the relationships between specialized skills, actions, and the specialization of the brain has been very helpful in diagnosing the location of brain injuries and wounds, although today this is less important because of electronic brain-imaging techniques, such as computed tomography (CT) scans, that permit precise computerized localization.

On a theoretical level, there is a much better understanding of how the areas of the brain generate abilities and consciousness. Before they knew much about the specialization of many brain parts, scientists tried to identify functions by stimulating brain areas with electrodes or by removing brain areas. Some regions did not show obvious reactions to these techniques, and early researchers did not know that these were areas specialized for thinking and associating. They labeled the brain parts the silent areas and thought that they had no functions. It is now known that there is no surplus or silent brain area. All parts of the brain perform vital functions; when any brain part is injured, modern techniques can identify deficits in the performance of those functions.

Studies of lateralized brain functions have raised the question of why bilaterally symmetrical brains evolved lateralization. Most current thinking is that use of tools and the beginnings of speech put a premium on processing rapid, precise sequences of actions or perception. The hemisphere controlling the dominant hand, which is usually the left hemisphere, already had some of these abilities. The development of speech centers in turn gave an evolutionary advantage to individuals with more specializations of the left hemisphere.

Being able to localize brain damage may help with designing the best kinds of tasks for a patient in a rehabilitation program. It can also help in detecting hidden, subtle problems. As scientists have learned more about the complex interrelationships of different brain parts, most attempts to solve problem behaviors by removing brain tissue have stopped.

Before and after World War II, an operation called prefrontal lobotomy was common. The surgeon would either remove or damage the front-most part of the cerebral cortex or cut the connections between those areas and lower brain centers. Now it is known that damage to the left prefrontal lobe leaves a person unable to anticipate details and makes a person act as if depressed, but with no real sadness. Damage to the right prefrontal lobe leaves a person unable to anticipate patterns, and people with such damage do socially inappropriate things, such as public belching. Knowledge about these side effects helped make these operations rare.

In the 1970's, some prominent brain scientists proposed the theory that education centered on verbal lecture was only educating students' left hemispheres. They suggested that education of the dominated right hemispheres was needed to increase intuition, creativity, and other useful abilities. Books were written advocating learning to draw with the right brain, and claims were made about freeing the right hemisphere from the control of the left. As the right hemisphere is better understood, it is clear that its abilities are used even in a highly verbal culture. Reading facial expressions, for example, requires the right hemisphere, and when a person's expression does not match his or her words, people are more likely to believe the person's face. On the other hand, there is some recent evidence that after damage to the left hemisphere, some people (who are more likely to be left-handed or female) can perhaps develop some right hemisphere speech abilities. This may lead to better treatments for patients who lose language abilities, a condition called aphasia.

BRAIN EXPERIMENTATION

Physiological psychology developed within a classic experimental psychology model. Most early work was with animals, much of it with rats. Simultaneously, physicians working with brain-damaged patients began to generate a broad range of data about the relationship between human brain anatomy and behavioral deficits. Psychologists developed testing procedures more sophisticated than those developed by neurologists. As a result, many neurologists and neurosurgeons hired psychologists to administer psychological tests to their patients to detect subtle changes in abilities and behaviors. Today the best neurodiagnostic approaches combine psychological

testing techniques with clinical medical techniques, including those developed by Luria in Russia.

Psychologists understand refined experimental and testing procedures; physicians can be authorized to do brain surgery. Once Sperry found that cats appeared to have two minds after he separated their two cerebral hemispheres, the next step was for psychologists to work with doctors, who could perform medically justified human operations. The step after that was to use psychological techniques to understand the very subtle changes in behavior that resulted. Using experimental procedures developing in the study of perception, learning, and cognition, Sperry, Michael Gazzaniga, and others were able to show that each hemisphere understood the world in its own way. Later they were able to show lateralized abilities in people with intact brains.

Physiological psychology in American psychology departments is becoming less oriented toward animal experimentation and more oriented toward human clinical studies. The cooperative efforts of psychologists (sometimes called psychoneurodiagnosticians) and medical doctors generate more precise information about how human brains work. This means that there is less need for animal models of how human brains function. New data about brain functioning are being incorporated into current learning, cognitive, clinical, and computer-related psychology theories.

SOURCES FOR FURTHER STUDY

Changeux, Jean-Pierre. *Neuronal Man: The Biology of Mind.* Translated by Laurence Garey. New York: Pantheon Books, 1985. The author reviews the history of human investigation of the nervous system and how ideas about mind and body have changed as a result of greater knowledge. It is written for the layperson. Educates about a wide range of current neurological and biochemical discoveries and philosophical issues.

Gardner, Howard. *The Shattered Mind: The Person After Brain Damage.* New York: Alfred A. Knopf, 1975. A very readable account of how brain damage to various regions and connections of the brain changes a person. Excellent clinical descriptions of symptoms and how these interact with the person. Teaches the anatomy of the cerebral hemispheres in a painless and accurate way.

Kolb, Bryan, and Ian Q. Whishaw. *Fundamentals of Human Neuropsychology.* 4th ed. New York: W. H.

Freeman, 1995. An excellent text. This book logically guides the reader through the fundamentals of brain and neuron function to detailed descriptions of research on the purposes of all major brain areas. Provides a general model to understand the brain and functional systems like memory or language. The material is designed to be understood at different levels.

Luria, Aleksandr R. "The Functional Organization of the Brain." *Scientific American* 196 (March, 1970): 66-78. Luria was a dominant force in Russian neuropsychology. In this classic article he presents a simple but profound model of the organization of the human brain. The frontal lobes involve action and planning, the hind parts of the cortex involve memory and sensation, and lower brain areas organize motivation, emotion, and reflex.

Springer, Sally P., and Georg Deutsch. *Left Brain, Right Brain.* 5th ed. New York: W. H. Freeman, 1997. A good review of the literature and experimental work on lateralized brain functions. It is evenhanded and reviews the more speculative theories about special right-hemisphere abilities carefully and fairly. Most extreme ideas, such as claiming that the left hemisphere is the overly logical male brain and the right hemisphere the intuitive, female, artistic brain, are rejected. There is a very good section on the origins and meaning of left-handedness.

Leland C. Swenson

SEE ALSO: Aphasias; Brain damage; Brain structure; Cognitive ability: Gender differences; Language; Learning; Motor development; Nervous system; Neuropsychology; Psychosurgery; Split-brain studies; Thought: Study and measurement; Visual system.

Brain structure

TYPE OF PSYCHOLOGY: Biological bases of behavior
FIELDS OF STUDY: Biological influences on learning; nervous system; thought

Different areas of the brain have specialized functions that control activities ranging from basic biological processes to complex psychological operations. Understanding the distinctive features of different neurological areas provides insight into why people and other animals act, feel, and think as they do.

KEY CONCEPTS
- cerebral cortex
- cerebral hemispheres
- forebrain
- hindbrain
- lobes
- midbrain
- neural tube
- neurons

INTRODUCTION

About two weeks after conception, a fluid-filled cavity called the neural tube begins to form on the back of the human embryo. This neural tube will sink under the surface of the skin, and the two major structures of the central nervous system (CNS) will begin to differentiate. The top part of the tube will enlarge and become the brain; the bottom part will become the spinal cord. The cavity will persist through development and become the fluid-filled central canal of the spinal cord and the four ventricles of the brain. The ventricles and the central canal contain cerebrospinal fluid, a clear plasmalike fluid that supports and cushions the brain and also provides nutritive and eliminative functions for the CNS. At birth the average human brain weighs approximately 12 ounces (350 grams), a quarter of the size of the average adult brain, which is about 3 pounds (1,200 to 1,400 grams). Development of the brain in the first year is rapid, with the brain doubling in weight in the first six months.

The development of different brain areas depends on intrinsic and extrinsic factors. Internally, chemicals called neurotrophins promote the survival of neurons (the basic cells of the nervous system that are specialized to communicate electrochemically with one another) and help determine where and when neurons will form connections and become diverse neurological structures. Externally, diverse experiences enhance the survival of neurons and play a major role in the degree of development of different neurological areas. Research has demonstrated that the greater the exposure a child receives to a particular experience, the greater the development of the neurological area involved in processing that type of stimulation. While this phenomenon occurs throughout the life span, the greatest impact of environmental stimulation in restructuring and reorganizing the brain occurs in the earliest years of life.

Experience can alter the shape of the brain, but its basic architecture is determined before birth. The brain consists of three major subdivisions: the hindbrain (rhombencephalon, or "parallelogram-brain"), the midbrain (mesencephalon, or "mid-brain"), and the forebrain (prosencephalon, or "forward brain"). The hindbrain is further subdivided into the myelencephalon ("marrow-brain") and the metencephalon ("after-brain"), while the forebrain is divided into the diencephalon ("between-brain") and the telencephalon ("end-brain"). To visualize roughly the locations of these brain areas in a person, one can hold an arm out, bend the elbow 90 degrees, and make a fist. If the forearm is the spinal cord, where the wrist enlarges into the base of the hand corresponds to the hindbrain, with the metencephalon farther up than the myelencephalon. The palm of the hand, enclosed by the fingers, would be the midbrain. The fingers would be analogous to the forebrain, with the topmost surface parts of the fingers being the telencephalon.

One can take the analogy a step further. If a fist is made with the fingers of the other hand and placed next to the fist previously made, each fist would represent the two cerebral hemispheres of the forebrain, with the skin of the fingers representing the forebrain's cerebral cortex, the six layers of cells that cover the two hemispheres. Finally, like close-fitting gloves, the meninges cover the cortex. The three layers of the meninges play a protective and nutritive role for the brain.

The more advanced the species, the greater the development of the forebrain, in general, and the cortex, in particular. The emphasis here is placed on a neuroanatomical examination of the human brain, beginning with a look at the hindbrain and progressing to an investigation of the cerebral cortex. The terms "anterior" ("toward the front") and "posterior" ("toward the back") will be used frequently in describing the location of different brain structures. Additionally, the words "superior" ("above") and "inferior" ("below") will be used to describe vertical locations.

THE HINDBRAIN

As the spinal cord enters the skull, it enlarges into the bottommost structure of the brain, the medulla (or medulla oblongata). The medulla controls many of the most basic physiological functions for survival, particularly breathing and the beating of the heart. Reflexes such as vomiting, coughing, sneezing, and salivating are also controlled by the medulla. The medulla is sensitive to opiate and amphetamine drugs, and overdoses of these drugs can impair its normal functioning. Severe impairment can lead to a fatal shutdown of the respiratory and cardiovascular systems.

Just above the medulla lie the pons, parts of the reticular formation, the raphe system, and the locus coeruleus. All these structures play a role in arousal and sleep. The pons plays a major role in initiating rapid eye movement (REM) sleep. REM sleep is characterized by repeated horizontal eye movements, increased brain activity, and frequent dreaming. The reticular system (sometimes called the reticular activating system, or RAS) stretches from the pons through the midbrain to projections into the cerebral cortex. Activation of the reticular system, by sensory stimulation or thinking, causes increases in arousal and alertness in diverse areas of the brain. For the brain to pay attention to something, there must be activation from the reticular formation. The raphe system, like the reticular system, can increase the brain's readiness to respond to stimuli. However, unlike the reticular formation, the raphe system can decrease alertness to stimulation, decrease sensitivity to pain, and initiate sleep. Raphe system activity is modulated somewhat by an adjacent structure called the locus coeruleus. Abnormal functioning of this structure has been linked with depression and anxiety.

The largest structure in the metencephalon is the cerebellum, which branches off from the base of the brain and occupies a considerable space in the back of the head. The cerebellum's primary function is the learning and control of coordinated perceptual-motor activities. Learning to walk, run, jump, throw a ball, ride a bike, or perform any other complex motor activity causes chemical changes to occur in the cerebellum that result in the construction of a sort of program for controlling the muscles involved in the particular motor skills. Activation of specific programs enables the performance of particular motor activities. The cerebellum is also involved in other types of learning and performance. Learning language, reading, shifting attention from auditory to visual stimuli, and timing (such as in

The Anatomy of the Brain

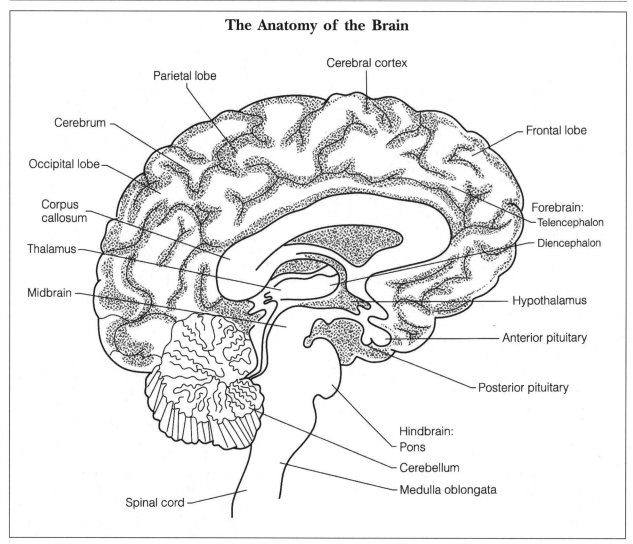

(Hans & Cassidy, Inc.)

music or the tapping of fingers) are just a few tasks for which normal cerebellar functioning is essential. Children diagnosed with learning disabilities often are found to have abnormalities in the cerebellum.

THE MIDBRAIN

The superior and posterior part of the midbrain is called the tectum. There are two enlargements on both sides of the tectum known as the colliculi. The superior colliculus controls visual reflexes such as tracking the flight of a ball, while the inferior colliculus controls auditory reflexes such as turning toward the sound of a buzzing insect. Above and between the colliculi lies the pineal gland, which con-

tains melatonin, a hormone that greatly influences the sleep-wake cycle. Melatonin levels are high when it is dark and low when it is light. High levels of melatonin induce sleepiness, which is one reason that people sleep better when it is darker. Another structure near the colliculi is the periaqueductal gray (PAG) area of the ventricular system. Stimulation of the PAG helps to block the sensation of pain.

Beneath the tectum is the tegmentum, which includes some structures involved in movement. Red nucleus activity is high during twisting movements, especially of the hands and fingers. The substantia nigra smooths out movements and is influential in maintaining good posture. The characteristic limb trembling and posture difficulties of Parkinson's disease are attributable to neuronal damage in the substantia nigra.

THE FOREBRAIN

Right above the midbrain, in the center of the brain, lies the thalamus, which is the center of sensory processing. All incoming sensory information except for the sense of smell goes to the thalamus first before it is sent on to the cerebral cortex and other areas of the brain. Anterior to and slightly below the thalamus is the hypothalamus. Hypothalamic activity is involved in numerous motivated behaviors such as eating, drinking, sexual activity, temperature regulation, and aggression. It does so largely through its regulation of the pituitary gland, which is attached beneath the hypothalamus. The pituitary gland controls the release of hormones that circulate in the endocrine system.

SUBCORTICAL STRUCTURES. Numerous structures lie beneath the cerebral cortex in pairs, one in each hemisphere. Many of these structures are highly interconnected with one another and are therefore seen to be part of a system. Furthermore, most of the subcortical structures can be categorized as belonging to one of two major systems. Surrounding the thalamus is one system called the basal ganglia, which is most prominently involved in movements and muscle tone. The basal ganglia deteriorate in Parkinson's and Huntington's diseases, both disorders of motor activity. The three major structures of the basal ganglia are the caudate nucleus and putamen, which form the striatum, and the globus pallidus. The activities of the basal ganglia extend beyond motor control. The striatum, for instance, plays a significant role in the learning of habits as well as in obsessive-compulsive disorder, a disorder of excessive habits. In addition, disorders of memory, attention, and emotional expression (especially depression) frequently involve abnormal functioning of the basal ganglia.

The nucleus basalis, while not considered part of the basal ganglia, nevertheless is highly interconnected with those structures (and the hypothalamus) and receives direct input from them. Nucleus basalis activity is essential for attention and arousal.

The other major subcortical system is the limbic system. The limbic system was originally thought to be involved in motivated or emotional behaviors and little else. Later research, however, demonstrated that many of these structures are crucial for memory formation. The fact that people have heightened recall for emotionally significant events is likely a consequence of the limbic system's strong involvement in both memory and motivation or emotion.

Two limbic structures are essential for memory formation. The hippocampus plays the key role in making personal events and facts into long-term memories. For a person to remember information of this nature for more than thirty minutes, the hippocampus must be active. In people with Alzheimer's disease, deterioration of the hippocampus is accompanied by memory loss. Brain damage involving the hippocampus is manifested by amnesias, indecisiveness, and confusion. The hippocampus takes several years to develop fully. This is thought to be a major reason that adults tend to remember very little from their first five years of life, a phenomenon called infantile amnesia.

The second limbic structure that is essential for learning and memory is the amygdala. The amygdala provides the hippocampus with information about the emotional context of events. It is also crucial for emotional perception, particularly in determining how threatening events are. When a person feels threatened, that person's amygdala will become very active. Early experiences in life can fine-tune how sensitive a person's amygdala will be to potentially threatening events. A child raised in an abusive environment will likely develop an amygdala that is oversensitive, predisposing that person to interpret too many circumstances as threatening. Two additional limbic structures work with the amygdala in the perception and expression of threatening events, the septal nuclei and the cingulate gyrus. High activity in the former structure inclines one to an interpretation that an event is not threatening. Activity in the latter structure is linked to positive or negative emotional expressions such as worried, happy, or angry looks.

Other major structures of the limbic system include the olfactory bulbs and nuclei, the nucleus accumbens, and the mammillary bodies. The olfactory bulbs and nuclei are the primary structures for smell perception. Experiencing pleasure involves the nucleus accumbens, which is also often stimulated by anything that can become addictive. The mammillary bodies are involved in learning and memory.

CORTICAL LOBES. The most complex thinking abilities are primarily attributable to the thin layers that cover the two cerebral hemispheres—the cortex. It is this covering of the brain that makes for the greatest differences between the intellectual capabilities of humans and other animals. Both hemispheres are typically divided into four main lobes, the distinct cortical areas of specialized functioning. There are, however, many differences between people not only in the relative size of different lobes but also in how much cerebral cortex is not directly attributable to any of the four lobes.

The occipital lobe is located at the back of the cerebral cortex. The most posterior tissue of this lobe is called the striate cortex, due to its distinctive striped appearance. The striate cortex is also called the primary visual cortex because it is there where most visual information is eventually processed. Each of the layers of this cortical area is specialized to analyze different features of visual input. The synthesis of visual information and the interpretation of that result involve other lobes of the brain. The occipital lobe also plays the primary role in various aspects of spatial reasoning. Activities such as spatial orientation, map reading, or knowing what an object will look like if rotated a certain amount of degrees all depend on this lobe.

Looking down on the top of the brain, a deep groove called the central sulcus can be seen roughly in the middle of the brain. Between the central sulcus and the occipital lobe is the parietal lobe. The parietal lobe's predominate function is the processing of the bodily sensations: taste, touch, temperature, pain, and kinesthesia (feedback from muscles and joints). A parietal band of tissue called the postcentral gyrus that is adjacent to the central sulcus (posterior and runs parallel to it) contains the somatosensory cortex in which the surface of the body is represented upside down in a maplike fashion. Each location along this cortical area corresponds to sensations from a different body part. Furthermore, the left side of the body is represented on the right hemisphere and vice versa. Damage to the right parietal cortex usually leads to sensory neglect of the left side of the body—the person ignores sensory input from that side. However, damage to the left parietal cortex causes no or little sensory neglect of the right side of the body.

The parietal lobe is involved with some aspects of distance sensation. The posterior parietal lobe plays a role in the visual location of objects and the bringing together of different types of sensory information, such as coordinating sight and sound when a person looks at someone who just called his or her name. Some aspects of the learning of language also engage the operation of the parietal cortex.

On the sides of each hemisphere, next to the temples of the head, reside the temporal lobes. The lobes closest to the ears are the primary sites of the interpretation of sounds. This task is accomplished in the primary auditory cortex, which is tucked into a groove in each temporal lobe called the lateral sulcus. Low-frequency sounds are analyzed on the outer part of this sulcus; higher-pitched sounds are represented deeper inside this groove. Closely linked with auditory perception are two other major functions of the temporal lobe: language and music comprehension. Posterior areas, particularly Wernicke's area, play key roles in word understanding and retrieval. More medial areas are involved in different aspects of music perception, especially the planum temporale.

The temporal cortex is the primary site of two important visual functions. Recognition of visual objects is dependent on inferior temporal areas. These areas of the brain are very active during visual hallucinations. One area in this location, the fusiform gyrus, is very active during the perception of faces and complex visual stimuli. A superior temporal area near the conjunction of the parietal and occipital lobes is essential for reading and writing.

The temporal lobe is in close proximity to, and shares strong connections with, the limbic system. Thus, it is not surprising that the temporal lobe plays a significant role in memory and emotions. Damage to the temporal cortex leads to major deficits in the ability to learn and in maintaining a normal emotional balance.

The largest cerebral lobe, comprising one-third of the cerebral cortex, is the frontal lobe. It is involved in the greatest variety of neurological functions. The frontal lobe consists of several anatomically distinct and functionally distinguishable areas that can be grouped into three main regions. Starting at the central sulcus (which divides the parietal and frontal lobes) and moving toward the anterior limits of the brain, one finds, in order, the precentral cortex, the premotor cortex, and the prefrontal cortex. Each of these areas is responsible for different types of activities.

In 1870, German physicians Gustav Fritsch and Eduard Hitzig were the first to stimulate the brain electrically. They found that stimulating different regions of the precentral cortex resulted in different parts of the body moving. Subsequent research identified a "motor map" that represents the body in a fashion similar to the adjacent and posteriorly located somatosensory map of the parietal lobe. The precentral cortex, therefore, can be considered the primary area for the execution of movements.

The premotor cortex is more responsible for planning the operations of the precentral cortex. In other words, the premotor cortex generates the plan to pick up a pencil, while the precentral cortex directs the arm to do so. Thinking about picking up the pencil, but not doing so, involves more activity in the premotor cortex than in the precentral cortex. An inferior premotor area essential for speaking was discovered in 1861 by Paul Broca and has since been named for him. Broca's area, usually found only in the left hemisphere, is responsible for coordinating the various operations necessary for the production of speech.

The prefrontal cortex is the part of the brain most responsible for a variety of complex thinking activities, foremost among them being decision making and abstract reasoning. Damage to the prefrontal cortex often leads to an impaired ability to make decisions, rendering the person lethargic and greatly lacking in spontaneous behavior. Numerous aspects of abstract reasoning, such as planning, organizing, keeping time, and thinking hypothetically are also greatly disturbed by injuries to the prefrontal cortex.

Research with patients who have prefrontal disturbances has demonstrated the important role of this neurological area in personality and social behavior. Patients with posterior prefrontal damage exhibit many symptoms of depression: apathy, restlessness, irritability, lack of drive, and lack of ambition. Anterior abnormalities, particularly in an inferior prefrontal region called the orbitofrontal area, result in numerous symptoms of psychopathy: lack of restraint, impulsivity, egocentricity, lack of responsibility for one's actions, and indifference to others' opinions and rights.

The prefrontal cortex also contributes to the emotional value of decisions, smell perception, working memory (the current ability to use memory), and the capacity to concentrate or shift attention.

Children correctly diagnosed with attention-deficit hyperactivity disorder (ADHD) often have prefrontal abnormalities.

HEMISPHERIC DIFFERENCES. The two cerebral hemispheres are connected by a large band of fibers called the corpus callosum and several small connections called commissures. In the early 1940's, American surgeon William van Wagenen, in order to stop the spread of epileptic seizures from crossing from one hemisphere to the other, performed the first procedure of cutting the 200 million fibers of the corpus callosum. The results were mixed, however, and it was not until the 1960's that two other American surgeons, Joe Bogen and P. J. Vogel, decided to try the operation again, this time also including some cutting of commissure fibers. The results reduced or stopped the seizures in most patients. However, extensive testing by American psychobiologist Roger Sperry and his colleagues demonstrated unique behavioral changes in the patients, called split-brain syndrome. Research with split-brain syndrome and less invasive imaging techniques of the brain, such as computed tomography (CT) and positron-emission tomography (PET) scans, has demonstrated many anatomical and functional differences between the left and right hemispheres.

The degree of differences between the two cerebral hemispheres varies greatly depending on a number of factors. Males develop greater lateralization—larger differences between the hemispheres—and develop the differences sooner. Those with a dominant right hand have greater lateralization than left- or mixed-handers. Therefore, when there is talk of "left brain versus right brain," it is important to keep in mind that a greater degree of difference exists in right-handed males. A minority of people, usually left-handers, show little differences between the left and right hemispheres.

The right hemisphere (RH) tends to be larger and heavier than the left hemisphere (LH), with the greatest difference in the frontal lobe. Conversely, several other neurological areas have been found to be larger in the LH: the occipital lobe, the planum temporale, Wernicke's area, and the Sylvian fissure. An interesting gender difference in hemispheric operation is that the LH amygdala is more active in females whereas the RH amygdala is more active in males.

The left-brain/right-brain functional dichotomy has been the subject of much popular literature.

While there are many differences in operation between the two hemispheres, it is important to realize that many of the differences are subtle, and in many regards both hemispheres are involved in the psychological function in question, only to different degrees.

The most striking difference between the two hemispheres is that the RH is responsible for sensory and motor functions of the left side of the body and the LH controls those same functions for the body's right side. This contralateral control is found to a lesser degree for hearing and, due to the optic chiasm, not at all for vision.

In the domain of sound and communication, the LH plays a greater role in speech production, language comprehension, phonetic and semantic analysis, visual word recognition, grammar, verbal learning, lyric recitation, musical performance, and rhythm keeping. A greater RH contribution is found in interpreting nonlanguage sounds, reading Braille, using emotional tone in language, understanding humor and sarcasm, expressing and interpreting nonverbal communication (facial and bodily expressions), and perceiving music. Categorical decisions, the understanding of metaphors, and the figurative aspects of language involve both hemispheres.

Regarding other domains, the RH plays a greater role in mathematical operations, but the LH is essential for remembering numerical facts and the reading and writing of numbers. Visually, the RH contributes more to mental rotation, facial perception, figured/ground distinctions, map reading, and pattern perception. Detail perception draws more on LH resources. The RH is linked more with negative emotions such as fear, anger, pain, and sadness, while positive affect is associated more with the LH. Exceptions are that schizophrenia, anxiety, and panic attacks have been found to be related more to increases in LH activity.

SUMMARY

It has been estimated that the adult human brain contains 100 billion neurons forming more than 13 trillion connections with one another. These connections are constantly changing, depending on how much learning is occuring and on the health of the brain. In this dynamic system of different neurological areas concerned with diverse functions, the question arises of how a sense of wholeness and stability emerges. In other words, where is the "me" in the mind? While some areas of the brain, such as the frontal lobe, appear more closely linked with such intimate aspects of identity as planning and making choices, it is likely that no single structure or particular function can be equated with the self. It may take the activity of the whole brain to give a sense of wholeness to life. Moreover, the self is not to be found anyplace in the brain itself. Instead, it is what the brain does—its patterns of activity—that defines the self.

SOURCES FOR FURTHER STUDY

Goldberg, Stephen. *Clinical Neuroanatomy Made Ridiculously Simple.* Miami: MedMaster, 2000. One of a series of books intended to help students in the medical professions by presenting an abbreviated version of various medical subjects. The use of mnemonic devices, humor, and case studies makes the book accessible to a college-educated audience.

Hendleman, Walter J. *Atlas of Functional Neuroanatomy.* Boca Raton, Fla.: CRC Press, 2000. Hendleman presents a visual tour of the brain through drawings, photographs, and computer-generated illustrations. Three-dimensional images of the brain can be observed by using the accompanying CD-ROM.

Kalat, James W. *Biological Psychology.* 7th ed. Belmont, Calif.: Wadsworth/Thomson Learning, 2001. A top-selling book in the area of physiological psychology. While intended for college students, this engaging, easy-to-read text is accessible to general audiences. Chapters 4 and 5 contain excellent overviews of brain anatomy and functioning.

Ornstein, Robert. *The Right Mind: Making Sense of the Hemispheres.* Fort Washington, Pa.: Harvest Books, 1998. The man who helped popularize the left-brain/right-brain dichotomy in *The Psychology of Consciousness* (1972) reexamines the functioning of the two hemispheres in this book. The result is an easy-to-read, entertaining view of hemispheric lateralization that dispels many myths about differences in hemispheric functioning.

Ornstein, Robert, Richard F. Thompson, and David Macaulay. *The Amazing Brain.* Boston: Houghton Mifflin, 1991. This is one of the best introductory books about the brain, written with a light and humorous touch. The lay reader will enjoy the accessibility of the text, the excellent (and unique) sketches, and the fanciful flare the authors use in examining a complicated subject.

Paul J. Chara, Jr.

SEE ALSO: Adrenal gland; Animal experimentation; Brain damage; Brain specialization; Consciousness; Consciousness: Altered states; Endocrine system; Endorphins; Gonads; Hormones and behavior; Memory; Memory: Animal research; Memory: Empirical studies; Memory: Physiology; Nervous system; Neurons; Neuropsychology; Pituitary gland; Psychobiology; Split-brain studies; Synaptic transmission; Thyroid gland; Visual system.

Breuer, Josef

BORN: January 15, 1842, in Vienna, Austria
DIED: June 20, 1925, in Vienna, Austria
IDENTITY: Austrian physiologist, physician, and pioneer of psychoanalysis
TYPE OF PSYCHOLOGY: Psychopathology; psychotherapy
FIELDS OF STUDY: Anxiety disorders; evaluating psychotherapy; models of abnormality; personality disorders; psychodynamic therapies; sexual disorders; stress and illness

After making important physiological discoveries, Breuer, with Sigmund Freud, helped found psychoanalysis.

Josef Robert Breuer was born in Vienna and spent his entire life there. His mother died when he was four, and his father, who educated him until he was eight, became his inspirational model. His formal schooling began at the Akademisches Gymnasium, and after his graduation in 1858, he entered the University of Vienna where, in 1859, he began his medical studies. After receiving a medical degree in 1867, he married Matilda Altmann, a union that produced five children.

Breuer achieved his first recognition through research in physiology. Working with the German physiologist Ewald Hering, Breuer discovered how a certain nerve regulated respiration (the Hering-Breuer reflex). He then studied, on his own, the inner ears of fish, reptiles, birds, and mammals, concluding, in

Josef Breuer. (Library of Congress)

1873, that the inner ear's semicircular canals regulate the animal's balance. Though his successful physiological research assured him of a scientific career at the University of Vienna, he refused to become an Extraordinary Professor, deciding instead to devote himself to his successful medical practice, which included university professors and well-known politicians.

One of his patients serendipitously led to another of his great scientific discoveries. In 1880, Breuer began treating "Anna O.," a young woman whose symptoms included paralysis and an aversion to drinking water. Breuer, who interpreted her illness as hysteria, decided to use hypnosis to get at the emotional roots of her problems. When the emotional event behind the problem was made conscious and Anna O.'s repressed feelings were fully expressed, this catharsis cured her symptoms.

Reluctant to generalize from a single case, Breuer did not publish his observations, but in 1882 he told Sigmund Freud about them. Freud himself did not use this new therapeutic technique until 1889, and he and Breuer did not fully publish their results until 1895, with *Studienüber Hysterie* (*Studies in Hysteria*, 1950). Soon after this book appeared, their relationship ended, perhaps due to Freud's insistence that every hysteria had a sexual cause whereas Breuer believed that psychoses had other causes.

Breuer's later work centered on his medical practice. His skill as a diagnostician and his deep humaneness brought him numerous patients from all walks of life, some of whom (colleagues and the destitute) he treated for free. An exceptionally cultured man, he was a lover of art, music, and literature. He counted among his friends the composer Hugo Wolf, the writer and physician Arthur Schnitzler, and the philosopher and priest Franz Brentano. Even in his old age he kept abreast of recent medical discoveries. According to his friends, he maintained his critical acumen and personal warmth until his death, which occurred in Vienna in 1925.

SOURCES FOR FURTHER STUDY

Dimen, Muriel, and Adrienne Harris, eds. *Storms in Her Head: Freud and the Construction of Hysteria.* New York: Other Press, 2001. A series of articles reconsidering the impact of Breuer and Freud's *Studies on Hysteria* in light of the later development of psychology.

Ellenberger, Henri. *The Discovery of the Unconscious: The History and Evolution of Dynamic Psychiatry.* New York: Basic Books, 1970. By using unpublished information provided by Breuer's family, Ellenberger provides fresh interpretations of the Freud-Breuer relationship.

Jones, Ernest. *The Life and Work of Sigmund Freud, Volume 1: The Formative Years and the Great Discoveries, 1856-1900.* New York: Basic Books, 1953. Though scholars have discovered faults of fact and interpretation in Jones's work, it still contains much useful information about the Breuer-Freud collaboration.

Sulloway, Frank J. *Freud, Biologist of the Mind: Beyond the Psychoanalytic Legend.* New York: Basic Books, 1979. This intellectual biography by a historian of science reassesses Freud's life and work, including Freud's relationship with Breuer.

Robert J. Paradowski

SEE ALSO: Freud, Sigmund; Hypnosis; Psychotherapy: Historical approaches.

Brief therapy

TYPE OF PSYCHOLOGY: Psychotherapy
FIELDS OF STUDY: Behavioral therapies; cognitive therapies; psychodynamic therapies

Brief therapy is a time-limited treatment that encourages change in the way a person behaves and thinks. This form of psychotherapy improves a person's coping skills and can improve self-esteem. Brief therapy is designed for those who are already functioning fairly well occupationally and have some positive relationships. The person needs a good motivation level for successful brief therapy.

KEY CONCEPTS
- brief focal psychotherapy
- forced choice questions
- short-term psychotherapy
- time-limited psychotherapy
- trial interpretations

INTRODUCTION

Brief therapy is a fairly recent trend in the practice of psychotherapy that uses short-term treatment methods as a way to help people handle current life problems and crises. The distinctive features of brief therapy include a focus on specific problems and topics and a time limit. During brief therapy, the therapist takes an active role in directing the participant to specific issues and limiting the exploration of other aspects of the person's life. This approach contrasts with traditional open-ended therapy, which seeks to explore numerous topics when they are uncovered during psychotherapy.

Although brief therapy is time-limited, there is no consensus concerning the exact number of therapy sessions for this form of treatment. It may last from one session to a maximum of twenty-five meetings with a therapist. Brief therapy is also known as time-limited psychotherapy or short-term psychotherapy. Consensus is also lacking for identifying the type of person who benefits most from this form of therapy. Sometimes focusing on a particular problem may bring forth additional problems that cannot be addressed in the time-limited format.

Because of the time-limited nature of brief therapy, the costs associated with psychotherapy are less than with traditional forms. Brief therapy has become popular with managed care organizations, as it helps to contain treatment costs.

HISTORICAL TRENDS

The foundations for brief therapy were laid by Franz Alexander and Thomas French in 1946, when they identified the critical elements for a time-limited form of psychotherapy. They suggested that new ways of thinking, acting, and feeling could be promoted in individuals through the establishment of a corrective emotional experience during treatment. If individuals were selected who had a high motivation for change and worked effectively with a therapist, they could achieve change in a short time.

In the 1950's, Daniel Malan, working in London, developed brief focal psychotherapy as a time-limited treatment. In this type of therapy, the patient and therapist formulate a focus for the treatment and set a termination date before the therapy begins. The average number of sessions for this treatment is twenty meetings. In order to be selected for this therapy, a person must be able to think in feeling terms, have a high motivation level, and respond to the trial interpretations from the therapist. Trial interpretations are explanations provided by the therapist about why a person is behaving in a certain manner.

Also developed in the 1950's was short-term anxiety-provoking psychotherapy. Peter Sifneos identified individuals who could select a specific problem in their lives and have the motivation to solve the problem in therapy. For those persons, Sifneos confronted the problem using forced-choice questions. This type of question does not permit a person to avoid problems or ideas that may be upsetting. The focus of this form of brief therapy is on anything related to the identified problem that provokes worry and anxiety.

James Mann produced time-limited psychotherapy in the 1970's from his work at Boston University. Mann selected individuals for this treatment who had an easily identifiable central conflict in their lives. He limited treatment to only twelve sessions. The conflicts usually relate to problems with maturation and psychological development. For example, a young man may be having difficulty moving away from his parents and be afraid of living alone. This conflict of independence versus dependence would become the central focus of the time-limited psychotherapy. The treatment would then focus on possible solutions to this conflict.

CURRENT ISSUES

One of the major similarities between all brief therapies is the importance of the therapist's behavior during the sessions. In brief therapy, the therapist is very active in the process of focusing on specific problems and confronting the patient to solve his or her problem. Since the therapist is very direct with the patient, there is a dynamic interaction between them designed to obtain solutions in the least amount of time. Today, brief therapy utilizes many cognitive and behavioral techniques to facilitate the changes sought from the person seeking treatment. Cognitive techniques focus on modifying how a person thinks about the surrounding environment. Behavioral techniques attempt to reinforce desired behaviors and remove actions that are causing problems in a person's life. Specific exercises are performed to solve problems and to improve interpersonal skills. Research investigations of brief therapy have shown that it is effective for a specific range of mental health problems. However, controversy has emerged over the extensive use of brief therapy.

Brief therapy has been found to be the treatment of choice for managed care organizations, which often discourage long-term treatments. Outpatient psychotherapy is usually approved for six to eight sessions of brief therapy. Critics charge that the mental health profession is being driven by economic considerations rather than the needs of its patients. The development of brief therapy and the support that it is receiving from managed care organizations have created a conflict among those providing psychotherapy that may take years to resolve.

SOURCES FOR FURTHER STUDY

Engler, J., and D. Goleman. *The Consumer's Guide to Psychotherapy.* New York: Fireside, 1992. The authors provide a classic description of the various forms of psychotherapy and show how a person can choose a treatment best suited for his or her needs.

Horowitz, M. *Personality Styles and Brief Psychotherapy.* New York: Basic Books, 1997. A good book that provides details on the effectiveness of brief therapy for persons with different personality characteristics. The reader would need to understand some basic concepts of personality development.

Lazarus, A. *Brief but Comprehensive Psychotherapy*. New York: Springer, 1997. The author makes the case that long-term psychotherapy will soon be available only to the wealthy. If people are not able to pay directly for psychotherapy, they will receive only short-term treatment. The author provides a good resource for a debate on the positives and negatives of brief therapy.

MacKenzie, K. "Principles of Brief Intensive Psychotherapy." *Psychiatric Annals* 2 (1991): 123-155. A good review of how brief therapy takes place. The author describes the conditions that are needed for brief therapy to be effective. The article provides the specific information on the process of treatment.

Piper, W., and A. Joyce. "A Consideration of Factors Influencing the Utilization of Time-Limited Short Term Group Therapy." *International Journal of Group Psychotherapy* 46 (1996): 331-332. Brief therapy techniques have been adapted for group psychotherapy. This article comments on the usefulness of this practice.

Frank J. Prerost

SEE ALSO: Behavior therapy; Behavioral family therapy; Cognitive behavior therapy; Cognitive therapy; Couples therapy; Drug therapies; Gestalt therapy; Group therapy; Music, dance, and theater therapy; Observational learning and modeling therapies; Person-centered therapy; Play therapy; Psychotherapy: Children; Psychotherapy: Effectiveness; Psychotherapy: Goals and techniques; Psychotherapy: Historical approaches; Rational-emotive therapy; Reality therapy; Shock therapy.

Bystander intervention

TYPE OF PSYCHOLOGY: Social psychology
FIELDS OF STUDY: Group processes; prosocial behavior

The study of the psychology of bystander intervention has led to an understanding of the processes that often prevent witnesses to an incident from offering needed assistance, even if an emergency is involved; such events may have tragic consequences, and knowledge of the dynamics of these situations may sometimes keep them from occurring.

KEY CONCEPTS
- audience inhibition
- bystander effect
- confederate
- diffusion of responsibility
- social influence

INTRODUCTION

In early 1964, Kitty Genovese was stabbed to death in front of her New York City apartment building as she returned from work around 3:30 A.M. The assault was particularly brutal, actually consisting of three separate attacks stretching over a period of more than half an hour. Perhaps most shocking about this tragedy, however, was a troubling fact that emerged in the police department's subsequent investigation: Thirty-eight of the woman's neighbors had witnessed the incident without intervening. No one had even called the police during the episode.

This case was only one of several similar occurrences that took place in the mid-1960's, attracting considerable attention and prompting much commentary. The remarks of newspaper columnists, magazine writers, and the like focused on such notions as "alienation," "apathy," "indifference," and "lack of concern for our fellow humans." Bibb Latan and John Darley, social psychologists who at the time were professors at universities in New York City, reasoned that ascribing such personality characteristics to bystanders who fail to help is not the key to understanding how onlookers can remain inactive while another individual is victimized. Rather, one must look to the situation itself to uncover the powerful social forces that inhibit helping.

Latan and Darley thus embarked on a program of research that culminated in their classic 1970 book *The Unresponsive Bystander: Why Doesn't He Help?* They began their analysis of the "bystander effect" by recognizing several good reasons that one should not necessarily expect bystanders to offer help in an emergency. For example, most people are not prepared to deal with emergencies, which tend to happen quickly and without warning. In addition, direct intervention may involve real physical danger, as in the Genovese incident. Finally, becoming involved in such situations may lead to court appearances or other legal consequences.

Latan and Darley also proposed a model describing a sequence of cognitive events that must occur before a bystander will offer assistance in an emergency. First, a bystander must notice the event. Second, he or she must interpret that event as an emergency. Third, the bystander must decide that it is his or her responsibility to do something. At this point, two steps in the process still remain: The bystander must decide exactly what to do, and then he or she must successfully implement that decision. It is important to recognize that a negative outcome at any of these steps in the decision-making process will prevent helping. In light of this cognitive process and the other reasons that people fail to intervene in emergencies, it is perhaps surprising, Latan and Darley suggested, that bystanders ever help.

FACTORS THAT PREVENT ASSISTANCE

Remarkably (and ironically), one situational factor is primarily responsible for the social inhibition of helping: the presence of other people. Latan and Darley proposed three social psychological processes to explain precisely how the presence of others inhibits helping. Each operates within the decision-making framework described earlier, and all three appear to be necessary to account completely for the bystander effect.

The first of these processes is audience inhibition, which refers to people's general reluctance to do things in front of others. When people are aware that their behavior is on public display and are concerned about what other people think, they may be hesitant to offer help for fear of appearing incompetent. Furthermore, a bystander who decides to offer help will be embarrassed if it turns out that he or she has misinterpreted the situation when it is not really an emergency. For example, how might a person feel if he or she stepped out of the crowd to administer CPR to a man lying unconscious on the ground, only to roll him over and realize that he is merely intoxicated? Risks of this sort are greater when larger numbers of other people are present.

The second process, social influence, frequently contributes to the social inhibition of helping by leading bystanders to misinterpret the event. Emergencies are often ambiguous, and a person confronted with ambiguity will look to the behavior of other people for clues about how to behave. While the person is attempting to appraise the reactions of other people, he or she will probably attempt to remain calm. That person, then, is likely to see a group of others doing exactly the same: appearing calm and doing nothing while trying to figure out

whether a true emergency is taking place. Each person will be fooled by the inaction of everyone else into thinking that the situation is less serious than it really is and that not intervening is the appropriate course of action. The ultimate result is a sort of group behavioral paralysis, and the victim goes without help.

The final process, the most powerful of the three, was probably the main force at work in the Genovese incident (social influence was probably not involved, since witnesses remained isolated from one another in their own apartments). This phenomenon, known as diffusion of responsibility, occurs when an individual knows that others are available to help. While a lone bystander at an emergency bears the total responsibility for helping, those in a group share the responsibility equally with the others present. Thus, the larger the number of other witnesses, the smaller is each individual's obligation to act. As a result, individuals in groups are likely to assume that someone else will intervene.

SOCIAL PSYCHOLOGICAL RESEARCH

Latan and Darley tested their ideas in a number of ingenious experiments, several of which are considered classic examples of social psychological research. In one of these, Columbia University students arrived individually at a laboratory to take part in a study that they believed would involve an interview. Each subject was sent to a waiting room to complete a preliminary questionnaire. Some of them found two other people already seated in the room, while others sat down alone.

Soon after the subject began working on the questionnaire, smoke began filling the room through a wall vent. The smoke could hardly be ignored; within four minutes the room contained enough smoke to interfere with vision and breathing. Latan and Darley were primarily interested in how frequently subjects simply got up and left the room to report the emergency. Most (75 percent) of the subjects who were waiting alone reported the smoke, but those in groups were far less likely to do so. Groups consisting of three naïve (never tested) subjects reported it only 38 percent of the time; when the subject waited (unknowingly) with two confederates who were instructed to do nothing, only 10 percent responded. In a social psychological experiment, a confederate is a person instructed to behave in a certain way.

Observations of the unresponsive subjects supported the researchers' notion that the social influence process in groups would inhibit helping by leading people to misinterpret the situation. Interviews with these participants revealed that they had produced a variety of explanations for the smoke: air conditioning vapor, steam, smog, and even "truth gas." In other words, lone subjects for the most part behaved responsibly, but those in groups were generally led by the inaction of others to conclude almost anything but the obvious—that a legitimate emergency was taking place. It is important to realize that social influence, as demonstrated in this experiment, is most potent when bystanders in groups do not communicate with one another; such was the case in this experiment, and such tends to be the case with analogous groups in real life. Simply talking to the others present can clarify what really is happening, thus eliminating the bystander effect.

DIFFUSION-OF-RESPONSIBILITY RESEARCH

A second classic study demonstrates the power of the diffusion-of-responsibility process. In this experiment, college students thought they were participating in a group discussion about the difficulties of adjusting to college. In order to reduce the discomfort that could be associated with discussing personal matters, each subject was ushered to a private cubicle from which he or she would communicate with other group members through an intercom system. In each case, however, there was only one actual subject; the other "group members" had been previously tape recorded. Thus, Latan and Darley were able to manipulate the size of the group as perceived by the subject.

Each "member" of the group talked for two minutes, with the actual subject speaking last. A second round then began, and the first "group member" to speak began suffering a frighteningly severe epileptic seizure, choking and pleading for help. Since the subject had no idea where the other "group members" were located, the only available course of helping action was to leave the cubicle and report the emergency to the person in charge.

On the basis of the diffusion-of-responsibility concept, Latan and Darley expected that the likelihood of helping would decrease as the perceived size of the group increased. When the subject was part of a two-person group (only the subject and the victim, thus making the subject the only person available to help), 85 percent of the participants reported the seizure. When the subject believed that he or she was in a group of three, 62 percent responded. Only 31 percent of those who thought they were in a six-person group offered help. Without question, the responsibility for acting in this emergency was perceived to be divided among everyone believed to be available to help.

The circumstances of this experiment correspond directly to those of the Kitty Genovese murder. Most important, the subjects in this study were not in a face-to-face group, just as the witnesses to the Genovese murder were isolated in their own apartments; consequently, social influence could not lead to a misinterpretation of the event (which was not ambiguous anyway). In short, simply knowing that others are available to respond acts as a powerful deterrent to helping. It is also significant that this experiment demonstrated that bystanders who fail to intervene are usually not the least bit apathetic or indifferent. Rather, the typical unresponsive subject showed clear signs of distress over the plight of the victim; nevertheless, the belief that others were present still tended to suppress intervention.

Diffusion of responsibility is a very common social force and is not restricted to serious situations. Anyone who has failed to work as hard as possible on a group task, heard a doorbell go unanswered at a party, or experienced a telephone ringing seven or eight times even though the entire family is at home has probably fallen victim to the same process.

POWER OF SITUATIONAL FORCES

The work of Latan and Darley attracted much attention and acclaim. From a methodological standpoint, their experiments are still regarded as some of social psychology's most clever and intriguing. Their findings, however, were even more remarkable: Demonstrating consistently the social inhibition of helping, they destroyed the common belief in "safety in numbers." This research also provides a powerful illustration of one of the major lessons of social psychology—that situational forces affecting behavior can be overpowering, eliminating at least temporarily the influence of personality. The work of Latan and Darley showed convincingly that a person cannot rely on human nature, kindness, or any other dispositional quality if he or she should become the victim of an emergency.

This program of research also provided the impetus for much work on helping that has been conducted by other investigators. Various kinds of precipitating incidents were examined, as were differences between experiments conducted in laboratories and those performed in natural settings. Other studies investigated the effects of a wide range of different characteristics of the subjects, victims, and other bystanders involved. It was discovered, for example, that people are more likely to offer assistance when someone else has already modeled helping behavior and if the victim is particularly needy, deserving, or somehow similar to the helper; certain transitory mood states, such as happiness and guilt, were also found to increase helping.

Despite the large assortment of factors investigated, many of these other studies included a manipulation of the variable that had been the principal concern of Latan and Darley: group size. Two major articles published by Latan and his colleagues in 1981 reviewed nearly one hundred different instances of research comparing helping by individuals in groups with that by lone bystanders. They found, almost without exception in these studies, that people were less likely to help in groups than when they were alone, suggesting that the bystander effect is perhaps as consistent and predictable as any within the domain of social psychology.

Although incidents such as the murder of Kitty Genovese do not occur every day, it is important to recognize that scores of them have been reported over the years, and they continue to occur regularly. Unfortunately, the understanding provided by the research has not led to strategies for avoiding these tragedies. (Considering the ability of situational forces to override personality influences, one should not be too surprised by this.) There is, however, one bit of hope: At least one study has demonstrated that students who have learned about the bystander effect in a psychology class are more likely to intervene in an emergency than those who have not been exposed to that material.

SOURCES FOR FURTHER STUDY

Batson, C. D. "Prosocial Motivation: Is It Ever Truly Altruistic?" In *Advances in Experimental Social Psychology*, edited by Leonard Berkowitz. San Diego, Calif.: Academic Press, 1987. A very thorough examination of what happens psychologically within the person who helps, with a special focus on the role of empathy in determining the helping response. This chapter is somewhat high-level, but it does convey the flavor of this area of research.

Cialdini, Robert B. *Influence: Science and Practice.* 4th ed. Boston: Allyn & Bacon, 2000. An extremely interesting book dealing generally with the issue of social influence. Contains an excellent chapter analyzing the bystander effect, with emphasis on the role of other people in helping to define a social situation. Cialdini presents some provocative examples and offers advice about how to prevent oneself from becoming a victim.

Latan, Bibb, and John M. Darley. *The Unresponsive Bystander: Why Doesn't He Help?* New York: Appleton-Century-Crofts, 1970. The classic source on bystander intervention in emergencies, detailing all of Latan and Darley's original research on the problem. The clever methodology of many of their experiments and their engaging writing style make this a fascinating and readable book.

Latan, Bibb, S. A. Nida, and D. W. Wilson. "The Effects of Group Size on Helping Behavior." In *Altruism and Helping Behavior: Social, Personality, and Developmental Perspectives*, edited by J. Phillipe Rushton and Richard M. Sorrentino. Hillsdale, N.J.: Lawrence Erlbaum, 1981. Reviews the research on the relationship between group size and helping, including a discussion of the methodological problems involved. Contains not only a good summary of Latan and Darley's original theoretical ideas but also some subsequent developments, such as Latan's general model of group behavior known as social impact theory.

Macaulay, Jaqueline, and Leonard Berkowitz, eds. *Altruism and Helping Behavior: Social Psychological Studies of Some Antecedents and Consequences.* New York: Academic Press, 1970. A classic volume reporting much of the earliest work on the social psychology of helping. Not all the chapters deal directly with bystander intervention, but the book does contain two separate chapters by Bibb Latan and John M. Darley that provide excellent summaries of much of their original work.

Rushton, J. Phillipe, and Richard M. Sorrentino, eds. *Altruism and Helping Behavior: Social, Personality, and Developmental Perspectives.* Hillsdale, N.J.: Lawrence Erlbaum, 1981. Presents a range of articles reflecting the different directions established in the study of helping behavior following the initial exploration of bystander intervention in emergencies. Some of the chapters deal not with bystander intervention per se but with helping or altruism in the broader sense (such as how altruism is learned).

Staub, Ervin. "Helping a Distressed Person: Social, Personality, and Stimulus Determinants." In *Advances in Experimental Social Psychology*, edited by Leonard Berkowitz. New York: Academic Press, 1974. Another important and frequently cited chapter from an earlier point in the history of research in this area. Although social psychologists rarely take issue with Bibb Latan and John M. Darley's analysis of bystander intervention, Staub offers a somewhat different perspective, placing more emphasis on personality influences. He also presents some interesting research with children.

Steve A. Nida

SEE ALSO: Altruism, cooperation, and empathy; Attitude-behavior consistency; Crowd behavior; Group decision making; Groups; Helping.

C

California Psychological Inventory (CPI)

DATE: First published in 1957
TYPE OF PSYCHOLOGY: Personality assessment
FIELDS OF STUDY: Personality

The California Psychological Inventory is a paper-and-pencil personality test used to assess normal people in terms of a wide range of personality characteristics. Although the test has been criticized for overlap among subscales and cultural bias, it is considered among the best validated and most useful of such tests.

KEY CONCEPTS
- empirical criterion keying
- externality-internality
- folk concepts
- norm favoring versus norm questioning
- norm group
- realization
- structural scales

INTRODUCTION

The California Psychological Inventory (CPI) is a paper-and-pencil test designed for a comprehensive analysis of traits that describe a normal adult personality. The test itself consists of 462 statements about feelings and opinions, ethical and social attitudes, personal relationships, and characteristic behavior. The testee responds to each item as "true" or "false." Responses to these statements are analyzed, first of all, according to how well they fit twenty different patterns, each of which correspond to a specified personality characteristic. The personality characteristics that are assessed include such everyday traits as sociability, dominance, independence, responsibility, self-control, tolerance, and achievement. The individual test-taker's scores on each scale are evaluated by how these scores com-

pare with the range of scores established by a nationwide comparison group or norm group. Such comparisons also permit evaluating the test-taker on three structural scales that summarize patterns underlying the twenty primary scales at a more abstract and basic level: externality-internality (self-confident assertive extraversion versus introversion), norm-favoring versus norm-questioning (allegiance to the conventional social rules versus its lack), and the degree of one's "realization" of these tendencies, an index of self-fulfillment or satisfaction.

DEVELOPMENT

Harrison Gough, the author of the CPI, began assembling items relevant to the measurement of everyday personality characteristics in the late 1940's. It was 1957, however, before the completed eighteen scales of the CPI were published by Consulting Psychologist Press. In 1987, modest revisions in the scale were initiated. At this time, a few items were modified to reflect cultural changes, and two new primary scales, independence and empathy, were added to the original eighteen. The most important change, however, was the addition of the three summary, structural scales.

Two important principles governed the CPI's development. The first of these was Gough's interest in measuring "folk concepts," characteristics which in many cultures and over centuries made sense to ordinary people. This principle was in contrast to many existing tests that assessed concepts based upon psychiatric diagnosis or academic personality theories or were abstracted from a mathematical procedure called factor analysis.

A second guiding principle was that of empirical criterion keying, which means that the validity of items upon scales, as well as the scales themselves, should be established by actual research. In such research, items and scales are tested to assure that people who are show evident differences in real-life functioning answer the item or the scale in the different ways one would expect. For example, the socialization scale was conceived to measure moral uprightness in the sense of observing society's rules and customs. One would expect that convicted felons would answer questions on this scale in ways different from Eagle Scouts, and felons would be expected to score much lower on this scale. Research verifying this difference supported the validity of the item and the scale. Hundreds of such predictions derived from the meaning of various CPI scales were tested. Only thereafter was the test considered valid.

EVALUATION

A major criticism of the CPI is that there is much overlap between highly similar scales. Dominance and capacity for status, for example, seem to involve only slightly nuanced measurements of almost the same thing. It has been argued, therefore, that the essential information could be gleaned from fewer, simpler scales. Gough answered this criticism by pointing out that everyday descriptions of others by ordinary folk also show this sort of overlap. He also pointed out that the structural scales, added in 1987, permit such simple, efficient description of a personality without depriving the test-taker of the refined and detailed analysis offered by assessing twenty primary traits.

It has also been charged that the CPI is often employed beyond the uses for which its validity has been established. Clinicians are prone to apply the test to abnormal populations for which validity data is incomplete. The test has also been frequently used for people from cultures outside the United States and for minorities within the United States. While Gough selected his "folk concepts" for their apparent cross-cultural relevance, validity studies in minority and Third World subcultures have been neglected. Interpreting the test results of those from different cultural backgrounds must, therefore, be done with caution.

These admitted limitations could be addressed by adding more studies of minority or clinical populations to the already impressive research with this instrument. For over a half century, the CPI has served such purposes as predicting vocational choice, academic success, and antisocial behavior. Few other personality tests have been as thoroughly validated. Its many scales permit a detailed description of a person in language that makes sense. Useful and much used, the CPI remains one of the very best personality tests for normal populations.

SOURCES FOR FURTHER STUDY

Anastasi, Anne, and Susana Urbina. *Psychological Testing*. Upper Saddle, N.J.: Prentice Hall, 1997. Chapters on personality inventories in general texts are useful in putting the CPI in a comparative context. The text is especially thorough.

Bolton, B. "Review of the California Psychological Inventory, Revised Edition." In *Eleventh Mental Measurements Yearbook*, edited by J. J. Framer and J. C. Conly. Lincoln, Neb.: Buros Institute of Mental Measurements, 1992. This influential and objective review awards many accolades. Comments such as "more reliable than the manual advertises" and "with outstanding interpretative information" are typical.

Gough, H. G. "The California Psychological Inventory." In *Testing in Counseling Practice*, edited by C. E. Walker and V. L. Campbell. Hillsdale, N.J.: Lawrence Erlbaum, 1992. An excellent account by the test's author of the application of the CPI to counseling.

Gough, H. G., and P. Bradley. "Delinquent and Criminal Behavior as Assessed by the Revised California Psychological Inventory." *Journal of Clinical Psychology* 48 (1992): 298-308. An example of a validity study that supports the usefulness of the test in discriminating between felonious and normal populations.

Groth-Marnat, Gary. *Handbook of Psychological Assessment*. 3d ed. New York: John Wiley & Sons, 1997. Chapter 8 thoroughly covers the CPI, including its development, validation, interpretation, and uses.

Megargee, E. I. *The California Psychological Inventory Handbook*. San Francisco: Jossey-Bass, 1972. Summarizes the wealth of research validating each of the eighteen scales of the original CPI.

Thomas E. DeWolfe

SEE ALSO: Beck Depression Inventory (BDI); Children's Depression Inventory (CDI); Clinical interviewing, testing, and observation; Depression; Diagnosis; *Diagnostic and Statistical Manual of Mental Disorders* (DSM); Minnesota Multiphasic Personality Inventory (MMPI); Personality: Psychophysiological measures; Personality interviewing strategies; Personality rating scales; State-Trait Anxiety Inventory; Thematic Apperception Test (TAT).

Cannon, Walter B.

BORN: October 19, 1871, in Prairie du Chien, Wisconsin
DIED: October 1, 1945, in Franklin, New Hampshire
IDENTITY: American physiologist
TYPE OF PSYCHOLOGY: Biological basis of behavior
FIELDS OF STUDY: Experimental methodologies

Cannon was an American physiologist, known for a series of experimental investigations into the process of digestion, the nervous system, and the body's self-regulating mechanisms.

Walter Bradford Cannon was born in Prairie du Chien, Wisconsin, in 1871. He earned his bachelor's, master's, and medical degrees from Harvard University, where he became a professor of physiology. Cannon served as chair of Harvard's physiology department from 1906 to 1942.

Cannon began his investigations in 1896, one year after German physicist Wilhelm Conrad Roentgen discovered X rays. Cannon used X rays to observe the process of digestion in laboratory animals. Using an instrument called a fluoroscope, he watched the progress of food and waste through the body. During these experiments, he noticed that when an animal was under stress, its digestive processes halted. This led him to wonder about the body's response to danger, fear, and trauma.

Using mainly surgical and chemical means, Cannon investigated the response of the heart, the sympathetic nervous system, and the adrenal gland to unnatural circumstances. He also studied the body's self-regulating mechanisms, and especially the work of nineteenth century French physiologist Claude Bernard, who investigated carbohydrate metabolism in humans as well as the function of the autonomic nervous system. The basis of health, according to Bernard, is the organism's success in maintaining a dynamic internal equilibrium. Cannon named this dynamic state "homeostasis" and showed that the body could adjust to meet serious external danger through such processes of the human body as internal regulation of body heat and alkalinity of the blood and preparation of the body for defense by the secretion of epinephrine (also called adrenaline) in the adrenal gland.

Beginning in 1931, Cannon suffered from cancer associated with the X-ray exposures that he underwent early in his career. He remained active in national scientific circles, however, overseeing the organization of research for the effective treatment of shock and blood loss during World War II. He died in 1945.

SOURCES FOR FURTHER STUDY

Benison, Saul, Elin L. Wolfe, and A. Clifford Barger. *Walter B. Cannon: The Life and Times of a Young Scientist.* Harvard University Press, 1987. The first volume of a biography of Cannon, covering his childhood, training, and early years as a scientist.
Wolfe, Elin L., Saul Benison, and A. Clifford Barger. *Walter B. Cannon: Science and Society.* Cambridge, Mass.: Harvard University Press, 2000. The second volume of Cannon's biography, taking up the story from World War I through the end of his life.

Mary E. Carey

SEE ALSO: Adrenal gland; Animal experimentation; Fight-or-flight response; General adaptation syndrome; Stress: Physiological responses; Stress-related diseases.

Career and personnel testing

TYPE OF PSYCHOLOGY: Personality
FIELDS OF STUDY: Ability tests; intelligence assessment; personality assessment

The popularity of career and personnel testing reflects the trend toward the utilization of interest surveys, ability and aptitude tests, and personality tests for the systematic development of personal careers.

KEY CONCEPTS
- achievement tests
- aptitude tests
- intelligence tests
- interest inventories
- personality tests
- value tests

INTRODUCTION

Psychologists have developed more than thirty-five hundred testing devices for assessing human capabilities. The groups of tests that have been utilized most frequently for career and personnel purposes have been those measuring interests, abilities and aptitudes, personality, and values.

Inventories that survey interest patterns are useful in providing indications of the areas in which individuals might work. Research by psychologist E. K. Strong, Jr., has shown that people in the same line of work also tend to have similar hobbies, like the same types of books and magazines, and prefer the same types of entertainment.

Psychological research by John L. Holland concluded that most occupations can be grouped into six vocational themes reflecting certain employment preferences: "realistic," favoring technical and outdoor activities such as mechanical, agricultural, and nature jobs; "investigative," interested in the natural sciences, medicine, and the process of investigation; "artistic," favoring self-expression and dramatics such as the musical, literary, and graphic art occupations; "social," reflecting an interest in helping others, as in teaching and social service; "enterprising," interested in persuasion and political power, as in management, sales, politics, and other areas of leadership; and "conventional," including enjoyment of procedures and organization such as office practices, clerical, and quantitative interest areas.

Tests that measure ability include intelligence tests, achievement tests, and aptitude tests. Intelligence tests purport to measure objectively a person's potential to learn, independent of prior learning experiences. Attempting such objective measurement is a highly complex task; whether it can truly be achieved is open to debate. The very concept of "intelligence," in fact, has been controversial from its inception. The two most highly developed tests of individual intelligence are the fourth revision of the Stanford-Binet (1984), a scale originally developed in 1916, and the Wechsler Adult Intelligence Scale-Revised (1981), a version of a scale originally developed in 1939.

Achievement tests are designed to measure how much a person has learned of specific material to which he or she has been previously exposed. Aptitude tests measure a personal ability or quality (such as musical or mechanical aptitude) in order to pre-dict some future performance. For example, the military would like to be able to predict the likelihood that a given candidate for pilot training will successfully complete the complicated and expensive course of training. Flying a plane requires good physical coordination and a good sense of mechanical matters, among other things. Therefore, candidates for flight training are given a battery of aptitude tests, which include tests of mechanical aptitude and eye-hand coordination, in order to estimate later performance in flight training. People who score poorly on such aptitude tests tend to fail pilot training.

Psychologists recognize that it is important to understand a person's interests and abilities—and personality tendencies—if a thorough appraisal of career potentials is to be made. Personality tests measure dispositions, traits, or tendencies to behave in a typical manner. Personality tests are described as either objective (a structured test) or subjective (a projective personality test). Objective tests are structured by providing a statement and then requiring two or more alternative responses, such as in true-or-false questions in the Woodworth Personal Data Sheet). In contrast, projective personality tests ask open-ended questions or provide ambiguous stimuli that require spontaneous responses (as in the Rorschach inkblot test). The two types of personality test evoke different information about the respondent.

The development of objective personality tests was greatly improved when studies showed that personality tests did not have to rely completely upon face validity, or the apparent accuracy of each test question. Through empirical research, the accuracy of a question can be tied to the likelihood of a question being associated with certain behavior. Consequently, it does not matter whether a person answers the question "I am not aggressive" as either "true" or "false." What does matter is whether that question is accurately associated with aggressive or nonaggressive behavior for a significant number of people who answer it in a particular way. This approach is referred to as criterion keying: The items in a test are accurately associated with certain types of behavior regardless of the face validity of each question.

Beginning with Gordon Allport's Study of Values, psychologists have recognized that personal values affect individual career choices. Allport found six general values that are important to most individuals: theoretical, economic, aesthetic, social, political, and religious. Occupational values represent a grouping of needs, just as abilities represent a grouping of work skills. Renee Dawis and Lloyd Lofquist found that there are six occupational values: achievement, comfort, status, altruism, safety, and autonomy.

TESTING IN PRACTICE

In order for people to enter careers that will be satisfactory for them, it is desirable to make an effort to match their personal interests with the day-to-day activities of the careers they will eventually choose. Interest inventories are one method of helping people make career choices that compare their interest patterns with the activities of persons in the occupation they hope to enter.

The Strong Vocational Interest Blank (SVIB) was developed by E. K. Strong, Jr. It matches the interests of a person to the interests and values of a criterion group of employed people who were happy in the careers they have chosen. This procedure is an example of criterion keying. Strong revised the SVIB in 1966, using 399 items to relate to fifty-four occupations for men and a separate form for thirty-two occupations for women. The reliability of this test to measure interests is quite good, and validity studies indicate that the SVIB is effective in predicting job satisfaction.

The Strong-Campbell Interest Inventory (SCII) was developed by psychologist D. T. Campbell as a revision of the SVIB. In this test, items from the men's and women's forms were merged into a single scale, reducing the likelihood of sex bias, a complaint made about the SVIB. Campbell developed a theoretical explanation of why certain types of people like working in certain fields; he based it on Holland's theory of vocational choice. Holland postulated that interests are an expression of personality and that people can be classified into one or more of six categories according to their interests and personality. Campbell concluded that the six personality factors in Holland's theory were quite similar to the patterns of interest that had emerged from many years of research on the SVIB. Therefore, Holland's theory became incorporated into the SCII. The SCII places individuals into one of the six Holland categories, or groupings of occupations, with each group represented by a national sample. There are now dozens of occupational

scales with both male and female normative comparisons.

The Kuder Occupational Interest Survey (KOIS) was first developed in 1939. This survey also examines the similarity between the respondent's interests and the interests of people employed in different occupations. It can provide direction in the selection of a college major. Studies on the predictive validity of the KOIS indicate that about half of a selected group of adults who had been given an early version of the inventory when they were in high school were working in fields that the inventory suggested they enter. The continuing development of this measure suggests that it may be quite useful for guidance decisions for high school and college students.

The Self-Directed Search (SDS) was developed by Holland as means of matching the interests and abilities of individuals with occupations that have the same characteristics. Holland uses a typology that groups occupations in the categories of realistic, investigative, artistic, social, enterprising, and conventional. There are three forms of the SDS: Form E is designed for use with middle-school students or older individuals with limited reading ability; Form R is for use with high school students, college students, or adults; and Form CP is designed for use with college students and adults. The test is also available in other languages, such as Spanish.

Several ability and aptitude tests have been used in making decisions concerning employment, placement, and promotion. The Wonderlic Personnel Test (WPT) was based on the Otis Self-Administering Tests of Mental Ability. The WPT is a quick (twelve-minute) test of mental ability in adults. Normative data are available for more than fifty thousand adults between twenty and seventy-five years of age. The Revised Minnesota Paper Form Board Tests (RMPFBT) is a revision of a study in the measurement of mechanical ability. The RMPFBT is a twenty-minute speed test consisting of sixty-four two-dimensional diagrams cut into separate parts. The test seems to measure those aspects of mechanical ability requiring the capacity to visualize and manipulate objects in space. It appears to be related to general intelligence.

The U.S. Department of Labor developed an instrument to measure abilities entitled the General Aptitude Test Battery (GATB). The GATB measures nine specific abilities: general learning, verbal ability, numerical ability, spatial ability, eye-hand coordination, finger dexterity, and manual dexterity. Another ability test that was developed by the U.S. government is the Armed Services Vocational Aptitude Battery (ASVAB). The ASVAB is used by the Department of Defense to assist individuals in identifying occupations that match their personal characteristics. The occupations are grouped into the six categories espoused by Holland.

Personality tests were developed in an effort to gain greater understanding about how an individual is likely to behave. As tests have been improved, specific traits and characteristics have been associated with career development, such as leadership propensities or control of impulses. Several personality tests have been used in career and personality development. The Minnesota Multiphasic Personality Inventory II (MMPI-2) is the 1989 version of a scale developed in 1943 by S. R. Hathaway and J. C. McKinley. The test was designed to distinguish normal from abnormal behavior. It was derived from a pool of one thousand items selected from a wide variety of sources. It remains the premier objective personality test. The California Psychological Inventory (CPI) was developed by Harrison Gough in 1957 and was revised in 1987. Although about one third of the 462 items on the CPI are identical to items on the MMPI, it is regarded as a good measure for assessing normal individuals for interpersonal effectiveness and internal controls.

The 16 Personality Factor Questionnaire (16PF) was developed by Raymond Cattell in 1949 and was revised in 1970. Considerable effort has been expended to provide a psychometrically sound instrument to measure personality, and it remains an exemplary illustration of the factor-analytic approach to measuring personality traits. The Personality Research Form (PRF) was developed by Douglas Jackson in 1967. It was based on Henry Murray's theory of needs. The PRF includes two validity scales and twenty multidimensional scales of personality traits. It has been favorably reviewed for its psychometric rigor and is useful in relating personality tendencies to strengths and weaknesses in working within a corporate or employment setting.

Tests to measure occupational values include the Minnesota Importance Questionnaire (MIQ) by David Weiss, Renee Dawis, and Lloyd Lofquist and the Values Scale (VS) by Doris Nevill and Donald Super. The MIQ compares individual needs with reinforc-

ers found in occupations. The VS measures work values that are commonly sought by workers, such as personal development and achievement. The values in the test are also cross-referenced with the occupational groups found in Holland's typology.

An alternative to paper-and-pen tests is the use of computerized career guidance systems. These systems include computer software systems such as SIGI PLUS and DISCOVER and online programs such as Bridges. The common elements of these systems include the utilization of an assessment instrument, the provision of an individualized detailed occupational profile, and instructions on how to use the information in career planning.

FUNCTIONS OF TESTING

These instruments are examples of tests that are frequently used for career and personnel assessment. The range of psychological assessment procedures includes not only standardized ability tests, interest surveys, personality inventories and projective instruments, and diagnostic and evaluative devices but also performance tests, biographical data forms, scored application blanks, interviews, experience requirement summaries, appraisals of job performance, and estimates of advancement potential. All these devices are used, and they are explicitly intended to aid employers who make hiring decisions in order to choose, select, develop, evaluate, and promote personnel. Donald N. Bersoff notes that the critical element in the use of any psychological test for career and employment purposes is that employers must use psychometrically sound and job-relevant selection devices. Such tests must be scientifically reliable (appropriate, meaningful, or useful for the inferences drawn from them) and valid (measuring what they claim to measure).

Each of the test procedures previously described would be used for different purposes. Ability tests can be used to determine whether a person has the potential ability to learn a certain job or specific skills. Ability tests are used for positions that do not have a minimum educational prerequisite (such as high school, college, or professional degree). They are also used to select already employed individuals for challenging new work assignments and for promotion to a more demanding employment level. The United States Supreme Court has held that the appropriate use of "professionally developed ability tests" is an acceptable employment practice; however, the employer must demonstrate a relationship between the relevance of the selection test procedure to job qualification. This requirement is to ensure that the ability test provides a fair basis for selection and is nondiscriminatory. The goal of Title VII of the Civil Rights Act of 1964 was to eliminate discrimination in employment based on race, color, religion, sex, or national origin in all of its forms. The use of a selection procedure or test must meet this standard.

Interest tests have been developed to identify a relationship between the activities a person enjoys and the activities of a certain occupation. For example, a salesperson should enjoy meeting people and persuading others to accept his or her viewpoint. An interest inventory can validly link a person's preferences and interests with associated social activities and can thereby identify sales potential. Interest inventories are frequently given when an employer seeks more information that could lead to a good match between a prospective employee and a job's requirements. Interest inventories typically survey a person's interests in leisure or sports activities, types of friends, school subjects, and preferred reading material.

Personality, or behavior traits, can be identified by test inventories and related to requisite employment activities. Once again, these personality dimensions must be demonstrated to be job-related and must be assessed reliably from a performance appraisal of the specific position to be filled. For example, behavior traits such as "drive" or "dependability" could be validated for use in promoting individuals to supervisory bank teller positions if demonstrated to be job-related and assessed reliably from a performance appraisal.

The use of psychological tests has grown immensely since the mid-twentieth century. Increased public awareness, the proliferation of different tests, and the use of computer technology with tests indicate that continually improving career and personnel tests will emerge. Yet these developments should proceed only if testing can be conducted while protecting the human rights of consumers—including their right not to be tested and their right to know test scores and how test-based decisions will affect their lives. Psychological testing must also be nondiscriminatory and must protect the person's right to privacy. Psychologists are ethically and legally bound to maintain the confidentiality of their clients.

Making a selection among the many published psychological tests is a skill requiring experienced psychologists. In personnel selection, the psychologist must determine if the use of a psychological test will improve the selection process above what is referred to as the base rate, or the probability of an individual succeeding at a job without any selection procedure. Consequently, the use of a test must be based on its contributing something beyond chance alone. This requirement necessitates that a test be reasonably valid and reliable, in that it consistently tests what it was designed to test. Consequently, the use of a test is only justified when it can contribute to the greater likelihood of a successful decision than would be expected by existing base rates.

Existing theories of career selection have related career choices to personal preferences, developmental stages, and the type of relationship a person has had with his or her family during childhood. More extensive research will continue to assess other relationships between one's psychological makeup and successful career selection. This positive beginning should eventually result in more innovative, more objective, and more valid psychological tests that will greatly enhance future career and personnel selection.

SOURCES FOR FURTHER STUDY

American Psychological Association. "Ethical Principles of Psychologists." *American Psychologist* 36 (1981): 633-638. Documents psychologists' ethical responsibilities concerning human rights, particularly pertaining to the right or privacy.

Bersoff, Donald N., Laurel P. Malson, and Donald B. Verrilli. "In the Supreme Court of the United States: *Clara Watson v. Fort Worth Bank and Trust.*" *American Psychologist* 43 (December, 1988): 1019-1028. This brief was submitted to inform the Supreme Court of the state of current scientific thought regarding validation of personnel assessment devices.

Buros Institute of Mental Measurement. *The Fourteenth Mental Measurements Yearbook.* Lincoln: University of Nebraska Press, 1999. This source is one of the most comprehensive reviews of testing materials. It contains information on the reliability and validity of vocational tests.

Campbell, D. T. *Manual for the Strong-Campbell Interest Inventory.* Stanford, Calif.: Stanford University Press, 1977. This manual describes the SCII instrument and its uses. It represents a progression in the use of interest inventories, because it is merged with John L. Holland's vocational themes.

Committee to Develop Standards for Educational and Psychological Testing. *Standards for Educational and Psychological Testing*. Washington, D.C.: American Psychological Association, 1985. This document provides a framework for the evaluation and validation of testing and other assessment devices.

Darley, John M., Samuel Glucksberg, and Ronald A. Kinchia. *Psychology*. 5th ed. Englewood Cliffs, N.J.: Prentice-Hall, 1991. This introductory psychology text discusses the relationship between an aptitude test and the prediction of future performance, providing examples to aid in differentiating aptitude from achievement.

Holland, John L. *Manual for the Self-Directed Search*. Palo Alto, Calif.: Consulting Psychologists Press, 1985. Describes Holland's vocational classification system, including work activities, general training requirements, and occupational rewards. Holland's theory of vocational choice is basic to a number of tests used for career development.

Kapes, Jerome T., Marjorie Moran Mastie, and Edwin A. Whitfeld. *A Counselor's Guide to Career Assessment Instruments*. Alexandria, Va.: National Career Development Association, 1994. This resource contains descriptions of more than fifty tests. In addition to test descriptions, it also provides publisher information, test review, and critiques.

Murphy, L. L, J. C. Imparce, and B. S. Plake. *Tests in Print V*. Lincoln: University of Nebraska Press, 1999. This resource contains information such as publishing sources on a variety of tests. It is periodically updated.

Zunker, Vernon. *Using Assessment Results for Career Development*. Pacific Grove, Calif.: Brooks/Cole, 2001. This book contains explanations of various types of tests such as aptitude and achievement instruments. Specific tests, including computerized systems, are described as well.

Robert A. Hock;
updated by Debra S. Preston

SEE ALSO: Ability tests; Assessment; Career Occupational Preference System (COPS); Creativity: Assessment; General Aptitude Test Battery (GATB); Human resource training and development; Intelligence tests; Interest inventories; Kuder Occupational Interest Survey (KOIS); Scientific methods; Stanford-Binet test; Strong Interest Inventory (SII); Survey research: Questionnaires and interviews; Testing: Historical perspectives; Wechsler Intelligence Scale for Children-Third Edition (WISC-III).

Career Occupational Preference System (COPS)

DATE: The 1960's forward

TYPE OF PSYCHOLOGY: Intelligence and intelligence testing

FIELDS OF STUDY: Ability tests; intelligence assessment

Career interests such as the COPS have been developed to assist people make career planning decisions. COPS purports to assess certain abilities, interests, and other characteristics and matches them with characteristics of jobs, occupations, college majors, and careers. These selections imply that an individual can make better decisions with the help of an interest inventory.

KEY CONCEPTS
• career
• interest inventory
• job choice

INTRODUCTION

The Career Occupational Preference System (COPS), an interest inventory, presents 168 job-related items that can be grouped into fourteen job-determinant scores: science, professional; science, skilled; technology, professional; technology, skilled; consumer economics; outdoor; business, professional; business, skilled; clerical; communication; arts, professional; arts, skilled; service, professional; and service, skilled. The descriptor "professional" can be best characterized as those job choices that require at least four years of college education and lead to a career, as opposed to those that do not.

The person completing the inventory is asked to rate the 168 job-related items as to whether these are things they like very much, like moderately, dislike moderately, or dislike very much. The person completing the inventory would use the scale to answer preferences concerning a number of different job activities.

The COPS was first developed in the late 1960's and has undergone several editions and revisions. Editions in foreign languages are available. While the test is untimed, most individuals who take the test finish in less than one hour. The scores recorded by the COPS can be used to enter most occupational information systems. Both professionals and nonprofessionals can benefit from information received from the COPS. However, like most reference or interest systems, the COPS should be used to guide exploration and not judge respondants. Given the reading level of the inventory and the types of information solicited, it would be appropriate for the COPS to be used in junior high schools, senior high schools, community colleges, and four-year colleges and universities.

TECHNICAL ASPECTS

The COPS has been developed and interpreted through the statistical procedure of multiple-factor analysis. The purpose of this type of analysis is to understand which sets of variables match up or correlate best with one another. For example, are the "professional" and "skilled" items the same or different? If the cluster of items is the same, reporting and interpreting the scores would be influenced one way; however, if the cluster of items is different, reporting and interpreting would be very different. With that in mind, it is possible to suggest that all fourteen clusters present as "different" when using this statistical procedure.

In addition to the statistical procedure of multiple-factor analysis of the variables in the cluster, it is equally important to understand whether the items themselves are relevant to the world of work. Additionally, the specific descriptions used in the clusters should match up, specifically, to the world of work. For example, descriptions of skills used in the clerical cluster should generally deal with clerical duties and specifically detail expected clerical duties. Without this type of matching, much of the usefulness of the COPS would be compromised. The 168 items used in the COPS do match both the general and the specific nature of clusters. This provides further evidence that individual scores do match what might be expected during the accomplishment of the fourteen general clusters.

Of equal importance is whether the COPS can be considered statistically reliable, whether it is internally consistent (demonstrated by concurrent statistical correlation studies) and can be relied upon to give the same results over time (demonstrated by time-sequential statistical correlation studies). If internal consistency cannot be demonstrated, it is difficult to place much confidence in a survey which does not hold together. If the temporal stability does not exist, it is difficult to place much confidence in an instrument that does not give the same results over time.

The COPS does well on both counts of reliability considerations. Reports of internal consistency, parallel forms (different items for the same clusters from completely different, independent tests), and tests given after time periods ranging from one week to one year all point to the usefulness of the COPS. In fact, COPS scores do seem to point to a similarity between attained scores and choices of college major, actual job location, and actual job title.

CRITIQUE

In order for individuals to enter an appropriate career, they must begin to identify specific interests and examine the relative importance of those interests. Some individuals will need little guidance in making career choices; others will need the guidance of a survey instrument such as the COPS interest inventory. In the more than seventy-five years since the introduction of the first interest inventory, millions of people have received important information to use in decision making. Caution is always expressed by the authors of these inventories that no decision should be made on the basis of the results determined by one inventory. The COPS interest inventory is one of eighty interest inventories currently in use.

SOURCES FOR FURTHER STUDY

Bauernfeind, R. H. "COPSystem Interest Inventory." *Test Critiques*. Vol. 5. Kansas City, Mo.: Test Corporation of America, 1986. An important critique of the COPS. Presents statistics about its reliability and validity.

Murphy, L. L., and J. C. Conoley, eds. *Tests in Print IV*. Vol. 1. Lincoln, Neb.: Buros Institute of Mental Measurements, 1994. Introduces the COPS. A resource for detailed research items.

Daniel L. Yazak

Career selection, development, and change

TYPE OF PSYCHOLOGY: Developmental psychology
FIELDS OF STUDY: Adulthood

The world of work is changing at an increasingly rapid rate, and many working people find themselves forced to find new careers. By examining their personal interests and needs as well as the possibilities for financial rewards in a given field, those people selecting or changing careers can be more certain of career satisfaction and success.

KEY CONCEPTS
- career
- career choice
- career development
- career transition
- re-careering
- redirection

INTRODUCTION

A review of theories prominent in the psychology of career development points to their profound preoccupation with the idea that adults must work. The average adult spends more time working than performing any other waking activity. Satisfaction in one's career has been found empirically to have the potential for fulfilling such needs as productivity, competition, altruism, functioning as a team member, and independence. It is the most important avenue for fulfilling one's dreams. These studies also reveal that both personality traits and career interest change over time.

The definitions of career, career choice, and career development emphasize the idea that careers unfold throughout the life span and therefore require that individuals have the skills to adapt to these changes. According to Carl McDaniels in Rich Feller's and Garry Walz's *Career Transitions in Turbulent Times* (1997), a career is defined as the totality of work and leisure experiences over a life span. Career choice refers to the decisions that individuals make at any point in their careers. Career development encompasses the total constellation of psychological, sociological, educational, physical, economic, and chance factors that combine to shape the career of any given individual over the life span. Thus, individuals are constantly in a state of career development that often results in career change.

CAREER CHOICE AND CHANGE

The reasons individuals select certain occupations are varied. Frank Parsons's trait factor model of the early 1900's matched personal traits to job characteristics. Its assumptions included the idea that people possess stable and persistent traits, among them interests, talents, and intelligence. A related assumption was that jobs could be differentiated in terms of their needs for differing skills and levels of ability. The person with certain traits could therefore be matched with certain job needs, and the individual would be satisfied forever. Psychological tests became prominently used to measure traits and to classify occupations.

Parsons's basic tenets were expanded by John L. Holland in 1959. Over five hundred studies have supported his contention that individuals in similar jobs have similar interests and abilities. His highly respected and useful research resulted in the development of six categories of persons and jobs: realistic (R), investigative (I), artistic (A), social (S), enterprising (E), and conventional (C). Holland assumes that most people have a dominant type and one or two other types of some, but lesser, importance. To reflect this belief, he arranged the typology in a clockwise order around a hexagon, as R, I, A, S, E, C. He argues empirically that some types are more compatible and some are less compatible. The closer they are on the hexagon, the more compatible. For instance, RI, AS, and EC are examples of consistent types and have higher job achievement and satisfaction and more stable choices and personalities. RS, AC, and IE would be examples of those, therefore, who would have lower job achievement and satisfaction and less stable choices and personalities.

Holland leaves room, however, for change to occur. His basic belief is that personality type stabilizes between ages eighteen and thirty and is thereafter rather difficult to change. The more consistent a person's type is, the more he or she will find a satisfactory job environment. Consistent types, he says, will more often deal with job dissatisfaction by altering the work environment rather than by changing their own personalities. The need for a new repertoire of skills, new training, and new credentialing when making drastic career changes tends to reduce the amount of personality change people must make. In other words, changing careers, even when this requires reeducation, may be preferred over major changes in personality.

DEVELOPMENT AND TRANSITION

McDaniels has converged the works of Parsons, Holland, and Donald Edwin Super into an approach called developmental trait factor. From this point of view, career development consists of a continuous interaction of work and leisure across the life span in a series of transitional situations. Career choices are made that reflect the individual's interests and abilities at a certain point in time, but the choices will need to be reevaluated periodically as the individual grows and the surrounding world changes.

Nancy Schlossberg stated that individuals are more likely than not to experience a career transition at some point in their lives. She defined a transition as any event or nonevent that results in change in relationships, routines, assumptions, and/or role within self, work, family, health, and/or economics. A unique aspect of transitions as defined by Schlossberg is that nonevents can result in life changes. Examples of nonevents are anticipated promotions that did not occur and unexpected job layoffs. Thus, transitions, whether anticipated or not, involve a process of continuing and changing reactions over time that are linked to the individual's continuous and changing appraisal of self in the situation.

An important contributor to the psychology of careers is Donald Super, who states that career choice develops in five stages: growth (birth through age fourteen), exploration (ages fourteen through twenty-five), establishment (ages twenty-five through forty-five), maintenance (ages forty-five through sixty-five), and decline or disengagement (age sixty-six and older). He refers to this long-term developmental process as the "maxicycle." He emphasizes, however, that as a person matures and becomes more realistic, the possibility of career change may direct the individual into a new job or even an entirely new career. The maxicycle may then be repeated from the beginning in a very brief time frame, in "minicycle" form. In changing to the new position, the person experiences growth, exploration, establishment, and maintenance, but focused into days, weeks, or months rather than years.

CAREER SATISFACTION

Major psychological theories of career development recognize the possibility, and even probability, of change. The change may be in job choices within a particular career, a process of redirecting one's energies with a minimum of reschooling. The change may, however, involve more than redirection and move into major re-careering. The reasons for this shift are especially important to psychologists who believe that career satisfaction invades all facets of psychological wholeness. They believe that adults work for more than a livelihood. Otherwise, the rich would cease working and those who could perform high-paying jobs would not choose work that pays much less than their earnable income.

Super studied numerous lists of human motives, of reasons for working and of reasons people like or dislike jobs. These lists emanated from the research of a variety of students of human nature. His comparison and reduction of these lists pointed to three major needs for which satisfaction is sought: human relations, the work itself, and livelihood. Human relations involve the recognition of the person, independence, fair treatment, and status. Work means that the activity is interesting, is an opportunity for self-expression, and has a satisfying physical work situation and conditions. Livelihood refers to adequate earnings and security. Although Super's work is a product of the 1950's, it is regularly updated. He added self-realization to his motives for working, a common term used in humanistic psychology to emphasize the integration or wholeness that Carl Rogers believed achievable by the "fully functioning individual." Work has the potential for satisfying personal determinants that are psychological and biological, as well as satisfying situational determinants that are historical and socioeconomic.

From Super's lengthy and impressive research, the implications for change in careers are noteworthy. The frustration of any one or a combination of the three basic satisfactions sought in work (human relations, interesting work, and livelihood) that hinders one from achieving self-realization is sufficient motivation for change. To say it negatively, one may feel frustration in human relations because of lack of recognition, in work because tasks fail to maintain interest, or in livelihood because of insufficient earnings and security.

Super's work dealing with change based on changing interests and circumstances includes the idea that new careers emerge with changing times. The worker today has literally hundreds of new careers to consider. For example, S. Norman Feingold and Norma Reno Miller address this idea in their book *Emerging Careers: New Occupations for the Year 2000 and Beyond* (1983). Their finding was that scores of occupations are disappearing from the American scene and that scores of new jobs are being added that did not exist twenty-five years ago. The shift from industrial jobs to high-tech jobs was underscored by labor forecasters such as Carl McDaniels in *The Changing Workplace* (1989) and John Naisbett and Patricia Aburdene in *Megatrends 2000* (1990). The changing workplace necessitates changing job skills.

RE-CAREERING

The idea of changing careers, or re-careering, is a contemporary phenomenon. Since the 1980's, hundreds of books have centered on the topic. A valuable asset to the reader of such books is a strong statistical message: People change jobs or careers several times during their tenure of work. Dick Goldberg suggests that the average rate of career change is three to four times in a lifetime and that some 40 million out of 100 million people in the workforce are in some stage of career transition at any given time. One example of such a change might be a bank employee who moves to another bank but fills an entirely new position, with new requirements and job description (redirection). The job has actually changed. Redirection does not refer to the person who works in a bank and then moves to another bank in an identical position but at a higher salary. Career change includes both redirec-

tion and re-careering. Another, more drastic example is of a social worker with a master's degree in social work. After nine years of listening to people's problems, she is burned out; she also finds the pay increments to be insufficient for her needs. She begins exploring the possibility of combining her interest in helping people with her developing interest in investment counseling (re-careering).

Richard N. Bolles, author of *What Color Is Your Parachute?* (32d ed., 2001), regularly emphasizes that career change and job hunting are repetitive activities for every working person in the United States. According to statistics, the average job in the United States, at least when people are new to the job market, lasts about 3.6 years. "The average person," says Bolles, "will have ten employers in his or her lifetime and three distinct careers." A very practical suggestion, then, emerges from his writing: "You must learn how to conduct the search, for you are surely going to have to do it again!"

Career change requires methodology. Self-help books on career change provide valuable advice as to the methods of re-careering. They provide practical ideas on reassessing one's assets and liabilities, narrowing one's choices, determining one's career preferences, packaging or repackaging oneself, writing a resume, and negotiating the career change. Such changes are often more easily executed within the same career. The individual, for example, who is in business marketing may, as he or she matures, decide that management rather than marketing would provide a greater challenge and better financial security. Such a career may not require reschooling as much as it does repackaging oneself as to interests, strengths, and desired goals. An actor who tires of acting may find new excitement in the areas of directing and producing.

One example of career change involves a man who began as a high school science teacher. He later became a high school principal. Still later, he changed to become a consultant for the Ohio State Board of Education. Finally, he took an administrative position at a liberal arts college. In his case, re-careering involved additional graduate work and the meeting of certain requirements. He took all the suggested steps of reassessment, determining preferences, repackaging himself, interviewing, and negotiating the change. The necessary further education and meeting of certification requirements along the way seemed to be well worth the effort to him.

The result is a professional educator with an obviously renewed zest for life because of the challenges of attaining desired goals. He was very excited about his original job as high school science teacher, but as he changed, so did his interests and goals.

The literature, whether in the form of vocational guidance and career development, in the psychology of career counseling, or in the practical paperbacks that teach concrete steps to be taken, all carries the same theme: Career change is a skill that can be learned and applied with considerable success. Individuals are told in various ways, whether by noted theorists such as Super and Holland, or by practitioners such as McDaniels, Feingold, and others, to identify and communicate transferable skills or to acquire new job-related skills.

Ronald L. Krannich states that re-careering is a process that means repeatedly acquiring marketable skills and then changing careers in response to one's own interests, needs, and goals, as well as in response to the changing needs and opportunities of a technological society. The standard careering process must be modified with three new careering emphases: acquiring new marketable skills through retraining on a regular basis, changing careers several times during a lifetime, and utilizing more efficient communication networks for finding employment. Sigmund Freud said very little about adulthood except that it is the time "to love and to work." A large segment of life's satisfaction derives from satisfaction in one's work and will, no doubt, carry over to enhance the chances of one's ability to love.

CAREER TESTING AND RESOURCES

Several tests have been developed to assist in the process of matching individual traits to comparable work environment traits. One example is Holland's Self-Directed Search (SDS). As a result of completing the SDS, users are assigned a two- or three-letter code (such as RI, AS, ECR) that will lead them to a list of occupations that should reflect their interests and abilities. Some tests have been developed that integrate matching traits with a developmental approach. An example is the Career Exploration Inventory (CEI) by John Liptak, which contains an interest inventory and also includes a career planning component.

Several career information resources have been developed to provide individuals with information on the world of work. One of the first of these resources is the Dictionary of Occupational Titles (DOT). The DOT was developed in 1972 by the U.S. Employment Service and is regularly updated. It is a compendium of over twelve thousand occupations, each one described and classified. The Occupational Outlook Handbook is another source created by the U.S. government. It contains information on work environments, earnings, and job outlooks for specified occupations.

This theoretical emphasis on the complexity of human change had to be coupled with the societal phenomenon of dynamic technological change. More and greater changes are to come, as attested by the suggestions of researchers that future workers should be equipped with skills, flexibility, and the keen notion that their options should remain open throughout life. One cannot now fathom what new occupations will arise in the future. The Occupational Outlook Handbook, published by the U.S. Department of Labor, is unable to update itself fast enough. The O'NET is a resource available online that is expected to replace the DOT. The O'NET provides the same occupational information as the DOT, but it can be more quickly updated. Newspapers have published career supplements in which advertisements appear for specialists in robot behavior, ocean hotel management, and subquarkian physics. The horizon is filled with possibilities.

SOURCES FOR FURTHER STUDY

Bolles, Richard. *What Color Is Your Parachute?* 32d ed. San Francisco: Ten Speed Press, 2001. This self-help book is updated biannually. It is designed to assist job changers and covers topics such as where to find jobs, how to write a resume, and how to conduct oneself during an interview.

Feingold, S. Norman, and Norma Reno Miller. *Emerging Careers: New Occupations for the Year 2000 and Beyond.* Garret Park, Md.: Garret Park Press, 1983. The authors study the professional literature on new, emerging careers and survey more than five hundred colleges and universities as to new courses being offered related to emerging careers. Shows the astounding changes in career choices, with hundreds being eliminated and new ones being added. A futuristic view of emerging career fields and the need to adapt to them.

Feller, Rich, and Garry Walz, eds. *Career Transitions in Turbulent Times.* Greensboro, N.C.: ERIC/CASS,

1997. A collection of essays written by prominent career theorists. A variety of topics are explored, including the developmental trait factor approach to career development by Carl McDaniels, changing concepts of careers by A. G. Watts, and how to manage career plateaus by Frederick Hudson.

Krannich, Ronald L. *Re-careering in Turbulent Times: Skills and Strategies for Success in Today's Job Market.* Manassas, Va.: Impact, 1983. Discusses the methodology of career development, redirection, and re-careering. Recognizes the need to prepare for an uncertain future by linking work skills to job search skills. Outlines how one can re-career in the decades ahead.

Lewis, Adele Beatrice, and Bill Lewis, with Steve Radlaver. *How to Choose, Change, Advance Your Career.* Woodbury, N.Y.: Barron's Educational Series, 1983. From the vantage point of professionals in the marketplace. The authors emphasize the importance of the career person's participation in the process. Their thirty years in the personnel business affords excellent help to the individual seeking a sense of direction.

Schlossberg, Nancy, and S. P. Robinson. *Going to Plan B: How You Can Cope, Regroup, and Start Your Life on a New Path.* New York: Simon and Schuster, 1996. The authors explain the theory of career transitions. Many personal narratives from workers in a transition are imparted in the book. The authors also include strategies for working through a transition.

Super, Donald Edwin. *The Psychology of Careers: An Introduction to Vocational Development.* New York: Harper, 1957. After Frank Parsons's early text *Choosing a Vocation* (1909), this is possibly the next volume incorporating the results of significant research of psychologists, sociologists, and economists during the interim of almost fifty years. It served as a catalyst to launch the important work of researchers in recent decades. Super is still active in structuring his developmental theory to meet contemporary needs.

U.S. Department of Labor. *Dictionary of Occupational Titles.* Washington, D.C.: Employment and Training Administration, 1991. This source contains the official definitions for more than twelve thousand occupations. Each definition lists the major tasks that are associated with the occupation as well as worker traits that are needed for proficiency in the occupation.

_____. *Occupational Outlook Handbook.* Washington, D.C.: Author, 2000. This reference source contains details about the work environment, training needs, earnings, job outlooks, and related occupations for the occupations that are defined in the DOT. Oftentimes the DOT and the OOH are used as companions to each other. The OOH also contains labor force projections such as the fastest growing occupations. It is also assessable through the Bureau of Labor Statistics Web site.

F. Wayne Reno; updated by Debra S. Preston

SEE ALSO: Ability testing; Coaching; Human resource training and development; Interest inventories; Midlife crises; Self-actualization; Work motivation.

Case-study methodologies

TYPE OF PSYCHOLOGY: Psychological methodologies
FIELDS OF STUDY: Descriptive methodologies

Case-study methodologies represent a number of techniques for studying people, events, or other phenomena within their natural settings. Typically, case studies involve careful observations made over an extended period of time in situations where it is not possible to control the behaviors under observation. The results and interpretation of the data are recorded in narrative form.

KEY CONCEPTS
- extraneous variable
- independent variable
- laboratory setting research
- naturalistic observation
- quasi-experiments

INTRODUCTION

According to social scientist Robert Yin, case-study research is one of the most frequently misunderstood methods used to study behaviors. Yin, in his book *Case Study Research: Design and Methods* (1984), points out that misconceptions have come about because of the limited coverage that case-study research receives in the average textbook on research methods. In addition, most texts typically confuse the case-study approach with either qualitative research methods or specific types of quasi-experimental designs (experiments that do not allow subjects to be assigned randomly to treatment conditions).

Yin defines a case study as a method for studying contemporary phenomena within their natural settings, particularly when the behaviors under study cannot be manipulated or brought under the experimenter's control. Thus, unlike studies that are performed in the sometimes rigidly sterile laboratory setting (in which phenomena are studied in an artificial environment with rigorous procedures in place to control for outside influences), the case-study approach collects data where the behaviors occur in real-life contexts. Although behavior in natural settings can lead to a wealth of data waiting to be mined, it also has its drawbacks. Someone using this approach needs to recognize that the lack of control over extraneous variables can compound the difficulty associated with trying to identify the underlying variables that are causing the behaviors. Extraneous variables can be defined as those that have a detrimental effect on a research study, making it difficult to determine if the result is attributable to the variable under study or to some unknown variable not controlled for. Despite this concern, case-study methods are seen as valuable research tools to help unlock the mysteries behind events and behaviors. The approach has been used by psychologists, sociologists, political scientists, anthropologists, historians, and economists, to name a few.

HISTORY OF CASE STUDIES
Long before the scientific community began to formalize the procedures associated with conducting case studies, scientists, philosophers, and physicians were studying phenomena in their natural contexts by making direct observations and later systematically recording them. Although it is difficult to pinpoint how long this method has been used, there are a number of documented cases dating back to the second and third centuries. Galen, a leading physician in Rome in the second century, spent five years as a surgeon to the gladiators in the Roman Colosseum. During this time, he made painstaking observations correlating head injuries that the gladiators received with loss of intellectual abilities. In a sense, this was a prelude to the case study of today.

Psychology has been heavily influenced by the natural sciences. Since the natural sciences gave birth to the scientific method—a particular technique for gaining knowledge which includes the testing of hypotheses in ways that can be verified—it is not surprising that psychology adopted a modified version of the scientific method that could be applied to the study of people and other organisms. It soon became apparent, however, that not all situations lend themselves to study by an experiment. Thus, it was important for alternative methodologies to be developed and used. The case study is an outgrowth of this quest to find alternative methods for studying complex phenomena.

DESIGN TYPES AND PURPOSES
Yin suggests that case-study designs vary according to two distinct dimensions. One dimension accounts for the number of "cases" being studied: the presence of either single- or multiple-case designs. A second dimension allows for case studies to be either "holistic" (studying the entire unit of analysis as a single global entity) or "embedded" (allowing multiple units of analysis to be studied for the purpose of understanding their interworkings). According to Yin, this classification system leaves the researcher with a choice among four different design types: single-case (holistic) design, single-case (embedded) design, multiple-case (holistic) design, and multiple-case (embedded) design. Choosing among these designs involves the kinds of research questions that the researcher is attempting to answer.

Case-study methods are initiated for a variety of reasons, one of which is to serve as a vehicle for exploratory research. As a new research area begins to develop, the initial uncharted territory is sometimes best studied (particularly when the research questions are ill-defined) using a case-study method to determine which direction should be pursued first. This method has therefore been commonly misperceived as being able to contribute only in a limited exploratory capacity; however, the case study can, and should, be used not only to help focus initial research questions but also to describe and explain behaviors. As Yin makes clear, both "how" questions and "why" questions can be answered by this approach.

EXPERIMENTS VERSUS CASE STUDIES
A frequently asked question is, "When should one choose to conduct a case study, rather than an experiment?" To answer this question, it is important

to understand some basic differences between case-study methods and experimental designs. Experiments allow the researcher to manipulate the independent variables (those under the control of the experimenter) that are being studied.

For example, in a study to determine the most effective treatment approach for severe depression, subjects could be randomly assigned to one of three different treatments. The treatments are under the control of the researcher in the sense that he or she determines who will get a particular treatment and exactly what it will be. On the other hand, case studies are used in situations where the variables cannot be manipulated. Experiments typically, although not exclusively, are performed in a laboratory setting. Case studies occur in naturalistic settings, a research environment in which, in contrast to laboratory research, subjects are studied in the environment in which they live, with little or no intervention on the part of the researcher. Experiments are characterized as having rigorous control over extraneous variables. Case studies typically lack such control. Experiments place a heavy emphasis on data-analysis procedures that use numbers and statistical testing. Case studies emphasize direct observation and systematic interviewing techniques, and they are communicated in a narrative form. Experiments are designed so that they can be repeated. Case studies, by their very nature, can be quite difficult to repeat.

SINGLE-CASE VERSUS MULTIPLE-CASE STUDIES

One of Yin's dimensions for classifying case studies involves single-case versus multiple-case studies. In some instances, only a single-case study is necessary or at times even possible; this is true when a unique case comes along that presents a valuable source of information. For example, a social scientist wanting to explore the emotional impact of a national tragedy on elementary school children might choose to study the *Challenger* space shuttle disaster or the World Trade Center attacks, as a single-case study.

Eminent Russian psychologist Aleksandr Luria, in his book *The Mind of a Mnemonist: A Little Book About a Vast Memory* (1968), has, in a most engaging style, described a single-case (holistic) study. The case involved a man by the name of Shereshevskii (identified in the book as subject "S") who possessed an extraordinary memory. Luria began to observe "S" systematically in the 1920's after "S" had asked him to test his memory. Luria was so astounded

by the man's ability to study information for brief periods of time and then repeat it back to him without an error that he continued to observe and test "S" over the next thirty years. Luria was convinced that this man possessed one of the best memories ever studied.

Because of the nature of the phenomenon—an unusually vast memory—and the fact that this man was capable of performing memory feats never before witnessed, a single-case (holistic) study was begun. When studying rare phenomena, as in this instance, it is not possible to find the number of subjects typically required for an experiment; thus, the case-study approach presents the best alternative. Over the next thirty years, Luria carefully documented the results of literally hundreds of memory feats. In some instances, Luria presented "S" with a list of words to memorize and asked him to recall them immediately. At other times, without any forewarning, Luria asked "S" to recall words from lists given more than fifteen years before. In most of these instances, "S" recalled the list with only a few errors. Luria commented on much more than the results of these memory tests; he also carefully studied the personality of "S." Luria wanted to understand him as a whole person, not only as a person with a great memory. Closely involved with his subject, Luria personally gave the instructions and collected the data. Whereas the data from the memory tasks provided some degree of objectivity to the study, most of the information came from the subjective observations and judgments made by Luria himself. The study was reported in a book-length narrative.

HAWTHORNE STUDIES

A second example involves a case study that was part of a larger group known as the Hawthorne studies, conducted at the Western Electric Company, near Chicago, in the 1920's. One particular study, called the Bank Wiring Observation Room Study, was initiated to examine the informal social interactions that occur within a small group of employees in an industrial plant.

A group of fourteen men was moved to a self-contained work room that simulated the plant environment; a psychologist was assigned to observe the behavior of the group. No manipulation of any variables occurred; there was only passive observation of the employees' behavior. As might be expected, the presence of the observer discouraged many of the men from behaving as they normally would if someone were not present. The men were suspicious that the psychologist would inform their supervisor of any behaviors that were not allowed on the job. After a month passed, however, the men became accustomed to the observer and started to behave as they normally did inside the plant. (One should note the length of time needed to begin observing "normal" work behaviors; most experiments would have been terminated long before the natural behaviors surfaced.) The informal social interactions of this group were studied for a total of eight months.

This study was significant in that it exposed a number of interesting social phenomena that occur in a small division at work. One finding was that informal rules were inherent in the group and were strictly enforced by the group. For example, workers always reported that the same number of units were assembled for that day, regardless of how many were actually assembled. This unspoken rule came from a group that had considerable influence over the rate of production. Also, despite a company policy that forbade an employee to perform a job he was not trained to do, men frequently rotated job assignments to counteract the boredom that typically occurs in this kind of work.

This study was important because it systematically observed the naturally occurring relationships and informal social interactions that exist in an industrial setting. The case-study method proved to be very effective in bringing this information to light.

CASE STUDY CRITICISMS

Over the years, case-study methods have not received universal acceptance, which can be seen in the limited exposure that they receive in social science textbooks on methodology; it is not uncommon for a textbook to devote only a few paragraphs to this method. This attitude is attributable in part to some of the criticisms raised about case-study designs. One criticism is that this technique lends itself to distortions or falsifications while the data are being collected. Since direct observation may rely on subjective criteria, in many instances based on general impressions, it is alleged that this data should not be trusted. A second criticism is that it is difficult to draw cause-and-effect conclusions because of the lack of control measures to rule out alternative rival

hypotheses. Third, the issue of generalization is important after the data have been collected and interpreted. There will often be a question regarding the population to which the results can be applied.

In the second half of the twentieth century, there appears to have been a resurgence of the use of case-study methods. Part of the impetus for this change came from a reactionary movement against the more traditional methods that collect data in artificial settings. The case-study method plays a significant role in studying behavior in real-life situations, under a set of circumstances that would make it impossible to use any other alternative.

SOURCES FOR FURTHER STUDY

Baker, Therese L. *Doing Social Research.* 3d ed. New York: McGraw-Hill, 1998. Gives the reader a general introduction to field research, observational studies, data collection methods, survey research, and sampling techniques, as well as other topics which will help the reader evaluate "good" field experiments from those that are poorly constructed.

Berg, Bruce L. *Qualitative Research Methods for the Social Sciences.* 4th ed. Boston: Allyn & Bacon, 2000. Discusses a field strategy used by anthropologists and sociologists to study groups of people; in addition, discusses the ethical issues that arise while conducting research. Looks at the dangers of covert research and provides the guidelines established by the National Research Act.

Griffin, John H. *Black Like Me.* Reprint. New York: Signet, 1996. This excellent book, first published in 1962, is a narrative of the author's experiences traveling around the United States observing how people react to him after he takes on the appearance of a black man. This monumental field study, which contributed to an understanding of social prejudice, provides the reader with an excellent example of the significance of and need for conducting field research.

Luria, Aleksandr R. *The Mind of a Mnemonist: A Little Book About a Vast Memory.* 1968. Reprint. Cambridge, Mass: Harvard University Press, 1988. A fascinating case study written by a founder of neuropsychology and one of the most significant Russian psychologists. Directed toward a general (nonspecialist) audience. The case study focuses on his subject Shereshevskii (subject "S") and the extraordinary memory that he possessed.

Singleton, Royce, Jr., et al. *Approaches to Social Research.* 3d ed. New York: Oxford University Press, 1999. This well-written text discusses various aspects of field experimentation such as how to select a research setting and gather information, how to get into the field, and when a field study should be adopted. The chapter on experimentation can be used to contrast "true" experiments with field studies.

Spradley, James. *Participant Observation.* New York: International Thompson Publishing, 1997. A guide to constructing and carrying out a participant observation study, from a chiefly anthropological perspective.

Yin, Robert K. *Case Study Research: Design and Methods.* 2d ed. Thousand Oaks, Calif.: Sage Publications, 1994. This rare volume is perhaps the finest single source on case-study methods in print. Yin shows the reader exactly how to design, conduct, analyze, and even write up a case study. Approximately forty examples of case studies are cited with brief explanations. Not highly technical.

Bryan C. Auday

SEE ALSO: Animal experimentation; Archival data; Data description; Experimental psychology; Experimentation: Ethics and subject rights; Experimentation: Independent, dependent, and control variables; Field experimentation; Hypothesis development and testing; Observational methods; Sampling; Scientific methods; Statistical significance tests; Survey research: Questionnaires and interviews.

Causal attribution

TYPE OF PSYCHOLOGY: Social psychology
FIELDS OF STUDY: Social perception and cognition

Causal attribution concerns the explanations people offer about the causes of their own or other people's behavior. It has contributed to an understanding of emotions as well as people's reactions to failures, and the reasons that they give for those failures.

KEY CONCEPTS
- consensus information
- consistency information
- distinctiveness information
- external causes
- internal causes
- stable causes
- unstable causes

INTRODUCTION

When one hears about the behavior of a serial killer, sees a person shoplift, or is rejected by a friend, one may ask oneself why such behaviors or events occurred. Identifying the causes of behaviors may help people learn what kind of behaviors they can expect. People speculate about the causes of positive behaviors as well. For example, one may want to understand why a great athlete has set a number of records, why someone received a job promotion, or why one did well on a test.

The study of causal attribution focuses on the explanations that people make about the causes of their own or other people's behavior. Researchers in this area have gone beyond identifying attributions to trying to understand why people make the attributions that they do. Research on causal attribution has contributed to an understanding of many other aspects of people's behavior, such as attitude change, interpersonal attraction, and helping behavior.

CLASSIFICATIONS

Causal attributions are classified in a number of ways. One of the most important classifications is whether the attribution is made to an internal state or an external force. Internal attributions are made to causes internal to the person, such as individual personality characteristics, moods, and abilities. For example, one may attribute the cause of a shoplifter's behavior to kleptomania, of a friend's rejection to one's own lack of social skills, and of an athlete's records to his or her ability. External attributions, on the other hand, are made to causes external to the person, characteristics of the environment. Thus, the shoplifter's behavior might be perceived to be caused by a broken home, a friend's rejection by some characteristic of the friend (for example, lack of loyalty), and the athlete's record to the efforts of the team.

Causal attributions are also classified according to their stability. Stable causes are relatively permanent and are consistent across time. Unstable causes fluctuate across time. Internal and external causes

This drawing from 1885 illustrates the nineteenth century attitude toward causal attribution: "The sins of the drunken father are visited on the heads of the children—a thief and woman of shame visit their lunatic father in the criminal lunatic asylum." (Library of Congress)

may be either stable or unstable. For example, a person's ability is usually considered internal and stable, whereas effort is internal and unstable. Laws are external and stable, whereas the weather is external and unstable. If shoplifting is attributed to kleptomania, the cause is internal and stable, whereas if shoplifting is attributed to a dare from someone, the cause is external and unstable.

Bernard Weiner includes a third classification for causal attributions, that of controllability/uncontrollability: Some causes are within a person's control, whereas other causes are beyond a person's control. In this approach, controllability can exist with any combination of the internal/external and stable/unstable dimensions. Thus, ability—an internal, stable cause—is largely perceived as an uncontrollable cause. For example, people have little control over whether they have the ability to distinguish

green from red. On the other hand, effort—an internal, unstable cause—is perceived as controllable. A student can choose whether to study hard for a test.

KELLEY'S THEORY

Psychological research on causal attributions has gone beyond the classification of attributions. Psychologists have developed theories that help predict the circumstances under which people make various attributions. In this regard, Harold Kelley's theory has been extremely useful in making predictions about how people make internal and external attributions. From Kelley's perspective, attributions are made on the basis of three kinds of information: distinctiveness, consensus, and consistency.

Information about distinctiveness is derived from knowing the extent to which a person performs a certain behavior only in a certain situation. For example, the behavior of a person who only steals items from stores has higher distinctiveness than the behavior of a person who steals from stores, people's homes, and people on the street. According to Kelley, a behavior low in distinctiveness is likely to elicit an internal attribution. Thus, the behavior of a person who steals in a number of situations is more likely to be explained by an internal attribution (kleptomania) than by an external one.

Information about consensus is derived from knowing the way in which other people respond to the stimulus object. If the behavior is shared by a large number of people—if everyone steals items from stores, for example—the behavior has higher consensus than if few people steal from stores. A behavior high in consensus is likely to elicit an external attribution. If everyone steals from a certain store, there might be something about the store that elicits shoplifting.

Finally, information about consistency is derived from knowing the way in which the person responds over time. If the person shoplifts much of the time that he or she shops, the behavior has higher consistency than if the person shoplifts occasionally. According to Kelley, behaviors high in consistency are likely to elicit internal attributions. Thus, the behavior of a person who shoplifts much of the time is likely to be explained by an internal attribution (kleptomania).

Kelley's theory has generated many more predictions than those described here. His theory, along with those of other attribution researchers, assumes that people have a need to predict behavior. If behavior is predictable, the world becomes a more controllable place in which to live.

ROLE OF EMOTIONS

One of the earlier applications of the research on causal attributions by social psychologists was in understanding emotions. Stanley Schachter and Jerome Singer proposed that perceptions of emotions are influenced by the physiological arousal that a person feels and by the cognitive label that the person uses (for example, "I'm jealous" or "I'm angry"). They argued that the physiological arousal is the same for all emotions. For example, a rapid heart rate can be the result of intense love or intense anger. According to Schachter and Singer, when someone feels physiologically aroused, the person looks to the situation to label his or her feelings. If someone is unaware of the true source of his or her arousal, it is possible for him or her to misattribute that arousal to a plausible cause.

An example can illustrate this approach. When "George" began drinking coffee as a teenager, he was unaware of the physiologically arousing effects of caffeine. He can recall drinking too much coffee one morning and getting in an argument about some issue. The caffeine created arousal; however, because George was in an argument, he labeled the arousal as caused by his being angry. As a result of that attribution, he acted in an angry manner. Thus, George misattributed the physiological arousal produced by the caffeine to a feeling of anger.

Psychological investigations of the emotions of love and crowding have used this attributional approach. In an experiment on romantic attraction by Gregory White, Sanford Fishbein, and Jeffrey Rutsein, male subjects ran in place for 120 seconds (high physiological arousal) or 15 seconds (low physiological arousal) and were presented with a picture of an unattractive or attractive woman. Subsequently, the subjects were asked to evaluate the woman in terms of romantic attractiveness. Male subjects with high physiological arousal indicated that they were more romantically attracted to the attractive woman than did the male subjects with less physiological arousal. Similarly, in an experiment on crowding by Stephen Worchel and Charles Teddie, subjects sat close (high physiological arousal) or far apart (low physiological arousal). For some of the subjects, there were pictures on the wall; for other subjects, there were no pictures on the wall. Subsequently, subjects were asked how crowded they felt. For the subjects with high physiological arousal, those with no pictures on the wall indicated that they felt more crowded than did those with pictures on the wall. Without pictures on the wall, the subjects could only attribute their arousal to other people. In each of these examples, the subjects used an external cue to label their internal state (emotion).

LEARNED HELPLESSNESS

Causal attributions have also been used to understand the phenomenon of learned helplessness. Martin E. P. Seligman has demonstrated in a number of experiments that people take longer to solve soluble problems after they have tried and failed to solve a series of insoluble problems than if they had not been presented with the insoluble problems. Seligman initially proposed that people did not try harder on the soluble problems because they learned that their outcomes (failures on the insoluble problems) were independent of what they did. From an attributional perspective, however, the argument would be that people do not try harder on the soluble problems because it is less damaging to their self-esteem to attribute their failure on the insoluble problems to the lack of effort, an internal, unstable cause, rather than to an internal, stable cause, such as ability. People can then retain the belief that they can always do better next time if they try harder. Research favors the attributional interpretation of learned helplessness, as is indicated by the research of Arthur Frankel and Melvin Snyder.

EXCUSE THEORY

An area in which causal attribution has played a crucial role is in excuse theory as proposed by C. R. Snyder. People make excuses to protect themselves from their failure experiences. Excuses help people feel that they are not totally responsible for their failures. Kelley's attribution theory has been influential in the development of Snyder's model of excuse making. Thus, people can excuse a poor performance by using consensus-raising excuses, consistency-lowering excuses, or distinctiveness-raising excuses.

When people employ distinctiveness-raising excuses, they claim that the poor performance is specific to one situation and not generalizable to others ("I performed poorly only in this class"). When people employ consistency-lowering excuses, they claim that they have a poor performance occasionally, not frequently ("This was the only time I performed poorly"). Finally, when people employ consensus-raising excuses, they claim that everyone performed as poorly as they did ("This test was so hard that everyone did poorly on it"). George Whitehead and Stephanie Smith have examined the impact of an audience on the use of consensus-raising excuses. They found that people are less likely to use consensus-raising excuses in public than in private. Thus, one is more likely to say, "This test was hard, and everyone did poorly on it," to oneself than to one's teacher, who knows how everyone else performed.

EVOLUTION OF RESEARCH

The basic ideas for causal attribution were presented by Fritz Heider in his 1958 book *The Psychology of Interpersonal Relations*. From the richness of Heider's writings, a number of social psychologists have generated different attributional theories. One problem with this research area, as with other research areas in social psychology, is that no single theory effectively encompasses all the different ideas proposed by causal attribution theorists. Nevertheless, causal attribution research has played an important role in the history of psychology because of its emphasis on cognition—how people think.

In the late 1950's, when Heider wrote his book, and in the early 1960's, when Schachter and Singer did their experiment regarding emotion, psychology was heavily influenced by behaviorism, and had been for many years. From a behavioristic perspective, the study of thinking was in disrepute because it involved processes that were largely unobservable. Theorizing about causal attribution involved theorizing about the way in which people think about the causes of behavior. Today, as can be seen from the amount of research on causal attribution and other cognitive processes, psychologists' interest in cognition has broadened.

Early research on causal attribution often tested the theories. Research generally supported the theories but often found that they had limitations as well. For example, research on Kelley's attribution theory found that people do use information about distinctiveness, consensus, and consistency when making attributions. Kelley's theory further suggests that each type of information should be considered equally important in the attribution process. Subsequent research, however, indicated that consensus information may be underutilized in certain circumstances. Further theoretical research on causal attributions will be of continuing interest to psychologists.

Researchers will want to know the influence of culture on causal attributions. Much of the theorizing and empirical research on causal attribution has been done in the United States. It is important to know whether the phenomena that psychologists have documented with people in the United States generalize to people from other cultures. Evidence from several sources has indicated that people from the United States attribute outcomes more to internal causes than do people from Third World nations. This finding is believed to reflect different cultural traditions, but more cross-cultural research on causal attribution is needed.

Once the causal attributions that people make are understood, research can focus on the consequences of these attributions. For example, when people excuse a poor performance, they should feel better about themselves. Also, when people attribute their positive outcomes to internal factors, their feelings about themselves should be better than when they attribute their positive outcomes to external factors. This area is one of many that is likely to receive more attention from social psychological researchers in the future.

SOURCES FOR FURTHER STUDY

Fiske, Susan T., and Shelley E. Taylor. *Social Cognition.* 2d ed. New York: McGraw-Hill, 1991. Reviews the various attribution theories and the research these theories have generated. Attribution theories are also presented within the broader context of social cognition.

Frankel, Arthur, and Melvin L. Snyder. "Poor Performance Following Unsolvable Problems: Learned Helplessness or Egotism?" *Journal of Personality and Social Psychology* 36, no. 12 (1978): 1415-1423. This experiment is typical of the research that tests the competing explanations for the performance deficit following failure. The article provides a review of each explanation and shows how attributions can protect people's positive image of themselves.

Heider, Fritz. *The Psychology of Interpersonal Relations.* New York: John Wiley & Sons, 1958. Included is the chapter that stimulated theorizing about causal attribution. Also presents ideas about social behavior that stimulated research on balance theory. The book is extremely thought provoking.

Schachter, Stanley, and Jerome Singer. "Cognitive, Social, and Physiological Determinants of Emotional State." *Psychological Review* 69, no. 5 (1962): 379-399. This experiment is considered a classic by some psychologists. It presents the paradigm that is so often utilized in research on the misattribution of arousal, as exemplified by the work of Stephen Worchel and Charles Teddie and of Gregory White, Sanford Fishbein, and Jeffrey Rutsein. Most general psychology textbooks include this experiment in their chapter on emotions.

Seligman, Martin E. P. *Helplessness: On Depression, Development, and Death.* 1975. Reprint. San Francisco: W. H. Freeman, 1992. Defines helplessness, presents experiments on helplessness, and integrates them into a theory. The experiments utilize a diversity of subjects, including dogs and people. Also compares helplessness to depression and proposes a therapeutic strategy for depression. Nicely illustrates how a theory is developed.

Snyder, C. R., Raymond L. Higgins, and Rita J. Stucky. *Excuses: Masquerades in Search of Grace.* New York: John Wiley & Sons, 1983. Presents a theory of excuse making and delineates different types of excuses. A number of research studies are also marshaled to support the theory. Highly readable; includes many examples of adaptive and maladaptive excuses.

White, Gregory L., Sanford Fishbein, and Jeffrey Rutsein. "Passionate Love and the Misattribution of Arousal." *Journal of Personality and Social Psychology* 41, no. 1 (1981): 56-62. This experiment nicely illustrates the misattribution-of-arousal paradigm and shows how a hypothesis about the development of passionate love can be tested empirically.

Whitehead, George I., III, and Stephanie Smith. "Competence and Excuse-Making as Self-Presentational Strategies." In *Public Self and Private Self,* edited by Roy F. Baumeister. New York: Springer-Verlag, 1986. Presents the authors' hypothesis and research regarding when and why particular excuses are utilized. This research follows from the excuse-making theory as proposed by C. R. Snyder, Raymond Higgins, and Rita Stucky.

Worchel, Stephen, and Charles Teddie. "The Experience of Crowding: A Two-Factor Theory." *Journal of Personality and Social Psychology* 34, no. 1 (1976): 30-40. This experiment nicely illustrates the misattribution-of-arousal paradigm. In addition, it was an important experiment in environmental psychology because it showed that population density and crowding are not necessarily the same.

George I. Whitehead III and Stephanie Smith

SEE ALSO: Abnormality: Psychological models; Attributional biases; Cognitive maps; Emotions; Learned helplessness; Motivation.

Child abuse

TYPE OF PSYCHOLOGY: Developmental psychology
FIELDS OF STUDY: Adolescence; infancy and childhood

*The experience of physical or psychological abuse in
childhood can have a profound, long-term, deleterious effect upon a person's social development and
emotional well-being. Child abuse places a youngster
at increased risk to develop a variety of psychological
problems, including low self-esteem, anxiety, depression, behavior disorders, educational difficulties,
and distorted relationships with peers and adults.*

KEY CONCEPTS
- neglect
- physical abuse
- psychological abuse
- sexual abuse

INTRODUCTION

It is difficult to imagine anything more frightening
to a child than being rejected, threatened, beaten,
or molested by an adult who is supposed to be his or
her primary source of nurturance and protection.
Yet throughout human history, children have been
abandoned, incarcerated, battered, mutilated, and
even murdered by their caregivers. Although the
problem of child maltreatment is an old one, both
the systematic study of child abuse and the legally
sanctioned mechanisms for child protection are relatively new and gained momentum in the last half
of the twentieth century.

In the United States, child abuse and neglect are
defined in both federal and state legislation. The
federal legislation provides a foundation for states
by identifying a minimum set of acts or behaviors
that characterize maltreatment. This legislation also
defines what acts are considered physical abuse, neglect, and sexual abuse.

The Child Abuse Prevention and Treatment Act
(CAPTA) of 1974 as amended in 1996 defines child
abuse and neglect as, at a minimum, any recent act
or failure to act on the part of a parent or caretaker
that results in death, serious physical or emotional
harm, or sexual abuse or exploitation or an act or
failure to act that presents an imminent risk of serious harm.

When applied by legal and mental health profes-

sionals in real-world situations, however, the definition of abuse may vary according to the developmental age of the child victim, the frequency or
intensity of the behaviors regarded as abusive, the
degree of intentionality, and a consideration of extenuating circumstances. In general, however, child
abuse includes any act or omission on the part of
a parental figure that damages a child's physical
or psychological well-being or development that is
nonaccidental or the result of a habitual behavioral
pattern. A broad spectrum of behaviors are considered to be abusive, ranging from the more easily
recognizable physical abuse to more subtle forms of
maltreatment including neglect, sexual abuse, and
emotional abuse.

TYPES OF ABUSE

Physical abuse is characterized by the infliction
of physical injury as a result of punching, beating,
kicking, biting, burning, shaking, or otherwise harming a child. The parent or caretaker may not have
intended to hurt the child; rather, the injury may
have resulted from overdiscipline or physical punishment. Child neglect is characterized by failure
to provide for the child's basic needs. Neglect can
be physical, educational, or emotional. Physical neglect includes refusal of, or delay in, seeking health
care; abandonment; expulsion from the home or
refusal to allow a runaway to return home; and inadequate supervision. Educational neglect includes
the allowance of chronic truancy, failure to enroll a
child of mandatory school age in school, and failure
to attend to a special educational need. Emotional
neglect includes such actions as marked inattention
to the child's needs for affection; refusal of or failure to provide needed psychological care; spouse
abuse in the child's presence; and permission of
drug or alcohol use by the child. The assessment of
child neglect requires consideration of cultural values and standards of care, as well as recognition that
the failure to provide the necessities of life may be
related to poverty.

Sexual abuse includes fondling a child's genitals,
intercourse, incest, rape, sodomy, exhibitionism, and
commercial exploitation through prostitution or the
production of pornographic materials. Many experts
believe that sexual abuse is the most underreported
form of child maltreatment because of the secrecy
or "conspiracy of silence" that so often characterizes
these cases.

A Highway Patrol officer walks through cutouts of children on the steps of the Kansas Statehouse. The cutouts, on which were listed child abuse statistics for each county in the state, were part of a program to recognize Child Abuse Prevention Month. (AP/Wide World Photos)

Emotional abuse (psychological or verbal abuse, or mental injury) includes acts or omissions by the parents or other caregivers that have caused, or could cause, serious behavioral, cognitive, emotional, or mental disorders. In some cases of emotional abuse, the acts of parents or other caregivers alone, without any harm evident in the child's behavior or condition, are sufficient to warrant Child Protective Services (CPS) intervention. For example, the parents or caregivers may use extreme or bizarre forms of punishment, such as confinement of a child in a dark closet. Less severe acts, such as habitual scapegoating, belittling, or rejecting treatment, are often difficult to prove. Therefore, CPS may not be able to intervene without evidence of harm to the child.

EXTENT OF ABUSE

Estimates of the extent of child abuse in the United States have ranged from two hundred thousand to four million cases per year. The most widely accepted incidence figure comes from the National Committee for the Prevention of Child Abuse, which estimated that in 1999, 826,000 children were "severely abused," including more than one thousand abuse-related deaths. It is important, when considering the actual magnitude of the problem of child maltreatment, to remember that the estimates given most likely underestimate the true incidence of child abuse, both because of the large number of cases that go unreported and because of the lack of agreement as to precisely which behaviors constitute "abuse" or "neglect." In addition, abusive treatment of children is rarely limited to a single episode, and it frequently occurs within the context of other forms of family violence.

Certain forms of maltreatment seem to appear with greater regularity within certain age groups. Neglect is most often reported for infants and toddlers, with incidence declining with age. Reports of sexual abuse and emotional maltreatment are most common among older school-aged children and adolescents. Physical abuse seems to be reported equally among all age groups; however, children less than five years old and adolescents have the highest rates of actual physical injury. Victimization rates by race and ethnicity ranged from a low of 4.4 Asian/Pacific Islander victims per 1,000 children of the same race in the population, to 25.2 African American victims per 1,000 children.

Although research studies generally conclude that there is no "typical" child abuse case consisting of a typical abused child and a typical abusive parent or family type, certain characteristics occur with greater regularity than others. For example, there is considerable evidence that premature infants, low-birthweight infants, and children with problems such as hyperactivity, physical handicaps, and mental retardation are at particularly high risk for being abused by their caregivers. Physical abuse and neglect are reported with approximately equal frequency for girls and boys, while sexual abuse against girls is reported four times more frequently than is sexual abuse against boys.

Contrary to the once-held stereotype of abusive parents, only a small proportion (5 to 10 percent) of abusive parents suffer from a severe psychiatric disorder. While female caregivers are the perpetrators in approximately 60 percent of all reported cases of child maltreatment, male caregivers are more likely to inflict actual physical injury, and they are the primary perpetrators in cases of sexual abuse of both male and female children. Although no single abusive personality type has been identified, research has revealed a number of areas of psychological functioning in which abusive parents often differ from nonabusive parents. Abusive parents tend to exhibit low frustration tolerance and express negative emotions (for example, anger or disappointment) inappropriately. They are more socially isolated than are nonabusive parents. Abusive parents also tend to have unrealistic expectations of their children, to misinterpret their children's motivations for misbehaving, to utilize inconsistent and inflexible parenting skills, and to view themselves as inadequate or incompetent as parents.

Research also indicates that marital conflict, unemployment, large and closely spaced families, overcrowded living conditions, and extreme household disorientation are common in abusive homes. Statistics regarding race, education level, and socioeconomic status of abusive families are somewhat controversial in that there exists the possibility of an underreporting bias favoring the white, middle- to upper-class family; however, like several other negative outcomes in childhood (for example, underachievement, criminality, teen pregnancy), child abuse is associated with poverty, underemployment, insufficient education, and the increased experience of unmanageable stress and social isolation that coexists with these sociodemographic variables.

CONSEQUENCES OF ABUSE

Abused children are believed to be at much greater risk of developing some form of pathology in childhood or in later life. When considered as a group and compared to nonabused youngsters, abused children exhibit a variety of psychological difficulties and behavioral problems. Yet no single emotional or behavioral reaction is consistently found in all abused children. It is important, when investigating the impact of child abuse, to view the abuse within a developmental perspective. Given a child's different developmental needs and capabilities over the course of his or her development, one might expect that both the psychological experience and the impact of the abuse would be quite different for an infant than if the same maltreatment involved an eight-year-old child or an adolescent. One should also note that the abuse occurs within a particular psychological context, and that the experience of the abuse per se may not be the singular, most powerful predictor of the psychological difficulties found in abused children. Rather, the child's daily exposure to other, more pervasive aspects of the psychological environment associated with an abusive family situation (for example, general environmental deprivation, impoverished parent-child interactions, or chronic family disruption and disorganization) may prove to be more psychologically damaging. Finally, it is important not to view the range of symptoms associated with abused children solely as deficits or pathology. These "symptoms" represent an abused child's best attempt at coping with an extremely stressful family environment given the limited psychological resources and skills he or she has available at that particular time in his or her development.

From the home environment, and from parents in particular, children learn their earliest and perhaps most influential lessons about how to evaluate themselves as valuable, loveable, and competent human beings. They learn about controlling their own actions and about successfully mastering their environment. They learn something about the goodness of their world and how to relate to the people in it. Growing up in an abusive home distorts these early lessons, often resulting in serious interference with the most important dimensions of a child's development: the development of a healthy sense of self, the development of self-control and a sense of mastery, the capacity to form satisfying relationships, and the ability to utilize one's cognitive capacities to solve problems.

In general, research has shown that abused children often suffer from low self-esteem, poor impulse control, aggressive and antisocial behaviors, fearfulness and anxiety, depression, poor relationships with peers and adults, difficulties with school adjustment, delays in cognitive development, lowered academic achievement, and deficits in social and moral judgment. The way in which these difficulties are expressed will vary according to a child's stage of development.

SIGNS OF ABUSE

In infancy, the earliest sign of abuse or neglect is an infant's failure to thrive. These infants show growth retardation (weight loss can be so severe so as to be life-threatening) with no obvious physical explanation. To the observer, these infants appear to have "given up" on interacting with the outside world. They become passive, socially apathetic, and exhibit little smiling, vocalization, and curiosity. Other abused infants appear to be quite irritable, exhibiting frequent crying, feeding difficulties, and irregular sleep patterns. In either case, the resulting parent-child attachment bond is often inadequate and mutually unsatisfying.

Abused toddlers and preschoolers seem to lack the infectious love of life, fantasy, and play that is characteristic of that stage of development. They are typically anxious, fearful, and hypervigilant. Their emotions are blunted, lacking the range, the spontaneity, and the vivacity typical of a child that age. Abused toddlers' and preschoolers' ability to play, particularly their ability to engage in imaginative play, may be impaired; it is either deficient or preoccupied with themes of aggression. Abused children at this age can either be passive and over-compliant or oppositional, aggressive, and hyperactive.

School-aged children and adolescents exhibit the more recognizable signs of low self-esteem and depression in the form of a self-deprecating attitude and self-destructive behaviors. They are lonely, withdrawn, and joyless. Behaviorally, some act in a compulsive, overcompliant, or pseudomature manner, while others are overly impulsive, oppositional, and aggressive. Problems with school adjustment and achievement are common. With the school-aged child's increased exposure to the larger social environment, deficits in social competence and interpersonal relationships become more apparent. Progressing through adolescence, the manifestations of low self-esteem, depression, and aggressive, acting-out behaviors may become more pronounced in the form of suicide attempts, delinquency, running away, promiscuity, and drug use.

These distortions in self-esteem, impulse control, and interpersonal relationships often persist into adulthood. There has been much concern expressed regarding the possibility of an intergenerational transmission of abuse—of the experience of abuse as a child predisposing a person to becoming an abusive parent. Research indicates that abused children are six times more likely to abuse their own children than are members of the general population.

EXPLANATIONS

Child maltreatment is a complex phenomenon that does not have a simple, discrete cause, nor does it affect each victim in a predictable or consistent manner. Since "battered child syndrome" gained national attention in the early 1960's, theories attempting to explain child maltreatment have evolved from the simplistic psychiatric model focusing on the abuser as a "bad" parent suffering from some form of mental illness to a view of child abuse as a multidetermined problem, with anyone from any walk of life a potential abuser.

Perhaps the most comprehensive and widely accepted explanation of child abuse is the ecological model. This model views abuse as the final product of a set of interacting factors including child-mediated stressors (for example, temperamental difficulties, or a mental or physical handicap), parental predispositions (for example, history of abuse as a child, emotional immaturity), and situational stresses (for example, marital conflict, insufficient social support, or financial stress) occurring within a cultural context that inadvertently supports the mistreatment of children by its acceptance of corporal punishment and tolerance for violence, and its reluctance to interfere with family autonomy. Utilizing this ecological framework, one can imagine how an abusive situation can develop when, for example, an irritable, emotionally unresponsive infant is cared for by an inexperienced, socially isolated mother in a conflict-filled and financially strained household embedded within a larger cultural context in which the rights and privileges of childhood do not necessarily include freedom from violence.

Knowledge regarding the impact of child abuse has also changed over the years, from a view of maltreated children as almost doomed to develop some form of psychopathology to an acknowledgment that child abuse, like other major childhood stressors, can result in a broad spectrum of adaptive consequences, ranging from psychological health to severe psychiatric disorder. Some children actually do well in their development despite their experience with extreme stress and adversity. For example, while adults who were abused as children are more likely than nonabused individuals to become child abusers, nearly two-thirds of all abused children do not become abusive parents. The important questions to be answered are why and how this is so. Research on "stress-resistant" individuals such as these nonabusers has shifted the focus away from pathology to the identification of factors within the individual (for example, coping strategies) and within the environment (for example, social support) that appear to serve a protective function.

Finally, while the treatment of abused children and their abusive caregivers remains an important goal in the mental health field, a focus on the prevention of child abuse has also gained momentum. Many abused children and their families can be helped with proper treatment; however, the existing need for services far exceeds the mental health resources available. An increased understanding of the factors that protect families against engaging in abusive behaviors has resulted in the creation of successful preventive interventions. These prevention programs seek to reduce the incidence of new cases of child abuse by encouraging the development and strengthening of competencies, resources, and coping strategies that promote psychological well-being and positive development in parents, children, and families.

The problem of child abuse does not occur in isolation. It coexists with other abhorrent problems facing American children such as poverty, lack of guaranteed adequate medical care, insufficient quality daycare, and unequal educational resources. Child abuse, like these other problems, can be prevented and eradicated. People have come a long way in terms of their understanding of child maltreatment; yet until the needs of children truly become a national priority, child abuse will continue, brutally and unnecessarily, to rob children of their childhood.

SOURCES FOR FURTHER STUDY

Briere, John N. *Child Abuse Trauma*. Newbury Park, Calif.: Sage Publications, 1992. Considers the unique and overlapping long-term effects of all major forms of child abuse. Includes information on seven types of child abuse and neglect—ranging from sexual and physical abuse to mistreatment by alcoholic or drug addicted parents.

Cicchetti, Dante, and Vicki Carlson, eds. *Child Maltreatment: Theory and Research on the Causes and Consequences of Child Abuse and Neglect*. New York: Cambridge University Press, 1989. Edited chapters by leading experts in the field providing a state-of-the-art evaluation of what is known about the causes and consequences of child maltreatment. Describes the history of child maltreatment and intervention strategies designed to prevent or remediate the negative consequences of abuse.

Clark, Robin E., and Judith Freeman Clark. *The Encyclopedia of Child Abuse*. 2d ed. New York: Facts on File, 2000. In encyclopedic form, provides comprehensive information regarding all forms of child maltreatment. Includes discussions of causation, consequences, treatment, and prevention. Entries reflect a range of disciplines including psychology, law, medicine, sociology, economics, history, and education. An extensive bibliography also included.

Conte, Jon R., ed. *Critical Issues in Child Sexual Abuse: Historical, Legal, and Psychological Perspectives*. Newbury Park, Calif.: Sage Publications, 2000. Intended to describe what is known and what is not known (but needs to be known) in several specific areas of childhood abuse. Each author emphasizes the most critical unknowns in his or her area. Chapters focus on sexual offenders, children's memory, adult memory for trauma, children as victims, treatment challenges of traumatized victims, victims in court, and treatment of dissociate identity clients.

Garbarino, James, and Gwen Gilliam. *Understanding Abusive Families*. Lexington, Mass.: Lexington Books, 1980. Presents an ecological and developmental perspective on child abuse. Explores the interrelated contributions of child characteristics, parental characteristics, and the community context to the development of an abusive parent-child relationship. Considers the way in which the causes, dynamics, and consequences of abuse may change from infancy through adolescence.

Kantor, Glenda, K., and Jana L. Jasinski, eds. *Out of the Darkness: Contemporary Perspectives on Family Violence*. Newbury Park, Calif.: Sage Publications, 1997. Features information on family violence from the international arena. Integrates the work of emerging scholars and key figures in the field. Provides a comprehensive and interdisciplinary package of the newest generation of investigation and theory. Explores controversial topics including international studies; theory, methods, assessment, and interventions; and ethical and cultural issues related to both child and partner abuse.

Wolfe, David A. *Child Abuse: Implications for Child Development and Psychopathology*. 2d ed. Newbury Park, Calif.: Sage Publications, 1999. Presents a thorough review of facts and issues regarding the abuse of children, emphasizing topics such as sociodemographic risk factors, variations in family socialization practices, factors associated with healthy versus abusive parent-child relationship, psychological characteristics of the abusive parent, and a developmental perspective on the abused child.

Judith Primavera;
updated by Shelley A. Jackson

SEE ALSO: Aggression; Attachment and bonding in infancy and childhood; Battered woman syndrome; Domestic violence; Ego defense mechanisms; Gender-identity formation; Psychoanalytic psychology and personality: Rape and sexual assault; Sigmund Freud; Separation and divorce: Children's issues.

Childhood disorders

TYPE OF PSYCHOLOGY: Psychopathology
FIELDS OF STUDY: Childhood and adolescent disorders

Childhood disorders involve significant behavioral or psychological patterns associated with distress, disability, an important loss of freedom, or significantly increased risk of death, pain, or disability that affect infants, children, or adolescents.

KEY CONCEPTS
- attention-deficit and disruptive disorders
- communication disorders
- elimination disorders
- feeding and eating disorders
- learning disorders
- mental retardation
- motor coordination disorders
- pervasive developmental disorders
- tic disorders

INTRODUCTION

The concept of mental disorder, like many other concepts in science and medicine, lacks a consistent operational definition that covers all situations. A useful tool to evaluate mental disorders is the American Psychiatric Association's *Diagnostic and Statistical Manual of Mental Disorders* (DSM). Revised about every ten years, a revised fourth edition called the DSM-IV-TR was published in 2000. It is coordinated with the *International Statistical Classification of Diseases and Related Health Problems* (ICD), developed by the World Health Organization for all diseases. A comprehensive manual, the DSM conceptualizes mental disorders as clinically significant behavioral or psychological syndromes or patterns. These patterns must be more than expected and culturally sanctioned responses to a particular event, for example the death of a loved one.

The DSM contains a separate section for disorders that are usually first diagnosed in infancy, childhood, or adolescence. Grouped in this section are mental retardation, learning disorders, motor skills disorders, pervasive developmental disorders, attention-deficit and disruptive behavior disorders, feeding and eating disorders, tic disorders, elimination disorders, and other disorders associated with infancy, childhood, or adolescence. Other disorders are associated with adults, but children may have them as well. This second group includes organic disorders, schizophrenia, mood disorders, anxiety disorders, somatoform disorders, factitious disorders, dissociative disorders, sleep disorders, impulse-control disorders, and adjustment disorders.

MENTAL RETARDATION

Mental retardation means that the child has significantly below average intellectual functioning. On an intelligence quotient (IQ) test, significantly below average functioning would mean a score below 70, which is two standard deviations below the mean and below the score of about 98 percent of the population. A mistake that people sometimes make with intelligence tests is to assume that they represent an absolute trait. A low score on an intelligence test might reflect below-average functioning but might also reflect illness, distraction, a native language different from that used by the examiner, sociocultural background, or other features.

In mental retardation, in addition to low scores on intelligence tests, the child also has impaired adaptive functioning in at least two important life skills. These life skills are communication, self-care, home living, social-interpersonal skills, use of com-

munity resources, self-direction, functional academic skills, work, leisure, health, and safety. In an assessment of intellectual functioning, it is useful to gather evidence from reliable independent sources, such as an intelligence test, a teacher, a parent, and/or medical records.

Four degrees of retardation can be specified. In the largest group, mild retardation, intelligence scores are about 55 to 70, and the person by late teens can function up to about a sixth-grade academic level. As adults, these individuals can live successfully in the community, although they may need supervision when they are in unusual or stressful situations. In moderate mental retardation, intelligence scores are about 40 to 55, and the person can profit from vocational training and, with supervision, attend to personal care. In severe retardation, intelligence scores are about 25 to 40, and the person may be able to learn the alphabet and some simple numbers and can adapt well to supervised life in the community or a group home. In profound retardation, intelligence scores are about 10 to 25, and the person can perform simple tasks in closely supervised and sheltered settings.

In 30 to 40 percent of individuals with mental retardation, no clear cause can be determined. In other individuals, causes for retardation include he-

---

DSM-IV-TR Criteria for Feeding and Eating Disorders of Infancy or Early Childhood

FEEDING DISORDER OF INFANCY OR CHILDHOOD (DSM CODE 307.59)

Feeding disturbance manifested by persistent failure to eat adequately with significant failure to gain weight or significant loss of weight over at least one month

Disturbance not due to an associated gastrointestinal or other general medical condition such as esophageal reflux

Symptoms not better accounted for by another mental disorder (such as Rumination Disorder) or by lack of available food

Onset before age six

PICA (DSM CODE 307.52)

Persistent eating of nonnutritive substances for a period of at least one month

Eating of nonnutritive substances inappropriate to developmental level

Behavior not part of a culturally sanctioned practice

If symptoms occur exclusively during the course of another mental disorder (such as mental retardation, a pervasive developmental disorder, schizophrenia), they are sufficiently severe to warrant independent clinical attention

RUMINATION DISORDER (DSM CODE 307.53)

Repeated regurgitation and rechewing of food for a period of at least one month following a period of normal functioning

Behavior not due to an associated gastrointestinal or other general medical condition such as esophageal reflux

Behavior does not occur exclusively during the course of Anorexia Nervosa or Bulimia Nervosa

If symptoms occur exclusively during the course of mental retardation or a pervasive developmental disorder, they are sufficiently severe to warrant independent clinical attention

redity, early problems in embryonic or perinatal development, environmental influences, mental disorders, and medical conditions.

LEARNING DISORDERS

In learning disorders, the child's achievement in reading, mathematics, or written expression is substantially below that expected for age, schooling, and level of intelligence. The learning problems significantly interfere with academic achievement or daily living. Approximately 5 percent of United States public school students have a learning disorder. Learning disorders are different from normal variations in academic achievement and from lack of opportunity, poor teaching, or cultural factors. Impaired vision or hearing may affect learning ability, and so should be investigated if a learning disorder is suspected.

Learning disorders can involve problems with reading, mathematics, written expression, or some combination of these areas. In reading disorder, a family pattern is often present, and 60 to 80 percent of affected children are boys. In mathematics and written expression disorder, parents or teachers typically notice a problem as early as second or third grade but not earlier, because most children are exposed to little mathematics or formal writing instruction before then.

MOTOR COORDINATION DISORDERS

Motor coordination disorders involve performance in daily activities that is substantially below that expected given the child's age and intelligence. They include marked delays in achieving motor milestones (such as sitting), clumsiness, and poor performance in handwriting or sports.

DSM-IV-TR Criteria for Tic Disorders

CHRONIC MOTOR OR VOCAL TIC DISORDER (DSM CODE 307.22)

Single or multiple motor or vocal tics (sudden, rapid, recurrent, nonrhythmic, stereotyped motor movements or vocalizations), but not both, at some time during the disorder

Tics occur many times a day nearly every day or intermittently throughout a period of more than one year; during this period, no tic-free periods of more than three consecutive months

Disturbance causes marked distress or significant impairment in social, occupational, or other important areas of functioning

Onset before age eighteen

Disturbance not due to direct physiological effects of a substance (such as stimulants) or a general medical condition (such as Huntington's disease or postviral encephalitis)

Criteria for Tourette's Disorder never met

TOURETTE'S DISORDER (DSM CODE 307.23)

Both multiple motor and one or more vocal tics (sudden, rapid, recurrent, nonrhythmic, stereotyped motor movements or vocalizations) at some time during the disorder, although not necessarily concurrently

Tics occur many times a day (usually in bouts) nearly every day or intermittently throughout a period of more than one year; during this period, no tic-free periods of more than three consecutive months

Onset before age eighteen

Disturbance not due to direct physiological effects of a substance (such as stimulants) or a general medical condition (such as Huntington's disease or postviral encephalitis)

TRANSIENT TIC DISORDER (DSM CODE 307.21)

Single or multiple motor and/or vocal tics (sudden, rapid, recurrent, nonrhythmic, stereotyped motor movements or vocalizations)

Tics occur many times a day, nearly every day for at least four weeks, but for no longer than twelve consecutive months

Disturbance causes marked distress or significant impairment in social, occupational, or other important areas of functioning

Onset before age eighteen

Disturbance not due to direct physiological effects of a substance (such as stimulants) or a general medical condition (such as Huntington's disease or postviral encephalitis)

Criteria for Tourette's Disorder or Chronic Motor or Vocal Tic Disorder never met

TIC DISORDER NOT OTHERWISE SPECIFIED (DSM CODE 307.20)

To qualify for a diagnosis of motor coordination disorder, the problem is not due to a general medical condition or pervasive developmental disorder. If the child is mentally retarded, the motor difficulties exceed those associated with the retardation.

COMMUNICATION DISORDERS

Communication disorders include problems with expressive or receptive language, phonology, stuttering, or some combination of these areas. Aspects of these problems vary depending on their severity and the child's age.

When the problem involves expressive language, the features may include limited speech, limited vocabulary, difficulty acquiring new words, and simplified sentences. Nonlinguistic functioning and comprehension, however, are within normal limits. When the problem involves difficulties with both expressive language and receptive language, the child also has difficulty understanding words, sentences, or specific types of words. When the problem involves phonology, the child fails to use developmentally expected speech sounds. Severity ranges from little to completely unintelligible speech, and lisping is particularly common. When the problem involves stuttering, the child has a disturbance in the normal fluency and time patterning of speech.

PERVASIVE DEVELOPMENTAL DISORDERS

Pervasive developmental disorders are characterized by severe, pervasively impaired social interaction or communication skills or by stereotyped behavior, interests, and activities. These disorders include autism, Asperger's disorder, Rett's disorder, childhood integration disorder, or some combination of these symptoms. These disorders are usually evident in the first years of life and are often associated with some degree of mental retardation. They are sometimes observed with a diverse group of other general medical conditions, including chromosomal abnormalities, congenital infections, and structural central nervous system abnormalities.

Autism involves markedly abnormal social interactions and communication and a markedly restricted repertoire of activity and interests. The child may fail to maintain eye-to-eye contact or share enjoyment, interests, or achievements spontaneously with others and may develop no age-appropriate peer relationships. The child also shows qualitative impair-

ment in communication, such as delay in developing spoken language, inability to initiate or sustain a conversation, or stereotyped, repetitive use of language. Children with this disorder may be oblivious to other children, including siblings. Onset is prior to age three years. Asperger's disorder involves similar social deficits but no delays in language acquisition, though subtler forms of communication may be affected.

Rett's disorder and childhood integrative disorder involve multiple specific deficits following a period of normal functioning after birth. In Rett's disorder, which has been diagnosed only in girls, head growth decelerates between four and forty-eight months. The child loses previously acquired hand skills and develops poorly coordinated gait or trunk movements. Also, he or she loses social engagement and has impaired expressive and receptive language. Childhood integrative disorder involves similar deterioration, but the period of normal development is longer. The deficits in expressive or receptive language, social skills, bowel or bladder control, play, or motor skills occur after age two but before age ten. Childhood integrative disorder is more common in boys than in girls.

ATTENTION-DEFICIT AND DISRUPTIVE BEHAVIOR DISORDERS

These disorders include attention-deficit hyperactivity disorder (ADHD), conduct disorder, and oppositional defiant disorder. ADHD involves persistent inattention and/or hyperactivity-impulsivity that is more severe than is typical for the child's age. Symptoms are present before age seven, persist for at least six months, and are present in at least two settings, such as school and home. Most children show a combined set of problems, including both inattention and hyperactivity. A few children show either the inattention symptoms or the hyperactivity-impulsivity symptoms.

Conduct disorder involves repetitive, persistent behavior that violates the basic rights of others or major age-appropriate social norms. Children with conduct disorder may cause or threaten harm to people or animals, cause property loss or damage, display deceitfulness or theft, or seriously violate rules. Oppositional defiant disorder involves recurrent negative, defiant, disobedient, and hostile behavior toward authority figures. Conduct disorder may develop in childhood or adolescence; oppositional defiant disorder typically develops before age eight years. In both cases, the behavior pattern is usually present in a variety of settings.

FEEDING AND EATING DISORDERS

These disorders include persistent feeding and eating disturbances. They include pica, rumination, feeding disorder, anorexia, and bulimia.

Pica involves persistently eating one or more nonnutritive substances, such as paint or dirt. The behavior is developmentally inappropriate and not part of a culturally sanctioned practice.

Rumination involves repeated regurgitation and rechewing of food after feeding. Infants may develop rumination after a period of normal functioning, and it lasts for at least one month. The infant shows no apparent nausea, retching, disgust, or associated gastrointestinal disorder. Age of onset is between three months and twelve months.

Feeding disorder involves persistent failure to eat adequately without a gastrointestinal or other general medical explanation. Infants with this disorder may be more irritable and difficult to console during feeding than other infants. Age of onset is before six years.

Anorexia nervosa, often called simply anorexia, involves refusing to maintain a minimally normal body weight (85 percent less than expected), being intensely afraid of gaining weight, and having a distorted body image. Anorexia is most characteristic of middle-class, white adolescent girls in industrial societies in which attractiveness is linked to thinness. These teenaged girls typically have such a low body weight that they stop having menstrual periods.

Bulimia nervosa, often called simply bulimia, involves binge eating and inappropriate compensatory methods to prevent weight gain, such as purging or using laxatives excessively. Episodes of binging and purging occur at least twice a week for at least three months. Individuals with this disorder experience a lack of control over eating, and their self-evaluation is unduly influenced by body shape and weight. Bulimia is also most typical of adolescent girls from industrialized societies.

TIC DISORDERS

A tic is a sudden, rapid, recurrent, nonrhythmic, stereotyped motor movement or vocalization. For example, the person may have an eye tic that involves small, jerky, involuntary movement of the muscles surrounding the eye. All children and adults experience mild tics, but a tic disorder means that the tics are frequent, recurrent, and not due to substances or medical conditions.

Simple motor tics are movements such eye blinking, nose wrinkling, or neck jerking that usually last less than several hundred milliseconds. Complex motor tics include hand gestures, jumping, stomping, and squatting that last seconds or longer. Vocal tics may involve various words or sounds such as clicks, grunts, yelps, barks, or sniffs. Tourette's syndrome and transient tic disorder are two types of tic disorders.

Tourette's disorder involves multiple motor tics and one or more vocal tics that occur many times a day, recurrently throughout at least one year. The individual never has a tic-free period of more than three consecutive months. Onset is before age eighteen years, and, in a small minority of cases (less than 10 percent), the individual involuntarily utters obscenities. Transient tic disorder means that the individual has single or multiple motor or vocal tics that occur many times a day, nearly every day for at least four weeks, but for no longer than twelve consecutive months.

ELIMINATION DISORDERS

Elimination disorders involve age-inappropriate soiling (encopresis) or wetting (enuresis). Most often the behavior is involuntary, but occasionally it may be intentional. The incontinence must not be due to substances or a general medical condition.

Encopresis involves passage of feces into inappropriate places such as clothing or the floor that occurs at least once a month for at least three months. The child must be at least four years old. Most commonly, there is evidence of constipation and feces are poorly formed. Less often, there is no evidence of constipation and feces are normal. Encopresis is more common with boys than with girls.

Enuresis involves repeated voiding of urine into bed or clothes that occurs at least twice per week for at least three months or else causes clinically significant distress or impairment. The child must be at least five years old. Nocturnal enuresis occurs only at night and is most common. Diurnal enuresis occurs only during the day and more often with girls than with boys. It is uncommon after age nine.

DSM-IV-TR Criteria for Elimination Disorders

ENCOPRESIS

- With Constipation and Overflow Incontinence (DSM code 787.6)
- Without Constipation and Overflow Incontinence (DSM code 307.7)

Repeated passage of feces into inappropriate places such as clothing or floor (whether involuntary or intentional)

At least one such event a month for at least three months

Chronological age of at least four years (or equivalent developmental level)

Behavior not due exclusively to direct physiological effects of a substance (such as laxatives) or a general medical condition, except through a mechanism involving constipation

ENURESIS (DSM CODE 307.6)

Repeated voiding of urine into bed or clothes (whether involuntary or intentional)

Behavior is clinically significant as manifested by one of the following:

- frequency of twice a week for at least three consecutive months
- presence of clinically significant distress or impairment in social, academic (occupational), or other important areas of functioning

Chronological age of at least five years (or equivalent developmental level)

Behavior not due exclusively to direct physiological effect of a substance (such as a diuretic) or a general medical condition (such as diabetes, spina bifida, seizures)

Types: Nocturnal Only, Diurnal Only, Nocturnal and Diurnal

OTHER CHILDHOOD DISORDERS

A few other disorders are more characteristic of children than adults. They include separation anxiety disorder, selective mutism, reactive attachment disorder, and stereotypic movement disorder.

Although most children experience some transient anxiety when separated from a loved one, children with separation anxiety disorder have excessive anxiety when separated from the home or from their attachment figures. The anxiety lasts for at least four weeks, begins before age eighteen years, and causes clinically significant distress or impairment.

Children with selective mutism persistently fail to speak in specific social situations (such as school or with playmates) where speaking is expected, despite speaking in other situations. The disturbance interferes with educational or occupational achievement or with social communication. Selective mutism lasts for at least one month and is not limited to the first month of school, when many children may be shy and reluctant to speak.

Reactive attachment disorder involves markedly disturbed and developmentally inappropriate social relatedness in most contexts. It begins before age five and is associated with grossly pathological care. In inhibited attachment, the child persistently fails to initiate and respond to most social interactions in a developmentally appropriate way. In disinhibited attachment, the child shows indiscriminate sociability or a lack of selectivity in the choice of attachment figures. Thus, the child has diffuse attachments and shows excessive familiarity with relative strangers.

Stereotypic movement disorder involves motor behavior that is repetitive, seemingly driven, and nonfunctional. For example, the child may repeatedly strike a wall. The motor behavior markedly interferes with normal activities or results in self-inflicted bodily injury that would require medical treatment if unprotected.

ADULT DISORDERS IN CHILDREN

In addition to disorders associated with infancy, childhood, or adolescence, children may have behavioral or psychological disorders that are typically associated with adults. They include organic disorders, schizophrenia, mood disorders, anxiety, somatoform disorders, factitious disorders, dissociative disorders, sleep disorders, impulse-control disorders, and adjustment disorders.

Organic disorders are behavioral or psychological problems caused by substances such as cocaine or amphetamines or by medical conditions such as encephalitis. They include such symptoms as delirium, dementia, amnesia, and cognitive deficits.

Schizophrenia involves delusions, hallucinations, disorganized speech, or disorganized or catatonic behavior. It lasts for at least six months. Onset is typically late teens to mid-thirties.

Mood disorders include depression and bipolar disorder. Depression involves at least two weeks of depressed mood or loss of interest or pleasure in nearly all activities. Additional symptoms include changes in appetite, sleep, or activity; decreased energy; feelings of worthlessness or guilt; difficulty thinking, concentrating, or making decisions; and recurrent thoughts of death or suicide. Bipolar disorder involves at least one episode of mania as well as at least one episode of depression.

Anxiety disorders include panic disorder with or without agoraphobia, specific phobias, social phobias, obsessive-compulsive disorder, post-traumatic stress disorder, acute stress disorder, and generalized anxiety disorder. Panic attacks can occur in the context of any of these disorders.

Somatoform disorders involve physical symptoms that are not fully explained by a general medical condition or a substance. One somatoform disorder is somatization, which involves a combination of pain, gastrointestinal, sexual, and pseudoneurological symptoms. Another somatoform disorder is conversion, which involves physical symptoms that have no medical explanation. Other somatoform disorders are pain disorder, hypochondriasis (preoccupation with serious disease), and dysmorphic disorder (preoccupation with a defect in appearance).

Factitious disorders are characterized by intentionally produced physical or psychological symptoms. The motivation is to assume the sick role. In malingering, in contrast, the motivation is obvious when the environmental circumstances are known (such as avoiding a test at school).

Dissociative disorders involve disruptions in consciousness, memory, identity, or perception that are more than ordinary forgetfulness. One dissociative disorder is nonorganic amnesia, which involves an inability to recall important personal information, usually of a traumatic or stressful nature. An extreme form of memory loss is fugue, which involves an inability to recall one's past and confusion about personal identity. Fugue typically is characterized by sudden, unexpected travel away from home or loved ones. Another is dissociative identity disorder, formerly called multiple personality disorder, which is characterized by two or more distinct identities. Still another dissociative disorder is depersonalization, which involves a persistent or recurrent feeling of being detached from one's mental processes or body.

Sleep disorders may be due to other mental disorders, medical conditions, or substances. Primary sleep disorders that are presumed to arise from abnormalities in the ability to generate or time sleep-wake cycles. Conditioning often complicates primary sleep disorder. Symptoms of sleep disorder may include insomnia (difficulty initiating or maintaining sleep), hypersomnia (excessive sleepiness), narcolepsy (irresistible attacks of sleep), nightmares, sleep terror, or sleepwalking.

Impulse-control disorders may involve intermittent explosive episodes, kleptomania, pyromania, pathological gambling, or trichotillomania (hair-pulling). The essential feature of impulse-control disorders is a failure to resist an impulse, drive, or temptation to perform an act that is harmful to self or others.

Adjustment disorders involve a psychological response to an identifiable stressor that results in emotional or behavioral symptoms. As with other disorders, one must consider cultural setting in evaluating for the possibility of this disorder.

SOURCES FOR FURTHER STUDY

American Psychiatric Association. *Diagnostic and Statistical Manual of Mental Disorders: DSM-IV-TR.* Rev. 4th ed. Washington, D.C.: Author, 2000. The most comprehensive manual for diagnosing mental disorders.

Barkley, R. A. "Attention-Deficit Hyperactivity Disorder." *Scientific American,* September, 1998, 66-71. An expert covers the topic with insight and compassion.

Costello, C. G. *Symptoms of Schizophrenia.* New York: John Wiley & Sons, 2000. A good overview of schizophrenia.

Howlin, P. *Autism: Preparing for Adulthood.* London: Routledge, 1997. A good overview of autism.

Levy, T. M., and M. Orlans. *Attachment, Trauma, and Healing: Understanding and Treating Attachment Disorder in Children and Families.* Washington, D.C.: Child Welfare League of America, 1998. Describes holding therapy, a treatment for reactive disorders that requires parents to initiate physical contact with their child, by force if necessary.

Schwartz, S. *Abnormal Psychology: A Discovery Approach.* Mountain View, Calif.: Mayfield, 2000. One of the many good, basic abnormal psychology textbooks.

Shapiro, A. K., E. S. Shapiro, J. G. Young, and T. E. Feinberg. *Gilles de la Tourette Syndrome.* New York: Lippincott-Raven, 1998. A good compilation of the literature on Tourette's syndrome.

Lillian M. Range

SEE ALSO: Anxiety disorders; Attachment and bonding in infancy and childhood; Attention-deficit hyperactivity disorder (ADHD); Bed-wetting; Child abuse; Dyslexia; Family life: Children's issues; Father-child relationship; Juvenile delinquency; Learning disorders; Mother-child relationship; Parental alienation syndrome; Piaget, Jean; Prenatal physical development; Psychotherapy: Children; Schizophrenia: High-risk children; Separation and divorce: Children's issues; Sibling relationships; Stepfamilies; Stuttering; Teenage suicide; Violence by children and teenagers.

Children's Depression Inventory (CDI)

DATE: 1977 forward
TYPE OF PSYCHOLOGY: Psychopathology
FIELDS OF STUDY: Depression; childhood and adolescent disorders

The Children's Depression Inventory is a self-report questionnaire that allows children to report on their feelings of sadness and depression. This widely used questionnaire can be completed by children and adolescents themselves.

KEY CONCEPTS
• multiple informants
• norm
• psychometric properties

INTRODUCTION

The Children's Depression Inventory (CDI) was first developed in 1977 by Maria Kovacs. It was based on the Beck Depression Inventory, which is a self-report measure for depression for adults. The CDI was designed to assess depression in children and adolescents from the ages of seven to seventeen. The measure has twenty-seven items that ask children to report on their possible depressive experiences, such as feeling sad, crying a lot, not having fun anymore, being tired, not wanting to live, having trouble sleeping, experiencing low self-esteem, and having difficulties with friends.

The CDI is worded so that children and adolescents can read the questions themselves and write down their own answers. Each item offers three statements that signify varying levels of severity (from no problems to severe problems). Children and adolescents are asked to choose the statement that is most reflective of how they have been feeling within the past two weeks.

For example, one item gives children the following three options: I am sad once in a while. I am sad many times. I am sad all the time. Children are asked to put a mark by the sentence that describes their feelings. The first sentence (I am sad once in a while) is something that even people who are not depressed would be likely to endorse, whereas the third sentence (I am sad all the time) is more reflective of depression.

There is no specific item that confirms a diagnosis of depression. Instead, all of the items on the CDI are added together to provide an overall picture of how the child feels. The measure has been normed so that a child's responses are compared against other children of that age and gender. The idea is that children's answers should be compared with what is average or normative for that age and gender. Through this norming process, professionals can be sure not to diagnose a child who is just feeling normal amounts of distress. Overall, the CDI can help professionals gain a better understanding of children's and adolescents' feelings of depression and related concerns.

STRENGTHS AND WEAKNESSES

One of the primary strengths of the CDI is that it is very widely used throughout many countries. This commonality allows easy communication between professionals. The norms and standardization sample of the CDI allow professionals to have confidence in their interpretations of children's and adolescents' depressive symptoms. The strong psychometric properties suggest that the CDI is reliable (that is, stable) and valid (that is, meaningful). In addition, the CDI is very practical to use because it is easy to administer and to score, and it is not expensive for professionals to purchase.

Even with these strengths, the CDI has some limitations. Although it was originally meant to assess depression only, there is now research to suggest that it assesses other problems as well as depression. For example, children who have difficulty with school or who have problems with peers because of excessive fighting might receive high scores on the CDI. Thus, it is important for professionals to assess many aspects of the child's life rather than relying on the CDI alone to help diagnose depression.

OTHER METHODS TO ASSESS CHILDHOOD DEPRESSION

Even with a well-respected measure such as the CDI, it is standard practice for professionals to use a variety of measures before diagnosing depression in children and adolescents. In addition to the CDI, professionals could conduct a structured diagnostic interview (such as the Diagnostic Interview Schedule for Children) with the child to assess for symptoms of depression and other psychological difficulties. Professionals may also want to observe the child (either in their office or in the classroom) to evaluate how the child interacts with others and to assess for depressive symptoms such as withdrawal or crying.

In addition to gathering information from the child directly, it is incumbent on professionals to utilize multiple informants (such as parents and teachers) to assess depression. The term "multiple informants" is used to suggest that other individuals in the child's life can provide useful information about the child's psychological symptoms. Structured diagnostic interviews can be conducted with parents about their child and both parents and teachers can complete behavior checklists that might shed more light on the child's psychological functioning. Many widely used behavior checklists (such as the Child Behavior Checklist and the Teacher Report Form, both developed by Tom Achenbach) can be used in conjunction with the CDI. Professionals should try to get an overall view of the child's functioning and the family's functioning, rather than using the CDI by itself to diagnose depression.

SOURCES FOR FURTHER STUDY

Cole, David A., Kit Hoffman, Jane M. Tram, and Scott E. Maxell. "Structural Differences in Parent and Child Reports of Children's Symptoms of Depression and Anxiety." *Psychological Assessment* 12, no. 2 (2000): 174-185. Describes a study that compares children's responses on the CDI and a parent-report version of the CDI. This study shows a strong design for investigating the meaning of the CDI.

Gladstone, Tracy R. G., and Nadine J. Kaslow. "Depression and Attributions in Children and Adolescents: A Meta-analytic Review." *Journal of Abnormal Child Psychology* 23, no. 5 (1995): 597-606. Provides an overview of the connections between the CDI and children's thoughts related to depression.

Kovacs, Maria. *Children's Depression Inventory Manual.* North Tonawanda, N.Y.: Multi-health Systems, 1992. This manual provides the entire history and current use of the CDI. Professionals who use the CDI often consult this manual for clarifications regarding scoring and interpretation of the CDI.

Liss, Heidi, Vicky Phares, and Laura Liljequist. "Symptom Endorsement Differences on the Children's Depression Inventory with Children and Adolescents on an Inpatient Unit." *Journal of Personality Assessment* 76, no. 3 (2001): 396-411. This study explores the use of the CDI in an ethnically diverse sample of children who were severely troubled. The study found that issues other than depression (such as conduct problems, school problems) are assessed by the CDI.

Petersen, Anne C., Bruce E. Compas, Jeanne Brooks-Gunn, Mark Stemmler, Sydney Ey, and Kathryn E. Grant. "Depression in Adolescence." *American Psychologist* 48, no. 2 (1993): 155-168. This article is considered a classic description of depression in children and adolescents. The article is especially good for readers interested in finding out more about depression in childhood and adolescence.

Vicky Phares

SEE ALSO: Beck Depression Inventory (BDI); Depression.

Circadian rhythms

TYPE OF PSYCHOLOGY: Biological bases of behavior; consciousness; stress

FIELDS OF STUDY: Biology of stress; depression; endocrine system; nervous system; sleep

Circadian rhythms are cyclical variations in biological processes or behavior with a duration of about one day. The sleep-wake cycle, body temperature, mental abilities and many other physiological functions show circadian rhythms. The severity of many human diseases, such as asthma and hypertension, also fluctuates in a diurnal pattern. Shift-work problems, jet lag, and seasonal affective disorder are examples of disorders caused by alterations in circadian rhythms initiated by external environmental changes.

KEY CONCEPTS
- chronobiology
- circadian rhythm
- free-running rhythm
- jet lag
- melatonin
- seasonal affective disorder
- suprachiasmatic nucleus
- Zeitgeber

INTRODUCTION

Circadian rhythms are a fundamental characteristic of life. "Circadian" refers to rhythms that are about a day in length (from the Latin *circa*, "about," and *diem*, "day"); the term was coined by Franz Halberg. Although historically many of the early observations were made on plants and animals, the examples cited here come primarily with humans.

The most obvious rhythm of human activity is the sleep-wake cycle. Each day, humans are most active during the daylight hours, then sleep for much of the dark period. A species with this schedule is called "diurnal" (animals active during the dark period are termed "nocturnal"). People are essentially diurnal, but shift workers may adapt completely over a period of weeks to a nocturnal schedule of activity.

This pattern is such a natural part of human lives that its role in human physiology is underappreciated and underinvestigated. It is known that the sleep-wake cycle is not determined as rigidly as many other physiological rhythms. For example, one can choose not to sleep for several days and thereby temporarily abolish the pattern. A more fundamental and less easily modified rhythm is the

circadian rhythm of body temperature. In this case, there is a daily fluctuation of slightly more than 1 degree centigrade over the course of twenty-four hours, with the lowest body temperature occurring around 4:00 A.M. to 5:00 A.M. Of importance is the fact that the temperature rhythm continues its fluctuation, although somewhat dampened, even if a person stays awake for several days.

There are additional characteristics of circadian rhythms that are surprising. For example, the rhythms behave as though they are endogenous—that is, oscillations are produced within the organism rather than originating from the outside. An area of the brain called the hypothalamus has a cluster of nerve-cell bodies called the suprachiasmatic-nuclei, which, if destroyed, will abolish various rhythms, including the temperature rhythm in some animals. (Several of the body's circadian rhythms are believed to be regulated by this part of the brain.) An additional source of evidence that circadian rhythms are basically endogenous is the fact that when living organisms, including humans, are kept in constant conditions, the rhythms free-run and show a period, or length, which is different from exactly twenty-four hours.

Free-running rhythms, those that are not synchronized by an environmental signal, are observed in humans if the individual lives for many days or weeks in an isolated cave or bunker where possible time cues such as the light-dark cycle or other factors have been eliminated. The famous cave explorer Michel Siffre found that he had a sleep-wake cycle of twenty-four hours, thirty-one minutes when he lived alone in a cave without time cues for two months. Similar studies in the more controlled environments of World War II bunkers were carried out by the German scientist Jürgen Aschoff. In each case, it was found that the body's rhythms gradually drifted out of phase with the actual time of day when watches and the natural cycle of light changes were eliminated. Aschoff termed factors which maintain a circadian periodicity Zeitgebers, or "time givers." Individual subjects were found to have their own unique period, or length, for their free-running rhythms—for example, 24.3, 24.5, 24.7, or 24.9 hours. It has been well documented that various rhythms such as the sleep-wake cycle, body temperature, blood pressure, respiration rate, and urinary excretion of sodium, under constant conditions, will show slightly different period lengths and will therefore become desynchronized. Desynchronization, which may occur in the elderly under normal living conditions, is thought by some scientists to lead to various disease states. For example, episodes of mania in people with bipolar illness can be triggered by travel to a geographical zone with increased sunlight.

Various mental abilities in humans have been shown to be subject to circadian variations. One's ability to estimate time duration varies during the day inversely to the daily change in temperature. The ability to memorize numbers is better in the morning than in the afternoon, and one's ability to add random numbers is better in the morning than in the afternoon. Eye-hand coordination changes with a circadian rhythm, with skills better during the day and performance reduced at night. The existence of these rhythms has many implications, and the further study of such rhythmic factors remains a vital common ground between physiology and psychology.

The hypothalamus, located just above the pituitary gland in the brain, is thought to regulate many human rhythms. Its cell clusters, or nuclei, receive input from various sense organs and brain areas. In response, they secrete "releasing hormones," which travel to glands in the body and stimulate release of other, second and third downstream hormonal systems that modulate body processes. These hypothalamic nuclei and secondary hormones are active in many cyclical patterns. For example, female sex hormones from the pituitary gland follow characteristic circadian patterns, monthly patterns that develop the female ovum (egg) and regulate each menstrual cycle, and lifetime patterns that initiate sexual maturation and menopause.

These hormones act on many body organs, which therefore also show circadian rhythms. Heart rate, blood pressure, metabolism, and body temperature are all lower at night than during the day. Triggered by a surge of cortisol, another pituitary hormone, in the early morning hours, heart rate and blood pressure rise. This pattern stresses the cardiovascular system and is likely responsible for the clear increased incidence of heart attacks during these hours.

Manipulating Circadian Rhythms

The most familiar way humans apply their understanding of body clocks is to adjust to external changes in the sleep-wake cycle. A person can willfully avoid sleep for hours without a parallel increase in fatigue, as is attested by students who get a "second wind" once they study past 3:00 to 4:00 A.M. Some researchers envision an underlying circadian rhythm of alertness and fatigue that enhances one's ability to awaken in the morning and to fall asleep in the late evening. In general, it is easier to awaken in the morning, when one's body temperature is increasing, and it is easier to fall asleep in the late evening, when one's temperature is falling. So-called owls and larks do exist in the human population; persons who fall into these two groups differ in when their body temperature peaks, with larks peaking earlier.

The detailed makeup of sleep also shows periodicity. Brain waves measured with an electroencephalograph (EEG) record four distinct waves, each associated with a type and depth of sleep that repeats two to five times each night. The pattern changes with age; children sleep most deeply on initiation of sleep, while adults sleep most deeply just before waking. Rapid eye movement (REM) sleep, associated with dreaming, occurs more frequently later during the sleep period. Most major cities now have sleep laboratories in which scientists monitor the sleep of patients and apply theories involving circadian rhythms to improve the type and timing of medications.

Shift Work and Jet Lag

When people are forced to change their sleep-wake schedule, for either work or travel, shift-work problems and jet lag can result. Shift work is required in circumstances in which around-the-clock services are either essential or economically beneficial. These include medical, police, military, utility, transportation, and other essential services, as well as tasks in the chemical, steel, petroleum, and various other manufacturing industries. Work is done and days off are given according to many different schedules. A number of catastrophic events, such as the Three Mile Island nuclear accident (1979), the chemical explosion in Bhopal, India (1984), and the Chernobyl nuclear accident (1986) happened during the late-evening or night shift, when fatigue of ill-adapted workers may have been a factor. Within the population, there are "owls" who can adapt to night shift work without the physical problems experienced by their comrades. It is known that physiological and behavioral rhythms will shift to a new schedule only if the schedule is kept the same for a period of weeks. Shift workers who stay on their schedule of night work and day sleep will quickly shift their sleep-wake cycle and eventually shift their various behavioral and more fundamental physiological rhythms such as body temperature. Because the body's circadian rhythms are more than twenty-four hours in length, it is easier to start work later on successive days than it is to start work earlier.

What later became known as jet lag was first experienced by Wiley Post and Harold Gatty on their 1931 around-the-world airplane trip. By the 1950's, increasing numbers of tourists, diplomats, flight crews, and pilots were suffering from the general malaise, headaches, fatigue, disruptions of the sleep-wake cycle, and gastrointestinal disorders that can occur when people cross several time zones within a few hours. As for shift work, there have been catastrophic accidents that may have been caused in part by the inability of workers to adjust rapidly to a new time frame. The effects are worse on eastward flights than on westward flights, perhaps because the circadian rhythms can undergo an adjustment to a lengthening in timing better than to a shortening. A night flight from New York to Paris results in a six-hour time shift, with breakfast coming six hours early according to one's nonshifted circadian rhythms. Within a few days, one's sleep-wake cycle adjusts, but deeper physiological rhythms may take two or more weeks to shift to the new time zone.

Various means have been used to reduce the effects of jet lag. Most experienced diplomats or business persons plan to arrive at the site of negotiations a few days early so that they will have a chance to adjust. It can also help to begin to shift one's activities and sleep pattern a few hours in the direction of the anticipated shift a day or two before one leaves home. Mild sedatives can be used effectively to induce sleep, but the efficacy of complicated diets and most other regimens recommended in the popular press has not been supported by studies performed on humans.

SEASONAL AFFECTIVE DISORDER

Another application of chronobiology is in the study and treatment of seasonal affective disorder (SAD). People with SAD typically experience clinical depression in March and April, at the end of the win-

ter months of shorter daylight. This depression is unlike the more common melancholic depression, which is characterized by loss of sleep and appetite, in that it is accompanied by increased eating, particularly of carbohydrates, and increased sleep, up to sixteen hours per day. It is also distinguished from the winter blues, which occurs in one of four individuals, usually earlier in the winter. While SAD is not considered a variant of bipolar disorder, it resembles bipolar disorder in the type of depressive symptoms and its relationship to sunlight. Many highly creative individuals, such as artist Vincent Van Gogh, writers Tennessee Williams and Edgar Allan Poe, President Abraham Lincoln, and many others have suffered either bipolar illness or SAD, describing the "seasons of the mind" in their work.

Circadian rhythms are fundamental to the pathophysiology and treatment of SAD. Response to daylight is modulated by a pea-sized organ midline under the cerebral hemispheres of the brain called the pineal gland. In darkness, the pineal gland secretes melatonin and possibly other substances. Information about light, transmitted along specific nerve pathways from the eyes, inhibits release of melatonin. While it is not clear exactly how loss of daylight leads to seasonal depression, bright light therapy can reverse or prevent it, possibly by altering circadian rhythms such as those influencing mood, sleep, and appetite via secondary effects of melatonin.

Psychiatrists treat SAD by having a person sit in front of a light box for thirty to sixty minutes early in the morning and at dusk. The light box emits 1,500 lux light at a frequency that mimics sunlight. This treatment is usually effective within a week. Those with recurrent episodes can also use the light box prophylactically or schedule vacations in sunny climates during their most vulnerable periods.

The severity of other illnesses also follows a circadian rhythm. Stomach acid secretion peaks in the late afternoon and just after midnight, leading to worsened symptoms of peptic ulcers at these times. Drugs that inhibit acid secretion are given at night to take advantage of this phenomenon. Similarly, asthma exacerbations tend to occur at night; predictably, oral medications for asthma produce better results if given before bedtime. Some types of high blood pressure peak at night, others in the morning; again, drugs should be given so that peak drug levels coincide with peak blood pressure readings.

Scientists are just beginning to understand cellular and genetic biorhythms. As they do, treatment will become increasingly specific and effective. Already, chemotherapy is given for cancer at more exact times to coincide with the most vulnerable period of cancer cell division, allowing for lower doses, fewer side effects, and better treatment results. As circadian rhythms are better understood, many aspects of health and daily life may be managed with greater ease.

CIRCADIAN RHYTHM RESEARCH

In 1729, a French astronomer, Jean Jacques d'Ortous de Mairan, reported his observations on the leaf movements of a "sensitive" heliotrope plant that continued to open and close its leaves approximately every twenty-four hours even when it was kept in continuous dark. This was the first demonstration of a free-running rhythm. Studies on humans included those by Sanctorius, who in the seventeenth century constructed a huge balance upon which he was seated in a chair and studied circadian rhythms in body weight. Julian-Joseph Virey, a Parisian pharmacist, postulated endogenous biological clocks modified by environmental input in his 1814 doctoral thesis, and is credited with formally establishing the field of chronobiology. Yet despite these early studies, it was the 1950's before circadian rhythms were more widely studied and research on humans began to be more common.

In psychology, Nathaniel Kleitman and Eugene Aserinsky in the 1940's discovered rapid eye movement, or REM, sleep. The rhythmic patterns in REM sleep and their relation to the circadian sleep-wake cycle have remained an active area for research. The psychobiologist Curt Richter carried out work on the activity rhythms in rats. Richter also identified the general area in which the suprachiasmatic nuclei are found as a region of the hypothalamus important in controlling circadian rhythms. Simon Folkard and colleagues have studied various human performance tests and have found numerous circadian rhythms. They found that the circadian rhythms in memory tests peaked at different times, depending on the complexity of the number to be memorized. There remains a need for more research by psychologists who incorporate variation due to circadian rhythm into their research design.

SOURCES FOR FURTHER STUDY

Ahlgren, Andrew, and Franz Halberg. *Cycles of Naure: An Introduction to Biological Rhythms.* Washington, D.C.: National Science Teachers Association, 1990. An easy-to-read introduction to biological rhythms written expressly for the high school student. Contains simple experiments, some of which would make ideal science-fair projects or classroom demonstrations. Very nicely illustrated and well written, this booklet covers most of the fundamental characteristics of circadian rhythms. Highly recommended to students and teachers alike.

Binkley, Sue A. *Biological Clocks: Your Owner's Manual.* Amsterdam: Harwood Academic Publishers, 1997. A wide-ranging discussion of historical, personal, zoological and human topics in chronobiology. A pleasurable read for the advanced high school student or layperson, with an annotated bibliography to direct further research.

Coleman, Richard. *The Twenty-Four-Hour Business: Maximizing Productivity Through Round-the-Clock Operations.* New York: American Management Association, 1995. This international authority on shift-work scheduling writes practical guidelines for anyone involved in business planning on how to address safety and alertness issues while maximizing productivity.

Minors, D. S., and J. M. Waterhouse. *Circadian Rhythms and the Human.* Boston: John Wright, 1981. A comprehensive textbook that reviews hundreds of research reports to give an outstanding overview of the field. Written for the college level and above. A classic.

Redfern, Peter H, and Bjorn Lemmer, eds. *Physiology and Pharmacology of Biological Rhythms.* New York: Springer-Verlag, 1997. An advanced textbook for the postgraduate level and above.

Rosenthal, Norman E. *Winter Blues: Seasonal Affective Disorder—What It Is and How to Overcome It.* New York: Guilford, 1998. An update to his prior excellent books on the symptoms and treatment of SAD by the director of light therapy research at the National Institute for Mental Health. Includes listings of resource centers and detailed descriptions of dietary, drug and light treatments.

Siffre, Michel. *Beyond Time.* New York: McGraw-Hill, 1964. An enthralling account of the adventures of a cave explorer who stays without a clock alone in caves for months at a time and carefully notes his physiological and psychological changes.

Written for the general public, this book generated wide interest in such isolation experiments. Fascinating reading.

Winfree, Arthur T. *The Timing of Biological Clocks.* New York: Scientific American Library, 1987. A beautifully illustrated book that covers philosophical concepts of time and clocks as well as the nature of circadian and other biological rhythms. Some sections are rather mathematical, but these are well worth the effort to understand and appreciate. Recommended for the college-level or motivated high school student.

John T. Burns;
updated by Elizabeth Haase

SEE ALSO: Bipolar disorder; Dreams; Ethology; Health psychology; Insomnia; Seasonal affective disorder; Sleep.

Clinical depression

TYPE OF PSYCHOLOGY: Psychopathology
FIELDS OF STUDY: Depression

Clinical depression is an emotional disorder characterized by extreme sadness or a loss of ability to experience pleasure. Its clinical features also include symptoms that are cognitive (for example, low self-worth), behavioral (for example, decreased activity level), and physical (for example, fatigue). Depression is a frequently diagnosed disorder in both inpatient and outpatient mental health settings.

KEY CONCEPTS
• anhedonia
• Beck Depression Inventory (BDI)
• Children's Depression Inventory (CDI)
• cognitive therapy for depression
• dysphoria
• dysthymic disorder
• helplessness
• monoamine oxidase inhibitors (MAOIs)
• tricyclics

INTRODUCTION

Clinical depression is a severe emotional disorder that is characterized by four classes of symptoms:

emotional, cognitive, behavioral, and physical. The major emotional symptoms, at least one of which is necessary for the diagnosis of depression, are dysphoria (extreme sadness or depressed mood) and anhedonia (lack of capacity to experience pleasure). Depressed individuals also experience cognitive symptoms. They may have feelings of worthlessness or excessive or inappropriate guilt. Some may have recurrent thoughts of death or suicidal ideation; others actually attempt suicide or create a specific plan for doing so. Behavioral symptoms of depression may include either restlessness or agitation, diminished ability to think or concentrate, and indecisiveness. Depressed individuals also experience several physical symptoms. They become easily fatigued, experience a loss or gain in appetite, show significant weight loss or gain, and experience sleep disturbances, such as insomnia (an inability to fall asleep) or hypersomnia (excessive sleepiness).

PREVALENCE

Depression is one of the more commonly experienced mental disorders. For example, in 1985, psychologists John Wing and Paul Bebbington examined research that used psychological tests to measure the prevalence of (or lifetime risk for) depression in the general population. They found that estimates of the prevalence of depression generally ranged from about 5 to 10 percent. Interestingly, all the studies examined by Wing and Bebbington agreed that depression was more common in women than in men. Estimates of the prevalence of depression ranged from 2.6 to 4.5 percent in men and from 5.9 to 9.0 percent in women.

Depression is also related to other characteristics. Risk for depression increases with age. The evidence is clear that depression is more common in adults and the elderly than in children or adolescents. Interest in childhood depression has increased since the early 1970's, however, and the number of children and adolescents who have been diagnosed as depressed has increased since that time. Depression is also related to socioeconomic status. In general, people who are unemployed and who are in lower income groups have higher risks for depression than others. This may be a result of the higher levels of stress experienced by individuals in lower-income groups. Finally, family history is related to depression. That is, clinical depression tends to run in

Many of the psychosocial stressors associated with old age, such as the deaths of loved ones and chronic illnesses, are common causes of clinical depression. (PhotoDisc)

families. This is consistent with both biological and psychological theories of depression.

Psychologists face several difficulties when attempting to determine the prevalence of depression. First, the symptoms of depression range in severity from mild to severe. It may not always be clear at which point these symptoms move from the mild nuisances associated with "normal" levels of sadness to significant symptoms associated with clinical depression. Since the early 1970's, clinical psychologists have devoted an increased amount of attention to depressions that occur at mild to moderate levels. Even though these milder depressions are not as debilitating as clinical depression, they produce significant distress for the individual and so warrant attention. In 1980, the term "dysthymic disorder" was introduced to describe depressions which, although mild to moderate, persist chronically.

Another complication in determining the prevalence of depression is that it may occur either as a primary or as a secondary problem. As a primary problem, depression is the initial or major disorder which should be the focus of clinical intervention. On the other hand, as a secondary problem, depression occurs in reaction to or as a consequence of another disorder. For example, many patients experience such discomfort or distress from medical or mental disorders that they eventually develop the symptoms of depression. In this case, the primary disorder and not depression is usually the focus of treatment.

TREATMENT APPROACHES

There are several major approaches to the treatment of clinical depression, each focusing on one of the four classes of symptoms of depression. Psychoanalytic therapists believe that the cause of depression is emotional: underlying anger which stems from some childhood loss and which has been turned inward. Psychoanalysts therefore treat depression by helping the client to identify the cause of the underlying anger and to cope with it in a more effective manner.

Psychiatrist Aaron T. Beck views depression primarily as a cognitive disorder. He holds that depressives have negative views of self, world, and future, and that they interpret their experiences in a distorted fashion so as to support these pessimistic views. A related cognitive model of depression is that of Martin E. P. Seligman. He argues that depression

---

DSM-IV-TR Criteria for Major Depression

MAJOR DEPRESSIVE EPISODE

Five or more of the following symptoms present during the same two-week period and representing a change from previous functioning:

- depressed mood or loss of interest or pleasure (at least one); does not include symptoms clearly due to a general medical condition, mood-incongruent delusions, or hallucinations
- depressed mood most of the day, nearly every day, as indicated by either subjective report or observation made by others; in children and adolescents, can be irritable mood
- markedly diminished interest or pleasure in all, or almost all, activities most of the day, nearly every day, as indicated by either subjective account or observation made by others
- significant weight loss (when not dieting) or weight gain or decrease/increase in appetite nearly every day; in children, consider failure to make expected weight gains
- insomnia or hypersomnia nearly every day
- psychomotor agitation or retardation nearly every day observable by others, not merely subjective feelings of restlessness or being slowed down
- fatigue or loss of energy nearly every day
- feelings of worthlessness or excessive or inappropriate guilt (which may be delusional) nearly every day, not merely self-reproach or guilt about being sick
- diminished ability to think or concentrate, or indecisiveness, nearly every day, either by subjective account or as observed by others
- recurrent thoughts of death (not just fear of dying), recurrent suicidal ideation without a specific plan, or suicide attempt or specific plan for committing suicide

Criteria for Mixed Episode not met

Symptoms cause clinically significant distress or impairment in social, occupational, or other important areas of functioning

Symptoms not due to direct physiological effects of a substance or general medical condition

Symptoms not better accounted for by bereavement, persist for longer than two months, or characterized by marked functional impairment, morbid preoccupation with worthlessness, suicidal ideation, psychotic symptoms, or psychomotor retardation

MAJOR DEPRESSIVE DISORDER, SINGLE EPISODE (DSM CODE 296.2X)

Presence of single Major Depressive Episode

Major Depressive Episode not better accounted for by Schizoaffective Disorder and not superimposed on Schizophrenia, Schizophreniform Disorder, Delusional Disorder, or Psychotic Disorder Not Otherwise Specified

No Manic Episodes, Mixed Episodes, or Hypomanic Episodes, unless all manic-like, mixed-like, or hypomanic-like episodes are substance- or treatment-induced or due to direct physiological effects of a general medical condition

Specify for current or most recent episode: Severity/Psychotic/Remission Specifiers; Chronic; with Catatonic Features; with Melancholic Features; with Atypical Features; with Postpartum Onset

MAJOR DEPRESSIVE DISORDER, RECURRENT (DSM CODE 296.3X)

Presence of two or more Major Depressive Episodes; with an interval of at least two consecutive months in which criteria not met for Major Depressive Episode

Major Depressive Episodes not better accounted for by Schizoaffective Disorder and not superimposed on Schizophrenia, Schizophreniform Disorder, Delusional Disorder, or Psychotic Disorder Not Otherwise Specified

No Manic Episodes, Mixed Episodes, or Hypomanic Episodes, unless all manic-like, mixed-like, or hypomanic-like episodes are substance- or treatment-induced or due to direct physiological effects of a general medical condition

Specify for current or most recent episode: Severity/Psychotic/Remission Specifiers; Chronic; with Catatonic Features; with Melancholic Features; with Atypical Features; with Postpartum Onset

Specify: Longitudinal Course Specifiers (with and Without Interepisode Recovery); with Seasonal Pattern

results from the perception that one is helpless or has little or no control over the events in one's life. Seligman has shown that laboratory-induced helplessness produces many of the symptoms of depression. Cognitive therapy for depression, which Beck described in 1979, aims at helping depressed clients identify and then change their negative and inaccurate patterns of thinking.

Behavioral therapists view depression as the result of conditioning. Psychologist Peter Lewinsohn suggests that depression results from low amounts of reinforcement. His behavioral therapy for depression aims at increasing reinforcement levels, through scheduling pleasant activities and improving the client's social skills.

Biologically oriented therapies exist as well. Two classes of antidepressant medications, monoamine oxidase inhibitors (MAOIs) and tricyclics, are effective both in treating clinical depression and in preventing future episodes of depression. Electroconvulsive (shock) therapy (ECT) has also been found to be effective in treating severe depression. Although the reasons the biological treatments work have not been conclusively identified, it is thought that they are effective because they increase the activity or amount of norepinephrine and serotonin, two neurotransmitters which are important in the transmission of impulses in the nervous system.

DEPRESSION MEASURES

In 1983, Eugene Levitt, Bernard Lubin, and James Brooks reported the results of the National Depression Survey, which attempted to determine the prevalence and correlates of depression in the general population. They interviewed more than 3,000 people, including 622 teenagers, who were randomly selected to be a representative sample of the entire United States population. Subjects completed a brief self-report measure of depression and answered questions concerning their age, occupation, education, religion, and other variables.

Levitt, Lubin, and Brooks found that slightly more than 3 percent of the population was experiencing depression that was severe enough to warrant clinical intervention and so could be termed clinical depression. This figure is similar to that found by other investigators. In addition, Levitt, Lubin, and Brooks found that depression was related to sex, age, occupational status, and income. Depression was higher for subjects who were female, older,

lower in occupational status, and either low or high in income (earning less than $6,000 or more than $25,000).

One of the most widely used measures of depression is the Beck Depression Inventory (BDI). Beck introduced this test in 1961 to assess the severity of depression in individuals who are known or suspected to have depression. The BDI has twenty-one items, each concerning a symptom of depression (for example, weight loss, suicidal thinking) which is rated for severity. The BDI can be self-administered or can be completed by an interviewer.

Since its introduction, the BDI has become one of the most widely used measures of depression for both research and clinical purposes. Many studies have shown that the BDI is an accurate and useful measure of depression. For example, BDI scores have been found to be related to both clinicians' ratings of the severity of a client's depression and clinical improvements during the course of treatment for depression, and to be able to discriminate between the diagnosis of clinical depression and other conditions.

Psychologist Maria Kovacs developed the Children's Depression Inventory (CDI) by modifying the BDI for use with children. Similar in format to the BDI, the CDI contains twenty-eight items, each of which concerns a symptom of depression that is rated for severity. Research has supported the utility of the CDI. CDI ratings have been found to be related to clinicians' ratings of childhood depression. CDI scores have also been found to discriminate children hospitalized for depression from children hospitalized for other disorders. The CDI (along with other measures of childhood depression) has contributed to psychology's research on and understanding of the causes and treatment of childhood depression.

DEPRESSION RESEARCH

Many research projects since the 1970's have examined the effectiveness of cognitive and behavioral treatments of depression. Beck and his colleagues have demonstrated that cognitive therapy for depression is superior to no treatment whatsoever and to placebos (inactive psychological or medical interventions which should have no real effect but which the client believes have therapeutic value). In addition, this research has shown that cognitive therapy is about as effective as both antidepressant medications and behavior therapy. Similarly, Lewinsohn and others have shown the effectiveness of behavior therapy on depression by demonstrating that it is superior to no treatment and to placebo conditions.

One of the most important studies of the treatment of depression is the Treatment of Depression Collaborative Research Program, begun by the National Institute of Mental Health (NIMH) in the mid-1980's. A group of 250 clinically depressed patients was randomly assigned to four treatment conditions: interpersonal psychotherapy, cognitive behavioral psychotherapy, tricyclic antidepressant medication, and placebo medication. Treatment was presented over sixteen to twenty sessions. Patients were assessed by both self-report and a clinical evaluator before treatment, after every fourth session, and at six-, twelve-, and eighteen-month followups after the end of treatment.

This study found that patients in all four treatment conditions improved significantly over the course of therapy. In general, patients who received antidepressant medication improved the most, patients who received the placebo improved the least, and patients who received the two forms of psychotherapy improved to an intermediate degree (but were closer in improvement to those receiving antidepressant medication than to those receiving the placebo). This study also found that, for patients in general, there was no significant difference between the effectiveness rates of the antidepressant medication and the two forms of psychotherapy.

For severely depressed patients, however, antidepressant medication and interpersonal psychotherapy were found to be more effective than other treatments; for less severely depressed patients, there were no differences in effectiveness across the four treatment conditions.

THEORIES

Clinical depression is one of the most prevalent psychological disorders. Because depression is associated with an increased risk for suicide, it is also one of the more severe disorders. For these reasons, psychologists have devoted much effort to determining the causes of depression and developing effective treatments.

DSM-IV-TR Criteria for Dysthymic Disorder (DSM code 300.4)

Depressed mood for most of the day, more days than not, indicated either by subjective account or observation by others, for least two years

In children or adolescents, mood can be irritable and duration must be at least one year

Presence, while depressed, of two or more of the following:
- poor appetite or overeating
- insomnia or hypersomnia
- low energy or fatigue
- low self-esteem
- poor concentration or difficulty making decisions
- feelings of hopelessness

During this two-year period (one year in children or adolescents), person has never been without symptoms for more than two months at a time

No Major Depressive Episodes during this two-year period (one year in children or adolescents)

Disturbance not better accounted for by chronic Major Depressive Disorder or Major Depressive Disorder, in Partial Remission

Previous Major Depressive Episode is possible, provided there was full remission (no significant signs or symptoms for two months) before development of Dysthymic Disorder

After initial two years (one year in children or adolescents) of Dysthymic Disorder, superimposed episodes of Major Depressive Disorder are possible; in that case, both diagnoses may be given when criteria are met for Major Depressive Episode

No Manic Episodes, Mixed Episodes, or Hypomanic Episodes

Criteria not met for Cyclothymic Disorder

Disturbance does not occur exclusively during the course of a chronic Psychotic Disorder, such as Schizophrenia or Delusional Disorder

Symptoms not due to direct physiological effects of a substance or general medical condition

Symptoms cause clinically significant distress or impairment in social, occupational, or other important areas of functioning

Specify: Early Onset (before age twenty-one) or Late Onset (age twenty-one or older)

Specify for most recent two years: with Atypical Features

Theories and treatments of depression can be classified into four groups: emotional, cognitive, behavioral, and physical. In the first half of the twentieth century, the psychoanalytic theory of depression, which emphasizes the role of the emotion of anger, dominated clinical psychology's thinking about the causes and treatment of depression. Following the discovery of the first antidepressant medications in the 1950's, psychologists increased their attention to physical theories and treatments of depression. Since the early 1970's, Beck's and Seligman's cognitive approaches and Lewinsohn's behavioral theory have received increased amounts of attention. By the 1990's, the biological, cognitive, and behavioral theories of depression had all surpassed the psychoanalytic theory of depression in terms of research support for their respective proposed causes and treatments.

Another shift in emphasis in psychology's thinking about depression concerns childhood depression. Prior to the 1970's, psychologists paid relatively little attention to depression in children; classical psychoanalytic theory suggested that children had not yet completed a crucial step of their psychological development that psychoanalysts believed was necessary for a person to become depressed. Thus, many psychologists believed that children did not experience depression or that, if they did become depressed, their depressions were not severe. Research in the 1970's demonstrated that children do experience depression and that, when depressed, children exhibit symptoms similar to those of depressed adults. Since the 1970's, psychologists have devoted much effort to understanding the cause and treatment of childhood depression. Much of this work has examined how the biological, cognitive, and behavioral models of depression, originally developed for and applied to adults, may generalize to children.

Another shift in psychology's thinking about depression concerns the attention paid to mild and moderate depressions. Since the 1960's, clinical psychology has been interested in the early detection and treatment of minor conditions in order to prevent the development of more severe disorders. This emphasis on prevention has influenced the field's thinking about depression. Since the early 1970's, psychologists have applied cognitive and behavioral models of depression to nonpatients who obtain high scores on measures of depression. Even though these individuals are not clinically depressed, they still experience significant distress and so may benefit from the attention of psychologists. By using cognitive or behavioral interventions with these individuals, psychologists may prevent the development of more severe depressions.

SOURCES FOR FURTHER STUDY

Beck, Aaron T., A. J. Rush, B. F. Shaw, and G. Emery. *Cognitive Therapy of Depression.* 1979. Reprint. New York: Guilford Press, 1987. Summarizes the cognitive theory of depression and describes how this model can be applied in the treatment of depressed clients.

Beutler, Larry E., John F. Clarkin, and Bruce Bongar. *Guidelines for the Systematic Treatment of Depressed Patients.* New York: Oxford University Press, 2000. Summarizes the current state of research and extracts treatment principles that can be applied by mental health professionals from a wide range of theoretical backgrounds.

Blazer, Dan. *Depression in Late Life.* 3d ed. New York: Springer, 2002. A comprehensive review of the treatment of depression among the elderly. Covers epidemiology, pharmacology, depression and cognitive impairment, unipolar and bipolar disorders, bereavement, and existential depression.

Hammen, Constance. *Depression.* New York: Psychology Press, 1997. A modular course presenting research-based information on the diagnosis and treatment of depression. Written for students and mental health professionals.

Lewinsohn, Peter M., Rebecca Forster, and M. A. Youngren. *Control Your Depression.* Rev. ed. New York: Simon & Schuster, 1992. A self-help book for a general audience. Describes Lewinsohn's behavioral therapy, which has been found to be an effective treatment for depression.

Nezu, Arthur M., George F. Ronan, Elizabeth A. Meadows, and Kelly S. McClure, eds. *Practitioner's Guide to Empirically Based Measures of Depression.* New York: Plenum, 2000. Reviews and compares more than ninety measures of depression in terms of requirements, suitability, costs, administration, reliability, and validity.

Seligman, Martin E. P. *Helplessness: On Depression, Development, and Death.* Reprint. San Francisco: W. H. Freeman, 1992. Seligman explains the learned helplessness theory of depression, describing his early research and comparing the symptoms of laboratory-induced helplessness to those of clinical depression.

Michael Wierzbicki

SEE ALSO: Bipolar disorder; Cognitive behavior therapy; Cognitive therapy; Depression; Diagnosis; Drug therapies; Mood disorders; Seasonal affective disorder; Shock therapy; Suicide; Teenage suicide.

Clinical interviewing, testing, and observation

DATE: The early twentieth century forward
TYPE OF PSYCHOLOGY: Personality
FIELDS OF STUDY: Personality assessment

Clinical interviewing, testing, and observation are the three major components of a comprehensive assessment used to develop a formulation of person's personality, make a diagnosis, and develop a plan of treatment. Each of these components contributes to the development of an integrative view of the patient, which is focused on the referral question or why the assessment was requested.

KEY CONCEPTS
- chief complaint
- clinical formulation
- clinical interviewing
- cognitive assessment
- compulsions
- delusions
- hallucinations
- mental status exam
- neuropsychological assessment
- obsessions
- personality assessment
- phobias
- psychological testing

INTRODUCTION
The purpose of clinical interviewing, testing, and observation is to obtain a clear, comprehensive, balanced view of the patient, which is termed a clinical formulation, and to develop a rational treatment plan to address the patient's difficulties. Clinical interviewing, in combination with observation, is the backbone of all mental health professions, a creative and dynamic process that represents a somewhat elusive set of complex skills, including integrating a large amount of information about a person into a clinically useful formulation, developing a diagnosis, and making recommendations for treatment based on the clinical assessment. Today the clinician is required to perform many types of interviews suited to the clinical task at hand, including assessments in settings as diverse as an inpatient psychiatric unit; an inpatient medical unit; a psychotherapy practice, a consultation and liaison setting; and an emergency room. Psychological testing may also be needed to gain additional information and to validate a diagnosis developed during the clinical interview and observations.

CLINICAL INTERVIEWING AND OBSERVATION
The clinical interview can be structured, semistructured, or unstructured. In the structured interview, the clinician covers the topics in a consistent way, using one of several published guidelines. In the semistructured interview, only part of the interview uses a published interview schedule. Most clinicians use a free-flowing, unstructured exchange between the clinician and patient. No matter what format is used, the clinician will work to develop rapport with the patient so that the essential information needed to help the patient can be obtained. Observation of the patient's verbal and nonverbal behavior is also noted during the interview.

Whether the interview is structured, semistructured, or unstructured, the clinician must produce a written record of the interview. This report is focused on the referral question, which is the reason the assessment was requested. Most clinicians begin by presenting identifying information such as the patient's name, age, marital status, sex, occupation, race or ethnicity, place of residence and circumstances of living, and referral information. The chief complaint or the problem for which the patient seeks professional help is usually described next and is stated in the patient's own words. The intensity and the duration of the problem are noted, including any possible precipitating events, such as the loss of a loved one. Symptoms associated with the chief complaint are assessed and noted in the report.

Current and past health history, for both physical and psychological problems, is important to review. There are physical illnesses that may affect the patient's psychological state and vice versa. Prior episodes of emotional and mental disturbances should be described. The clinician needs to inquire about and report prescribed medication and alcohol and drug use.

Personal history may include information about the patient's parents and other family members and any family history of psychological or physical problems. The account of the patient's own childhood and noteworthy experiences can be very detailed. Educational and occupational history are outlined, along with social, military, legal, and marital experiences. The mental status exam is also part of the clinical interview and written report.

THE MENTAL STATUS EXAM

The mental status exam is simply the clinician's evaluation of the patient's current mental functioning. It is a staple of the initial mental health examination. The mental status exam may be viewed as consisting of two major parts: the behavioral observation aspects and the cognitive aspects.

The behavioral observation aspects include noting general appearance and behavior, mood, and flow of thought of the patient. General appearance and behavior are assessed by noting such things as the patient's apparent age in relation to stated age (for instance, does the patient look younger or older than he or she actually is?), body posture, degree of alertness, hygiene, motor activity, facial expressions, and voice quality. Anything that seems outside the general norm would be noted (for instance, agitation). The clinician should also note any physical difficulties such as the need to wear glasses. The basic quality of mood is closely monitored and noted during the interview. The basic moods can be boiled down to anger, anxiety, contentment, disgust, fear, guilt, irritation, joy, sadness, shame, and surprise. Finally, the flow of the patient's thoughts must be described if it is unusual in any way.

It is important to clearly delineate any noteworthy aspects of the person's appearance, behavior, mood, or thought content rather than just providing a summary statement. For example, the clinician may write in the report that the person had a sad face and appeared to be about to cry, yet claimed to be happy. Another patient may have jumped from topic to topic and seemed unaware that there appeared to be no connection between topics. Attitude toward the clinician is also important. For example, some patients might be openly hostile while others are very cooperative. All the findings made in this first portion of the mental status exam are generally discovered by observation alone.

The second part of the mental status exam, the cognitive aspect, is determined by asking the patient certain types of questions. Some clinicians fail to assess the cognitive aspects of the mental status exam, despite the critical importance of this information to the overall evaluation of the patient. These clinicians may believe that it may be insulting to ask obvious questions of a patient who appears unimpaired. The clinician can prepare the patient for such questions by explaining that these questions are just a routine part of the clinical interview. The initial questions assess the person's orientation to person, place, and time. That is, does the patient know who he or she is, where he or she is (city, state, facility), and what the date is? Then the patient is asked to memorize three common objects. Serials sevens are conducted, a task in which the patient is asked to subtract seven from one hundred, and then subtract seven from the result and so on toward zero. After that task is completed, the patient is asked to name the three objects memorized earlier. Other tasks may include naming objects the clinician points to, such as a pencil, following three-stage commands, and copying simple designs. These tasks assess attention, concentration, language, and short-term memory. Abstract thinking ability can be assessed by asking the patient to interpret proverbs (for instance, "What does it mean when someone says that people that live in glass houses shouldn't throw stones?" or explain likenesses and differences (such as, "How are an orange and an apple alike?").

In this part of the mental status exam, the patient's content of thought is noted, particularly bizarre ideas. A delusion is a fixed, false belief that cannot be explained by the patient's culture and education. Types of delusions include delusions of grandeur (such as believing that one is a musical virtuoso when one actually has little musical ability), body change (for instance, believing that one's insides are rotting), reference (such as believing that others are always talking about one), and thought broadcasting (for instance, believing that one's thoughts can be transmitted across the world). Hallucinations are false sensory perceptions that occur in the absence of a related sensory stimulus. Any of the five senses can be involved in hallucinations, but it is the auditory or visual modalities that are typically involved. For example, a patient may see someone who is not there. A phobia is an unreasonable and intense fear associated with some object (such as spiders) or some situation (such as closed spaces). Finally, the presence of obsessions and compulsions needs to be assessed. An obsession is a belief, idea, or thought that dominates the patient's thought content, while a compulsion is an impulse to perform an act repeatedly in a way that the patient realizes is neither appropriate nor useful.

INTERVIEWING INFORMANTS

While most patients will tell clinicians all they need to know, it is often useful to obtain information about the patient's present difficulties from other sources such as relatives, friends, and other mental health professionals. In some instances, verifying data or seeking additional information is essential. For example, information gained from children, adolescents, and adults who are psychotic or have limited cognitive ability may need to be verified and supplemented. Having a personality disorder may not particularly bother the patient, but family and friends suffer and can offer specific examples of problems involving the patient. Informants can also give information about cultural norms, childhood health history, and other relevant facts. Therefore, valuable information can be gained from people who know the patient well.

Interviewing informants will provide the opportunity to gain additional insight into the patient's interpersonal relationships. The extent and quality of emotional and tangible support available to the patient may also be determined. Emotional support is having someone to talk to about problems, everyday occurrences, and triumphs. Types of tangible support include financial assistance, a place to live, and transportation to work and doctors' appointments.

PSYCHOLOGICAL TESTING

Testing may be requested by the mental health professional to clarify issues that came up in the clinical interview and to validate a diagnostic impression. Psychological testing is essentially assessing a sample of behavior using an objective and standardized measure. While all mental health professionals are trained to conduct clinical interviews, typically, applied psychologists conduct and interpret the testing required. Applied psychologists include school, clinical, and counseling psychologists. The type of testing requested depends on what information is needed to answer the referral question or questions. For example, if there were some question about the patient's level of intelligence, cognitive testing would be needed. The types of testing requested may include personality assessment, cognitive assessment, and assessment of specific abilities or interests. Personality assessment is the measurement of affective aspects of a person's behavior such as emotional states, motivation, attitudes, interests, and interpersonal relations using standardized instruments. Cognitive assessment includes intelligence, achievement, and neuropsychological testing. Neuropsychological testing is used to assess brain dysfunction. The measurements of specific abilities or interests include assessing multiple aptitudes such as the potential to do well in a certain type of job (such as mechanical skills) and the measurement of values and interests. Information gathered from the clinical interview, observations, and the results of the tests are integrated into a formal report usually written by a psychologist.

While some instruments can be administered by those trained by a psychologist, others require rather extensive training. For example, most pencil and paper instruments such as the well-known Minnesota Multiphasic Personality Inventory II (MMPI-2), a comprehensive personality assessment instrument, require little training to administer. Others, such as individual intelligence tests and most projective instruments (such as the Rorschach inkblot test), require extensive advanced training to administer. Interpretation of psychological tests needs to be done by doctoral-level applied psychologists.

Behavioral observations are also done during the testing process. How does the patient approach the task? For example, one patient may approach a task in a careful, systemic way, while another patient may use a trial-and-error approach. Verbalizations during testing are noted and may reveal a pattern of behavior. Some patients, for example, may consistently make excuses for what they perceive as poor performance on tests. Signs of anxiety, restlessness, boredom, anger, or other noteworthy reactions are important data.

Information gleaned from various psychological tests, the clinical interview, and behavioral observations are formed into a comprehensive and useful report with a diagnosis and specific recommendations for treatment. Writing this type of psychological report is a highly developed skill formed in graduate-level coursework and during extensive supervised experience.

THE DSM

The results of the clinical interview, observations, and any psychological testing are used to develop a clinical formulation and to decide on a diagnosis. The *Diagnostic and Statistical Manual of Mental Disorders: DSM-IV-TR* (rev. 4th ed., 2000) is the primary diagnostic system used by all mental health professionals. In the DSM-IV-TR, the clinical formulation is summarized on five axes. Axis I consists of all clinical syndromes and V codes (conditions that are not attributable to a mental disorder, but are a focus for therapeutic intervention) except for personality disorders and developmental disorders, which are noted on Axis II. While there are a large number of mental disorders that can be noted on Axis I or II, they can be categorized into seventeen general categories, such as mood disorders, schizophrenia and related disorders, personality disorders, and anxiety disorders. Examples include academic problems, occupational problems, and uncomplicated bereavement. Axis II lists diagnoses only from the personality disorders and developmental disorders categories. There are several personality disorders including narcissistic, paranoid, avoidant, and dependent. Developmental disorders include mental retardation and autistic disorder. Axis III summarizes any physical disorders or conditions the patient currently has which are relevant to the mental disorder. Axis IV lists psychosocial and environmental problems that are grouped into nine categories, such as problems with primary support group, economic problems, and problems related to the legal system/crime. Finally, Axis V is a global assessment of functioning. Ratings are to be made by combining symptoms and occupational and interpersonal functioning on a 100-point scale, with 100 as the highest level. This rating measure is called the Global Assessment of Functioning scale or GAF

scale. Two GAF ratings are made. The first rating is the highest level of functioning over the past year that was sustained for at least a two-month period. This rating may help to predict the outcome of treatment. The current level of functioning is reflected in the second rating.

SOURCES FOR FURTHER STUDY

American Psychiatric Association. *Diagnostic and Statistical Manual of Mental Disorders: DSM-IV-TR*. Rev. 4th ed. Washington, D.C.: Author, 2000. The renowned and well-regarded DSM-IV-TR is indispensable for a thorough understanding of current diagnostic thinking. There are descriptions of each mental disorder with specific criteria for diagnosis along with associated features, specific cultural, age and gender patterns, prevalence rates, and course of the mental illness.

Gladding, Samuel T. *Counseling: A Comprehensive Profession*. 4th ed. Upper Saddle River, N.J.: Prentice Hall, 2000. This text describes in an interesting and informative manner the historical foundations of counseling, counseling process and theory, and skills and specialties in the practice of counseling. The chapter on building a counseling relationship includes a thorough description of conducting the initial interview with an empathic stance.

Goldstein, Gerald, and Michel Hersen. *Handbook of Psychological Assessment*. 2d ed. New York: Pergamon, 1990. This edited book contains three excellent chapters on clinical interviewing. The first is an overview and includes the history of interviewing techniques, how to diagnosis and how to conduct a mental status exam. The other two chapters focus on structured interviews for children, adolescents, and adults. There are also useful chapters on behavioral assessment, the use of psychological assessment in treatment and the psychological assessment of minority group members.

Morrison, James. *The First Interview: A Guide for Clinicians*. 2d ed. New York: Guilford, 1995. This is an excellent introductory text for students in psychology, psychiatry, social work, counseling, medicine, and nursing. It describes how to elicit information for a clinical interview from even the most challenging patient. Numerous clinical vignettes are provided to fully illustrate these effective techniques. This text also provides detailed instructions on how to integrate the information obtained into a useful report.

Reik, Theodore. *Listening with the Third Ear.* New York: Farrar, Straus, 1952. This book is a classic. It focuses on the free-format style of interviewing and contains a variety of insights concerning issues such as conscious and unconscious observation, free-floating attention, and the therapist-patient working alliance.

Karen D. Multon

SEE ALSO: Beck Depression Inventory (BDI); California Psychological Inventory (CPI); Children's Depression Inventory (CDI); Diagnosis; *Diagnostic and Statistical Manual of Mental Disorders* (DSM); Minnesota Multiphasic Personality Inventory (MMPI); Personality interviewing strategies; Personality: Psychophysiological measures; Personality rating scales; State-Trait Anxiety Inventory; Thematic Apperception Test (TAT).

Coaching

DATE: The 1970's forward
TYPE OF PSYCHOLOGY: Social psychology
FIELDS OF STUDY: Adulthood; attitudes and behavior; interpersonal relations

Coaching is a strategy, most commonly used in business-related organizations, to help executives increase their personal effectiveness and manage their careers.

KEY CONCEPTS
- coaching practice
- content coaching
- developmental coaching
- external versus internal coaching
- feedback coaching

INTRODUCTION

Executives in most organizations, regardless of their level of responsibility, are challenged with the impact of technology, competitive markets, consumer demands, the expectations of a diverse workforce, and the problems associated with leadership. The practice of executive coaching, as an intervention, has been used in business settings since the 1970's. During this period, executives were enrolled in short-term programs to learn skills such as business etiquette and employee relations. In the 1980's, more sophisticated programs were developed that also focused on personal effectiveness. By the late 1990's, executive coaching was considered one of the fastest growing areas in consulting, with the number of coaches estimated in the tens of thousands.

The increased popularity of coaching is linked to its efficiency and cost-effectiveness. It is intended to be a goal-focused, personal plan for managers to improve performance, enhance a career, or work through organizational issues. The one-on-one, targeted approach of coaching adds to its appeal.

MODELS OF COACHING

Coaching can be categorized into three areas: feedback coaching, developmental coaching and content coaching. Each is delivered differently and variations are based on company needs. However, all types of coaching are designed to help managers enhance their skills or improve in a specific area. Feedback coaching involves helping managers create a plan that addresses a particular need and giving them a responsive evaluation. An assessment instrument is used to identify strengths and areas needing improvement. Coaching usually occurs through several in-person conversations over a one- to six-month period. It begins with a planning meeting and is followed by subsequent sessions that assess progress and challenges and provide encouragement. The final meeting is used to conduct a mini-assessment and update the development plan. At this point, there also may be an option to continue coaching.

In-depth coaching generally lasts between six months and one year. This type of coaching is characterized as a close, intimate relationship between the executive and the coach. The information collection and analysis phase are extensive and typically involve interviews with the executive's staff, colleagues, and in some instances, clients, vendors, and family members. Multiple assessment tools are used to measure competencies, interests, and strengths. The coach may even observe the executive at work.

These data are reviewed during an intensive feedback session, which may last up to two days, and it results in the creation of a development plan. The coach continues to be involved during the implementation phase of the plan to determine progress, discuss roadblocks, and offer support. This work continues until the development plan has been completely implemented and the executive has made noticeable improvements.

Content coaching distinguishes itself from the other types of coaching because its goal is to help managers learn about specific areas of knowledge or develop a certain skill. For example, a manager may need to know more about global marketing or how to improve presentation skills. Content coaches, as experts in specialized fields, may require managers to read books to increase their content knowledge about a topic and participate in follow-up discussions. Other forms of coaching may involve analyzing videotaped role-playing or demonstrations and attending seminars or one-on-one meetings. The manager's skill level and the desired outcome determine the duration of the coaching.

EXTERNAL VERSUS INTERNAL COACHES

The cornerstones of the coaching relationship are trust and confidentiality. The degree of a coach's involvement with the organization whose members are being coached is the source of debate, especially regarding whether a coach should be external or internal. External coaches offer a safe place for the coaching process. As outside resources, they have no appearance of a conflict of interest. Since they have no company-related interest in the outcome, the managers can speak freely without fear of reprisal.

Internal coaches have the dual role of serving both the company and the employee. An advantage is that the internal coach knows the organization's policies and people. This knowledge can serve to benefit the overall organizational and individual goals. However, the sense of anonymity is lost, which could result in a compromise of the coaching relationship. In either instance, the integrity of the coaching relationship contributes to its success.

THE FUTURE OF COACHING

Although coaching is characterized by the individual nature of the relationship between the executive and the coach, it occurs within the context of an organization. Many coaches believe that merely helping executives to change is insufficient, because these executives have created organizations that reflect their own personalities and inadequacies. Therefore, the responsibilities of the coach must broaden to encourage the executive to implement changes in a way that will benefit the entire organization. The notion of coaching can then be extended to that of coaching organizations. In this way, team building and performance support techniques enable employees to manage themselves and their own behavior with increasing competence.

SOURCES FOR FURTHER STUDY

Cook, M. *Effective Coaching*. New York: McGraw-Hill, 1999. Employees will work harder and produce more when they believe they are appreciated, valued, and understood. The author explains how to apply good coaching methods in the workplace and quickly establish the discipline needed to create a cooperative, nonthreatening environment.

Flaherty, J. *Coaching: Evoking Excellence in Others*. Boston: Butterworth-Heinemann, 1999. Starting from the premise that one must understand people before one can coach, the author examines coaching from a sociological/psychological perspective. The book provides operating principles, assessment models, and sample coaching conversations.

Gilley, J. W. *Stop Managing, Start Coaching: How Performance Coaching Can Enhance Commitment and Improve Productivity*. New York: McGraw-Hill, 1997. The author suggests that managers should be performance coaches. This occurs through mentoring, career coaching, confrontation, and training.

Goldsmith, M., L. Lyons, and A. Freas, eds. *Coaching for Leadership: How the World's Greatest Coaches Help Leaders Learn*. San Francisco: Jossey-Bass/Pfeiffer, 2000. Written by executive coaches, this book provides an understanding of how and why coaching works and how managers can make the best use of the coaching process.

Markle, G. L. *Catalytic Coaching: The End of the Performance Review*. Westport, Conn.: Quorum Books, 2000. The author provides forms, instruments, and detailed instructions to operationalize this system which focuses on positive behavior change, motivation, retention, internal promotion, and the prevention of lawsuits.

O'Neill, M. *Executive Coaching with Backbone and Heart: A Systems Approach to Engaging Leaders with*

Their Challenges. San Francisco: Jossey-Bass, 2000. Effective coaches require courage, compassion, and initiative. This guidebook offers a four-phase methodology to manage the coach-client relationship.

Anna Lowe

SEE ALSO: Achievement motivation; Career selection, development, and change; Motivation; Sport psychology; Work motivation.

Codependency

TYPE OF PSYCHOLOGY: Psychopathology
FIELDS OF STUDY: Personality theory; substance abuse

Codependency is characterized by a lack of a stable self-concept, which manifests itself in a troubled perception of self and disturbed relationships with others. By compulsively taking care of others and denying their own needs, often to the point of serious self-neglect, codependents seek an identity through achieving a favorable image in the eyes of others.

KEY CONCEPTS
- addiction
- compulsion
- identity development
- self-concept
- systems theory

INTRODUCTION

At the foundation of codependency is a pervasive lack of identity development. Codependents look to others for thoughts, feelings, and values that would normally come out of a well-developed sense of self. For example, when asked to offer an opinion on the death penalty, a typical codependent might respond by waiting for the group consensus and then offering a "safe" response—one that would be most in keeping with the thoughts of the group. This is often done subconsciously and is in contrast to the healthy reaction of offering an honest personal viewpoint.

In truth, codependents do not withhold their feelings as much as they are unaware of what they feel, because of their incomplete development of a separate self: They cannot reveal what they literally do not know. Since their self-perceptions are composites of the reflections they have received from others, how they present themselves will vary, often markedly, depending on who is with them. Codependents have difficulty recognizing and articulating feelings, and they often hold back their feelings out of fear. Though they may not be aware of their feelings, their feelings do, nevertheless, influence them. Their needs remain unmet in their desire to please others, or at the very least to avoid disapproval. As a result, they accumulate anger and rage for which they have no healthy outlet. Depression is also common, particularly a low-grade, chronic depression that would be relieved if they could focus on their own needs.

CHARACTERISTICS

Codependents have high, and often unrealistic, expectations for themselves, and they tend to be perfectionists. An exaggerated fear of failure drives them, as does a barely conscious sense of being defective or somehow incomplete as a person. As the result of this poor evaluation of themselves, codependents fear getting close to others because others may judge them as harshly as they judge themselves. To guard against being "found out," they keep emotionally distant, though their behaviors may appear to others as genuinely warm and intimate. In truth, their real selves are closely guarded and available to no one—including themselves.

They often channel this backlog of unmet emotional needs into addictive or compulsive behaviors. When the pressure builds, codependents may seek diversion in shopping, gambling, work, chemicals, overeating, or other addictions. Instead of experiencing the emotional development that occurs from facing and overcoming interpersonal problems, codependents retreat further from their feelings through the quick "fix" of indulging in addictive behaviors. The effect of their inattention to their needs is cumulative and progressive and interferes with interpersonal relationships. Codependents take care of others, both emotionally and physically, to feel needed as caretakers. Their focus is primarily external, so they pay close attention to how others are feeling and behaving, then adjust how they act to receive the approval they crave.

Since codependents cannot be sure they are interpreting others' wants and needs correctly, their efforts to achieve approval are often unsuccessful. They have unrealistic perceptions of their abilities to control the environment, and when faced with normal limitations, they may frantically increase their efforts in the aim for perfection. As with all their efforts, the goal is self-esteem through external approval. Even when the approval is forthcoming, ironically, the satisfaction is small, because the approval is for a false representation of self. This leaves them feeling that if others really knew them, they would not be accepted. Codependents typically channel this feeling, as they do most other feelings, into more controlling and caretaking behaviors in an attempt to bolster self-esteem.

IDENTITY ISSUES

Because codependents have not developed clear identities, the interdependence between two persons that is characteristic of healthy relationships is not possible. Getting close brings fears of losing what little identity they have. Typically codependents move closer to others to achieve intimacy, then retreat when they fear the closeness will overwhelm them. They fear abandonment as well, so when the emotional distance from others seems too great, they move closer to others and again face their fears of intimacy overwhelming them. This dance between intimacy and distance is ultimately not satisfying and leaves the codependent feeling even more alone.

Codependency originates in settings where individuals feel unwilling or unable to display their true identities. Most typically, codependency occurs in addictive family systems where the family members' needs are secondary to the needs of the addicted individual. Family members cope with and adapt to the addiction in an attempt to stabilize the family system. Individual members' needs are not met if they conflict with the central need of keeping the family in balance and denying the effects of the addiction. Children in these family systems fail to develop separate identities because so much of their energy goes to controlling the environment. The adults in the family also may have failed to develop identities as children, or they may have abandoned their identities as adults under the pressure of keeping the family stable. In other words, codependency can be the result of the failure of normal identity development or of the abandonment of an already developed identity under the pressure of a dysfunctional family system.

FAMILY AND IDENTITY

A look at identity development in a healthy family system provides a clear picture of codependency. Theorist Erik Erikson proposed in 1963 that identity formation occurs through the resolution of crises throughout the life cycle. According to Erikson, as the individual masters the tasks of the various stages of development, he or she moves on to the next stage. Failure to work through the tasks of any stage results in incomplete development for the person. In a healthy family that meets a child's basic needs, he or she receives support and guidance to pass through the early stages of identity formation, as outlined by Erikson.

Stage one, trust versus mistrust, occurs from birth through the age of eighteen months; the second stage, autonomy versus shame and doubt, occurs between eighteen months and three years. Stage three, initiative versus guilt, lasts from the age of three to the age of six. Industry versus inferiority, the fourth stage, lasts from the age of six to age eighteen. The emerging identity is built upon the basic sense of trust the child develops in the early years of life. If experience teaches the child that others are not trustworthy, then the child's sense of self will be weak. Therefore, efforts to move through the later developmental stages will be hampered. In short, trust is essential to all the later developmental work.

In a family in which trust is not easily developed, such as in an addictive family system, the children direct most of their energy toward achieving a feeling of relative safety. The children learn to look to others to provide the sense of safety they could not develop internally. As they take care of other family members' needs, the family system remains stable, which provides a type of security, though the children's individual needs are not recognized and met. This external focus is adaptive in the short term, as the children are meeting some of their safety and security needs, but ultimately, mature identity development is thwarted. The more stable and emotionally healthy the parents are, the more likely it is that the child will successfully move through the later developmental stages. With the mastery of the developmental tasks, the child begins to feel like a competent individual in a stable and predictable environment. This emerging identity then forms the core of the self as a distinct individual.

ROLES AND IDENTITIES

Claudia Black (1981) identified roles that children adopt in alcoholic families in order to get some of their needs met. These roles have been found to be applicable to other dysfunctional family systems as well. The "responsible one," who is often the oldest child, functions as an adult by taking care of many basic needs of the family members, sometimes including the parents. The "adjuster" adapts to whatever the family system needs and avoids calling attention to himself or herself. The "placater" brings comfort and diversion to the family and takes on the responsibility for the family members' emotional stability. A final role is the "acting-out child," who keeps the family focused on his or her problem behaviors and receives punishment, criticism, and predominantly negative attention.

These roles can overlap so that the "responsible one" may alternate his or her overly mature behaviors with periods of acting out that direct the family's attention to the current problem and away from the fact that the whole family system is in trouble. The family can then console itself that without "the problem," it would be fine. The "placater" also might shift roles and take care of physical needs and responsibilities that would be more appropriately handled by the adults in the family. The "acting-out child" does not always act out; she or he can stop delinquent behaviors if they are not needed. The important issue for the development of codependency is not that children put the needs of the family ahead of their own but that they fill these roles to achieve safety emotionally and physically and fail to develop their own individual thoughts, needs, and feelings. Their development gets lost in their efforts to maintain the family balance.

This ability of codependents to adopt roles and cope despite how they feel is a major strength in certain settings, such as in an alcoholic or other unpredictable family setting. The adapting and responding to others becomes a problem when it is not a choice but is the only way that the codependent knows how to react. As adults, their behavioral repertoire is limited, as their response to demands is to adapt and take care of what everyone else needs first.

The picture is not as bleak as it may seem. Basic personality traits for such occupations as teaching, nursing, and counseling include empathy and the ability to "read" others, which are typically highly developed skills for codependents. On the whole, codependents are resourceful people who learned to survive in difficult circumstances by being acutely aware of the needs and viewpoints of others. The focus of treatment for these individuals is not to reconstruct their personalities but to help them expand their range of behavioral and emotional options.

THERAPY AND CODEPENDENCY

The term "codependency" originated in the 1970's in the alcohol-treatment field to describe individuals whose lives had become unmanageable because of their relationships with alcoholics. Prior to that time the term used was "co-alcoholic" or "para-alcoholic," which described a cluster of symptoms

---

Characteristics of Codependent People

- an exaggerated sense of responsibility for the actions of others
- a tendency to confuse love and pity, with the tendency to "love" people they can pity and rescue
- a tendency to do more than their share, all of the time
- a tendency to become hurt when people do not recognize their efforts
- an unhealthy dependence on relationships; the codependent will do anything to hold on to a relationship, to avoid a feeling of abandonment
- an extreme need for approval and recognition

- a sense of guilt when asserting themselves
- a compelling need to control others
- lack of trust in self and/or others
- fear of being abandoned or alone
- difficulty identifying feelings
- rigidity/difficulty adjusting to change
- problems with intimacy/boundaries
- chronic anger
- lying/dishonesty
- poor communication
- difficulty making decisions

Source: National Mental Health Association (NMHA) factsheet "General Mental Health Issues: Co-Dependency," 1997.

that the family members of the alcoholic displayed that included depression, anxiety, and interpersonal difficulties. The introduction of the term "codependency" helped to define the cluster of symptoms more clearly so that codependency became a legitimate focus for treatment. Families began receiving treatment targeted at their needs, at times completely independent of the alcoholic's treatment. Research showed that this focus on the family's need resulted in longer-term sobriety for the alcoholic.

In the 1980's, clinicians became aware that while codependency most obviously arose from alcoholic families or relationships, it also occurred where other addictions or serious dysfunctions were present. Thus, the model for understanding codependency began to be applied by professionals to diverse problems such as eating disorders, gambling, and other addictions. Codependency as an issue began to gain the attention of professionals beyond the addictions field and in other treatment disciplines.

Many traditional clinicians and researchers have been slow to accept codependency as a legitimate treatment issue since the theory has not been grounded in the scholarly research considered necessary for establishing new trends in the field. Clinicians who treat clients for codependency issues maintain, however, that it is not necessary to wait for research to verify what has already been shown to be useful in clinical practice. Their position is that when a treatment modality helps people, it is ethical to continue the treatment concurrently with the research that should ultimately validate their work. Treatment for codependency has been multifaceted and is apparently most effective when it includes some combination of individual or group therapy, self-help groups, workshops, and educational resources. Through the various treatment strategies, codependents begin to recognize the positive aspects of their personalities, such as adaptiveness and the ability to intuit what others need. In time they can learn to extend to themselves the same attention and caretaking they previously gave only to others.

A common fear of codependents is that if they stop being "caretakers" of others they will become uncaring individuals. This fear is usually unfounded, since greater intimacy and depth of emotion are possible in relationships in which individuals give to others by choice rather than through the continuing sacrifice of their own needs. Codependent personalities develop out of dysfunctional family, community, or other systems; when left untreated, this situation results in a continued poor self-concept and in disturbed relationships with others. Treatment has apparently been effective in helping codependents make significant changes. Recognition of codependent traits can therefore be a springboard for personal growth and development rather than a cause for despair.

SOURCES FOR FURTHER STUDY

Ackerman, Robert J., ed. *Growing in the Shadow: Children of Alcoholics.* Pompano Beach, Fla.: Health Communications, 1986. A collection of brief essays by leaders in the adult children of alcoholics and codependency recovery movements. Includes an outline of the causes and treatments of codependency as well as cross-cultural and family treatment considerations. Valuable to the professional yet readily comprehensible by the lay reader.

Beattie, Melody. *Codependent No More.* 2d ed. New York: Harper/Hazelden, 1996. A comprehensive overview of codependency that is complete with clear examples. A bestseller for many months and probably the most frequently read book in the codependency recovery movement. The majority of the book is devoted to selfhelp principles for codependents.

Black, Claudia. *It Will Never Happen to Me!* 1981. Reprint. New York: Ballantine, 1991. A brief book designed to introduce family members to the dysfunctional rules and roles of the alcoholic family.

Cermak, Timmen L. *Diagnosing and Treating Codependence.* Minneapolis: Johnson Institute Books, 1986. A proposal to have "codependency" declared a diagnostic category by the American Psychiatric Association. Aimed at a professional audience, but may be of interest to the lay reader.

Erikson, Erik H. *Identity, Youth, and Crisis.* 1968. Reprint. New York: W. W. Norton, 1994. Erikson's theory on the development of identity throughout the stages of the life cycle. A highly theoretical work.

Friel, John. *Adult Children: Secrets of Dysfunctional Families.* Deerfield Beach, Fla.: Health Communications, 1988. A comprehensive overview of dysfunctional family systems and their predictable effects on family members. Clearly written, a valuable resource for both general and professional audiences.

Schaef, Anne Wilson. *Co-dependence: Misunderstood-Mistreated.* Reprint. San Francisco: Harper & Row, 1992. An integration of the principles of the chemical dependency and mental health fields. Covers the history and development of the concept of codependence. Mostly written for a general audience; some chapters are directed toward professionals.

Linda E. Meashey

SEE ALSO: Addictive personality and behaviors; Alcohol dependence and abuse; Identity crises; Personality theory; Self-esteem; Substance use disorders.

Cognitive ability
Gender differences

TYPE OF PSYCHOLOGY: Cognition; developmental psychology

FIELDS OF STUDY: Adolescence; biological influences on learning; cognitive development; cognitive learning; cognitive processes; problem solving; thought

Cognitive differences between men and women have been attributed to both biological and social learning differences. Most differences are quite small; others can be reduced by educational and social intervention. Furthermore, different cognitive styles may encourage diverse solutions to important problems.

KEY CONCEPTS
- academic achievement
- adolescence
- cognition
- gender
- psychobiology

INTRODUCTION

The study of differences between men and women includes biological, emotional, social, and cognitive variables. Cognitive psychologists study the ways in which people process information, including perceiving, attending, learning and memory, and thinking and language. A pioneer review of all the studies concerning gender differences by Eleanor Maccoby and Carol Jacklin, published in 1974, concluded that the two sexes are more alike than different. Published studies note that there is considerable overlap between men's and women's performance, no matter what is being measured. An individual male or female may be much better than most of the opposite sex on any characteristic that is studied. The term "gender differences" refers to differences between groups, rather than between particular individuals. The degree of difference necessary to be considered significant does not necessarily have to be great, but the observed differences must be reliable.

Studies of cognitive abilities typically include assessments of verbal skills, including the ability to use and understand words and sentences; mathematical skills, including the ability to manipulate abstract symbols; and spatial skills or the ability to manipulate objects in space. Psychologists Janet Shibley Hyde, Nita McKinley, Paula and Jeremy Caplan, Mary Crawford, and Roger Chaffin have done extensive reviews of published studies on gender differences in cognition and have reported the following overall findings: There are no consistent gender differences in verbal abilities, except that females tend to perform better than males in speech production. Males tend to perform better on spatial abilities, but the sizes of these observed differences are highly dependent on what is required on each specific test. There are no consistent differences in mathematical abilities, with the exception that adolescent males tend to perform better than females on tests of mathematical problem solving. Finally, differences between men and women in science achievement are minute, and the sizes of such differences vary depending on the specific area of science being tested.

Many attempts have been made to determine whether gender differences are caused by biological or environmental factors. Traditionally, psychologists have referred to attempts to separate these causal factors as the "nature versus nurture" debate. However, biologist Anne Fausto-Sterling has said that biological and environmental influences on human development are inseparable. Attempts to separate these effects "both oversimplify biological development and downplay the interactions between an organism and its environment."

EDUCATIONAL SETTINGS

In educational settings, infants and preschool children are typically tested and observed on a one-to-one basis in the areas of verbal development and spatial ability. Differences before age six are relatively minor, but girls do have a slight advantage in verbal development. Some people believe that this occurs because their central nervous systems mature somewhat earlier than boys' nervous systems. Other studies have found that adults talk to girls more than to boys, perhaps changing the environment for the two sexes and thus their developing abilities.

In grade school, girls typically outperform boys, although boys receive more attention from teachers. Girls do at least as well at mathematics, and usually better in verbal activities, such as reading, writing, and spelling. Boys' relatively poorer performance has been attributed to the predominantly feminine atmosphere of the early school years and to their somewhat slower rate of neurological development. Boys tend to perform more extremely than girls. They are placed more often in special education classes for learning disabled or gifted children. Boys may also be more vulnerable to conditions such as attention-deficit hyperactivity disorder (ADHD) that may interfere with their academic achievement.

In adolescence, gender differences are at their most extreme. Girls who did quite well in school before adolescence often show a drop in grades as well as standardized test performance. Boys do much better, particularly in the areas of mathematics and science. A few researchers have suggested that increased amounts of testosterone, a male sex hormone, may be related to the teenage boy performing better in mathematics and related studies. However, the nature of the relationship between hormonal levels and the development of cognitive abilities is unknown. Psychologist Janet Hyde, however, has emphasized that cultural pressure to conform to traditional gender roles be-

Girls and boys may have different ways of solving problems. (CLEO Photography)

comes stronger in adolescence. The adolescent female is socialized to believe that achievement, particularly in male-dominated disciplines such as math and science, is gender inappropriate. This culturally imposed belief in "femininity-achievement incompatibility" puts girls "in a situation in which two equally important systems of value are in conflict." Thus, for a girl to continue to achieve in traditionally masculine disciplines is unfeminine. When they are younger, girls may be encouraged to get good grades and excel academically in all subjects, but this reward system may change abruptly when they reach adolescence when societal pressure to conform to the traditional feminine role gets stronger.

In adulthood, test-score differences tend to diminish. Janet Hyde has concluded that there are no verbal differences between the genders. Males, however, have traditionally accomplished more and have more often received social acknowledgments, such as the Nobel Prize. This seems to be a difference in performance rather than ability. It is caused by social expectations of appropriate gender roles—expectations of what is appropriate for each sex to do.

Cognitive style, or the way in which people solve problems, represents another area of gender differences. Jean Piaget studied cognitive development in children and noted that adolescent boys used more formal operational thinking than did adolescent girls. In formal operational thinking, people approach problems in a precisely logical way. In 1970, William Perry published a study of the cognitive development of undergraduates at Harvard, beginning at the time they entered college until graduation. While his study included few women, he found the intellectual development of both genders was fairly similar. In the mid-1980's, Mary Field Belenky, Blythe McVicker Clinchy, Nancy Rule Goldberger, and Jill Mattuck Tarule did a similar study based on personal interviews with 130 women, 90 of whom were college students. These researchers were able to identify five "ways of knowing" among these women; however, they were careful to point out that these categories are not necessarily fixed, exhaustive, or universal and that they are similar to categories, seen in men's thinking. They concluded that any gender differences observed were due to socialization and experiences in traditional educational institutions.

TESTING DIFFERENCES

Male and female differences have been noted in achievement tests such as the Scholastic Aptitude Test (SAT) and the American College Test (ACT). The tests are designed not to benefit one sex more than the other, but gender differences are still found. Males are more likely to have extremely high scores and to do better in mathematics. For example, a study of mathematically precocious youth surveyed forty thousand seventh-graders who scored extremely well on the Scholastic Aptitude Test, a test usually taken by college-bound eleventh- and twelfth-graders. Of the 280 children who scored above 700, only 20 were female. However, some researchers have found that, when the number of advanced math classes taken in high school is taken into account, such differences diminish. In 1991, the American Association of University Women released a report titled *Shortchanging Girls, Shortchanging America*, which stated that gender inequities in the classroom contribute to gender differences in academic achievement. For example, in male-dominated disciplines, such as math and science, girls were often discouraged from taking advanced courses. When girls did take these courses, teacher expectations of high achievement were lower for girls than for boys. Teachers called on boys to answer questions more often and challenged them more in class.

Differences in mathematics ability have been used to explain why some occupations are male-dominated and some are mostly female. For example, there are many more male scientists and engineers than female scientists and engineers. Both genders need to be introduced to the many unknown accomplishments of high achieving females in male dominated fields. An example of such invisible contributions included those of scientist Rosalind Franklin to the discovery of the structure of deoxyribonucleic acid (DNA), which is commonly attributed to Francis Crick and James Watson. Educators and school counselors can emphasize the merits of all career opportunities, regardless of gender. For example, boys can be encouraged to explore traditionally female professions, such as nursing and elementary education, while girls can be encouraged to pursue careers in engineering and computer science.

Differences in male and female abilities have interested educators as they try to maximize the potential of all their students. It is vitally important that both boys and girls receive encouragement to excel in all areas of thinking. In grade school, boys need male teachers to imitate. In later years, girls need to have contact with female scientists, engineers, and mathematicians. Counselors should be especially aware of the need to allow adolescents to explore fully different careers, and they should not limit children's options.

Training is an important factor in gender differences. Mathematics scores are directly related to the number of mathematics classes a person has taken. Gender differences on tests of spatial perception can also be eliminated by training. Paul Tobin used the embedded figures test, which requires people to pick out a drawing hidden within another drawing. He gave the test to teenage boys and girls, finding that boys performed better. After one practice session, however, the gender differences were eliminated.

Family and sociocultural contexts also influence cognitive abilities. In their study of women's cognitive styles, Belenky and associates did intensive interviews with women of various backgrounds and ages. They found that some women did not believe that they could think things out for themselves. One group of women were called "silent" and had typically been physically or emotionally abused. These "silent" women did not believe that they could understand anything. In addition, both William Perry, who studied mostly male undergraduates, and Mary Field Belenky and her colleagues observed a stage in which some young women and men look to external sources, such as experts and authorities, for "right answers" and "truth." However, many of the men seemed to identify with the experts and authorities in a way that women often did not. It was as though the men saw themselves as "potential experts." This gender difference in self-perceptions can be explained by the predominance of males in positions of power and authority in our society.

CONCLUSIONS

Interest in gender differences is common to most societies, but only recently have scientists begun to ask about the origins of such differences. Many researchers are questioning the usefulness of the study of group comparisons in general. Such studies of "difference" are often based on a dominant "standard" group that is then used as a frame of reference to assess how other groups deviate from this standard.

An increased demand for social justice that arose during the 1960's renewed interest in the question of gender differences. Eleanor Maccoby and Carol Jacklin surveyed every research report on male and female cognitive differences up to 1970 and concluded that the research supported very few real differences. Further studies have suggested that social influences are at least as important as biological influences, if not more so.

One reason women have been found to be inferior to men is that male behavior has traditionally been used as the standard. If women behave differently from men, it is concluded that they are inferior. In the area of personality, Sigmund Freud came to the conclusion that women are innately psychologically inferior. Karen Horney, however, considered the role of culture in shaping perceptions of women. She pointed out that women's perceived weaknesses were based on the experiences of men, a more powerful social group.

Overall, research shows that there is much more variability in cognitive performance within each gender than between them. Gender differences in academic achievement are, however, sometimes observed during adolescence, when societal pressures to conform to traditional gender roles are strong. All social groups, such as males and females, are heterogeneous. Individual differences within such groups are caused by the continuous interplay between the biology of the organism and its experience in the environment.

SOURCES FOR FURTHER STUDY

Belenky, Mary Field, et al. *Women's Ways of Knowing: The Development of Self, Voice, and Mind.* New York: Basic Books, 1986. Describes an intensive series of interviews with more than ninety women, and identifies five types of cognitive styles that were used by these women. Individual descriptions and quotations make the book interesting reading. A copy of the survey is included in the book.

Bleier, Ruth. *Science and Gender.* New York: Pergamon Press, 1984. Describes the reasons there are more men than women in science and engineering, and reports on other studies concerning male and female abilities.

Fausto-Sterling, Anne. *Myths of Gender: Biological Theories About Women and Men.* Rev. ed. New York: Basic Books, 1992. A critical review of the research on biological explanations of gender differences.

Hare-Mursten, Rachel T., and Jeanne Marecek. "The Meaning of Difference: Gender Theory, Post-Modernism, and Psychology." *American Psychologist* 43 (June, 1988): 455-464. This article is serious reading, but it is not intended for specialists. Presents theories on gender differences developed in the 1980's.

Hyde, Janet Shibley. *Half the Human Experience.* 5th ed. Lexington, Mass.: Heath, 1996. This excellent book reviews research and theory pertaining to all aspects of gender differences. An accessible text for college students that many high school students also could use. Includes many references to other authors and researchers. Particularly valuable as it relates differences in cognitive development to social and biological factors.

Hyde, Janet Shibley, and Marcia C. Linn, eds. *The Psychology of Gender: Advances Through Meta-Analysis.* Baltimore: The Johns Hopkins University Press, 1986. A collection of scholarly articles that reanalyze many research efforts. Should be read by advanced undergraduates for a complete understanding of gender differences.

Jacklin, Carol. "Female and Male: Issues of Gender." *American Psychologist* 44 (February, 1989): 127-133. The coauthor of the pioneering work on sex differences (noted below) summarizes research between 1974 and 1989.

Maccoby, Eleanor E., and Carol Nagy Jacklin. *The Psychology of Sex Differences.* Stanford, Calif.: Stanford University Press, 1974. Reviews all research on gender differences to the early 1970's. This book is somewhat scholarly but is useful, as it presents the most comprehensive and balanced review of the research up to its publishing date.

Mary Moore Vandendorpe;
updated by Cathy J. Bogart

SEE ALSO: Ability tests; Achievement motivation; Brain specialization; Cognitive development: Jean Piaget; College entrance examinations; Gender-identity formation; Gilligan, Carol; Horney, Karen; Intelligence; Intelligence tests; Moral development; Sexism; Women's psychology: Carol Gilligan; Women's psychology: Karen Horney; Women's psychology: Sigmund Freud.

Cognitive behavior therapy

TYPE OF PSYCHOLOGY: Psychotherapy
FIELDS OF STUDY: Behavioral therapies

A number of approaches to therapy fall within the scope of cognitive behavior therapy. These approaches all share a theoretical perspective that assumes that internal cognitive processes, called thinking or cognition, affect behavior; that this cognitive activity may be monitored; and that desired behavior change may be effected through cognitive change.

KEY CONCEPTS
- behavior therapy
- cognition
- cognitive restructuring
- cognitive therapy
- depression

INTRODUCTION

The cognitive behavior therapies are not a single therapeutic approach, but rather a loosely organized collection of therapeutic approaches that share a similar set of assumptions. At their core, cognitive behavior therapies share three fundamental propositions: Cognitive activity affects behavior; cognitive activity may be monitored and altered; and desired behavior change may be effected through cognitive change.

The first of the three fundamental propositions of cognitive behavior therapy suggests that it is not the external situation which determines feelings and behavior, but rather the person's view or perception of that external situation that determines feelings and behavior. For example, if one has failed the first examination of a course, one could appraise it as a temporary setback to be overcome or as a horrible loss. While the situation remains the same, the thinking about that situation is radically different in the two examples cited. Each of these views will lead to significantly different emotions and behaviors.

The third cognitive behavioral assumption suggests that desired behavior change may be effected through cognitive change. Thus, while cognitive behavior theorists do not reject the notion that rewards and punishment (reinforcement contingencies) can alter behavior, they are likely to emphasize that there are alternative methods for behavior change, one in particular being cognitive change. Many approaches to therapy fall within the scope of cognitive behavior therapy as it is defined above. While these approaches share the theoretical assumptions described above, a review of the major therapeutic procedures subsumed under the heading of cognitive behavior therapy reveals a diverse amalgam of principles and procedures, representing a variety of theoretical and philosophical perspectives.

RATIONAL THERAPIES

Rational-emotive therapy, developed by psychologist Albert Ellis, is regarded by many as one of the premier examples of the cognitive behavioral approach; it was introduced in the early 1960's. Ellis proposed that many people are made unhappy by their faulty, irrational beliefs, which influence the way they interpret events. The therapist will interact with the patient or client, attempting to direct the patient to more positive and realistic views. Cognitive therapy, pioneered by Aaron T. Beck, has been applied to such problems as depression and stress. For stress reduction, ideas and thoughts that are producing stress in the patient will be questioned; the therapist will get the patient to examine the validity of these thoughts; thought processes can then be restructured so the situations seem less stressful. Cognitive therapy has been found to be quite effective in treating depression, as compared to other therapeutic methods. Beck held that depression is caused by certain types of negative thoughts, such as devaluing the self or viewing the future in a consistently pessimistic way.

Rational behavior therapy, developed by psychiatrist Maxie Maultsby, is a close relative of Ellis's rational-emotive therapy. In this approach, Maultsby combines several approaches to include rational-emotive therapy, neuropsychology, classical and operant conditioning, and psychosomatic research; however, Maultsby was primarily influenced by his association with Albert Ellis. In this approach, Maultsby attempts to couch his theory of emotional disturbance in terms of neuropsychophysiology and learning theory. Rational behavior therapy assumes that repeated pairings of a perception with evaluative thoughts lead to rational or irrational emotive and behavioral reactions. Maultsby suggests that self-talk, which originates in the left hemisphere of the brain, triggers corresponding right-

hemisphere emotional equivalents. Thus, in order to maintain a state of psychological health, individuals must practice rational self-talk that will, in turn, cause the right brain to convert left-brain language into appropriate emotional and behavioral reactions.

Rational behavior therapy techniques are quite similar to those of rational-emotive therapy. Both therapies stress the importance of monitoring one's thoughts in order to become aware of the elements of the emotional disturbance. In addition, Maultsby advocates the use of rational-emotive imagery, behavioral practice, and relaxation methods in order to minimize emotional distress.

SELF-INSTRUCTIONAL TRAINING

Self-instructional training was developed by psychologist Donald Meichenbaum in the early 1970's. In contrast to Ellis and Beck, whose prior training was in psychoanalysis, Meichenbaum's roots are in behaviorism and the behavioral therapies. Thus Meichenbaum's approach is heavily couched in behavioral terminology and procedures. Meichenbaum's work stems from his earlier research in training schizophrenic patients to emit "healthy speech." By chance, Meichenbaum observed that patients who engaged in spontaneous self-instruction were less distracted and demonstrated superior task performance on a variety of tasks. As a result, Meichenbaum emphasizes the critical role of "self-instructions"—simple instructions such as "Relax. . . Just attend to the task"—and their noticeable effect on subsequent behavior.

Meichenbaum developed self-instructional training to treat the deficits in self-instructions manifested in impulsive children. The ultimate goal of this program was to decrease impulsive behavior. The way to accomplish this goal, as hypothesized by Meichenbaum, was to train impulsive children to generate verbal self-commands, to respond to their verbal self-commands, and to encourage the children to self-reinforce their behavior appropriately.

The specific procedures employed in self-instructional training involve having the child observe a model performing a task. While the model is performing the task, he or she is talking aloud. The child then performs the same task while the model gives verbal instructions. Subsequently, the child performs the task while instructing himself or herself aloud, then while whispering the in-structions. Finally, the child performs the task co-vertly. The self-instructions employed in the pro-gram included questions about the nature and demands of the task, answers to these questions in the form of cognitive rehearsal, self-instructions in the form of self-guidance while performing the task, and self-reinforcement. Meichenbaum and his asso-ciates have found that this self-instructional train-ing program significantly improves the task perfor-mance of impulsive children across a number of measures.

SYSTEMATIC RATIONAL RESTRUCTURING

Systematic rational restructuring is a cognitive be-havioral procedure developed by psychologist Marvin Goldfried in the mid-1970's. This procedure is a variation on Ellis's rational-emotive therapy; how-ever, it is more clearly structured than Ellis's method. In systematic rational restructuring, Goldfried sug-gests that early social learning experiences teach individuals to label situations in different ways. Fur-ther, Goldfried suggests that emotional reactions may be understood as responses to the way individu-als label situations, as opposed to responses to the situations themselves. The goal of systematic ratio-nal restructuring is to train clients to perceive situa-tional cues more accurately.

The process of systematic rational restructuring is similar to systematic desensitization, in which a subject is to imagine fearful scenes in a graduated order from the least fear-provoking to the most fear-provoking scenes. In systematic rational restructur-ing, the client is asked to imagine a hierarchy of anxiety-eliciting situations. At each step, the client is instructed to identify irrational thoughts associated with the specific situation, to dispute them, and to reevaluate the situation more rationally. In addition, clients are instructed to practice rational restructur-ing in specific real-life situations.

STRESS INOCULATION

Stress inoculation training incorporates several of the specific therapies already described. This proce-dure was developed by Meichenbaum. Stress inoc-ulation training is analogous to being inoculated against disease. That is, it prepares clients to deal with stress-inducing events by teaching them to use coping skills at low levels of the stressful situation, and then gradually to cope with more and more

stressful situations. Stress inoculation training in-volves three phases: conceptualization, skill acqui-sition and rehearsal, and application and follow-through.

In the conceptualization phase of stress inocula-tion training, clients are given an adaptive way of viewing and understanding their negative reactions to stressful events. In the skills-acquisition and re-hearsal phase, clients learn coping skills appropri-ate to the type of stress they are experiencing. With interpersonal anxiety, the client might develop skills that would make the feared situation less threaten-ing (for example, learning to initiate and maintain conversations). The client might also learn deep muscle relaxation to lessen tension. In the case of anger, clients learn to view potential provocations as problems that require a solution rather than as threats that require an attack. Clients are also taught to rehearse alternative strategies for solving the prob-lem at hand.

The application and follow-through phase of stress inoculation training involves the clients practicing and applying the coping skills. Initially, clients are exposed to low levels of stressful situations in imag-ery. They practice applying their coping skills to handle the stressful events, and they overtly role-play dealing with stressful events. Next, the client is given homework assignments that involve gradual exposure to actual stressful events in his or her ev-eryday life. Stress inoculation training has been ef-fectively applied to many types of problems. It has been used to help people cope with anger, anxiety, fear, pain, and health-related problems (for exam-ple, cancer and hypertension). It appears to be suit-able for all age levels.

PROBLEM-SOLVING THERAPY

Problem-solving therapy, as developed by psycholo-gists Thomas D'Zurilla and Marvin Goldfried, is also considered one of the cognitive behavioral ap-proaches. In essence, problem-solving therapy is the application of problem-solving theory and research to the domain of personal and emotional problems. Indeed, the authors see the ability to solve problems as the necessary and sufficient condition for emo-tional and behavioral stability. Problem solving is, in one way or another, a part of all psychotherapies. Cognitive behavior therapists have taught general problem-solving skills to clients with two specific aims: to alleviate the particular personal problems for which clients have sought therapy, and to provide clients with a general coping strategy for personal problems.

The actual steps of problem solving that a client is taught to carry out systematically are as follows. First, it is necessary to define the dilemma as a problem to be solved. Next, a goal must be selected which reflects the ultimate outcome the client desires. The client then generates a list of many different possible solutions, without evaluating their potential merit (a kind of brainstorming). Now the client evaluates the pros and cons of each alternative in terms of the probability that it will meet the goal selected and its practicality, which involves considering the potential consequences to oneself and to others of each solution. The alternative solutions are ranked in terms of desirability and practicality, and the highest one is selected. Next, the client tries to implement the solution chosen. Finally, the client evaluates the therapy, assessing whether the solution alleviated the problem and met the goal, and, if not, what went wrong—in other words, which of the steps in problem solving needs to be redone.

Problem-solving therapies have been used to treat a variety of target behaviors with a wide range of clients. Examples include peer relationship difficulties among children and adolescents, examination and interpersonal anxiety among college students, relapse following a program to reduce smoking, harmony among family members, and the ability of chronic psychiatric patients to cope with interpersonal problems.

SELF-CONTROL THERAPY

Self-control therapy for depression, developed by psychologist Lynn Rehm, is an approach to treating depression which combines the self-regulatory notions of behavior therapy and the cognitive focus of the cognitive behavioral approaches. Essentially, Rehm believes that depressed people show deficits in one or some combination of the following areas: monitoring (selectively attending to negative events), self-evaluation (setting unrealistically high goals), and self-reinforcement (emitting high rates of self-punishment and low rates of self-reward). These three components are further broken down into a total of six functional areas.

According to Rehm, the varied symptom picture in clinically depressed clients is a function of different subsets of these deficits. Over the course of ther-

apy with a client, each of the six self-control deficits is described, with emphasis on how a particular deficit is causally related to depression, and on what can be done to remedy the deficit. A variety of clinical strategies are employed to teach clients self-control skills, including group discussion, overt and covert reinforcement, behavioral assignments, self-monitoring, and modeling.

STRUCTURAL PSYCHOTHERAPY

Structural psychotherapy is a cognitive behavioral approach that derives from the work of two Italian mental health professionals, psychiatrist Vittorio Guidano and psychologist Gianni Liotti. These authors are strongly persuaded by cognitive psychology, social learning theory, evolutionary epistemology, psychodynamic theory, and cognitive therapy. Guidano and Liotti suggest that for an understanding of the full complexity of an emotional disorder and subsequent development of an adequate model of psychotherapy, an appreciation of the development and the active role of an individual's knowledge of self and the world is critical. In short, in order to understand a patient, one must understand the structure of that person's world.

Guidano and Liotti's therapeutic process utilizes the empirical problem-solving approach of the scientist. Indeed, the authors suggest that therapists should assist clients in disengaging themselves from certain ingrained beliefs and judgments, and in considering them as hypotheses and theories subject to disproof, confirmation, and logical challenge. A variety of behavioral experiments and cognitive techniques are utilized to assist the patient in assessing and critically evaluating his or her beliefs.

OTHER THERAPIES

As can be seen, the area of cognitive behavior therapy involves a wide collection of therapeutic approaches and techniques. The approaches described here are but a representative sample of possible cognitive behavioral approaches. Also included within this domain are anxiety management training, which comes from the work of psychologist Richard Suinn, and personal science, from the work of psychologist Michael Mahoney.

The cognitive behavioral approaches are derived from a variety of perspectives, including cognitive theory, classical and operant conditioning approaches, problem-solving theory, and developmental theory.

All these approaches share the perspective that internal cognitive processes, called thinking or cognition, affect behavior, and that behavior change may be effected through cognitive change.

These approaches have several other similarities. One is that all the approaches see therapy as time-limited. This is in sharp distinction to the traditional psychoanalytic therapies, which are generally open-ended. The cognitive behavior therapies attempt to effect change rapidly, often with specific, preset lengths of therapeutic contact. Another similarity among the cognitive behavior therapies is that their target of change is also limited. For example, in the treatment of depression, the target of change is the symptoms of depression. Thus, in the cognitive behavioral approaches to treatment, one sees a time-limited focus and a limited target of change.

EVOLUTION

Cognitive behavior therapy evolved from two lines of clinical and research activity: First, it derives from the work of the early cognitive therapists (Albert Ellis and Aaron Beck); second, it was strongly influenced by the careful empirical work of the early behaviorists.

Within the domain of behaviorism, cognitive processes were not always seen as a legitimate focus of attention. In behavior therapy, there has always been a strong commitment to an applied science of clinical treatment. In the behavior therapy of the 1950's and 1960's, this emphasis on scientific methods and procedures meant that behavior therapists focused on events that were directly observable and measurable. Within this framework, behavior was seen as a function of external stimuli which determined or were reliably associated with observable responses. Also during this period, there was a deliberate avoidance of such "nebulous" concepts as thoughts, cognitions, or images. It was believed that these processes were by their very nature vague, and one could never be confident that one was reliably observing or measuring these processes.

It is important to note that by following scientific principles, researchers developed major new treatment approaches which in many ways revolutionized clinical practice (among them are systematic desensitization and the use of a token economy). Yet during the 1960's, several developments within behavior therapy had emphasized the limitations of

a strict conditioning model to understanding human behavior.

In 1969, psychologist Albert Bandura published his influential volume *Principles of Behavior Modification*. In this volume, Bandura emphasized the role of internal or cognitive factors in the causation and maintenance of behavior. Following from the dissatisfaction of the radical behavioral approaches to understanding complex human behavior and the publication of Bandura's 1969 volume, behavior therapists began actively to seek and study the role of cognitive processes in human behavior.

SOURCES FOR FURTHER STUDY

D'Zurilla, Thomas J., and Arthur M. Nezu. "Social Problem-Solving in Adults." In *Advances in Cognitive-Behavioral Research and Therapy*, edited by Philip C. Kendall. Vol. 1. New York: Academic Press, 1982. An excellent summary of problem-solving therapy. As indicated by its title, the Kendall book in which this article appears also contains other informative articles dealing with cognitive behavior therapy.

Goldfried, Marvin R. "The Use of Relaxation and Cognitive Relabeling as Coping Skills." In *Behavioral Self-Management: Strategies, Techniques, and Outcomes*, edited by Richard B. Stuart. New York: Brunner/Mazel, 1977. A description of systematic rational restructuring by Marvin Goldfried, who developed the technique; reveals its similarities to and differences from rational-emotive therapy.

Maultsby, Maxie C., Jr. *Rational Behavior Therapy*. Englewood Cliffs, N.J.: Prentice-Hall, 1984. An excellent summary of rational behavior therapy, as developed by Maultsby; discusses self-talk and its emotional and behavioral consequences.

Meichenbaum, Donald. *Cognitive Behavior Modification*. New York: Plenum, 1977. A well-written introduction to Meichenbaum's approaches, with clear examples of the applications of self-instructional training to impulsive children and schizophrenic patients.

_____. *Stress Inoculation Training*. New York: Pergamon, 1985. This short training manual presents a clear, useful overview of stress inoculation training, along with a detailed account of the empirical research completed in testing the approach.

Donald G. Beal

SEE ALSO: Behavioral family therapy; Cognitive social learning: Walter Mischel; Cognitive therapy; Existential psychology; Rational-emotive therapy; Transactional analysis.

Cognitive development
Jean Piaget

TYPE OF PSYCHOLOGY: Developmental psychology
FIELDS OF STUDY: Cognitive development

Piaget, in one of the twentieth century's most influential development theories, proposed a sequence of maturational changes in thinking. From the sensorimotor responses of infancy, the child acquires symbols. Later, the child begins relating these symbols in such logical operations as categorizing and quantifying. In adolescence, abstract and hypothetical mental manipulations become possible.

KEY CONCEPTS
- concrete operations stage
- conservation
- egocentric
- formal operations stage
- operations
- preoperational stage
- schema (*pl.* schemata)
- sensorimotor stage

INTRODUCTION

Jean Piaget (1896-1980), a Swiss psychologist, generated the twentieth century's most influential and comprehensive theory of cognitive development. Piaget's theory describes how the maturing child's interactions with the environment result in predictable sequences of changes in certain crucial understandings of the world about him or her. Such changes occur in the child's comprehension of time and space, quantitative relationships, cause and effect, and even right and wrong. The child is always treated as an actor in his or her own development. Advances result from the active desire to develop concepts or schemata which are sufficiently similar to the real world that this real world can be fitted or assimilated into these schemata. Schemata can be defined as any process of interpreting an object or event, including habitual responses, symbols, or mental manipulations. When a schema ("Cats smell nice") is sufficiently discrepant from reality ("That cat stinks"), the schema itself must be accommodated or altered ("That catlike creature is a skunk"). For children everywhere, neurologically based advances in mental capacity introduce new perceptions that make the old ways of construing reality unsatisfactory and compel a fundamentally new construction of reality—a new stage of development. Piaget conceptualizes four such stages: sensorimotor (in infancy), preoperational (the preschool child), concrete operational (the school-age child), and formal operational (adolescence and adulthood).

SENSORIMOTOR STAGE

In the sensorimotor stage, the infant orients himself or herself to objects in the world by consistent physical (motor) movements in response to those sensory stimuli that represent the same object (for example, the sight of a face, the sound of footsteps, or a voice all represent "mother"). The relationship between motor responses and reappearing objects becomes progressively more complex and varied in the normal course of development. First, reflexes such as sucking become more efficient; then sequences of learned actions that bring pleasure are repeated (circular reactions). These learned reactions are directed first toward the infant's own body (thumb sucking), then toward objects in the environment (the infant's stuffed toy).

The baby seems to lack an awareness that objects continue to exist when they are outside the range of his or her senses. When the familiar toy of an infant is hidden, he or she does not search for it; it is as if it has disappeared from reality. As the sensorimotor infant matures, the infant becomes convinced of the continuing existence of objects that disappear in less obvious ways for longer intervals of time. By eighteen months of age, most toddlers have achieved such a conviction of continuing existence, or object permanence.

PREOPERATIONAL STAGE

In the preoperational stage, the preschool child begins to represent these permanent objects by internal processes or mental representations. Now the development of mental representations of useful objects proceeds at an astounding pace. In symbolic play, blocks may represent cars and trains. Capable of deferred imitation, the child may pretend to be a cowboy according to his memory image of a motion-picture cowboy. The most important of all representations are the hundreds of new words the child learns to speak.

As one might infer from the word "preoperational," this period, lasting from about age two through ages six or seven, is transitional. The preschool child still lacks the attention, memory capacity, and mental flexibility to employ his or her increasing supply of symbolic representations in logical reasoning (operations). It is as if the child remains so focused upon the individual frames of a motion picture that he or she fails to comprehend the underlying plot. Piaget calls this narrow focusing on a single object or salient dimension "centration." The child may say, for example, that a quart of milk he or she has just seen transferred into two pint containers is now "less milk" because the child focuses upon the smaller size of the new containers. Fido is seen as a dog, not as an animal or a mammal. The child uncritically assumes that other people, regardless of their situation, share his or her own tastes and perspectives. A two-year-old closes his eyes and says, "Now you don't see me, Daddy." Piaget calls this egocentrism.

CONCRETE OPERATIONS STAGE
The concrete operations stage begins at age six or seven, when the school-age child becomes capable of keeping in mind and logically manipulating several concrete objects at the same time. The child is no longer the prisoner of the momentary appearance of things. In no case is the change more evident than in the sort of problem in which a number of objects (such as twelve black checkers) are spread out into four groups of three. While the four-year-old, preoperational child would be likely to say that now there are more checkers because they take up a larger area, to the eight-year-old it is obvious that this transformation could easily be reversed by regrouping the checkers. Piaget describes the capacity to visualize the reversibility of such transformations as "conservation." This understanding is fundamental to the comprehension of simple arithmetical manipulations. It is also fundamental to a second operational skill: categorization. To the concrete-operational child, it seems obvious that while Rover the dog can for other purposes be classified as a

household pet, an animal, or a living organism, he will still be a "dog" and still be "Rover." A related skill is seriation: keeping in mind that an entire series of objects can be arranged along a single dimension, such as size (from smallest to largest). The child now is also capable of role-taking, of understanding the different perspective of a parent or teacher. No longer egocentric (the assumption that everyone shares one's own perspective and the cognitive inability to understand the different perspective of another), the child becomes able to see himself as others see him and to temper the harshness of absolute rules with a comprehension of the viewpoints of others.

FORMAL OPERATIONS STAGE
The formal operations stage begins in early adolescence. In childhood, logical operations are concrete ones, limited to objects that can be visualized, touched, or directly experienced. The advance of the early adolescent into formal operational thinking involves the capacity to deal with possibilities that are purely speculative. This permits coping with new classes of problems: those involving relationships that are purely abstract or hypothetical, or that involve the higher-level analysis of a problem by the systematic consideration of every logical (sometimes fanciful) possibility. The logical adequacy of an argument can be examined apart from the truth or falsity of its conclusions.

Concepts such as "forces," "infinity," or "justice," nowhere directly experienced, can now be comprehended. Formal operational thought permits the midadolescent or adult to hold abstract ideals and to initiate scientific investigations.

ILLUSTRATING STAGE DEVELOPMENT
Piaget was particularly clever in the invention of problems which illustrate the underlying premises of the child's thought. The crucial capability that signals the end of the sensorimotor period is object permanence, the child's conviction of the continuing existence of objects that are outside the range of his or her senses. Piaget established the gradual emergence of object permanence by hiding from the child familiar toys for progressively longer periods of time, with the act of hiding progressively less obvious to the child. Full object permanence is not considered achieved until the child will search for a familiar missing object even

when he or she could not have observed its being hidden.

The fundamental test of concrete operational thought is conservation. In a typical conservation task, the child is shown two identical balls of putty. The child generally affirms their obvious equivalence. Then one of the balls of putty is reworked into an elongated, wormlike shape while the child watches. The child is again asked about their relative size. Younger children are likely to say that the wormlike shape is smaller, but the child who has attained conservation of mass will state that the size must still be the same. Inquiries concerning whether the weights of the differently shaped material (conservation of weight) are the same and whether they would displace the same amount of water (conservation of volume) are more difficult questions, generally not answerable until the child is older.

STANDARDIZED TESTS

Since Piaget's original demonstrations, further progress has necessitated the standardization of these problems with materials, questions, procedures, and scoring so clearly specified that examiners can replicate one another's results. Such standardization permits the explanation of the general applicability of Piaget's concepts. Standardized tests have been developed for measuring object permanence, egocentricity, and role-taking skills. The Concept Assessment Kit: Conservation, for example, provides six standard conservation tasks for which comparison data (norms) are available for children in several widely diverse cultures. The relative conceptual attainments of an individual child (or culture) can be measured. It is encouraging that those who attain such basic skills as conservation early have been shown to be advanced in many other educational and cognitive achievements.

IMPLICATIONS FOR EDUCATION

Piaget's views of cognitive development have broad implications for educational institutions charged with fostering such development. The child is viewed as an active seeker of knowledge. This pursuit is advanced by his or her experimental engagement with problems which are slightly more complex than those problems successfully worked through in the past. The teacher is a facilitator of the opportunities for such cognitive growth, not a lecturer or a drillmaster. The teacher provides physical materials that

can be experimentally manipulated. Such materials can be simple: Blocks, stones, bottle caps, and plastic containers all can be classified, immersed in water, thrown into fire, dropped, thrown, or balanced. Facilitating peer relationships and cooperation in playing games are also helpful in encouraging social role-taking and moral development.

Since each student pursues knowledge at his or her own pace, and in his or her own idiom, great freedom and variety may be permitted in an essentially open classroom. The teacher may nudge the student toward cognitive advancement by presenting a problem slightly more complex than that already comprehended by the student. A student who understands conservation of number may be ready for problems involving the conservation of length, for example. Yet the teacher does not reinforce correct answers or criticize incorrect ones. Sequencing is crucial. The presentation of knowledge or skill before the child is ready can result in superficial, uncomprehended verbalisms. Piaget does not totally reject the necessity of the inculcation of social and cultural niceties (social-arbitrary knowledge), the focus of traditional education. He would maintain, however, that an experimentally based understanding of physical and social relationships is crucial for a creative, thoughtful society.

FINESSING PIAGET'S RESEARCH

Piaget hypothesized sequences of age-related changes in ways of dealing with reality. His conclusions were based on the careful observation of a few selected cases. The voluminous research since Piaget's time overwhelmingly supports the sequence he outlined. The process almost never reverses. Once a child understands the conservation of substance, for example, his or her former conclusion that "Now there is more" seems to the child not simply wrong but absurd. Even within a stage, there is a sequence. Conservation of mass, for example, precedes conservation of volume.

Post-Piagetian research has nevertheless led to a fine-tuning of some of his conclusions and a modification of others. Piaget believed that transitions to more advanced cognitive levels awaited neurological maturation and the child's spontaneous discoveries. Several researchers have found that specific training in simplified and graded conservation and categorization tasks can lead to an early ripening of these skills. Other research has called into question

Piaget's timetable. The fact that, within a few months of birth, infants show subtle differences in their reactions to familiar versus unfamiliar objects suggests that recognition memory for objects may begin earlier than Piaget's age for object permanence. If conservation tasks are simplified—if all distraction is avoided, and simple language and familiar materials are used—it can be shown that concrete operations also may begin earlier than Piaget thought. Formal operations, on the other hand, may not begin as early or be applied as universally in adult problem solving as suggested by Piaget's thesis. A significant percentage of older adolescents and adults fail tests for formal operations, particularly in new problem areas.

More basic than readjustments of his developmental scheduling is the reinterpretation of Piaget's stages. The stage concept implies not only an invariant sequence of age-related changes but also developmental discontinuities involving global and fairly abrupt shifts in an entire pattern or structure. Yet the prolonged development and domain-specific nature of many operational skills, cited above, suggest a process that is neither abrupt nor global. An alternative view is that Piaget's sequences can also be understood as the results of continuous improvements in attention, concentration, and memory. Stages represent only transition points on this continuous dimension. They are more like the points of a scale on a thermometer than the stages of the metamorphosis of a caterpillar into a moth.

PIAGET'S IMPACT

Even with the caveat that his stages may reflect, at a more fundamental level, an underlying continuum, Piaget's contributions can be seen as a great leap forward in approximate answers to one of humankind's oldest questions: how human beings know their world. The eighteenth century philosopher Immanuel Kant described certain core assumptions, such as quantity, quality, and cause and effect, which he called "categories of the understanding." Human beings make these assumptions when they relate specific objects and events to one another—when they reason. Piaget's work became known to a 1960's-era American psychology that was dominated by B. F. Skinner's behavioral view of a passive child whose plastic nature was simply molded by the rewards and punishments of parents and culture. The impact of Piaget's work shifted psychology's focus back to a Kantian perspective of the child as an active reasoner who selectively responds to aspects of culture he or she finds relevant. Piaget himself outlined the sequence, the pace, and some of the dynamics of the maturing child's development of major Kantian categories. Such subsequent contributions as Lawrence Kohlberg's work on moral development and Robert Selman's work on role-taking can be viewed as an elaboration and extension of Piaget's unfinished work. Piaget, like Sigmund Freud, was one of psychology's pivotal thinkers. Without him, the entire field of developmental psychology would be radically different.

SOURCES FOR FURTHER STUDY

Piaget, Jean. *The Psychology of the Child.* Translated by Helen Weaver. New York: Basic Books, 2000. Piaget's seminal presentation of his theories on children's cognitive development from infancy to adolescence.

Scholnik, Ellin Kofsky, ed. *Conceptual Development: Piaget's Legacy.* Hillsdale, N.J.: Lawrence Erlbaum, 1999. A collection of papers presented at the centenary of Piaget's birth at the Jean Piaget Society's annual symposium, assessing his legacy and effect on the understanding of children's cognitive development.

Serulnikov, Adriana. *Piaget for Beginners.* New York: Writers and Readers, 2000. A condensed overview of Piaget's theories for the general public. Part of the well-known For Beginners series.

Singer, Dorothy G., and Tracey A. Robinson. *A Piaget Primer: How a Child Thinks.* Rev. ed. New York: Plume, 1996. An introduction to Piaget's theories aimed at educators, child psychologists, and parents, using examples and illustrations from classic children's literature and popular children's television programming.

Smith, Lesley M., ed. *Critical Readings on Piaget.* New York: Routledge, 1996. A collection of essays assessing Piaget's theories and their impact, all originally published between 1990 and 1995. A follow-up to the same editor's *Piaget: Critical Assessments* (1992), which covered the period 1950-1990.

Thomas E. DeWolfe

SEE ALSO: Adolescence: Cognitive skills; Cognitive ability: Gender differences; Cognitive psychology; Development; Language; Moral development.

Cognitive dissonance

TYPE OF PSYCHOLOGY: Social psychology
FIELDS OF STUDY: Attitudes and behavior

Cognitive dissonance theory examines the effects of inconsistencies between attitudes and behaviors. It has evolved into an important theory of attitude change and has offered insights into diverse topics such as the effects of rewards, punishment, and choice on attitudes.

KEY CONCEPTS
- attitude
- cognition
- consonance
- dissonance
- external justification

INTRODUCTION

Cognitive dissonance theory, developed by social psychologist Leon Festinger, suggests that there is a basic human tendency to strive for consistency between and among cognitions. Cognitions are defined as what people know about their attitudes and behaviors. An attitude is defined as one's positive or negative evaluations of a person, place, or thing. If an inconsistency does arise—for example, if an individual does something that is discrepant with his or her attitudes—cognitive dissonance is said to occur. Dissonance is an uncomfortable state of physiological and psychological tension. It is so uncomfortable, in fact, that when individuals are in such a state, they become motivated to rid themselves of the feeling. This can be done by restoring consistency to the cognitions in some way.

What exactly does dissonance feel like? Although it is very difficult to describe any kind of internal state, the reactions one has when one hurts the feelings of a loved one or when one breaks something belonging to someone else are probably what Festinger meant by dissonance.

RESTORING CONSONANCE

When in a state of dissonance, there are three ways a person can restore consistency or (in the language of the theory) consonance. Consonance is defined as the psychological state in which cognitions are not in conflict. One way to create consonance is

to reduce the importance of the conflicting cognitions. The theory states that the amount of dissonance experienced is a direct function of the importance of the conflicting cognitions. Consider, for example, a man who actively pursues a suntan. The potential for dissonance exists with such behavior, because the cognition "I am doing something that is increasing my chances for skin cancer" may be in conflict with the cognition "I would like to remain healthy and live a long life." To reduce dissonance, this person may convince himself that he would rather live a shorter life filled with doing enjoyable and exciting things than live a longer, but perhaps not so exciting, life. The inconsistency still exists, but the importance of the inconsistency has been reduced.

A second way to reduce dissonance is to add numerous consonant cognitions, thus making the discrepancy seem less great. The suntanner may begin to believe he needs to be tan to be socially accepted because all of his friends have tans. The tanner may also begin to believe that suntanning makes him look more attractive and healthier and, indeed, may come to believe that suntanning does promote health.

The last way that Festinger proposed that people could reduce dissonance is the simplest, but it is the one that caught the attention of many social psychologists. It is simply to change one of the discrepant cognitions. The suntanner could either stop suntanning or convince himself that suntanning is not associated with an increased risk of skin cancer. In either case, the inconsistency would be eliminated.

This latter possibility intrigued social psychologists because it offered the possibility that people's behaviors could influence their attitudes. In particular, it suggested that if someone does something that is inconsistent with his or her attitudes, those attitudes may change to become more consistent with the behavior. For example, imagine that a woman wanted a friend to favor a particular candidate in an upcoming election, and the friend favored the opposing candidate. What would happen if this woman convinced the friend to accompany her to a rally for the candidate the friend did not support? According to the theory, the friend should experience some degree of dissonance, as the behavior of attending a rally for candidate X is inconsistent with the attitude "I do not favor candidate

X." To resolve the inconsistency, the friend may very well begin to convince herself that candidate X is not so bad and actually has some good points. Thus, in an effort to restore consonance, the friend's attitudes have changed to be more consistent with behavior.

DISSONANCE-INDUCED ATTITUDE CHANGE

Changes in behavior cannot always be expected to lead to changes in attitudes. Dissonance-induced attitude change—that is, attitudes that change in an effort to be consistent with a behavior—is likely to happen only under certain conditions. For one, there must not be any external justification for the behavior. An external justification is an environmental cause that might explain the inconsistency. If the friend was paid a hundred dollars to attend the rally for the candidate or was promised a dinner at a fancy restaurant, she most likely would not have experienced dissonance, because she had a sufficient external justification. Dissonance is most likely to occur when no external justification is present for a behavior.

Second, dissonance is most likely to occur when individuals believe that the behavior was done of their own free will—that is, when they feel some sort of personal responsibility for the behavior. If the friend had been simply told that she was being taken out for an exciting evening and was not told that she was going to this candidate's rally until she got there, she most likely would not have experienced dissonance.

Third, dissonance is more likely to occur when the behavior has some sort of foreseeable negative consequences. If the friend knew that when attending the rally, each person was required to pay a donation or was required to hand out pamphlets for the candidate, and she still elected to go, she would probably have experienced considerable dissonance; now she is not only attending a rally for a candidate she opposes but also actively campaigning against her preferred candidate.

EFFECT OF REWARDS

Perhaps the most-researched application of dissonance theory concerns the effects on attitudes of rewarding people for doing things in which they do not believe. In one study, Festinger and J. M. Carlsmith had students perform a boring screw-turning task for one hour. They then asked the stu-

dents to tell another student waiting to do the same task that the task was very interesting. In other words, they asked the students to lie. Half the students were offered twenty dollars to do this; the other half were offered one dollar. After the students told the waiting student that the task was enjoyable, the researchers asked them what they really thought about the screw-turning task. The students who were paid twenty dollars said they thought the screw-turning task was quite boring. The students who were paid only one dollar, however, said that they thought the task was interesting and enjoyable.

Although surprising, these findings are precisely what dissonance theory predicts. When a student informed a waiting student that the task was enjoyable, the possibility for dissonance arose. The cognition "This task was really boring" is inconsistent with the cognition "I just told someone that this task was quite enjoyable." The students paid twenty dollars, however, had a sufficient external justification for the inconsistency. Hence, there was no dissonance and no need to resolve any inconsistency. The students paid one dollar, however, did not have the same external justification; most people would not consider a dollar to be sufficient justification for telling a lie, so these students were in a real state of dissonance. To resolve the inconsistency, they changed their attitudes about the task and convinced themselves that the task was indeed enjoyable, thereby achieving consonance between attitudes and behavior. Thus, the less people are rewarded for doing things they might not like, the more likely it is that they will begin to like them.

EFFECT OF PUNISHMENT

Dissonance theory makes equally interesting predictions about the effects of punishment. In a study by Elliot Aronson and Carlsmith, a researcher asked preschool children to rate the attractiveness of toys. The researcher then left the room, but, before leaving, he instructed the children not to play with one of the toys they had rated highly attractive. This became the "forbidden" toy. The researcher varied the severity of the punishment with which he threatened the children if they played with the forbidden toy. For some children, the threat was relatively mild. The researcher said he would be upset. For others, the threat was more severe. The researcher said that he would be angry, would pack up the toys and leave, and would consider the child a baby.

Both threats of punishment seemed to work, as no children played with the forbidden toy. When the researcher asked the children later to rerate the attractiveness of the toys, however, it was apparent that the severity of the threat did make a difference. For children who were severely threatened, the forbidden toy was still rated as quite attractive. For the mildly threatened children, however, the forbidden toy was rated as much less attractive.

By not playing with the forbidden toy, children were potentially in a state of dissonance. The cognition "I think this is an attractive toy" is inconsistent with the cognition "I am not playing with the toy." Those in the severe threat condition had a sufficient external justification for the discrepancy. Hence, there was no dissonance and no motivation to resolve the inconsistency. Those in the mild threat condition had no such external justification for the inconsistency, so they most likely felt dissonance, and they resolved it by convincing themselves that the toy was not so attractive. Thus, perhaps surprisingly, the more mild the threats used to get children not to do something, the more likely it is that they will come to believe that it is not something they even want to do.

ROLE OF DECISION MAKING

A last type of everyday behavior for which dissonance theory has implications is decision making. According to the theory, many times when one makes a decision, particularly between attractive alternatives, dissonance is likely to occur. Before making a decision, there are probably some features of each alternative that are attractive and some that are not so attractive. When the decision is made, two sets of dissonant cognitions result: "I chose something that has unattractive qualities" and "I did not choose something that has attractive qualities." To resolve this dissonance, people tend to convince themselves that the chosen alternative is clearly superior to the unchosen alternative. So, although before the decision was made, each alternative was seen as equally attractive, after the decision, the chosen alternative is seen as much more attractive. For example, Robert Knox and James Inkster went to a racetrack and asked a sample of people who were waiting in line to place their bets how confident they were that their horse was going to win. They then asked a sample of

people who were leaving the betting window the same question.

As might have been predicted by now, a bettor was much more confident about a horse's chances after having placed the bet. Before placing a bet, there is no dissonance. After actually placing money on the horse, the potential for dissonance ("I placed money on a horse that might lose and I didn't bet on a horse that might win") arises. To avoid or resolve this dissonance, bettors become much more confident that their horse will win and, by default, more confident that other horses will not.

PROMINENT INFLUENCE IN PSYCHOLOGY

Cognitive dissonance theory was introduced in 1957, at a time when interest in the motives underlying people's attitudes and behaviors was at a peak in social psychology. Although dissonance theory has emerged as perhaps the best-known and most-researched theory in social psychology, when it was first developed it was one of a handful of theories, now collectively known as cognitive consistency theories, that proposed that people are motivated to seek consistency among and between thoughts, feelings, and behaviors.

There are numerous explanations as to why cognitive dissonance theory has become as important as it has, but two seem particularly intriguing. One concerns the intellectual climate in psychology during the time the theory was introduced. At the time, research in most fields of psychology, including social psychological research on attitude change, was influenced by learning theory. Learning theory suggests that behavior is a function of its consequences: People do those things for which they are rewarded and do not do those things for which they are not rewarded or for which they are punished. Therefore, according to this perspective, to change significantly any form of behavior, from overt actions to attitudes and beliefs, some kind of reward or incentive needs to be offered. The bigger the incentive, the more change can be expected (similarly, the stronger the punishment, the more change can be expected). Research on attitude change, therefore, also focused on the role of rewards and punishment. What made dissonance theory stand out was its prediction that sometimes *less* reward or incentive will lead to more change. This counterintuitive prediction, standing in stark contrast to the generally accepted ideas about the roles of rewards and punishment, brought immediate attention to dissonance theory not only from the social psychological community but also from the psychological community in general; it quickly vaulted the theory to a position of prominence.

A second reason dissonance has become such an important theory has to do with its particular influence on the field of social psychology. Before the theory was introduced, social psychology was identified with the study of groups and intergroup relations. Dissonance theory was one of the first social psychological theories to emphasize the cognitive processes occurring within the individual as an important area of inquiry. As a result, interest in the individual waxed in social psychology, and interest in groups waned. Indeed, the study of groups and intergroup relations began, in part, to be considered the province of sociologists, and the study of the individual in social settings began to define social psychology. Thus, dissonance theory can be credited with significantly changing the focus of research and theory in social psychology.

SOURCES FOR FURTHER STUDY

Aronson, Elliot. "The Theory of Cognitive Dissonance." In *Advances in Experimental Social Psychology*. Vol. 4, edited by Leonard Berkowitz. New York: Academic Press, 1969. This chapter by one of the leading dissonance researchers critically examines the original theory and offers a revised version of the theory based on empirical findings. Clearly written and easily accessible to nonpsychologists.

Festinger, Leon. *A Theory of Cognitive Dissonance*. Stanford, Calif.: Stanford University Press, 1957. Festinger's seminal work represents the formal introduction of the theory. Theory and data on decision making, attitude change, and exposure to attitude-discrepant information are addressed. It is interesting to compare this original work with later versions of the theory, such as Aronson's chapter.

Harmon-Jones, Eddie, ed. *Cognitive Dissonance: Progress on a Pivotal Theory in Social Psychology*. Washington, D.C.: American Psychological Association, 1999. A collection of papers assessing current thought on the concept of cognitive dissonance and suggestions for future research directions.

McClure, John. *Explanations, Accounts, and Illusions: A Critical Analysis*. New York: Cambridge University Press, 1991. A survey of the major ways in which social psychology explains human self-awareness and social cognition, including a discussion of cognitive dissonance.

Kenneth G. DeBono

SEE ALSO: Attitude-behavior consistency; Attitude formation and change; Causal attribution; Motivation; Self-perception theory.

Cognitive maps

TYPE OF PSYCHOLOGY: Cognition; learning; memory; social psychology
FIELDS OF STUDY: Cognitive learning; cognitive processes; social perception and cognition

A cognitive map is the representation of one's social and cultural environment. Individuals from different cultures may have different perceptions of the world due to their cognitive maps. These differences can influence how they interact with their surrounding environment. In a more specific sense, a cognitive map is the development of an internal representation of spatial relationships between items, allowing for navigation through an environment, acquired through actual experience or through other means.

KEY CONCEPTS
• cognition
• competence
• context
• culture
• expectancy
• latent learning
• performance

INTRODUCTION

Edward C. Tolman first identified what he later named cognitive maps as a result of a series of experiments conducted in the 1920's and 1930's. In these experiments, Tolman sought to discover whether learning occurred that might not be immediately reflected in performance—what he came to term "latent learning."

In a typical experiment, Tolman constructed an intricate maze. Three groups of hungry rats ran the maze once a day for twelve days. The first group, the rewarded control group, received food for successfully completing the maze. The second group, the nonrewarded control group, received no food; its members investigated the maze. The third group, the experimental group, also received no food for the first ten days of the experiment, and its members simply surveyed the maze. On the eleventh day, the experimental group was provided with food; on the twelfth day, this group performed as well as the rewarded control group.

The conclusion was that latent learning had taken place and that under the appropriate conditions, the experimental group reflected this learning through its performance—the successful completion of the maze. Tolman asserted that the rats had formed "cognitive maps" that enabled them to solve the maze.

Learning (defined here as the construction of cognitive maps), therefore, is not the same as performance. Although learning is reflected in performance, Tolman's work strongly suggests that the appropriate context is necessary to elicit that performance. In the case of the experimental group, it was the food the experimenters provided on the eleventh day of a twelve-day experiment. The rats, Tolman inferred, anticipated that successful completion of the maze on the next attempt would result in their receiving the desired food.

Research has supported Tolman's pioneering work. In 1978, Emil W. Menzel, for example, used chimpanzees to illustrate the spatial dimensions of cognitive maps. He hid food in a field and then carried a chimpanzee around the field with him. He did not allow the ape either to eat or approach the food, preventing both instrumental conditioning and primary reinforcement from taking place. Later, the chimpanzee that had been shown the food's hiding places and five experimental chimpanzees that had not seen them were released in the field. Invariably, the first chimpanzee went directly to the food. The experimental animals found their food through scrutinizing the area near the chimpanzee that had been shown the hidden supply of food or begging food from this chimpanzee.

In 1976, David S. Olton and Robert J. Samuelson demonstrated spatial memory (cognitive maps) in rats through employment of a radial maze. Each arm of the maze had food at the end of it. Through a series of manipulations, the experimenters demonstrated that the rats remembered which arms they had explored and at which arms they had been fed. They eliminated the possibility that the animals used smell to locate the food through altering the animals' sense of smell. Furthermore, other researchers moved the maze to note whether other factors, such as tactile clues, influenced the rats. In each variation of the experiment, the rats behaved as if they were responding to spatial location and not tactile clues. The implication of the studies goes beyond rats. In 1985, William Roberts and Nelly Van Veldhuizen demonstrated that pigeons, as well as rats, can work the radial maze.

LEARNING THEORIES

Cognitive theories in learning have gained in popularity. Tolman's pacesetting work established the concepts of cognitive map, internal spatial memories of the animal's relevant environment, and expectancy, an animal's anticipation of a sequence of events in time. Tolman's work, supported and developed through additional research, further established the distinction between learning and performance. Linguists such as Noam Chomsky express this distinction as one between competence and performance.

Cognitive anthropologists, influenced by Tolman's work, have applied his concept to the learning of individuals within sociocultural systems. Cognitive maps, in their view, provide guides to cultural behavior through organizing the psychological, social, and cultural landscape in terms of its relevant characteristics for members of any given society. Two famous covers of *The New Yorker* magazine, for example, illustrate the point. One cover is a New Yorker's view of the West. In that view, the entire center of the United States comprises an area smaller than Midtown Manhattan. The view to the east is little better: The Atlantic Ocean becomes a puddle, and the geography of Europe is greatly distorted. The point is not that New Yorkers are more ethnocentric than other people; it is that all people exaggerate those aspects of their landscapes or environments that are most important to them, and they neglect those features that they consider unimportant.

A number of factors enter into perceptions of what is most relevant and what is not. Some of these are personal, such as age, gender, likes, and dislikes; others are social—class, ethnic group, occupation. All factors, however, fit into a cultural context and take on meanings within that context. Anyone attempting to understand the manner in which people learn and demonstrate that learning through adequate and appropriate performance must take into account these factors and how they help shape an individual's cognitive map.

In education, the "prior learning" approach has sought to come to grips with these issues and to apply them to instructional ends. Essentially, this perspective maintains that it cannot be assumed that learning has not taken place merely because a student does not demonstrate the desired performance. William Labov demonstrated, for example, that the presumed inarticulateness of African American street youths was a function of the setting in which people had tested them. In more natural settings, Labov determined that they were, in fact, highly articulate.

Tolman's insight that rats in a maze will demonstrate latent learning through performance when an appropriate stimulus is present has influenced cognitive therapy. This therapy is based on the hypothesis that people base their behavior on cognitive maps and expectancies. These internal representations of spatial relationships and anticipated sequences of events, based on past experiences—psychological, social, and cultural—form individuals' perceptions of reality even though these stimuli are not materially present.

Cognitive motivation theory is a "pull theory" of motivation. It is based on the hypothesis that people's expectancies provide incentives for behavior. There are positive-incentive and negative-incentive motivations. Working for a promotion along paths anticipated to achieve that desired goal is an example of positive-incentive motivation. In contrast, a youngster who is developing his martial arts skills in order to deal with bullies who beat him each time he encounters them provides an example of negative-incentive motivation.

Values enter intimately into cognitive motivation theory. In order to motivate people, incentives must be valued. If people do not value an incentive, such as a promotion, they are less likely to perform the actions they associate with receiving that incentive. If they receive the goal without performing the behavior (for example, if someone receives a promotion undeservedly), they are less likely to value the goal. In sum, there is an intrinsic relationship between expectancies and value.

Moreover, relief and frustration enter the picture. Relief refers to not receiving an expected negative result (a person does not fail a test for which he or she did not study). Frustration involves failure to attain a goal for which a person has prepared. Failure to receive a promotion to which a person is entitled is an example of frustration. Relief is an example of positive-incentive motivation, and frustration is an example of negative-incentive motivation.

Albert Bandura and others have advocated cognitive behavior therapy based on the application of positive and negative incentives. Such therapy seeks to alter the expectancies and relational maps of clients. Thus, clients can relearn their environment through redrawing cognitive maps and altering their expectancies. There are many techniques employed to bring about these changes in spatial and event expectations.

Therapists who employ Albert Ellis's rational-emotive therapy, for example, believe that the therapist should take a strong interventionist role in the therapy, aggressively confronting the client whenever he or she exhibits examples of irrational thought. These confrontations seek to force clients to learn new, more rational ways of thinking and, therefore, behaving.

Cognitive behavioral therapists seek to change a person's inappropriate thoughts to more effective ones. They first learn what their clients are thinking and then relate these thoughts to inappropriate behavior. They seek to help their clients learn new thoughts that will result in more appropriate behavior. Patients are taught to "talk to themselves," substituting good thoughts for bad. Rather than dwelling on failure, patients concentrate on success or positive aspects of their lives. A student taking an examination, for example, would stop thoughts of failure and remind himself or herself about how well test preparation had gone. Self-encouragement would replace self-disparagement.

Each of these applications is based on the theory that people's behavior is based on internal representations of the world. Each person's representations differ in some way from that of others. These representations influence both the way in which one learns about the world and the manner in which one represents that world. The application of Tolman's work on cognitive maps and their related internal representations, or expectancies, has led to a deeper understanding of learning.

RELEVANCE OF COGNITIVE MAPS TO PSYCHOLOGY

One of the important issues for the field of cognitive psychology is the issue of representation. In general terms, how do humans store information in the brain? Allen Paivio, in 1969, presented the dual code theory, which suggests that both analogical and verbal codes are used for representing information. Some information maybe stored in an image like form (analogue) while other information is stored in a verbal format. Zenon Phylyshyn, in 1973, advocates the propositional hypothesis, which suggests that concepts are stored in an abstract form that captures the underlying relationship between ideas. People may experience images, but this experience is simply a by-product, an epiphenomenon, of the retrieval of information. Research into cognitive maps may provide some insight into the issue of representation.

SOURCES OF INFORMATION FOR A COGNITIVE MAP

The development of a cognitive map may include in the representation information from a variety of sources, including landmarks, route information, and survey information. This information may be incorporated into a cognitive map over time and is not necessarily mutually exclusive. Salient features such as landmarks, distinctive objects that stand out from the rest of the environment, provide a point of reference for orientation and navigation within an environment. Route knowledge is specific information regarding how to navigate from one location to another. The directions one gives to allow another to navigate from one location to another would be similar to route information. Survey knowledge provides an overview of the relationships between locations. This perspective has a better grasp of the global relationship between various locations. This type of knowledge is acquired from maps by traversing the environment from a number of different perspectives.

In addition to the type of information available, a number of other factors can influence the development of a cognitive map, such as angle, shape, and orientation. These factors may lead to distortions in generating a map. For example, streets that cross each other at an odd angle tend to be drawn closer to a 90 degree angle than they really are. Still other factors that are not spatial in nature may affect the retrieval of information. In 1991, Keith Clayton and Ali Habibi discussed the confounding of time and space. Locations experienced close together in space are often experienced close together in time. Retrieval of information, in some cases, may be due to temporal proximity versus spatial proximity. Other such factors in this category may include semantic clustering (grouping together of similar items) and route knowledge (grouping of items spatially and temporally).

METHODS FOR ASSESSING COGNITIVE MAPS

A variety of methods have been used to test spatial knowledge, including location judgment (whether a location is closer to one reference point or another), recognition (whether the item was part of the map or not), distance estimations (how far between two locations), drawing a map, providing directions, and pointing (what direction would one travel from a given location to another specific location). In a 1986 study, Timothy McNamara discusses the merits of using tasks such as location judgment and recognition that allow one to look at priming, which taps into automatic processes. These tasks may be informative in terms of how spatial information is organization in long-term memory. Other tasks, such as pointing, may be more informative in terms of strategies that are used to answer spatial questions.

In 1978, Albert Stevens and Patty Coupe asked subjects which is farther west, Reno, Nevada, or San Diego, California. Many incorrectly inferred that San Diego is farther west than Reno, since California is farther west than Nevada. In actuality, the state of California curves under the state of Nevada, making Reno farther west. This implies the use of information such as relative position within categories (states) rather than actual spatial information between the two locations.

OTHER AREAS OF RESEARCH IN COGNITIVE MAPS

Research suggests that the ability to form and use a cognitive map begins to develop around the age of three. Judy DeLoache, in her 1987 experiments, used a scaled model of a larger room to test children's spatial knowledge. Children of various ages were asked to find a small, hidden toy in the model. After finding the small toy, children were then asked to find the larger toy, which was hidden in the same location in the larger room. This task required the child to use the information from the scaled model to find the object in the larger environment. DeLoache suggested that the younger children had a difficult time using the scaled model of a room as a basis for a representation of the larger room. Research in this area continues to look at the application and development of these skills over time.

Studies on gender differences in spatial knowledge have focused on strategies such as wayfinding and direction pointing. The use of such spatial strategies tends to be gender-specific. It appears that women prefer to use a strategy of wayfinding based on the use of landmarks, while men tend to prefer using more of a global or survey strategy. Ward and colleagues (1986) suggest that these differences may be due to preferred strategies versus actual differences in acquisition of spatial knowledge.

REALITY REPRESENTATION AND BEHAVIOR

Tolman's concept of the cognitive map grew out of a recognition that internal representations of reality influence behavior. Moreover, learning is not indistinguishable from performance—the two processes are analytically distinct. An organism may have learned behavior without demonstrating that behavior through performance. This latent learning can be elicited through the presentation of adequate incentives.

Tolman's work in the 1920's and 1930's did much to advance the field of cognitive psychology at a time when behavioral psychology dominated the schools. It provided an additional dimension to learning, advancing the position of internal representations of reality. The empirical evidence offered to support cognitive theory has been impressive, and its status in psychology has advanced accordingly; it is often combined with behavioral concepts, as in the work of Bandura.

That combination has enabled educators and therapists to bring about behavioral changes based on changes in the manner in which students and patients perceive their worlds. New internal representations of the external environment can be brought about through changes in cognitive maps and expectancies. In turn, these changes alter the bases of decisions that influence an individual's future behavior.

Tolman's work has influenced linguistics, anthropology, sociology, and other social and behavioral sciences. Scholars in these areas have applied the concept of the cognitive map cross-culturally and within cultures to members of subgroups. Future work will apply it to the manner in which each individual negotiates his or her way within cultural and social systems. Continuing work in anthropology and sociology in the negotiated nature of sociocultural systems draws heavily on cognitive maps. Prior learning theory is based on the idea of latent learning, and future work will continue to extract applications of significant value to education.

Future advances will likely occur in studies that investigate field dependence and independence in cognition as related to other aspects of culture, such as child-rearing patterns and subsistence practices. The continuing interest in the relationship between language and the cultural organization of reality holds promise for further advances in understanding and applying cognitive maps. The role of choice in the individual's construction of these maps is also an area of intensive investigation.

SOURCES FOR FURTHER STUDY

Bandura, Albert. *Social Foundations of Thought and Action: A Social-Cognitive Theory.* Englewood Cliffs, N.J.: Prentice-Hall, 1986. Presents a clear and concise exposition of Bandura's combination of behavioral and cognitive perspectives in psychology. Advocates an approach that sees behavior resulting from cognitive maps and expectancies.

Bukatko, Danuta, and Marvin W. Daehler. *Child Development: A Thematic Approach.* 3d ed. Boston: Houghton Mifflin, 1998. Provides a summary of the research discussing the development of spatial knowledge in children from landmark to route to configurational knowledge.

Chomsky, Noam. *Language and Mind.* New York: Harcourt Brace Jovanovich, 1972. The influential inventor of transformational grammar presents his views on the relationship of language and mind, as well as presenting another extension of Edward C. Tolman's concepts.

Fromkin, Victoria, and Robert Rodman. *An Introduction to Language.* New York: Holt, Rinehart and Winston, 1988. An introductory book that discusses the field of linguistics, including theoretical developments. Demonstrates the manner in which cognitive concepts are being developed in linguistics.

Gallistel, C. R. *The Organization of Learning.* Cambridge, Mass.: MIT Press, 1990. Discusses spatial knowledge from a number of perspectives including the spatial abilities of various animals.

Labov, William. *The Social Stratification of English in New York City.* Washington, D.C.: Center for Applied Linguistics, 1982. Persuasive argument that in appropriate circumstances, the assumed inarticulateness of young African American men disappears. Example of latent learning forming the basis for adequate performance in a setting that elicits appropriate behavior.

Matlin, Margaret W. *Cognition.* 5th ed. Fort Worth, Tex.: Harcourt, 2002. See Matlin's discussion about cognitive maps and the number of factors that effect them. Also talks about the importance of representation in general, including prepositional versus analogical representation.

Menzel, Emil W. "Cognitive Mapping in Chimpanzees." In *Cognitive Processes in Animal Behavior,* edited by Stewart H. Hulse, Harry Fowler, and Werner K. Honig. Hillsdale, N.J.: Lawrence Erlbaum, 1978. Adds significantly to the research on cognitive mapping through reporting on Menzel's carefully controlled experiment with chimpanzees and hidden food.

Olton, David S., and Robert J. Samuelson. "Remembrance of Places Passed: Spatial Memory in Rats." *Journal of Experimental Psychology: Animal Behavior Process* 2, no. 2 (1976): 97-116. Research that reports on rats in a radial maze, further establishing the validity of cognitive maps and strengthening their place in learning theory.

Roberts, William A., and Nelly Van Veldhuizen. "Spatial Memory in Rats on the Radial Maze." *Journal of Experimental Psychology: Animal Behavior Processes* 11, no. 2 (1985): 241-260. Extends earlier findings of cognitive maps in rats on the radial maze to pigeons. Careful attention to method, allowing psychologists to extend their findings beyond confines of the research, should be noted.

Tolman, Edward Chace. "Cognitive Maps in Rats and Men." *Psychological Review* 55 (1948): 189-209. Summarizes Tolman's earlier experiments with rats in a clear and comprehensive manner. Applies the theory of cognitive maps to humans and suggests applications of the theory.

_____. *Purposive Behavior in Animals and Men.* New York: Century, 1932. The first book to report Tolman's finding regarding cognitive maps. Serves as the initial source for understanding cognitive maps.

Frank A. Salamone;
updated by Michael S. Bendele

SEE ALSO: Cognitive psychology; Cognitive social learning: Walter Mischel; Cognitive therapy; Concept formation; Decision making; Incentive motivation; Learning; Motivation.

Cognitive psychology

TYPE OF PSYCHOLOGY: Cognition
FIELDS OF STUDY: Cognitive processes; thought

Cognitive psychology is concerned with the scientific study of human mental activities involved in the acquisition, storage, retrieval, and utilization of information. Among its wide concerns are perception, memory, reasoning, problem solving, intelligence, language, and creativity; research in these areas has widespread practical applications.

KEY CONCEPTS
- artificial intelligence
- cognitive behavioral therapy
- cognitive science
- episodic memory
- long-term memory
- metamemory
- prospective memory
- semantic memory
- short-term memory
- working memory

INTRODUCTION

Cognitive psychology is that branch of psychology concerned with human mental activities. A staggering array of topics fit under such a general heading. In fact, it sometimes seems that there is no clear place to end the catalog of cognitive topics, as mental operations intrude into virtually all human endeavors. As a general guideline, one might consider the subject matter of cognitive psychology as those mental processes involved in the acquisition, storage, retrieval, and utilization of information.

Among the more specific concerns of cognitive psychologists are perception, attention, memory, and imagery. Studies of perception and attention might be concerned with how much of people's vast sensory experience they can further process and make sense of, and how they recognize incoming information as forming familiar patterns. Questions regarding the quality of memory include how much information can be maintained, for how long, and under what conditions; how information is organized in memory and how is it retrieved or lost; and how accurate the memory is, as well as what can be done to facilitate a person's recall skills. Cognitive researchers concerned with imagery are interested in people's ability to "see" in their minds a picture or image of an object, person, or scene that is not physically present; cognitive researchers are interested in the properties of such images and how they can be manipulated.

In addition to these concerns, there is great interest in the higher-order processes of planning, reasoning, problem solving, intelligence, language, and creativity. Cognitive psychologists want to know, for example, what steps are involved in planning a route to a destination or a solution to a problem, and what factors influence people's more abstract ability to reason. They seek to understand the importance of prior knowledge or experience, to discover which strategies are effective, and to see what obstacles typically impede a person's thinking. They are interested in the relationships between language and thought, and between creativity and intelligence.

The following exchange is useful in illustrating some of the topics important to cognitive psychologists. Imagine that "Jacob" and "Janet" are two children on a busy playground:

Jacob: Do you want to play some football?

Janet: Sure! Tell me where the ball is and I'll go get it.

Jacob: The football's in my locker in the equipment room. Go back in the building. Go past our classroom, turn right at the water fountain, and it's the second door on your left. My locker is number 12, and the combination is 6-21-13.

Janet: Okay, it'll just take me a couple of minutes. [As she runs to get the ball, Janet repeats over and over to herself, "12; 6, 21, 13. . . ."]

Jacob: [*shouting*] The football field's being watered; meet me in the gym.

Even such a simple encounter involves and depends upon a rich assortment of cognitive skills. At a basic level, Jacob and Janet have to be aware of each other. Their sensory systems allow the detec-

tion of each other, and their brains work on the raw data (information) from the senses in order to perceive or interpret the incoming information. In this case, the data are recognized as the familiar patterns labeled "Jacob" and "Janet." During the course of the brief conversation, the children must also attend to (concentrate on) each other, and in doing so they may be less attentive to other detectable sights and sounds of their environment.

This scenario illustrates the use of more than one type of memory. Janet stores the locker number and combination in short-term memory (STM), and she maintains the information by rehearsing it. After Janet retrieves the ball and redirects her attention to choosing teams for the football game, she may forget this information. Jacob does not need to rehearse his combination continually to maintain it; rather, his frequent use of his combination and the meaningfulness of this information have helped him to store it in long-term memory (LTM). If someone later asks Janet where she got the football, she will retrieve that information from her episodic LTM. Episodic memory holds information about how things appeared and when they occurred; it stores things that depend on context. The language comprehension of the children also illustrates another type of LTM. Semantic LTM, or semantic memory, holds all the information they need in order to use language; it includes not only words and the symbols for them, their meaning and what they represent, but also the rules for manipulating them. When Janet hears the words "football," "water fountain," and "locker," she effortlessly retrieves their meanings from LTM. Furthermore, metamemory, an understanding of the attributes of one's own memories, is demonstrated. Janet knows to rehearse the combination to prevent forgetting it.

Jacob probably employed mental imagery and relied on a cognitive map in order to direct Janet to the equipment room. From his substantial mental representation of the school environment, Jacob retrieved a specific route, guided by a particular sequence of meaningful landmarks. In addition to their language capabilities and their abilities to form and follow routes, a number of other higher-level mental processes suggest something of the intelligence of these children. They appear to be following a plan that will result in a football game. Simple problem solving is demonstrated by Janet's calculation of how long it will take to retrieve the football and in Jacob's decision to use the gym floor as a substitute for the football field.

THEORETICAL AND METHODOLOGICAL APPROACHES

To understand cognitive psychology, one must be familiar not only with the relevant questions—the topic matter of the discipline—but also with the approach taken to answer these questions. Cognitive psychologists typically employ an information-processing model to help them better understand mental events. An assumption of this model is that mental activities (the processing of information) can be broken down into a series of interrelated stages and scientifically studied. A general comparison can be made between the information processing of a human and a computer. For example, both have data input into the system, humans through their sense organs and computers via the keyboard. Both systems then translate and encode (store) the data. The computer translates the keyboard input into electromagnetic signals for storage on a disk. People oftentimes translate the raw data from their senses to a linguistic code which is retained in some unique human storage device (for example, a piercing, rising-and-falling pitch may be stored in memory as "baby's cry"). Both humans and computers can manipulate the stored information in virtually limitless ways, and both can later retrieve information from storage for output. Although there are many dissimilarities between how computers and humans function, this comparison accurately imparts the flavor of the information-processing model.

In addition to constructing computational models that specify the stages and processes involved in human thought, cognitive psychologists use a variety of observational and experimental methods to determine how the mind works. Much can be learned, for example, from the study of patients with neuropsychological disorders such as the progressive dementias, including Alzheimer's disease. The "lesion," or brain injury, study is the oldest and most widely used technique to study brain function. Examining what happens when one aspect of cognition is disrupted can reveal much about the operation of the remaining mechanisms.

Behavioral studies—in contrast to "lesion" studies—examine cognitive function in healthy subjects, using a variety of experimental methods developed throughout the twentieth century. One of the continuing challenges of cognitive psychology is the construction of experiments in which observable behaviors accurately reveal mental processes. Researchers bring volunteers into the laboratory and measure, for example, the time it takes for subjects to judge whether a word they are shown had appeared in a list of words they had earlier studied.

Other researchers study human cognition in more naturalistic settings called field studies. In one such study, the average score of grocery shoppers on a paper-and-pencil arithmetic test was 59 percent, but their proficiency in the supermarket on analogous tasks reached ceiling level (98 percent). Much of what is done in the laboratory could be thought of as basic research, whereas field approaches to the study of cognition could be characterized as applied research.

APPLIED RESEARCH IN COGNITIVE PSYCHOLOGY

For many psychologists, the desire to "know about knowing" is sufficient reason to study human cognition; however, there are more tangible benefits. Examples of these widespread practical applications may be found in the fields of artificial intelligence and law, and in the everyday world of decision making.

Artificial intelligence (AI) is a branch of computer science that strives to create a computer capable of reasoning, processing language, and, in short, mimicking human intelligence. While this goal has yet to be obtained in full, research in this area has made important contributions. The search for AI has improved the understanding of human cognition; it has also produced applied benefits such as expert systems. Expert systems are computer programs that simulate human expertise in specific domains. Such programs have been painstakingly developed by computer scientists who have essentially extracted knowledge in a subject area from a human expert and built it into a computer system designed to apply that knowledge. Expert systems do not qualify as true artificial intelligence, because, while they can think, they can only do so very narrowly, on one particular topic.

A familiar expert system is the "chess computer." A computerized chess game is driven by a program that has a vast storehouse of chess knowledge and the capability of interacting with a human player, "thinking" about each game in which it is involved. Expert systems are also employed to solve problems

A schoolteacher leads a second-grader in cognitive learning exercises designed to help students connect the left and right sides of their brains, thus improving reading ability. (AP/Wide World Photos)

in law, computer programming, and various facets of industry. A medical expert system has even been developed to consult interactively with patients and to diagnose and recommend a course of treatment for infectious diseases.

There are legal implications for the cognitive research of Elizabeth Loftus and her colleagues at the University of Washington. Some of their experiments demonstrate the shortcomings of human long-term memory, research relevant to the interpretation of eyewitness testimony in the courtroom. In one study, Loftus and John Palmer showed their subjects films of automobile accidents and asked them to estimate the speeds of the cars involved. The critical variable was the verb used in the question to the subjects. That is, they were asked how fast the cars were going when they "smashed," "collided," "bumped," "hit," or "contacted" each other. Interestingly, the stronger the verb, the greater was the speed estimated. One interpretation of these findings is that the nature of the "leading question" biased the

answers of subjects who were not really positive of the cars' speeds. Hence, if the question employed the verb "smashed," the subject was led to estimate that the cars were going fast. Any astute attorney would have no trouble capitalizing on this phenomenon when questioning witnesses to a crime or accident.

In a second experiment, Loftus and Palmer considered a different explanation for their findings. Again, subjects saw filmed car accidents and were questioned as to the speeds of the cars, with the key verb being varied as previously described. As before, those exposed to the verb "smashed" estimated the fastest speeds. In the second part of the experiment, conducted a week later, the subjects were asked additional questions about the accident, including, "Did you see any broken glass?" Twenty percent of the subjects reported seeing broken glass, though none was in the film. Of particular interest was that the majority of those who made this error were in the group which had been exposed to the strongest verb, "smashed."

Loftus and Palmer reasoned that the subjects were melding actual information that they had witnessed with information from another source encountered after the fact (the verb "smashed" presented by the questioner). The result was a mental representation of an event that was partly truth and partly fiction. This interpretation also has implications for the evaluation of eyewitness testimony. Before testifying in court, a witness will likely have been questioned numerous times (and received many suggestions as to what may have taken place) and may even have "compared notes" with other witnesses. This process is likely to distort the originally experienced information.

Consider next the topic of decision making, an area of research in cognitive psychology loaded with practical implications. Everyone makes scores of decisions on a daily basis, from choosing clothing to match the weather, to selecting a college or a career objective. Psychologists Amos Tversky and Daniel Kahneman are well known for their research on decision making and, in particular, on the use of heuristics. Heuristics are shortcuts or rules of thumb that are likely, but not guaranteed, to produce a correct decision. It would seem beneficial for everyone to appreciate the limitations of such strategies. For example, the availability heuristic oftentimes leads people astray when their decisions involve the estimating of probabilities, as when faced with questions such as, Which produces more fatalities, breast cancer or diabetes? Which are more numerous in the English language, words that begin with *k* or words that have *k* as the third letter? Experimental subjects typically, and incorrectly, choose the first alternative. Kahneman and Tversky's research indicates that people rely heavily on examples that come most easily to mind—that is, the information most available in memory. Hence, people overestimate the incidence of breast-cancer fatalities because such tragedies get more media attention relative to diabetes, a more prolific but less exotic killer. In a similar vein, words that begin with *k* come to mind more easily (probably because people are more likely to organize their vocabularies by the initial sounds of the words) than words with *k* as the third letter, although the latter in fact outnumber the former. One's decision making will doubtless be improved if one is aware of the potential drawbacks associated with the availability heuristic and if one is able to resist the tendency to estimate probabilities based upon the most easily imagined examples.

COGNITIVE CONTEXTS

The workings of the human mind have been pondered throughout recorded history. The science of psychology, however, only dates back to 1879, when Wilhelm Wundt established the first laboratory for the study of psychology in Leipzig, Germany. Although the term was not yet popular, Wundt's primary interest was clearly in cognition. His students laboriously practiced the technique of introspection (the careful attention to, and the objective reporting of, one's own sensations, experiences, and thoughts), as Wundt hoped to identify through this method the basic elements of human thought. Wundt's interests remained fairly popular until around 1920. At that time, John B. Watson, a noted American psychologist and behaviorist, spearheaded a campaign to redefine the agenda of psychology. Watson was convinced that the workings of the mind could not be objectively studied through introspection and hence mandated that the proper subject matter for psychologists should be overt, observable behaviors exclusively. In this way, dissatisfaction with a method of research (introspection) led to the abandonment of an important psychological topic (mental activity).

In the 1950's, a number of forces came into play that led to the reemergence of cognitive psychology in America. First, during World War II, considerable research had been devoted to human-factors issues such as human skills and performance within, for example, the confines of a tank or cockpit. After the war, researchers showed continued interest in human attention, perception, decision making, and so on, and they were influenced by a branch of communication science, known as information theory, that dealt abstractly with questions of information processing. The integration of these two topics resulted eventually in the modern information-processing model, mentioned above.

Second, explosive gains were made in the field of computer science. Of particular interest to psychology were advances in the area of artificial intelligence. It was a natural progression for psychologists to begin comparing computer and brain processes, and this analogy served to facilitate cognitive research.

Third, there was growing dissatisfaction with behavioral psychology as defined by Watson and with its seeming inability to explain complex psychological phenomena. In particular, Noam Chomsky, a well-known linguist, proposed that the structure of language was too complicated to be acquired via the principles of behaviorism. It became apparent to many psychologists that to understand truly the diversity of human behavior, internal mental processes would have to be accepted and scientifically studied.

Working memory emerged as an important theoretical construct in the 1980's and 1990's. Everyday cognitive tasks—such as reading a newspaper article or calculating the appropriate amount to tip in a restaurant—often involve multiple steps with intermediate results that need to be kept in mind temporarily to accomplish the task at hand successfully. "Working memory" refers to the system or mechanism underlying the maintenance of task-relevant information during the performance of a cognitive task. As the "hub of cognition," working memory has been called "perhaps the most significant achievement of human mental evolution." According to Alan Baddeley, working memory comprises a visuospatial sketchpad; a phonological loop, concerned with acoustic and verbal information; a central executive that is involved in the control and regulation of the system; and an episodic buffer that combines information from long-term memory with that from the visuospatial sketchpad and the phonological loop. Prospective memory is also emerging as an important domain of research in cognitive psychology. This type of memory involves the intention to carry out an action in the future: for instance, to pick up dry cleaning after work.

Cognitive psychology is now a vibrant subdiscipline that has attracted some of the finest scientific minds. It is a standard component in most undergraduate and graduate psychology programs. More than half a dozen academic journals are devoted to its research, and it continues to pursue answers to questions that are important to psychology and other disciplines as well. The cognitive perspective has heavily influenced other subfields of psychology. For example, many social psychologists are interested in social cognition, the reasoning underlying such phenomena as prejudice, altruism, and persuasion. Some clinical psychologists are interested in understanding the abnormal thought processes underlying problems such as depression

and anorexia nervosa; a subspecialty—cognitive behavioral therapy—treats mental illness using methods that attempt to directly treat these abnormal thoughts.

The burgeoning field of cognitive science represents a contemporary union of cognitive psychology, neuroscience, computer science, linguistics, and philosophy. Cognitive scientists are concerned with mental processes but are particularly interested in establishing general, fundamental principles of information processing as they may be applied by humans or machines. Their research is often heavily dependent on complex computer models rather than experimentation with humans. With fast-paced advances in computer technology, and the exciting potential of expertise shared in an interdisciplinary fashion, the field of cognitive science holds considerable promise for answering questions about human cognition.

SOURCES FOR FURTHER STUDY

Ashcraft, Mark H. *Human Memory and Cognition.* Glenview, Ill.: Scott, Foresman, 1989. A fine textbook, geared for college students who have had some background in psychology but accessible to the inquisitive layperson. Ashcraft writes informally and provides chapter outlines and summaries, a glossary of key terms, and suggested supplemental readings. Perception and attention, memory, language, reasoning, decision making, and problem solving are all well covered.

Baddeley, Alan D. "The Cognitive Psychology of Everyday Life." *British Journal of Psychology* 72, no. 2 (1981): 257-269. An interesting journal article in which Baddeley describes his research conducted outside the laboratory environment. Considers such practical topics as absentmindedness, alcohol effects, and the effectiveness of saturation advertising. A must for those who question the ecological validity (the real-life applicability) of cognitive research.

Berger, Dale E., Kathy Pezdek, and William P. Banks, eds. *Applications of Cognitive Psychology.* Hillsdale, N.J.: Lawrence Erlbaum, 1987. Five chapters each on three topics: educational applications, teaching of thinking and problem solving, and human-computer interactions. The chapters range in sophistication and accessibility, so this book should appeal to readers of diverse backgrounds. There are helpful name and subject indexes.

Hochberg, Julian. *Perception and Cognition at Century's End*. San Diego, Calif.: Academic Press, 1998. This book reviews research findings over the past half-century in broad areas of perception and other aspects of cognitive functioning.

Kahneman, Daniel, Paul Slovic, and Amos Tversky, eds. *Judgment Under Uncertainty: Heuristics and Biases*. New York: Cambridge University Press, 1982. A comprehensive source on heuristics and decision making with an easy-to-understand introductory chapter by the editors. A four-chapter section is devoted to the availability heuristic, and there is an interesting chapter on probabilistic reasoning in clinical medicine.

Kendler, Howard H. *Historical Foundations of Modern Psychology*. Chicago: Dorsey Press, 1987. A well-written account of the emergence of cognitive psychology and the contributions of other disciplines such as linguistics, engineering, and computer science. Approachable for the layperson; provides a fine historical backdrop. It is of limited use, beyond review, for the upper-level college student.

Miyake, Akira, and Priti Shah, eds. *Models of Working Memory: Mechanisms of Active Maintenance and Executive Control*. New York: Cambridge University Press, 1999. This volume compares and contrasts existing models of working memory. It does so by asking each contributor to address the same comprehensive set of important theoretical questions on working memory. The answers to these questions provided in the volume elucidate the emerging general consensus on the nature of working memory among different theorists and crystallize incompatible theoretical claims that must be resolved in future.

Pinker, Steven. *How the Mind Works*. New York: W. W. Norton, 1997. Pinker, one of the world's leading cognitive scientists, discusses what the mind is, how it evolved, and how it allows us to see, think, feel, laugh, interact, enjoy the arts, and ponder the mysteries of life. He explains the mind by "reverse-engineering" it—figuring out what natural selection designed it to accomplish in the environment in which we evolved. The mind, he writes, is a system of "organs of computation" that allowed our ancestors to understand and outsmart objects, animals, plants, and each other.

Sternberg, Robert J., and Talia Ben-Zeev. *Complex Cognition: The Psychology of Human Thought*. New York: Oxford University Press, 2001. This book reviews of the key concepts and research findings within the field of cognitive psychology. The authors offer a synthesis of the two dominant approaches in cognitive studies—normative reference and "bounded rationality"—combining the best elements of each to present an inclusive new theory that emphasizes multiple points of view, including both the objective and subjective views of the self and others.

Wells, Gary L., and Elizabeth F. Loftus, eds. *Eyewitness Testimony: Psychological Perspectives*. New York: Cambridge University Press, 1984. A fourteen-chapter source with heavy consideration of laboratory research, but with references to courtroom cases as well. There is nice coverage of research on children as witnesses, as well as on "earwitness" testimony and the use of hypnosis as a memory aid.

Mark B. Alcorn;
updated by Allyson M. Washburn

SEE ALSO: Artificial intelligence; Attention; Cognitive ability: Gender differences; Cognitive development: Jean Piaget; Cognitive maps; Computer models of cognition; Decision making; Language; Logic and reasoning; Pattern recognition.

Cognitive social learning
Walter Mischel

TYPE OF PSYCHOLOGY: Personality
FIELDS OF STUDY: Behavioral and cognitive models; personality theory

Mischel's social learning theory presents a cognitive-social alternative to traditional personality theories. He posits that behavior is determined by a complex interaction of situational and cognitive variables and cannot be predicted from a few widely generalized traits. Consistent features in behavior result from cognitive person variables, defined as acquired and relatively stable modes of information processing.

KEY CONCEPTS
- construction competencies
- encoding strategy

- expectancies
- person variable
- personal construct
- personality trait
- prototype
- stimulus value

INTRODUCTION

Psychologist Walter Mischel developed a cognitive social learning approach to personality that presents a serious challenge to traditional theories and their central tenet that behavior can be predicted from a few widely generalized traits. In his influential book *Personality and Assessment* (1968), Mischel reviewed the literature on personality traits. Personality traits can be defined as a stable disposition to behave in a given way over time and across situations. Although Mischel found impressive consistencies for some attributes such as intelligence, the vast majority of behavior patterns were not consistent, even in highly similar situations. Mischel concluded that behavior is largely determined by situational variables that interact in complex ways with individual modes of information processing. Stable features in behavior result from acquired cognitive person variables (relatively stable individual differences that influence how people interact with their world).

PERSON VARIABLES

Cognitive and behavioral construction competencies represent the first of the person variables. Mischel terms them "competencies" to emphasize that they represent potentials—that is, what people *can* do, rather than what they do. Referring to their "constructive" quality implies that people do not passively store but actively construct their experiences by transforming and synthesizing incoming information in novel ways. Another of these person variables involves encoding strategies and personal constructs. People encode information and classify events in personalized, unique ways. For different individuals, traitlike constructs such as intelligence or honesty may therefore have some overlapping features but may also have many idiosyncratic ones. This explains why two people can witness and process the same event but interpret it differently. Both people only attend to stimuli consistent with their own personal construct systems and ignore discrepant information.

Mischel maintains that besides knowing people's potentials and how they construct events, to predict behavior people must also know their expectations. One type, termed stimulus-outcome expectancies, develops when people form associations between two events and begin to expect the second event as soon as the first occurs. For example, if a child learns to associate parental frowning with being scolded or spanked, any angry face alone may soon instill anxiety.

A second type, termed response-outcome expectancies, refers to learned "if-then rules," in which specific actions will result in certain outcomes. Outcome expectancies can have a significant influence on what people do. When expectations are inconsistent with reality, they can lead to dysfunctional behavior. Expecting relief from alcohol, when drinking actually leads to multiple problems, illustrates this point.

Subjective stimulus values—subjective values or worth that a person attributes to an object or event—are another type of person variable. In spite of holding identical outcome expectancies, people may behave differently if they do not attribute equal value to this outcome. For example, many believe that practice makes perfect, but not everyone values achievement. Furthermore, the worth of a given outcome often depends on its context. Even an avid skier might cancel a ski trip on an icy, stormy winter day.

Self-regulatory systems and plans are yet another kind of person variable. Besides being affected by external rewards and punishments, people are capable of regulating their own behavior. They set goals and mediate self-imposed consequences, depending on whether they meet their own standards. These self-regulatory processes produce individual differences in behavior independently from the effects of extrinsically imposed conditions.

More recently, Mischel and his colleagues have proposed that people also classify events based on cognitive prototypes. These are analogous to templates, and they contain only the best or most typical features of a concept. Although prototypes facilitate the classification of input information, they carry with them the danger of stereotyping. Anyone who, for example, has mistaken a female business executive for the secretary can appreciate the problem resulting from inaccurate classification.

In summary, with the concept of person variables, Mischel can explain behavioral consistency and at the same time take into account the environment as an important determinant of human actions. In psychologically strong situations, person variables play a minimal role (at a church service, for example, all people behave similarly). In psychologically weak situations (such as a cocktail party), however, individual differences are pronounced, because there are no consistent cues to signal what behaviors are deemed appropriate. Therefore, whether or how much cognitive dispositions influence behavior varies with the specific situation.

DISPOSITIONAL AND SITUATIONAL VARIABLES

Despite a widespread tendency among people to describe themselves and others in traitlike terms (intelligent, friendly, aggressive, domineering, and so forth), research has shown that a person's behavior cannot be predicted from a few broadly generalized personality traits. This does not mean that behavior is totally inconsistent, but that dispositions alone are insufficient to explain consistency and that dispositional, as well as situational, variables need to be taken into account for a complete analysis.

To separate the effects of person and situation variables on behavior, Mischel and his colleagues conducted a series of experiments. In one study, the experimenters assessed adolescents' dispositions toward success or failure. Weeks later they had them solve skill-related tasks and, regardless of their actual performance, gave one group success, a second group failure, and a third group no feedback on their performance. Then the adolescents had to choose between a less desirable reward, one for which attainment was independent of performance on similar tasks, and a preferred reward, for which attainment was performance-dependent. In both bogus feedback conditions, the situational variables had a powerful effect and completely overrode pre-existing dispositions toward success or failure. Adolescents who believed they had failed the tasks more often selected the noncontingent reward, while those who believed they had succeeded chose the contingent reward. For subjects in the no-feedback condition, however, the preexisting expectancy scores were highly accurate predictors of their reward choices. This study illustrates how dispositions emerge under weak situational cues but play a trivial role when the setting provides strong cues for behavior. Therefore, Mischel (1973) considers it more

meaningful to analyze "behavior-contingency units" that link specific behavior patterns to those conditions in which they are likely to occur, rather than looking only at behavior. In other words, instead of labeling people "aggressive," it would be more useful to specify under what conditions these people display aggressive behaviors. Such precise specifications would guard against an oversimplified trait approach and highlight the complexities and idiosyncrasies of behavior as well as its interdependence with specific stimulus conditions.

SELF-CONTROL

Mischel and his colleagues also have conducted extensive research on self-control. Their work has been summarized in an article published in 1989 in the journal *Science*. In several experiments, the researchers attempted to clarify why some people are capable of self-regulation, at least in some areas of their lives, while others fail in such attempts. They found enduring differences in self-control as early as the preschool years. In one study, for example, they showed young children pairs of treats, one less and one more desirable (for example, two versus five cookies or one versus two marshmallows). The children were told that the experimenter would leave the room and that they could obtain the more valuable treat if they waited until he or she returned. They could also ring the bell to bring the experimenter back sooner, but then they would receive the lesser treat. During the waiting period, which lasted a maximum of fifteen minutes, the children were unobtrusively observed. Later, the children's strategies to bridge the waiting period were analyzed. It became apparent that self-control increased when the children used behavioral or cognitive strategies to bridge the delay, such as avoiding looking at the rewards, distracting themselves with singing, playing with their fingers, or cognitively transforming the rewards (for example, thinking of marshmallows as clouds). Interestingly, a follow-up study more than ten years later revealed that those preschool children who had displayed more self-control early were socially and academically more competent, more attentive, more verbal, and better able to cope with stress than their peers as adolescents. In a related study, the length of delay time in preschool proved to be correlated with the adolescents' Scholastic Aptitude Test (SAT) scores, suggesting that greater self-control is related to superior academic achievement.

These studies provide an excellent illustration of how cognitive person variables sometimes can have very stable and generalized effects on behavior. The early acquisition of effective cognitive and behavioral strategies to delay gratification had a positive influence on the children's long-term adjustment. Thus, self-control fulfills the requirements of a "personality disposition" in Mischel's sense, because it constitutes an important mediating mechanism for adaptive social behavior throughout the life cycle.

Although the examples presented above lend support to Mischel's theory, one might argue that children's behavior under the constraints of a research setting is artificial and may not reflect what they normally do in their natural environment. While this argument is plausible, it was not supported in a later study with six- to twelve-year-old children in a summer residential treatment facility. Observing children under naturalistic circumstances in this facility led to comparable results. Children who spontaneously used effective cognitive-attentional strategies for self-regulation showed greater self-control in delay situations and were better adjusted than their peers.

An unanswered question is how best to teach children effective information-processing skills. If these skills acquire dispositional character and influence overall adjustment, their attainment would indeed be of vital importance to healthy development.

EVOLUTION OF RESEARCH

Until the late 1960's, the field of personality psychology was dominated by trait and state theories. Their central assumption, that people have traits that produce enduring consistencies in their behavior, went unchallenged for many years. The widespread appeal of these trait assumptions notwithstanding, since the late 1960's personality and social psychologists have been entangled in the "person-situation debate," a controversy over whether the presumed stability in behavior might be based more on illusion than reality. While doubts about the existence of traits were already raised in the middle of the twentieth century, the work of Walter Mischel was instrumental in bringing the controversy into the forefront of academic psychology. In reviewing a voluminous body of literature, Mischel showed in 1968 that virtually all so-called trait measures, except intelligence, change substantially over time and

even more dramatically across situations. Traits such as honesty, assertiveness, or attitudes toward authority typically showed reliability across situations of .20 to .30. This means that if the correlation of behavior presumably reflecting a trait in two different situations is .30, less than one-tenth ($.30 \times .30 = .09$, or 9 percent) of the variability in the behavior can be attributed to the trait. Mischel therefore concluded that perceptions of behavioral stability, while not arbitrary, are often only weakly related to the phenomenon in question.

FUNCTIONAL ANALYSIS

There is consensus, however, that human actions show at least some degree of consistency, which is evidenced most strongly by the sense of continuity people experience in their own selves. How can people reconcile the inconsistency between their own impressions and the empirical data? Mischel's cognitive social learning perspective presents one possible solution to this dilemma. Rather than trying to explain behavior by a few generalized traits, Mischel has shifted the emphasis to a thorough examination of the relationship between behavior patterns and the context in which they occur, as the following example illustrates. Assume that parents are complaining about their child's demanding behavior and the child's many tantrums. After observing this behavior in various situations, a traditional personality theorist might conclude that it manifests an underlying "aggressive drive." In contrast, a social learning theorist might seek to identify the specific conditions under which the tantrums occur and then change these conditions to see if the tantrums increase or decrease. This technique, termed "functional analysis" (as described in Mischel in 1968), systematically introduces and withdraws stimuli in the situation to examine how the behavior of interest changes as a function of situational constraints.

The controversy sparked by Mischel's work has not been completely resolved. Few psychologists today, however, would assume an extreme position and either argue that human actions are completely determined by traits or advocate a total situation-specificity of behavior. As with so many controversies, the truth probably lies somewhere in the middle.

SOURCES FOR FURTHER STUDY

Lieber, Robert M., and Michael D. Spiegler. *Personality: Strategies and Issues.* 7th ed. Monterey, Calif.:

Brooks/Cole, 1996. Chapter 21 persents a read-able synopsis of Mischel's cognitive social-learning theory and reviews the concept of person variables, Mischel's work on delay of gratification, and his position on the interaction of emotion and cognition. Highly recommended as an easy introduction to Mischel's work.

Mischel, Harriet N., and Walter Mischel, eds. *Readings in Personality*. New York: Holt, Rinehart and Winston, 1973. Presents a collection of papers by different authors on some of the central topics and viewpoints in personality psychology. Provides in-depth analyses of various trait, state, and social theories of personality. Several chapters by Walter Mischel present his views on social learning, personality, and his empirical work on self-control.

Mischel, Walter. *Personality and Assessment*. 1968. Reprint. Mahwah, N.J.: Lawrence Erlbaum, 1996. Classic exposition of Mischel's early work, containing a compelling critique of traditional trait and state approaches to personality. Discusses issues relevant to the assessment and modification of maladaptive social behavior. Should be available in many public and all university libraries.

_____. "Toward a Cognitive Social Learning Reconceptualization of Personality." *Psychological Review* 80, no. 4 (1973): 252-283. Written in response to the many reactions Mischel's 1968 book provoked in the research community. Clarifies several common misunderstandings of Mischel's position (for example, the situation-specificity issue) and gives a thorough presentation of his five personality variables. No specialized knowledge in psychology or personality theory is necessary for the reader to be able to follow the author's main arguments.

Mischel, Walter, Yuichi Shoda, and Monica L. Rodriguez. "Delay of Gratification in Children." *Science* 244, no. 4907 (1989): 933-938. Presents an excellent, brief summary of Mischel's work on self-control and delay of gratification spanning almost two decades. Discusses a number of stable individual differences in information-processing and strategic behaviors used by preschool children that were predictive of adult social adjustment.

Edelgard Wulfert

SEE ALSO: Cognitive behavior therapy; Cognitive psychology; Cognitive therapy; Learning; Personal constructs: George A. Kelly; Social learning: Albert Bandura.

Cognitive therapy

TYPE OF PSYCHOLOGY: Psychotherapy
FIELDS OF STUDY: Cognitive therapies

Cognitive therapy holds that emotional disorders are largely determined by cognition or thinking, that cognitive activity can take the form of language or images, and that emotional disorders can be treated by helping patients modify their cognitive distortions. Treatment programs based on this model have been highly successful with depression, panic disorder, generalized anxiety disorder, and other emotional problems.

KEY CONCEPTS
• arbitrary inference
• automatic thoughts
• cognitive specificity hypothesis
• cognitive triad
• schemata
• selective abstraction

INTRODUCTION

Cognitive therapy, originally developed by Aaron T. Beck (born in 1921), is based on the view that cognition (the process of acquiring knowledge and forming beliefs) is a primary determinant of mood and behavior. Beck developed his theory while treating depressed patients. He noticed that these patients tended to distort whatever happened to them in the direction of self-blame and catastrophes. Thus, an event interpreted by a normal person as irritating and inconvenient (for example, the malfunctioning of an automobile) would be interpreted by the depressed patient as another example of the utter hopelessness of life. Beck's central point is that depressives draw illogical conclusions and come to evaluate negatively themselves, their immediate world, and their future. They see only personal failings, present misfortunes, and overwhelming difficulties ahead. It is from these cognitions that all the other symptoms of depression derive.

It was from Beck's early work with depressed patients that cognitive therapy was developed. Shortly thereafter, the concepts and procedures were applied to other psychological problems, with notable success.

AUTOMATIC THOUGHTS AND SCHEMATA

Two concepts of particular relevance to cognitive therapy are the concepts of automatic thoughts and schemata (schemata is the plural of schema). Automatic thoughts are thoughts that appear to be going on all the time. These thoughts are quite brief—only the essential words in a sentence seem to occur, as in a telegraphic style. Further, they seem to be autonomous, in that the person made no effort to initiate them, and they seem plausible or reasonable to the person (although they may seem far-fetched to somebody else). Thus, as a depressed person is giving a talk to a group of business colleagues, he or she will have a variety of thoughts. There will be thoughts about the content of the material. There is also a second stream of thoughts occurring. In this second channel, the person may experience such thoughts as: "This is a waste of time," or "They think I'm dumb." These are automatic thoughts.

Beck has suggested that although automatic thoughts are occurring all the time, the person is likely to overlook these thoughts when asked what he or she is thinking. Thus, it is necessary to train the person to attend to these automatic thoughts. Beck pointed out that when people are depressed, these automatic thoughts are filled with negative thoughts of the self, the world, and the future. Further, these automatic thoughts are quite distorted, and finally, when these thoughts are carefully examined and modified to be more in keeping with reality, the depression subsides.

The concept of schemata, or core beliefs, becomes critical in understanding why some people are prone to having emotional difficulties and others are not. The schema appears to be the root from which the automatic thoughts derive. Beck suggests that people develop a propensity to think crookedly as a result of early life experiences. He theorizes that in early life, an individual forms concepts—realistic as well as unrealistic—from experiences. Of particular importance are individuals' attitudes toward themselves, their environment, and their future. These deeply held core beliefs about oneself are seen by Beck as critical in the causation of emo-

tional disorders. According to cognitive theory, the reason these early beliefs are so critical is that once they are formed, the person has a tendency to distort or view subsequent experiences to be consistent with these core beliefs. Thus, an individual who, as a child, was subjected to severe, unprovoked punishment from a disturbed parent may conclude "I am weak" or "I am inferior." Once this conclusion has been formulated, it would appear to be strongly reinforced over years and years of experiences at the hands of the parent. Thus, when this individual becomes an adult, he or she tends to interpret even normal frustrations as more proof of the original belief: "See, I really am inferior." Examples of these negative schemata or core beliefs are: "I am weak," "I am inferior," "I am unlovable," and "I cannot do anything right." People holding such core beliefs about themselves would differ strongly in their views of a frustrating experience from those people who hold a core belief such as "I am capable."

Another major contribution of cognitive therapy is Beck's cognitive specificity hypothesis. Specifically, Beck has suggested that each of the emotional disorders is characterized by its own patterns of thinking. In the case of depression, the thought content is concerned with ideas of personal deficiency, impossible environmental demands and obstacles, and nihilistic expectations. For example, a depressed patient might interpret a frustrating situation, such as a malfunctioning automobile, as evidence of his or her own inadequacy: "If I were really competent, I would have anticipated this problem and been able to avoid it." Additionally, the depressed patient might react to the malfunctioning automobile with: "This is too much, I cannot take it anymore." To the depressed patient, this would simply be another example of the utter hopelessness of life.

PATTERNS OF THOUGHT

While the cognitive content of depression emphasizes the negative view of the self, the world, and the future, anxiety disorders are characterized by fears of physical and psychological danger. The anxious patient's thoughts are filled with themes of danger. These people anticipate detrimental occurrences to themselves, their family, their property, their status, and other intangibles that they value.

In phobias, as in anxiety, there is the cognitive theme of danger; however, the "danger" is confined to definable situations. As long as phobic sufferers are able to avoid these situations, they do not feel threatened and may be relatively calm. The cognitive content of panic disorder is characterized by a catastrophic interpretation of bodily or mental experiences. Thus, patients with panic disorder are prone to regard any unexplained symptom or sensation as a sign of some impending catastrophe. As a result, their cognitive processing system focuses their attention on bodily or psychological experience. For example, one patient saw discomfort in the chest as evidence of an impending heart attack.

The cognitive feature of the paranoid reaction is the misinterpretation of experience in terms of mistreatment, abuse, or persecution. The cognitive theme of the conversion disorder (a disorder characterized by physical complaints such as paralysis or blindness, where no underlying physical basis can be determined) is the conviction that one has a physical disorder. As a result of this belief, the patient experiences sensory and/or motor abnormalities that are consistent with the patient's faulty conception of organic pathology.

CHANGING THE PATIENT'S MIND

The goal of cognitive therapy is to assist the patient to evaluate his or her thought processes carefully, to identify cognitive errors, and to substitute more adaptive, realistic cognitions. This goal is accomplished by therapists helping patients to see their thinking about themselves (or their situation) as similar to the activity of a scientist—that they are engaged in the activity of developing hypotheses (or theories) about their world. Like a scientist, the patient needs to "test" his or her theory carefully. Thus, patients who have concluded that they are "worthless" people would be encouraged to test their "theories" rigorously to determine if this is indeed accurate. Further, in the event that the theories are not accurate, patients would be encouraged to change their theories to make them more consistent with reality (what they find in their experience).

A slightly different intervention developed by Beck and his colleagues is to help the patient identify common cognitive distortions. Beck originally identified four cognitive distortions frequently found in emotional disorders: arbitrary inference, selective abstraction, overgeneralization, and magnification or minimization. These were later expanded to ten or more by Beck's colleagues and students.

Arbitrary inference is defined as the process of drawing a conclusion from a situation, event, or experience when there is no evidence to support the conclusion or when the conclusion is contrary to the evidence. For example, a depressed patient on a shopping trip had the thought, "The salesclerk thinks I am a nobody." The patient then felt sad. On being questioned by the psychologist, the patient realized that there was no factual basis for this thought. Selective abstraction refers to the process of focusing on a detail taken out of context, ignoring other, more salient features of the situation, and conceptualizing the whole experience on the basis of this element. For example, a patient was praised by friends about the patient's child-care activities. Through an oversight, however, the patient failed to have her child vaccinated during the appropriate week. Her immediate thought was, "I am a failure as a mother." This idea became paramount despite all the other evidence of her competence.

Overgeneralization refers to patients' patterns of drawing a general conclusion about their ability, their performance, or their worth on the basis of a single incident. For example, a student regards his poor performance on the first examination of the semester as final proof that he "will never make it in college." Magnification and minimization refer to gross errors in evaluation. For example, a person, believing that he has completely ruined his car (magnification) when he sees that there is a slight scratch on the rear fender, regards himself as "good for nothing." In contrast, minimization refers to minimizing one's achievements, protesting that these achievements do not mean anything. For example, a highly successful businesswoman who was depressed concluded that her many prior successes "were nothing . . . simply luck." Using the cognitive distortions, people are taught to examine their thoughts, to identify any distortions, and then to modify their thoughts in order to eliminate the distortions.

THERAPEUTIC TECHNIQUES

In terms of the therapeutic process, the focus is initially on the automatic thoughts of patients. Once patients are relatively adept at identifying and modifying their maladaptive automatic thoughts, the therapy begins to focus on the maladaptive underlying beliefs or schemata. As previously noted, these beliefs are fundamental beliefs that people hold about themselves. These beliefs are not as easy to identify as the automatic thoughts. Rather, they are identified in an inferential process. Common patterns are observed; for example, the person may seem to be operating by the rule: "If I am not the best _____, then I am a failure," or "If I am not loved by my spouse or mate, then I am worthless." As in the case of the earlier cognitive work with automatic thoughts, these beliefs are carefully evaluated for their adaptability or rationality. Maladaptive beliefs are then modified to more adaptive, realistic beliefs.

A variety of techniques have been developed by cognitive therapists for modifying maladaptive cognitions. One example of these techniques is self-monitoring. This involves the patient's keeping a careful hour-by-hour record of his or her activities, associated moods, or other pertinent phenomena. One useful variant is to have the patient record his or her mood on a simple zero-to-one-hundred scale, where zero represents the worst he or she has ever felt and one hundred represents the best. In addition, the patient can record the degree of mastery or pleasure associated with each recorded activity.

A number of hypotheses can be tested using self-monitoring, such as: "It does not do any good for me to get out of bed," "I am always miserable; it never lets up," and "My schedule is too full for me to accomplish what I must." By simply checking the self-monitoring log, one can easily determine if one's miserable mood ever ceases. A careful examination of the completed record is a far better basis for judging such hypotheses than is the patient's memory of recent events, because his or her recollections are almost always tainted by the depression.

As therapy progresses and patients begin to experience more elevated moods, the focus of treatment becomes more cognitive. Patients are instructed to observe and record automatic thoughts, perhaps at a specific time each evening, as well as recording when they become aware of increased dysphoria. Typically, the thoughts are negative self-referents ("I am worthless"; "I will never amount to anything"), and initially, the therapist points out their unreasonable and self-defeating nature. With practice, patients learn "distancing," that is, dealing with such thoughts objectively and evaluating them

rather than blindly accepting them. Homework assignments can facilitate distancing: The patient records an automatic thought, and next to it he or she writes down a thought that counters the automatic thought, as the therapist might have done. According to Beck, certain basic themes soon emerge, such as being abandoned, as well as stylistic patterns of thinking, such as overgeneralization. The themes reflect theaforementioned rules, and the ultimate goal of therapy is to assist the patient to modify them.

Finally, cognitive therapy has been applied to a variety of psychological disorders with striking success. For example, studies from seven independent centers have compared the efficacy of cognitive therapy to antidepressant medication, a treatment of established efficacy. Comparisons of cognitive therapy to drugs have found cognitive therapy to be superior or equal to antidepressant medication. Further, follow-up studies indicate that cognitive therapy has greater long-term effects than drug therapy. Of special significance is the evidence of greater sustained improvement over time with cognitive therapy.

Cognitive therapy has been successfully applied to panic disorder, resulting in practically complete reduction of panic attacks after twelve to sixteen weeks of treatment. Additionally, cognitive therapy has been successfully applied to generalized anxiety disorder, eating disorders, and inpatient depression.

DEPRESSION AND COGNITIVE THERAPY

Cognitive theory and cognitive therapy originated in Aaron T. Beck's observation and treatment of depressed patients. Originally trained in psychoanalysis, Beck observed that his patients experienced specific types of thoughts, of which they were only dimly aware, that they did not report during their free associations. Beck noticed that these thoughts were frequently followed by an unpleasant effect. Further, he noted that as the patients examined and modified their thoughts, their mood began to improve.

At the time of the emergence of the cognitive model, the treatment world was dominated primarily by the psychoanalytic model (with its heavy emphasis on the unconscious processes) and to a lesser extent by the behavioral model (with its emphasis on the behavioral processes, to the exclusion of thought). The psychoanalytic model was under attack, primarily because of a lack of careful empirical support. In contrast, behavior therapists were actively demonstrating the efficacy of their approaches in carefully designed studies. Beck and his students began to develop and test cognitive procedures systematically, and they have developed an impressive body of research support for the approach.

SOURCES FOR FURTHER STUDY

Beck, Aaron T. *Cognitive Therapy and the Emotional Disorders.* New York: International Universities Press, 1976. An easy-to-read book that presents a general overview of the cognitive model and illustrates the cognitive model of different psychological disorders.

Beck, Aaron T., and Gary Emery. *Anxiety Disorders and Phobias: A Cognitive Perspective.* Reprint. New York: Basic Books, 1990. Presents the cognitive theory and model of anxiety disorders, as well as the clinical techniques used with anxious patients.

Beck, Aaron T., A. J. Rush, B. F. Shaw, and Gary Emery. *Cognitive Therapy of Depression.* Reprint. New York: Guilford, 1987. Presents the cognitive theory of depression and actual techniques used with depressed patients. Both makes a theoretical contribution and serves as a clinical handbook on depression.

Burns, David D. *Feeling Good: The New Mood Therapy.* Rev. ed. New York: Avon, 1999. Readable introduction to the major concepts and techniques of cognitive therapy; written by one of Beck's students.

Emery, Gary, Steven D. Hollom, and Richard C. Bedrosian, eds. *New Directions in Cognitive Therapy: A Casebook.* New York: Guilford, 1981. Contains cases presented by major cognitive therapists. Focuses on the application of cognitive therapy to a wide range of presenting problems (such as loneliness and agoraphobia), as well as diverse populations (such as adolescents, the elderly, and the psychologically naïve).

Donald G. Beal

SEE ALSO: Cognitive behavior therapy; Cognitive social learning: Walter Mischel; Personal constructs: George A. Kelly; Rational-emotive therapy; Reality therapy; Transactional analysis.

College entrance examinations

TYPE OF PSYCHOLOGY: Intelligence and intelligence testing

FIELDS OF STUDY: Ability tests; intelligence assessment; methodological issues

College entrance examinations are one of several measures used by American colleges and universities to select candidates for admission. The examinations purport to measure aptitude for college work, and they are widely used. College entrance examinations have been strongly criticized, however, and these criticisms raise crucial methodological and ethical issues regarding the use of standardized tests for admission selection.

KEY CONCEPTS

- aptitude
- bogie score
- cognates
- homographs
- informed consent
- percentile
- raw score
- validity

INTRODUCTION

American colleges and universities consider a variety of factors when selecting students for admission. These factors may include, but are not necessarily limited to, high school grades, class rank, difficulty of courses taken, personal interviews, letters of reference, and samples of students' written works. In addition, most colleges and universities require students to submit test scores from one or more of several nationally administered standardized tests. Known collectively as college entrance examinations, the most commonly used tests in the United States are the American College Test (ACT) and the Scholastic Aptitude Test (SAT). Some students also may take Achievement Tests (ATs), the Preliminary Scholastic Aptitude Test/National Merit Scholarship Qualifying Test (PSAT/NMSQT), and Advanced Placement examinations (APs). Advanced Placement examinations are not used in admission decisions but are given to students who wish to receive college credit for classes taken in high school.

ACT

The ACT (originally the American College Test) is created and administered by the American College Testing Assessment Program (ACTAP). According to the ACTAP, the ACT is not content-specific. That is, students are not asked to recall specific information learned in high school. Rather, the ACT asks students to demonstrate their reasoning ability in four fields: English, mathematics, reading, and scientific reasoning. In each of these fields, students are required to think, reason, solve problems, and make inferences.

Each section of the ACT is timed. The complete test contains 215 multiple-choice questions, and students are given two hours and fifty-five minutes to complete these items. Students receive scores on a scale of 1 (low) to 36 (high) for each of the four skill areas, and a composite score. In addition, students receive scores on a scale of 1 (low) to 18 (high) for each of the seven subsections of the test. Student scores are also presented as percentiles.

The English test of the ACT asks students to read five prose passages and answer seventy-five questions based on the readings. Students are given forty-five minutes to complete the English test. The English test is designed to measure grammar, punctuation, sentence structure, style, organization, and writing strategy. Performance is reported as a total score and as two subscores: usage/mechanics and rhetorical skills. The mathematics test consists of sixty questions and is designed to measure skills in basic mathematics, algebra, geometry, and trigonometry. Students are allowed sixty minutes to complete the mathematics test. Performance is reported as a total score and as three subscores: prealgebra/elementary algebra; intermediate algebra/coordinate geometry; plane geometry/trigonometry.

The reading test requires students to read a passage and answer ten questions for each of four fields of study within a thirty-five-minute period. The four fields of study are prose fiction, humanities, social science, and natural science. Besides a total score, student performance is presented as two subscores: art/literature and social studies/sciences. Students are allowed thirty-five minutes to complete the forty-question scientific reasoning test. Questions are drawn from all natural science disciplines (biology, chemistry, physics, earth science, astronomy, and meteorology). Students are presented materials in one of three formats (data representation, research summaries, and conflicting viewpoints) and are asked to evaluate conclusions or make predictions based on the material presented.

SAT AND PSAT

The Scholastic Aptitude Test, created and developed by the Educational Testing Service (ETS), is administered in cooperation with the College Entrance Examination Board (CEEB), commonly known as the College Board. Like the ACT, the SAT is designed to measure skills necessary for college-level work. The SAT tests two basic skill areas, verbal ability and mathematical reasoning, using a multiple-choice format.

In June, 2002, the College Board announced a major restructuring of the SAT to be administered beginning in 2005. The test had been revised in 1994 to eliminate antonyms from the verbal exam and to allow some open-ended answers (rather than multiple choice) and the use of calculators in the math exam. This version contained two verbal sections, both of which contained multiple-choice questions involving analogies, sentence completion, and reading comprehension. The 2005 revision will condense these two parts into one exam called the SAT Critical Reading Exam, which would eliminate the analogies section and add short reading sections to the original long reading sections. A new SAT section called the SAT Writing Exam will be added, containing multiple choice questions on grammar and, for the first time, a written essay. The SAT Math Exam, which originally contained questions involving problem solving and quantitative comparisons requiring only a mastery of Geometry and Algebra I, will be expanded to cover material from Algebra II as well, while eliminating the quantitative comparisons questions. Each of these skill areas (verbal ability and mathematical reasoning) is scored on a scale of 200 (low) to 800 (high). Composite and percentile scores are provided.

The SAT II: Subject Tests exam was instituted to replace Achievement Tests and the test of standard written English. Content areas include American history, European history, French, German, Hebrew, Latin, Spanish, Japanese, Chinese, biology, chemistry, physics, English composition, English literature, higher-level mathematics, and English and math placement tests. On the SAT II, the test of standard written English is combined with the English composition test (an Achievement Test). The new writing test of the SAT II contains a series of multiple-choice questions testing grammar and usage, as well as an essay section.

In addition to taking the ACT and SAT, some students may take the PSAT/NMSQT. Administered primarily during the junior year in high school, this test contains sections testing verbal skills and mathematical reasoning in a multiple-choice format. Students are allowed fifty minutes per section to complete the PSAT/NMSQT. Test scores are used to award National Merit Scholarships, National Achievement Scholarships, and Achievement Scholarships.

As noted, college entrance examination scores are only one factor used by American colleges and universities in selecting potential students. While some colleges and universities do not require ACT or SAT scores, relying on other measures for determining a student's eligibility for admission, most institutions do require submission of college entrance examination scores as part of the admissions process. In addition, almost three hundred American colleges and universities have minimum score requirements for admission to their institutions.

GENDER, ETHNIC, AND ECONOMIC BIAS

Despite their importance and wide use, college entrance examinations are not without their flaws or their critics. The two main organizations that create college entrance examinations, Educational Testing Service and the American College Testing Assessment Program (renamed simply ACT in 1996), work to maintain and improve the validity and reliability of the tests and to avoid bias. Nevertheless, the tests have been subjected to some serious criticisms, and it is because of the tests' very importance that such criticism must be considered. Criticisms focus on six basic issues of testing: the existence of bias and flawed questions, testing procedures, and accusations of lack of due process, violation of privacy, and misuse of test results.

Critics have argued that standardized college entrance examinations are biased against women, the poor, minorities, students from rural areas, and students for whom English is not their first or primary language. Bias charges are serious because they call into question the validity of the tests and, if true, mean that some students may be unfairly denied admission to the college of their choice.

Other things being equal, high test scorers should perform better in college than low test scorers. Na-

tional SAT test score averages have consistently showed that men perform better on the test than women. The gender gap in test scores varies by year; in 2001, women scored an average of 35 points lower than men on the math exam and 3 points lower on the verbal. A similar pattern exists regarding PSAT/NMSQT. ACT scores show a far smaller gender gap; in 2001, women's composite scores averaged only 0.2 points lower than men's scores. If standardized college entrance examinations accurately predict future academic success, men should have higher average grades in college than women. Yet, at least during the first year, the reverse is true: Women have higher average grades during their freshman year than men.

Educational Testing Service states that women's scores are lower because greater numbers of women have been taking the test since 1970 than took it in previous decades. Consequently, the test pool for women is increasingly less selective and includes a greater number of low scorers, reducing the overall average. Ruth Ekstrom, Marilane Lockheed, and Thomas Donlon, however, have found that the structure of test questions influences gender performance. Women are less likely to answer a test item correctly if the question contains only, or refers primarily to, male characters. A survey of the reading comprehension passages contained in SAT examinations showed that 93 percent of the characters to which the passages referred were male. Gender differences in test performance may be, in part, a consequence of test structure. In addition, evidence indicates that college entrance examinations place more emphasis on subject areas in which men have traditionally outperformed women (science and mathematics). Accordingly, test content selection may account for some of the gender differences in test scores.

Phyllis Rosser notes that compared to men, women answer fewer questions on the SAT, are less likely to guess at questions, and answer a higher percentage of questions correctly. The SAT awards one raw point score for every correct answer but deducts only one-quarter point for an incorrect answer. On average, it is better to make educated guesses on the SAT than it is not to answer a question. Consequently, women's lower test scores may be the result of gender differences regarding test-taking strategies. The ACT does not penalize students for guessing. Scores are determined on the basis of correct answers. Other factors, not yet clearly identified, must account for gender differences regarding test scores on the ACT.

There is strong evidence that test performance on college entrance examinations is influenced by socioeconomic status. In the case of the SAT, students from high-income families have test-score averages over two hundred points higher than the average scores of students from families living at or below the poverty level. Proportionally similar disparities are found in ACT scores. These patterns may stem from differences in educational opportunities rather than differences in aptitude. Additionally, less affluent students may be unable to afford test preparation courses, which can significantly increase scores on college entrance examinations.

Minority students score lower on college entrance examinations than whites, although differences vary by group and over time. The difference in average scores between African American and white students is comparable to the difference between the average scores of poverty-level and upper-income students; the differences between average scores of Asian American and white students is negligible. There is also evidence that college entrance examinations may contain bias against students from rural areas and students for whom English is not their first or primary language. James Loewen found that incoming University of Vermont students from rural areas had SAT scores that averaged 100 points lower than those of students from urban areas; however, the actual academic performance of the two groups was similar. Alicia Schmitt found that Hispanic students who took the SAT were much more likely to answer incorrectly questions which contain cognates and/or homographs. Consequently, differences in test scores between Hispanics and whites may be partially the result of language differences, not differences in aptitude for college work.

FACTUAL ACCURACY AND VALIDITY

In addition to bias, critics have charged that college entrance examinations contain flawed questions (questions that have more than one meaning or more than one answer), which may unfairly penalize test takers. For example, in 1981, Daniel Lowen successfully challenged an answer to a PSAT/NMSQT question. That same year, Michael Galligan successfully challenged an answer to an SAT question and

forced the ETS to raise the test scores of thousands of students. More than forty additional students received New York State Regents Scholarships because of this change.

Critics have also charged the ETS with using unethical testing procedures, lack of due process protection, and invasion of privacy. John Weiss, Barbara Beckwith, and Bob Schaeffer claim the experimental questions on the SAT are fundamentally unfair because they violate the principle of informed consent and are flawed. In addition, no due process protection exists for students who are accused of cheating on the examination. Students may appeal to the ETS, but the ETS has sole discretion in determining guilt or innocence in cases of suspected cheating. Finally, Weiss et al. argue that the confidentiality of personal information on test takers collected by the ETS is not protected under the current system, and say that the ETS should be required to obtain consent before the release of any such data.

THE RISE OF STANDARDIZED TESTING

Until the creation of standardized college entrance examinations, many American colleges and universities used their own tests to assess the merits of potential students. These tests varied in quality. Scoring was frequently subjective, and because each institution used a different test, test scores from one school could not be used to apply for admission to another. Recognizing the need for uniformity in admission testing, the "committee of ten," a group of prominent American educators, created the College Entrance Examination Board in 1900. The board's function was to establish a centralized organizational structure for admission evaluation and to bring some degree of uniformity and objectivity to the selection process. The board quickly developed the College Board Examination, and it was first administered in 1901.

In the 1920's, as colleges and universities became more selective in their admission standards, use of the College Board Examination increased. Realizing the need for further refinement, the College Board appointed Carl Brigham chair of a committee to review and evaluate the board's test instruments and testing procedures. A former student of Robert Yerkes, a pioneer in the development of American intelligence testing, Brigham had long been interested in the standardization and mass application of testing procedures. In his *A Study of American Intelligence* (1923), for example, Brigham advocated the application of psychometrics to national immigration policy. Under Brigham's direction, a new college entrance examination was developed. Completed in 1926, the new test was called the Scholastic Aptitude Test.

While on the faculty of Princeton University, Brigham helped develop a formula through which SAT scores and high school grades could be used to produce a "bogie grade"—an estimate of the grade average of a potential applicant after one year at Princeton. The formula was gradually adopted by other institutions and became an important component in the admission decision process. Variations of this formula are still widely used today. With the success of the SAT, Brigham established a psychometric laboratory at Princeton. Development of the Achievement Tests was proposed in 1936. Under a plan presented by the president of Harvard, the College Board and other testing organizations were consolidated into the Educational Testing Service in 1947. Today, Educational Testing Service and its chief competitor, the American College Testing Assessment Program, dominate the creation and production of standardized college entrance examinations.

Standardized testing has become an established feature of American life. Millions of standardized tests are administered each year. Despite their flaws, college entrance examinations provide a systematic and relatively objective means to select candidates for admission. For schools that receive large numbers of applications for admission each year, test scores provide a relatively inexpensive and time-effective way to screen candidates. Realizing the flaws in standardized testing and the danger of overreliance on test scores, some institutions have developed alternatives to the traditional selection process. Some have made submission of test scores optional. Other schools allow students to select, from a series of options, which test scores they will submit. Evidence indicates that these alternatives to the traditional admission selection process work well and deserve consideration for adoption by other institutions.

SOURCES FOR FURTHER STUDY

Hoffmann, Banesh. *The Tyranny of Testing.* 1962. Reprint. Westport, Conn.: Greenwood, 1978. Dated but still relevant critique of standardized tests and their use in admission selection. Examines the problem of defective or ambiguous test questions and looks at issues regarding the validity and reliability of standardized tests.

Leman, Nicholas. *The Big Test: The Secret History of the American Meritocracy.* New York: Farrar, Straus, and Giroux, 2000. The first third of this book on the fight against anti-affirmative action measures in California deals with the history of standardized college admissions tests.

Nairn, Allan. *The Reign of ETS: The Corporation That Makes Up Minds.* Washington, D.C.: Ralph Nader Report on the Educational Testing Service, 1980. Presents an excellent discussion of the history of the Educational Testing Service and the development of standardized tests in America. Also provides a detailed critique of the Scholastic Aptitude Test and its use.

Owen, David, and Marilyn Doerr. *None of the Above: The Truth Behind the SATs.* Rev. ed. Lanham, Md.: Rowman & Littlefield, 1999. An exposé of the Educational Testing Service that challenges the validity of the SAT as a measurement of academic achievement.

Rosser, Phyllis. *Sex Bias in College Admissions Tests: Why Women Lose Out.* 3d ed. Cambridge, Mass.: The Center, 1989. Charges that standardized college entrance examinations are biased against women. Discusses the impact of testing bias on admission selection and scholarship allocation.

Weiss, John G., Barbara Beckwith, and Bob Schaeffer. *Standing Up to the SAT.* New York: Arco, 1989. Describes the structure of the Scholastic Aptitude Test and presents relevant criticisms of the test and its testing procedures. Also discusses alternatives to standardized college entrance examinations.

Charles V. Smedley

SEE ALSO: Ability tests; Cognitive ability: Gender differences; Feminist psychotherapy; Intelligence quotient (IQ); Intelligence tests; Race and intelligence; Sexism; Testing: Historical perspectives.

Community psychology

TYPE OF PSYCHOLOGY: Social psychology
FIELDS OF STUDY: Attitudes and behavior; social perception and cognition

Community psychology is dedicated to the development of a knowledge base that can be used to implement and evaluate culturally congruent human-services programs. Community psychology is associated with the community mental health movement, and community psychologists have a particular interest in research and services that focus on prevention.

KEY CONCEPTS
- action-oriented research
- culturally congruent services
- ecology
- epidemiology
- incidence
- person-environment fit
- prevalence
- primary prevention
- secondary prevention
- tertiary prevention

INTRODUCTION

Community psychology is founded on the following precepts: an emphasis on the competence of persons and communities; an appreciation of personal and cultural diversity; an orientation that promotes prevention; a preference for organizational, community- and/or systems-level intervention; and a belief in the need for an ecologically valid database with which to determine the appropriateness and value of human-service interventions.

Community psychology emphasizes social, environmental, and cultural factors as significant elements influencing the development and expression of behaviors commonly identified as signs of maladjustment. Community psychology demands a respect for human diversity—people have a right to be different. Requiring that people fit into a particular mold or conform to a particular standard increases the probability that some will be considered failures or maladjusted individuals. Instead of focusing on how to motivate "deviant" people to adjust, the community psychologist attempts to increase behavioral options, expand cultural and environmental choices, redistribute resources, and foster the acceptance of variability.

From a community-psychology perspective, it is not the weakness of the individual that causes psychopathology but a lack of person-environment fit. The concept of person-environment fit is founded in ecology. Ecology posits that each organism is in constant interaction with all aspects of its environment, including all things animate and inanimate. From the ecological perspective, it is the unique interaction of species with the environmental milieu that dictates survival. In relation to people, ecology requires an appreciation not only for the ambient environment but also for social, psychological, personal, and cultural factors that interact and influence an individual's adjustment and survival.

Community psychologists use their knowledge of ecological principles to create culturally congruent interventions that maximize service effectiveness. To develop services that are culturally congruent requires an appreciation for the history, aspirations, belief systems, and environmental circumstances of the community or group with which one is to work. Knowing that interactions and the fit between persons and environments are of primary importance, community psychologists work to promote changes at a systems level rather than only working to change the individual. Community psychologists know, however, that even systems-level changes will be of little value—and will perhaps even lead to harm—if they are not personally and culturally relevant to the persons they are designed to help.

There is considerable diversity in the training and orientation of community psychologists. Still, as a general rule, community psychologists can be expected to have knowledge and expertise in the following areas: program development, resource utilization, community organization, consultation, community mental health programming, preventive interventions, program evaluation, grant writing, needs assessment, advocacy, crisis intervention, direct service delivery, manpower training, systems analysis, and the political ramifications of social change. Community psychologists use their knowledge of these areas as they work within the framework of one of the following models: clinical/community, community/clinical, community activist, academic/research, prevention, social ecology, evaluation/policy analysis, or consultation.

COMMUNITY MODELS

Psychologists trained in the clinical/community model have expertise in individual assessment and psychotherapy. They are likely to work within community mental health centers or other human-services programs as direct service providers. They differ from traditionally trained clinical psychologists in having an orientation that is directed toward crisis intervention, public health, and prevention.

The community/clinical model leads to a primary emphasis of working with community groups to enable the development, implementation, and administration of human-services initiatives. This model is very similar to the community-activist model; persons with a community/clinical orientation, however, are more likely to work within the system than outside it.

Persons following the community-activist model draw on their training in psychology to enable them to confront social injustice and misallocation of resources. These individuals are versed in grass-roots community organization, the realities of social confrontation, and advocacy.

The academic/research model of community psychology is founded on the principles of action-oriented research. Here the researcher is directed to work on real-world problems using ecologically valid methods. Furthermore, action-oriented research requires that recommendations that follow from the researcher's findings be implemented.

Psychologists who advocate the prevention model use epidemiological data—information concerning the rates and distribution of disorders—to enable the development of programs designed to prevent mental health problems. Primary prevention programs—undertakings that attempt to keep problems from forming—are the preferred initiatives.

Persons trained in the social-ecology model participate in the development of research and interventions based on an ecological perspective. Here an appreciation of the complexities and the myriad interactions of communities and social organizations is paramount.

The evaluation/policy-analysis model requires that adherents be versed in program evaluation methods—techniques related to the assessment of the quality, efficiency, and effectiveness of service initiatives. This model dictates that information obtained from program evaluation be fed back into the system in the form of policy recommendations.

The consultation model provides a framework for the dissemination of knowledge. To be an effective consultant, the community psychologist must be cognizant of various consultation methods. Furthermore, she or he must have specialized expertise founded in one of the preceding models.

Regardless of the model followed, community psychology demands a commitment to the community, group, or individual served. The job of the community psychologist is to foster competence and independence. The ideal client, whether the client is an individual or a community, is the client who no longer needs the psychologist.

PREVENTION PROGRAMS

Community psychology has played a major role in sensitizing human-services professionals to the need for services oriented toward prevention. Many of the assumptions and principles of prevention are taken from the field of public health medicine. Public health officials know that disease cannot be eradicated by treatment alone. Furthermore, the significant gains in life expectancy that have occurred over the last one hundred years are not primarily the result of wonder drugs, transplants, or other marvels of modern medicine. Instead, improved sanitation, immunizations, and access to an adequate food supply have been the key factors in conquering diseases and increasing the human life span.

In order to design and implement effective prevention-oriented programs, one must have an understanding of epidemiology, incidence, and prevalence. Epidemiology is the study of the rates and distributions of disorders as these data pertain to causes and prevention. Incidence is the number of new cases of a disorder that occur in a given population in a specific period. Prevalence is either the total number of cases of a disorder in a given population at a specific point in time or the average number of cases during a specific period. By combining information concerning epidemiology, incidence, and prevalence, it is possible to arrive at insights into the causes of a disorder, likely methods of transmission, prognosis, and intervention methods that may prove fruitful.

Community psychologists identify prevention activities as falling into one of three classifications: primary prevention, secondary prevention, and tertiary prevention. Although some have argued that only primary prevention activities should be recognized as prevention, all three classifications have a place.

In tertiary prevention, the underlying disorder is not directly treated or eliminated; instead, tertiary prevention focuses on mitigating the consequences of a disorder. Tertiary prevention has no effect on incidence rates and little or no effect on prevalence rates. Reducing the stigma associated with the label "mental illness," increasing the self-help skills of persons who have mental retardation, promoting the independence of persons with chronic mental disorders, and developing programs to provide cognitive retraining for persons who have suffered head injuries are examples of tertiary-prevention activities.

An example of a tertiary-prevention program is the community lodge program developed by George Fairweather, which has come to be known as the Fairweather Lodge Program. The program was begun as an attempt to solve a problem that arose in an experiment in giving psychiatric patients the power to direct their treatment by means of self-governing groups. Although it was quite effective, the program suffered because many of its gains did not carry over after patients were discharged. The community lodge program was developed to deal with this problem. During their hospital stays, patients were encouraged to form small support groups. Prior to discharge, members of these support groups would be introduced to the lodge concept. The lodge concept called for former patients to live together, pool their resources, and work as a team in a lodge-owned enterprise. This program, which began in the early 1960's, has been replicated on numerous occasions. Data show that patients discharged to a community lodge are more likely to maintain gainful employment and are less likely to be readmitted to the hospital than are patients discharged to a traditional community mental health program.

Secondary prevention has its basis in the belief that prevalence rates can be reduced if disorders are identified and treated as early as possible. Diversion programs for youths who manifest predelinquent behavior, acute care for persons with mental disorders, employee assistance programs, and psychological screenings for schoolchildren are examples of secondary prevention.

An example of a secondary-prevention program is the Primary Mental Health Project (PMHP) developed by Emory Cowen in the late 1950's. The PMHP was founded on the basis of the idea that maladjustment in early school grades is associated with the development of behavioral and emotional problems later in life. The program was designed to provide early detection so that interventions could be introduced before significant dysfunction had an opportunity to develop. Furthermore, consultation and competency building—rather than traditional therapeutic techniques—were viewed as the most effective interventions. Although the PMHP has not had a demonstrated effect in reducing later psychiatric disorders, the program has been shown to have other beneficial effects.

Primary prevention is aimed at the eradication of the causes of disorders and/or the development of interventions that can be initiated before pathology develops. Primary prevention results in a lowering of both incidence and prevalence rates. Psychological services for disaster victims, genetic screening, parenting classes, reducing exposure to toxins, immunization for rubella, and maternal nutrition programs are examples of primary-prevention activities. Another example of primary prevention is community education programs designed to teach safe sex and/or to reduce the sharing of contaminated needles. To the extent that these programs reduce the spread of acquired immunodeficiency syndrome (AIDS), they will also decrease the incidence of AIDS dementia complex.

Community psychologists are involved in many service activities besides prevention-oriented enterprises. These initiatives include the training and utilization of paraprofessionals, the promotion of self-help groups and natural helping networks, advocacy, community consultation, program evaluation, the planning and implementation of new human-services programs, crisis intervention, and mental health education.

AN EMERGING FIELD

Community psychology had its origins in the 1960's, a time of radical ideas, antiestablishment attitudes, and a belief in the perfectibility of humankind. In 1965 in Swampscott, Massachusetts, a meeting was called to ascertain how psychology could most effectively contribute to the emerging community mental health movement.

A transformation in treatment focus was taking place at the time of the Swampscott meeting. This change had been provided with a blueprint for its development in a report by the Joint Commission on Mental Illness and Health written in 1961. The Joint Commission report, *Action for Mental Health*, called for a shift from treating psychiatric patients in large state mental hospitals to the provision of care through outpatient community mental health clinics and smaller inpatient units located in general hospitals. Additionally, the report included the following recommendations: increasing support for research, developing "aftercare," providing partial hospitalization and rehabilitation services, and expanding mental health education to ensure that the public became more aware of mental disorders and to reduce the stigmatization associated with mental illness.

On February 5, 1963, President John F. Kennedy became the first president of the United States to address Congress regarding the needs of the mentally ill and the mentally retarded. President Kennedy called for a "bold new approach" that would include funding for prevention, expanding the knowledge base regarding causes of disorders and treatment alternatives, and creating a new type of treatment facility that, independent of the ability to pay, would provide high-quality comprehensive care in the local community—the creation of community mental health centers.

In October of 1963, President Kennedy signed into law the Community Mental Health Centers Act. The law required that programs funded through the act provide five essential services: inpatient care, outpatient treatment, emergency services, partial hospitalization, and consultation and education.

Although the initial purpose for convening the Swampscott meeting had been to determine how psychology could contribute to the staffing needs of community mental health centers, the conferees took a broader perspective and chose to view the community mental health movement as addressing a limited aspect of a larger set of social problems. As a consequence, the meeting failed to address adequately the training needs of psychologists who would be working in the new community mental health centers; intead, the most significant result of the meeting was the birth of community psychology.

In the ensuing years, community psychology and community psychology training programs have varied in the degree to which they involve the educational needs of psychologists employed by community mental health centers. Still, there is no doubt that the research and service initiatives that community psychologists have developed in regard to crisis intervention, consultation, prevention, empower- ment, the use of paraprofessionals, program planning, resource development, and program evaluation serve as valuable models and contribute to the successful operation of community mental health programs and a variety of other human-services activities.

SOURCES FOR FURTHER STUDY

Caplan, Gerald. *Principles of Preventive Psychiatry.* New York: Basic Books, 1964. Caplan was a key figure in directing attention to the need to be informed concerning biological, psychological, and sociocultural factors as they influence psychopathology. Furthermore, Caplan's call for an emphasis on primary prevention antedated the origin of community psychology.

Heller, Kenneth, et al. *Psychology and Community Change: Challenges of the Future.* 2d ed. Homewood, Ill.: Dorsey Press, 1984. Describes how knowledge of groups, organizations, and communities can be applied in addressing social problems. Ecological approaches and prevention-oriented interventions are the primary substance of the text.

Levine, Murray, and David V. Perkins. *Principles of Community Psychology: Perspectives and Applications.* 2d ed. New York: Oxford University Press, 1996. The authors provide an extended discussion of social problems, the conceptual foundations of community psychology, and the application of community-psychology principles to promote effective change. Substantial portions of the text are devoted to labeling theory and the effects of crises.

Mann, Philip A. *Community Psychology: Concepts and Applications.* New York: Free Press, 1978. The origins of community psychology and the relevance of the concept of community are described. Additionally, the assumptions and implications of four models are detailed: the mental health model, organizational model, social-action model, and ecological model.

Rappaport, Julian. *Community Psychology: Values, Research, and Action.* New York: Holt, Rinehart and Winston, 1977. Rappaport provides a comprehensive survey of the paradigms, principles, and practice of community psychology. The book focuses attention on the social roots of pathology and the need for systems-level interventions that are culturally congruent.

Rappaport, Julian, and Edward Seidman, eds. *Handbook of Community Psychology*. New York: Plenum, 2000. A massive reference work (nearly one thousand pages) covering every topic relevant to the theory and practice of community psychology.

Scileppi, John A., Robin Diller Torres, and Elizabeth Lee Tead. *Community Psychology: A Common Sense Approach to Mental Health*. Upper Saddle River, N.J.: Prentice Hall, 1999. An introductory textbook, covering classic and contemporary theories in the field; the ecological model; the concept of prevention; crisis and coping; social support and self-help; consultation; program evaluation; the politics of intervention and empowerment; strategies for change; the changing community in the information age; and the future of community psychology.

Bruce E. Bailey

SEE ALSO: Environmental psychology; Human resource training and development; Juvenile delinquency; Mental health practitioners; Psychology: Fields of specialization; Testing: Historical perspectives.

Complex experimental designs

TYPE OF PSYCHOLOGY: Psychological methodologies
FIELDS OF STUDY: Experimental methodologies

Complex experimental designs in psychology research investigate the effects of two or more variables on an individual's behavior; when the effects of these variables combine to predict the behavior, rather than acting independently, this is called an interaction. Knowledge of interactions contributes to an ability to understand research observations.

KEY CONCEPTS
- analysis of variance
- experimental variable
- main effect
- statistical significance
- subject variable

INTRODUCTION

Psychology seeks to predict and understand the behavior of individuals, whether humans or other animals. To produce general rules about individual behavior, its research methods usually involve making large numbers of observations of behavior of different individuals or of the same individual at different times.

At the simple level of design, psychological research measures a single behavior repeatedly and summarizes these observations—for example, describing the mean amount of practice needed to learn a task, the percentage of people who express a particular attitude, or the mean reaction time to answer a question. Such research can show what typically happens, but it does not predict when this behavior will occur, suggest how it can be altered, or explain what causes it.

At an intermediate level of design, research in psychology is concerned with how one measured characteristic or experience of an individual human or animal relates to some behavior of that same individual which the researcher is trying to predict or understand. In a post facto intermediate research design, the predictor variable is some quality or characteristic of the individual which already exists, called a subject variable. In an experimental intermediate research design, the predictor variable is some recent experience or current stimulus, called a manipulated variable, which the psychologist performing the research has selected and administered.

Behavior is called a variable because it can differ (or vary) among individuals or in the same individual at different times. Subject variables, such as gender, self-consciousness, age, and birth order, also differ among individuals and, in some cases, within the same individual over time. Manipulated variables include psychoactive drugs, persuasive arguments, sensory isolation, and psychotherapy. They vary in the sense that the researcher exposes different individuals, or the same individual at different times, to different levels or amounts of that treatment.

FACTORIAL RESEARCH DESIGNS

Complex (or factorial) research designs investigate how two or more predictor variables are related to the individual's behavior. An example would be studying how a number of subject variables, such as age, ethnicity, religion, gender, and intelligence test scores, all combine to predict political attitudes. In this case, one has a post facto complex research design. If the predictor variables are all manipulated by the experimenter—the amount of an administered drug varied, differing anxiety-inducing instructions given, and tasks of contrasting difficulties presented—then this is an experimental complex research design. The most common approach combines the measurement of subject variables with the manipulation of variables for the purpose of learning whether the effects of the manipulation have the same effects on all kinds of individuals. This is the mixed complex research design. An example of the latter design would be the measurement of gender and age followed by the manipulation of the kind of message used to persuade individuals about the importance of recycling waste; later, the individuals' recycling behavior would be observed.

In this last example, the three factors being measured to see if they are related to recycling behavior may yield between zero and seven statistically significant results from an analysis of variance of the data. An analysis of variance is defined as a statistical technique, commonly abbreviated as ANOVA, used in inferential statistics to determine which behaviors that are measured are related to differences in other variables. Of the significant results, three may be main effects, meaning that the differences in observed behavior occur for any of the variables when averaged across all levels of the other variables. Any effects which are not main effects are interactions, meaning that the effect on behavior of one or more variables may be affected by a change in another variable.

In other words, if one message was found to be more effective than the other for boys but not for girls, an interaction would be said to exist. The effect of the message on recycling behavior would not be the same for all people, but rather would depend on the gender of the listener. When such an interaction occurs, it can be said that the effect of one variable on the measured behavior depends on the level of the other variable.

In this three-factor example, there are four possible interactions. One of them is the three-way interaction, since there is a possibility that the behavior for each combination of the factors cannot be predicted merely by adding the independent main effects for each factor. This means that the three factors contribute to behavior in some manner such that they interact, so that they are not independent of one another. An example would be if one of the messages is less appealing to older girls than it is to younger girls, or to boys of any age. The

other three possible interactions in this experiment are all possible pairings of the variables: gender and age, gender and message, and age and message.

VARYING RESEARCH FACTORS

Imagine the example given above concerning recycling first as a simple research design. In this case, measurement (in some carefully defined and described manner) of behavior alone might find that 15 percent of all people practice recycling. To learn more about the causes of recycling, one might shift to an experimental intermediate research design. By measuring the effects of varying the message about recycling, one might find the results shown in the left panel of the accompanying figure. This shows that message B produced more recycling (24 percent) than did message A (17 percent).

One should be wary of such a conclusion, however, whether it is found in published research or in one's own investigations. The mixed complex research design can make further measurements on subject variables to see whether these findings are the same for all individuals, or whether there is some personal characteristic which predicts the effect of the manipulated variable.

The right panel of the figure shows what might be found if gender were measured as well. Because equal numbers of boys and girls were assigned to each group, the mean recycling for each message remains the same (24 percent for message B, and 17 percent for message A), but it can be seen that the effect of each message was very different depending on the gender of the individual. Here an interaction, which was not evident in the simple or intermediate research designs, can be seen. It is an important interaction because it shows that the effect of the messages on recycling behavior is different depending on whether the listener is a boy or a girl.

Now imagine that another subject variable, age, was also measured. The children were grouped into two categories, ages six to ten and ages eleven to fourteen. Thus, there were four groups, differentiated by gender and age: younger girls, older girls, younger boys, and older boys. Keeping the numbers in each group equal, it might be found that there are no effects of age on which message influences recycling behavior except in the girls who heard message B. In this group, young girls showed 23 percent recycling, and older girls 13 percent. Thus,

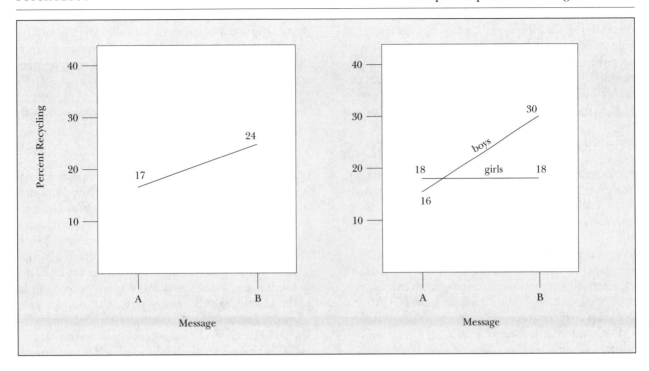

there would be a three-way interaction, in which both gender and age were dependent on each other to determine the effect of the message on behavior.

PRACTICAL AND THEORETICAL APPLICATIONS

Psychological researchers want to know about such interaction effects for both practical and theoretical purposes. An example of a practical application might be environmentalists reading this research to learn how best to improve recycling by children. Whether through television commercials broadcast during programs with a known audience, or through messages in the schools, environmentalists can tailor the message which will be the most effective for a given audience.

Basic researchers are trying to develop theories to understand more general behavior, such as attitude change or motivational processes. These theories may become sophisticated enough to make predictions for practical purposes such as the recycling program mentioned here, changing people's behavior in therapy. In the present example, the interactions observed may cause the researcher to look at the content of message B to attempt to understand why it was more effective for all boys and for younger girls but was rejected by older girls. If the researcher noted that the message used a popular car-

toon action figure as a role model for recycling, then possibly it is only boys and younger girls who identify with that action figure.

From further reading in the field of developmental psychology, the researcher may hypothesize that older girls would identify more with romantic fictional characters, and so design a recycling message which would have more appeal to them. The test of this new message would be an example of how complex research designs work to build cumulatively on previous research to produce more precise practical applications and also to improve theories about the sources of individual behavior.

ANALYZING COMPLEX BEHAVIOR

Complex experimental designs were developed to answer detailed questions about individual behavior. Simple and intermediate research designs provide some information, but the experience of psychological researchers is that behavior is not simple. Behavior has multiple causes, which do not always act independently of one another. Thus there is the necessity for complex research designs, advanced statistical techniques, and sophisticated theories.

These methods are used in a great many areas of research in psychology. Therefore, the individual who wishes to know, at a professional level, about the behavior of humans and other animals must be able to understand the reports of the psychologists who do this research. Others can learn about psychology at a more general level by relying on secondary accounts written for a broader audience. Much of this research depends on the statistical technique of analysis of variance. This is often performed by using a computer software package designed for this purpose. These statistical software packages are great labor savers; at the same time, however, they can mislead a researcher into incorrect conclusions about behavior if he or she is not familiar with experimental methodology.

Subject Versus Manipulated Variables

It is especially important when drawing conclusions to discriminate between subject variables and manipulated variables. The reason is causality. Subject variables are measured after the fact (post facto) and consist of characteristics which the individual already possesses. Logically, subject variables cannot be assured to be part of a cause-and-effect connection with the behavior of interest. They may possibly be the cause—for example, a measured trait of anxiety may affect reactions to stress—but characteristics such as age and gender may instead be contributors to socialization, experiences, hormonal changes, or peer pressures. Other subject variables such as education or social class may be a result of behavior rather than its cause. When subject variables are found in research to be related to behavior, they may be a cause of that behavior, but the research does not provide evidence to justify that conclusion. Only manipulated variables, in a careful controlled experiment, may be assumed to cause the behavior which they precede.

A Range of Behavioral Influences

It is also important that the researcher remember that the variables selected only represent a few of the possible influences on behavior. In some cases, the subject variables are only related to more powerful variables yet to be discovered. For the example used here, it was suggested that gender and age were predictors of the most effective persuasive message. Perhaps what was most important was that these were approximate predictors of which individuals prefer action figures over romantic figures. An analysis of how the persuasive messages are working may find that the answer to a question such as "Which figures do you prefer for playing?" would be a much more accurate predictor of the behavior in this situation than the mere assumption that boys and girls separate along lines of gender in every preference and psychological process. Awareness of these and similar research refinements comes with experience and training.

Sources for Further Study

Edwards, Allen Louis. *Experimental Design in Psychological Research.* 5th ed. New York: Holt, Rinehart and Winston, 1984. Presents discussions of interactions and complex experimental designs through the use of concrete examples. More than most other statistics books, Edwards's is concerned with presenting the probabilistic basis for the concepts discussed, especially the probabilities of finding differences between groups as a result of accident or chance.

Martin, David W. *Doing Psychology Experiments.* 5th ed. Belmont, Calif.: Wadsworth, 1999. An important book about the design, execution, interpretation, and reporting of psychological research, written in a clear and engaging manner. Does not provide instructions for making statistical calculations; more for helping the reader or consumer of psychological research understand what was done and what it means. Exceptional sections on theory and on research ethics.

Myers, Jerome L. *Fundamentals of Experimental Design.* 3d ed. Boston: Allyn & Bacon, 1979. Provides excellent examples of graphing higher-order interactions and of calculational methods. Contains discussions of designing an experiment and interpreting statistics. Has an important section on the further data analyses for simple main effects which should be performed after an interaction has been found.

Sprinthall, Richard C. *Basic Statistical Analysis.* 6th ed. Boston: Allyn & Bacon, 1999. Offers a comprehensive introduction to a wide variety of experimental and statistical procedures at the beginning university level. Notable for its discussions of cause and effect, nonparametrics, and computers in research. Better than average for its treatment of drawing and evaluating graphical representations of data.

Winer, B. J. *Statistical Principles in Experimental Design.* 3d ed. New York: McGraw-Hill, 1991. A widely recognized standard in the field of experimental design and statistical analysis. May be overly technical in spots for some readers, but also has very readable explanations of the meaning of interactions and how they can be understood. May be useful for understanding some of the methods and conclusions of research articles.

Roger A. Drake

See also: Animal experimentation; Archival data; Case-study methodologies; Data description; Experimental psychology; Experimentation: Ethics and participant rights; Experimentation: Independent, dependent, and control variables; Field experimentation; Hypothesis development and testing; Observational methods; Quasi-experimental designs; Sampling; Scientific methods; Statistical significance tests; Survey research: Questionnaires and interviews; Within-subject experimental designs.

Computer models of cognition

Type of psychology: Cognition
Fields of study: Cognitive processes; nervous system

The nervous system is the basis for all cognitive and mental activity. The nervous system can be viewed as processing information received from the environment. Computer models of cognition based on the actual structure of the human nervous system show great promise for elucidating the relationship between cognition and the nervous system.

Key concepts
• architecture
• natural intelligence
• netware
• neural network
• neurocomputer
• parallel distributed processing
• processing elements
• training law
• transfer function
• weights

Introduction
Human cognition depends upon the operation of the neural anatomy that forms the nervous system.

Essentially, the brain is composed of some 100 billion neurons. Roger Penrose has divided the brain into three areas: primary, secondary, and tertiary. Each of these three areas has a sensory and motor component. The primary areas are the visual, olfactory, somatosensory, and motor areas. These areas handle the input and output functions of the brain. The secondary areas lie near the primary regions and process the input received by the primary areas. Plans of action are developed in the secondary areas, and these actions are translated into movements of the muscular system by the primary cortex. The tertiary area makes up the rest of the brain. The most complex, abstract, sophisticated, and subtle activity of the brain occurs here. Information from the different sensory areas is received, collected, integrated, and analyzed. As Penrose says, "memories are laid down, pictures of the outside world are constructed, general plans are conceived and executed, and speech is understood or formulated." Thus, information or stimulation from the environment is received or inputted at the primary sensory areas. This information is then processed in increasingly complex and sophisticated ways in the secondary and tertiary sensory areas. The processed sensory information is sent to the tertiary motor area in the form of a grand plan of action, and it is then refined into plans for specific actions at the secondary and primary motor regions.

Models of Information Processing
The question for psychologists to solve is how to represent or model this complex activity that is the basis for human thought and action in the three regions of the brain. The theory of information processing contends that human cognition can be successfully modeled by viewing the operation of the brain as analogous to the operation of a computer. Penrose observed that the brain presents itself as "a superb computing device." More specifically, Robert J. Baron stated:

> The fundamental assumption is that the brain is a computer. It is comprised of some 100 billion computational cells called neurons, which interact in a variety of ways. Neurons are organized into well defined and highly structured computational networks called neural networks. Neural networks are the principal computational systems of the brain.

A field known as neurocomputing or computational neuroscience holds great promise for providing such a computer-based model. The particular kind of computer to be used is a neurocomputer, which is modeled on the actual structure or architecture of the brain. The unit of the neurocomputer is the processing element, or neurode, which corresponds to a biological neuron. The neurocomputer is constructed of many neurodes that are interconnected to each other to form a neural network. Each neurode can receive a number of inputs, either externally or from other neurodes, and each input has a weight or strength given to it. These weights are all summed, and a single output results. This output can then act as an input to other neurodes to which it is interconnected. If the output is excitatory, it will encourage firing of the interconnected neurodes; if the output is inhibitory, it will discourage firing of the interconnected neurodes. The neurocomputer processes all the inputs and outputs in a parallel manner (that is, all of the neurodes can potentially operate simultaneously). The software that runs the neurocomputer is called netware. The netware provides the interconnections between neurodes, how the neural network will react to the input it receives (training law), and how the input and output are related to each other (transfer function). Neurocomputers are drastically different from any other kind of computer because their architecture and operation are modeled after the human brain. Thus, neurocomputers can perform human functions, such as being taught to learn new behaviors. Maureen Caudill refers to these computers as being "naturally intelligent," as opposed to the serial computer used with "artificial intelligence."

Because neurocomputers are constructed as analogues of the human nervous system, they are particularly adept and useful for solving the kinds of problems that the human brain can solve. Conventional computers would have great difficulty solving these problems because they are constructed to perform certain kinds of tasks very quickly and efficiently (for example, processing large amounts of numbers very rapidly), tasks which the human brain cannot do nearly as well. The following two applications of neurocomputers and neural networks are discussed in a book by Caudill and Charles Butler called *Naturally Intelligent Systems* (1990).

USES OF ARTIFICIAL INTELLIGENCE

A machine called the vectorcardiograph was found, in tests, to be able to detect heart problems better than cardiologists were. The usual electrocardiograph records signals received from up to twelve leads placed on different parts of the body. Each recording is made separately and in a particular sequential order. In contrast, the vectorcardiograph records signals from only three locations (front-back, head-foot, right-left), and it records all three sources of data simultaneously. This parallel processing of the information suits the vectorcardiograph very nicely to neural networks.

Essentially, the vectorcardiograph was trained in three stages to differentiate between normal and abnormal electrocardiograms, much as a human is trained to discriminate or distinguish between two stimuli. In the first stage, the system was trained to recognize all the normal cases presented to it and a portion of the abnormal cases presented to it. The input weights were then set at the appropriate values and training continued. In the second stage, the neural network was trained also to recognize all normal cases and a portion of the remaining abnormal cases. Again, the input weights were set at their appropriate values. The third stage of training commenced, and training continued until the system could recognize the remaining abnormal cases. The training set consisted of vectorcardiographs from 107 people, half of whom were judged to be normal and the other half of whom were judged to be abnormal. When the vectorcardiograph was presented with sixty-three new cases never before presented, it correctly diagnosed 97 percent of the normal and 90 percent of the abnormal cases. Trained clinicians were able to identify, respectively, 95 percent and 53 percent of the cases. The diagnostic capabilities of the vectorcardiograph demonstrate the capabilities and potentials of neural networks.

A neural network known as the Multiple Neural Network Learning System (MNNLS) can be trained to make decisions to accept or reject a mortgage application. The system uses twenty-five areas of information that are divided into four categories: cultural (credit rating, number of children, employment history); financial (income, debts); mortgage (amount, interest rate, duration); and property (age, appraised value, type).

The MNNLS is a system of nine separate neural networks that are divided into three different layers, with three networks in each area. Each layer is analogous to a panel of three experts. One expert in each of the three layers concerns itself only with financial information, the second only with cultural and mortgage information, and the third with all four categories. When presented with a mortgage application, the first layer attempts to arrive at a decision. If the three "experts" all agree, the mortgage is accepted or rejected; however, if one of the experts disagrees with another, then the application goes to the second layer of experts, and the same process is repeated. The MNNLS is useful because it is very efficient and accurate. It is efficient because it is able to process a wide variety of problems, since the neural networks correspond to different experts. The first layer effectively handles simple decisions, whereas the second and third layers can handle increasingly difficult decisions. MNNLS agreed with decisions made by humans about 82 percent of the time. In those cases where the MNNLS disagreed with the human decision, the MNNLS was in fact nearly always correct. This happens because the MNNLS is a neural network that insists upon consensus of a panel of experts (that is, consensus between separate neural networks). It would be economically unfeasible to have a panel of humans evaluate mortgages; however, a single person evaluating applications is more likely to make a mistake than a panel of evaluators.

METAPHORS OF MODELING

Stephen J. Hanson and David J. Burr astutely observed that "the computer metaphor has had a profound and lasting effect on psychological modeling." The influence of the computer can be seen especially in its use in artificial intelligence and in computer metaphors of learning and memory, in which information is processed, encoded, stored, and retrieved from three distinct memory stores (sensory, short-term, and long-term memory). The particular computer that has been used as the metaphor of the human mind and cognition has been the digital or serial computer.

It eventually became apparent to cognitive scientists, however, that the digital computer is actually a poor analogy for the human mind, because this computer operates in a decidedly nonhuman way. For example, the digital computer operates much too fast—much faster than the human mind can process information. It also processes much more

data than the human mind can process. If the software is sound, the digital computer is perfect and operates error-free. Human problem solving, on the other hand, is characterized by mistakes. The digital computer is not capable of autonomous learning. It does only what it is told to do by the program; it cannot teach itself new things, as can a human. The digital computer is very poor at pattern recognition tasks, such as identifying a human face, something an infant can do very rapidly. The digital computer provides no information about the underlying structure (the nervous system) that makes human cognition and information processing possible.

A number of cognitive scientists have argued that the fields of artificial intelligence and traditional cognitive science have reached dead ends because of their reliance on the digital computer analogy of the mind, which is limited and largely inaccurate. Cognitive science and neurophysiology are now striking out in a promising new direction by using neural networks and neurocomputers as the analogue of the human mind. The human mind is closely related to the human brain; many would argue that the mind is equivalent to the brain. Therefore, in order to study the mind and cognition, one must build a computer that is modeled on the architecture of the brain. The neurocomputer is modeled on the human brain, and the digital computer is not.

Unlike digital computers, neurocomputers operate in a manner consistent with the operation of the human nervous system and human cognition. Neurocomputers provide a potentially promising way to understand cognition, as well as providing a productive connection and interrelationship with neurophysiology.

SOURCES FOR FURTHER STUDY

AI Expert, 1986-1995. Most issues contain one or two informative articles on developments in neural networks.

Allman, William F. *Apprentices of Wonder: Inside the Neural Network Revolution*. New York: Bantam Books, 1989. Readable, nontechnical discussion of neural networks that presents their various aspects and features interviews with several key researchers in this field.

Baron, Robert J. *The Cerebral Computer: An Introduction to the Computational Structure of the Human Brain*. Hillsdale, N.J.: Lawrence Erlbaum, 1987.

Compelling argument for viewing the human nervous system as a computer. The first chapters provide a good discussion of the relationship between neurophysiology and computers.

Caudill, Maureen, and Charles Butler. *Naturally Intelligent Systems.* Cambridge, Mass.: MIT Press, 1990. Provides a thorough introduction to neural networks—the different types and their uses. Among the applications discussed are those for the vectorcardiograph and for the Multiple Neural Network Learning System.

Hanson, Stephen J., and David J. Burr. "What Connectionist Models Learn: Learning and Representation in Connectionist Networks." *Behavioral and Brain Sciences* 13, no. 3 (1990): 471-518. The first several pages provide good background on cognitive psychology's use of computer analogues of the mind and their relationship to neural networks.

Harnish, Robert. *Minds, Brains, Computers: An Historical Introduction to Cognitive Science.* New York: Blackwell, 2002. Approaches the history of cognitive science from the perspective of two models, the digital computer and the neural network. Intended as a textbook for introductory cognitive science classes.

Penrose, Roger. *The Emperor's New Mind: Concerning Computers, Minds, and the Laws of Physics.* New York: Oxford University Press, 1989. Presents a somewhat different slant on the relationship between the brain and cognition, and the human mind as a computer; the author is a physicist.

Schneider, Walter. "Connectionism: Is It a Paradigm Shift for Psychology?" *Behavior, Research Methods, Instruments, and Computers* 19, no. 2 (1987): 73-83. Schneider's presidential address to the Psychonomic Society. Presents a good introduction to neural networks and the impact they can be expected to have on cognitive psychology.

Stillings, Neil A., et al. *Cognitive Science: An Introduction.* Cambridge, Mass.: MIT Press, 1987. A standard textbook on cognitive psychology, with emphasis on neurophysiology. Also features one of the first presentations on neural networks and cognition to appear in a textbook.

Laurence Miller

SEE ALSO: Artificial intelligence; Brain structure; Cognitive psychology; Neurons; Neuropsychology; Synaptic transmission.

Concept formation

TYPE OF PSYCHOLOGY: Cognition
FIELDS OF STUDY: Cognitive processes; thought

In order to think and communicate about the endless objects, living things, and events in the world, a person simplifies those things by mentally grouping them and organizing them based on relationships and features they have in common. The process of constructing rules about how things go together is called concept formation, and it is a powerful mental tool.

KEY CONCEPTS
- artificial concepts
- concept
- concept formation
- fuzzy borders
- natural concepts
- prototype
- stimulus materials

INTRODUCTION

Humans are faced with the task of making sense of a world that contains a seemingly endless array of unique objects and living things. In order to reduce this endless uniqueness to something that is mentally manageable, people form concepts. A concept can be defined as an abstract idea based on grouping objects or events according to their common properties. Concepts guide thoughts and behaviors, so it is important to understand both the nature of those concepts and how people construct them. Animals of all types also have the ability to form concepts. Animals form concepts at a much more fundamental level than humans, but they have been shown to differentiate among various colors and various geometric patterns, for example. Throughout its long history, research on concept formation has used animals, such as pigeons and rats, as well as human subjects.

In daily life, the term "concept" is used in a way that is different from the way in which psychologists use it. Whereas psychologists say that a concept exists when two or more things are grouped on the basis of a common feature or property of each, everyday language uses the term "concept" to refer to abstract ideas, such as the concept of "integrity," or to a mental picture in one's mind; for example, "I have a concept of how I want my room to look." The term is used here as psychologists use it. Psychologists also frequently use the word "category" as a synonym for "concept."

Psychologists have had to be very innovative when designing experiments to study concept formation, because there is no way to observe the way in which people think or form concepts directly. The techniques vary from study to study, but subjects are typically asked to choose which of several items fits a particular concept.

The early researchers in the area, including Jerome Bruner, Jacqueline Goodnow, and George Austin, used materials in their experiments that have since been referred to as "artificial" stimuli or concepts, because they used geometric figures such as circles and squares of various sizes and shapes that were deliberately devised to have only a certain number of alterable characteristics or features. Years later, researchers such as Eleanor Rosch became interested in "natural" concepts, based on complex real world objects, in which partial membership in a category is a possible alternative.

TECHNIQUES OF STUDY

In a typical study on artificial concept formation, a psychologist would construct visual patterns that would not normally be encountered in daily life. The patterns would be printed on cards to create the stimulus materials, or anything presented to a subject during the course of an experiment that requires that subject to make a response. These visual patterns would vary in terms of size, shape, number, or color, for example, and would be referred to as dimensions. Basically, a dimension is any changeable characteristic of the stimulus. A dimension can have two or more values, and the value is determined by the number of sizes, shapes, numbers, or colors being utilized.

In this example, each dimension can have three values. In other words, there would be objects of small, medium, and large size; circular, triangular, and square shapes; one, two, or three items; and purple, red, and green colors. Varying those dimensions and values, the particular stimulus patterns presented to the subject would be things such as two large green squares, three small red triangles, or perhaps one medium purple circle. The concept to be learned is selected by the researcher beforehand and is kept secret from the subject, because the sub-

ject must discover the concept. The concept might be something such as "purple triangles of any size and any number." Thus, in this case, the specific concept to be learned would be "purple and a triangle."

In a concept formation task, the stimuli are usually presented to the subjects in one of two ways: the reception method or the selection method. In the reception technique, the subject is shown a single card and is asked to state whether that card displays the concept that the experimenter had in mind. The experimenter then tells the subject whether the response is correct or incorrect. The subject is then shown another card.

In the selection technique, by contrast, the entire set of cards is simultaneously displayed to the subject in one large array. The number of cards in the entire set is determined by the combination of all possible dimensions and values. The subject selects a particular card from the array, stating whether it displays the concept to be learned. Following each selection and judgment, the experimenter informs the subject about correctness.

USE OF RULES AND CATEGORIES

Some tasks require subjects to discover the values, the rule, or both. A rule tells how the values must be combined. The two most common kinds of rules are called conjunction and disjunction. The conjunction rule uses the word "and," as in "all figures that are both purple and triangles." Thus, a subject learning a concept involving the conjunction rule would learn to respond yes to all purple triangles and no to all other figures. The disjunction rule uses the word "or," as in "all figures that are purple or a triangle or both."

An important development in research on concepts involves natural concepts or real-life categories. Rosch pointed out that the artificial-concept learning tasks use materials unlike those encountered in the everyday world. Most concepts in the everyday world do not fall into neatly defined categories. Many have fuzzy borders—conceptual borders that appear ill defined and shift according to the context in which the category member occurs—that involve some uncertainty. For example, is a tomato a fruit or a vegetable? Rosch theorized that people decide whether an item belongs to a particular category by comparing that item with a prototype or best example for that category. An apple is highly prototypical of the fruit category, whereas a coconut is a less typical example.

MAKING SENSE OF ONE'S ENVIRONMENT

If a person understands the concept of sunglasses, he or she can recognize something as a pair of sunglasses even though they may look different from all the other sunglasses the person has seen before. A new pair of sunglasses with iridium-coated lenses can be included within the concept because the pair has qualities that are common to the entire class of objects that people refer to as sunglasses. They have earpieces, they block out the sun to some degree, and they cover the eyes. Sunglasses belong to the even larger conceptual category of eyewear. Concepts such as eyewear, cookware, furniture, and vehicles are very useful. It would be impossible to think intelligently without the ability to form concepts. Without that ability, every time a person encountered something that was slightly different from other things, it would be necessary to learn about that object as if it were completely new.

A person would then primarily function instinctually because, according to Michael Eysenck, it would be impossible to relate prior learning to new situations. By applying concepts, a person can develop an immediate understanding of new objects or ideas, because they can be related to a general class of similar objects and ideas that are familiar. A person knows what to expect from an object, even when it is encountered for the first time. In this way, thinking beings save an amazing amount of work. Concepts reduce the complexity of the environment and eliminate the need to learn constantly.

IMPLICATIONS FOR EDUCATION

The development and refinement of some concepts take place over a long period of time. A person can have general concepts about some things, precise concepts about others, and also be in the process of refining vague concepts. In the course of life, a person's understanding of a particular concept develops and expands with additional experience, advanced training, and new information. Understanding this has ramifications for formal education.

Much teaching is directed toward the development of concepts. In fact, it would be almost impossible to use the vast amount of mental information that is available to human beings to solve problems,

make decisions, understand language, and communicate without the ability to simplify the world by means of conceptualization. One of the principal objectives of formal education is to allow students to formulate a hypothesis, or tentative guess, about how some attribute contributes to a concept. Students are then encouraged to test the hypothesis. If it is wrong, they can adopt a new hypothesis that incorporates different attributes or the same attributes but with different rules, based on feedback they receive from an instructor.

Researchers have identified a number of factors involved in concept learning that apply to the process of education. One factor is the number of attributes. It is easier to learn a concept if there are only one or two relevant attributes, rather than several. Another factor is salience. It is easier to learn a concept if the relevant attributes are salient, or obvious. A third factor is positive examples. People tend to make better use of positive examples, although it is sometimes helpful and even necessary to give some negative examples. For example, imagine teaching a young child the concept of "housecat" by using examples that are all positive. One shows the child pictures of a Persian, a Siamese, and a Russian Blue. From the viewpoint of a teacher, it is desirable to highlight or emphasize the relevant features of the concepts to make them salient, such as mentioning that the creatures in all the pictures have fur. The child learns to say "cat" to each picture. A teacher cannot, however, be certain which aspects of the pictures determine the child's response. For all the teacher knows, the child considers a picture of a cat to be another example of a "dog." For this reason, it is important to include relevant negative examples. In general, negative examples tend to be more useful in later stages of training.

ARTIFICIAL INTELLIGENCE

As science fiction becomes fact, it is becoming desirable to be able to "teach" computers how to form concepts. This type of investigation is conducted in the field of artificial intelligence. In order to develop artificial ways of duplicating human thought and intelligence, it is important to know how the thought process is accomplished by humans. Imagine a task in which a computer is asked to identify whether something is a triangle. A computer could be programmed to learn the concept, but it would take a very sophisticated program. In comparison, it is easy for humans to recognize immediately what constitutes a triangle, based on vast experience with other triangular objects. Concept formation in computers provides the foundation for the ability to recognize handwriting, fingerprints, speech, and many other things electronically.

One of the problems for computers is that, although some concepts are well defined, most are not: This is Rosch's point. In addition, human experience and context play an important role in concept formation, which poses difficulties for computers. Even more troublesome for a computer is the fact that many conceptual categories are based on human imagination. Because people have knowledge about the world and how it operates, they adjust their conceptual categories to fit reality. Unless computers have human knowledge and experience, their concepts will not be exactly like those of humans.

CONCEPT THEORIES

Throughout the history of the scientific study of concept formation, three main types of theories have become apparent. They are association theory, hypothesis-testing theory, and information-processing theory. In the associationistic view, the organism passively receives information from the environment. Each example of the concept that has yet to be learned provides the organism with an additional piece of information. In this way, relevant features are reinforced, whereas irrelevant features disappear. This approach requires nothing from the organism except a memory of previous examples. This approach was in vogue in the first half of the twentieth century. According to associationistic views, stimuli gradually become associated with some response by means of a complex form of discrimination learning. By means of discrimination learning, discriminable aspects of stimulus patterns are detected and labeled. Later modifications of association theory introduced the idea of mediation, assuming that concepts are formed because of an intervening step in the mind of the learner, which connects the stimuli with the response.

A second line of theory development, hypothesis testing, views the subject as an active participant in the process of concept learning. According to this line of thought, the organism always has some hypothesis regarding the unknown concept. Incoming information is used to check the current hypothesis and is used as the basis for modifying that hypothesis if it is incompatible with existing evidence. Eventually, the organism hits on the correct hypothesis and forms the concept. The research of Bruner, Goodnow, and Austin, which was first published in 1956, adhered to the view of the organism as an active hypothesis tester.

Finally, theories were developed that emphasized the information-processing nature of concept formation. These theories view the process in terms of a sequence of decisions made by the learner. The learner is seen as accepting external information, or stimuli, processing the information in a variety or ways, and producing some final response. One of the earliest attempts to produce an information-processing model for the learning of concepts was made by Earl Hunt in 1962.

SOURCES FOR FURTHER STUDY

Bourne, Lyle E., Jr. *Human Conceptual Behavior.* Boston: Allyn & Bacon, 1966. A short book of definite historical importance that summarizes the work on concept formation up to 1966. The writing style is enjoyable, and the book is clearly written, although the ideas it expresses are complex.

Bourne, Lyle E., Jr., Roger L. Dominowski, and Elizabeth Loftus. *Cognitive Processes.* 2d ed. Englewood Cliffs, N.J.: Prentice-Hall, 1986. A thorough textbook on the psychology of thinking. The chapter on concept formation is insightful and clear. The reading level is appropriate for psychologists and nonpsychologists alike.

Bruner, Jerome S., Jacqueline J. Goodnow, and George A. Austin. *A Study of Thinking.* New York: John Wiley & Sons, 1956. This book is a classic. The first three chapters provide an insightful introduction to concepts and concept formation in general. The latter chapters describe research and provide a methodological analysis of performance, beginning a tradition in concept formation that has now been discarded as a result of new findings and updated theoretical views. A pioneering book in the area of concept formation.

Eysenck, Michael W., and Mark T. Keane. *A Handbook of Cognitive Psychology.* 4th ed. Hillsdale, N.J.: Lawrence Erlbaum, 2000. Provides a readable introduction to the entire area of thinking, of which concept formation is one part. The section on categorization provides an overall perspective and succinctly summarizes the research.

Hunt, Earl B. *Concept Learning: An Information Processing Problem.* New York: John Wiley & Sons, 1962. Another historically relevant book that emphasizes the mathematical and probabilistic process of concept acquisition. Hunt's view of concept formation provided a theoretical breakthrough at the time. A substantial section of the book discusses concept acquisition as it relates to the area of artificial intelligence, which was a very new field of inquiry when the book was written.

Rosch, Eleanor H. "Classification of Real-World Objects: Origins and Representation in Cognition." In *Thinking: Readings in Cognitive Science*, edited by P. N. Johnson-Laird and P. C. Wason. Cambridge, England: Cambridge University Press, 1975. The chapter by Eleanor Rosch is important reading; she was one of the first people to break away from research using artificial concepts and begin to explore natural ones. The chapter is quite understandable.

Deborah R. McDonald

SEE ALSO: Cognitive psychology; Decision making; Learning; Logic and reasoning; Pattern recognition; Thought: Inferential; Thought: Study and measurement.

Conditioning

TYPE OF PSYCHOLOGY: Learning

FIELDS OF STUDY: Instrumental conditioning; Pavlovian conditioning

Conditioning and learning are roughly synonymous terms. Both refer to changes in behavior resulting from experience, but conditioning has a more specific meaning, referring to changes in behavior that are the direct result of learning relationships between environmental events. Two types of relationships are studied by learning psychologists. The first involves learning the relationship between environmental events that consistently occur together. The second involves learning the environmental consequences of behavior. These two learning scenarios correspond to classical and operant conditioning respectively.

KEY CONCEPTS
- behavioral approach
- conditioned stimulus (CS)
- conditioned response (CR)
- contiguity
- Law of Effect
- operant response (R)
- reinforcing stimulus (S^r)
- schedules of reinforcement
- shaping
- unconditioned stimulus (US)
- unconditioned response (UR)

INTRODUCTION

Learning refers to any change in behavior or mental processes associated with experience. Traditionally psychologists interested in learning have taken a behavioral approach which involves studying the relationship between environmental events, and resulting behavioral changes, in detail. Though the behavioral approach typically involves studying the behavior of nonhuman subjects in controlled laboratory environments, the results that have been found in behavioral research have often found wide application and use in human contexts. Since the early twentieth century behavioral psychologists have extensively studied two primary forms of learning, classical and operant conditioning.

CLASSICAL CONDITIONING

Classical conditioning is also referred to as associative learning or Pavlovian conditioning, after its primary founder, the Russian physiologist Ivan Pavlov (1849-1936). Pavlov's original studies involved examining digestion in dogs. The first step in digestion is salivation. Pavlov developed an experimental apparatus that allowed him to measure the amount of saliva the dog produced when presented with food. Dogs do not need to learn to salivate when food is given to them—that is an automatic, reflexive response. However, Pavlov noticed that, with experience, the dogs began to salivate before the food was presented, suggesting that new stimuli had acquired the ability to elicit the response. In order to examine this unexpected finding Pavlov selected specific stimuli, which he systematically presented to the dog just before food was presented. The classic example is the ringing of a bell, but there was nothing special about the bell per se. Dogs do not salivate in response to a bell ringing under normal circumstances. What made the bell special was its systematic relationship to the delivery of food. Over time, the dogs began to salivate in response to the ringing of the bell even when the food was not presented. In other words, the dog learned to associate the bell with food so that the response (salivation) could be elicited by either stimulus.

In classical conditioning terminology, the food is the unconditioned stimulus (US). It is unconditioned (or unlearned) because the animal naturally responds to it before the experiment is begun. The sound of the bell ringing is referred to as the conditioned stimulus (CS). It is not naturally effective in eliciting salivation—learning is required in order for it to do so. Salivating in response to food presentation is referred to as the unconditioned response (UR) and salivating when the bell is rung is referred to as the conditioned response (CR). Though it would seem that saliva is saliva, it is important to differentiate the conditioned from the unconditioned response, because these responses are not always identical. More important, one is a natural, unlearned response (the UR) while the other requires specific learning experiences in order to occur (the CR).

Classical conditioning is not limited to dogs and salivation. Modern researchers examine classical conditioning in a variety of ways. What is important is the specific pairing of some novel stimulus (the CS) with a stimulus that already elicits the response (the US). One common experimental procedure examines eye blink conditioning in rabbits, where a brief puff of air to the eye serves as the US and the measured response (UR) is blinking. A tone, a light, or some other initially ineffective stimulus serves as the CS. After many pairings in which the CS precedes the air puff, the rabbit will begin to blink in response to the CS in the absence of the air puff. Another common behavior that is studied in classical conditioning research is conditioned suppression. Here a CS is paired with an aversive US, such as a mild electric shock. Presentation of the shock disrupts whatever behavior the animal is engaged in at the time, and with appropriate pairing over time the CS comes to do so as well. A final example that many humans can relate to is taste aversion learning. Here a specific taste (CS) is paired with a drug or procedure that causes the animal to feel ill (US). In the future, the animal will avoid consuming (CR) the taste (CS) associated with illness (US). Taste aversions illus-

trate the fact that all forms of conditioning are not created equal. To learn a conditioned eye blink or salivation response requires many CS-US pairings, while taste aversions are often learned with only one pairing of the taste and illness.

UNDERLYING FACTORS

Psychologists have long studied the factors that are necessary and sufficient for producing classical conditioning. One important principle is contiguity, which refers to events occurring closely together in space and/or time. Classical conditioning is most effective when the CS and US are more contiguous, though precisely how closely together they must be presented depends upon the type of classical conditioning observed. Taste aversion conditioning, for example, will occur over much longer CS-US intervals than would be effective with other conditioning arrangements. Nevertheless, the sooner illness (US) follows taste (CS), the stronger the aversion (CR) will be.

Though seemingly necessary for classical conditioning, contiguity is not sufficient. A particularly clear demonstration of this fact is seen when the CS and US are presented at the exact same moment (a procedure called simultaneous conditioning). Though maximally contiguous, simultaneous conditioning is an extremely poor method for producing a CR. Furthermore, the order of presentation matters. If the US is presented before the CS, rather than afterward as is usually the case, then inhibitory conditioning will occur. Inhibitory conditioning is seen in experiments in which behavior can change in two directions. For example, with a conditioned suppression procedure, inhibitory conditioning is seen when the animal increases, rather than decreases, its ongoing behavior when the CS is presented.

These findings have led modern researchers to focus on the predictive relationship between the CS and the UCS in classical conditioning. An especially successful modern theory of classical conditioning, the Rescorla-Wagner Model, suggests that CS's acquire associative strength in direct proportion to how much information they provide about the upcoming US. In addition to providing a quantitative description of the way in which CRs are learned, the Rescorla-Wagner model has predicted a number of counterintuitive conditioning phenomena, such as blocking and overshadowing. Taken as a whole, the newer theoretical conceptions of classical conditioning tend to view the learning organism less as a passive recipient of environmental events than as an active analyzer of information.

Does classical conditioning account for any human behaviors? At first glance, these processes might seem a bit simplistic to account for human behaviors. However, some common human reactions are quite obviously the result of conditioning. For instance, nearly everyone who has had a cavity filled will cringe at the sound of a dentist's drill, because the sound of the drill (CS) has been paired in the past with the unpleasant experience of having one's teeth drilled (US). Cringing at the sound of the drill would be a conditioned response (CR). Psychologists have found evidence implicating classical conditioning in a variety of important human behaviors, from the emotional effects of advertising to the functioning of the immune system to the development of tolerance in drug addiction.

OPERANT CONDITIONING

At about the same time that Pavlov was conducting his experiments in Russia, an American psychologist named Edward L. Thorndike (1874-1949) was examining a different form of learning that has come to be called instrumental or operant conditioning. Thorndike's original experiments involved placing cats in an apparatus he designed, which he called a puzzle box. A plate of food was placed outside the puzzle box, but the hungry cat was trapped inside. Thorndike designed the box so that the cat needed to make a particular response, such as moving a lever or pulling a cord, in order for a trap door to be released, allowing escape and access to the food outside. The amount of time it took the cat to make the appropriate response was measured. With repeated experience, Thorndike found that it took less and less time for the cat to make the appropriate response.

Operant conditioning is much different from Pavlov's classical conditioning. As was stated before, classical conditioning involves learning "what goes with what" in the environment. Learning the relationship changes behavior, though behavior does not change the environmental events themselves. Through experience, Pavlov's dogs began to salivate when the bell was rung, because the bell predicted food. However, salivating (the CR) did not cause the food to be delivered. Thorndike's cats, on the other

hand, received no food until the appropriate response was made. Through experience, the cats learned about the effects of their own behavior upon environmental events. In other words, they learned the consequences of their own actions.

To describe these changes, Thorndike postulated the Law of Effect. According to the Law of Effect, in any given situation an animal may do a variety of things. The cat in the puzzle box could walk around, groom itself, meow, or engage in virtually any type of feline behavior. It could also make the operant response, the response necessary to escape the puzzle box and gain access to the food. Initially, the cat may engage in any of these behaviors and may produce the operant response simply by accident or chance. However, when the operant response occurs, escape from the box and access to the food follows. In operant conditioning terminology, food is

Ivan Pavlov, the Russian behavioral scientist whose studies on dogs formed the basis of classical, or Pavlovian, conditioning. (Library of Congress)

the reinforcer (S^r, or reinforcing stimulus) and it serves to strengthen the operant response (R) that immediately preceded it. The next time the animal finds itself in the puzzle box, its tendency to produce the operant response will be a bit stronger as a consequence of the reinforcement. Once the response is made again, the animal gains access to the food again—which strengthens the response further. Over time, the operant response is strengthened, while other behaviors that may occur are not strengthened and thus drop away. So, with repeated experience, the amount of time that it takes for the animal to make the operant response declines.

SKINNERIAN CONDITIONING

In addition to changing the strength of responses, operant conditioning can be used to mold entirely new behaviors. This process is referred to as shaping and was described by American psychologist B. F. Skinner (1904-1990), who further developed the field of operant conditioning. Suppose that the experiment's objective was to train an animal, such as a laboratory rat, to press a lever. The rat could be given a piece of food (S^r) each time it pressed the lever (R), but it would probably be some considerable time before it would do so on its own. Lever pressing does not come naturally to rats. To speed up the process, the animal could be "shaped" by reinforcing successive approximations of lever-pressing behavior. The rat could be given a food pellet each time that it was in the vicinity of the lever. The Law of Effect predicts that the rat would spend more and more of its time near the lever as a consequence of reinforcement. Then the rat may be required to make some physical contact with the lever, but not necessarily press it, in order to be rewarded. The rat would make more and more contact with the lever as a result. Finally, the rat would be required to make the full response, pressing the lever, in order to get food. In many ways, shaping resembles the childhood game of selecting some object in the room without saying what it is, and guiding guessers by saying "warmer" as they approach the object, and as they move away from it, saying nothing at all. Before long, the guessers will use the feedback to zero in on the selected object. In a similar manner, feedback in the form of reinforcement allows the rat to "zero in" on the operant response.

Skinner also examined situations where reinforcement was not given for every individual response

but was delivered according to various schedules of reinforcement. For example, the rat may be required to press the lever a total of five times (rather than once) in order to get the food pellet, or the reinforcing stimulus may be delivered only when a response occurs after a specified period of time. These scenarios correspond to ratio and interval schedules. Interval and ratio schedules can be either fixed, meaning that the exact same rule applies for the delivery of each individual reinforcement, or variable, meaning that the rule changes from reinforcer to reinforcer. For example, in a variable ratio-five schedule, a reward may be given after the first five responses, then after seven responses, then after three. On average, each five responses would be reinforced, but any particular reinforcement may require more or fewer responses.

To understand how large an impact varying the schedule of reinforcement can have on behavior, one might consider responding to a soda machine versus responding to a slot machine. In both cases the operant response is inserting money. However, the soda machine rewards (delivers a can of soda) according to a fixed-ratio schedule of reinforcement. Without reward, one will not persist very long in making the operant response to the soda machine. The slot machine, on the other hand, provides rewards (delivers a winning payout) on a variable-ratio schedule. It is not uncommon for people to empty out their pockets in front of a slot machine without receiving a single reinforcement.

SUPERSTITIOUS PIGEONS

As with classical conditioning, exactly what associations are learned in operant conditioning has been an important research question. For example, in a classic 1948 experiment, Skinner provided pigeons with food at regular intervals regardless of what they were doing at the time. Six of his eight pigeons developed stereotyped (consistent) patterns of behavior as a result of the experiment despite the fact that the pigeons' behavior was not really necessary. According to the Law of Effect, some behavior would be occurring just prior to food delivery and this behavior would be strengthened simply by chance pairing with reinforcement. This would increase the strength of the response, making it more likely to occur when the next reward was delivered—strengthening the response still further. Ultimately, one behavior would dominate the pigeons' behavior in that experimental context. Skinner referred to this phenomenon as superstition. One need only observe the behavior of baseball players approaching the plate or basketball players lining up for a free-throw shot to see examples of superstition in human behavior.

Superstition again raises the issue of contiguity—simply presenting reinforcement soon after the response is made appears to strengthen it. However, later studies, especially a 1971 experiment conducted by J. E. R. Staddon and V. Simmelhag, suggested that it might not be quite that simple. Providing food rewards in superstition experiments changes a variety of responses, including natural behaviors related to the anticipation of food. In operant conditioning, animals are learning more than the simple contiguity of food and behavior; they are learning that their behavior (R) causes the delivery of food (S^r). Contiguity is important, but is not the whole story.

In addition, psychologists have explored the question "What makes a reinforcer reinforcing?" That is to say, is there some set of stimuli that will "work" to increase the behaviors they follow in every single circumstance? The answer is that there is not some set of rewards that will always increase behavior in all circumstances. David Premack was important in outlining the fact that reinforcement is a relative, rather than an absolute, thing. Specifically, Premack suggested that behaviors in which an organism is more likely to engage serve to reinforce behaviors in which they are less likely to engage. In a specific example, he examined children given the option of playing pinball or eating candy. Some children preferred pinball and spent more of their time playing the game than eating the candy. The opposite was true of other children. Those who preferred pinball would increase their candy-eating behavior (R) in order to gain access to the pinball machine (S^r). Those who preferred eating candy would increase their pinball-playing behavior (R) in order to gain access to candy (S^r). Behaviors that a child initially preferred were effective in reinforcing behaviors that the child was less likely to choose—but not the other way around.

NEGATIVE CONSEQUENCES

Positive or rewarding outcomes are not the only consequences that govern behavior. In many cases, people respond in order to avoid negative outcomes or stop responding when doing so produces unpleasant events. These situations correspond to the operant procedures of avoidance and punishment. Many psychologists have advocated using reinforcement rather than punishment to alter behavior, not because punishment is necessarily less effective in theory but because it is usually less effective in practice. In order for punishers to be effective, they should be (among other things) strong, immediate, and consistent. This can be difficult to accomplish in practice. In crime, for example, many offenses may have occurred without detection prior to the punished offense, so punishment is not certain. It is also likely that an individual's court hearing, not to mention his or her actual sentence, will be delayed by weeks or even months, so punishment is not immediate. First offenses are likely to be punished less harshly than repeated offenses, so punishment gradually increases in intensity. In the laboratory, such a situation would produce an animal that would be quite persistent in responding, despite punishment.

In addition, punishment can produce unwanted side effects, such as the suppression of other behaviors, aggression, and the learning of responses to avoid or minimize punishing consequences. Beyond this, punishment requires constant monitoring by an external authority, whereas reinforcement typically does not. For example, parents who want to punish a child for a dirty room must constantly inspect the room to determine its current state. The child certainly is not going to point out a dirty room that will cause punishment. On the other hand, if rewarded, the child will bring the clean room to the parents' attention. This is not to suggest that punishment should necessarily be abandoned as one tool for controlling behavior. Rather, the effectiveness of punishment, like reinforcement, can be predicted on the basis of laboratory results.

INTERACTIONS AND BIOLOGICAL CONSTRAINTS

Though the distinction between classical and operant conditioning is very clear in principle, it is not always so clear in practice. This makes sense if one considers real-life learning situations. In many circumstances events in the environment are associated (occur together) in a predictable fashion, and behavior will have consequences. This can be true in the laboratory as well, but carefully designed experiments can be conducted to separate out the impact of classical and operant conditioning on behavior.

In addition, the effectiveness of both classical and operant conditioning is influenced by biological factors. This can be seen both in the speed with which classically conditioned taste aversions (as compared with other CRs) are learned and in the stimulation of natural food-related behaviors in operant superstition experiments. Related findings have demonstrated that the effects of rewarding behavior can be influenced by biology in other ways that may disrupt the conditioning process. In an article published in 1961, Keller and Marian Breland described their difficulties in applying the principles of operant conditioning to their work as animal trainers in the entertainment industry. They found that when trained with food reinforcement, natural behaviors would often interfere with the trained operant response—a phenomenon they called instinctive drift. From a practical point of view, their research suggested that to be successful in animal training, one must select operant responses that do not compete with natural food-related behaviors. From a scientific point of view, their research suggested that biological tendencies must be taken into account in any complete description of conditioning processes.

APPLICATIONS OF CONDITIONING TECHNOLOGY
Beyond being interesting and important in its own right, conditioning research also serves as a valuable tool in the psychological exploration of other issues. In essence, conditioning technology provides a means for asking animals questions—a way to explore interesting cognitive processes such as memory, attention, reasoning, and concept formation under highly controlled laboratory conditions in less complex organisms.

Another area of research is the field of behavioral neuroscience, a field that combines physiological and behavioral approaches in order to uncover the neurological mechanisms underlying behavior. For example, the impact of various medications and substances of abuse on behavior can be observed by administering drugs as reinforcing stimuli. It is interesting to note that animals will produce operant responses in order to receive the same drugs to which humans become addicted. However, in animals, the neurological mechanisms involved in developing addictions can be studied directly, using both behavioral and physiological experimental techniques in a way that would not be possible with human subjects, due to ethical considerations.

In addition, the principles of classical and operant conditioning have been used to solve very real human problems in a variety of educational and therapeutic settings, a strategy called applied behavior analysis. The principles of operant conditioning have been widely applied in settings where some degree of control over human behavior is desirable. Token economies are situations where specified behaviors, such as appropriate classroom behavior, are rewarded according to some schedule of reinforcement. The reinforcers are referred to as tokens because they need not have any rewarding value in and of themselves, but they can be exchanged for reinforcers at some later time. According to the principles of operant conditioning, people should increase the operant response in order to gain the reinforcers, and if the token economy is developed properly, that is exactly what occurs. If token economies sound rather familiar it is for good reason. Money is an extremely potent token reinforcer for most people, who perform operant responses (work) in order to receive token reinforcers (money) that can later be exchanged for primary reinforcers (such as food, clothing, shelter, or entertainment).

Finally, learning principles have been applied in clinical psychology in an effort to change maladaptive behaviors. Some examples include a procedure called systematic desensitization, in which the principles of classical conditioning are applied in an effort to treat phobias (irrational beliefs), and social skills training, in which operant conditioning is used to enhance communication and other interpersonal behaviors. These are only two examples of useful applications of conditioning technology to treat mental illness. Such applications suggest the need for ongoing research into basic conditioning mechanisms. We must fully understand conditioning principles in order to appropriately apply them in the effort to understand and improve the human condition.

SOURCES FOR FURTHER STUDY
Domjan, Michael. *Domjan and Burkhard's "The Principles of Learning and Behavior."* 3d ed. Pacific Grove, Calif.: Brooks/Cole, 1993. An extremely useful and complete textbook presenting classi-

cal as well as up-to-date research in the areas of operant and classical conditioning.

Schwartz, Barry, ed. *Psychology of Learning: Readings in Behavior Theory.* New York: W. W. Norton, 1984. A collection of reprinted articles on conditioning and learning.

Skinner, B. F. *Beyond Freedom and Dignity.* New York: Alfred A. Knopf, 1971. The influential B. F. Skinner outlines his philosophical views on conditioning and its importance in confronting world problems.

Linda R. Tennison

SEE ALSO: Aversion, implosion, and systematic desensitization; Behaviorism; Habituation and sensitization; Learned helplessness; Learning; Operant conditioning therapies; Pavlovian conditioning; Phobias; Reflexes.

Conduct disorder

TYPE OF PSYCHOLOGY: Psychopathology

FIELDS OF STUDY: Childhood and adolescent disorders

Children with conduct disorder show a deficit in social behavior. They are overtly hostile, disobedient, physically and verbally aggressive, vengeful, and destructive toward the property of others. Many of these children are diagnosed with antisocial personality disorder in adulthood. Genetic and environmental factors appear to interact as causative factors in the development of the disorder.

KEY CONCEPTS

- antisocial personality
- cohesive family model
- juvenile delinquency
- oppositional defiant disorder
- self-perpetuating cycle

INTRODUCTION

Conduct disorder is a psychiatric disorder that is first diagnosed during childhood or adolescence. It is characterized by a continuing pattern of antisocial behaviors that violate the rights of other people. The prevalence of conduct disorder is believed to be around 3 to 10 percent of the child and adoles-cent population. It is four to five times more common in males than in females. Conduct disorder in adolescence is considered to have serious consequences for society, as it contributes to the high rate of criminal offenses found in that age category. Although many children and adolescents engage in antisocial acts, persons with conduct disorder engage in the behavior in a repetitious and persistent fashion.

Actions that are associated with conduct disorder include bullying, lying, fighting, temper tantrums, destruction of property, stealing, setting fires, cruelty to both animals and people, physical assaults, truancy, and sexual assault. Early signs of conduct disorder can involve excessive arguments with parents, stubbornness, refusing to cooperate with adults, substance abuse, and vandalism. The prognosis for conduct disorder is poor, as it may lead to adult criminal behavior and problems in occupational and marital roles. Many persons with conduct disorder become involved with illegal drugs and excessive alcohol use.

A key factor associated with long-term negative outcomes for the child is the level of aggression shown by the individual. A particularly negative sign for long-term prognosis is the commission of sexual assaults. Highly aggressive children tend to remain aggressive over time and typically develop an antisocial personality in adulthood. About 25 to 40 percent of children with a conduct disorder that began before the age of ten have been found to develop an antisocial personality in adulthood. As adults, these individuals have a lack of remorse for hurting, mistreating, or stealing from other people. They do not conform to social norms nor do they care about other people. The adult with an antisocial personality acts in an impulsive fashion with disregard for the rights of others.

Another psychiatric disorder, oppositional defiant disorder, often precedes the development of conduct disorder. Oppositional defiant disorder is defined by a pattern of negativistic, defiant, disobedient, and hostile behavior toward authority figures. This disorder begins around six years of age, while conduct disorder typically does not begin until age nine. The specific signs of oppositional defiant disorder, according to the American Psychiatric Association, include often losing one's temper, often arguing with adults, actively defying or refusing an adult's requests, deliberately annoying people, blaming others for mistakes, being easily annoyed by others, being often angry and resentful, and being spiteful. The behaviors need to be present for at least six months to make the diagnosis. Almost all children with conduct disorder showed the signs of oppositional defiant disorder. Neither of these psychiatric disorders should be confused with juvenile delinquency, which is a legal term referring to violations of the law by minors.

DIAGNOSIS

According to the American Psychiatric Association, a diagnosis of conduct disorder is appropriate when a child shows a persistent and repetitive pattern of behavior in which the basic rights of others or societal norms and rules are violated. The pattern of behavior has to be shown in the following areas: aggression to people and animals, destruction of property, deceitfulness or theft, or serious violations of rules. Specific examples in these categories include intimidation of others, initiating physical fights, using weapons, stealing while confronting a victim, forcing someone into sexual activity, fire setting, deliberately destroying property, running away from home, and school truancy. The disturbances in behavior must cause significant impairment in social, academic, or occupational functioning. The pattern of misconduct must last for at least six months to warrant the diagnosis. Two types of conduct disorder are recognized. The childhood onset type occurs when the disruptions take place before age ten. An adolescent onset type is reserved for those persons who show the behavior after that age. Usually the early onset type of conduct disorder is related to serious outcomes and long-term problems.

CAUSAL FACTORS

The development of a conduct disorder appears to be the result of a combination of genetic and environmental factors. A genetic predisposition toward low verbal intelligence, mild psychoneurological problems, and a difficult temperament appears to set the stage for an early onset of conduct disorder in childhood. A self-perpetuating cycle emerges in the families of children with conduct disorder. The young child's difficult temperament can lead to problems in parent-child bonding. The mild psychoneurological deficits may make it difficult for the child to attain self-control of impulsive behav-

iors. As the child interacts with the environment, a lack of parental bonding and difficulty in controlling impulses leads to poor social skills and rejection from others. By the time the child is school age, readiness has not been attained for that structured setting. Consequently, when school is begun, the teacher cannot focus sufficient attention on the child to overcome the deficits in learning already experienced by the child. The cycle continues as disruptive behaviors grow in intensity in the new environments and further rejection takes place. Other children begin to exclude the aggressive and oppositional child with the conduct disorder, and this enhances the sense of isolation for that child. Soon the child is drawn to other children, typically older peers, who have already been isolated for their conduct problems. The child with conduct disorder may then seek companionship from peers who are antisocial. Associating with such individuals reinforces the disruptive behaviors. The combination of rejection by parents, peers, and teachers leads these children toward continuing isolation and alienation. Antisocial acts against people and property escalate as the children with conduct disorders band together.

Researchers have noted that the family situation of children with conduct disorder is filled with conflict and disharmony. Family discord and hostility are commonly expressed between family members. Frequently, the parents have an unstable marital relationship and experience disturbed emotional expression. They do not provide the child with a consistent pattern of guidance, acceptance, or affection. The parents are ineffective in their parenting behavior and provide little effective supervision or discipline. Children in these households do not learn respect for authority, nor do they learn how to succeed academically. As the child grows older, the parents withdraw from the child as they become fearful of demanding anything from their son or daughter. Basically, the children in these home environments are trained by family members in an indirect fashion to have antisocial tendencies.

A negative home environment is a powerful factor in the development of children who become violent. Research has shown that the biological parents of children with conduct disorder have a high rate of antisocial tendencies and criminal records. Frustrating and unstructured home environments promote the development of an early-onset form of

---

DSM-IV-TR Criteria for Oppositional Defiant Disorder (DSM code 313.81)

Pattern of negativistic, hostile, and defiant behavior

Lasts at least six months, with four or more of the following:
- often loses temper
- often argues with adults
- often actively defies or refuses to comply with adults' requests or rules
- often deliberately annoys others
- often blames others for his or her mistakes or misbehavior
- often touchy or easily annoyed by others
- often angry and resentful
- often spiteful or vindictive

Criterion met only if the behavior occurs more frequently than is typically observed in individuals of comparable age and developmental level

Behaviors cause clinically significant impairment in social, academic, or occupational functioning

Behaviors do not occur exclusively during the course of a psychotic or mood disorder

Criteria for Conduct Disorder not met

If the individual is age eighteen or older, criteria for Antisocial Personality Disorder not met

---

conduct disorder. Parents who are themselves antisocial provide inadequate models for healthy emotional growth. Children may find an environmental pull toward negative behaviors as they grow in a home environment that is frustrating and produces a sense of malaise. Negative environmental influences become greatest on the child with a genetic vulnerability and poor home situation.

TREATMENT OPTIONS
The focus for treatment is on the dysfunctional patterns of behavior found in the families of children with conduct disorder. One approach is called the cohesive family model of treatment. This method targets the ineffective parenting strategies found in these families. The child with conduct disorder has not been socialized to behave in socially accepted ways. Children learn to escape or avoid parental criticism by increasing their negative actions. When this happens, the parents show increasing amounts of anger, which serves as a model for the child to imitate. During treatment, cooperation from parents is needed in order to teach the most effective methods to control the child's negative actions. Behav-

ioral techniques based upon learning principles are used to train parents in parenting skills. Parents are taught to consistently accept and reward only positive behaviors shown by their children. The parents must learn to stop focusing their attention on the negative actions. Specific skills are taught so that parents learn how to establish appropriate rules for the child and implement appropriate consequences for breaking rules.

Children can be taught to improve their verbal skills as a way to enhance their participation in groups and educational settings. Problem-solving skills are promoted in the child so that problem behaviors can be identified and alternatives can be selected. Family therapy permits a therapist to witness inappropriate interactions between family members and suggest ways to effectively interact with one another.

In some cases, the child with a conduct disorder is removed from the home environment. Foster homes or institutional settings may be recommended as the last resort to stop the detrimental effects of the home setting on the child. The goal then becomes to intervene with the parents to teach effective parenting skills and then return the child when progress has been made. A problem with this strategy is that the child often perceives the foster home as an additional rejection by both parents and society. The new setting must have a pronounced atmosphere of acceptance in order to counteract this possible sense of rejection.

SOURCES FOR FURTHER STUDY
Biederman, J., S. Farone, and R. Russell. "Is Childhood Oppositional Defiant Disorder a Precursor to Adolescent Conduct Disorder? Findings from a Four-Year Follow-up of Children with ADHD." *Child and Adolescent Psychiatry* 47 (1996): 1193-1204. The role of oppositional defiant disorder in the development of conduct disorder is reviewed. The signs and symptoms associated with this disorder are described by the authors.

Cadoret, R., L. Leve, and E. Devor. "Genetics and Aggressive Behavior." *Psychiatric Clinics of North America 20 (1997): 301-322.* This article provides extensive details about behavior and genetic studies. The information is technical and knowledge of brain anatomy is useful.

Chamberlain, P., and J. Rosicky. "The Effectiveness of Family Therapy in the Treatment of Adolescents with Conduct Disorders and Delinquency." *Journal of Marital and Family Therapy* 21 (1995): 441-459. This article describes the importance of identifying dysfunctional patterns of family interactions in treating children with conduct disorder. Behavioral techniques are used to produce effective patterns of disciplining a child with this disorder.

Frick, P. *Conduct Disorders and Severe Antisocial Behavior.* New York: Plenum, 1998. This is an excellent resource for details about conduct disorder. The book provides extensive information about possible causes and an extended discussion about the antisocial actions associated with the disorder.

Grilo, C., D. Becker, and T. McGlashan. "Conduct Disorder, Substance Use Disorders, and Coexisting Conduct and Substance Use Disorders in Adolescent Inpatients." *American Journal of Psychiatry* 153 (1996): 914-920. Children with a conduct disorder are at risk of developing a number of other problem behaviors, including substance abuse. This article describes the possible coexisting problems to this disorder.

Hindshaw, S., and C. Andeson. "Conduct and Oppositional Defiant Disorder." In *Child Psychopathology*, edited by E. Mash and R. Barkley. New York: Guilford, 1996. This is a good exploration

---

DSM-IV-TR Criteria for Conduct Disorder

Repetitive and persistent pattern of behavior violating the basic rights of others or major age-appropriate societal norms or rules

Manifested by three or more of the following criteria in the past year, with at least one in the past six months:

AGGRESSION TO PEOPLE AND ANIMALS
- often bullies, threatens, or intimidates others
- often initiates physical fights
- has used a weapon that can cause serious physical harm
- has been physically cruel to people
- has been physically cruel to animals
- has stolen while confronting a victim (such as mugging, purse snatching, armed robbery)
- has forced someone into sexual activity

DESTRUCTION OF PROPERTY
- has deliberately engaged in fire setting with the intention of causing serious damage
- has deliberately destroyed others' property (other than by fire setting)

DECEITFULNESS OR THEFT
- has broken into someone else's house, building, or car
- often lies to obtain goods or favors or to avoid obligations
- has stolen items of nontrivial value without confronting a victim (such as shoplifting, forgery)

SERIOUS VIOLATIONS OF RULES
- often stays out at night despite parental prohibitions, beginning before age thirteen
- while living in parental or parental surrogate home, has run away from home overnight at least twice or once without returning for a lengthy period
- often truant from school, beginning before age thirteen

Behavior causes clinically significant impairment in social, academic, or occupational functioning

If the individual is age eighteen or older, criteria for Antisocial Personality Disorder not met

Severity:
- Mild: Few if any conduct problems exceeding those required for diagnosis or conduct problems causing only minor harm to others
- Moderate: Number of conduct problems and effect on others intermediate between "mild" and "severe"
- Severe: Many conduct problems exceeding those required for diagnosis or conduct problems causing considerable harm to others

DSM code based on age at onset:
- Childhood-Onset Type (DSM code 312.81): At least one criterion prior to age ten
- Adolescent-Onset Type (DSM code 312.82): Absence of any criteria prior to age ten
- Unspecified Onset (DSM code 312.89): Unknown

of the long-term consequences of conduct disorder. The authors provide information about the various outcomes seen in adulthood for persons with the diagnosis.

Kadzin, A. E. *Conduct Disorder in Childhood and Adolescence*. Newbury Park, Calif.: Sage, 1994. The author emphasizes the importance of the family and social context in the development of conduct disorder. Children's confusion over the parent-child relationship is considered to be a major cause of conduct disorder.

Frank J. Prerost

SEE ALSO: Anxiety disorders; Attachment and bonding in infancy and childhood; Attention-deficit hyperactivity disorder (ADHD); Bed-wetting; Child abuse; Childhood disorders; Dyslexia; Family life: Children's issues; Father-child relationship; Juvenile delinquency; Learning disorders; Misbehavior; Mother-child relationships; Parental alienation syndrome; Piaget, Jean; Prenatal physical development; Psychotherapy: Children; Schizophrenia: High-risk children; Separation and divorce: Children's issues; Sibling relationships; Stepfamilies; Stuttering; Teenage suicide; Violence by children and teenagers.

Confidentiality

TYPE OF PSYCHOLOGY: Psychological methodologies; psychotherapy

FIELDS OF STUDY: Ability tests; behavioral therapies; biological treatments; classic analytical themes and issues; cognitive therapies; evaluating psychotherapy; experimental methodologies; general constructs and issues; group and family therapies; humanistic therapies; intelligence assessment; interpersonal relations; methodological issues; organic disorders; personality assessment; psychodynamic therapies

Confidentiality is special state of protection designed to limit unauthorized disclosure of and ensure secrecy about certain types of relationships, communication, and other information.

KEY CONCEPTS
- competency
- consent
- duty to protect
- duty to warn
- ethics
- federal certificate of confidentiality
- institutional review board

INTRODUCTION

Confidentiality is important to psychologists in both its legal meaning and its ethical meaning. The legal meaning covers relevant federal, state, and local laws that may affect how much confidentiality can or must be maintained by a mental health practitioner. Ethics refers to moral principles or values; ethically, psychologists may choose to disclose or refuse to disclose information. Such values may be in conflict with the law but in the best interest of the individual research participant, therapeutic client, consultant client, or other party whose information, data, or relationships to the psychologist are being protected.

When individuals enter into a professional relationship with a psychologist, the psychologist provides information to the individual informing them of the limits of confidentiality pertaining to their relationship. In research projects, this takes place during the consent process, when the individual participant is giving permission and agreement to participate in the project proposed. Typically, the consent process is overseen by an institutional review board, a group of individuals who ensure that the rights of participants are properly addressed and protected. In therapy, this takes place during the intake process, before treatment begins. In any case, an individual may always disclose personal information as he or she wishes.

Legally, professionals such as psychologists are not allowed to disclose protected information unless given permission to do so by the client. However, some exceptions to this general rule exist. One exception is when clients admit that they may commit harm to themselves. In this situation, the psychologist takes appropriate action to prevent any harm coming to the individual. The obligation to do so is known as a duty to protect. A second exception is when clients admit that they may commit harm to another person. In this situation, the psychologist takes appropriate action to prevent harm coming to the individual identified as the target of harm. Typically this activity by the psychologist is understood as a duty to warn. It should be noted though that even with these duties, the information shared is only that necessary to achieve the duties to protect or warn. In either situation, what is imperative is that the individual entering into any agreements with the psychologist be competent. Competency refers to the legal fitness of the individual to make such a decision. This means the individual is mentally able to understand the consequences of the decision, can make a free choice in the decision, and is choosing to enact the decision.

IMPORTANCE

Confidentiality is an important protection for a number of reasons. First, confidentiality is important because it protects therapeutic clients, research participants, their private information, and their interests. Second, such protection allows free participation in therapeutic activities, research, and other programs without fear of having private information disclosed without permission. This encourages honesty and trust. Particularly for research endeavors, confidentiality maintains the integrity of the scientific work at hand by dissuading participants from altering their information so as to protect themselves, which could inadvertently damage the research.

Such concerns about confidentiality in research have led to the development of special certificates of confidentiality for government-funded research projects, such as those sponsored by the National Institutes of Health. With a federal certificate of confidentiality, data collected from an individual for the purpose of research are given special protection from forced disclosure (such as with a subpoena). The certificate allows study investigators and their research institutions to refuse to disclose identifying information about participants that could have adverse consequences for the participant if it were disclosed. Information protected could include name, address, identifying numbers such as a social security number, criminal history, fingerprints, voiceprints, photographs, history of mental health problems, alcohol or drug use history, human immunodeficiency virus (HIV) status, pregnancy termination, or other sensitive medical data, such as bodily tissues or genetic information. These protections allow participants to avoid potential consequences such as problems related to reputation, employability, financial standing, and insurability, among others. This protection extends to any type of proceeding (civil, legislative, administrative, or criminal), whether at the federal, state, or local level of government.

CONTEXT

In the United States, the Fourth Amendment to the Constitution asserts that people have a right to be secure in their persons, houses, papers, and effects, and protected against searches and seizures that are unreasonable or not founded in probable cause. With events such as the terrorist attacks of September 11, 2001, in the United States, concerns over confidentiality and the protection of private information were heightened. Debate raged over the need to balance individual desire for privacy with a strong need for information to protect national security.

In this same context, there are increasing requests for information from marketing companies, health care management organizations, and even the government for the purpose of federally funded research. At the same time, technology is increasing to the point that information shared by one individual could affect that person's entire family across generations. For instance, one person providing genetic information about family history of illness could affect the ability of that individual's family members to be insured or to be eligible for certain benefits. Confidentiality therefore is likely to develop as a more complex legal and ethical issue over time, as its relevance to whole systems of people, not just individuals, is recognized.

SOURCES FOR FURTHER STUDY

Alderman, Ellen, and Caroline Kennedy. *The Right to Privacy.* New York: Knopf, 1995. Describes privacy legally and informs readers of their basic privacy rights.

Dennis, Jill Callahan. *Privacy and Confidentiality of Health Information.* San Francisco: Jossey-Bass, 2000. Focuses on protecting private health information.

Givens, Beth, and the Privacy Rights Clearinghouse. *The Privacy Rights Handbook: How to Take Control of Your Personal Information.* New York: Harper-Collins, 1997. This book gives practical information about how to manage one's private information.

Smith, Robert Ellis, and Sangram Majumdar. *Ben Franklin's Web Site: Privacy and Curiosity from Plymouth Rock to the Internet.* Providence, R.I.: Privacy

Journal, 2000. This book provides a historical overview of privacy issues.

Nancy A. Piotrowski

SEE ALSO: Addictive personality and behaviors; Alcohol dependence and abuse; Behavior therapy; Behavioral family therapy; Brief therapy; Cognitive behavior therapy; Cognitive therapy; Couples therapy; Drug therapies; Gestalt therapy; Group therapy; Observational learning and modeling therapy; Person-centered therapy; Psychotherapy: Children; Psychotherapy: Effectiveness; Psychotherapy: Goals and techniques; Psychotherapy: Historical approaches; Rational-emotive therapy; Reality therapy; Shock therapy; Substance use disorders.

Consciousness

TYPE OF PSYCHOLOGY: Consciousness
FIELDS OF STUDY: Cognitive processes; sleep; thought

Consciousness refers to a number of phenomena, including the waking state; experience; and the possession of any mental state. Self-consciousness includes proneness to embarrassment in social settings; the ability to detect one's own sensations and recall one's recent actions; self-recognition; awareness of awareness; and self-knowledge in the broadest sense.

KEY CONCEPTS
- awareness
- alternate state of consciousness
- developmental aspects of consciousness
- evolution of consciousness
- history of consciousness study

INTRODUCTION

Many scientists have ignored the phenomena associated with consciousness because they deem it inappropriate for empirical investigation. However, there is clear evidence that this position is changing. Researchers in the fields of psychology, neurobiology, philosophy, cognitive science, physics, medicine, anthropology, mathematics, molecular biology, and art are now addressing major issues relating to consciousness. These researchers are asking such questions as what constitutes consciousness,

whether it is possible to explain subjective experience in physical terms, how scientific methods can best be applied to the study of consciousness, and the neural correlates of consciousness.

Moreover, new methods of brain imaging have helped clarify the nature and mechanisms of consciousness, leading to better understanding of the relationship between conscious and unconscious processes in perception, memory, learning, and other domains. These and other questions have led to a growing interest in consciousness studies, including investigations of properties of conscious experience in specific domains (such as vision, emotion, and metacognition) and a better understanding of disorders and unusual forms of consciousness, as found in blindsight, synesthesia, and other syndromes.

HISTORY OF CONSCIOUSNESS STUDY

The definition of consciousness proposed by English philosopher John Locke (1632-1704)—"the perception of what passes in a man's own mind"—has been that most generally accepted as a starting point in understanding the concept. Most of the philosophical discussions of consciousness, however, arose from the mind-body issues posed by the French philosopher and mathematician René Descartes (1596-1650). Descartes raised the essential questions that until recently dominated consciousness studies. He asked whether the mind, or consciousness, is independent of matter, and whether consciousness is extended (physical) or unextended (nonphysical). He also inquired whether consciousness is determinative or determined. English philosophers such as Locke tended to reduce consciousness to physical sensations and the information they provide. European philosophers such as Gottfried Wilhelm Leibniz (1646-1716) and Immanuel Kant (1724-1804), however, argued that consciousness had a more active role in perception.

The nineteenth century German educator Johann Friedrich Herbart (1776-1841) had the greatest influence on thinking about consciousness. His ideas on states of consciousness and unconsciousness influenced the German psychologist and physiologist Gustav Theodor Fechner (1801-1887), as well as the ideas of Sigmund Freud (1856-1939) on the nature of the unconscious.

The concept of consciousness has undergone significant changes since the nineteenth century, and the study of consciousness has undergone serious challenge as being unscientific or irrelevant to the real work of psychology. Nineteenth century scholars had conflicting opinions about consciousness. It was either a mental stuff different from everyday material or a physical attribute like sensation. Sensation, along with movement, separates humans and other animals from nonsensate and immobile lower forms of life. Scholars viewed consciousness as different from unconsciousness, such as occurred in sleep or under anesthesia. Whatever the theory, these scholars generally employed the same method, that of introspection.

EXPERIMENTAL STUDY

It was the German psychologist Wilhelm Max Wundt (1832-1920) who began the experimental study of consciousness in 1879 when he established his research laboratory. Wundt saw the task of psychology as the study of the structure of consciousness, which extended well beyond sensations and included feelings, images, memory, attention, duration, and movement. By the 1920's, however, behavioral psychology had become the major force in psychology. John Broadus Watson (1878-1958) was the leader of this revolution. He wrote in 1913, "I believe that we can write a psychology and never use the terms consciousness, mental states, mind . . . imagery and the like." Between 1920 and 1950, consciousness was either neglected in psychology or treated as a historical curiosity. Behaviorist psychology led the way in rejecting mental states as appropriate objects for psychological study. The inconsistency of introspection as method made this rejection inevitable. Neurophysiologists also rejected consciousness as a mental state but allowed for the study of the biological underpinnings of consciousness. Thus, brain functioning became part of their study. The neural mechanisms of consciousness that allow an understanding between states of consciousness and the functions of the brain became an integral part of the scientific approach to consciousness. Brain waves—patterns of electrical activity—correlate with different levels of consciousness. These waves measure different levels of alertness. The electroencephalograph provides an objective means for measuring these phenomena.

Beginning in the late 1950's, however, interest in the subject of consciousness returned, specifically in those subjects and techniques relating to altered states of consciousness: sleep and dreams, meditation, biofeedback, hypnosis, and drug-induced states. When a physiological indicator for the dream state was found, a surge in sleep and dream research followed. The discovery of rapid eye movement (REM) helped to generate a renaissance in consciousness research. Thus, during the 1960's there was an increased search for "higher levels" of consciousness through meditation, resulting in a growing interest in the practices of Zen Buddhism and yoga from Eastern cultures.

This movement yielded such programs as Transcendental Meditation, and these self-directed procedures of physical relaxation and focused attention led to biofeedback techniques designed to bring body systems involving factors such as blood pressure or temperature under voluntary control. Researchers discovered that people could control their brain-wave patterns to some extent, especially the alpha rhythms generally associated with a relaxed, meditative state. Those people interested in consciousness and meditation established a number of "alpha training" programs.

Hypnosis and psychoactive drugs also received great attention in the 1960's. Lysergic acid diethylamide (LSD) was the most prominent of these drugs, along with mescaline. These drugs have a long association with religious ceremonies in non-Western cultures. Fascination with these altered states of consciousness led to an increased interest in research on consciousness. As the twentieth century progressed, the concept of consciousness began to come back into psychology. Developmental psychology, cognitive psychology, and the influence of cognitive philosophy each played a role in influencing the reintroduction of the concept, more sharply etched, into the mainstream of psychology.

JEAN PIAGET

Jean Piaget, the great developmental psychologist, viewed consciousness as central to psychological study. Therefore, he sought to find ways to make its study scientific. To do so, Piaget dealt in great detail with the meaning of the subject-object and mind-body problems. Piaget argued that consciousness is not simply a subjective phenomenon; if it were, it would be unacceptable for scientific psychology. Indeed, Piaget maintained that conscious phenomena play an important and distinctive role in human behavior. Moreover, he directed research to examine the way in which consciousness is formed, its origins, stages, and processes. Consciousness is not an epiphenomenon, nor can psychologists reduce it to physiological phenomena. For Piaget, consciousness involves a constructed subjective awareness. It is a developmentally constructed process, not a product. It results from interaction with the environment, not from the environment's action on it: "[T]he process of becoming conscious of an action scheme transforms it into a concept; thus becoming conscious consists essentially in conceptualization."

There are two relationships necessary for the understanding of consciousness. The first is that of subject and object. The second is the relationship between cognitive activity and neural activity. Both are essential to getting at the process of cognition and its dynamic nature.

MEMORY AND ALTERED STATES

A variety of studies and experiments have explored the effects of certain variables on consciousness. For instance, it is important to ascertain the way in which variables that increase memorability in turn influence metamemory. Results have been inconsistent. However, it was found that when experimenters directed subjects to remember some items and forget others, there was an increase in recalling those items that experimenters were directed to remember. There was, nevertheless, no effect on the accuracy of what was remembered.

Sleep and dreams, hypnosis, and other altered states have provided another intriguing area of study for those interested in consciousness. The relationship of naps to alertness later in the day has proved of great interest to psychologists. In one study, nine healthy senior citizens, seventy-four to eighty-seven years of age, experienced nap and no-nap conditions in two studies each. Napping was for one and one-half hours, from 1:30 to 3:00 P.M. daily. The no-nap condition prohibited naps and encouraged activity in that period. Various tests were used to measure evening activity as well as record sleep. Aside from greater sleep in the twenty-four-hour period for those who had the ninety-minute nap, there was no difference on any other measure.

The threat simulation theory of dreaming holds that dreams have a biological function to protect the dream self. This dream self behaves in a defensive fashion. An empirical test of this theory con-

firmed the predictions and suggests that the theory has wide implications regarding the functions of consciousness.

The study of consciousness, then, has elucidated understanding of perception, memory, and action, created advances in artificial intelligence, and illustrated the philosophical basis of dissatisfaction with the dualistic separation of mind and body. Electrical correlates of states of consciousness have been discovered, as well as structures in the brainstem that regulate the sleep cycle. Other studies have looked at neural correlates in various states such as wakefulness, coma, the persistent vegetative state, the "locked-in" syndrome, akinetic mutism, and brain death. There are many other areas of consciousness in which neuroscience has made major advances.

An important problem neglected by neuroscientists is the problem of meaning. Neuroscientists are apt to assume that if they can see that a neuron's firing is roughly correlated with some aspect of the visual scene, such as an oriented line, then that firing must be part of the neural correlate of the seen line. However, it is necessary to explain how meaning can be expressed in neural terms as well as how the firing of neurons is connected to the perception of a face or person.

IMAGERY

Imagery is associated with memory, perception, and thought. Imagery occurs in all sensory modes. However, most work on imagery has neglected all but visual imagery. Concerns with imagery go back to the ancient Greek philosophers. Plato (c. 428-348 B.C.E.) and Aristotle (384-322 B.C.E.), for example, compared memory to a block of wax into which one's thoughts and perceptions stamp impressions. Aristotle gave imagery an important place in cognition and argued that people think in mental images. Early experimental psychologists, such as Wundt, carried on this notion of cognition.

Around 1901, Oswald Külpe (1862-1915) and his students at the University of Würzburg in Germany challenged these assumptions. However, these experiments employed introspective techniques, which Wundt and other attacked as being inconclusive. The controversy led to a rejection of mental imagery, introspection, and the study of consciousness itself. In the twentieth century, a movement toward seeing language as the primary analytical tool and a rejection of the old dominance of imagery came into fashion. The phenomenology of French philosopher and writer Jean-Paul Sartre (1905-1980) also led to a decline of interest in imagery.

A revival of research on imagery followed the cognitive science revolution of the 1960's and 1970's, contributing greatly to the rising scientific interest in mental representations. This revival stemmed from research on sensory deprivation and on hallucinogenic drugs. Studies in the role of imagery mnemonics also contributed to this reemergence of imagery studies.

CONCLUSION

As the concept of a direct, simple linkage between environment and behavior became unsatisfactory in the late twentieth century, the interest in altered states of consciousness helped spark new interest in consciousness. People are actively involved in their own behavior, not passive puppets of external forces. Environments, rewards, and punishments are not simply defined by their physical character. There are mental constructs involved in each of these. People organize their memories. They do not merely store them. Cognitive psychology, a new division of the field, has emerged to deal with these interests.

Thanks to the work of developmental psychologists such as Piaget, great attention is being given to the manner in which people understand, or perceive, the world at different ages. There are advances in the area of animal behavior stressing the importance of inherent characteristics that arise from the way in which a species has been shaped to respond adaptively to the environment. There has also been the emergence of humanistic psychologists, concerned with the importance of self-actualization and growth. Clinical and industrial psychology have demonstrated that a person's state of consciousness in terms of current feelings and thoughts is of obvious importance. Although the role of consciousness was often neglected in favor of unconscious needs and motivations, there are clear signs that researchers are interested in emphasizing once more the nature of states of consciousness.

SOURCES FOR FURTHER STUDY

Brann, E. T. H. *The World of the Imagination: Sum and Substance.* Savage, Md.: Rowman & Littlefield, 1991. This work discusses the role of imagination in cognition.

Chalmers, D. *The Conscious Mind: In Search of a Fundamental Theory.* New York: Oxford University Press, 1995. This study presents a clear summary of various theories of consciousness.

Greenfield, S. A. *Journey to the Centers of the Mind.* New York: W. H. Freeman, 1995. This is a study of biological influences in cognition.

Libet, B. *Neurophysiology of Consciousness: Selected Papers and New Essays by Benjamin Libet.* Boston: Birkhäuser, 1993. This work clearly presents the role of neurophysiology in conscious thought.

Weiskrantz, L. *Consciousness Lost and Found.* New York: Oxford University Press, 1997. A study of modes of consciousness and the manner in which psychologists have rediscovered the importance of the concept.

Frank A. Salamone

SEE ALSO: Consciousness: Altered states; Dementia; Dreams; Hallucinations; Hypnosis; Insomnia; Meditation and relaxation; Synesthesia; Thought: Inferential; Thought: Study and measurement; Virtual reality.

Consciousness: Altered states

TYPE OF PSYCHOLOGY: Consciousness
FIELDS OF STUDY: Cognitive processes

The investigation of altered states of consciousness began in psychology with the recognition that consciousness is not a fixed, unvarying state, but is in a continual state of flux. Consciousness can be altered by many chemical and nonchemical means, and there is some evidence to indicate that certain altered states are necessary for normal psychological functioning.

KEY CONCEPTS
- biofeedback
- circadian rhythm
- electroencephalogram (EEG)
- hypnagogic and hypnopompic states
- hypnosis
- meditation

- psychoactive drugs
- restricted environmental stimulation (RES)

INTRODUCTION

The great psychologist William James, in his 1890 textbook *The Principles of Psychology*, made the following now-famous observation regarding states of consciousness:

> Our normal waking consciousness, rational consciousness as we call it, is but one special type of consciousness, whilst all about it, parted from it by the filmiest of screens, there lie potential forms of consciousness entirely different.

James went on to say that the understanding of human psychological functioning would never be complete until these alternate states were addressed. Most psychologists would now acknowledge that a person's normal waking consciousness is readily subject to changes. These changes are referred to as altered states of consciousness. What constitutes a genuine altered state and how many such states may exist are both subjects of some controversy.

States of consciousness have always been central to the attempt to understand human nature. For example, every society of which any record exists has possessed both chemical and nonchemical means of altering consciousness.

From a historical point of view, Sigmund Freud (1856-1939) may have done more than any other theorist to stimulate interest in states of consciousness. Freud's psychoanalytic theory of personality held that there were three primary levels of consciousness: consciousness, preconsciousness, and unconsciousness. The conscious level includes mental activities of which one is unaware. The preconscious level consists of mental material of which one is currently unaware but that can be voluntarily recalled—roughly equivalent to memory. The unconscious level, which held the greatest interest for Freud, contains thoughts, feelings, memories, and drives that are blocked from awareness because they are unpleasant or arouse anxiety. In addition to his interest in these three levels of consciousness, Freud's interest in altered states at various points in his career was manifested in investigations of cocaine, hypnosis, and the analysis and interpretation of dreams.

In the early twentieth century, with the growth of behaviorism, which insisted that in order to be a science psychology should confine itself to investigating only objective, observable behavior, the study of altered states of consciousness fell out of favor. Events in the larger culture during the 1960's and 1970's, however, helped stimulate interest in altered states within psychology. During this period, efforts to expand consciousness by means of drugs, meditation, Eastern religious practice, and new ways of relating to oneself and others led to the active study of altered states of consciousness. The attempts of psychologists to study altered states of experience will perhaps be viewed in the future as a landmark in the development of psychology as a science. The willingness of psychology to explore the novel realms that altered states represent may help to expand the understanding of both consciousness and reality.

VARIATIONS IN CONSCIOUSNESS

Physiological psychologist Karl Pribram lists the following states of consciousness: states of ordinary perceptual awareness; states of self-consciousness; dream states; hypnagogic and hypnopompic states (the transition states, characterized by vivid dreamlike imagery, that occur as one goes into and comes out of sleep); ecstatic states (such as the orgiastic experience); socially induced trance or trancelike states; drug-induced states; social role states; linguistic states (for example, a multilingual person thinking in one, rather than another, language); translational states (as when one linguistic universe is being recorded or translated in another); ordinary transcendental states (such as those experienced by an author in the throes of creative composition); extraordinary transcendental states that are achieved by special techniques; other extraordinary states (such as those that allow "extrasensory awareness"); meditational states; dissociated states, as in the case of pathological multiple personality; and psychomotor states manifest in temporal-lobe epilepsies. To that list could be added the following additional states: sleep; the hyperalert state, characterized by increased vigilance while one is awake; the lethargic state, characterized by dulled, sluggish mental activity; states of hysteria, with intense feeling and overpowering emotion; regressive states, such as senility; daydreaming with rapidly occurring thoughts that bear little relation to the external environment; coma; sleep deprivation; sensory overload or deprivation; and prolonged strenuous exercise. This list is by no means exhaustive.

Some of these states clearly represent greater degrees of alteration of the "normal" consciousness than others. There is, however, no universal agreement on what constitutes the normal state of consciousness. Charles Tart and other authors have suggested that what is usually called "normal" consciousness is not a natural, given state, but a construction based mainly on cultural values and inputs. In any case, some altered states of consciousness are experienced on a daily basis by everyone, while others are much more rare and may require great effort or special circumstances to achieve.

INFLUENCES ON ALTERED CONSCIOUSNESS
Some alterations in conscious functions are induced by daily changes in biological rhythms. Bodily events that occur in roughly a twenty-four-hour cycle are referred to as circadian rhythms, from the Latin *circa* ("about") and *dies* ("day"). It is thought that these cycles are created by natural events, such as the light-dark cycle, and by other cues in the daily routine, such as mealtimes. The sleeping-waking cycle is the major circadian rhythm, but there are others, such as fluctuations in body temperature. This daily body-temperature cycle appears to be directly related to levels of mental activity. When all external cues are removed, circadian rhythms extend to about twenty-five hours. As a result of prolonged isolation, the cycle can become completely distorted, with periods of up to forty hours of waking followed by periods of up to twenty-two hours of sleep. When the change is gradual in this way, the individual has a distorted sense of time and believes that he or she is experiencing normal periods of sleep and waking. Abrupt changes in circadian rhythms, as when one crosses several time zones, are what lead to that sleepy, uncomfortable feeling known as jet lag.

In addition to biological rhythms, there are other regular daily variations in consciousness. On the way to sleep each night, people enter a kind of "twilight" period known as the hypnagogic state. The state of consciousness that is entered immediately before waking is called the hypnopompic state. In both these states, one is partially asleep and partially continuing to process environmental stimuli. Both are characterized by vivid imagery, and many people have reported creative insight during these periods.

STAGES OF SLEEP
Sleep itself is not a unified state, but consists of five distinct stages: one stage of rapid eye movement (REM) sleep and four stages of nonrapid eye movement (NREM) sleep. During a typical night's sleep, one moves in and out of these stages four or five times. REM sleep is primarily associated with periods of dreaming. Sleeping subjects awakened during a period of REM sleep report having just experienced a dream about 80 percent of the time, compared with less than 10 percent when NREM sleep is interrupted. Psychologists are still unclear on exactly why humans need to sleep, but the need for periods of REM sleep might be part of the reason. When sleeping subjects are deprived of REM sleep (and their NREM sleep is undisturbed), they often show many of the symptoms of not having slept at all. Also, when later given the opportunity for uninterrupted sleep, they spend a greater percentage of time in the REM stage, as if they were trying to make up for the lost REM sleep (this is referred to as the REM-rebound effect). The REM-rebound effect is lessened if the individual is encouraged to engage in an increased amount of daydreaming, which indicates a possible connection between day and night dreams.

PSYCHOACTIVE DRUGS
The use of psychoactive drugs is a common method for altering consciousness. These drugs are chemical substances that act on the brain to create psychological effects and are typically classified as depressants, stimulants, narcotics (opiates), hallucinogens, or antipsychotics. Several drugs, such as nicotine, caffeine, and alcohol, are so much a part of the lifestyle in modern society that users may not even think of them as drugs. The use of many psychoactive drugs can lead to physical and/or psychological dependence, or addiction, as the body/mind develops a physiological/psychological need for the drug. The body can also build up a tolerance for a drug, which means that higher and higher doses are necessary to produce the same effects. Once addiction has been established, discontinuing the use of the drug can lead to withdrawal symptoms, such as nausea, fever, convulsions, and hallucinations, among others, which can sometimes be fatal.

The type of altered state produced by a psychoactive drug depends on the class to which the drug belongs. Depressants, such as alcohol, barbiturates, and tranquilizers, depress central nervous system functioning and usually produce relaxation, anxiety reduction, and—eventually—sleep. Narcotics (opiates), such as heroin, morphine, and codeine, depress activity in some areas of the cortex but create excitation in others, producing feelings of euphoria and providing relief from pain. Stimulants, such as amphetamines, cocaine, caffeine, and nicotine, stimulate central nervous system activity, producing feeling of alertness and euphoria and lack of appetite. Hallucinogens, such as lysergic acid diethylamide (LSD), mescaline, and psilocybin, can produce hallucinations, delusions, exhilaration, and, in some cases, quasi-mystical experiences.

Hypnosis and Meditation

Two popular nonchemical techniques for altering consciousness are hypnosis and meditation. Hypnosis was first discovered in the eighteenth century by Franz Mesmer, and its history has been full of controversy ever since. An altered state is induced in hypnosis by the suggestive instructions of the hypnotist, usually involving progressive relaxation. The hypnotized subject often appears to be asleep but remains alert inside, exhibiting varying degrees of responsiveness to the suggestions of the hypnotist. Only about 10 percent of the population can enter the deepest hypnotic state, while another 10 percent cannot be hypnotized at all. The rest of the population can achieve some degree of hypnotic induction. Psychologists argue about whether hypnosis is a genuine altered state or simply a form of role playing.

There is less controversy regarding meditation as a true altered state. Since the mid-1960's, there has been extensive research on the physiological changes that occur during meditation. Some of the findings include a decrease in oxygen consumption of 16 percent during meditation (compared with an 8 percent drop during the deepest stage of sleep), a cardiac output decrease of 25 percent, and an average slowing of the heart rate by five beats per minute. During meditation, electroencephalogram (EEG) patterns are dominated by the alpha rhythm, which has been associated with relaxation. An EEG is a graphic recording of the electrical activity of brain waves. Researchers R. K. Wallace and Herbert Benson believed that there was sufficient physiological evidence to justify calling the meditative state a "fourth major state of consciousness" (along with waking, dreaming, and sleeping), which they termed a "wakeful, hypometabolic [reduced metabolic activity] state." Beginning meditators usually report feelings of relaxation and "ordinary thoughts," while advanced practitioners sometimes report transcendental experiences of "consciousness without content."

Applications of Hypnosis

Research on altered states of consciousness has led to many benefits. The analgesic properties of hypnosis were verified in research conducted by Ernest Hilgard at Stanford University. He found that hypnotic suggestion could be used to reduce or eliminate experimentally induced pain. Even though subjects were not consciously aware of the pain, Hilgard found that, with the right questions, he could uncover a "hidden observer," a dissociated aspect of the subject's conscious awareness that did monitor the feelings of pain. Hilgard reports that hypnotic relief from pain has been reported for the chronic pain of arthritis, nerve damage, migraine headaches, and cancer. For individuals who are unable to be anesthetized because of allergic reactions or fear of needles, hypnosis is often used as an effective substitute for the control of pain. It has been effectively applied in cases involving dental work, childbirth, burns, abdominal surgery, and spinal taps. Hypnotic suggestion has also been effective in reducing the nausea associated with cancer chemotherapy.

The use of hypnosis to recover forgotten memories is much more controversial. One dramatic phenomenon displayed with certain hypnotic subjects is age regression, in which the individual not only is able to recall vividly childhood memories but also seems to reenact behaviors from childhood, including body postures, voice, and handwriting characteristics of a given age. There is no way of knowing, however, whether this represents true recall or is simply a type of fantasy and role playing. Hypnosis has also been used to enhance the memories of crime witnesses in court proceedings. There is evidence, however, that actual recall does not become more accurate and that the witness may be unintentionally influenced by the suggestions of the hypnotist, which could lead to inaccuracies and distortions in the "remembered" events. For this reason, courts in many states automatically disqualify testimony obtained by means of hypnosis.

BENEFITS OF MEDITATION

Research on the physiological effects of meditation led to the application of meditative techniques as a treatment to combat stress-related illnesses. Meditators have often experienced significant decreases in such problems as general anxiety, high blood pressure, alcoholism, drug addiction, insomnia, and other stress-related problems. Researchers have also found that the scores of meditators on various psychological tests have indicated general mental health, self-esteem, and social openness. Many psychologists argue, however, that these effects are not unique to meditation and can be produced by means of other relaxation techniques. Meditation researcher Robert Ornstein has suggested that the long-term practice of meditation may induce a relative shift in hemispheric dominance in the brain from the left hemisphere, which is associated with such linear processes as language and logical reasoning, to the right hemisphere, which is associated with nonlinear processes such as music perception and spatial reasoning. Consistent with this idea are findings that meditators are better on certain right-hemispheric tasks such as remembering musical tones but worse on verbal problem-solving tasks that involve the left hemisphere.

Early research on advanced meditators in India indicated that they could exhibit control over what are normally autonomic processes in the body—for example, speeding up or slowing down the heart rate at will, stopping the heart for up to seventeen seconds, controlling blood flow to different areas of the body, and controlling brain-wave patterns at will. At first, these results were met with skepticism, but it is now known that humans and animals can learn to control previously involuntary processes by using a technique known as biofeedback. Through biofeedback training, an individual who is connected to a special measuring device can monitor autonomic events such as blood pressure, skin temperature, and muscle tension. Having this information can allow the individual gradually to gain control over these autonomic processes. Biofeedback techniques have been applied to an enormous variety of clinical problems. EEG biofeedback, for example, has been used to train epileptics to emit brain-wave patterns that are incompatible with those that occur during brain seizures. Other disorders that have been successfully treated by means of biofeedback include cardiac disorders, high blood pressure, tension headaches, anxiety, and neuromuscular disorders such as cerebral palsy.

SENSORY DEPRIVATION

Other applications have grown out of research on altered states of consciousness produced by restricting sensory stimulation from the environment. Researchers in the 1950's completed extensive studies on the effects of prolonged sensory deprivation. Subjects placed in soundproof isolation chambers with translucent goggles to eliminate vision and padded arm tubes to minimize touch sensation often experienced negative psychological effects after about a day. Most subjects suffered from extreme boredom, slowed reaction time, and impaired problem-solving ability. Some subjects reacted to sensory deprivation by creating their own internally generated sights and sounds in the form of hallucinations. These results led to the institution of special procedures to help reduce the effects of sensory deprivation in certain occupations: for example, airline pilots on long night flights, astronauts living for prolonged periods in tiny space capsules, and individuals working in isolated weather stations. A controlled form of sensory deprivation known as restricted environmental stimulation therapy (REST) has been used to reduce the effects of overarousal and hyperactivity. REST sessions usually involve floating in heavily salted warm water in a dark, soundproof tank. Most subjects find this floating sensation very pleasant, and there have been many reports of long-term reductions in high blood pressure and other stress-related problems.

ARGUMENT FOR STATE-SPECIFIC SCIENCES

Although traditional scientific methods are poorly suited to the study of consciousness, many beneficial tools that can be used to measure the physiological correlation of altered states, such as the electroencephalograph, have been developed as an outgrowth of the study of states of consciousness.

Psychologist Charles Tart suggested the creation of state-specific sciences. In reaching this conclusion, he argues that any particular state of consciousness (including ordinary waking) is a semiarbitrary construction—a specialized tool that is useful for some things but not for others and that contains large numbers of structures shaped by a particular culture's value judgments. Thus, science is observation and conceptualization carried out within the highly selective framework provided by a culturally determined ordinary state of consciousness. Tart suggests that, since altered states of consciousness often represent radically different ways of organizing observations and reworking conceptualizations of the universe (including oneself), if the scientific method were applied to developing sciences within various states of consciousness, there would be sciences based on radically different perceptions, logics, and communications, and thus science as a whole would gain new perspectives that would complement the existing one.

Regardless of whether this suggestion is taken seriously, it is clear that the study of states of consciousness has achieved legitimacy in scientific psychology. The investigation so far has revealed that human consciousness is much more diverse and varied than many psychologists previously believed.

SOURCES FOR FURTHER STUDY

Flannagan, Owen J. *Dreaming Souls: Sleep, Dreams, and the Evolution of the Mind.* New York: Oxford University Press, 1999. A professor of philosophy, experimental psychology, and neurobiology proposes that dreams are an unplanned side effect of the evolution of a human mind designed to "have experiences." Reviews current research and theory on the nature and functions of dreaming as well as presenting his own thesis.

Hilgard, Ernest Ropiequet. *Divided Consciousness: Multiple Controls in Human Thought and Action.* Expanded ed. New York: John Wiley & Sons, 1986. A discussion of consciousness by one of the most respected experimental psychologists. Included are discussions on the hidden observer phenomenon in hypnosis and on other dissociation phenomena such as multiple personality, amnesia, and fugue states.

Hobson, J. Allen. *The Dream Drugstore: Chemically Altered States of Consciousness.* Cambridge, Mass.: MIT Press, 2001. Discusses the natural and voluntarily altered chemistry of the brain and its effects on human consciousness. Despite the somewhat psychedelic tone of the title, Hobson addresses the contemporary reliance on antidepressants such as Prozac as well as the "recreational" drugs of underground culture, and presents the possible connections between dreaming

states, drug-induced states, and mental illnesses in a nonjudgmental fashion.

Ornstein, Robert Evan, ed. *The Nature of Human Consciousness.* San Francisco: W. H. Freeman, 1973. This anthology contains essays by many of the pioneers in the psychological study of altered states of consciousness, including Carl Jung, Roberto Assagioli, Arthur Deikman, and many others. Topics include meditative states, psychosynthesis, Sufism, and synchronicity.

_____. *The Psychology of Consciousness.* 2d rev. ed. New York: Penguin Books, 1986. This is considered a classic text on altered states of consciousness. It provides in-depth discussions of the psychology of meditation and the relationship of altered states to hemispheric differences in the brain.

Ward, Colleen A., ed. *Altered States of Consciousness and Mental Health: A Cross-cultural Perspective.* Thousand Oaks, Calif.: Sage Publications, 1989. A collection of papers assessing the mental health value and use of altered states of consciousness from a non-Western perspective.

Wolman, Benjamin B., and Montague Ullman, ed. *Handbook of States of Consciousness.* New York: Van Nostrand Reinhold, 1986. This is an excellent sourcebook on psychological theory and research on altered states of consciousness. Discusses, in addition to the topics covered in this article, trance states, lucid dreams, ultradian rhythms, and many other things.

Oliver W. Hill, Jr.

SEE ALSO: Circadian rhythms; Consciousness; Dementia; Dreams; Hallucinations; Hypnosis; Insomnia; Meditation and relaxation; Synesthesia; Thought: Inferential; Thought: Study and measurement; Virtual reality.

Constructivist psychology

TYPE OF PSYCHOLOGY: Psychotherapy
FIELDS OF STUDY: Adulthood; behavioral and cognitive models; behavioral therapies; cognitive therapies; personality theory

Constructivist psychology recognizes that people actively create the realities to which they respond. Peo-

ple organize their experience by actively constructing templates of meaning that help them interpret their past, negotiate their present, and anticipate their future.

KEY CONCEPTS
- conversation
- meanings
- narratives
- philosophy
- psychotherapy

INTRODUCTION

One tenet of constructivist thought is that the narratives that people tell serve two functions. One, they are organizational, allowing people to account for the plot structure of their past. Two, they are anticipatory, orienting people toward a meaningful future. Our stories are who we are.

Another tenet of constructivist thought is that the nuances of people's construction of the world are what is important, not whether this construction is right or wrong. A constructivist emphasizes developing a viable, workable construction of people, things, and events, rather than an accurate representation of absolute reality. People can construct multiple meanings for the events in their lives, each meaning may help them to understand and respond creatively to their experience. The *Journal of Constructivist Psychology*, formerly the *International Journal of Personal Construct Psychology*, contains empirical research, conceptual analyses, critical reviews, and occasionally case studies that further explore aspects of constructivist psychology.

ROOTS

There is no single founder of constructivist psychology, but it has roots in philosophy. Some early contributors are the German philosopher Immanuel Kant (1724-1804), British psychologist Frederic C. Bartlett (1886-1969), and Swiss psychologist Jean Piaget (1896-1980).

Kant believed that experience and sensation were not passively written into a person, but rather that the mind is an active, form-giving structure that transforms and coordinates data into integrated thought. For example, a man may believe that all women are inferior to all men. At committee meetings, this man ignores women, devalues their contributions, and forgets that women made helpful suggestions or recommendations. This man has inadvertently constructed a world that fits his preconceived ideas.

Bartlett applied constructivist concepts in his investigations of human memory. In classical research on remembering, Bartlett maintained that memories were reconstructed out of bits and pieces of recollected information. For example, when a person witnesses a crime, she does not store intact, unchangeable photographs of it. Rather, her impressions are ongoing, and can be shaped by subsequent questioning, comments, and other information such as what she reads in the newspaper.

Piaget chronicled how children's cognitive schemas change as a function of maturation. Piaget documented how children do more than simply learn facts; they actually change the way they think as they mature. For example, a four-year-old will look at one set of ten pennies in a widely spaced row and believe that they are more pennies than a second set of fifteen closely spaced pennies, even though this child can count accurately. At age seven, in contrast, this same child will grasp that the pennies are unchanged by how closely they are packed together, and will know that the second set contains more pennies.

PSYCHOTHERAPY

Seen through a constructivist lens, psychotherapy involves a quest for relatedness, connection, and mutuality of meaning in spite of uniqueness. The psychotherapist must join with the client to develop a refined map of his or her often inarticulate constructions by focusing on personal meanings, the constructions of roles, and the relationship between client and therapist.

Constructivists distrust highly standardized procedures for modifying human behavior. Likewise, constructivists oppose applying universal categories of disorders that fail to capture the richness and subtlety of any given individual. For example, a constructivist would resist using a diagnosis of major depression because this dry category fails to convey any information about how the patient makes meaning out of life. Treatment or diagnostic manuals cannot accommodate the individual person or the specific relationship.

Further, constructivists resist viewing the therapist as an expert who makes the client more functional or adaptive. Rather, constructivists grant that therapist and client are both experts, and no one knows the client's world or experience better than the client. The constructivist recognizes that because the client's constructions are working fictions rather than established facts, they are amenable to alternative interpretations.

Because emotional adjustment is a not simply a straightforward matter of making one's thoughts realistic and in line with the observable world, constructivist therapists draw the client's attention to troubling discrepancies between working models of self and world, and moment-to-moment experiencing. For example, the client views herself as calm and rational, yet she speaks in a pressured way, grips the chair strongly, and has a frown on her face, all of which suggest anger or another strong emotion. One goal is not to dispute negative emotions, but to intensively explore the emotions and extend her self-awareness in the direction of greater complexity and integration. Another goal is to develop new meanings. For example, the therapist might ask her to speak aloud in the critical voice of her conscience. As she angrily delineates shortcomings, she might realize the resemblance to her mother's criticisms. Therapy might help her synthesize her self-contempt and her need for comfort into a new self-acceptance.

Constructivist therapists who treat the entire family view therapy as a conversation whose goal is to alter the whole system. The therapist functions not as an expert who gives answers, but more as a conversation manager who promotes exchanges between family members that dissolve old problems by helping people talk about them in new ways and reach new perspectives.

In a constructivist view, human knowing is more than simply developing realistic mental maps of an external world. Rather, a person actively creates a narrative by binding past experiences and ongoing life events into meaningful units across time, themes, and persons.

SOURCES FOR FURTHER STUDY

Lyddon, William J. "Forms and Facets of Constructivist Psychology." In *Constructivism in Psychotherapy*, edited by Robert A. Neimeyer and Michael J. Mahoney, 1990. An academic looks at the background and forms of constructivism.

Neimeyer, Greg J., ed. *Constructivist Assessment: A Casebook*. Newbury Park, Calif.: Sage Publications, 1993. Specific examples help clarify assessment issues in constructivism.

Neimeyer, Robert A. "Constructivist Psychotherapies." In *Encyclopedia of Psychology*. Washington, D.C.: American Psychological Association, 2000. An overview with background about the philosophical roots of constructivism.

Neimeyer, Robert A., and Alan E. Stewart. "Constructivist and Narrative Psychotherapies." In *Handbook of Psychological Change*, edited by C. R. Snyder and Rick E. Ingram. New York: Wiley, 2000. Gives a clear, thorough overview of constructivist and narrative psychotherapy.

Lillian M. Range

SEE ALSO: Behavior therapy; Cognitive therapy; Emotions; Memory; Personality theory; Piaget, Jean.

Consumer psychology

TYPE OF PSYCHOLOGY: Cognition

FIELDS OF STUDY: Attitudes and behavior; cognitive processes; thought

Psychologists have investigated many aspects of consumer behavior; the ultimate goal of nearly all research on consumers is to understand how consumers obtain and process information and why they choose some goods and services and not others.

KEY CONCEPTS

- attitude
- behavioral intention
- belief
- compensatory rules
- subjective norm

INTRODUCTION

The decision-making approach to understanding consumer behavior follows from the assumption that the consumer is someone who seeks and takes in information from numerous sources, processes it, and then makes a selection from a set of alternatives. A major proponent of this view is James R. Bettman. The essence of his theory, presented in *An Information Processing Theory of Consumer Choice* (1979), is an explanation of how consumers react to information—from advertisers, friends, family, salespeople, and so on. The theory integrates six components of information processing: limitations in the human capacity to process information; the motivation to move from some initial state to a desired state; attention to and perceptual encoding of information; the search for information from memory and the external environment, and the evaluation of this information; decision processes; and the effects of consumption and learning. All these components are related through the construct of choice. Put another way, one becomes motivated, pays attention, obtains and evaluates information, learns, and compares alternatives in order to reach a goal. Because of its comprehensive nature, Bettman's theory of consumer choice has been highly influential in the academic and marketing communities.

The information-processing and decision-making perspectives on consumer purchases stand in sharp contrast to an alternative view, called behavioral influence, which presumes that consumers respond directly to pressures of the environment and give little or no conscious thought to their purchases. There is some evidence that consumer purchase decisions can be influenced by factors (such as music) of which they are unaware. Hence, consumers can be influenced by factors that they cannot evaluate and weigh in a decision process. This raises special concerns about methods of protecting consumers.

Perhaps the most useful and enduring theory to explain consumer behavior is Martin Fishbein and Icek Azjen's theory of reasoned action. This theory states that behavior results from an intention. For example, the purchasing of a product is a consequence of an intention to purchase that product. Thus, what is important to understand is how people form intentions. Consumers form intentions by taking into account two types of information. One is their overall evaluation of the product. The other is the subjective norms supporting purchase of the product. According to this theory, people plan to purchase a product if they evaluate it positively and believe that their purchase of it would be approved by those who are important to them. Because this theory emphasizes attitudes concerning a behavior toward an object and not only the object itself, it has successfully predicted many behaviors that attitudes alone could not.

In reality, the extent to which information is sought, evaluated, and weighed in a decision process on the part of a consumer depends greatly on the extent to which the consumer is involved in the process. The complexity of the decision process varies with consumer involvement. If the consumer is relatively uninvolved, the search for information is likely to be limited, with little evaluation of alternatives. With such routine decision making, there is little opportunity for the formation of attitudes toward the product—until after purchase or consumption. Involvement is thought to be a result of the personality of the consumer, the nature of the product, and characteristics of the situation. Consumers who are more self-confident, younger, educated, or less experienced with the product category tend to engage in a more extensive information search. Consumers show greater information search for products with higher perceived financial, performance, social, or physical risk. Situational factors such as amount of time, quantity of product, or store alternatives also help determine the extent of information search.

The consumer's decision to buy involves two major components: what brand to buy and where to purchase it. The decision process used to purchase a product can be classified as either compensatory or noncompensatory. With a compensatory rule, only the overall evaluation is important. This means that high evaluations on one dimension can compensate for low ones on another. In contrast, a noncompensatory rule results in a product being eliminated if it falls below an acceptable level on one dimension, regardless of its standing on other dimensions.

The decision process has been monitored by a variety of techniques to learn whether compensatory or noncompensatory rules are being used. Another objective of studying the consumer-choice process is to learn how information is selected and used. Researchers have used eye-movement monitors, computerized information displays, and information boards to track the order and extent of information search. Research by cognitive psychologists has shown that people tend to compare products on a single attribute rather than forming overall evaluations of each product and then making comparisons. This points to the value of displaying information such as unit price or nutritional values, which facilitates comparisons across products.

THE DIFFICULTIES OF PREDICTION

The prediction of behavior on the basis of attitudes has always been very complex. While it is true that people who have a positive attitude toward a product buy more of it than those who do not, other hypothesized links between attitudes and behavior simply do not hold. For example, lifestyle surveys have shown an increasing trend toward the belief that meal preparation should take as little time as possible. Yet during the same time period in which these surveys were conducted, sales of frozen pizza remained constant, and sales of frozen dinners fell.

Along similar lines, attitudes toward advertisements do not necessarily correlate with attitudes toward the product being advertised, let alone with purchase of the product. Even a specific attitude may fail to predict behavior toward an object. To demonstrate this, one might ask a friend to describe her attitude toward a Mercedes (or Porsche) and toward a Ford Pinto. The attitude of many people toward the former is far more favorable, but in reality they are less likely to purchase their preferred make of automobile.

One reason the theory of reasoned action has been successful is that it does not attempt to link attitudes to behaviors in general. Because of this, the prediction of specific behaviors toward "attitude objects" can be achieved. This theory can also be applied to changing specific behaviors. For example, if a person does not intend to engage in a safety practice, a traditional attitude-change approach would attempt to persuade the person of the value of the practice. Fishbein and Azjen's theory, however, suggests an alternative: persuading the person of the existence of subjective norms supporting the safety practice. This approach is not suggested by any other theoretical perspective on consumer behavior.

The debates about information and consumer decision making have had an impact on public policy and regulatory activities. William Wilkie identifies three concerns in the policy arena, all of them relating to the type, amount, and form of information that should be provided to consumers. First is the goal of providing consumers with complete information. Only by being fully informed can people spend their time, money, and effort in their best interest. Yet complete information may be impossible, and, even if it is available, the consumer may be unwilling or unable to process it all in decision making.

The second objective of public policy is to provide information that is "choice-neutral." Since the marketing community presents information that will favor particular brands, public policy provides balance with an emphasis on objective information. The last, and most difficult, public policy application concerns trade-offs between the freedom of marketers to control information dissemination and the costs and benefits of information to consumers. This is likely to remain a politically controversial matter.

An understanding of the decision rules used by consumers can be applied effectively in marketing. The use of noncompensatory rules is encouraged by product ratings of critical factors such as safety. It is easy to eliminate those brands that do not possess a certain rating or "seal of approval" from further consideration. Another application of this principle can be seen in attempts to create the belief that consideration of a particular attribute should dominate the choice process. By stressing price and only price, the marketer is in effect telling the consumer that no other attributes are relevant. No matter how competing brands may be evaluated on other attributes, they cannot compensate for inferior positions on the price dimension.

A good illustration of strategies to promote noncompensatory decision rules can be seen in the environmental movement. By focusing consumers on the environmental impact of their purchases, marketers prevent other attributes from being taken into consideration. Sometimes this can lead to the purchase of one product over another, as in the case of cloth rather than disposable diapers; or one brand of the product may be chosen over alternatives, as in the case of nonchlorine rather than chlorine bleach or a high- rather than a low-energy-efficient appliance. In the most extreme cases, noncompensatory rules in decision making can lead to "negative purchases": If all brands of tuna fish are obtained through techniques that kill dolphins, no brand is bought. Similarly, consumption of products with possible health hazards falls if a single dimension dominates information search and noncompensatory rules are used by consumers. No price reduction or rebate will induce one to purchase any brand if the product itself is judged unacceptable along the health dimension. One way of inhibiting such negative purchase decisions is to create ambiguity about the actual health hazards of the product or about information on product risks. With an overload of information that is difficult to process effectively, the consumer may become more reluctant to deem a product below the threshold necessary for purchase.

ADVERTISING AND CONSUMPTION

There have historically been three independent forces stimulating research on consumer behavior. One arises from the desire to influence consumers. Consumer decision-making research combines with advertising and marketing to create desires for products, preferences for brands, and patterns of consumption. An opposing force encouraging consumer behavior research is the desire to protect consumers; organizations committed to consumer rights have identified their own agendas for research on the decision-making processes of consumers. The third group interested in consumer behavior consists of scientists with a fundamental interest in human behavior as it occurs in the marketplace. The field on the whole is neutral with respect to the interests of consumers or those who wish to influence them.

The strong emphasis on decision making in the field of consumer psychology has, as in many areas in psychology, been encouraged by the cognitive revolution. Although researchers continue to recognize that people respond to affective and emotional appeals, they have become more attuned to consumers' conscious processing of information. This trend can be expected to continue. The need to gather and evaluate information will grow as products and services become more diverse and complex. Another reason that consumer psychology will continue to place an emphasis on decision making is consumers' demand for more complete and accurate information about goods and services.

One of the limitations of the cognitive theories of consumer decision making is that they typically fail to take into account differences between individuals and groups of people. Consumer psychology is likely to become increasingly concerned with market segmentation as the ability to understand the diverse needs of various groups develops. Further specialization of research on the aged and children as consumers is also predictable. Among emerging global

trends is an increased interest in marketing to women around the world. The rise of Internet shopping has also made enormous changes in consumer behavior, diminishing the face-to-face interaction of consumer and salesperson and vastly increasing the ease of comparison shopping.

SOURCES FOR FURTHER STUDY

Acuff, Daniel S. *What Kids Buy and Why.* New York: Free Press, 1997. Written for marketers aiming at children, describes the developmental processes of childhood psychology and how to utilize it in product development and advertising.

Bettman, James R. *An Information Processing Theory of Consumer Choice.* Reading, Mass.: Addison-Wesley, 1979. A scholarly presentation of an integrated theory of consumer choice from an information-processing perspective. Numerous propositions are formulated, with frequent reference to empirical research.

Fenwick, Ian, and John A. Quelch, eds. *Consumer Behavior for Marketing Managers.* Boston: Allyn & Bacon, 1984. Reviews of the consumer-behavior research literature on issues concerning current applications. Of special interest is chapter 3, on the consumer decision-making process. Topics covered are the information overload controversy, low-involvement consumer information processing, and the view that consumer behavior involves the making of decisions.

Jacoby, Jacob, and Jerry C. Olson, eds. *Perceived Quality: How Consumers View Stores and Merchandise.* Lexington, Mass.: Lexington Books, 1985. A set of articles contributed by various specialists in perceptions of quality. Presents the views of retailers, manufacturers, and consumers; discusses regulatory and economic perspectives on quality.

Solomon, Michael R., and Nancy J. Rabolt. *Consumer Behavior: In Fashion.* Upper Saddle River, N.J.: Prentice Hall, 2002. Explores the social psychology of buying clothing, using multicultural examples. Written for fashion marketers and the general public interested in the underlying mechanisms of their consumer behavior.

Wilkie, William L. *Consumer Behavior.* 3d ed. New York: John Wiley & Sons, 1994. A textbook stressing concepts, findings, and applications in the broad area of consumer psychology. Balanced and informative treatment of research, theory, and practice. Good coverage of the cognitive aspects of consumer behavior, including learning, information processing, perception, and decision making.

Janet A. Sniezek

SEE ALSO: Advertising; Attitude-behavior consistency; Attitude formation and change; Cognitive maps; Field experimentation; Group decision making; Motivation; Survey research: Questionnaires and interviews.

Cooperation, competition, and negotiation

TYPE OF PSYCHOLOGY: Social psychology
FIELDS OF STUDY: Group processes; interpersonal relations

Cooperation, competition, and negotiation are social processes central to the functioning of a group. They influence the effectiveness of a group in making decisions, completing tasks, and resolving differences, and they have a major impact on interpersonal relationships among group members.

KEY CONCEPTS
- competitive social situations
- contriently interdependent goals
- principled negotiation
- prisoner's dilemma
- social trap
- strategic negotiation

INTRODUCTION
The terms "cooperation," "competition," and "negotiation" are fairly common words used to describe frequent interpersonal experiences. Most people can immediately draw to mind experiences of each type. This discussion will focus primarily on dynamics within a group setting. Since a group is commonly defined by social scientists as two or more people exerting influence on one another, discussion of each term can be understood as describing a process among informal groups, such as friends, spouses, business partners, coworkers, and classmates, as well as more formally established

groups, such as appointed or elected committees, boards of directors, faculty, and members of an organization.

When people cooperate with one another, it is assumed that members of the group have similar goals; when they compete with one another, it is assumed they have different (and often conflicting) goals. This distinction is illustrated in definitions offered by Morton Deutsch, a leading researcher in group processes. Deutsch suggested that in cooperative situations, goals are "contriently interdependent," which means simply that goal achievement by one group member facilitates goal achievement by other members. In competitive situations, goal achievement by one group member hinders goal achievement by other members. It is often under conditions of competition that the process of negotiation enters. Cooperation and competition (with resulting negotiation) are central factors influencing group characteristics such as cohesiveness, effectiveness, and interpersonal relationships.

SELF-INTEREST AND SOCIAL DILEMMAS
Researchers have been interested in studying behavior when long-term interests are served by cooperation but short-term interests are served by looking out for oneself. In fact, these dilemmas are frequently involved with issues threatening the future of society, such as waste recycling, pollution control, and the depletion of natural resources. The question left to answer is how one reconciles self-interest (for example, not spending money to fix the damaged pollution-control device on one's automobile) with societal well-being (the necessity of reducing pollutants).

Psychologists have used laboratory games to study such social dilemmas. Perhaps the most frequently used game is called the prisoner's dilemma. In this game, a subject (here named John) is one of two criminal suspects who have been working in tandem. The two subjects are being questioned separately by a district attorney (DA) about a crime that has been committed; both are guilty. The DA, however, has only enough evidence to convict both of a lesser crime. The DA offers each suspect a chance to confess. If John confesses and his cohort does not, John will be granted immunity and the DA will have enough evidence to convict his partner of the more serious offense. This is the best scenario for John but the worst for his partner. If the partner confesses and John does not, the partner is granted immunity and John receives the heavier sentence. This is the worst scenario for John but the best for his cohort. If neither confesses, each will receive a light sentence for the lesser crime; this is the second-best scenario for each individual but the best scenario for the overall partnership. Finally, if both confess, each will receive a moderate sentence for the lesser offense. This is the third-best scenario for each individual but a bad option for the partnership.

It has been found that, in the prisoner's dilemma, most people will confess, although not confessing is the most cooperative approach with one's partner; confession is considering self-interest first, even at the expense of one's partner. If John adopts only an individualistic perspective and does not worry about the collective good, confessing is the better strategy; after all, if his partner does not confess, then he is free. If the partner does confess, John will receive a moderate sentence rather than risking a severe sentence by not confessing.

There is, however, a catch in this situation: Both prisoners will think the same way; hence, both will receive a moderate sentence. If both had not confessed and, in a sense, cooperated with each other, both would receive a light sentence. By looking out for self-interest, both partners lose.

Variations of this dilemma have been developed around themes more relevant to the typical citizen, especially the college student (such as negotiation for bonus points in a course). Each variant of the game is structured so that each party is better off individually by not cooperating. Yet by *mutually* not cooperating, both parties end up worse off than if they had cooperated.

STRATEGIC NEGOTIATION

There are ways for persons or groups to avoid such social traps, or situations in which, by mutually not cooperating, conflicting parties end up worse off than if they had cooperated.

One approach is to employ strategic negotiation, a reciprocal communication process in which parties with conflicting interests can examine specific issues and make, as well as consider, offers and counteroffers. Negotiation involves the ability to communicate, which may not always be available in situations of conflict (including some of the laboratory games employed by psychologists).

Sometimes negotiation is viewed solely as a process of protecting self-interests. Some people, often called hard bargainers, talk tough, even employing threatening tactics. The person who threatens to sue or claims that there is nothing to be negotiated would be an example of a hard bargainer. Soft bargainers, on the other hand, are willing to bend, even to the point of sacrificing self-interests. Such individuals often believe that their good faith approach is a model for the other negotiator, thereby promoting reconciliation while still hoping for important concessions. In group settings, soft bargainers may be concerned about group cohesion and make concessions contrary to self-interest. The extent to which hard ver-

Team sports provide children with valuable experience of both competition and cooperation. (CLEO Photography)

sus soft bargaining is effective is a complex matter, depending on many factors present in the negotiation process. Thus, it is neither easy nor necessarily accurate to claim that one technique is better than another.

FOUR ELEMENTS OF EFFECTIVE NEGOTIATION

Despite the hard-bargaining tone of the title *Getting to Yes: Negotiating Agreement Without Giving In* (1981; revised 1991), the authors, Roger Fisher and William Ury, drawing on research as part of the Harvard Negotiation Project (a project dealing with all levels of conflict resolution, ranging from marital relationships to global disputes), promote what they call principled negotiation. Their approach identifies four basic elements of effective negotiation and problem solving. First, they recommend that negotiators separate the people from the problem. By focusing on the problem rather than the intentions or motives of the people involved, participants are more likely to see themselves as working together, attacking the problem rather than each other. Second, the authors recommend that negotiators focus on interests by identifying underlying issues rather than by negotiating specific positions. They claim that position taking often obscures what the participants really want. Third, before trying to reach agreement, the negotiators should individually and collectively generate a variety of options, especially identifying options that may produce mutual gain. By adopting this strategy, the negotiation is transformed into a group problem-solving process. Finally, negotiators should insist that the eventual resolution be based on some objective criteria considered fair by both parties. The principled negotiator is thus neither hard nor soft, but is able to reach agreement without, as the title of the book says, giving in.

One of the key elements of Fisher and Ury's approach is the process of getting people to attack problems rather than each other, thus fostering a sense of cooperative teamwork. What is implied is that working cooperatively makes the task at hand more manageable and the negotiating process more enjoyable, with a more effective outcome resulting.

RESEARCH

A series of studies conducted by Deutsch during the 1940's and 1950's generally supports these assertions. Small groups of five people met over a five-week period, some working in cooperative situations, others in competitive situations. Members of the cooperative groups, where all group members would be equally rewarded for a combined effort, indicated that they liked their group and its individual members better, reacted more favorably to other members' contributions, and generally rated the overall experience higher than did members of competitive groups (in which group members were told that the amount and quality of their individual contributions to the task at hand would be rank-ordered).

More recent studies provide additional support demonstrating the superiority of cooperation. In one study, members of cooperative groups found the atmosphere more relaxing and felt greater freedom to contribute to the group process than did members of competitive groups. In general, it can be said without equivocation that interpersonal relationships are more positive in cooperative than in competitive group situations.

One might ask, however, whether cooperative groups are more effective in achieving goals or in making good decisions than are competitive groups. Results of several studies generally support, as expected, the notion that when group members coordinate their efforts, the outcome is more successful than when group members compete with one another. One study compared two groups of interviewers in a public employment agency. Interviewers in a cooperative atmosphere, in which interviewers worked together to place applicants in job settings, were more successful than interviewers in a more competitive atmosphere.

Is competition ever healthy in a group setting? Most of the research that stresses the advantages of a cooperative atmosphere has involved highly interdependent tasks. That is, in order to reach a goal, group members must rely on one another for success. Thus, it should not be surprising that teams in a sport that requires considerable teamwork (for example, basketball or volleyball) should perform better when players get along with one another. For sports in which teamwork is less important (for example, cross-country track or skiing), however, a sense of harmony among team members may be less beneficial, especially if recognition is provided on an individual basis. Thus, although research has rarely documented advantages of a competitive atmosphere, there appear to be some conditions in which a sense of competition among group members is not particularly disruptive. The key is whether the task requires a highly interdependent effort among group members.

Some surprising sex differences have been found with regard to individual cooperation and competition, especially in laboratory studies involving games such as the prisoner's dilemma. While the traditional sex-role stereotype for women is to be cooperative and accommodating in an attempt to maintain harmony, research seems to indicate that women sometimes demonstrate a more competitive nature than men. One explanation of this finding is that women are more likely to make choices that are consistent with the interpersonal setting. If the interpersonal setting suggests competition (as it does in the prisoner's dilemma game), women compete at least as hard as men; if it suggests cooperation, women cooperate at least as much as men.

CONTRIBUTIONS OF DEUTSCH AND SHERIF

Much of the work on cooperation and competition must be credited to Morton Deutsch's classic studies of the 1940's and 1950's. Deutsch's mentor was the respected social psychologist Kurt Lewin at the Massachusetts Institute of Technology. The relationship between Lewin and Deutsch was more than that of teacher and student. Lewin later founded the Commission on Community Interrelations. As a member of that commission, Deutsch was one of the first researchers to employ scientific methodology in studying societal effects of racially integrated housing. Undoubtedly, Lewin's work on leadership had a major impact on Deutsch. Just as Lewin's research suggested that leaders who facilitate a cooperative climate among group members in decision-making processes maximize group productivity and member satisfaction, Deutsch's research clearly stresses the superiority of a cooperative versus competitive intragroup atmosphere.

In the late 1950's, Muzafer Sherif also studied the comparative processes of competition and cooperation by creating such conditions in real-life settings. Sherif discovered that the social dynamics of preadolescent boys in a camp setting were very similar to patterns of group behavior among adults. Groups functioned well in a cooperative atmosphere, especially under conditions of intergroup competition. The most striking finding in Sherif's research was how the conflicting groups could overcome their differences when presented superordinate goals—

that is, goals that were compelling for both groups but that could not be attained without the help of the other group.

REAL-LIFE APPLICATIONS

Cooperation is not always easily attained. Much of the research discussed, particularly regarding negotiation, suggests that the unbridled pursuit of self-interest is detrimental to the collective good. This may help explain why history is replete with examples of military escalation between opposing countries and why mutual disarmament is so difficult. One-sided disarmament, leaves that side vulnerable to exploitation, which, from that side's perspective, is the worst predicament in which to be.

Research conducted on group processes, including research on cooperation, competition, and negotiation, may help people further understand such important real-life issues as how a board of directors can most efficiently run a corporation or what atmosphere is most conducive to good decision making—whether that decision is about a family vacation, a neighborhood plan to fight crime, or an international dispute. In an age of international tensions, interracial conflicts, labor-management disputes, and domestic friction, the study of group processes is crucial.

SOURCES FOR FURTHER STUDY

Duffy, Karen Grover, James W. Grosch, and Paul V. Olczak, eds. *Community Mediation: A Handbook for Practitioners and Researchers.* New York: Guilford, 1991. Takes much relevant research and applies it to the topic of community mediation. As the title implies, it is meant for a wide audience; it is scholarly but not overly technical. Easily readable by the college undergraduate.

Fisher, Roger, and William Ury. *Getting to Yes: Negotiating Agreement Without Giving In.* 2d ed. New York: Penguin, 1991. A very practical, short (160-page) paperback. This was a national best-seller for a good reason. The authors translate high-powered research and communicate it in very understandable language; they make a reasonable case for principled negotiation, though some of their suggestions and examples seem a bit unrealistic.

Jandt, Fred Edmund. *Win-Win Negotiating: Turning Conflict into Agreement.* New York: John Wiley & Sons, 1987. A very readable book designed for anyone involved in negotiation. Typical of popular books in that many bold claims are unsubstantiated, but the author has considerable experience as a consultant and seminar leader in conflict management and is a good writer. Highly readable at the high school level.

Pruitt, Dean G., and Jeffrey Z. Rubin. *Social Conflict: Escalation, Stalemate, and Settlement.* New York: Random House, 1986. Blends good scholarship with practical considerations, though the emphasis is much more on the former. Though not a lengthy book, it does a good job of reviewing the literature on conflict.

Ury, William. *Getting Past No: Negotiating Your Way from Confrontation to Cooperation.* Rev. ed. New York: Bantam Doubleday Dell, 1993. A continuation of the approaches offered in *Getting to Yes,* focused on persuasion of a hostile counterpart to a negotiation.

Peter C. Hill

SEE ALSO: Affiliation and friendship; Altruism, cooperation, and empathy; Cooperative learning; Group decision making; Groups; Intergroup relations; Leadership; Parenting styles; Social identity theory; Social perception.

Cooperative learning

TYPE OF PSYCHOLOGY: Social psychology
FIELDS OF STUDY: Group processes; prejudice and discrimination

Cooperative learning refers to a variety of ways in which individuals work together to produce or obtain some defined goal. Research supports the effectiveness of cooperative learning strategies in the areas of achievement, positive interactions with others, and self-esteem development.

KEY CONCEPTS
- dyad
- group investigation
- student teams-achievement divisions (STAD)
- task specialization
- teams-games-tournament (TGT)

INTRODUCTION

Cooperative learning involves working in small groups toward some desired end. Groups, in and of themselves, do not have to be cooperative. Group members may compete for benefits, or an individual group member may assume all the responsibility for a group task. Neither of these group situations is cooperative. In cooperative learning, individuals depend on one another to receive benefits. Cooperative learning methods can be contrasted with competitive methods, which have individuals work against one another to reach a goal, and individualistic methods, which encourage each person to work toward a goal without regard for the performance or behaviors of others.

Informal group activities such as sharing ideas can be considered cooperative learning. Some psychologists believe that even simple cooperative interactions between individuals can be associated with enhanced cognitive and social development. Most of the research on cooperative learning, however, reflects a more formal, structured approach.

JIGSAW LEARNING TECHNIQUE

One of the first structured cooperative learning techniques, "jigsaw," was developed by social psychologist Elliot Aronson and his colleagues. Aronson envisioned an academic environment in which a heterogeneous mix of students could achieve success and learn to appreciate one another through equal-status contact. In jigsaw, students are placed in small groups that mix characteristics such as race, gender, and ability. The teacher assigns a common task, such as learning about Christopher Columbus, to the entire class. The assignment is broken down into subtopics. For example, the assignment on Columbus might include a review of Columbus's early life, information on his voyages, a description of life in and around North America when Columbus set sail, and a review of Columbus's later life. Each student in a group assumes responsibility for one of the subtopics of the assignment. Students then meet with members from other groups who share the same subtopic. At this point, students have formed new, specialized groups in which individuals with the same information can help one another master the subtopic. Afterward, the members of the specialized groups return to their original groups to teach the material they have mastered and to learn the information on the other subtopics from other group members. Achievement is measured by testing students individually on all the information for the assignment. Jigsaw also includes extensive team-building and communication-training activities.

USE OF GROUP REWARDS

Although Aronson and his colleagues had high expectations for the cognitive and social benefits of jigsaw, reviews of the effects have been mixed. Cooperative learning methods that have emphasized group rewards over the individual rewards associated with jigsaw have shown more consistent benefits for learners. For example, Robert Slavin and his colleagues at The Johns Hopkins University have developed several successful group-reward cooperative learning methods, including student teams-achievement divisions (STAD) and teams-games-tournament (TGT). In STAD, the teacher presents a lesson and students study worksheets in small, heterogeneous groups. Afterward, students take individual quizzes. Group scores are computed based on how much each group member improves over previous performance; group scores are reported in a class newsletter. TGT differs by having group members compete against members of other teams with similar records of past performance; group scores are based on the competition.

Two techniques developed by other research teams, learning together and group investigation, also use group rewards. Learning together emphasizes the development of social skills such as trust, conflict resolution, and accurate communication. Students work together to complete a single piece of work and are rewarded for working cooperatively and for task performance. In group investigation, small groups of students choose topics from a unit that the class is studying. Group members then choose a subtopic for each member to investigate. Like jigsaw, group investigation uses task specialization—the dividing up of responsibility among group members for separate aspects of the group activity. Unlike jigsaw, in group investigation, group members work together to prepare a presentation for the entire class and are rewarded for group work.

BENEFITS

Taken together, the various cooperative learning methods illustrate that there are benefits to cooperative learning methods over traditional competitive or individualistic approaches to instruction. Cooperative learning is also credited with increasing positive social interactions. Researchers report greater interaction between members of different racial or ethnic groups, greater acceptance of mainstreamed students, and greater friendship among students. Teachers and students in cooperative classrooms report more positive attitudes toward school. Finally, students in cooperative learning studies often show increased levels of self-esteem.

IMPLICATIONS FOR EDUCATION

Because of the clear relevance of cooperative learning techniques for the education of children, cooperative strategies have been investigated in a number of long-term school projects. A good example is the Riverside Cooperative Learning Project. One part of the project involved training student teachers in cooperative learning techniques and evaluating the effects of the training on their students. Elementary school student teachers were randomly assigned to either a traditional classroom structure, a STAD-structured classroom, or a TGT-structured classroom. STAD was considered the purest example of cooperative learning in the study because TGT contains a competitive element; in that group, members compete against members of other groups in order to gain points for their own group (team). Thus, TGT is a combination of cooperation and competition. TGT is still considered to be more of a cooperative method than the traditional classroom, which is oriented toward competitive and individualistic activities.

The academic gains that students made under the three classroom structures varied in the Riverside project based on the race of the students. African American students made the greatest gains in the STAD classroom, the classroom considered to be the clearest example of cooperative learning. Students of European descent did best in the TGT (cooperative-competitive) classroom. Mexican American students made the greatest gains in the traditional classroom. These results are important because they add support to the belief that some of the racial differences that occur in performance in schools may be related to cultural preferences for one type of classroom structure over another.

In this study, the authors were surprised that the Mexican American students did not do better in the cooperative classrooms, since studies on ethnic differences suggest that Mexican American culture is oriented toward cooperation over competition. The Mexican American children in the Riverside project, however, were third-generation Americans with little knowledge of Spanish. Before the study began, they tested like the European American students in terms of cooperation; the African American students, on the other hand, tested higher than the Mexican American and the European American students on cooperation. Knowing which classroom structure will be best for a student, then, is not as simple as determining the student's racial or ethnic heritage.

Classroom climate was more positive in the cooperative classrooms than in the traditional classroom, particularly for the Mexican American and African American students. Cooperativeness was higher among students in cooperative classrooms, and students in cooperative classes were more democratic in choosing friends. Schools that want to emphasize social change, then, might prefer cooperative learning methods. Yet while cooperative techniques seemed better overall, the Riverside project also demonstrated that a variety of classroom structures may be necessary in schools to optimize performance for a majority of students.

EFFECTS IN THE WORKPLACE

Cooperative learning methods have also been investigated in laboratory studies with adult learners. Such studies are important for understanding the extent of the effects of cooperative learning methods and for evaluating whether these methods might be useful with older students and with materials that might be found in work environments. If the effects of cooperative methods on achievement transfer to work environments, employers might begin to train people differently and increase job performance. If the effects of cooperative methods on social interactions transfer to work environment, employers might improve organizational climates and also enhance job performance. Since the workforce is becoming more diversified, information on reactions to cooperative learning methods by different groups of people should be beneficial. A diversified environment also puts increased pressure on organizations to determine the best ways to get people to work together for increased productivity.

Preliminary studies on adults suggest that cooperative learning benefits can be obtained with dyads (a pair of persons working together on a task); that individual accountability and external rewards may not be as critical as they are in the school setting; and that personality differences and the type of material being learned may be more important.

CULTURAL AND ETHNIC CONSIDERATIONS

The topic of cooperation has been an important one for psychologists almost since the origins of psychology as a science in the late nineteenth century. John Dewey (1859-1952), a philosopher and educator who discussed the importance of cooperation in education, and Kurt Lewin (1890-1947), the psychologist who influenced the study of group dynamics in the 1940's, are both seminal figures in the study of cooperation. Most of the current research on structured cooperative methods, however, can be traced to studies in the 1970's. Some of those early researchers were particularly concerned with the changing demographic patterns in schools that made schools seem more heterogeneous than had been the case in the past. Civil rights legislation ordering desegregation contributed to changes in the makeup of some schools. Mainstreaming also added variety to the composition of classrooms. Around the same time, an increase in research on ethnicity seemed to indicate that cultural differences between groups that considered themselves to be disenfranchised (for example, African Americans and Mexican Americans) and the European American majority culture were not going to disappear. If anything, the nation was becoming more diverse, and the probability of intergroup conflict seemed even more likely if people did not learn to work together.

Some theoreticians also speculated that differences in achievement between different racial and ethnic groups might be related to clashes between cultural values and classroom structures. In essence, classroom structure might serve as a tool for discriminating against some potentially capable students. The traditional classroom atmosphere in the United States continues to be highly competitive and individualistic. Students compete for higher grades, often at the expense of others. Cooperation is for the most part discouraged because teachers are asked to evaluate the work of the individual for grades. Yet the increasing ethnic diversity of the United States means that better understanding of ethnic groups and procedures that enhance learning for as many students as possible are important considerations for educators and employers.

Since researchers and theoreticians of cooperative learning methods have addressed the cognitive, social, and personal effects of cooperative methods, they will be increasingly influential in a number of settings.

SOURCES FOR FURTHER STUDY

Aronson, Elliot, et al. *The Jigsaw Classroom.* 2d ed. Reading, Mass.: Addison-Wesley, 1996. A classic in the field. Discusses the rationale for developing this cooperative learning method, explains the jigsaw technique in detail, and presents the research findings.

Johnson, David W., and Roger T. Johnson. *Learning Together and Alone.* Boston: Allyn & Bacon, 1994. Aimed primarily at teachers. Contrasts cooperative, competitive, and individualistic learning methods and their appropriate uses.

Kagan, S., et al. "Classroom Structural Bias: Impact of Cooperative and Competitive Classroom Structures on Cooperative and Competitive Individuals and Groups." In *Learning to Cooperate, Cooperating to Learn,* edited by Robert E. Slavin et al. New York: Plenum, 1985. Only for those who want more information about the Riverside project. The project is described, and graphs are interpreted for the reader.

Sharan, Shlomo, ed. *A Handbook of Cooperative Learning Methods.* Westport, Conn.: Praeger, 1999. Aimed at teachers, offers an array of cooperative learning techniques and commentary on their use in the classroom.

Slavin, Robert E. *Cooperative Learning: Theory and Research.* 2d ed. Boston: Allyn & Bacon, 1994. Reviews various cooperative learning methods, some in detail, and the cognitive, social, and personal benefits associated with cooperative learning.

_____. "Research on Cooperative Learning: Consensus and Controversy." *Educational Leadership* 47, no. 4 (1989/1990): 52-54. A very readable discussion of areas of agreement and disagreement in the field. Only one among a variety of articles in this issue by major theoreticians and teachers of cooperative learning methods.

Judith L. Gay

SEE ALSO: Cooperation, competition, and negotiation; Educational psychology; Intergroup relations; Learning; Prejudice reduction.

Coping
Chronic illness

TYPE OF PSYCHOLOGY: Stress

FIELDS OF STUDY: Anxiety disorders; behavioral therapies; cognitive therapies; coping; critical issues in stress; depression; organic disorders; problem solving; schizophrenias; sexual disorders; stress and illness; substance abuse

When a chronic illness strikes a person, his or her entire life changes. Efforts that are undertaken to counteract these increased demands are called coping endeavors. Different people behave differently under such duress. However, certain coping styles have better outcomes, such as maintaining "positive outlook" or optimism, avoiding repressive coping, and obtaining social support.

KEY CONCEPTS
- appraisal
- crisis theory
- emotion-focused coping
- encounter
- hardiness
- optimism
- problem-focused coping
- retreat
- shock
- social support
- transactional model

INTRODUCTION

In modern times, chronic illnesses are becoming increasingly common. In the twenty-first century, the leading causes of death in the United States are chronic diseases, as opposed to the beginning of the previous century, when infectious diseases were more rampant. Chronic illnesses are diseases that are long in duration, have multiple risk factors, have a long latency period, are usually noncontagious, cause greater and progressive functional impairment, and are generally incurable. Examples of common chronic illnesses include heart diseases (such as coronary heart disease and hypertension), cancers (malignant neoplasms), chronic obstructive lung diseases (bronchial asthma, emphysema, and chronic bronchitis), cerebrovascular diseases (stroke), diabetes mellitus, kidney diseases (end-stage renal disease and renal failure), musculoskeletal disorders (rheumatoid arthritis and osteoarthritis), chronic mental illnesses, neurological disorders (epilepsy, Alzheimer's disease, Parkinson's disease, and multiple sclerosis), and accidents or injuries (traumatic brain injury, spinal cord injury, amputations, and burns). Dealing with these illnesses presents numerous challenges for patients and their family members and care providers. "Coping" is a term that is usually used to describe the process by which people manage demands in excess of the resources that are at their disposal. Therefore, in addition to medical treatment, management of chronic illnesses must address lifelong coping with these illnesses.

The interest in coping with chronic illnesses can be traced back to late 1960's, with the work of American physician Thomas Holmes and Richard Rahe, then a medical student, at the University of Washington. They constructed the Social Readjustment Rating Scale (SRRS) to assess the amount of stress to which an individual is exposed. Personal injuries or illnesses were rated as the sixth-most-important events in terms of their intensity in affecting one's life and increasing the chances of further illness in the subsequent year of life.

MODELS OF COPING

American psychologist Franklin Shontz, in his book *The Psychological Aspects of Physical Illness and Disability* (1975), described the phases of reaction to any illness. The first stage on being diagnosed with a chronic illness is what he described as the stage of shock, in which the person is in a bewildered state and behaves in an automatic fashion with a sense of detachment from all surroundings. In this stage, patients often describe themselves as observers rather than participants in what is happening around them. The second stage is the stage of encounter or reaction. In this stage, the person is feeling a sense of loss and has disorganized thinking. Emotions of grief, despair, and helplessness are common. In this stage, patients often describe the feeling of being overwhelmed by reality. The third stage is what Shontz calls retreat. In this stage, the feeling of denial becomes very strong, but this state cannot persist and the patient gradually begins to accept reality as the symptoms persist and functional impairments ensue.

In the 1980's, American psychologist Richard Lazarus, an emeritus professor at the University of California at Berkeley, proposed the famous coping model called the transactional model. This model has also been applied widely in understanding coping with chronic illnesses. According to the transactional model, all stressful experiences, including chronic illnesses, are perceived as person-environment transactions. In these transactions, the person undergoes a four-stage assessment known as appraisal. When confronted with a diagnosis of chronic illness, the first stage is the primary appraisal of the event. In this stage, the patient internally determines the severity of the illness and whether he or she is in trouble. If the illness is perceived to be severe or threatening, has caused harm or loss in the past, or has affected someone known to the person, then the stage of secondary appraisal occurs. If, on the other hand, the illness is judged to be irrelevant or poses minimal threat, then stress does not develop and no further coping occurs. The secondary appraisal determines how much control one has over the illness. Based upon this understanding, the individual ascertains what means of control are available. This is the stage known as coping. Finally, the fourth stage is the stage of reappraisal, in which the person determines whether the effects of illness have been negated.

According to the transactional model, there are two broad categories of coping. The first one is called problem-focused coping strategy, and the second one is called emotion-focused coping strategy. Problem-focused coping is based on one's capability to think about and alter the environmental event or situation. Examples of this strategy at the thought process level include utilization of problem-solving skills, interpersonal conflict resolution, advice-seeking, time management, goal-setting, and gathering more information about what is causing one stress. Problem solving requires thinking through various solutions, evaluating the pros and cons of different solutions, and then implementing a solution that seems most advantageous to reduce the stress. Examples of this strategy at the behavioral or action level include activities such as joining a smoking cessation program, complying a prescribed medical treatment, adhering to a diabetic diet plan, or scheduling and prioritizing tasks for managing time.

In the emotion-focused strategy, the focus is inward on altering the way one thinks or feels about a situation or an event. Examples of this strategy at the thought process level include denying the existence of the stressful situation, freely expressing emotions, avoiding the stressful situation, making social comparisons, or minimizing (looking at the bright side of things). Examples of this strategy at the behavioral or action level include seeking social support to negate the influence of the stressful situation; using exercise, relaxation, or meditation; joining support groups;, practicing religious rituals; and escaping through the use of alcohol and drugs.

CRISIS THEORY OF COPING

In the 1980's, American psychologist Rudolf Moos proposed the crisis theory to describe the factors that influence the crises of illnesses. He identified three types of factors that influence the coping process in illness. The first category of factors comprises the illness-related factors. The more severe the disease in terms of its threat, the harder is the coping. Examples of such severe threats include conditions such as burns that are likely to produce facial disfigurement, implantation of devices for excreting fecal or urinary wastes, or epileptic seizures. The second category of factors comprises background and personal factors. These factors include one's age, gender, social class, religious values, emotional maturity, and self-esteem. For example, men are often affected more if the illness threatens their ambition, vigor, or physical power, while children show greater resilience because of their relative naïveté and limited cognitive abilities. The third category of factors identified by Moos comprises physical and social environmental factors. Generally speaking, people who have more social support tend to cope better when compared to people who live alone and do not have many friends.

Moos proposed in his crisis theory that these three factors impinge on the coping process. The coping process begins with cognitive appraisal, in which the patient reflects on the meaning of the illness in his or her life. This leads to formulating a set of adaptive tasks. Moos identified three adaptive tasks for coping directly with the illness: dealing with the symptoms and functional impairment associated with the illness or injury; adjusting to the hospital environment or medical procedures; and developing relationships with care providers. He further identified four adaptive tasks as crucial for adapting to general psychosocial functioning: maintaining a sense of emotional balance and controlling negative affect; preserving a sense of mastery, competence, or self-image; sustaining meaningful

relationships with friends and family; and preparing for a future of uncertainty. The family members or long-term care providers who work with such patients also undergo these seven adaptive processes and must make these adjustments for effective coping. These adaptive tasks usually result in specific coping strategies. Moos described the following coping strategies: denial, or minimizing the seriousness of the illness (which is sometimes helpfu,l especially in the earlier stages); seeking information; learning medical procedures (which is sometimes helpful for self care, such as taking insulin shots); mastering adaptive tasks; recruiting family support; thinking about and discussing the future to decipher greater predictability; and finding a purpose in and positive impacts of the illness on one's life.

HEART DISEASES

Heart diseases or cardiovascular diseases have been the leading cause of death in the United States since the 1980's. Initial research on coping with heart disease was done on patients with myocardial infarction or heart attack. The research focused mainly on the role played by denial, which is a defense mechanism, described by the famous Austrian neurologist, Sigmund Freud (1856-1939), who is also called the father of psychoanalysis. Researchers using the "denial scale" classified patients into "denying" and "nondenying" groups and studied the outcomes of recovery. It was found that denial played an important role in decreasing anxiety and even in reducing deaths in the early stages of heart attack recovery. However, during the later phases of recovery, denial added to noncompliance with medical care, decreased seeking of information about the disease, and increased the risk of recurrence of heart attack. Recent research comparing the specific role of repression (or denial) and sensitization to the presence of disease supports the importance of sensitization in improving the solicitation of information, social functioning, and outcomes through the reduction of complications.

Recent research on coping and heart diseases has broadened its focus, improved coping measurement tools, and studied several other dimensions of coping. The first of these dimensions is the comparison between problem-focused strategies and emotion-focused strategies as described by Lazarus. In general, it has been found that people who use a problem-focused coping strategy report better social and psychological adjustment following hospital discharge, and these approaches are beneficial in the long run for improving disease outcomes. Emotion-focused strategies have been found to be of some utility in the short term in decreasing distress but have not been found to be useful in the long term. Further, people using emotion-focused strategies have reported greater incidence of anxiety and depression as a result of the heart disease. Another dimension of coping that researchers have studied pertains to optimism. American psychologist Charles Carver and his colleagues have found the beneficial effects of being optimistic when recovering from chronic heart disease. Similarly, researchers have found empirical evidence of what American psychologist Suzanne Kobasa described as hardiness, a term that comprises the trinity of control, commitment, and challenge, as being beneficial in improving psychosocial adjustment to heart disease and decreasing chances of anxiety and depression.

CANCERS

Cancers are a diverse group of diseases characterized by the uncontrolled growth and spread of abnormal cells in the body. At the start of the twenty-first century, cancers were the second leading cause of death in the United States. The lifetime probability of developing cancer was estimated at one in three, and it was estimated that cancers would soon be the leading cause of death and sickness. Cancers pose special challenges for coping, as these necessitate utilization of a wide range of coping options to deal with changing and often deteriorating functional abilities, medical challenges, treatment modalities (chemotherapy, surgery, and radiotherapy), and psychosocial reactions that the disease requires.

Like the earlier studies on coping with heart diseases, initial work on coping with cancers also focused on the role of defense mechanisms described by Freud. More recent research on coping and cancers has focused on personal disposition styles, coping strategies as described by Lazarus, and other special mechanisms. Results from disposition style studies suggest that internal locus of control and optimistic outlook are linked to lower levels of emotional distress and better psychological adaptation to cancer. On the other hand, avoidance or escapism has been associated with higher emotional distress. Problem-based coping strategies, as described by Lazarus, have also been found to be associated with

better psychosocial adaptation to cancer. On the other hand, disengagement-oriented strategies such as wishful thinking, blaming oneself, and adopting a fatalistic or resigned attitude have been found to be associated with higher levels of emotional distress and worse psychosocial adaptation to cancer. Likewise, acceptance of the diagnosis of cancer and resignation to this fact have also been found to be associated with worse psychosocial outcomes. Other coping strategies such as freely expressing feelings, denial, and seeking religion have yielded equivocal results.

CEREBROVASCULAR DISEASES

In 2002, cerebrovascular disease (CVD) was the third leading cause of death in the United States and represented about 7 percent of deaths from all causes. The most severe manifestation of CVD is stroke, with transient ischemic attack being a less severe clinically apparent variant. Stroke is a major cause of disability. Besides the usual generalized coping that goes with any chronic illness, coping with stroke specifically requires speech therapy, occupational therapy, and physiotherapy.

DIABETES

Diabetes mellitus is a disease in which the body is unable to sufficiently produce and/or properly use insulin, a hormone needed by the body to use glucose. The prevalence of this disorder has consistently risen in the United States, and it afflicted about 5 percent of the population in 2002. Besides the usual generalized coping that goes with any chronic illness, coping with diabetes specifically requires lifelong dietary changes, changes pertaining to physical activity patterns, and, in most cases, specific medicinal usage and compliance.

CHRONIC RESPIRATORY DISORDERS

Chronic lung diseases are a varied group of diseases that were, in 2000, identified as the fourth leading cause of death in the United States. Approximately 5 percent of the population had been diagnosed with these disorders. The most common chronic respiratory disorders are asthma, emphysema, and chronic bronchitis. Besides the compliance to medical treatment and the usual generalized coping that goes with any chronic illness, coping with respiratory disorders entails gradual buildup of exercise stamina and effective management of stress through relaxation techniques, since many acute attacks are both exaggerated and precipitated by stress.

CHRONIC MUSCULOSKELETAL DISORDERS

Arthritis and musculoskeletal disorders were the most common causes of physical disability in the United States in 2002, affecting approximately 15 percent of the population. Besides the usual generalized coping that goes with any chronic illness, these disorders require specific rehabilitative coping through physiotherapy, occupational therapy, and vocational rehabilitation.

CHRONIC MENTAL ILLNESSES

Poor and ineffective coping with stress often leads to persistent depression and anxiety. Besides these two common mental illnesses, other disorders such as schizophrenia, bipolar psychosis, variants of anxiety disorders, organic disorders (such as dementia and Alzheimer's disease), and other mental illnesses pose special coping challenges for patients and their family members. Besides the usual coping strategies, coping with mental disorders specifically involves long behavioral, psychological, and social challenges and therapies.

SOURCES FOR FURTHER STUDY

Allen, Jon G. *Coping with Trauma: A Guide to Self Understanding.* Washington, D.C.: American Psychiatric Press, 1995. A good self-help reference book for trauma victims, their friends, and family members. Coping with trauma and chronic illnesses are intricately related and the reader will find several topics of interest in this very readable book.

Helgeson, Vicki S., and Kristin Mickelson. "Coping with Chronic Illness Among the Elderly: Maintaining Self Esteem." In *Behavior, Health, and Aging,* edited by Stephen B. Manuck, Richard Jennings, Bruce S. Rabin, and Andrew Baum. Mahwah, N.J.: Lawrence Erlbaum, 2000. It has been found that distress following chronic illness reduces self-esteem. This chapter describes methods used in building one's self-esteem following chronic illness. The specific methods of social comparison, denial, and deriving meaning from the experience are discussed.

Livneh, Hanoch. "Psychosocial Adaptation to Cancer: The Role of Coping Strategies" *Journal of Rehabilitation* 66, no. 2 (2000): 40-50. A review article on the role of coping styles and strategies in the psychosocial adaptation to cancer. The article describes coping and its function in the context of coping with chronic illnesses with particular emphasis on cancers. A recommended reading for rehabilitation clinicians and researchers in the field.

_____. "Psychosocial Adaptation to Heart Diseases: The Role of Coping Strategies " *Journal of Rehabilitation* 65, no. 3 (1999): 24-33. A well-written review article that summarizes the research begun in the 1960's on psychosocial coping with heart diseases. The review captures a wide gamut of coping definitions, models, strategies, measurement issues, and levels of outcomes as they relate to heart diseases.

Moos, Rudolf H., ed. *Coping with Life Crises: An Integrated Approach.* New York: Plenum, 1986. A classic book compiling twenty-nine topical essays on coping with various life crises. The editor particularly elaborates on the crisis theory and its multifarious adaptive processes.

Romas, John, A., and Manoj Sharma. *Practical Stress Management: A Comprehensive Workbook for Managing Change and Promoting Health.* 2d ed. Needham Heights, Mass.: Allyn & Bacon, 2000. A practical workbook designed specifically for general public. Readers who are interested in applying some specific and effective coping techniques in their lives to combat chronic illness will find this workbook to be quite useful.

Manoj Sharma

SEE ALSO: Alzheimer's disease; Anxiety; Biofeedback and relaxation; Coping: Social support; Coping: Strategies; Coping: Terminal illness; Depression; Meditation and relaxation; Stress: Physiological responses; Stress-related diseases.

Coping
Social support

TYPE OF PSYCHOLOGY: Stress; social psychology
FIELDS OF STUDY: Coping; group processes; problem solving; stress and illness

Stress is a problem of modern society that everyone experiences at one time or another; people must de-

velop ways to deal with stressful events or risk being overwhelmed by them. Social support, which means turning to other people for support in times of personal crises, is one of the most-often-used coping strategies.

KEY CONCEPTS
- coping
- resources
- social comparison
- social support
- stress

INTRODUCTION

When there is a perceived discrepancy between environmental demands and one's ability to meet those demands, an individual is likely to feel stress. Stress has both psychological and physiological causes and effects. In order to continue to function in an adaptive way, everyone must learn to cope with stress. There are many ways to cope. At one extreme, some people avoid and/or deny the existence of stress. At the other extreme, some people seek out and directly confront the source of stress in order to overcome it. One of the most-often-used approaches in coping with stress is social support, which can be used on its own or combined with other coping strategies.

Social support has many meanings. Sometimes it is defined simply as information that one receives from others. This information could come from a variety of sources—from family, friends, coworkers, or even the family's faithful dog. For social scientists, social support is sometimes defined as the possibility of human interactions, and it can be measured by indicators such as marital status. In that case, it may be assumed that an individual who is married receives more social support than does one who is not married. This is often incorrect, however; there are many supportive relationships outside marriage—the parent-child relationship, for example.

Sidney Cobb in 1976 indicated that social support should be viewed as the receipt of information that one is cared for, is valued, and belongs to a mutually supportive social network. Parent-child relationships, and many others, would thus be possible sources of social support. This multidimensional view of social support has gained acceptance. Research in the area of social support has found common themes related to the perception of outcomes of in-

teractions among people. In this view, there are five major outcomes constituting social support: the perception of a positive emotion toward oneself from another; agreement with another person about one's beliefs or feelings; encouragement by another person to express one's beliefs or feelings in a non-threatening environment; the receipt of needed goods or services; and confirmation that one does not have to face events alone, that others will be there when needed. Viewing social support in terms of the subjective perception of an interaction rather than as the opportunity to interact with another is a useful way to conceptualize social support.

The perception of social support serves an important function in maintaining a positive sense of well-being by enabling one to cope with and adapt to stress. It has been shown to have a positive effect on physical as well as mental health. For example, the prognosis for an individual recovering from a heart attack or coping with a diagnosis of cancer is better for those with a good network of sources of social support. Research has shown that people who are depressed tend to have fewer and less supportive relationships with family members, coworkers, and friends than those who are not depressed.

There are different theories regarding the relationship between social support and stress. Some psychologists believe that social support has a buffering effect, while others believe that social support has a direct effect on stress. According to the buffering-effect model, social support is important when one is faced with a stressor because it comes between the individual and the source of stress, and thus it protects the individual from the negative effects of the stressor. In this case, social support acts as a safety net in much the same way that a physical safety net protects the trapeze artist from injury during a fall; unless there is a fall, the net does not serve any function. In contrast, the direct-effect model contends that social support is important regardless of the presence of a stressor. In this case, social support is seen as providing a generally positive effect on the individual, which would incidentally provide the individual with resources that can be called into play when faced with stress. For example, experiencing positive interactions can boost one's self-esteem in general. The high self-esteem is incorporated into the individual's self-concept, whether or not the person is currently dealing with a stressful event. However, when faced with stress, the self-esteem would then provide the individual with confidence to engage in problem-solving techniques to overcome the stressor. There is evidence to support both suggested mechanisms for social support, and it is likely that social support has both a buffering and a direct effect.

Despite the evidence indicating that social support helps people cope with stress, some studies show a negative effect. It seems that there are different types of social support, and it is important to match the type of support provided to the type of support needed. Tangible support is the providing of material aid in the form of goods and services. It is often needed but rarely given. One of the few instances in which it is commonly offered is following a death in the family, when friends and neighbors may bring over casseroles so that the grieving family can eat nutritious meals. Long-term tangible support is more likely to come either from impersonal sources, such as community-supported welfare programs, or from the most intimate source, the immediate family. The intermediate social network, consisting of friends and neighbors, is not likely to provide long-term tangible support.

Informational support is offered more freely by sources at all levels. This form of support serves an educational function, providing information relevant to coping with a problem. An example would be telling people whom to call when they have no heat in their apartments. The third form of social support is emotional support, which comes from the more intimate sources, one's family and close friends. This form of support involves expressing positive feelings toward an individual, acknowledging that person's worth, and accepting his or her expressions of beliefs and feelings.

A number of factors might influence whether social support is provided. One factor is the perception of the person needing help of the likelihood that the desired support would actually be provided. If a person believes that he or she will get the help that is needed, that person is more likely to seek out social support. Studies have shown that individuals who are reluctant to seek help are less likely to receive the very support they desperately need. Another factor that can influence the likelihood that social support will be provided is the person who could provide the desired support. That person has to perceive that there is an actual need on the part of the person requesting help. The individual also has to determine whether he or she can provide the

appropriate type of support. Finally, the person who needs help has to be willing to accept the offer of social support when it is made. It is important to remember that the receivers of social support are not the only potential beneficiaries of the interaction. Providers of social support can be also benefit from the interaction. In fact, studies show that even young children have a need to be helpful to others, particularly people in their families.

SUPPORT SETTINGS

Social support is applied in a variety of settings, both informal and formal. Informal settings for social support include the sharing of one's problems with friends and family. For example, an advertising executive may be under pressure to put together a campaign for the company's biggest client, who is considering changing firms. Informational support may come from the executive's coworkers over lunch. She might explain to her coworkers the problems she is facing designing the program. The coworkers might have faced similar problems, and they could tell the executive what they did to cope with the problems when they were experiencing them. The coworkers might provide tangible support by volunteering their time to work together on the campaign. Emotional support is more likely to come from the executive's family when she describes her day over dinner. The family members need to convey their love and respect to the executive. In this case, they need to indicate that their regard for the person is not dependent on the success of any advertising account. It might be counterproductive for the spouse to express confidence in the executive's ability to develop a successful campaign; the executive may then feel under more pressure, because now she not only has to worry about keeping the account but also may worry about disillusioning her spouse and losing that important source of support. Members of social networks need to be careful that they provide the correct form of social support, because providing support which does not match the needs of the recipient may be harmful.

Social support is important not only in a work setting but in a personal setting as well. For example, a man who is trying to lose weight would benefit from emotional support from his family and friends who let him know that they care about him and support his decision to lose weight. When dieting gets difficult, loved ones might be tempted to tell the dieter that they think he is fine just the way he is. That is not supportive of his decision to lose weight, however, and it works against his success. Informational support can be provided by giving the dieter information about ingredients and methods of meal preparation. This kind of support can be provided by a variety of people; waiters are generally quite willing to discuss this subject with restaurant patrons to give the needed information for a wise choice from the menu. This kind of support is requested so often, in fact, that many restaurants include such information on the menus themselves—an example of social support that is community based. Tangible support for weight loss can come from a diet or exercise partner who embarks on a weight-loss program with the dieter; another example would be a friend who provides low-calorie meals for the dieter.

Another informal setting in which social support is increasingly being provided is on the Internet. There has been a proliferation of Internet news and support groups that provide both informational and emotional support to individuals facing a number of physical and mental illnesses including diabetes, cancer, acquired immunodeficiency syndrome (AIDS), and depression. The use of support groups by the elderly in particular, many of whom may have been socially isolated prior to their use of the Internet, has increased significantly.

FORMAL SUPPORT

These examples of situations in which people need social support can also be used to illustrate support in a formal setting. The executive who is undergoing stress might seek professional help from a counselor. A counseling situation takes place in a supportive environment and is generally focused on emotional support; however, some therapy situations can also provide informational and tangible support. Behavior therapy can be a source of informational support, such as when the executive is given homework assignments to identify what specific behaviors or thoughts are triggers for her stress. A clear identification of the trigger will aid in setting up a program to combat the stress. Sometimes people take part in group therapy settings, where a counselor works with several clients at the same time. Participants in the session become a tight social network that provides emotional, informational,

and sometimes even tangible support. In this case, the executive might practice her presentation for the group, and the other members' critique might include new ideas or techniques which can be used to solve her problem. Constructive criticism of a presentation is a service that could be considered a form of tangible support, as well as informational and emotional support.

A dieter can get support in a formal setting by joining an organized group such as Weight Watchers or Overeaters Anonymous. Losing weight alone can be a difficult task, and research has demonstrated that successful weight loss reduction is more likely to occur in group settings. Emotional support comes from fellow dieters who understand exactly what the dieter is experiencing and accept him as he is. In this case, everyone has the same problem, so the dieter does not feel that he does not fit into society. Informational support comes from the group leader, who helps set goals and explains what behaviors need to be modified to achieve those goals. It also comes from other group members, who share recipes and advice on how to combat challenges. Tangible support comes in the form of the low-calorie meals provided by some weight-control programs or of a bond with a group member who can become an exercise partner. Social support from groups of people with common problems has been found to be so helpful that the number of such support, or self-help, groups is growing enormously. These groups are being founded for people with a wide range of problems: rape victims, people with alcohol dependency, spouses of military personnel stationed in a war zone, parents of sudden infant death syndrome (SIDS) victims, and caregivers of individuals with physical or mental illnesses. Formal social support groups, in a sense, act as the extended family that may be absent in a modern, mobile society.

Because positive social support has been associated with improved mental and physical health and overall well-being, interventions designed to promote positive health behaviors and to reduce adverse health behaviors have been targeted for not only individuals at risk but also their social support networks, which can play a significant role in influencing an individual's behavior. For example, in the attempt to reduce drinking and driving among young people, advertisers have used slogans such as "Friends don't let friends drive drunk," hoping to encourage peers to support responsible drinking and the use of designated drivers. Physicians have also discovered that patients are more likely to comply with their advice if spouses and children are involved in the treatment regimen, because these patients are more likely to practice safe health behaviors and comply with treatment if they feel they have the support of family and friends. Thus, the concept of social support can be useful not only in helping individuals cope when faced with stressful events in both formal and informal settings but also in enlisting the cooperation of an individual's social support network to promote successful behavioral health change.

THEORIES OF SUPPORT

Social support is best understood in the context of social comparison theory, first presented by Leon Festinger in 1954. People have a need to be "correct," to do the right thing, and to behave in a socially appropriate manner. It is not always easy to determine the correct position to hold in different situations. For example, how does someone decide what to wear to a party? Often an individual will call a friend who is also going to the party and ask what the friend is planning to wear. A person tends to make decisions in ambiguous situations by observing what other people are doing. In general, one feels comfortable when behaving, dressing, or thinking in a manner which is similar to those around one. A woman is likely to feel uncomfortable and underdressed if she wears a skirt and blouse to a party where everyone else is in formal attire. A skirt and blouse are perfectly acceptable articles of clothing for a woman and are no less functional at a party than a formal gown would be. She may have worn that outfit to a social gathering previously and felt perfectly comfortable. When everyone else is dressed differently, however, she feels that she stands out and therefore is not dressed correctly. Correctness is determined by majority standards. People learn by the process of socialization to conform to those around them. Social comparison is the process by which people learn norms, or social expectations, in different settings.

In the process of learning norms, one also learns the social benefits of conformity: acceptance by others. When an individual expresses an idea or behavior which is consistent with the ideas or behaviors of others, then the social group is comfortable around that person and permits that person to join the group. If that person deviates from the group norm, then that person may be ostracized by the group. This is the basis of peer pressure, which people learn to apply at a young age.

When people turn to others for informational social support, they often are looking for guidance to help fit in with a social norm—to do or think the right thing. Emotional social support tells one that one is like others and is valued and accepted by others. Tangible social support tells one that one's needs are acceptable and that other people will perform behaviors similar to one's own behavior in order to meet those needs. The goal of both social comparison and social support is to validate oneself by ensuring that one does not deviate from social expectations.

In an interesting experiment designed to test the role of social comparison in emotional reactions, subjects were asked to wait until it was their turn to participate in an experiment; the experiment was explained to some subjects in a way designed to create apprehension. Subjects were given the opportunity either to wait alone or to wait with others. Those who were made fearful tended to want to wait with others more than did subjects who were not made fearful. This preference demonstrated that fear creates a desire to affiliate. More important, however, subjects showed a preference to wait with others only if they were told that the others were waiting for the same experiment. In this context, it is easy to understand the growth of support groups for specific problems. When facing a stressful situation, people need to be around others who can really understand what they are going through—in other words, other people with the same problem. There is strength in numbers.

SOURCES FOR FURTHER STUDY

Pierce, Gregory R., Barbara R. Saranson, and Irwin G. Saranson, eds. *Handbook of Social Support and the Family*. New York: Plenum, 1996. The authors provide a comprehensive reference that explores and integrates the concept of social support within the context of the family. Research examining social support dimensions and the family are presented, and a number of real-world issues including the role of social support during pregnancy and how families tackle crises are presented.

Sarason, Barbara R., Irwin G. Sarason, and Gregory R. Pierce, eds. *Social Support: An Interactional View.* New York: John Wiley & Sons, 1990. The authors present a well-written, extensive reference tool examining social support from the perspective of personality processes. Results of research looking at individual differences in the impact of social interaction on stress are discussed.

Schaefer, C., J. C. Coyne, and R. S. Lazarus. "The Health-Related Functions of Social Support." *Journal of Behavioral Medicine* 4 (1981): 381-406. Describes the tangible, informational, and emotional categories of social support and the health-protective benefits to be reaped from their use. Useful in helping one understand the different forms of social support available.

Silver, R., and C. Wortman. "Coping with Undesirable Life Events." In *Human Helplessness*, edited by Judy Garber and Martin E. P. Seligman. New York: Academic Press, 1980. This chapter focuses on coping with stress and the resources available through interacting with other people. Social support is shown to be a multidimensional construct which is both productive and counterproductive in helping individuals cope with life events.

Suls, Jerry. "Social Support, Interpersonal Relations, and Health: Benefits and Liabilities." In *Social Psychology of Health and Illness*, edited by Glenn S. Sanders and Jerry Suls. Hillsdale, N.J.: Lawrence Erlbaum, 1982. An informative chapter that stresses the need to clarify what is meant by "social support" and suggests a more meaningful approach to understanding the concept. Presents research demonstrating both the benefits and problems arising from various forms of social support.

Vaux, Alan. *Social Support: Theory, Research, and Intervention.* New York: Praeger, 1988. This comprehensive book begins by helping the reader to conceptualize social support, then takes the reader from the theoretical level to the more practical levels of measurement, application, and outcomes. Despite limitations discussed in the book, this work shows the achievements to be made through the utilization of formal and informal social support networks.

Barbara A. Bremer;
updated by Leonie J. Brooks

SEE ALSO: Coping: Chronic illness; Coping: Strategies; Coping: Terminal illness; Health psychology; Social perception; Stress; Stress: Behavioral and psychological responses; Stress-related diseases; Support groups.

Coping
Strategies

TYPE OF PSYCHOLOGY: Stress

FIELDS OF STUDY: Behavioral therapies; cognitive therapies; coping; critical issues in stress; problem solving

In 1967, Psychological Abstracts *began utilizing coping as a separate entity, and since then more than ten thousand articles and books related to this concept have been published in psychology and health sciences. It is generally accepted that coping is the way in which people handle stress, and the term is usually used to denote the handling of more difficult stressful situations. Coping strategies are broadly classified in two types: problem-focused and emotion-focused.*

KEY CONCEPTS
- adaptation
- appraisal
- defense mechanisms
- emotion-focused coping
- hardiness
- mastery
- problem-focused coping
- sense of coherence
- social support
- transactional model

INTRODUCTION

The word "cope" is derived from the Latin word *colpus,* meaning "to alter" and, as defined in *Webster's Dictionary,* is usually used in the psychological paradigm to denote "dealing with and attempting to overcome problems and difficulties." In psychology, the word "coping," in addition to this behavioral application, has been used as a broad heuristic in several other domains, including as a thought process, as a personality characteristic, and in social context.

The concept of coping can be traced back to the defense mechanisms described in the psychoanalytical model by the famous Austrian neurologist Sigmund Freud (1856-1939). Freud described several methods that a person's mind uses to protect itself: introjection, isolation, projection reversal, reaction formation, regression, repression, sublimation, turning against the self, and undoing. While discussing all these terms is beyond the scope of the present discussion, it is worth noting that, according to Freud, mechanisms of defense are the devices that the mind uses in altering one's perception to situations disturbing the internal milieu or mental balance. He applied the concept in identifying sources of anxiety through free association.

One of Freud's associates, Austrian physician Alfred Adler (1870-1937), disagreed with Freud and described defense mechanisms as protective against external threats or challenges. Sigmund Freud's daughter, Anna Freud (1895-1982), herself a renowned psychologist, included both of these viewpoints and underscored the role of defense mechanisms as protective against both internal and external threats. She also extended the repertoire of defense mechanisms to include denial, intellectualization, ego restriction, and identification with the aggressor. Therefore, it appears that the concept of defense mechanisms was very similar to the present understanding of coping at the thought process level and preceded the concept of coping. However, psychologist Norma Haan, in her book *Coping and Defending* (1977), clearly distinguishes defense mechanisms from coping. She contends that coping is purposive and involves choices, while defense mechanisms are rigid and set. Coping, according to Haan, is more focused on the present, while defense mechanisms are premised on the past and distort the present.

Psychologist Robert White, in *Stress and Coping: An Anthology* (1985), contends that coping is derived from the larger biological concept of adaptation. The origin of all species is a result of adaptation mediated through the process of natural selection. This concept of adaptation is extended in the behavioral realm to include dealing with minor problems and frustrations, such as waiting in the grocery line, as well as more complex difficulties, such as dealing with the death of a spouse. In this context, coping is essentially an adaptation under more difficult conditions. White also talks about the term "mastery," which he contends is quite unpopular with psychologists because of its connotation with "superiority" and "winning and losing." However, mastery is another way of describing the concept of coping, whereby the anxiety or danger is mastered.

Perhaps the greatest impetus to the contemporary understanding of coping has come from the work of the American psychologist Richard Lazarus, an emeritus professor at the University of California at Berkeley, and his colleagues. Lazarus introduced the transactional model of stress and coping in his 1966 book *Psychological Stress and the Coping Process*. He elaborated this concept further in 1984 in the book *Stress, Appraisal, and Coping* (with coauthor Susan Folkman).

According to the transactional model, stressful experiences are perceived as person-environment transactions. In these transactions, the person undergoes a four-stage assessment known as appraisal. When confronted with any possible stressful situation, the first stage is the primary appraisal of the event. In this stage, based on one's previous experience, knowledge about oneself, and knowledge about the event, the person internally determines whether he or she is in trouble. If the event is perceived to be threatening or has caused harm or loss in the past, then the stage of secondary appraisal occurs. If, on the other hand, the event is judged to be irrelevant or poses no threat, then stress does not develop and no further coping is required. The secondary appraisal determines how much control one has over the situation or the event. Based upon this understanding, the individual ascertains what means of control are available. This is the stage known as coping. Finally, the fourth stage is the stage of reappraisal, in which the person determines whether the original event or situation has been effectively negated. The primary focus of Lazarus's conceptualization of coping is on coping as an application of thought processes and behavioral efforts to combat demands that exceed a person's resources. The hallmarks of this conceptualization are its focus on the process of coping as opposed to personality traits; the importance of specific stressful situations in inducing coping as opposed to a general physiological response; and a lack of reference to the outcome (whether positive or negative), as opposed to the mastery concept, which only emphasizes the positive aspects.

COPING STRATEGIES

According to the transactional model, there are two broad categories of coping. The first one is called problem-focused coping strategy, and the second one is called emotion-focused coping strategy. Problem-focused coping is based on one's capability to think about and alter the environmental event or situation. Examples of this strategy at the thought process level include utilization of problem-solving skills, interpersonal conflict resolution, advice-seeking, time management, goal-setting, and gathering more information about what is causing one stress. Problem-solving requires thinking through various solutions, evaluating the pros and cons of different solutions, and then implementing a solution that seems most advantageous to reduce the stress. Examples of this strategy at the behavioral or action level include activities such as joining a smoking cessation program, complying with a prescribed medical treatment, adhering to a diabetic diet plan, or scheduling and prioritizing tasks for managing time.

In the emotion-focused strategy, the focus is inward on altering the way one thinks or feels about a situation or an event. Examples of this strategy at the thought process level include denying the existence of the stressful situation, freely expressing emotions, avoiding the stressful situation, making social comparisons, or minimizing, (looking at the bright side of things). Examples of this strategy at the behavioral or action level include seeking social support to negate the influence of the stressful situation; using exercise, relaxation, or meditation; joining support groups; practicing religious rituals; and escaping through the use of alcohol and drugs.

Several predictive empirical studies done using this model have generally shown that problem-focused strategies are quite helpful for stressful events that can be changed, while emotion-focused strategies are more helpful for stressful events that cannot be changed. Some of these coping strategies are healthy, such as applying problem-solving skills; some are neither healthy nor unhealthy, such as practicing some religious rituals; and some are unhealthy or maladaptive, such as denying the existence of a stressful situation or escaping through the use of drugs.

Choice of coping strategy is influenced by the quantity and quality of available resources for coping that may be available to a person. These resources include knowledge (for example, knowledge of the functioning at a workplace), skills (such as analytical skills), attitudes (for example, self-efficacy or confidence in one's ability to perform a specific behavior), social resources (people with whom a person can exchange information), physical resources (such as health and stamina), material resources (money), and societal resources (policies and laws).

MEASUREMENT OF COPING STRATEGIES

Self-reported, paper-and-pencil tools are commonly used in measuring coping strategies. A popular assessment tool for measuring coping strategies is the Ways of Coping (WOC) Checklist developed by Lazarus and Folkman, which contains sixty-eight different items. These responses have been divided into eight categories: accepting of responsibility (such as criticizing or lecturing oneself), confrontational coping (expressing anger), distancing (trivializing the situation), escape avoidance (wishing that the situation would go away), planned problem-solving (making a plan of action and following it), positive reappraisal (changing or growing as a person in a good way), seeking of social support (talking to someone to find out about more about the situation), and self-controlling (keeping feelings to oneself). A further revision of this scale, the Ways of Coping Checkist-Revised, contains a list of forty-two coping behaviors.

American psychologist Charles Carver and his colleagues have designed the Coping Orientations to Problems Experienced (COPE) scale. The COPE scale has twelve component scales for types of coping strategies that include acceptance, active coping, denial, disengagement, humor, planning, positive reframing, religion, restraint, social support, self-distraction, and suppression of competing activities. Carver has also designed and tested a brief version of the COPE scale for use with other large protocols that has been found to be efficacious. Other scales have been developed to measure the daily utilization of coping.

PERSONALITY TRAITS AND COPING

The relationship between personality trait characteristics and coping has been suggested and studied by several researchers. American psychologist Suzanne Kobasa, in her 1977 University of Chicago doctoral dissertation, studied the role of personality and coping. Specifically, she examined the characteristics of highly stressed people among those who remained healthy and those who did not manifest any illness following stressful times. She coined the term "hardiness" to depict the personality profile of people who remained healthy. Her research found three general characteristics of hardiness: the belief of control or the ability to influence the events of one's experience; commitment to activities in life or a feeling of deep involvement; and challenge to further development or anticipation of change.

Israeli medical sociologist Aaron Antonovsky described the concept of "sense of coherence," also related to personality traits, as being central to coping. He described three components as being representative of this concept: comprehensibility, meaningfulness, and manageability. Comprehensibility means that the person believes that the world around him or her is making some sense, there is some set structure, and there is some level of predictability. Manageability implies the faith that a person has in his or her ability to meet the various demands in life in one way or another. Meaningfulness implies the belief that whatever one does has a purpose in life. Antonovsky proposed that people who possess a higher sense of coherence tend to cope better in life.

Another personality characteristic that has been studied in relation to coping is optimism. Optimism is the tendency to look at the brighter side of things and to expect positive outcomes from one's actions. Research has shown that optimism improves effective coping. Carver and his colleagues studied the effects of optimism in patients suffering from breast cancer, heart rehabilitation patients, and people in other stressful situations and have found the beneficial effect of optimism on coping.

American cardiologists Meyer Friedman and Ray Rosenman, in their observations of heart disease patients, described two types of personalities: Type A and Type B. Type A people are characterized by time urgency impatience, competitiveness, and hostility. Type B show the opposites of these characteristics, exemplified by no time urgency, and being cooperative and patient in their disposition. Type A personalities have been found to demonstrate negative coping styles in terms of showing more negative physiological and psychological outcomes.

SOCIAL ENVIRONMENT AND COPING

Coping does not occur in vacuum. Most stressful situations entail involvement with people. Therefore, social environment influences stress and coping. Social environment can be conceptualized at a broader level as the social structure, and it can also be conceptualized in a specific, narrow way as close social relationships. The latter are often described as social support and depict the most common way researchers have studied the social relationship in the context of coping. The broader effect of social structure on coping is rather obvious. For example, a person on the higher rung of the social ladder would have access to greater resources and thus would be able to apply a variety of coping resources, while a person at the bottom of the social ladder, living in poverty, would have less resources at his or her disposal.

Social support has been conceptualized from different perspectives. American sociologist James House, a professor at the University of Michigan, defined social support as the "aid and assistance that one receives through social relationships and interpersonal exchanges" and classified it into four types. The first is emotional social support, or the empathy, love, trust, and caring that one receives from others. The second kind is instrumental social support, or the tangible aid and service that one receives from others. The third type is informational social support, or the advice, suggestions, and information that one receives from others. The fourth type is appraisal social support, or the information that one receives for self-assessment. Social support has a direct effect on lowering stress levels and improving effective coping, as well as providing stress "buffering effects," or what statisticians call effect modulation. For example, a person undergoing stress may talk to a friend, who may provide a tangible aid to cope (direct effect), or may modify the receiver's perception of the stressful event, or enhance the receiver's belief that he or she can cope with the stressful event (buffering effect).

SOURCES FOR FURTHER STUDY

Bloona, Richard, ed. *Coping with Stress in a Changing World.* New York: McGraw Hill College Division, 1999. This is an applied textbook for college students in psychology, health sciences, nursing, business, and related fields. The book presents an applied framework for coping described as the four R's: rethink, reduce, relax, and re-lease.

Dewe, Philip. "Determinants of Coping: Some Alternative Explanations and Measurement Issues." *Psychological Reports* 88, no. 3 (2001): 832-834. A thought-provoking article about coping that promotes reflection on some theoretical and methodological issues. Theoretical issues discussed include the link between stress and coping and the relationship between personality and coping. Issues of methodological pluralism, the value of coping scores as derived through coping scales, varying interpretations of coping scores, and instructional details on coping scales are addressed.

Eckenrode, John, ed. *The Social Context of Coping.* New York: Plenum, 1991. This volume of contributions produced by the members of the Consortium for Research Involving Stress Processes (CRISP) focuses on the social dimensions of coping. Developmental issues, variations across life span, gender, specific role of social support, and research directions in coping are discussed.

Field, Tiffany M., Philip M. McCabe, and Neil Schneiderman, eds. *Stress and Coping.* Hillsdale, N.J.: Lawrence Erlbaum, 1985. This monograph includes a series of articles on psychophysiological, developmental, and psychosocial aspects of stress and coping. The psychosocial discussion pertaining to coping and anger and a multisystem model of coping discussed in the book are particularly relevant.

Lazarus, Richard, S., and Susan Folkman. *Stress, Appraisal, and Coping.* New York: Springer, 1984. This is a classic, landmark book on coping that is most frequently cited in the coping literature. A "must read" book on coping.

Monat, Alan, and Lazarus, Richard S., ed. *Stress and Coping: An Anthology.* 2d ed. New York: Columbia University Press, 1985. This is a compendium of twenty-six readings in the area of stress and coping. Topics in the areas of effects of stress, the link between environment and stress, the concept of coping, coping with stresses of everyday life, coping with death and dying, and stress management are discussed.

Rice, Virginia H., ed. *Handbook of Stress, Coping, and Health: Implications for Nursing Research, Theory, and Practice.* Lanham, Md.: Altamira Press, 1999. The authors of chapters in this book have taken special efforts to cater to the needs of graduate students in health fields. Includes a special section on theories that describe or explain the relationship of coping and health outcomes and the moderating influences thereof.

Romas, John, A., and Manoj Sharma. *Practical Stress Management. A Comprehensive Workbook for Managing Change and Promoting Health.* 2d ed. Needham Heights, Mass.: Allyn & Bacon, 2000. An applied workbook designed specifically for the general public and undergraduate students. The workbook is easy to read and is complemented by worksheets and thoughts for reflection to help readers examine coping in their lives from a personal health perspective.

Snyder, C. Richard, ed. *Coping: The Psychology of What Works.* New York: Oxford University Press, 1999. A treatise on coping that tries to bridge the gap between clinical, social, and personality psychologists. Contributors discuss the concept of coping, problem-focused strategies, emotion-focused strategies, the role of personality (including optimism and hoping), and coping with special situations. A good book but technical for the uninitiated.

Manoj Sharma

SEE ALSO: Biofeedback and relaxation; Coping: Chronic illness; Coping: Social support; Coping: Terminal illness; Decision making; Meditation and relaxation; Problem-solving stages; Stress; Stress: Behavioral and psychological responses; Stress: Physiological responses; Stress: Theories.

Coping
Terminal illness

TYPE OF PSYCHOLOGY: Cognition; consciousness; social psychology; stress

FIELDS OF STUDY: Aging; coping; depression; stress and illness

Terminal illness is perceived as a catastrophic threat to the continued existence of the self, one's relationships, and to all that is valued in this life. Successful coping depends on available medical, personal, social, and spiritual resources. The hospice move-

ment has introduced a humane and holistic approach to the support of the dying, treats the family as the unit of care, and is an alternative to the traditional, medical model.

KEY CONCEPTS
- death and dying
- death anxiety
- international hospice movement
- Lazarus and Folkman model of coping
- palliative care
- religious reframing
- self-help groups
- stages of dying
- terminal illness
- thanatology

INTRODUCTION

A terminal illness cannot be cured and, therefore, is recognized by the person dying as a catastrophic threat to the self, to one's relationships, and to one's body. In terms of the model of coping proposed by Richard Lazarus and Susan Folkman, death is the perceived threat or stressor causing stress and is evaluated by primary appraisal; the response or coping strategy depends on the person's secondary appraisal of available physical, psychological, social, and spiritual resources. The relationship between the perception of threat and the coping response is dynamic in that it changes over time. For example, the threat of death varies with physical or psychological deterioration and calls for changing strategies during the period of dying.

Anxiety and fear are typical of any crisis; however, when faced with the overwhelming crisis that death poses, a dying person is flooded with death anxiety or mortal fear of dying. Two classic views of death anxiety are Freudian and existential. Sigmund Freud (1856-1939) believed that it was impossible to imagine one's own death and that "death anxiety" is really fear of something else, whereas the existentialists believe that awareness of mortality is a basic condition of human existence and is the source of death anxiety. In 1996, Adrian Tomer and Grafton Eliason offered a contemporary "regrets" model, where death anxiety is a function of how much one regrets not having accomplished what one had hoped to accomplish in light of the time left. A major criticism of their work is that achievement takes precedence over social relationships and

other sources of meaning. In 2000, Robert J. Kastenbaum proposed an edge theory, where the response to extreme danger is distinct from the ordinary awareness of mortality. He suggested that death anxiety is the consequence of a heightened awareness of potential disaster at the edge of what is otherwise known to be relatively safe.

Thanatology, the study of death and dying, focuses on the needs of the terminally ill and their survivors. Some thanatologists distinguish between fear of the process of dying and fear of the unknown at death. For example, the Collett-Lester Scale, established in 1994, operationalizes these ideas by offering four subscales: death of self, death of others, dying of self, and dying of others. A major problem with studies of death anxiety is that researchers typically employ self-report questionnaires that measure conscious attitudes. In general, the construct validity of questionnaires is reduced when anxiety is confounded with unconscious denial or when death is confounded with dying.

HOSPICE AND PALLIATIVE CARE

From the beginning of the twentieth century until the 1970's, Americans with terminal illnesses usually died in hospitals. Medical treatment focused on pathology; control of pain with narcotics was limited, as most physicians were worried about consequent drug addiction. Efforts to save lives were machine-intensive and often painful. The psychological, social, and spiritual needs of the person were not as important as the heroic effort to preserve life at any cost. When Dame Cicely Saunders, a British nurse and physician, opened St. Christopher's Hospice in London in 1967, she introduced holistic reforms that treated both the dying person and his or her family and included regular administrations of morphine for the amelioration of pain. It was discovered that control of pain is better when dosing at regular intervals and that the total dosage may be less than if drugs are offered only in response to severe, acute pain. Saunders was a profound inspiration to the international hospice movement, as well as to the new field of palliative medicine. (The goal of palliative care is to relieve pain and symptoms and is different from traditional, curative care.)

Initially, hospices were hospital-based; however, toward the end of the twentieth century, home-based care became common. A full-service program provides an interdisciplinary team comprised of a physician, social worker, registered nurse, and pastor or counselor; round-the-clock care is available. Furthermore, after death, support services are offered to grieving families. In the United States, the National Hospice Reimbursement Act of 1983 offered financial support for full-service hospice care. A local hospice is an important coping resource for someone who chooses to forgo traditional medical treatment. It offers a means for preserving some control of the environment, as well as for maintaining personal dignity. Most important, a peaceful, pain-free death is possible.

STAGES OF DYING

About the time that the international hospice movement was gaining momentum, an important book titled *On Death and Dying* (1969) was published in America by the psychiatrist Elisabeth Kübler-Ross. She presented transcripts of interviews with dying patients who were struggling with common end-of-life concerns. What gripped American readers was her call for the treatment of dying people as human beings and her compelling, intellectual analysis of dying as a sequence of five stages: denial and isolation, anger, bargaining, depression, and acceptance. However, according to Robert J. Kastenbaum, there is no real empirical verification of her stage theory. Specifically, dying need not involve all stages and may not proceed in the sequence described by Kübler-Ross. Therapists point out that depression and anxiety are ever-present but change in intensity— sometimes manageable, sometimes overwhelming. While theoreticians argue about the scientific status of Kübler-Ross's stage theory, clinicians use her ideas to tailor therapeutic regimens depending on the current needs of their patients. One way to evaluate current status is in terms of how the patient is coping with various threats and challenges posed by dying.

The "stages" of dying may be thought of as emotion-focused coping behaviors for responding to death, a stressor that cannot be changed. In contrast, problem-focused coping behaviors are appropriate when an aspect of the stressor can be changed. When a dying mother is too weak to care for a child, she copes with the problem of her weakness by arranging for child care. When a husband is worried about the financial security of his wife, he draws up a will.

Denial is usually the first response to the shocking news of terminal illness. Denial of one's impending death is a way of coping with the threat of losing one's self and key relationships. The loss of one's self is characterized by the loss of what one values as personally defining. For example, death implies the ultimate loss of strength or of the capacity for meaningful work and ushers in a radical, unwanted change of self-concept. However, denial allows an acceptance of the facts at a slower, more manageable rate and is a way to cope emotionally with death anxiety.

Anger is a common venting response once denial is no longer consuming. (Other venting strategies include crying, yelling, sarcasm, and recklessness.) The private or public expression of anger is evidence that the person has moved beyond complete denial toward the recognition of death as a real threat.

Bargaining with fate or God is a futile but common coping strategy, whereby the person tries desperately to restore body integrity and self-concept. The efforts are sometimes heroic, as when a person has accepted that he or she is dying but tries to maintain some version of prior meaningful activities. The scope is limited and the places may change, but relationships and activities critical to self-concept continue for as long as possible.

Depression is marked by sorrow, grief for current and future losses, and diminished pleasure. It is different from the anxiety that arises when a person fears that what is necessary for an intact self is jeopardized; in contrast, depression occurs when the dying person is certain that he or she has lost what is necessary. Depression is the most common psychological problem in palliative-care settings. However, when ordinary depression becomes major, the treatable condition is often unrecognized and patients suffer needless emotional pain. Minor depression, an expected coping behavior, may be adaptive, whereas major depression is maladaptive and requires medical intervention.

Acceptance of one's terminal condition is viewed by many clinicians as a desired end-state because the possibility of a peaceful death comes with acceptance. The person has not given up emotionally but has reached a point of choosing not to struggle for survival. Therapists of various kinds interpret acceptance in the light of a particular worldview or theoretical paradigm. For example, the transpersonal counselor sees acceptance as evidence of an intrapsychic transformation of the self to a higher level of consciousness.

OTHER COPING STRATEGIES

Dying presents many threats and challenges, including psychological and spiritual distress, pain, exhaustion, loss of independence, loss of dignity, and abandonment. In addition to depression and anxiety, guilt is a response to believing that one must have been a bad person to deserve such a fate, or that one risked one's health in a way that brought on the illness. Sometimes people feel guilty because of anger and sarcasm vented on hapless family members, friends, helpers, or God. Thoughts of suicide may occur when depression is severe enough or if the pain is intolerable. Not all people suffer all these assaults, but each requires a strategy for coping.

It is not uncommon for friends and relatives to pull away from the dying person because of their own anxiety and discomfort. Witnessing the physical and emotional distress of a valued person poses

Psychiatrist Elisabeth Kübler-Ross gained fame as a specialist in the study of dying and bereavement. (AP/Wide World Photos)

a threat to successful, day-to-day management of mortal fears; one way to cope is by ignoring the dying. Unfortunately, physical or emotional distancing causes dreadful isolation and a sense of abandonment just when social support is most critically needed. The terminally ill in such a predicament may cope by turning to a pastoral counselor, therapist, self-help group, and/or local hospice.

Each type of therapist has a different focus. A psychoanalyst might encourage frank discussions of fears and anxieties. A cognitive-behavioral therapist might focus on changing maladaptive behavior by modifying negative thought patterns. A humanistic-existentialist might encourage a life review to help consolidate the patient's perceptions of the meaning of life and as a way to say "good-bye." A transpersonal counselor might focus on facilitating a meaningful transformation of self in preparation for death. A primary goal of therapy of any kind with dying patients is to promote physical and psychological comfort. Often, the therapist is an advocate acting as a liaison between the patient and the hospice, hospital, family, or friends. The therapist may provide helpful psychoeducational interventions, such as alleviating distress about an upcoming medical procedure by informing the patient about the rationale for the procedure, the steps involved, the predictable side effects, and the prognosis or forecast for the outcome. When the therapist also educates the family, the quality of their support is enhanced, thereby improving the well-being of the patient.

SELF-HELP GROUPS

Self-help groups provide significant mutual support to the terminally ill and to those in mourning. They are available in professional and nonprofessional settings. They are usually composed of peers who are in a similar plight and who, therefore, are familiar with the depression, anxiety, and guilt associated with dying. Access to a new, primary group counteracts common feelings of alienation and victimization by offering the opportunity for meaningful social support and information. Mutual disclosure reduces feelings of isolation and abandonment by building a community of peers. Sharing successful strategies for coping with secondary losses triggered by terminal illness restores hope. (For example, group members may know how to cope with the disfigurement of mastectomy or with confinement to a wheelchair.) Group participants also encourage one another to be active partners in their own medical care. Unreliable patterns of communication and reluctance to talk about dying are common outside the group; however, group members talk to one another openly, thereby reducing the dismay associated with patronizing exchanges with doctors and nurses or the silence of family and friends.

RELIGIOUS AND SPIRITUAL COPING

Psychologists emphasize the ways in which adversity may be conquered or controlled, but not every stressor is controllable. Certainly, dying brings into sharp relief the fact that humans are ultimately powerless in the face of death. At the end of life, people often turn to religion or spirituality for answers as to the purpose of their lives, the reasons for suffering, the destination of their souls, the nature of the afterlife—whether a life everlasting exists. Coping theorists may reduce the function of religion to "terror management," but others believe that the experience of the sacred cannot be understood empirically and that religion is more than an elaborate coping mechanism.

The psychologist of religion Kenneth I. Pargament studied the relationship between religion and coping. He defined religion functionally in terms of a search for significance in the light of the sacred. He described a typical belief system involving the event (in this case, death), the person, and the sacred. Core beliefs are that God is benevolent, the world is just or fair, and that the person is good. Dying jeopardizes the balance of this belief system; to cope, people turn to religious reframing as a way of conserving the significance or value of their core beliefs. For example, people facing a seemingly pointless death reframe its significance— death becomes an opportunity for spiritual growth or enlightenment; this preserves the beliefs that the person is good and that God is benevolent. Others reframe the nature of the person as being sinful, otherwise why does suffering exist? The result is that belief in a just world is preserved. Some reframe their beliefs regarding the sacred and consider God as punishing. However, several researchers have found that only a small proportion of people attribute their suffering to a vengeful, punishing God. Another way to reframe the nature of God is to reconsider His omnipotence. People may conclude that a loving God is constrained by forces in nature. This reframed belief preserves the idea that God is good.

Dying is not always the occasion for spiritual crisis; people of deep faith find solace in their relationship with God or with their understanding of the transcendent. The psychiatrist Harold G. Koenig reports in *The Healing Power of Faith* (1999) that faith, prayer, meditation, and congregational support mitigate fear, hopelessness, and the experience of pain. For people committed to a religious or spiritual belief system, God or spirit is a source of peace and hope while dying.

SOURCES FOR FURTHER STUDY

Cook, Alicia Skinner, and Kevin Ann Oltjenbruns. *Dying and Grieving: Life Span and Family Perspectives.* 2d ed. Fort Worth, Tex.: Harcourt Brace, 1998. Death and dying are discussed from a systems perspective with a special emphasis on consideration of developmental stage. Age is an important determinant of how death is understood and responded to by the dying person, family, and community. Hence, the authors present information separately for children, adolescents, and adults; they also discuss the needs of caregivers. This text is written for undergraduates.

Kastenbaum, Robert J. *Death, Society, and Human Experience.* 7th ed. Boston: Allyn & Bacon, 2001. This text is a very good overview of the field of thanatology written by an active researcher. Kastenbaum presents historical background, thoroughly covers the field of death studies, introduces theories about dying, and offers chapters on violent death (including murder, terrorism, and disaster), suicide, and euthanasia. Written for undergraduates.

Kübler-Ross, Elisabeth. *On Death and Dying.* New York: Macmillan, 1969. This is an important primary source in the field of thanatology. The interviews with dying patients are often quite moving. Kübler-Ross's book was a clarion call for reforms of common procedures for treatment of dying patients in hospital settings. Analyses of the stages of dying and the various coping responses of hospitalized patients are from a psychoanalyst's perspective.

Lair, George S. *Counseling the Terminally Ill: Sharing the Journey.* Washington, D.C.: Taylor & Francis, 1996. Lair is a transpersonal counselor who has written of the needs of a dying person in terms of holistic palliative care. The goal of transpersonal psychology is to facilitate wholeness, actualization, and growth even while dying. He considers that a good counseling relationship is like a shared journey and that a sensitive counselor takes her or his lead from the individual counseled.

Pargament, Kenneth I. *The Psychology of Religion and Coping: Theory, Research, Practice.* New York: Guilford, 1997. Pargament is a renowned psychologist who has written a perceptive and comprehensive text that explores the research literature on coping, religion, and their intersection. Somewhat demanding text with a very good bibliography. Highly recommended.

Tanja Bekhuis

See also: Coping: Chronic illness; Coping: Social support; Coping: Strategies; Health psychology; Death and dying; Depression; Stress; Stress: Behavioral and psychological responses; Stress-related diseases; Support groups.

Couples therapy

Type of psychology: Psychotherapy
Fields of study: Group and family therapies

Relationship distress represents one of the most common reasons that individuals seek psychological help in the United States. As a result, there is an increasing demand for treatment services which are both effective in altering destructive marital interactions and efficient in the use of the therapist's and client's time.

Key concepts
- cross-complaining loop
- domestic violence
- operant conditioning
- prevention programs
- validation loop

Introduction
Traditionally, marriage vows have represented pledges of mutual love and enduring commitment. Since the 1960's, however, marital relationships have

changed dramatically. In fact, while more than 90 percent of the United States population will marry at least once in their lifetime, it is anticipated that approximately 50 percent of first marriages and 60 percent of second marriages will end in divorce. Moreover, while the average first marriage in the United States will last only five to seven years, second marriages typically endure only for five years. It appears that a repetitive pattern of marriage, distress, and divorce has become commonplace. Such a cycle often results in considerable pain and psychological turmoil for the couple, their family, and their friends. These statistics dramatically indicate the need for effective ways to help couples examine and reapproach their relationships before deciding whether to terminate them.

Research has found evidence that links divorce and relationship distress to a wide variety of emotional disorders in spouses and their children. Depressive syndromes are evident in approximately half of female partners and nearly 15 percent of male partners in dysfunctional marriages. Almost half of all first admissions to state hospitals in the United States have relationship stress as a major factor. Evidence further reveals that suicide often follows marital discord, separation, and divorce. In fact, divorce and marital separation represent two of the most common significant stressors in adult life.

Interpersonal relationships are a highly complex yet important area of study and investigation. The decision to marry (or at least to commit to a serious intimate relationship) is clearly one of the most significant choices people make in their lives. Unfortunately, it is rare to find school curricula that offer any assistance, training, or education to help young people understand interpersonal relationships or make the decision to marry. Fortunately, advances in couples therapy have led to increased knowledge about interpersonal relationships and methods for improving relationship satisfaction. These advances have been documented in the scientific literature, and they extend to the treatment of cohabitating partners, premarital couples, remarried partners, gay or lesbian couples, separating or divorced couples, and stepfamilies. Moreover, couples-based treatment programs have shown effectiveness in the treatment of depression, anxiety disorders, domestic violence, sexual dysfunction, and a host of other problems.

COMMUNICATION AND CONFLICT RESOLUTION

Partners who seek couples therapy or counseling frequently have problems in two areas: communication and conflict resolution. These are the two major difficulties that most often lead to divorce. It has been shown that communication skills differentiate satisfied and dissatisfied couples more powerfully than any other factor. Indeed, communication difficulties are the most frequently cited complaint among partners reporting relationship distress.

Psychologist John M. Gottman, in his books *Marital Interaction: Experimental Investigations* (1979) and *A Couple's Guide to Communication* (Gottman et al., 1976), is one of many researchers who have highlighted the importance of communication problems within distressed relationships. Many characteristic differences between distressed and satisfied couples have been noted. Partners in distressed couples often misperceive well-intended statements from their partners, whereas satisfied couples are more likely to rate well-intended messages as positive; distressed partners also engage in fewer rewarding exchanges and more frequent punishing interactions than nondistressed couples. A partner in a distressed relationship is more immediately reactive to perceived negative behavior exhibited by his or her partner. There is generally a greater emphasis on negative communication strategies between distressed partners.

Distressed couples appear to be generally unskilled at generating positive change in their relationship. Gottman also reported that distressed couples are often ineffectual in their attempts to resolve conflicts. Whereas nondistressed couples employ "validation loops" during problem-solving exercises (one partner states the conflict and the other partner expresses agreement or support), distressed couples typically enter into repetitive, cross-complaining loops. These loops can be described as an interactional sequence wherein both individuals describe areas of dissatisfaction within the relationship yet fail to attend to their partners' issues. Moreover, as one spouse initiates aversive control tactics, the other spouse will typically reciprocate with similar behavior.

THERAPY FORMATS

Couples therapy attempts to alleviate distress, resolve conflicts, improve daily functioning, and prevent problems via an intensive focus on the couple as a unit and on each partner as an individual. Couples therapists are faced with a variety of choices regarding treatment format and therapeutic approach. Individual therapy focuses treatment on only one of the partners. Although generally discouraged by most practitioners, individual treatment of one partner can provide greater opportunities for the client to focus on his or her own thoughts, feelings, problems, and behaviors. Clients may feel less hesitant in sharing some details they would not want a spouse to hear, and individual treatment may encourage the client to take greater personal responsibility for problems and successes. In general, these advantages are outweighed by the difficulties encountered when treating relationship problems without both partners being present. In particular, interpersonal interactions are complex phenomena that need to be evaluated and treated with both partners present.

Concurrent therapy involves both partners being seen in treatment separately, either by the same therapist or by two separate but collaborating therapists. Advantages of the concurrent format include greater individual attention and opportunities to develop strategies to improve relationship skills by teaching each partner those techniques separately. Concurrent treatment, however, does not allow the therapist(s) to evaluate and treat the nature of the interpersonal difficulties with both partners present in the same room.

Conjoint format, on the other hand, involves both partners simultaneously in the therapy session. Conjoint treatment is widely used and generally recommended because it focuses intensively on the quality of the relationship, promotes dialogue between the couple, and can attend to the needs and goals of each partner as well as the needs and goals of the couple. The history of conjoint marital therapy begins, ironically, with Sigmund Freud's failures in this area. He believed firmly that it was counterproductive and dangerous for a therapist ever to treat more than one member of the same family. In fact, in 1912, after attempting to provide services simultaneously to a husband and wife, Freud concluded that he was at a complete loss about how to treat relationship problems within a couple. He also added that he had little faith in individual therapy for them.

Conjoint treatment is designed to focus intensively on the relationship in order to effect specific therapeutic change for that particular couple. Interventions can be tailor-made for the couple seeking treatment, regardless of the nature of the problem the couple describes (such as sexual relations, child rearing, household responsibilities). Moreover, couples are constantly engaged in direct dialogue, which can foster improved understanding and resolution of conflict. As compared with other approaches, conjoint marital therapy can focus on each of the specific needs and goals of the individual couple.

Group couples treatment programs have received increased attention and have shown very good to excellent treatment success. Advantages of group treatment for couples include opportunities for direct assessment and intervention of the relationship within a setting that promotes greater opportunity for feedback and suggestions from other couples experiencing similar difficulties. In fact, group therapy may promote positive expectations through witnessing improvements among other couples as well as fostering a sense of cohesiveness among couples within the group. In the group format, each partner has the opportunity to develop improved communication and conflict resolution approaches by learning relationship skills via interaction with the therapist(s), his or her spouse, and other group members. In addition, the cost of individual, concurrent, and conjoint therapy, in terms of time as well as dollars, has prompted several researchers and clinicians to recommend group couples therapy.

THERAPEUTIC APPROACHES

There are numerous approaches to the treatment of relationship problems practiced in the United States. Psychodynamic therapy focuses attention on the unconscious needs and issues raised during an individual's childhood. Phenomenological therapists focus on the here-and-now experiences of being in a relationship and have developed a variety of creative therapeutic techniques. Systems therapists view interpersonal problems as being maintained by the nature of the relationship structure, patterns of communication, and family roles and rules.

Behavioral marital therapy, however, is the most thoroughly investigated approach within the couples therapy field. Starting from a focus on operant conditioning (a type of learning in which behaviors are altered primarily by the consequences that follow them—reinforcement or punishment), behavioral marital therapy includes a wide range of asessment and treatment strategies. The underlying assumption that best differentiates behavioral treatments for distressed couples from other approaches is that the two partners are viewed as ineffectual in their attempts to satisfy each other. Thus, the goal of therapy is to improve relationship satisfaction by creating a supportive environment in which the skills can be acquired. Behavioral marital therapy incorporates strategies designed to improve daily interactions, communication patterns, and problem-solving abilities, and to examine and modify unreasonable expectations and faulty thinking styles.

BEHAVIORAL-EXCHANGE STRATEGIES

Psychologists Philip and Marcy Bornstein, in their book *Marital Therapy: A Behavioral-Communications Approach* (1986), described a sequential five-step procedure in the treatment of relationship dysfunction. These steps include intake interviewing, behavioral exchange strategies, communication skills acquisition, training in problem solving, and maintenance and generalization of treatment gains.

Intake interviewing is designed to accomplish three primary goals: development of a working relationship with the therapist, collection of assessment information, and implementation of initial therapeutic regiments. Because spouses entering treatment have often spent months, if not years, in conflict and distress, the intake procedure attempts to provide a unique opportunity to influence and assess the couple's relationship immediately. Since distressed couples often devote a considerable amount of time thinking about and engaging in discordant interpersonal interactions, it naturally follows that they will attempt to engage in unpleasant interactions during initial sessions. Information about current difficulties and concerns is clearly valuable, but improved communication skills and positive interactions appear to be of even greater merit early in treatment. Thus, couples are discouraged from engaging in cross-complaining loops and are encouraged to develop skills and implement homework procedures designed to enhance the relationship.

SKILL TRAINING

Building a positive working relationship between partners is viewed as essential in couples treatment programs. During training in behavioral exchange strategies, couples are aided in specifying and pinpointing behaviors that tend to promote increased harmony in their relationship. Couples engage in contracting and compromise activities in order to disrupt the downward spiral of their distressed relationship.

Training in communication skills focuses on practicing the basics of communication (such as respect, understanding, and sensitivity), and positive principles of communication (timeliness, marital manners, specification, and "mind reading"), improving nonverbal behaviors, and learning "molecular" verbal behaviors (such as assertiveness and constructive agreement). Improved communication styles are fostered via a direct, active approach designed to identify, reinforce, and rehearse desirable patterns of interactions. Clients are generally provided with specific instructions and "practice periods" during sessions in which partners are encouraged to begin improving their interactional styles. It is common that these sessions are audiotaped or videotaped to give couples specific feedback regarding their communication style.

Training in problem solving is intended to teach clients to negotiate and resolve conflicts in a mutually beneficial manner. Conflict resolution training focuses on learning, practicing, and experiencing effective problem-solving approaches. Couples receive specific instruction on systematic problem-solving approaches and are given homework assignments designed to improve problem-solving skills. Because the value of couples therapy lies in the improvement, maintenance, and use of positive interaction styles over time and across situations, treatment often aims to promote constructive procedures after the termination of active treatment. Thus, people are taught that it is generally easier to change oneself than one's partner, that positive interaction styles may be forgotten or unlearned if these strategies are not regularly practiced, and that new positive interactions can continue to develop in a variety of settings even as treatment ends.

COMPARATIVE RESEARCH

To highlight further the utility and effectiveness of behavioral-communications relationship therapy, Philip Bornstein, Laurie Wilson, and Gregory L. Wilson conducted an empirical investigation in 1988 comparing conjoint and behavioral-communications group therapy and group behavioral-communications therapies to a waiting-list control group (couples who were asked to wait two months prior to beginning treatment). Fifteen distressed couples were randomly assigned to experimental conditions and offered eight sessions of couples therapy. At the conclusion of treatment (as well as six months later), the couples in active treatment revealed significant alleviation of relationship distress. The conjoint and group couples revealed similar levels of improvement in communication skills, problem-solving abilities, and general relationship satisfaction. The waiting-list couples, on the other hand, revealed no improvement while they waited for treatment, indicating that relationship distress does not tend to improve simply as the result of the passage of time.

PREVENTION AND DISORDERS

Another line of couples research has focused on the utility of premarital intervention, or distress and divorce prevention programs. Unlike treatment programs, prevention programs intervene prior to the development of relationship distress. Prevention efforts are focused on the future and typically involve the training of specific skills which are viewed as useful in preventing relationship distress. Three major approaches to premarital intervention include the Minnesota Couples Communication Program, Bernard Guerney's relationship enhancement approach, and the Premarital Relationship Enhancement Program. Research is generally supportive of the effectiveness of these programs in helping partners learn useful skills which translate into improved relationships for at least three to eight years following the program. In addition, some evidence indicates that the alarming divorce rate in the United States can be decreased if partners participate in prevention programs prior to marriage; prevention programs that emphasize communication and conflict-resolution skills seem most advantageous.

There has also been considerable interest in the utility of couples-based treatment for various psychological disorders, including depression, anxiety disorders, and alcoholism. For example, the rationale for couples intervention as a viable treatment for depressed clients rests on the assumption that marital dysfunction is either causative or related to the maintenance of the depressed state. Since more than 50 percent of married couples seeking relationship therapy have at least one spouse who is depressed, and nearly 50 percent of women seeking depression treatment report marital discord, it appears that depression and marital dysfunction are not necessarily distinct problems. Thus, a primary advantage of marital therapy strategies in the resolution of depression is the simultaneous emphasis on and demonstrated effectiveness of such interventions in reducing relationship discord as well as depression.

IMPROVING TREATMENT

Since 1970, researchers and clinicians have witnessed large increases in the numbers of couples seeking treatment from therapists. As the demand for couples treatment has increased, more time and effort has been devoted to improving treatment methods. The behavioral approach has been shown to be highly effective in reducing relationship distress and preventing divorce; however, several investigations have demonstrated that cognitive components such as causal attributions and expectations are strongly related to satisfaction in the relationship. Moreover, it has been argued that dysfunctional cognitions may interfere with both the establishment and maintenance of positive behavior change. Evidence has prompted some researchers and practitioners to advocate a more systematic inclusion of strategies of cognitive behavior therapy within the behavioral marital therapy framework. Specifically, it is possible that the combination of cognitive and behavioral approaches will demonstrate increased utility if the two treatments are presented together in a singular, integrated treatment intervention. Such treatment would afford couples the opportunity to benefit from either one or both of the complementary approaches, depending on their own unique needs, at any time during the course of treatment. Moreover, such an integration of cognitive and behavioral tactics would parallel effective approaches already employed with depressed and anxious clients.

SOURCES FOR FURTHER STUDY

Beck, Aaron T. *Love Is Never Enough.* New York: Harper & Row, 1988. Written for couples everywhere, this text presents a review of cognitive therapy and includes many suggestions for couples wishing to improve their relationship. Through many clinical examples and dialogues with various couples in treatment, Beck highlights some of the key strategies for avoiding difficulties associated with misperceptions and miscommunication.

Bornstein, Philip H., and Marcy T. Bornstein. *Marital Therapy: A Behavioral-Communications Approach.* New York: Pergamon Press, 1986. Highlights some of the key research findings that differentiate distressed and satisfied partners in the areas of communication and conflict resolution. Also presents a clinical guide for counselors and therapists who work with couples to alleviate relationship dysfunction.

Gottman, John M., et al. *A Couple's Guide to Communication.* Champaign, Ill.: Research Press, 1979. A very useful guidebook for couples wishing to improve their communication and conflict-resolution skills. Suggestions for practicing improved interactions and increasing daily happiness are included.

Gurman, A. S. *Casebook of Marital Therapy.* New York: Guilford, 1985. Reviews various treatment strategies available for dealing with some of the most challenging difficulties in interpersonal relationships (including jealousy, sexual problems, and in-laws). Leaders from a variety of treatment approaches describe various aspects of their therapy approach.

Gurman, A. S., and D. P. Kniskern. *Handbook of Family Therapy.* Vol. 2. New York: Brunner/Mazel, 1991. A significant resource on the various models of treatment for couples and families. Presents a historical overview of marital and family therapy, describes various models and conceptualizations of treatment, and highlights special topics such as sex therapy and divorce interventions.

Jacobson, Neil S., and A. S. Gurman, eds. *Clinical Handbook of Couple Therapy.* 3d ed. New York: Guilford, 2002. Provides an overview and numerous clinical sections on the major models of relationship therapy and treatment suggestions for selected psychiatric disorders. Designed for clinicians and researchers alike, this edited text presents the views of most of the major figures in marital therapy.

Jacobson, Neil S., and Gayla Margolin. *Marital Therapy: Strategies Based on Social Learning and Behavior Exchange Principles.* New York: Brunner/Mazel,

1979. Presents a description of social learning theory and the methods typically employed in behavioral marital therapy. A landmark book in the history of marital therapy that still offers much candid clinical insight into the most effective methods for alleviating relationship distress.

Gregory L. Wilson

SEE ALSO: Behavioral family therapy; Cognitive behavior therapy; Group therapy; Midlife crises; Psychotherapy: Effectiveness; Separation and divorce: Adult issues; Separation and divorce: Children's issues; Strategic family therapy.

Creativity and intelligence

TYPE OF PSYCHOLOGY: Intelligence and intelligence testing

FIELDS OF STUDY: General issues in intelligence

Creativity and intelligence are two aspects of cognitive performance in humans. Creativity refers to having inventive, productive, and imaginative qualities; intelligence refers to having mental acuteness, the ability to understand, and the ability to act effectively to solve problems within one's environment. The areas of creativity and intelligence have provided insight into what it means to be gifted and talented.

KEY CONCEPTS
- analogy
- cognitive skills
- creativity
- giftedness
- intelligence
- problem solving
- problem solving by analogy

INTRODUCTION

Creativity and intelligence are two areas of cognitive functioning and performance which have been examined by researchers, educators, and others. Creativity can be defined as a person's cognitive abilities in areas such as fluency, flexibility, originality, elaboration, visualization, metaphorical thinking, problem definition, and evaluation. Intelligence is defined as the ability to perform various mental tasks which include reasoning, knowledge, comprehension, memory, applying concepts, and manipulating figures. The study of creativity and intelligence has developed based on studies in cognitive, developmental, and educational psychology. Given that psychology as a discipline may be defined as the systematic study of the mind and behavior, when one studies creativity and intelligence, one learns how to improve performance and lead those persons who are creative, gifted, and talented to new heights. Specifically, when one studies creativity, one gains information about students' abilities in imagination, discovery, and the ability to invent. When one studies intelligence, one gains information about students' abilities in logic, memory, and organization.

Creativity and intelligence have played a significant role in the history of psychology and an even greater role in the history of humankind. Progress in education is evident in at least three occurrences. First, interest in measuring individual differences has led to the development of tests to quantify creative and intellectual abilities. Second, attention to persons who have been identified as creative, gifted, talented, or highly intelligent has led to the development of special programs, learning experiences, and scholarships for these students. Third, the needs of these students have led to research on the students themselves. The results of numerous empirical students have been published to aid parents, educators, and even the gifted or creative individual in understanding the needs of those with special abilities.

Certain issues related to creativity and intelligence have evolved from discrepancies that have been found in obtaining relationships between creativity and intelligence. It is a mistake to lump creative and intelligent people together: Creative ability is not synonymous with intellectual ability. Many students who are very high in intelligence, as measured by a test, are not high in other intellectual functions, such as creativity. Many students who are high in creativity are not also high in intelligence.

DEFINING AND MEASURING CREATIVITY

Creativity refers to the process of being imaginative and innovative. A creative person is able to link existing information with new information in productive ways. Students who are creative may often be referred to as being gifted and/or talented.

Charles F. Wetherall has listed many characteristics of gifted, talented, and/or creative students. Creative students, for example, have a keen sense of observation and a desire to improve their abilities, produce a variety of possible solutions to problems, are curious and original, have the characteristic of persistence, are comfortable with ambiguity, are able to work independently, are able to analyze and synthesize information, demonstrate compulsivity and an urgency to complete a task or execute an idea, and have multiple latent abilities. Thus, when one's existing knowledge and information combine in a unique way, a creative product or idea is formed.

Many others have also sought to describe creativity. Characteristics of creative persons and creativity according to Gary A. Davis and Sylvia Rimm include valuing creative thinking, appreciating novel and far-fetched ideas, being open-minded and receptive to zany ideas, and being mentally set to produce creative ideas. Robert Sternberg describes creative people as those who have the ability and willingness to go beyond the ordinary limitations of themselves and their environment and to think and act in unconventional and perhaps dreamlike ways. Further, he states that creative people go beyond the unwritten canons of society, have aesthetic taste, and are inquisitive and intuitive. Major contributions have been made to many fields of endeavor as a result of creative enterprise.

Creativity has been studied through research that sought to examine personality and family issues related to creativity, the ecology of creativity, musical creativity, and creative ability in women. Research by Robert Albert that examined relationships between creativity, identity formation, and career choice led him to make six suggestions for parents and teachers to help students achieve maximally. This information would be beneficial both to students who are gifted and to those who are not. His suggestions include helping students experience emotions such as anger, joy, fear, and passion; teaching involvement rather than techniques to students; seeking to discover what people can do; allowing students to experience some novelty and flexibility; encouraging the students to ask the questions "What do I think?" "How do I think?" "What can I do?" and "How do I feel about it now that I have tried?"; and enhancing learning by being actively engaged with and taking chances with one another.

THEORIES OF INTELLIGENCE

Intelligence, according to Paul Kline, refers to a person's ability to learn, understand, and deal with novel situations. The intelligent person may be viewed as quick-witted, acute, keen, sharp, canny, astute, bright, and brilliant. Robert Sternberg, in *Intelligence Applied: Understanding and Increasing Your Intellectual Skills* (1986), describes intelligence as comprising a very wide array of cognitive and other skills; he does not see intelligence as a single ability.

After examining many theories of intelligence, Sternberg developed the triarchic (three-part) theory of intelligence. In the componential subtheory, the first part of the theory, intelligence is related to the external world of the individual. For example, a person who is intelligent in this area obtains high scores on standardized tests and is excellent in analytical thinking. The second part of the theory, the experiential subtheory, specifies intelligence in situations. A person who is intelligent in handling novel tasks with creativity but who may not have the best standardized test scores is demonstrating intelligence in this area. In the third part of the theory, the contextual subtheory, intelligence is related to the external world of the individual. For example, a person who is able to achieve success when interacting on the job or when influencing other people is demonstrating contextual intelligence.

ROLE OF ANALOGIES

Characteristics of intelligent persons include greater preference for, more attention to, and highly developed abilities for dealing with novelty; an ability to process information rapidly; an ability to ignore irrelevant information; and an ability to solve problems accurately. Problem-solving ability in intelligence may be observed in a person's ability to complete many tasks successfully. Among these tasks would be a person's ability to solve analogies.

Analogies are statements of a relationship between words, concepts, or situations. Problem solving by analogy occurs when students attempt to use the conditions and solution to one problem to assist them in understanding the conditions and solutions of another problem. Put another way, students use the relationships they see in one context or situation to assist them in understanding relationships in another context or situation. Many educators believe that solving analogies helps students to concretize their thinking, gauge how they understand information, tap and develop a facility for visual thinking, exercise and nurture creative and critical thinking, clarify and organize unfamiliar subject matter, and synthesize instructional material. Past research has pointed to an ability to solve analogies as one of the best predictors of intellectual ability. Intelligence has also been studied by examining the way in which students who have been identified as gifted (based on high intelligence test scores) solve problems. It was found that highly intelligent people are better able to separate relevant and irrelevant information.

ASSESSMENT TESTS

Both creativity and intelligence can be assessed by specialized tests designed for that purpose. One of the first people to examine the concept of intelligence in the United States was James McKeen Cattell (1860-1944). He is credited with the introduction of the use of the phrase "mental tests." After studying in Europe, Cattell developed and sought to refine tests which focused on the cognitive skills that he believed indicated intellectual ability: strength, reaction time, and sensory discrimination.

The first test to examine individual differences in intelligence was devised and published in France by Alfred Binet and Théodore Simon in 1905; it was called the Binet-Simon test. The Binet-Simon test was translated into English and went through a series of revisions by various people. The version of the Binet-Simon test most used in the United States is the Stanford-Binet, which was first published in 1916.

E. Paul Torrance developed the Torrance Tests of Creative Thinking; these tests seek to assess creativity as it relates to fluency, flexibility, originality, and elaboration. Each of these areas can be understood in the context of examples. Fluency in creativity is the ability one has to produce numerous original ideas that solve problems. For example, persons may demonstrate fluency when they can give multiple uses for a ballpoint pen. Flexibility in creativity is the ability to produce ideas that show a variety of approaches that may be used. Originality is the ability to create uncommon or unusual responses; for example, a unique or unconventional use of the ballpoint pen would be classified as original. Elaboration refers to a person's ability to add details to a basic idea. For example, if a common item such as a ballpoint pen is discussed in ex-

treme and minute details that do not focus on obvious aspects of the pen, elaboration is being demonstrated.

Intelligence tests consist of standardized questions and tasks that seek to determine the mental age of a person or the person's relative capacity to solve problems and absorb new information. Intelligence tests try to measure students' capacity to learn separate from their actual academic achievement.

Intelligence tests are either group-administered or individually administered; in group testings, large numbers of students can be assessed at the same time. According to Miles Storfer, individual intelligence tests such as the Stanford-Binet and the Wechsler series provide a good approximation of most people's abilities in the cognitive skills that the tests are designed to measure. These cognitive skills include being able to solve problems well, reasoning clearly, thinking logically, having a good vocabulary, and knowing an abundance of information in many areas.

IMPLICATIONS FOR SCIENCE AND TECHNOLOGY

Creative discovery has led to many technological breakthroughs and innovations in science and industry. Technological breakthroughs and success in science and industry have been evident in the extensive research into creative activity conducted by W. J. Gordon. He provides some source material that points to the relationship between invention, discovery, and learning. Creativity and analogies have led to breakthroughs in a wide variety of technological fields.

One example of the many technological breakthroughs and innovations in science and industry presented by Gordon occurred in 1865. John Boyd Dunlop was trying to think of a way to help his son be more comfortable when riding his bicycle over cobblestone streets. While watering his garden, he noticed how the hose resisted his fingers when he pressed his hand more firmly around it. He made the connections between the elastic resistance of the hose and how this type of elasticity would make his son more comfortable when biking. His first successful tire was made from a piece of garden hose.

SOURCES FOR FURTHER STUDY
Albert, Robert S. "Identity, Experiences, and Career Choice Among the Exceptionally Gifted and Emi-

nent." In *Theories of Creativity*, edited by Mark A. Runco and Robert S. Albert. Newbury Park, Calif.: Sage Publications, 1990. This twelve-chapter book on creativity is a compilation of the expertise of persons who have studied creativity in areas such as anthropology, behavior, cognition, development, and ecology. Topics are varied and include creativity in adolescents, creativity in women, relationships between emotional difficulties and creativity, and social factors that influence creativity.

Davis, Gary A., and Sylvia B. Rimm. *Education of the Gifted and Talented*. 4th ed. Boston: Allyn & Bacon, 1997. Presents various skills, behaviors, and characteristics of students who are gifted, talented, and/or creative. The abilities and skills involved in creative problem solving are explained in clear language. An excellent source to gain information on the educational needs of gifted, talented, or creative students.

Gordon, W. J. "Some Source Material in Discovery-by-Analogy." *Journal of Creative Behavior* 8, no. 4 (1974): 239-257. Focusing on an associative view of invention, discovery, and learning, Gordon cites thirty-eight examples of associative analogical connections which have triggered famous innovations and breakthroughs. A wide variety of technological fields are included. Interesting reading; gives the foundations of many items used in everyday life.

Kline, Paul. *Intelligence: The Psychometric View*. New York: Routledge, 1991. Provides a summary of studies focusing on the nature of intelligence and other human abilities. Topics include the history of the concept of intelligence, and ways to measure intelligence. The definitions of statistical and technical terms are presented in a clear and readable fashion.

Simenton, Dean Keith. *Origins of Genius: Darwinian Perspectives on Creativity*. New York: Oxford University Press, 1999. Explores the source of creativity in Darwinian properties of variation and selection.

Steptoe, Andrew, ed. *Genius and the Mind: Studies of Creativity and Temperament*. New York: Oxford University Press, 1998. A collection of case study essays on the psychology of creative "geniuses" such as Mozart, Byron, and Shakespeare.

Sternberg, Robert J. *Intelligence Applied: Understanding and Increasing Your Intellectual Skills*. Orlando, Fla.: Harcourt Brace Jovanovich, 1986. A training program based on the triarchic theory of intelligence that Sternberg has developed. Details effective strategies for solving various types of problems, including science insight problems and analogies. Exercises for practice are included.

Storfer, Miles D. *Intelligence and Giftedness: The Contributions of Heredity and Early Environment*. San Francisco: Jossey-Bass, 1990. Storfer presents information on the effects of nurture on intelligence, focusing on the nature and development of intellectual giftedness and the characteristics of intellectually gifted people. The concept of intelligence in different socioeconomic conditions, in enrichment programs, and in its varying types are highlighted in separate chapters. The factors that influence intelligence and giftedness are examined in detail.

Torrance, Ellis Paul. *Education and the Creative Potential*. Minneapolis: University of Minnesota Press, 1963. A compilation of seven papers and six experimental studies conducted by Torrance, who developed a test to measure creative thinking and conducted longitudinal studies on creativity. Information on topics such as developing creative potential in schoolchildren and factors that facilitate or inhibit creativity in children.

Weisberg, Robert W. *Creativity: Genius and Other Myths*. New York: W. H. Freeman, 1986. Weisberg discusses the behaviors, activities, and finished products of individuals who have been described as creative. Defines creativity by giving real-life examples and discusses the role that intense knowledge or expertise plays in creative problem solving.

Debra A. King-Johnson

SEE ALSO: Ability tests; Creativity: Assessment; Giftedness; Intelligence; Intelligence tests; Learning.

Creativity

Assessment

TYPE OF PSYCHOLOGY: Intelligence and intelligence testing

FIELDS OF STUDY: Ability tests; cognitive processes

Creativity is the ability to make something new that is widely valued. Various methods have been developed to assess this quality.

KEY CONCEPTS
- big "C" versus little "c" creativity
- convergent thinking
- creativity
- divergent thinking
- flexibility
- fluency
- intelligence
- originality
- problem finding
- problem solving

INTRODUCTION

The study of creativity has undergone many changes and developments, particularly since the early 1960's, and it has received recognition as a field in its own right. Creativity has traditionally been assessed via the finished products of the artist, musician, writer, poet, or inventor. The general consensus of the public has usually served as the final criterion of creativity. Any distinction between creativity and talent could be difficult to ascertain. The assessment of talent has usually been the province of people within a particular field. Musicians, artists, writers, and others in specific fields have assessed the skills of their students or protégés, either formally or informally; in some fields, specific tests do exist.

One generally accepted construct regarding creativity is divergent thinking. People who are considered creative seem to think in a more divergent mode. They see possibilities and options that are not perceived by most other people. If most people were to ask themselves the possible uses for a brick, they would probably list a few: to build a house, for example, or perhaps to use as a doorstop. Divergent thinkers may indicate that it could be used as a weapon, a hammer, a paperweight, a bookend, or a supportive device.

Commonly assessed components of divergent thinking include fluency, flexibility, elaboration, and originality. Fluency refers to the number of ideas that a person can generate to solve a given problem or produce a certain result. Flexibility is the ability to generate a number of different kinds of ideas. The amount of detail that one can supply for one's ideas is known as the amount of elaboration. Orig-

inality refers to the novelty or statistical infrequency of each idea. This concept has often been used as a synonym for creativity. If one person out of a hundred has an idea that no one else has, for example, that idea may be termed original. It might be strange, even bizarre, but it might also be positive.

Some theorists view creative thinking as a process or a series of stages. Finding a problem might be one stage, developing possible solutions would be another, and choosing a "best" solution would be another. Things may go wrong in any stage along the way. When difficulties are encountered, it is often effective to defer conscious thought for a period of time; often, this enables one to achieve a new insight into a problem. If one becomes fatigued, it is often best to rest and return to the problem when one is refreshed.

Some researchers have described different types of creativity. For example, Mihaly Csikszentmihalyi distinguished between everyday (little "c") creativity and extraordinary (big "C") creativity which transforms a domain. Little "c" creativity might be used to find a way to get to work faster, while big "C" creativity further develops a domain of knowledge or skill, often leading to eminence of the individual in that field. Other researchers have studied the relation between creativity and talent. Howard Gardner emphasized the role that specific aptitudes play in making something that is both new and valued. In his view, creativity can develop independently in one of eight "intelligences": linguistic, logical-mathematical, musical, spatial, bodily-kinesthetic, interpersonal, intrapersonal, and naturalistic. A creative writer (with linguistic intelligence) is not necessarily a creative musician, even if the writer also plays music.

Another aspect of creativity is validation. After one has created or invented something, one attempts to ascertain whether the idea, music, poem, or other creative endeavor truly has merit. The "test of time" is perhaps the ultimate element of validation. Sometimes an invention or creation is valued only for a time, then discarded; sometimes it is changed or improved upon. On the other hand, works such as the symphonies of Wolfgang Amadeus Mozart (1756-1791), the plays of William Shakespeare (1564-1616), and the artwork of Leonardo da Vinci (1452-1519) have stood the test of time and are still held in high esteem.

Intelligence has been thought to be an important aspect of creativity; a certain minimal amount of intelligence is certainly necessary. Mentally retarded people are, in general, not very creative. On the other hand, and more surprising, there are few people with very high intelligence quotient (IQ) scores who are creative. They appear to be preoccupied with finding the "right" answer; perhaps they naturally think more convergently. As previously noted, divergent thinking is a crucial aspect of creativity. If one is extremely intelligent, one may therefore need to make radical changes in order to think in divergent ways. Alternatively, intelligence as traditionally conceived and measured may not relate closely to domains (such as music or movement) where creativity emerges.

Personality has also been examined in terms of creativity. Research indicates that creative people seem to have a greater range of knowledge and interests than noncreative people. They seem to have an openness to new experience and have a willingness to try new types of things. They appear to value independence, as well as complexity. A good sense of humor is also noted. The creative personality is persistent and is willing to take risks. Many creative people are seen to have high energy and activity levels. Organization and abstraction skills are well developed. Creative people are able to tolerate ambiguity better than less-creative people; they seem to function well in ill-defined settings or situations and employ fairly unusual problem-solving strategies.

Sample Assessment Practices

A number of tests have been developed that attempt to measure creativity in school-age children. E. Paul Torrance became a leading figure in the field of creativity in the 1950's. His tests of divergent thinking have been used and researched extensively. There are two parts to the Torrance Tests of Creative Thinking (published by the Scholastic Testing Service), a verbal section and a "figural" section. There are several subtests in each area. In the verbal test, seven activities must be performed, including asking, guessing causes, guessing consequences, product improvement, unusual uses, unusual questions, and "just suppose." In the figural realm, there are three activities: picture construction, picture completion, and circles. There are complete manuals for administrative, scoring, and illustrative purposes.

A number of organizations offer computerized scoring services. Teachers or others who have not had special training are able to score the tests fairly reliably if they have invested the time to study the scoring guides carefully.

A test developed by Frank Williams, another researcher in the field of creativity, is the Exercises in Divergent Thinking and Divergent Feeling. The creative thinking part of the test offers a total score as well as subscores in fluency, flexibility, originality, and elaboration. On the creative feeling test, scores are offered on curiosity, imagination, complexity, and risk taking; again, a total score is offered. These tests represent the variables thought by Williams to be most important in creativity.

The parts of this test, in conjunction with the Williams scale, can help to identify children with creative potential. The Williams scale asks parents and teachers to rate children on a three-point scale in terms of their fluency, flexibility, originality, elaboration, curiosity, complexity, imagination, and risk taking. There are also four open-ended questions that allow parents and teachers to express specific concerns and offer salient information about the child. There is considerable specificity to the Williams scale, but there is also a ceiling effect in that some students can only earn a certain number of points; this may therefore give a limited vision of the test taker's skills and creative potential.

The Group Inventory for Finding Talent (GIFT), which allows children to rate their preferences for various activities, is also available. The GIFT has subscales for imagination, independence, and many interests. This test is computer-scored by the company rather than by the examiner or teacher. This test was developed by Gary Davis and Sylvia Rimm, two well-known experts in the field of gifted education. A major cross-cultural effort was undertaken by Hans Jellen and Klaus Urban. Their test, the Test for Creative Thinking and Drawing Production (TCT-DP), has been administered to subjects in eleven countries.

All these tests can help to discover creative potential in children, but few creativity researchers would advise that tests be used alone or argue that they are necessarily better predictors of creative potential than are alternative assessment techniques, such as expert judges' ratings of creative performances by children. One such alternative developed by Teresa Amabile is the consensual assessment technique, in which expert judges independently evaluate children's creative products. The assumption is that experts in a domain know what is creative when they see it. Other assessment alternatives offer more guidance by training judges to score products or portfolios according to subjective dimensions (such as aesthetic appeal or originality) or a scoring guide.

By adulthood, creativity has generally identified itself through a history of creative performances or products, so the problem of identifying creative talent is often not as acute as it was during the school years. Nevertheless, economic conditions may force a person to work at a job that provides no avenues or extra time to maximize creativity. Without help, some people may never find an outlet for their talents and skills. For this reason, adult personality assessments and interest inventories often include subscales that attempt to measure creativity, originality, or some similar construct. Scores on these measures can be used to develop self-understanding, find a suitable job placement, or increase work satisfaction.

DEVELOPING CREATIVITY

Everyone has some creative potential, but it may be difficult to discern exactly how much potential one has or in what field or domain it may lie. Creativity remains an elusive concept but one of great interest to many researchers; journals, conferences, and organizations are devoted to the subject.

Some psychologists and educators have been concerned with ways of enhancing creativity; one method is the idea of brainstorming. In this strategy, people offer ideas and suggestions regarding the clarification of or solution to a problem. All options are accepted, and no negativism is allowed; this enhances the climate of the group. Only later do the group members focus on which ideas are reasonable or possible. Some researchers have attempted to use behavioral reinforcement principles and procedures to promulgate creative responses; others have examined the effectiveness of creativity training. Methods have focused on either short-term or long-term programs.

Creativity in the classroom is another area that has been of concern. Some educators have worried in particular that educational reform movements may ultimately stifle creativity in the classroom. Psychologists John Glover and Roger Bruning have of-

fered suggestions for enhancing classroom creativity. Teachers, they suggest, should "try to find something positive in all ideas." Strange or unusual questions from students should not be discounted. Creativity should be rewarded systematically; it should also be expected. Creativity should be rewarded as extra credit when grades are given, and creative behaviors should be modeled by teachers. Teacher educator Alane Starko suggests that students be given the opportunity to find problems, rather than simply devising creative solutions. Content and lessons should expect students to question as well as answer, investigate as well as comprehend. Because creative people must ultimately identify new problems as well as provide new answers to problems, creativity must be investigated, assessed, and nurtured.

SOURCES FOR FURTHER STUDY

Csikszentmihalyi, Mihaly. *Creativity: Flow and the Psychology of Discovery and Invention.* New York: HarperCollins, 1996. A best-seller which reports the results of interviewing ninety-one famous individuals to identify commonalities in their experiences of creating.

Fishkin, Anne S., Bonnie Cramond, and Paula Olszewski-Kubilius, eds. *Investigating Creativity in Youth: Research and Methods*, Cresskill, N.J.: Hampton Press, 1999. Contributions to this volume include most contemporary perspectives on creativity research within the gifted education movement. The last six chapters focus on creativity assessment and models of creativity training.

Gardner, Howard. *Creating Minds.* New York: Basic Books, 1993. A best-seller which contains seven case studies of famous people, illustrating creativity in each domain of Gardner's theory of multiple intelligence.

Runco, Mark A., and Robert S. Albert, eds. *Theories of Creativity.* 2d ed. Cresskill, N.J.: Hampton Press, 2001. Runco and Albert have edited a text with chapters by the leading figures in the field. These twelve chapters are a gold mine for those interested in doing in-depth research in the field of creativity. Runco is also the editor of a major journal on the empirical study of creativity.

Starko, Alane Jordan. *Creativity in the Classroom: Schools of Curious Delight.* 2d ed. Mahwah, N.J.: Lawrence Erlbaum, 2000. Filled with excellent suggestions based on sound research. Chapter 8 focuses on assessing creativity.

Sternberg, Robert J. *Handbook of Creativity*. New York: Cambridge University Press, 1999. Technical chapters by leading experts provide valuable background information for understanding contemporary research on creativity and for conducting future studies.

Michael F. Shaughnessy;
updated by John F. Wakefield

SEE ALSO: Ability tests; Creativity and intelligence; Educational psychology; Giftedness; Intelligence; Intelligence quotient (IQ); Intelligence tests; Learning.

Crowd behavior

TYPE OF PSYCHOLOGY: Social psychology
FIELDS OF STUDY: Aggression; group processes; social motives

Crowd behavior is the study of how the behavior of people in groups differs from that of individuals. People in crowds often become much more focused on their social identity than on their own individual identity. As a result, they are much more influenced by the norms of the group.

KEY CONCEPTS
- bystander effect
- deindividuation
- diffusion of responsibility
- group norms
- social identity theory

INTRODUCTION

Crowds are groups of people who are together for short periods of time. The study of crowd behavior examines the actions that people in a crowd perform, and how these actions differ from the behavior of individuals acting alone. Crowd behavior became a focus of scholarly thought in the late nineteenth and early twentieth centuries in reaction to the social turmoil in Western Europe at that time. Italian criminologist Scipio Sighele (1868-1913) first wrote about crowd behavior. French psychologist Gustave Le Bon (1841-1931), the founder of crowd psychology, formalized and popularized

the concept with his book *The Crowd*, published in 1895. Le Bon's ideas reached a wide audience and are said to have influenced German dictator Adolf Hitler and Italian dictator Benito Mussolini as well as psychologists. Because crowds have performed many senseless and destructive acts, both historically and recently, understanding crowd behavior remains extremely important for psychologists.

The term "crowd" refers to a wide spectrum of human gatherings, varying in their complexity and the intention with which people join them. Some crowds are casual; people come together by happenstance (as a group of pedestrians standing on a sidewalk.) These tend to be simple, disorganized groups of people who do not know one another and will probably not see each other again. Others are conventionalized—the people have all chosen a common activity (for example, watching a parade or a sporting event) and express excitement in standard ways (cheering). Some crowds are purposive, choosing to be together for a common goal, such as a rally or political protest. These groups are often highly cohesive and highly organized.

Because crowds differ so much in their composition, organization, and purpose, there is also considerable variation in typical crowd behavior. Popular and scholarly attention has tended to focus on the situations in which crowd behavior is considered problematic. In these situations, the crowd often has an unusual problem to solve rapidly (for example, how to respond to a hostile police force). The occurrence of riots and violence attest to the fact that these sorts of problems are not always solved constructively by crowds. It should be noted, however that crowds are capable of behaving in positive ways as well.

UNDERLYING PSYCHOLOGICAL PROCESSES

Early theories of crowd behavior hypothesized that unruly crowds were made up of criminals or the mentally deficient. Proponents of this perspective assumed that crowd behavior could be explained by the makeup of the individual personalities of people in the crowd and that certain kinds of people were more likely to be found in a crowd. Le Bon provided a more psychological analysis of crowd behavior, recognizing that even people of high intelligence could become members of an unruly crowd. He believed that crowds transform people, obliterating their normal abilities to be rational and putting them in a hypnotic, highly suggestible state. Le Bon disapproved of crowd behavior in all forms. Consequently, in his book he painted an extremely negative picture of crowd behavior.

Modern social psychological research suggests that neither of these early viewpoints is a good description of the psychological forces underlying crowd behavior. Experimental research has determined that almost any individual could be influenced to behave in uncharacteristic ways under the right circumstances. Le Bon's perspective has also been greatly refined. Rather than relying on Le Bon's concepts of mass hypnosis and loss of rationality, modern researchers draw primarily from social identity theory to help explain crowd behavior. Social identity theory, originally developed by European psychologists Henri Tajfel and John Turner in the 1970's, posits that individuals derive an important part of their sense of identity from the groups to which they belong. Groups such as one's family, school, or religion can all provide positive sources of identity.

Under some circumstances, crowds can become a source of identity as well. A key psychological mechanism through which crowds become a source of identity is deindividuation, the loss of a person's sense of identity and weakening of inhibitions which occurs only in the presence of others. Crowds are especially likely to lead to deindividuation for a number of reasons. First, crowds lead individuals to feel less accountable for their actions; they are less likely to be singled out and feel less personally responsible for any act the crowd commits. Crowds also focus attention away from the self, so one's own values and internal standards become less influential. Thus, in line with social identity theory, deindividuation leads someone to become focused on social identity, rather than individual identity. When social identity is salient to an individual, that person becomes particularly susceptible to social influence. Group norms, or a group's standards and expectations regarding appropriate behavior, become especially important, and the individual is likely to conform strictly to those norms. In the short time frame of many crowd gatherings, the norm becomes whatever everyone else is doing.

It should be noted, however, that being amid a group of people does not always lead one to become deindividuated, nor does it always lead to the ascen-

dancy of social identity over individual identity. Often crowds do not engage in collective behavior at all. For example, on most city streets, pedestrians walking and milling about do not consider themselves to be part of a group, and do not draw a sense of identity from the people around them.

Eugen Tarnow noted that these wide variations in the effect of crowds on individuals can be best understood by identifying two phases, an individual phase and a conforming phase. During the individual phase, people move freely about. At these times, individuals are not particularly aware of their membership in a crowd and are not particularly influenced by those around them. In the conforming phase, however, individuals in a crowd are highly aware of the group of which they are a part, and they show high levels of conformity. During this phase, the group norms heavily influence each individual's behavior. Crowds typically alternate between these two phases, sometimes acting collectively, sometimes individually. For example, at a sporting event, fans are sometimes talking to their friends about topics of individual interest. However, when points are scored by the home team, the crowd responds collectively, as part of social group. At these moments spectators are not responding as individuals but as members of the social group, "fans."

The behaviors that members of a crowd perform will thus depend upon how strongly the crowd becomes a source of social identity, and the norms for behavior that become established among the group. Because these factors vary considerably from group to group, crowds cannot be characterized as wholly negative or uniformly simplistic, as Le Bon described them.

THE VIOLENT CROWD

Violent and destructive acts are among the most studied forms of crowd behavior. Many historical examples, from the French Revolution of 1789 to the Los Angeles riots of 1992, attest to the destructive power of crowds. A crowd of deindividuated people will not become violent, however, unless a group norm of violence becomes established. In riots, for example, there is usually an identifiable precipitating event (for example, one person smashing a window) that introduces a norm of violence. If a critical mass of people immediately follows suit, a riot ensues. Other crowds, such as lynch mobs, have the norm of violence previously established by their culture or by the group's previous actions.

Further, there is some evidence to suggest that the way in which a crowd of people is viewed by authorities can escalate crowd conflicts. For example, in 1998, European psychologists Clifford Stott and Stephen Reicher interviewed police officers involved with controlling a riot in Great Britain. Their analysis revealed that while police officers recognize that crowds contain subgroups of more dangerous or less dangerous members, they tend to treat all group members as potentially dangerous. The police officers' negative expectations often translate into combative behavior toward all crowd members. By acting on their negative expectations, authority figures often elicit the very behaviors they hope to prevent. This often leads to increased violence and conflict escalation.

Much evidence suggests that there is a direct relationship between degree of deindividuation and the extremity of a crowd's actions. For example, in 1986, Brian Mullen examined newspaper accounts of sixty lynchings occurring in the first half of the twentieth century. His analysis revealed that the more people present in the mob, the more violent and vicious was the event. Similarly, Leon Mann found in his analysis of twenty-one cases of threatened suicides that crowds watching were more likely to engage in crowd baiting (encouraging the person to jump from a ledge or bridge) when crowds were large and when it was dark. On a more mundane level, sports players are more aggressive when wearing identical uniforms than when dressed in their own clothes. Any factor that increases anonymity seems to increase deindividuation and increase the power of social identity, and thus increases the likelihood of extreme behavior.

In South Africa, psychological research on these phenomena has been presented in murder trials. People being tried for murder have argued that these psychological principles help explain their antisocial behavior. The use of psychological research findings for these purposes has sparked a great deal of controversy in the field.

THE APATHETIC CROWD

While crowds are most infamous for inciting people to rash action, sometimes crowds inhibit behavior. Research on helping behavior suggests that helping is much less likely to occur when there are many people watching. This well-established phenomenon, known as the bystander effect, was researched and described by American psychologists John Darley and Bibb Latane. In a typical experiment, participants overhear an "accident," such as someone falling off a ladder. Researchers observe whether participants go to help. Most people help when they are alone, but people are significantly less likely to help when they are with a crowd of other people. Darley and Latane argued that bystanders in a crowd experience a diffusion of responsibility. That is, each individual feels less personally responsible to act because each assumes that someone else will do so.

This phenomenon is exacerbated by the fact that in many situations, it is unclear whether an event is an emergency. For example, an adult dragging a screaming child out of a store could be a kidnapper making away with a child or a parent responding to a tantrum. Bystanders observe the reactions of others in the crowd to help them determine what the appropriate course of action is in an ambiguous situation. However, because the situation is ambiguous, typically each individual is equally confused and unsure. By waiting for someone else to act, bystanders convey the impression to others that they think nothing is wrong. Psychologists call this phenomenon pluralistic ignorance. People assume that even though others are behaving in exactly the same way as themselves (not acting), they are doing so for a different reason (knowing the situation is not an emergency). Thus, a social norm of inaction can also become established in a crowd.

THE PROSOCIAL CROWD

Despite the potential for great violence and destruction, most crowds that gather do so quite uneventfully. Further, sometimes crowd behavior is quite positive and prosocial. Research shows that sometimes deindividuation can lead to prosocial behavior. For example, nonviolent protests operate under an explicit norm of peaceful resistance and rarely lead to escalated violence on both sides. The power of prosocial norms was also experimentally established in a 1979 study conducted by psychologists Robert Johnson and Leslie Downing. Johnson and Downing had participants dress in either nurse's apparel or a white robe and hood like those worn by the Ku Klux Klan. Some from each group had their

The way in which individuals behave in a crowd has been a subject of increasing attention. (CLEO Photography)

individual identity made salient, while the rest did not. All participants were then given the opportunity to deliver an electric shock to someone who had previously insulted them. Among participants wearing the robes, those who were not identified delivered higher shock levels than those who were identified. Presumably these people were deindividuated and thus more strongly influenced by the violent cue of their costume. Of those in nurses' uniforms, the opposite was observed. Unidentified, deindividuated participants gave much less intense shocks than identified participants did. They were also more strongly influenced by the cues around them, but in this case the cues promoted prosocial action.

SOURCES FOR FURTHER STUDY

Coleman, A. M. "Crowd Psychology in South African Murder Trials." *American Psychologist* 46, no. 10 (1992): 1071-1079. This article describes how modern social psychological research on crowd behavior is being used to argue for extenuating factors in murder trials. The ethical issues raised from psychological testimony are discussed.

Gaskell, G., and R. Benewick, eds. *The Crowd in Contemporary Britain.* London: Sage, 1987. An excellent, comprehensive discussion of crowd behavior and political responses to it, drawing on work from scholars in several social scientific disciplines.

Le Bon, Gustave. *The Crowd.* New Brunswick, N.J.: Transaction Publishers, 1995. First published in 1895, this classic work explores the nature of crowd behavior and the places in modern life where crowd behavior holds sway.

McPhail, Clark. *The Myth of the Madding Crowd.* New York: Aldine De Gruyter, 1991. Authored by one of the major modern researchers on crowd behavior, this book summarizes and critiques Gustave Le Bon and earlier crowd theorists, and presents new formulations for understanding crowd behavior.

Mann, L. "The Baiting Crowd in Episodes of Threatened Suicide." *Journal of Personality and So-*

cial Psychology 41, no. 4 (1981): 703-709. In this paper, Mann provides a fascinating analysis of the factors that make crowds more likely to bait potential suicides.

_____. "'The Crowd' Century: Reconciling Practical Success with Theoretical Failure." *British Journal of Social Psychology* 35, no. 4 (1996): 535-553. Discusses the limits of Gustave Le Bon's crowd psychology theory and explores why, despite these limits, Adolf Hitler and Benito Mussolini were able to use his theory so successfully to manipulate crowds.

Reicher, S. *Crowd Behavior.* New York: Cambridge University Press, 2002. The most up-to-date scholarly perspectives on crowd behavior.

Van Ginneken, Jaap. *Crowds, Psychology, and Politics, 1871-1899.* New York: Cambridge University Press, 1992. Provides an historical perspective on the development of the field of crowd psychology, showing how early theories were shaped by current political events.

Cynthia McPherson Frantz

SEE ALSO: Bystander intervention; Community psychology; Group decision making; Group therapy; Groups; Intergroup relations.

Cultural competence

TYPE OF PSYCHOLOGY: All
FIELDS OF STUDY: All

Cultural competence is characterized by a set of skills and developmental experiences constituting an ongoing awareness of important differences among individuals from communities with different backgrounds related to biological, environmental, historical, political, psychological, religious, and other social aspects of heritage.

KEY CONCEPTS
- bias
- culture
- ethnicity
- norms
- prejudice
- racism

INTRODUCTION

When psychology is practiced, whether as a science or as a profession, it is practiced in a social and environmental context called culture. Culture is a characteristic of populations reflected in traditional beliefs, values, rituals, and other behaviors that are shared and transmitted from one generation to another. Culture is often thought of in terms of concepts such as ethnicity and norms. Ethnicity is generally described as a personal background characteristic connoting individual membership in a group that is defined by a common and distinctive linguistic, racial, national, and religious heritage. Norms are understood as the standard, average, or model behaviors, beliefs, or values people might have in a particular social grouping.

When psychologists speak of cultural competence, they are speaking about proper psychological practice that reflects an ongoing state of understanding, perceiving, and evaluating interactions among persons of differing cultural backgrounds. This can take place in therapeutic relationships, educational relationships, research endeavors, efforts to develop public policy, and even in the way information is presented. These interactions also may take place among individuals, families, communities, institutions, and nations. As such, this means that cultural competence must extend to these other levels of understanding human behavior and interactions.

Cultural competence also involves awareness and knowledge that there are many types of differences based on culture. Such awareness might include the varying values and importance assigned to different holidays, personal traits, language, standards of dress, standards of beauty, and even cultural icons by members of a particular cultural group. Other important dimensions of culture include differences in terms of preferred behavior states, for instance, being active or passive, or the types of interpersonal values that are preferred, for instance, cooperation versus competition. Still others are found in terms of preferences for acquiring knowledge (through teaching, through experience, or both), how time is seen (as linear, cyclical, or in terms of important events), and even for how reality is seen (objectively, subjectively, spiritually, or some combination of these ways of experience). This list is certainly incomplete, as cultures are constantly evolving. The things that make cultures distinct are dynamic in nature, and therefore achieving cultural competence is an ongoing process that requires constant self-awareness and self-evaluation.

IMPORTANCE

A good understanding of one's own culture and those of other individuals is important, as the points of interaction among cultures are where problems can develop. Bias, or an impartial or erroneous judgment or tendency to misperceive people or situations, may be activated by a lack of awareness of cultural issues. One familiar way bias may present itself is through prejudice. Prejudice is a judgment based on a bias and it is typically injurious or detrimental to the person misjudged and to the person doing the misjudging.

One particularly damaging type of prejudice that can result from a lack of cultural competence is racism, or prejudice based on race. Racism and prejudice may show up between individuals or groups, causing harm to one or both parties. However, racism may also show up not only at the level of individuals but also at the institutional level. For instance, some might call racial profiling an institutional form of racism. In health care, as an example, this might be evidenced in the form of individuals of a particular ethnic or cultural background being refused access to important health care services because of ill-informed beliefs about their need for responsiveness to such services, or it might develop because health care providers are not properly educated as to how different problems might present in culturally unique ways. Such a lack of identification would then result in a lack of referral for treatment services. The root cause of a lack of multicultural education at the point of identifying problems might be interpreted as a form of cultural incompetence at the individual and institutional levels. Some might go as far as to designate such consequences as a result of institutional racism. To some, this might seem an extreme judgment because the problems may result from a lack of awareness rather than deliberate discrimination, but this is at the heart of the concept of cultural competence: encouraging those in the social sciences and social services areas to always be on the alert for such potential problems.

CONTEXT

It is projected that by the year 2050, changes in both immigration and birthrate among individuals of different cultural backgrounds will mean that one out of three U.S. residents will be of a nonwhite racial background. Global communications are also increasing, as more forms of media become available to a wider audience through the Internet, television, and radio. Additionally, definitions of culture extend beyond race and ethnicity; cultures can be defined in terms of characteristics such as age, gender, sexual orientation, and socioeconomic status. As a result, the concept of cultural competence is likely to grow in importance as interactions among diverse cultures are likely to increase and foster as many opportunities for miscommunication as communication.

SOURCES FOR FURTHER STUDY

Diller, Jerry V. *Cultural Diversity: A Primer for the Human Services*. Belmont, Calif.: Wadsworth, 1999. An overview of cross-cultural counseling issues across a wide variety of populations. It also has many self-learning exercises.

Hampden-Turner, Charles M., Fons Trompenaars, and David Lewis. *Building Cross-Cultural Competence: How to Create Wealth from Conflicting Values*. New Haven, Conn.: Yale University Press, 2000. This book discusses the importance of cultural competence in business settings and provides practical tips on improving cross cultural interactions.

Leigh, James W. *Communicating for Cultural Competence*. Prospect Heights, Ill.: Waveland Press, 2001. Written for beginning interviewers. Provides tips for initial interactions with culturally diverse clients.

Sue, Derald Wing, and David Sue. *Counseling the Culturally Different: Theory and Practice*. 3d ed. New York: John Wiley & Sons, 1999. This book was written to challenge and inform those who work in multicultural counseling settings.

Nancy A. Piotrowski

SEE ALSO: Clinical interviewing, testing, and observation; Data description; Experimentation: Independent, dependent, and control variables; Observational methods; Prejudice; Prejudice reduction; Racism; Research ethics; Sexism.

MAGILL'S ENCYCLOPEDIA OF SOCIAL SCIENCE

PSYCHOLOGY

COMPLETE LIST OF ENTRIES

CATEGORIZED LIST OF ENTRIES

ABILITY TESTING

Ability tests
Career and personnel testing
College entrance examinations
Confidentiality
Creativity: Assessment
General Aptitude Test Battery
    (GATB)
Giftedness
Intelligence tests
Kuder Occupational Interest
    Survey (KOIS)
Peabody Individual Achievement
    Test (PIAT)
Stanford-Binet test
Strong Interest Inventory (SII)
Testing: Historical perspectives

Rape and sexual assault
Road rage
Separation and divorce: Adult issues
Sexism
Sibling relationships
Sport psychology
Violence and sexuality in the media
Violence by children and teenagers
Women's psychology: Carol Gilligan
Women's psychology: Karen Horney
Women's psychology: Sigmund Freud

METHODOLOGY
American Psychiatric Association
American Psychological Association
Animal experimentation
Archival data
Assessment
Beck, Aaron T.
Behaviorism
Case-study methodologies
Complex experimental designs
Confidentiality
Data description
Developmental methodologies
Diagnosis
Diagnostic and Statistical Manual of Mental Disorders (DSM)
Experimental psychology
Experimentation: Ethics and participant rights
Experimentation: Independent, dependent, and control variables
Eysenck, Hans
Field experimentation
Forensic psychology
Freud, Anna
Grammar and speech
Hypochondriasis, conversion, somatization, and somatoform pain

Hypothesis development and testing
International Classification of Diseases (ICD)
Kinsey, Alfred
Lewin, Kurt
Motivation
Observational methods
Psychoanalysis
Psychology: Definition
Psychosurgery
Quasi-experimental designs
Religiosity: Measurement
Research ethics
Rorschach, Hermann
Rorschach inkblots
Sampling
Scientific methods
Signal detection theory
Social networks
Statistical significance tests
Support groups
Survey research: Questionnaires and interviews
Teaching methods
Virtual reality
Watson, John B.
Within-subject experimental designs

MOTIVATION
Achievement motivation
Advertising
Affiliation and friendship
Affiliation motive
Allport, Gordon
Bandura, Albert
Beck Depression Inventory (BDI)
Crowd behavior
Denial
Dix, Dorothea
Drives
Eating disorders
Emotions
Evolutionary psychology
Eysenck, Hans
Field theory: Kurt Lewin
Forensic psychology
Helping

Homosexuality
Horney, Karen
Human resource training and development
Hunger
Hysteria
Incentive motivation
Industrial and organizational psychology
Instinct theory
Jealousy
Learning
Lorenz, Konrad
Love
Masters, William H., and Virginia E. Johnson
Motivation
Obesity
Optimal arousal theory
Parental alienation syndrome
Profiling
Psychoanalysis
Reinforcement
Religion and psychology
Religiosity: Measurement
Sex hormones and motivation
Sexual behavior patterns
Sport psychology
Substance use disorders
Support groups
Teaching methods
Thirst
Women's psychology: Carol Gilligan
Work motivation

NERVOUS SYSTEM
Artificial intelligence
Beck, Aaron T.
Behaviorism
Brain damage
Brain specialization
Brain structure
Circadian rhythms
Computer models of cognition
Defense reactions: Species specific
Drug therapies
Endorphins

Social psychological models:
  Karen Horney
Sport psychology

PSYCHOPATHOLOGY
Abnormality
Abnormality: Biomedical
  models
Abnormality: Legal models
Abnormality: Psychological
  models
Addictive personality and
  behaviors
Aggression
Aging: Cognitive changes
Agoraphobia and panic
  disorders
Alcohol dependence and abuse
Alzheimer's disease
Amnesia and fugue
Anorexia nervosa and bulimia
  nervosa
Antisocial personality
Anxiety disorders
Attention-deficit hyperactivity
  disorder (ADHD)
Autism
Battered woman syndrome
Beck, Aaron T.
Beck Depression Inventory
  (BDI)
Bed-wetting
Bipolar disorder
Borderline personality
Brain damage
Breuer, Josef
Childhood disorders
Children's Depression Inventory
  (CDI)
Clinical depression
Codependency
Conduct disorder
Dementia
Denial
Depression
*Diagnostic and Statistical Manual
  of Mental Disorders* (DSM)
Domestic violence
Down syndrome
Drug therapies

Eating disorders
Ego defense mechanisms
Grieving
Hallucinations
Histrionic personality
Hypochondriasis, conversion,
  somatization, and
  somatoform pain
Hysteria
Impulse control disorders
Incompetency
Insanity defense
*International Classification of
  Diseases* (ICD)
Jung, Carl G.
Kraepelin, Emil
Madness: Historical concepts
Minnesota Multiphasic
  Personality Inventory
  (MMPI)
Mood disorders
Multiple personality
Narcissistic personality
Neurotic disorders
Obsessive-compulsive disorder
Oedipus complex
Paranoia
Parental alienation syndrome
Parkinson's disease
Penis envy
Personality disorders
Phobias
Postpartum depression
Post-traumatic stress disorder
Psychopathology
Psychosomatic disorders
Psychotic disorders
Rape and sexual assault
Reactive attachment disorder
Rorschach, Hermann
Schizophrenia: Background,
  types, and symptoms
Schizophrenia: High-risk
  children
Schizophrenia: Theoretical
  explanations
Seasonal affective disorder
Separation anxiety
Sexual dysfunction
Sexual variants and paraphilias

Shyness
State-Trait Anxiety Inventory
Substance use disorders
Suicide
Support groups
Teenage suicide
Tourette's syndrome
Violence by children and
  teenagers

PSYCHOTHERAPY
Abnormality: Psychological
  models
American Psychiatric
  Association
Analytical psychotherapy
Anger
Archetypes and the collective
  unconscious
Aversion, implosion, and
  systematic desensitization
Battered woman syndrome
Beck Depression Inventory
  (BDI)
Behavior therapy
Behavioral family therapy
Bipolar disorder
Breuer, Josef
Brief therapy
Cognitive behavior therapy
Confidentiality
Constructivist psychology
Drug therapies
Ego defense mechanisms
Ellis, Albert
Feminist psychotherapy
Freud, Sigmund
Fromm, Erich
Gestalt therapy
Group therapy
Horney, Karen
Hysteria
Insanity defense
Jung, Carl G.
Kelly, George A.
Lacan, Jacques
Mental health practitioners
Miller, Neal E., and John Dollard
Music, dance, and theater
  therapy